VOLUME 1

Fundamental Accounting Principles

TENTH CANADIAN EDITION

VOLUME 1

Fundamental Accounting Principles

TENTH CANADIAN EDITION

Kermit D. Larson
University of Texas—Austin

Tilly Jensen
Northern Alberta Institute of Technology

Ray Carroll
Dalhousie University

Toronto Montréal Boston Burr Ridge, IL Dubuque, IA Madison, WI
New York San Francisco St. Louis Bangkok Bogota Caracas
Kuala Lumpur Lisbon London Madrid Mexico City Milan
New Delhi Santiago Seoul Singapore Sydney Taipei

McGraw-Hill
Ryerson Limited

A Subsidiary of The **McGraw·Hill** *Companies*

FUNDAMENTAL ACCOUNTING PRINCIPLES
Volume I
Tenth Canadian Edition

ISBN: 0-07-088984-8

1 2 3 4 5 6 7 8 9 10 TCP 0 9 8 7 6 5 4 3 2

Vice President and Editorial Director: *Patrick Ferrier*
Senior Sponsoring Editor: *Nicole Lukach*
Developmental Editor: *Glenn Turner/Burrston House; Katherine Goodes*
Senior Marketing Manager: *Jeff MacLean*
Manager, Editorial Services: *Kelly Dickson*
Senior Supervising Editor: *Margaret Henderson*
Copy Editor: *Laurel Sparrow*
Production Coordinator: *Nicla Dattolico*
Composition: *Karen Wolfe/ArtPlus Limited*
Interior Design: *Dave Murphy/ArtPlus Limited*
Cover Design: *Dave Murphy/ArtPlus Limited*
Cover Image: © *Andrew Judd/Masterfile*
Printer: *Transcontinental Printing Group*
Printed and bound in Canada

National Library of Canada Cataloguing in Publication Data

Larson, Kermit D.

Fundamental accounting principles

10th Canadian ed.

Includes index.
Contents: v. 1. Chapters 1-11 – v. 2. Chapters 12-20 –v. 3. Chapters 21-28.
ISBN 0-07-088984-8 (v. 1).—ISBN 0-07-088987-2 (v. 2).—
ISBN 0-07-088990-2 (v. 3)

1. Accounting. 2. Accounting—Problems, exercises, etc. I. Jensen, Tilly II. Carroll, Ray F. III. Title.

HF5635.L3268 2001 657 C2001-900564-4

Contents in Brief

Contents

What we're all about . . .

P

Welcome to the Tenth Canadian Edition of *Fundamental Accounting Principles*! We are Ray Carroll and Tilly Jensen, the new author team for the book, and we're really excited about sharing with you the details of the changes that make this text an invaluable learning tool and the best of its kind on the market ... the best because of the changes that were made and the source of those changes.

The first major change in the Tenth Edition was in the role of the authors. We became facilitators, incorporating into the Tenth Edition a wealth of suggestions made by an unprecedented number of instructors. To accumulate those data, our first priority was to listen and document the concerns and needs raised by financial accounting principles instructors from post-secondary institutions across Canada. Why pay attention to instructors? With student contact on a daily basis, instructors like us are in the best position to know exactly what students need and want, and what instructors require in terms of a textbook and support materials, to create the best possible learning environment.

After six stimulating focus group discussions held in major centres throughout Canada and attended by more than sixty instructors, three recurring themes became apparent:

1. *Emphasize the basics of accounting.* Instructors said that quality topic coverage means clear, concise explanations limited to the scope of a financial accounting principles course.
2. *Eliminate unnecessary features and marginal notations that distract the reader.* The optimum textbook was described as one that kept these to a minimum to help the reader maintain focus.

104 Part 1 Financial Reporting and the Accounting Cycle

For each journal entry, the usual process is to post debit(s) and then credit(s). The steps in posting are:

1. Identify the ledger account that was debited in the journal entry.
2. Enter the date of the journal entry in this ledger account.
3. Enter the source of the debit in the PR column, both the journal and page. The letter *G* shows it came from the General Journal.[6]
4. Enter the amount debited from the journal entry into the Debit column of the ledger account.
5. Compute and enter the account's new balance in the Balance column.
6. Enter the ledger account number in the PR column of the journal entry.

Repeat the six steps for credit amounts and Credit columns. Notice that posting does not create new information; posting simply transfers (or copies) information from the General Journal to the appropriate account in the ledger.

Step Six in the posting process for both debit and credit amounts of an entry inserts the account number in the journal's PR column. This creates a cross-reference between the ledger and the journal entry for tracing an amount from one record to another. It also readily shows the stage of completion in the posting process. This permits one to start and stop the posting process easily without losing one's place.

Posting in Computerized Systems

Computerized systems require no added effort to post journal entries to the ledger. These systems automatically transfer debit and credit entries from the journal to the ledger database. Journal entries are posted directly to ledger accounts. Many systems have programs that test the reasonableness of a journal entry and the account balance when recorded. For example, RecordLink's payroll program might alert a preparer to hourly wage rates that are greater than $100.

Answers—p. 110

11. When Maria Sanchez set up RecordLink, she invested $15,000 cash and equipment with a market value of $23,000. RecordLink also took responsibility for an $18,000 note payable issued to finance the purchase of equipment. Prepare the journal entry to record Sanchez's investment.
12. Explain what a compound journal entry is.
13. Why are posting reference numbers entered in the journal when entries are posted to accounts?

Trial Balance

LO9 Prepare and explain the use of a trial balance.

We know that double-entry accounting records every transaction with equal debits and credits. We also know that an error exists if the sum of debit entries in the ledger does not equal the sum of credit entries. This also means that the sum of debit account balances must equal the sum of credit account balances.

Step Four of the accounting cycle shown in Exhibit 3.1 requires the preparation of a trial balance to check whether debit and credit account balances are equal. A **trial balance** is a list of accounts and their balances at a point in time. Account balances are reported in the debit or credit column of the trial balance. Exhibit 3.14 shows the trial balance for Finlay Interiors after the fifteen entries described earlier in the chapter are posted to the ledger.

[6] Other journals are identified by their own letters. We discuss other journals later in the book.

Chapter 3 Analyzing and Recording Transactions 105

Another use of the trial balance is as an internal report for preparing financial statements. Preparing statements is easier when we can take account balances from a trial balance instead of searching the ledger. The preparation of financial statements using a trial balance is illustrated in the demonstration problem at the end of the chapter. We expand on this process in Chapter 4.

Exhibit 3.14

Trial Balance

FINLAY INTERIORS
Trial Balance
January 31, 2001

	Debit	Credit
Cash	$ 8,070	
Accounts receivable	-0-	
Prepaid insurance	2,400	
Supplies	3,600	
Furniture	26,000	
Accounts payable		$ 200
Unearned consulting revenue		3,000
Notes payable		6,000
Carol Finlay, capital		30,000
Carol Finlay, withdrawals	600	
Consulting revenue		3,800
Rental revenue		300
Rent expense	1,000	
Salaries expense	1,400	
Utilities expense	230	
Totals	$43,300	$43,300

Preparing a Trial Balance

Preparing a trial balance involves five steps:

1. Identify each account balance from the ledger.
2. List each account and its balance (in the same order as the Chart of Accounts). Debit balances are entered in the Debit column and credit balances in the Credit column.[7]
3. Compute the total of debit balances.
4. Compute the total of credit balances.
5. Verify that total debit balances equal total credit balances.

Notice that the total debit balance equals the total credit balance for the trial balance in Exhibit 3.14. If these two totals were not equal, we would know that one or more errors exist. Equality of these two totals does ***not*** guarantee the absence of errors.

Using a Trial Balance

We know that one or more errors exist when a trial balance does not *balance* (when its columns are not equal). When one or more errors exist, they often arise from one of the following steps in the accounting process:

[7] If an account has a zero balance, it can be listed in the trial balance with a zero in the column for its normal balance.

3. *Overhaul the problem material.* Develop single-topic problems, ensuring a balance and progression from a confidence-building level to more of a challenge. Instructors noted that accounting textbooks, including the Ninth Canadian Edition, have not fully recognized instructors' needs in the classroom. What's needed are single-topic questions at a level that will help build students' confidence (Quick Study) and move them gradually to the next level of learning (Exercises and then Problems).

Quick Study

QS 3-1
Identifying source documents

LO3

Select the items from the following list that are likely to serve as source documents:

- **a.** Income statement.
- **b.** Trial balance.
- **c.** Telephone bill.
- **d.** Invoice from supplier.
- **e.** Owner's withdrawals account.
- **f.** Balance sheet.
- **g.** Bank statement.
- **h.** Sales invoice.

Exercises

Exercise 3-1
Increases, decreases, and normal balances of accounts

LO4, 6

Complete the following table by: 1. Identifying the type of account listed on each line. 2. Entering *debit* or *credit* in the blank spaces to identify the kind of entry that would increase or decrease the account balance. 3. Identifying the normal balance of the account.

	Account	Type of Account	Increase	Decrease	Normal Balance
a.	Land				
b.	Harold Cooper, Capital				
c.	Accounts Receivable				
d.	Harold Cooper, Withdrawals				
e.	Cash				
f.	Equipment				
g.	Unearned Revenue				
h.	Accounts Payable				
i.	Postage Expense				
j.	Prepaid Insurance				
k.	Wages Expense				
l.	Fees Earned				

Problems

Problem 3-1A
Recording transactions in T-accounts

LO[7]

Check figure:
Cash balance = $18,600

Following are business transactions completed by Kevin Smith during the month of November 2001:

a. Kevin Smith invested $80,000 cash and office equipment with a $30,000 fair value in a new sole proprietorship named Apex Consulting.
b. Purchased land and a small office building. The land was worth $30,000, and the building was worth $170,000. The purchase price was paid with $40,000 cash and a long-term note payable for $160,000.
c. Purchased $2,400 of office supplies on credit.
d. Kevin Smith transferred title of his personal automobile to the business. The automobile had a value of $18,000 and was to be used exclusively in the business.
e. Purchased $6,000 of additional office equipment on credit.
f. Paid $1,500 salary to an assistant.
g. Provided services to a client and collected $6,000 cash.
h. Paid $800 for the month's utilities.
i. Paid account payable created in transaction (c).
j. Purchased $20,000 of new office equipment by paying $18,600 cash and trading in old equipment with a recorded cost of $1,400.
k. Completed $5,200 of services for a client. This amount is to be paid within 30 days.
l. Paid $1,500 salary to an assistant.
m. Received $3,800 payment on the receivable created in transaction (k).
n. Kevin Smith withdrew $6,400 cash from the business for personal use.

Required

1. Open the following T-accounts: Cash; Accounts Receivable; Office Supplies; Automobiles; Office Equipment; Building; Land; Accounts Payable; Long-Term Notes Payable; Kevin Smith, Capital; Kevin Smith, Withdrawals; Fees Earned; Salaries Expense; and Utilities Expense.
2. Record the effects of the listed transactions by entering debits and credits directly in the T-accounts. Use the transaction letters to identify each debit and credit entry.

This first phase of the research and development process provided the direction for the next part of the project: a two-stage review involving instructors from across the country, both users and non-users of the Ninth Edition. Stage-One reviewers critiqued the Ninth Canadian Edition, responding to directed questionnaires derived from the three-point theme described above. We took those reviews and completed a line-by-line analysis that provided the momentum for change in the first manuscript. Stage-Two reviewers then independently reviewed the first manuscript chapters and their suggestions were incorporated into the second manuscript. Some 200 reviews were completed. Burrston House (an independent auditor specializing in textbook revisions) then evaluated the final manuscript to ensure that Stage-Two reviewer comments had been incorporated. For some chapters, this part of the process meant that a third manuscript was needed.

It's been time consuming, but the result is the first truly Canadian financial accounting principles textbook. Because of the unprecedented research and development process described, the Tenth Edition is an instructor-driven textbook that has incorporated a wealth of instructors' knowledge and understanding about both accounting and the teaching of accounting. We've done what you asked!

What the reviewers said ...

A common concern with the Ninth Edition was summarized by one reviewer as follows:

> *"I am happy to see that the authors are removing some of the material from the book. The problem with a long-established text is that the authors want to improve on their product, and the tendency is to keep adding and adding and adding material. Unfortunately, there is constant pressure from our administration to reduce classroom hours, which means we can cover less not more material."*

Reviewers told us what to remove. For example, the majority of reviewers wanted all discussion of cash flows to be deleted from Volume I and restricted to Chapter 20 in Volume II. We took this direction, and it was validated by Stage-Two reviewers as follows:

> *"I was pleased that the major discussion of cash flows has been left to a later chapter."*

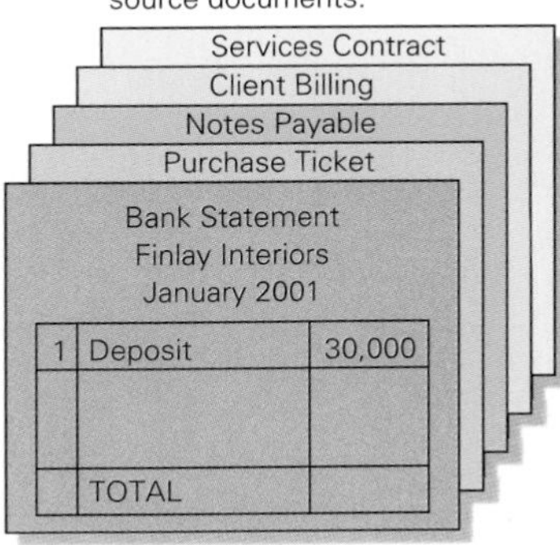

We included a brief introduction and exhibit of the accounting cycle in Chapter 3 based on a reviewer suggestion. The response to that and other Chapter 3 changes?

> *"Overall, I think this is a very good presentation of the material—probably the best of any text I have used."*

We made it a priority to support the more concise wording with new and improved exhibits. Stage-Two reviewers said of the changes made in the first draft:

> *"I like the condensation of information ..."*
>
> *"I am* **very** *pleased to see that most of the changes from the Ninth Edition involve leaving out or condensing wordy and overly detailed explanations and background information."*
>
> *"Bad debts topics have been extensively revised to simplify the topics.... Exhibit 10.6 (new) certainly shows the reader very clearly the topics involved.... This chapter in my current text is not bad but certainly not as good as this chapter."*

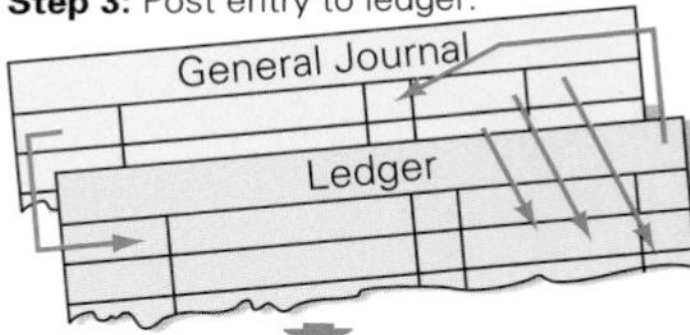

The exhibits referred to by these reviewers were suggested by Stage-One reviewers.

The call for more problems was addressed by creating material to satisfy specific reviewer requests:

> *"GIVE the students the unadjusted trial balance, so they will not be searching for it throughout written text."*
>
> *"More full work sheet problems with fewer and/or simpler adjustments are needed."*
>
> *"Would like to see more problem questions deal with the inventory shrinkage as an adjusting entry."*
>
> *"We need a few more exercises that involve ALL journals; most exercises only involve two journals at a time."*
>
> *"We need more bank reconciliation questions that use source documents."*

When asked to grade the problem material for the Tenth Edition in comparison to their current text, non-users said:

> *"The questions (new) are excellent. Tenth Edition: A; Current Text: B."*
>
> *"Definitely an A. Adding the new material has already improved what was a pretty good chapter to begin with. Current Text: B."*
>
> *"The problem/exercise material has been improved with the inclusion of several new. . . . Tenth Edition: A; Current Text: C."*

The end-of-chapter items were increased in number but also in quality. The Tenth Edition has achieved a balance between confidence building and more complex items as requested by reviewers. The revised distribution of the end-of-chapter material is shown below:

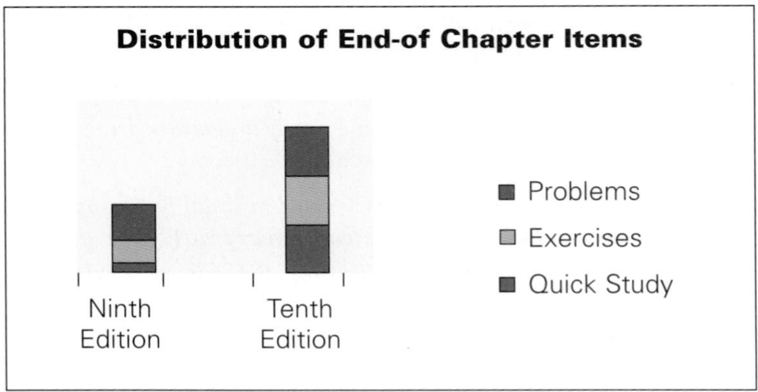

It is important to know that not all of the changes requested by reviewers were incorporated, because at times views conflicted. For example, the periodic versus perpetual issue was one where the majority of reviewers wanted perpetual in the chapter with the discussion of periodic kept to an appendix. After verifying that perpetual is the trend in Canadian business, we sided with the majority. We were able to satisfy the request for enhanced periodic problem material.

> *"The number of additional periodic inventory problems and exercises that the author has included in the manuscript has improved this section immensely."*

An exception to the standard of siding with the majority was the issue regarding ratios. Overwhelmingly, reviewers wanted all ratios moved out of individual chapters into Chapter 19 of Volume II. The first manuscript accommodated that request. But a Stage Two reviewer pointed out that for those courses where only Volume I is used, students would have no exposure to ratio analysis. As a result, we added select ratios back to Volume I in the form of appendices.

In summary, we listened!

What we did ... the details

For each chapter, the primary focus (in addition to the individual comments and suggestions of reviewers) was to:

1. *Go back to basics,*
2. *Eliminate distractions,* and
3. *Improve end-of-chapter material.*

This section of the preface includes a detailed list of the changes by chapter.

For all chapters, we did the following:

- Moved the "Beyond The Numbers" section at the end of each chapter to the Online Learning Centre to make room for end-of-chapter items
- Significantly reduced the "Did You Know?" and "Judgement Call" features
- Made the wording more concise
- Sequenced the end-of-chapter material in order of learning objective
- Relabelled end-of-chapter problems and alternate problems as "A" and "B" respectively
- Prefixed the end-of-chapter items relating to an appendix with an asterisk "*" in place of the superscripted "A"
- Revised T-account illustrations to resemble T-accounts
- Removed marginal accounting equations
- Moved detailed discussion of cash flows to Chapter 19
- Matched the format of solutions to the presentation of related material in the chapters.

For each chapter specifically, we did the following:

Chapter 1

- Included new chapter opening article describing the importance of accounting
- Added exhibits to reinforce opening article
- Moved accounting equation to Chapter 2
- Moved discussion of development of accounting principles and standards to Appendix 2A
- Added new appendix dealing with technology and accounting
- Included business with a net loss as opposed to net income to enhance reality
- Added 11 new end-of-chapter items
- Moved return on investment ratio to Chapter 20

Chapter 2

- Moved return on equity ratio to Chapter 20
- Enhanced discussion of accounting equation
- Consolidated discussion of development of accounting standards, including auditing and international standards, in Appendix 2A
- Added 17 new and modified end-of-chapter items

Chapter 3

- Introduced concept of accounting cycle in Chapter 3 along with exhibit, as opposed to it being buried in Chapter 5
- Added specific problems; two include beginning balances and two deal with correcting entries
- Increased emphasis on balance column ledger versus T-accounts in the end-of-chapter material
- Moved debt ratio to Chapter 20
- Improved presentation of debit–credit rules
- Eliminated Exhibit 3.13 of Ninth Edition
- Included alternative approach to correcting incorrect journal entries
- Added 26 new and modified end-of-chapter items

Chapter 4

- Provided new chapter opener to emphasize need for accurate financial information
- Improved discussion of amortization through clear exhibits
- Moved profit margin to Chapter 7
- Changed the end-of-chapter demonstration problem to be a continuation of the Chapter 3 problem
- Emphasized and reinforced accounting cycle through exhibit new to Chapter 4
- Provided 30 new end-of-chapter items

Chapter 5

- Added new mid-chapter demonstration problem demonstrating closing entries when there is a loss
- Reorganized chapter topics: work sheets are first, followed by closing entries, and finally classified balance sheet
- Rearranged work sheet acetates to conform with "turning pages in a book"
- Adjusted layout of exhibits regarding closing entries to improve clarity (side-by-side presentation)
- Moved current ratio to Appendix 5A
- Corrected errors in demonstration problem at end of chapter
- Reviewed accounting cycle rather than first introducing it in this chapter, after the fact
- Added 26 new end-of-chapter items

Chapter 6

- Reorganized chapter topics to match the accounting cycle (journal entries, adjustments, work sheet, income statement, closing entries)
- Included gross margin ratio in Appendix 6B
- Moved acid test ratio to Appendix 9A
- Added 18 new end-of-chapter items

Chapter 7

- Provided new chapter opener to emphasize importance and validity of perpetual inventory systems
- Moved inventory turnover and days' sales in inventory ratios to Appendix 7A
- Improved exhibits demonstrating inventory costing methods
- Arranged *inventory items and costs* to precede *assigning costs to inventory*
- Reduced discussion of lower of cost and market
- Moved discussion of inventory subsidiary ledgers to Chapter 8
- Deleted alternate method of calculating cost flow methods
- Arranged gross profit method of estimating inventory to precede retail method

- Introduced gross profit/margin ratio within the body of the chapter to correspond with the use of the term in estimating inventory using the gross profit method of estimating inventory; although the gross profit ratio is in Appendix 6B, the topic needs to be introduced in the contents of the chapter for those not using Appendix 6B
- Linked full disclosure principle to Appendix I at the end of the text
- Provided nine new end-of-chapter items and modified six others

Chapter 8

- Added brief discussion of inventory subsidiary ledgers that allows students to apply their understanding of Chapter 7 material
- Moved ratios to Chapter 20
- Moved discussion of GST/PST to end of the chapter
- Provided new discussion on accounting information systems and components of accounting systems and impact of new technologies
- Changed wording of "system principles" to "system standards" to eliminate confusion with "Generally Accepted Accounting Principles"
- Provided 15 new end-of-chapter items, including addition of inventory subsidiary ledgers and GST/PST

Chapter 9

- Provided new chapter opener to emphasize importance of internal controls over cash
- Significantly reduced discussion of cash equivalents
- Eliminated discussion of net purchase method
- Moved days' sales uncollected ratio to Appendix 10B
- Included acid-test ratio as Appendix 9B
- Improved petty cash and made it more concise
- Reduced discussion on internal control
- Incorporated real source documents to improve illustration of bank reconciliation process
- Improved mid-chapter demonstration problem
- Added real source documents to end-of-chapter demonstration problem for the preparation of a bank reconciliation
- Moved voucher system to appendix
- Eliminated use of "miscellaneous expense"
- Randomly ordered cheque numbering on bank statements
- Added 11 new end-of-chapter items

Chapter 10

- Moved converting receivables to cash before maturity to appendix
- Moved temporary investments to Chapter 18
- Moved accounts receivable turnover ratio and days' sales uncollected to appendix
- Rewrote section on bad debts; condensed, simplified and supported it by new illustrations
- Reordered direct write-off method to appear after allowance method of estimating bad debts
- Rewrote notes receivable section; condensed, simplified and supported it by examples
- Devised new exhibit to illustrate methods for writing off bad debts
- Eliminated installment accounts receivable section
- Provided new mid-chapter demonstration problem
- Supplied new end-of-chapter demonstration problem
- Added 27 new end-of-chapter items

Chapter 11

- Provided new chapter opener
- Supplied new mid-chapter demonstration problem
- Significantly reduced LO 1
- Included summary tables for EI and CPP rates
- Updated exhibits
- Included excerpts from tables in exhibits
- Included excerpts from tables at the end of the chapter for use with Quick Study and Exercises
- Amended LO 4 to include journal entry showing payment of payroll deductions
- Added 12 new end-of-chapter items and modified seven others

Chapter 12

- Supplied new chapter opener to provide example of capital intensive company
- Moved total asset turnover ratio to Chapter 20
- Rewrote and significantly reduced section on betterments, revenue and capital expenditures; it is now part of LO 2
- Consolidated three learning objectives into one (former LO 3, 4, 5)
- Split learning objective regarding partial period amortization and revised amortization into separate learning objectives

- Significantly condensed and moved to appendix complexities regarding exchanges
- Included new exhibits to clarify explanations
- Provided new mid-chapter demonstration problem
- Supplied new end-of-chapter demonstration problem
- Added 41 new end-of-chapter items and modified 16 others

Chapter 13

- Updated reference to Revenue Canada as CCRA in chapter opener
- Simplified definition of liabilities
- Clarified definition of current liabilities; it now includes reference to balance sheet date and specifies that payment is made using current assets
- Included order of liabilities in presentation
- Included real life examples of liabilities section
- Footnoted and explained key ratios affected by current versus long-term split of liabilities
- Clarified distinction between principal portion of liabilities and interest
- Provided numerical example and accompanying exhibits to clarify distinction between current and long-term portions of debt
- Expanded but simplified discussion of GST/PST and included more examples regarding entries
- Included more entries to demonstrate short-term notes payable
- Provided new exhibit to illustrate matching of interest expense across periods
- Devised new exhibit regarding contingent liability disclosure
- Moved times interest earned ratio to Chapter 20
- Eliminated PV section of chapter
- Moved discounting notes payable to appendix
- Moved lease liabilities to Chapter 17
- Minimized discussion regarding deferred income taxes
- Provided new mid-chapter demonstration problem, including amortization schedule
- Added 16 new end-of-chapter items and modified eight others

Chapter 14

- Enhanced exhibits regarding relationship between income allocation and closing of income summary
- Provided new illustration regarding liquidations
- Supplied new illustration showing fractional basis of allocating income
- Provided new demonstration of income allocation when there is a net loss
- Improved mid-chapter and end-of-chapter demonstration problems
- Added 13 new end-of-chapter items and modified eight others

Chapter 15

- Added new chapter opener regarding private corporations to increase discussion on topic
- Transferred cash dividends from Chapter 16 to Chapter 15
- Introduced Statement of Retained Earnings in Chapter 15 (was previously only in Chapter 16)
- Wrote new section on corporate financial statements beginning with income statement, then statement of retained earnings and finally the balance sheet, highlighting the differences/similarities for incorporated and unincorporated organizations
- Significantly reduced theory regarding characteristics, management, and organization of a corporation
- Included more real-life corporations as examples
- Illustrated shareholders' equity terminology in easy-to-follow exhibits
- Summarized shareholders' rights in a table
- Summarized advantages/disadvantages of corporations in a table
- Devised illustration of how shareholders' equity appears in the context of a balance sheet
- Deleted discussion of share subscriptions
- Included alternative approach to recording cash dividends (debit directly to retained earnings)
- Illustrated dividend preference for preferred shares in context of shareholders' equity section
- Condensed discussion of preferred share features
- Introduced closing entries for a corporation
- Moved par value to appendix
- Changed end-of-chapter problem to require the preparation of statement of retained earnings in addition to former requirements
- Moved book value per share calculation to Chapter 20
- Added 17 new end-of-chapter items and modified six others

Chapter 16

- Provided new chapter opener to demonstrate the change share capital can create for a corporation
- Made side-by-side illustrations of stock dividends and stock splits
- Deleted complex capital structure discussion
- Deleted statement of changes in shareholders' equity
- Moved ratios to Chapter 20 (except earnings per share)
- Simplified Exhibit 16.2 (comprehensive income statement) along with discussion to extent possible
- Inserted many "real" company examples to better demonstrate relevance of concepts and increase reader interest and awareness
- Included alternative for recording stock dividends (debit retained earnings directly)
- Moved treasury shares to appendix
- Explained why no gain is recorded regarding retirement of shares
- Provided new mid-chapter demonstration problem
- Improved exhibits regarding weighted average shares outstanding calculation
- Provided new exhibit illustrating how earnings per share presentation is determined
- Incorporated change in treatment of accounting changes and included journal entry; simplified example
- Added 18 new end-of-chapter items and modified seven others

Chapter 17

- Reorganized topics

Chapter 18

- Moved temporary investments from Chapter 10 to Chapter 18 based on reviewer request
- Added 17 new end-of-chapter items and modified 12 others

Chapter 19

- New chapter opener based on reviewer request

Chapter 20

- Deleted section on analysis reporting
- Moved book value per share calculation from Chapter 15 to Chapter 20
- Moved discussion of ratios from Chapter 16 to Chapter 20
- Moved all discussion of cash flow to this chapter based on reviewer feedback
- Added 26 new end-of-chapter items and modified 16 others

FAP features!

The strong pedagogy of *Fundamental Accounting Principles* (FAP) continues to address the ever-changing interests and needs in accounting education. A quick summary of the pedagogical areas follows.

Organization

Organization is crucial to effective learning, and FAP helps readers to organize and link accounting concepts, procedures, and analyses. A Chapter Preview introduces the importance and relevance of the material, and also links these materials to the opening article to motivate the reader. Here are additional materials to enhance learning effectiveness. From Chapter Previews and Learning Objectives to Flashbacks and the new cross-referencing feature, FAP remains the leader in successfully motivating students and guiding them through the accounting cycle in the business world.

Answers—p. 110

7. Does debit always mean increase and credit always mean decrease?
8. What kinds of transactions increase owner's equity? What kinds decrease owner's equity?
9. Why are most accounting systems called *double-entry*?
10. Double-entry accounting requires that:
    a. All transactions that create debits to asset accounts must create credits to liability or owner's equity accounts.
    b. A transaction that requires a debit to a liability account also requires a credit to an asset account.
    c. Every transaction must be recorded with total debits equal to total credits.

A series of Flashbacks in the chapter reinforce the immediately preceding materials. Flashbacks allow the reader to stop momentarily and reflect on the topics described. They give immediate feedback on the reader's comprehension before going on to new topics. Answers are provided.

Chapter Preview

We explained in Chapter 2 how the accounting equation P.45 helps us understand and analyze transactions and events. Analyzing financial transactions is the first step in the *accounting cycle*. Chapters 3 through 5 continue to explain and demonstrate each of the steps in the accounting cycle. All accounting systems use steps similar to those described here. These procedures are important because they lead to financial statements P.36. Maria Sanchez of RecordLink uses a Web-based system, but the steps in the accounting cycle are essentially identical for manual systems.

New to the Tenth Canadian Edition, the cross-referencing feature directs students to the page where the word or phrase is first explained.

Infographics and artwork aid in visual learning of key accounting and business topics. Photos, colour, highlighting and authentic documents all help with visual learning.

Motivation

Motivation drives learning. From the chapter's opening article and its focus on young entrepreneurs to the Judgement Call and demonstration problems, FAP motivates students. It brings accounting and business to life and demonstrates that this material can make a difference in the student's world.

Demonstration Problem

This demonstration problem is based on the same facts as the demonstration problem at the end of Chapter 2 except for two additional items: (b) August 1 and (j) August 18. The following events occurred during the first month of Barbara Schmidt's new haircutting business called The Cutlery:

a. On August 1, Schmidt put $3,000 cash into a chequing account in the name of The Cutlery. She also invested $15,000 of equipment that she already owned.

b. On August 1, Barbara paid $600 for six months of insurance effective immediately.

c. On August 2, she paid $600 cash for furniture for the shop.

d. On August 3, she paid $500 cash to rent space in a strip mall for August.

A Demonstration Problem appears at the end of the chapter. It illustrates important topics and shows how to apply concepts in preparing, analyzing and using information. A problem-solving strategy helps to guide the student. Most chapters also have a Mid-chapter Demonstration Problem with solution.

Answer—p. 109

Cashier

You are a cashier at a retail convenience store. When you were hired, the assistant manager explained the policy of immediately entering each sale into the cash register. Recently, lunch hour traffic has increased dramatically and the assistant manager asks you to take customers' cash and make change without recording sales in the cash register to avoid delays. The assistant manager says she will add up cash and enter sales equal to the cash amount after lunch. She says that in this way the register will always be accurate when the manager arrives at three o'clock. What do you do?

The Judgement Call feature requires students to make accounting and business decisions. It uses role-playing to show the interaction of judgement, the need for business awareness and the impact of decisions. Guidance answers are provided.

Technology

Technology continues to change business and accounting, creating new and exciting accounting opportunities. FAP is the leader in applying and showing technology in accounting. From the Excel® and Simply Accounting® icons and Web-based assignments to the Student Interactive eSource, FAP pushes the accounting frontier. The availability of content cartridges for course management platforms such as WebCT, Blackboard and PageOut make FAP accessible to *your* needs. As well, FAP is available in e-Book format.

To illustrate the growing importance of computers in accounting, select problems in the text have been designated for manual and computer study. In-text icons identify problems that can be worked out manually, or by using either Excel® or Simply Accounting® programs.

Free to adopters, PageOut helps you create your own custom, online course for your students.

FAP content is available in two of the most popular delivery platforms, WebCT and Blackboard. These platforms provide instructors with more user-friendly, flexible teaching tools.

Real world

Accounting is important to the information age. The features and assignments that highlight companies like WestJet and ClubLink show accounting in a modern, global context. FAP challenges students to apply learned knowledge in practical and diverse ways with analytical problems, research requirements and communication exercises. Other features — like Did You Know? — show that accounting is relevant to everyone.

Questions

1. Describe the fundamental steps in the accounting process.
2. What is the difference between a note receivable and an account receivable?
3. If assets are valuable resources and asset accounts have debit balances, why do expense accounts have debit balances?
4. Why does the bookkeeper prepare a trial balance?
5. Should a transaction be recorded first in a journal or the ledger? Why?
6. Are debits or credits listed first in general journal entries? Are the debits or the credits indented?
9. Review the WestJet balance sheet for fiscal year-end December 31, 1999 in Appendix I. Identify three accounts on the balance sheet that would carry debit balances and three accounts on the balance sheet that would carry credit balances.
10. Review the ClubLink balance sheet for fiscal year-end December 31, 1999 in Appendix I. Identify four different asset accounts that include the word "receivable" in the account title.

NHL Accounting

The Vancouver Canucks report the following major revenue and expense accounts:

Revenues:	**Expenses:**
Game ticket sales	Hockey operations
Radio and television	Merchandise and programs
Merchandise and programs	Administrative and marketing
Advertising and promotions	

SOURCE: Orca Bay Hockey Holdings' Financial Statements.

Social responsibility is important in the real world. Through the Did You Know? feature, FAP describes accounting's role in social responsibility by both reporting and assessing its impact.

Flexibility

FAP is the undisputed leader in offering a strong pedagogical support package. New this year is the Student Interactive eSource CD. Other support packages include Study Guide, Working Papers, Instructor's Manual, Test Bank, Computerized Test Bank and much, much more!

For the Instructor

Solutions Manual

To ensure complete accuracy, the Solutions Manuals have been technically checked at three different stages of development. The manuals contain solutions for the questions, exercises and problems.

Instructor's Resource Manual

Prepared by Jeanine Wall, Red River Community College, this manual contains materials for managing an active learning environment. Each chapter provides a Lecture Outline, a chart linking Learning Objectives to end-of-chapter material and transparency masters. For instructors' convenience, student copies of these visuals are provided in the Study Guide. If students do not acquire the Study Guide, adopters are permitted to duplicate these visuals for distribution.

Teaching Acetates

Teaching acetates enhance any instructor's teaching style. With 15+ acetates per chapter, Michael Hockenstein, Vanier College, created simple, step-by-step acetates to help instructors teach the course.

Test Bank

The Test Bank has been updated by Stephani Ibach, NAIT, to reflect the changes of the text. Approximately 20% of the questions are new in the Tenth Edition and have been sprinkled throughout the chapters. Volumes I and II are available in hard copy and a computerized version is available for the Test Bank's complete three volumes. Grouped according to Learning Objectives, the Test Bank contains a wide variety of questions—including true/false, multiple choice, matching, short essay, quantitative problems, and completion problems of varying levels of difficulty.

PowerPoint® Presentation Slides

Improved PowerPoint Presentation slides have been developed by Carol Bowman, Sheridan College, for the Tenth Edition to better illustrate chapter concepts. This package is available as a downloadable from the Online Learning Centre.

Online Learning Centre

This is an online resource that combines the best content with the flexibility and power of the Internet. For the instructor, the Online Learning Centre (OLC) offers:

- PowerPoint Presentation slides
- Downloadable supplements
- Solutions to OLC Internet exercises
- PageOut
- Additional problem material, including "Beyond the Numbers" exercises and problems

WebCT/Blackboard

For faculty requiring online content, FAP content is available in two of the most popular delivery platforms, WebCT and Blackboard. These platforms are designed for instructors who want complete control over course content and how it is presented to students. They provide instructors with more user-friendly and highly flexible teaching tools that enhance interaction between students and faculty.

PageOut

PageOut is a McGraw-Hill online tool that enables instructors to create and post class-specific Web pages simply and easily. No knowledge of HTML is required.

For the Student

Working Papers

Updated for the Tenth Edition, these volumes match end-of-chapter assignment material. They include papers that can be used to solve all of the Quick Studies, Exercises, Serial Problems and Comprehensive Problems. Each chapter contains one set of papers that can be used for either the problems or the alternate problems.

Study Guide

An essential study aid for students, the Study Guide volumes review the learning objectives and the summaries, outline the chapter, and provide a variety of practice problems and solutions. Prepared by Suzanne Coombs, Kwantlen University College.

Online Learning Centre

Organized by chapter, the Online Learning Centre offers the students the following features to enhance learning and understanding of fundamental accounting:

- Online quizzes
- Interactive true/false
- Interactive multiple choice
- Matching
- Fill-in-the-blanks
- Internet exercises
- Weblinks to companies mentioned in text
- PowerPoint Presentation slides
- Learning objectives
- Chapter outline
- Key terms

What about quality control?

The solid foundation of the Larson textbook is still a large part of the Tenth Edition, but with all of the changes made, we needed to be sure that the material was error free. To that end, the text went through technical checks at three different stages of development. We are confident that the Tenth Edition is of a standard that will satisfy quality-conscious users.

We couldn't have done it by ourselves...

A project as large as this requires an extensive team of dedicated individuals. We would like to convey special thanks to Richard Wright (Fanshawe College), Stephanie Ibach (Northern Alberta Institute of Technology), Lou Richards and Pauline Lutes (New Brunswick Community College Moncton), who spent countless hours performing technical and accuracy checks of the problem material and the solutions.

An unprecedented reviewing effort guided the Tenth Edition. The reviewers were pivotal to the entire process and we are grateful for their invaluable contributions. We know that many of them will recognize their suggestions in the form of a new exhibit, an innovative end-of-chapter problem or even in the absence of a topic. To acknowledge their involvement, we have listed all of the reviewers below. Thank you!

Robert Anderson	*University College of the Fraser Valley*
Cecile Ashman	*Algonquin College*
Cam Beck	*Holland College*
Maria Belanger	*Algonquin College*
Steve Blanchard	*NAIT*
Frank Alexander Boultbee	*Seneca College*
Carole Bowman	*Sheridan College*
Raymond Brookes	*Douglas College*
Rick Brown	*Niagara College*
Gillian Bubb	*University College of the Fraser Valley*
Charles Burke	*Lethbridge Community College*
Walt Burton	*Okanagan College*
Helen Carr	*Confederation College*
Michelle Causton	*Canadore College*
Scott Cawfield	*Centennial College*
Liang Chen	*Humber College*
Ray Chung	*Vancouver Community College*
Gerald Clayton	*New Brunswick Community College*
Roger Collins	*University College of Cariboo*
Louise Connors	*Nova Scotia Community College*
Suzanne Coombs	*Kwantlen College*
Sonny Costanzo	*Confederation College*
John Currie	*Humber College*
John Daye	*New Brunswick Community College*
Randy Dickson	*Red Deer College*
Carolyn Doni	*Cambrian College*
Dave Eliason	*SAIT*
Karen Erb	*New Brunswick Community College*
Colleen Evans	*Red River College*
Elizabeth Evans	*Nova Scotia Community College*
David Fleming	*George Brown College*
Reiner Frisch	*Georgian College*
Sam Garofalo	*Confederation College*
John Glendinning	*Centennial College*
Donna Grace	*Sheridan College*
Connie Hahn	*SAIT*
Elaine Hales	*Georgian College*
Ellen Hamer	*Langara College*
Mary Hamm	*BCIT*
Cliff Harrison	*SIAST*
Rob Harvey	*Algonquin College*
Sharon Hatten	*BCIT*
Rubin Hertzman	*Champlain College*
Elizabeth Hicks	*Douglas College*
Michael Hockenstein	*Vanier College*
John Holliday	*NAIT*
Ross Holmes	*Niagara College*
Patricia Hudson	*Humber College*
Alice Jardine	*New Brunswick Community College*
Jeremy Jarvis	*Kwantlen College*
Jo Ann Johnston	*BCIT*
Geraldine Joosse	*Lethbridge Community College*
Barbara Jordan	*Cambrian College*
Sandy Lagevin	*NAIT*
Roger Laliberte	*Champlain College*
Douglas Leatherdale	*Georgian College*
Stan Lee	*Vancouver Community College*
Valorie Leonard	*Laurentian University*
Dieter Loerick	*John Abbott College*
Edward Lowe	*Douglas College*
Pauline Lutes	*New Brunswick Community College*
Darla Lutness	*NAIT*
Dave MacFadyen	*Holland College*
Don MacMillian	*Algonquin College*
Marie Madill-Payne	*George Brown College*
Pat Margeson	*New Brunswick Community College*
Bonnie Martel	*Niagara College*
Steve Martin	*John Abbott College*
Jim McAllister	*New Brunswick Community College*
Scott McKellar	*Nova Scotia Community College*
Allen McQueen	*Grant MacEwan College*
Roger Melanson	*New Brunswick Community College*
David Mills	*Mount Royal College*

Rod Murray	*BCIT*
Jerry Mus	*Assiniboine College*
Hai-Binh Nguyen	*Champlain College*
M. Nicholson	*Okanagan College*
Tariq Nizami	*Champlain College*
Peter Norwood	*Langara College*
John O'Laney	*New Brunswick Community College*
Greg Peters	*Holland College*
Carson Rappell	*Dawson College*
Aziz Razwani	*Capilano College*
Traven Reed	*Canadore College*
Peter Richer	*John Abbott College*
Frank Ridley	*Seneca College*
Doug Ringrose	*Grant MacEwan College*
Jeffrey Rudolph	*Marianapolis College*
Brad Sacho	*Kwantlen College*
Dave Sale	*Kwantlen College*
Pina Salvaggio	*Dawson College*
Mike Sirtonski	*Assiniboine College*
Helen Stavaris	*Dawson College*
Ralph Sweet	*Durham College*
Helen Vallee	*Kwantlen College*
Jeanine Wall	*Red River College*
Judith Watson	*Capilano College*
John Western	*Kwantlen College*
John Wilson	*Capilano College*
Alison Wiseman	*Fanshawe College*
Elaine Womack	*St. Clair College*
Julie Wong	*Dawson College*
Richard Wright	*Fanshawe College*

In summary, instructors from across Canada were the driving force behind the Tenth Canadian Edition. We asked what was needed, we listened and then made changes. We've rolled out the red carpet and now invite you to enjoy the most market-driven financial accounting principles textbook ever published in Canada.

Welcome to the Tenth Edition!

McGraw-Hill Ryerson

Online Learning Centre

McGraw-Hill Ryerson offers you an online resource that combines the best content with the flexibility and power of the Internet. Organized by chapter, the LARSON Online Learning Centre (OLC) offers the following features to enhance your learning and understanding of Accounting:

- Online Quizzes
- Web Links
- Microsoft® PowerPoint® Presentations
- Internet Application Questions

By connecting to the "real world" through the OLC, you will enjoy a dynamic and rich source of current information that will help you get more from your course and improve your chances for success, both in accounting and in the future.

For the Instructor

Downloadable Supplements

All key supplements are available, password-protected for instant access!

PageOut

Create your own course Web page for free, quickly and easily. Your professionally designed Web site links directly to OLC material, allows you to post a class syllabus, offers an online gradebook, and much more! Visit www.pageout.net

Primis Online

Primis Online gives you access to our resources in the best medium for your students: printed textbooks or electronic ebooks. There are over 350,000 pages of content available from which you can create customized learning tools from our online database at www.mhhe.com/primis

Knowledge Gateway

Knowledge Gateway is a Web site–based service and resource for instructors teaching online. It provides instructional design services, and information and technical support for course management systems. It is located at http://mhhe.eduprise.com/

Higher Learning. Forward Thinking.™ 

ning Centre

For the Student

Online Quizzes

Do you understand the material? You'll know after taking an Online Quiz! Try the Multiple Choice and True/False questions for each chapter. They're auto-graded with feedback and the option to send results directly to faculty.

Web Links

This section references various Web sites, including all company Web sites linked from the text.

Microsoft® PowerPoint® Presentations

View and download presentations created for each text. Great for pre-class preparation and post-class review.

Internet Application Questions

Go online to learn how companies use the Internet in their day-to-day activities. Answer questions based on current organization Web sites and strategies.

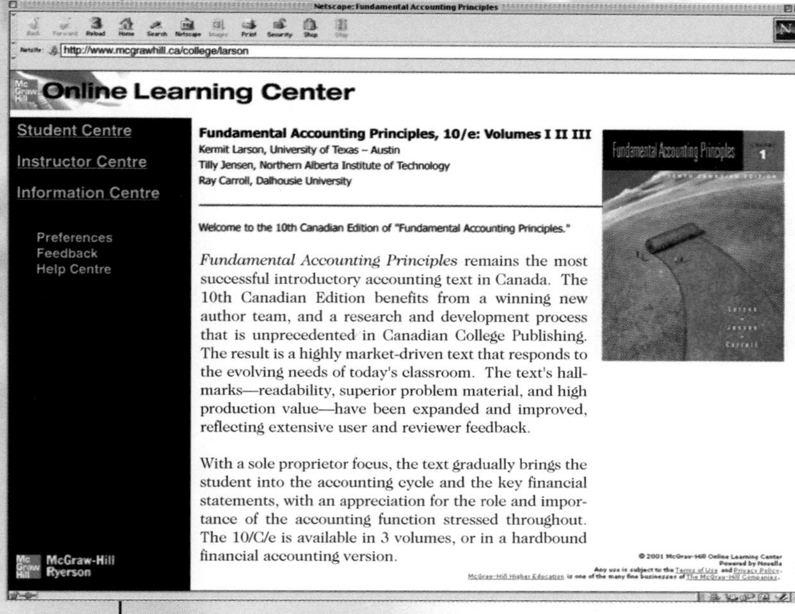

Your Internet companion to the most exciting educational tools on the Web!

The Online Learning Centre can be found at:
www.mcgrawhill.ca/college/larson

CHAPTER 1

Accounting: The Key to Success

Accounting Leads the Way

Wynne Powell is an accounting professional. He is also president and CEO of London Drugs, a business that has millions of dollars in revenues annually and a staff of approximately 6,000. It's a highly stressful position, he admits, but Wynne finds it stimulating. The excitement is in making things happen: taking money and making it grow, providing a return to the owners. "It's like a chess game; somebody makes a move and you carefully develop and adjust your strategy, positioning yourself for the win. It's fun!"

How do you make sure you win in business? According to Wynne, it's pretty basic: you need a thorough understanding of accounting figures; that's what allows a company to fail or flourish. The management team must fully understand how financial information is created; it's only then that they can use it to their advantage.

In Wynne's opinion, businesses begin to fail because of inappropriate or late financial figures. Advances in technology have ensured that accounting information can be available on a

Learning Objectives

LO1 Describe how technology is changing accounting.

LO2 Describe accounting and its goals and uses.

LO3 Describe profit and its two major components.

LO4 Identify forms of organization and their characteristics.

LO5 Identify users and uses of accounting.

LO6 Explain why ethics and social responsibility are crucial to accounting.

LO7 Identify opportunities in accounting and related fields.

real-time basis. Technology has also triggered the evolution of a new breed of accountant whose focus has expanded to every aspect of the business in every corner of the world.

"Accounting knowledge is the key," says Wynne Powell. "It is the *'language of business'* and as such is fundamental to your success in the business world." Accounting leads the way.

Chapter Preview

Accounting is at the heart of business: accounting information pulsates throughout an organization, feeding decision makers with details needed to give them an edge over competitors. Because of new technologies, the increasing speed and quantity of information available makes the task for accountants like Wynne Powell an ever-increasing challenge. Decision makers like Wynne cannot rely on hunches and guesses. Decision makers depend on their knowledge of accounting principles and practices to help identify and take advantage of opportunities discovered from reviewing large volumes of information. Through your studies of this book, you will learn about many of the accounting concepts, procedures and analyses common to both small and large businesses. This knowledge will provide you with the basics necessary to make better business decisions.

In this chapter, we describe accounting in the changing global economy, the forms of organizations, the users and uses of accounting information, the importance of ethics and social responsibility, and opportunities in accounting. This chapter provides a foundation for those students who have little or no understanding of business or the role of accounting in business. Chapter 2 will build on this foundation by focusing on transactions and financial statements.

Technology: Creating Change in Accounting

Describe how technology is changing accounting.

"The world is shrinking" ... "a global economy" ... both expressions are rooted in the advancement of communication and information technologies. Technology allows instant access to services, data, and news, as well as financial and non-financial information to aid business operations. For example, if a marine shop on the west coast requires a special part that is manufactured in Ontario, the order can be placed by phone, fax or e-mail, with the part conceivably being delivered by courier the next working day.

New forms of communication and resultant access to data have created an information superhighway that is redefining business communication. Global computer networks and telecommunications equipment allow access to all types of business information at the press of a button. Knowledge of the system is necessary to take advantage of opportunities available as a result of this information. The appendix to this chapter provides greater detail about aspects of the information superhighway that are relevant to accounting.

Over the past several years, demands on the accounting profession have expanded considerably because of technology. Spreadsheet and accounting software application skills are now essential. The need for accounting professionals to enhance their information technology (IT) knowledge and experience is growing because of new developments such as e-commerce.

Knowing how to utilize the new technologies increases job opportunities.

In the 1990s (1990 to 1999), the seasonally adjusted growth rate for all jobs in Canada was 10.6%. The seasonally adjusted growth rate for jobs in the sector that includes professional and technical services was 57.9% over the same period.
SOURCE: Statistics Canada Cat. No. 71-201-XPB.

This increased employment opportunity is driven by the growing need for individuals with the ability to understand and process information. It is this skill—the understanding and processing of information—which is the core of accounting. This skill will allow you to speak the language of business: accounting.

Show Me the Money!

By meeting the demands of change, accountants have not only been awarded increased job opportunities but they have also realized significant increases in salaries, as illustrated in Exhibit 1.1.

Exhibit 1.1

Growth of Average Annual Salaries for Accountants

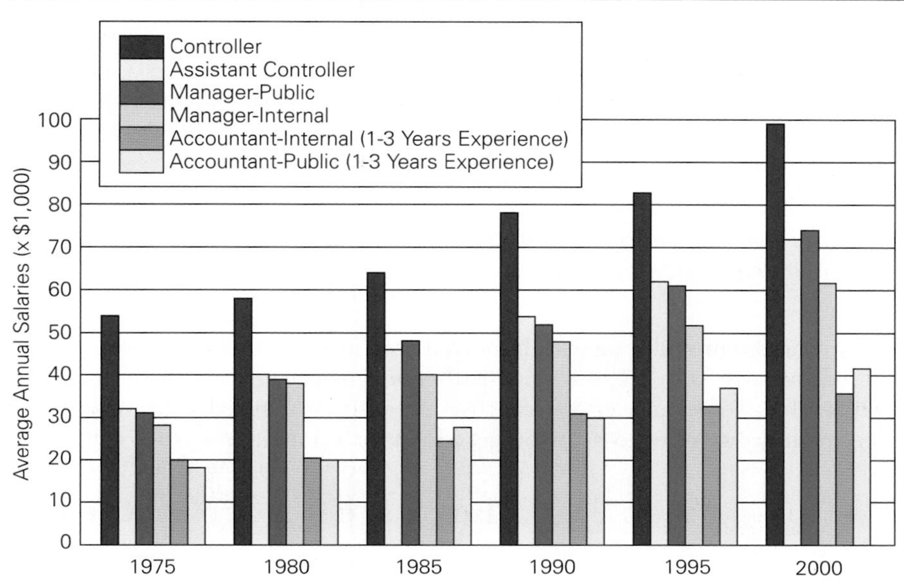

Source: 2000 Robert Half/Accountemps Salary Guide, p. 4.

What is Accounting?

Accounting knowledge is a powerful tool; it is your key to success, according to Wynne Powell. How does accounting knowledge give you power? What exactly is the focus of accounting? This section answers these fundamental questions.

Power of Accounting

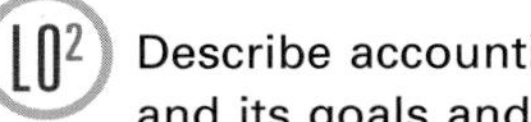

LO2 Describe accounting and its goals and uses.

Accounting is an information system that identifies, measures, records and communicates relevant, reliable, consistent and comparable information about an organization's economic activities. Its objective is to help people make better decisions. It also helps people better assess opportunities, products, investments, and social and community responsibilities. In addition to reporting on the performance of a business, what the business owns, and what it owes, accounting opens our eyes to new and exciting possibilities.

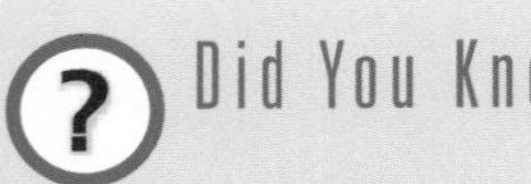

Power of Accounting Information in Small Business

Pete Seerden, owner of ECOF, used to pay thousands of dollars annually in leasing warehouse space to house his cabinet-making business. "Lease payments were eating into my profits big time. I looked at alternatives and crunched some numbers. I ended up buying my own warehouse. I knew that I was increasing my risk but the upside was that the money I used to pay for rent was now paying for my building. Now, I've expanded my warehouse and am leasing a part of it to somebody else."

Pete Seerden is not an accountant but was able to use his knowledge of accounting information to make a successful business decision.

Power of Accounting Information in Big Business

July 20, 2000—Toronto-Dominion (TD) Bank Teams Up with Starbucks to Create an Innovative Customer Experience. The TD Bank became the first major Canadian bank to combine banking with the services of a retailer in one of its branches. In the TD Bank branch at Queen and Bay Streets in downtown Toronto, you can purchase Starbucks products while doing your banking.

This innovative decision was made through an analysis of information from a variety of sources including the accounting information system. By increasing customer exposure for both parties, profits should be positively affected.

Accounting can provide you with important and interesting learning experiences. You will acquire knowledge and skills that will help you in both business and everyday life. For example, you can use accounting knowledge to make better investment decisions or to help you get a loan for a house.

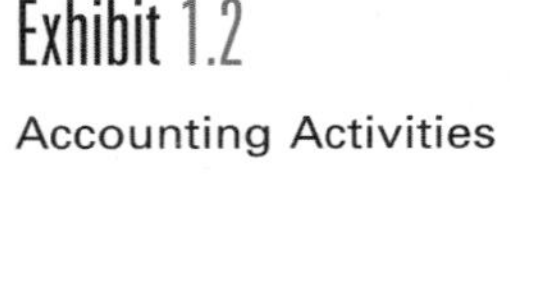

Accounting Activities

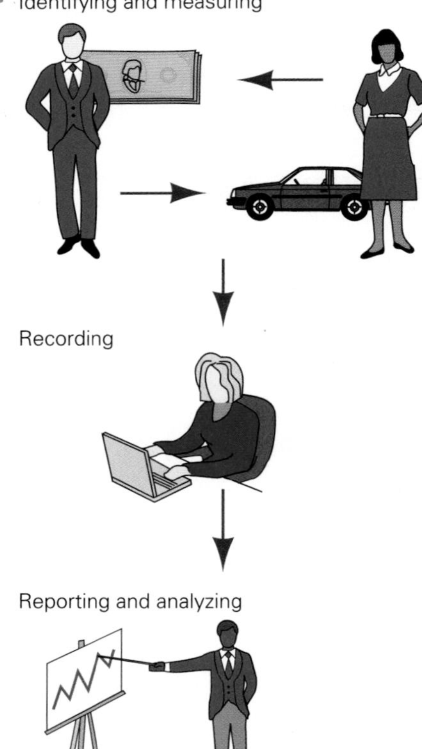

Focus of Accounting

Accounting affects many parts of life. Some examples of common contacts with accounting are through credit approvals, chequing accounts, tax forms and payroll. These experiences are limited and tend to focus on the *recordkeeping* (or *bookkeeping*) parts of accounting. **Recordkeeping**, or **bookkeeping**, is the recording of financial transactions and events, either manually or electronically, for the purpose of creating a reliable bank of data. Accounting *involves* the recordkeeping process but is *much* more.

The primary objective of accounting is to provide useful information for decision making. Accounting information results from the accounting activities of identifying, measuring, recording, reporting and analyzing economic events and transactions as shown in Exhibit 1.2. Accounting also involves designing information systems to provide useful reports to monitor and control an organization's activities. In order to use the reports effectively, decision makers must be able to interpret the information. The skills needed to understand and interpret accounting information come from an insight into each aspect of accounting, including recordkeeping. Because accounting is part of so much that we do in business and our everyday lives, you can enjoy greater opportunities if you understand and are able to use accounting information effectively.

Role of Accounting in Business

A **business** is one or more individuals selling products or services for profit. Products like athletic apparel (CCM, Bauer, NIKE, Reebok), computers (Dell, Hewlett-Packard, Apple) and clothing (Tilley, Levis, GAP) are part of our daily lives. Services like information communication (Sympatico, AOL Canada, CompuServe, Microsoft), dining (Tim Hortons, Harvey's, McDonald's, Burger King) and car rental (Tilden, Hertz, Budget) make our lives easier. A business can be as small as an in-home childcare service or as massive as the Hudson's Bay Company. Nearly 100,000 new businesses are started in Canada each year, with most of them being founded by people who want freedom from ordinary jobs, a new challenge in life, or the advantage of earning extra money. These people are interested in business profit!

Business Profit

LO3 Describe profit and its two major components.

Accounting can measure business *profit* and report details to interested individuals. **Profit**, also called **net income** or **earnings**, is the amount that a business earns after subtracting all *expenses* necessary to earn *revenues*. **Revenues**, also called **sales**, are the amounts earned from selling products and services. **Expenses** are the costs incurred in generating (or producing) revenues. Not all businesses make profits. A **net loss** arises when expenses are more than revenues. Many new businesses incur a **loss** in their first several months or years of business, yet no business can continually experience losses and stay in business.

Revenues − Expenses = Net Income
(when expenses less than revenues)
or
Revenues − Expenses = Net Loss
(when expenses greater than revenues)

To demonstrate how business profit is reported, let's look at the profit of an actual business. Cheapo Joe's Driving Range is located in Edmonton, Alberta and caters to golf enthusiasts. The profit breakdown for Cheapo Joe's Driving Range is illustrated in Exhibit 1.3. A bucket of balls at Cheapo Joe's costs $3.75 (or two for $6.50!); total revenues for the year ended December 31, 1999 were $87,689. Cheapo Joe's expenses were greater than revenues, causing a net loss of $10,271. Should the business be continued? What changes or opportunities might help Cheapo Joe's to realize a profit? These important questions can be considered only with an understanding of the accounting information available.

Exhibit 1.3

Cheapo Joe's 1999 Income Statement

Cheapo Joe's Driving Range
Income Statement
For Year Ended December 31, 1999

Revenues:		
Gross driving range revenue		$87,689
Operating expenses:		
Range balls expense	$ 6,522	
Range repairs and supplies expense	7,052	
Yard maintenance expense	3,626	
Fuel expense	2,848	
Golf supplies expense	5,255	
Snacks and miscellaneous expense	2,518	
Advertising and office expense	8,229	
Bank charges and interest expense	2,406	
Amortization expense	13,337	
Entertainment and promotion expense	304	
Insurance expense	300	
Professional fees expense	1,218	
Rent expense	10,050	
Salaries and benefits expense	31,365	
Utilities expense	2,930	
Total operating expenses		97,960
Net loss		$10,271

Did You Know?

The Top Three

What companies in Canada showed the fastest growing revenues over the five-year period 1994 to 1999? According to *PROFIT*, a Canadian magazine aimed at entrepreneurs, the top three are:

Rank	Company	Location	Description	1999 Revenue*	1994 Revenue*
1	Boardwalk Equities Inc.	Calgary, AB	Residential property manager	$185,972,000	$409,000
2	Cygnal Technologies Corp.	Oshawa, ON	Broadband network developer	$59,881,000	$143,000
3	DataMirror Corp.	Markham, ON	Data integration software	$42,174,000	$117,000

*rounded to nearest thousand

SOURCE: www.PROFITguide.com, accessed January 2, 2001.

Answers—pp. 20–21

1. What is a major aim of accounting?
2. Describe profit, revenues and expenses.
3. Distinguish between accounting and recordkeeping.

Mid-Chapter Demonstration Problem

A-1 Lawn Service provides yardcare to homeowners. During the month of April, Greg Alko, the owner and operator, mowed 83 lawns and charged each of his customers $20. He also rototilled 36 garden plots and received $25 for each. Greg spent $248 on gasoline and oil for equipment during the month, along with $702 for equipment rental. After paying a customer $40 to replace a flower planter that was accidentally broken, Greg is wondering if he is making a profit this month. Calculate the profit earned by A-1 Lawn Service during the month of April.

Planning the Solution

- Calculate the revenues.
- Calculate the expenses.
- Subtract expenses from revenues to determine the net income or net loss.

SOLUTION TO Mid-Chapter Demonstration Problem

Revenues = (83 lawns × $20 each) + (36 garden plots × $25 each)
= $1,660 + $900
= $2,560

Expenses = $248 for gasoline and oil + $702 for equipment rental
+ $40 flower planter
= $990

Revenues of $2,560 − Expenses of $990 = $1,570 Net Income or Profit

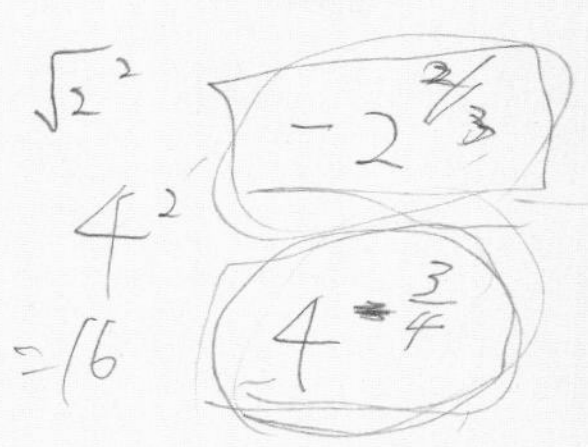

Forms of Organization

LO4 Identify forms of organization and their characteristics.

Not all organizations have profit as a primary goal. Business organizations typically strive for profit, but the performance of non-business organizations (such as government, schools, and churches) is measured not always in terms of profit but rather by how the organizations serve society.

Most organizations engage in economic activities. These can include the usual business activities of purchasing materials and labour, and selling products and services. They can also involve non-business activities like collecting money through taxes, dues, contributions, investments or borrowings. A common feature in all organizations, both business and non-business, is the power and use of accounting.

Business Organizations

Businesses take one of three forms: sole proprietorship, partnership, or corporation. For some of the characteristics of business organizations, see Exhibit 1.4.

Exhibit 1.4

Characteristics of Business Organizations

	Sole Proprietorship	Partnership	Corporation
Business entity	yes	yes	yes
Legal entity	no	no	yes
Limited liability	no	no	yes
Unlimited life	no	no	yes
Business taxed	no	no	yes
One owner allowed	yes	no	yes

Sole Proprietorship

A **sole proprietorship**, or **single proprietorship**, is a business owned by one person. No special legal requirements must be met in order to start this form of business, other than to file for a business licence and register the business name. While it is a separate entity[1] for accounting purposes, it is *not* a separate legal entity from its owner. This means, for example, that a court can order an owner to sell personal belongings to pay a proprietorship's debt. An owner is even responsible for debts that are greater than the resources of the proprietorship; this is known as **unlimited liability**, and is an obvious disadvantage of a sole proprietorship. Because tax authorities do not separate a proprietorship from its owner, the profits of the business are reported and taxed on the owner's personal income tax return. Small retail stores and service businesses often are organized as proprietorships.

Partnership

A **partnership** is owned by two or more persons called *partners*. Like a proprietorship, no special legal requirements must be met in order to start a partnership, other than to register the business name and obtain a business licence. To run the business together, the partners need an oral or written agreement that usually indicates how profits and losses are to be shared. A partnership, like a proprietorship, is not legally separate from its owners, therefore each partner's share of profits is reported and taxed on that partner's tax return. Partners are usually subject to *unlimited liability*.

There are two types of partnerships that limit liability. A **limited partnership** includes a general partner(s) with unlimited liability and a limited partner(s) with liability restricted to the amount invested. A **limited liability partnership** restricts partners' liabilities to their own acts and the acts of individuals under their control. This protects an innocent partner from the negligence of another partner, yet all partners remain responsible for partnership debts.

Corporation

A **corporation** is a business that is a separate legal entity chartered (or *incorporated*) under provincial or federal laws. A corporation is responsible for its own acts and its own debts. It can enter into its own contracts, and it can buy, own and sell property. It can also sue and be sued. Not only does separate legal status give a corporation an unlimited life, but it also entitles the corporation to conduct business with the rights, duties and responsibilities of a person. As a result, a corporation files a tax return and pays tax on its profits. A corporation acts through its managers, who are its legal agents. Separate legal status also means that the shareholders are

[1] The **business entity principle**, also known as the *economic entity principle* or simply the *entity principle*, is one of a group of accounting rules, the **Generally Accepted Accounting Principles (GAAP)**, which are discussed in detail in Chapter 2. This principle states that each economic entity or business of the owner must keep accounting records and reports separate from the owner and any other economic entity of the owner.

not personally liable for corporate acts and debts. Shareholders are legally distinct from the business and their loss is limited to what they invested. This **limited liability** is a key to why corporations can raise resources from shareholders who are not active in managing the business. Ownership, or equity, of all corporations is divided into units called **shares.** Owners of shares are called **shareholders** (the American term for shares is *stock* and for shareholders, *stockholders*). A shareholder can sell or transfer shares to another person without affecting the operations of a corporation. When a corporation issues (or sells) only one class of shares, we call them **common shares** or *capital stock.* Air Canada is an example of a Canadian corporation. As of March 31, 2000, Air Canada had issued a total of 79 million common shares to the public. This means that Air Canada's ownership is divided into 79 million units. A shareholder who owns 790,000 shares of Air Canada owns 1% of the company.

Non-business Organizations

Non-business organizations include not-for-profit and government organizations. They plan and operate not for profit but rather for other goals such as health, education, religious services, and cultural and social activities. Examples are public schools meeting the needs of citizens, and community care groups meeting the needs of the poor. Non-business organizations do not have an identifiable owner. Still, the demand for accounting information in these organizations is high since they are accountable to their sponsors. These organizations are accountable to taxpayers, donors, lenders, legislators, regulators and other constituents. Exhibit 1.5 lists a wide range of government and not-for-profit organizations that are affected by the power of accounting. This list is but a sampling of the roughly one-third of Canadian economic activity done by this type of organization. In all of these organizations, accounting captures key information about their activities and makes it available to users both internal and external to the organization.

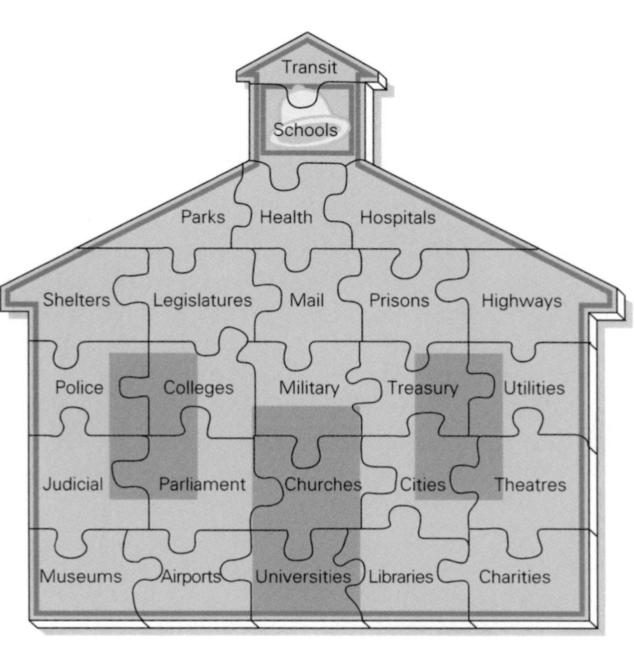

Exhibit 1.5

Partial List of Government and Not-for-profit Organizations

Answer—p. 20

Entrepreneur

You and a friend have developed a new design for mountain bikes that improves speed and performance by a remarkable 25% to 40%. You are planning to form a small business to manufacture and market these bikes. You and your friend are concerned about potential lawsuits from individuals who may become injured because of using the speed feature of the bikes with reckless abandon. What form of organization do you set up?

Answers—p. 21

4. What are the three common forms of business organizations?
5. Identify examples of non-business organizations.

Users of Accounting Information

LO5 Identify users and uses of accounting.

Accounting is a service activity: organizations set up accounting information systems to serve the decision-making needs of internal and external users. *Internal users* are found within the business, and *external users* are those outside of the business.

Did You Know?

Accounting Information at Work

The Multiple Sclerosis (MS) Society of Canada provides assistance and support to individuals with MS, in addition to funding research aimed at finding a cure. Accounting makes it possible for not-for-profit organizations like the MS Society of Canada to present to external users information like the following:

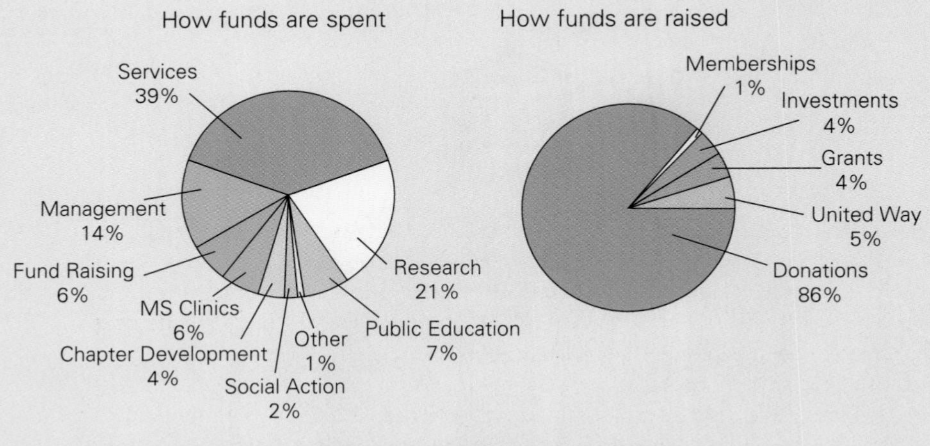

SOURCE: www.mssoc.ca, accessed January 2, 2001.

External Information Users

External users of accounting information are *not* directly involved in running the organization. They include shareholders, lenders, directors, customers, suppliers, regulators, lawyers, brokers and the press. Each external user has special information needs that depend on the kind of decision to be made. To make a decision, key questions need to be answered; this is often done using information available in accounting reports. The following table identifies several external users and decisions that require accounting information.

External User Group	Examples of Decisions to be Made	Questions That Require Accounting Information
Lenders (creditors) lend money or other resources to an organization	To lend money or not	Can current loans be repaid? Can additional loans be repaid? What is the future profit outlook?
Shareholders are the owners of a corporation	To invest or not	What is net income for current and past periods? Do loans seem large or unusual? Do expenses fit the level and type of revenues?
External auditors examine financial statements and provide assurance that they are prepared according to GAAP	To determine the reasonableness of a client's statements	Have all expenses been recorded? Do revenues include only those for the current period?
Employees of an organization, or their union representatives	To determine if wages are fair	Is net income large enough to support a request for increased pay?
Regulators, such as Canada Customs and Revenue Agency **(CCRA)**	To determine if payroll deductions are calculated properly	Are all employees being paid through the payroll system?
Others • Contributors to not-for-profit organizations	To continue financial support of the organization	Are funds being spent in an appropriate manner?
• Suppliers	To determine if goods should be supplied on credit	Is the purchaser able to pay for goods purchased?

External Reporting

Financial accounting is the area of accounting aimed at serving external users. Its primary objective is to provide external reports called *financial statements* to help users analyze an organization's activities. Because external users have limited access to an organization's information, their own success depends on getting external reports that are reliable, relevant, consistent and comparable. Some governmental and regulatory agencies have the power to get reports in specific forms, but most external users must rely on *general-purpose financial statements.* The term *general-purpose* refers to the broad range of purposes for which external users rely on these statements. Generally Accepted Accounting Principles (GAAP) are important in increasing the usefulness of financial statements to users. We discuss these principles along with the financial statements in Chapter 2.

Internal Information Users

Internal users of accounting information are those individuals directly involved in managing and operating an organization. The internal role of accounting is to provide information to help internal users improve the efficiency and effectiveness of an organization in delivering products or services.

Internal Reporting

Managerial accounting is the area of accounting aimed at serving the decision-making needs of internal users. Managerial accounting provides special-purpose reports customized to meet the information needs of internal users. An example of such a report is a listing of credit customers who are late in paying their accounts. Internal reports aim to answer questions like:

- What are the manufacturing expenses per unit of product?
- What is the most profitable mix of services?
- What level of revenues is necessary to show net income?
- Which service activities are most profitable?
- Which expenses change with a change in revenues?

This book will help you to learn the skills needed to use accounting information effectively to answer questions like these.

Exhibit 1.6

Internal Operating Functions

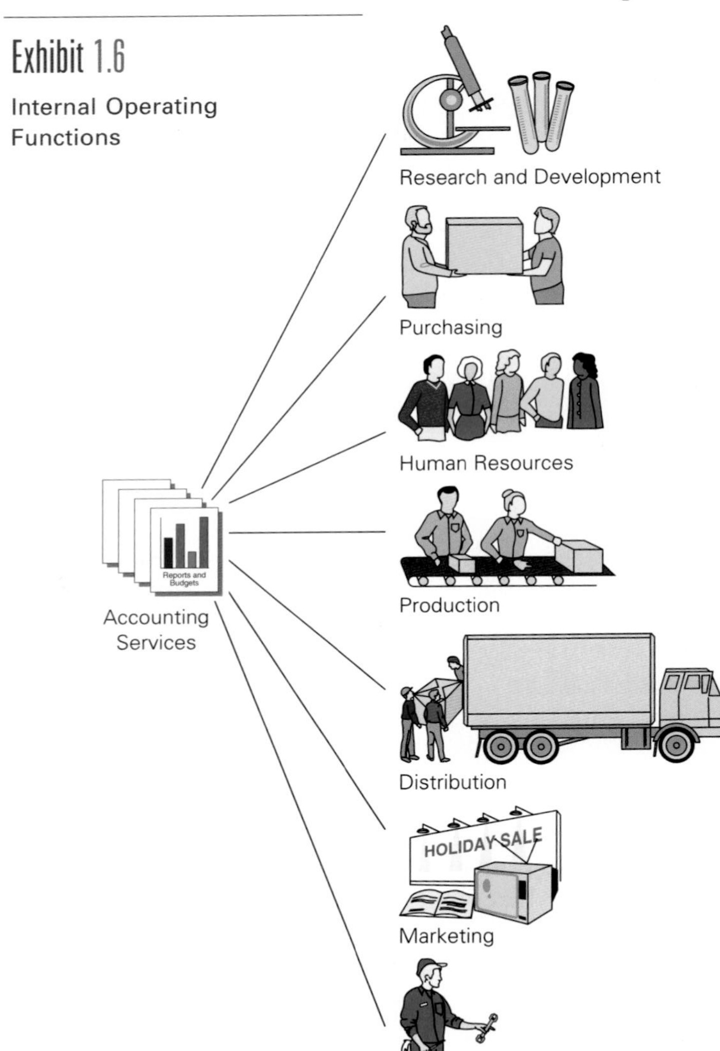

Internal Operating Functions

The responsibilities and duties of internal users extend to every function of an organization. There are at least seven functions common to most organizations, and accounting is essential to the smooth operation of each. The internal operating functions are shown in Exhibit 1.6.

Managers rely on **internal controls** to monitor operating functions. Internal controls are procedures set up to protect assets (like cash, equipment, and buildings), ensure that accounting reports are reliable, promote efficiency, and ensure that company policies are followed. For example, certain actions require verification, such as a manager's approval before materials enter production. Internal controls are crucial if accounting reports are to provide relevant and reliable information.

Ethics and Social Responsibility

LO6 Explain why ethics and social responsibility are crucial to accounting.

Ethics and ethical behaviour are important to the accounting profession and to those who use accounting information. We are reminded of this when we find stories in the media of cheating, or when we witness wrongful actions by individuals in business. A lack of ethics makes it harder for people to trust one another. If trust is missing, our lives are more difficult, inefficient and unpleasant. An important goal of accounting is to provide useful information for decision making. For information to be useful, it must be trusted; this demands ethics in accounting. Closely related to ethics is social responsibility. Both are discussed in this section.

Understanding Ethics

Ethics are beliefs that differentiate right from wrong. Ethics and laws often coincide, with the result that many unethical actions (such as theft and physical violence) are also illegal. Yet other actions are not against the law but are considered unethical, such as not helping people with certain needs or deliberately withholding critical information from the user.

Identifying the ethical path is sometimes difficult. The preferred ethical path is to take a course of action that avoids casting doubt on one's decision. For example, as a member of the board for a not-for-profit organization, you are involved in a decision where your brother's company could win a profitable contract to do work for the organization ... do you participate in the decision or do you remove yourself from the discussion? The ethical answer would be to avoid this conflict of interest by not participating. Accountants have ethical obligations in at least four general areas: they are expected to maintain a high level of professional competence, treat sensitive information as confidential, exercise personal integrity, and be objective in matters of financial disclosure.

Ethics are Timeless

Did You Know? 

The Rotary 4-Way Test, created by Herbert J. Taylor in 1932, is an internationally renowned guideline for making ethical business choices:

"Of the things we think, say or do:

1. Is it the Truth?
2. Is it Fair to all concerned?
3. Will it build goodwill and better friendships?
4. Will it be beneficial to all concerned?"

SOURCE: www.rotary.org, accessed January 2, 2001.

Organizational Ethics

Organizational ethics are likely learned through management example and leadership. Companies like Shell Canada, The Body Shop, Nortel Networks and Bank of Montreal work hard to convey the importance of ethics to employees. Ethical practices build trust, which promotes loyalty and long-term relationships with customers, suppliers and employees. Good ethics add to an organization's reputation and its success.

Accounting Ethics

Ethics are crucial in accounting. Providers of accounting information often face ethical choices as they prepare financial reports. Their choices can affect both the use and receipt of money, including taxes owed and money shared with owners. Accounting information can affect the price that a buyer pays and the wages paid to workers. It can even affect the success of products, services and divisions. Misleading information can lead to a wrongful closing of a division where workers, customers and suppliers are seriously harmed.

Because of the importance of accounting ethics, codes of ethics for accountants are set up and enforced. These codes include those of the Provincial Institutes of Chartered Accountants, the Provincial Societies of Management Accountants, and the Provincial Certified General Accountants' Associations. Samples from these codes are presented in Appendix II near the end of the book. These codes can be of help when one confronts ethical dilemmas.

Ethics codes are also useful when one is dealing with confidential information. For example, auditors have access to confidential salaries and an organization's strategies. Organizations can be harmed if auditors pass this information to others. To prevent this, auditors' ethics codes require them to keep information confidential. Internal accountants are also not to use confidential information for personal gain.

Ethical Challenge

In our lives, we encounter many situations requiring ethical decisions. We need to remember that accounting must be practised ethically if it is to be useful, and must always ensure that our actions and decisions are ethical.

Social Responsibility

Social responsibility is a concern for the impact of our actions on society as a whole. Organizations are increasingly concerned with their social responsibility, as there is significant pressure on them to contribute positively to society. Socially conscious employees, customers, investors, and others see to it that organizations follow claims of social awareness with actions. Exhibit 1.7 identifies an example of an organization trying to be socially responsible while conducting a business transaction.

Exhibit 1.7

Social Responsibility: Decision Making in Action

www.tdbank.ca

Identify issues. →	Analyze options. →	Make socially responsible decision.
Toronto-Dominion's (TD) acquisition of Canada Trust announced August 3, 1999. Issue: job loss associated with integration of two companies.	Lay employees off or retain.	A compromise decision was reached and TD announced a compensation guarantee for a period of 18 months from August 3, 1999.

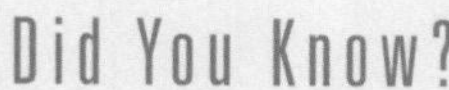

In Pursuit of Profit

How far can companies go in pursuing profits? In January of 1998, Eastern Ontario and parts of Quebec were battered by a tremendous ice storm. Countless people found themselves without electricity for extended periods. Many retailers of gas-powered generators raised the selling price of their product. Critics claimed that retailers were taking advantage of consumers in a time of crisis. It is important that companies balance profits with ethics and social responsibility.

Answers—p. 21

6. Who are the external and internal users of accounting information?
7. Why are internal controls important?
8. What are the guidelines to use in making ethical and socially responsible decisions?
9. Why are ethics and social responsibility valuable to organizations?
10. Why are ethics crucial to accounting?

Accounting Opportunities

LO7 Identify opportunities in accounting and related fields.

Exhibit 1.8 identifies the countless job opportunities in accounting by classifying accountants according to the kind of work that they perform. In general, accountants work in four broad fields:

- Financial
- Managerial
- Taxation
- Accounting-related

Exhibit 1.8

Opportunities in Practice

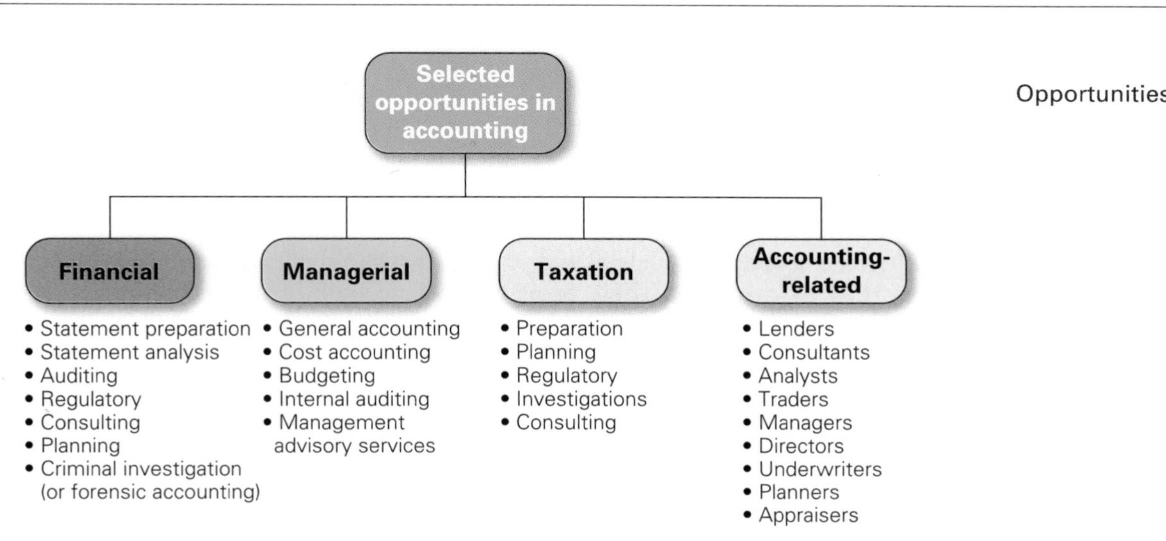

Another way to classify accountants is to identify the kinds of organizations in which they work. Most accountants are **private accountants** and work for a single employer, which is often a business. The services of **public accountants** are available to the public, which means that services are provided to many different clients. **Government accountants** work for local, provincial, and federal government agencies.

Financial Accounting

Financial accounting serves the needs of external users by providing financial statements. Many organizations, both business and non-business, issue their financial statements only after an audit. An **audit** is an independent review and test of an organization's accounting systems and records; it is performed to add credibility to the financial statements.[2] **External auditors** perform the audit function at the request of the board of directors to protect shareholder interests.

Managerial Accounting

Managerial accounting serves the needs of internal users by providing special-purpose reports. These special-purpose reports are the result of general accounting, cost accounting, budgeting, internal auditing, and management consulting.

General accounting	The task of recording transactions, processing the recorded data, and preparing reports for members of the management team such as the **controller** (the chief accounting officer of an organization).
Cost accounting	The process of accumulating the information that managers need about the various **costs** within the organization.
Budgeting	The process of developing formal plans for an organization's future activities.
Internal auditing	Function performed by auditors employed within the organization for the purpose of evaluating the efficiency and effectiveness of procedures.
Management consulting	Service provided by external accountants where suggestions are offered for improving a company's procedures; suggestions may concern new accounting and internal control systems, new computer systems, budgeting, and employee benefit plans.

Tax Accounting

Income tax raised by federal and provincial governments is based on the income earned by taxpayers. These taxpayers include both individuals and corporate businesses. Sole proprietorships and partnerships are not subject to income tax, but owners of these two non-corporate business forms must pay tax on income earned from these business forms. The amount of tax is based on what the laws define to be income. In the field of **tax accounting**, tax accountants help taxpayers comply with these laws by preparing their tax returns and providing assistance with tax planning for the future. The government (specifically, Canada Customs and Revenue Agency) employs tax accountants for collection and enforcement.

[2] To achieve this result, audits are performed by independent professionals who are public accountants. Little or no credibility would be added to statements if they were audited by a company's own employees.

Accounting-related Fields

Exhibit 1.8 lists several accounting-related opportunities. All of these professions are made easier with a working knowledge of accounting. This course provides that knowledge.

Professional Certification

Many accountants (financial, managerial, tax, and other) have professional accounting status. Accounting is a profession, like law and medicine, because accountants have special abilities and responsibilities. The professional status of an accountant is often indicated by one or more professional certifications. In Canada, there are several accounting organizations that provide the education and training required in order to obtain professional certification. These include the Institute of Chartered Accountants, the Certified General Accountants' Association, and the Society of Management Accountants. Successful completion of one of the prescribed programs leads to the following professional accounting designations: **Chartered Accountant (CA); Certified General Accountant (CGA); or Certified Management Accountant (CMA).**

For detailed information regarding professional accounting education programs and journals, refer to the following Web sites: www.cga-canada.org, www.cica.ca, and www.cma-canada.org.

The preceding discussions show how important accounting is for organizations. Regardless of your career goals, you will use accounting information because it is the language of business. The discussion also emphasizes the broad scope and growing number of opportunities available in accounting. This book will help you to take advantage of those opportunities.

11. What is the difference between private and public accountants?
12. What are the four broad fields of accounting?
13. What is the purpose of an audit?
14. Distinguish between managerial and financial accounting.

Answers—p. 21

Summary

LO1 **Describe how technology is changing accounting.** Technology has increased the access to, processing speed and quantity of accounting information. Accountants have had to enhance their information technology knowledge and experience in order to compete. However, accountants that possess strong information technology skills are in high market demand and, as a result, earn large salaries.

LO2 **Describe accounting and its goals and uses.** Accounting is an information and measurement system that aims to identify, measure, record and communicate relevant, reliable, consistent and comparable information about economic activities. It helps us better assess opportunities, products, investments, and social and community responsibilities. The power of accounting is in

Summary (continued)

opening our eyes to new and exciting opportunities. The greatest benefits of understanding accounting often come to those outside of accounting, because an improved understanding of accounting helps us to compete better in today's global and technologically challenging world.

LO3 **Describe profit and its two major components.** Profit is the amount that a business earns after subtracting all expenses from revenues (Revenues − Expenses = Profit). Revenues (sales) are the amounts earned from selling products and services. Expenses are the costs incurred in generating revenues. A loss arises when expenses are greater than revenues.

LO4 **Identify forms of organization and their characteristics.** Organizations can be classified either as businesses or non-businesses. Businesses are organized for profit, while non-businesses serve us in ways not always measured by profit. Businesses take one of three forms: sole proprietorship, partnership or corporation. These forms of organization have characteristics that hold important implications for legal liability, taxation, continuity, number of owners, and legal status.

LO5 **Identify users and uses of accounting.** There are both internal and external users of accounting. Some users and uses of accounting include: (a) management for control, monitoring and planning; (b) lenders for making decisions regarding loan applications; (c) shareholders for making investment decisions; (d) directors for overseeing management; and (e) employees for judging employment opportunities.

LO6 **Explain why ethics and social responsibility are crucial to accounting.** The goal of accounting is to provide useful information for decision making. For information to be useful, it must be trusted. This demands ethics and socially responsible behaviour in accounting. Without these, accounting information loses its reliability.

LO7 **Identify opportunities in accounting and related fields.** Opportunities in accounting and related fields are numerous. They encompass traditional financial, managerial and tax accounting, but also include accounting-related fields such as lending, consulting, managing and planning.

GUIDANCE ANSWER TO Judgement Call

Entrepreneur

You should probably form your business as a corporation if potential lawsuits are of prime concern. The corporate form of organization would protect your personal property from lawsuits directed at the business, and would place only the corporation's resources at risk. You should also examine the ethical and socially responsible aspects of starting a business where you anticipate injuries to others.

GUIDANCE ANSWERS TO Flashback

1. Accounting is an information and measurement system that identifies, measures, records and communicates relevant, reliable, consistent and comparable information to people that helps them in making better decisions. It helps people in business to identify and react to investment opportunities, and better assess opportunities, products, investments, and social and community responsibilities.
2. Profit is what a business earns after all expenses are subtracted from revenues. Revenues, also called sales, are the amounts earned from selling products and services. Expenses are the costs incurred for the purpose of creating revenues.

GUIDANCE ANSWERS TO  Flashback (continued)

3. Recordkeeping is the recording of financial transactions and events, either manually or electronically. While recordkeeping is essential to data reliability, accounting is this and much more. Accounting includes identifying, measuring, recording, reporting and analyzing economic events and transactions. It involves interpreting information, and designing information systems to provide useful reports that monitor and control an organization's activities.
4. The three common forms of business organizations are sole proprietorships, partnerships and corporations.
5. Non-business organizations include airports, libraries, museums, religious institutions, municipal governments, law enforcement organizations, postal services, colleges, universities, bus lines, utilities, highways, shelters, parks, hospitals and schools.
6. External users of accounting information are not directly involved in running the organization. Internal users of accounting information are those individuals directly involved in managing and operating an organization.
7. Internal controls are procedures set up to protect assets, ensure that accounting reports are reliable, promote efficiency, and encourage adherence to company policies. Internal controls are crucial if accounting reports are to provide relevant and reliable information.
8. The guidelines for ethical and socially responsible decisions are threefold: (1) identify ethical and/or social issue; (2) analyze options, considering both good and bad consequences for all individuals affected; and (3) make ethical/socially responsible decision, choosing the best option after weighing all consequences.
9. Ethics and social responsibility are important for people because, without them, existence is more difficult, inefficient and unpleasant. They are equally important to organizations, for this same reason. In addition, they often translate into higher profits and a better working environment.
10. Accounting aims to provide useful information for decision making. For information to be useful, it must be trusted. Trustworthiness of information demands ethics in accounting.
11. Private accountants work for a single employer, which is often a business. A public accountant is available to the public, which means that services are provided to many different clients.
12. The four broad fields of accounting are: financial, managerial, taxation, and accounting-related.
13. The purpose of an audit is to add credibility to the financial statements.
14. Managerial accounting is for internal users, while financial accounting is for external users.

APPENDIX

1A Accounting and Technology

LO8 Explain e-business and identify other technology applications useful to accounting.

Technology has become an integral part of modern society and business practice. *e-business* allows organizations to market themselves online as well as to conduct transactions over the Web. Internet technology provides access to all types of business-related information. Accounting software has advanced such that e-business transactions can be recorded and analyzed in conjunction with real-time information available on the Internet. Computing technology, in terms of accounting, had a very limited scope only five years ago. The technology is still responsible for reducing the time, effort and cost of recordkeeping while improving clerical accuracy. Because technology has changed the way we store, process and summarize large masses of data, accounting has been freed to expand its field … into *e-business.* Major consulting, planning and other financial services are quickly becoming part of this new technology wave. Now, more than ever, there is a need for people who can quickly sort through masses of data, interpret their meaning, identify key factors, and analyze their implications. Community leaders of today and tomorrow require accounting skills and support.

e-business

What is *e-business*? **e-business**, also known as **e-commerce**, is conducted when a business goes online. Going online does not necessarily mean that the business is selling over the Internet. According to a November 1999 study conducted by the Canadian Federation of Independent Business (CFIB), marketing products and services is the main online activity of almost half of smaller Canadian businesses.

> Skoki Lodge, hidden away in a pristine mountain valley in the Canadian Rockies is accessible only by foot or horseback in the summer and via cross-country skis in the winter. Skoki markets its lodging and mountaineering activities online at www.skokilodge.com. The company currently does not process bookings online but instead includes on its site a fax and telephone number along with an e-mail address.

Implications of e-business for Accounting

e-business has significant accounting implications. The accounting information system in place must be able to record transactions that occur online. The costs of acquiring and implementing this new technology must be assessed: will increased revenues justify the costs?

There are also the tax implications: one of the biggest challenges facing e-commerce businesses and government regulators is how to tax Internet business transactions. International Data Corp. announced that, in 1994, worldwide e-commerce sales approximated $0; by 1999, they were US $32 billion; and by 2003, projections are that they will be up to US $1 trillion. How can the CCRA, the Canadian taxation authority, ensure that it is collecting income taxes from all resident e-commerce businesses? There is no paper trail. How, then, can a tax auditor trace these transactions? Tax regulations will develop and accounting systems will need to adapt, which translates into the need for accounting personnel who are skilled and knowledgeable regarding related technology.

With technology, there is also the fear of unauthorized persons tampering with a computer system. Yahoo, eBay, and even the Government of Canada Web sites have made the headlines recently because of individuals using the Internet to illegally enter and cause damage to computer systems. Knowing how to protect your system effectively is just as important as knowing how to use it effectively. Steps need to be taken to ensure that once an accounting information system based on new technologies is in place, it is protected from potential compromise.

With e-commerce and the Internet, fraud on a global scale is on the increase. Accountants are providing their financial expertise to help uncover crimes involving technology.

Learning About the Technology

How does a student in introductory accounting deal with all of these technological issues? The answer: through exposure. By getting comfortable with the Internet through use and by learning to apply your accounting knowledge using an accounting software package, you will develop fundamental skills that will form the foundation for continued growth in the rapidly expanding area of technology.

This book will attempt to do two things in that regard:

1. Provide opportunities for you to enhance your learning through exploration on the Web; and
2. Expose you to the basic processes involved in an accounting software package.

To accomplish the first task, McGraw-Hill has a Web site with student resources that you can access; you'll find it at www.mcgrawhill.ca/college/larson. Also, throughout the text, Web sites will be highlighted in the margin as an invitation to explore a topic further. Examples of excellent sites are shown in the following section.

Daily events can have a major impact on a business. This kind of information is available through publications such as *The Globe and Mail*, *Profit Guide*, or *Canadian Business*, to name a few.

http://globeandmail.ca/hubs/rob.html

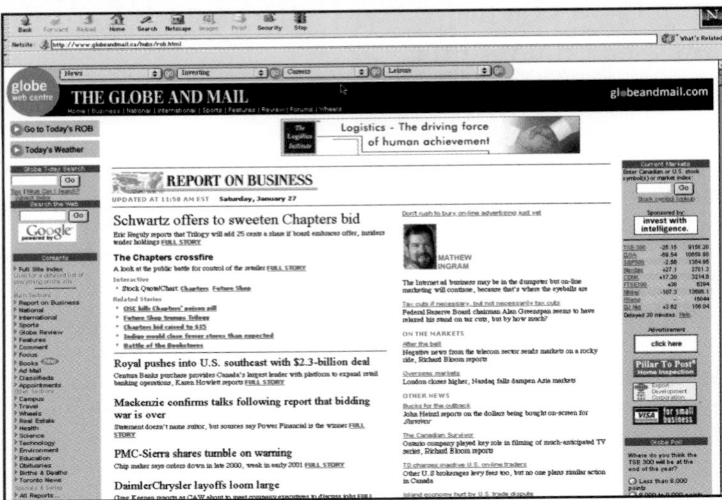

http://www.PROFITguide.com

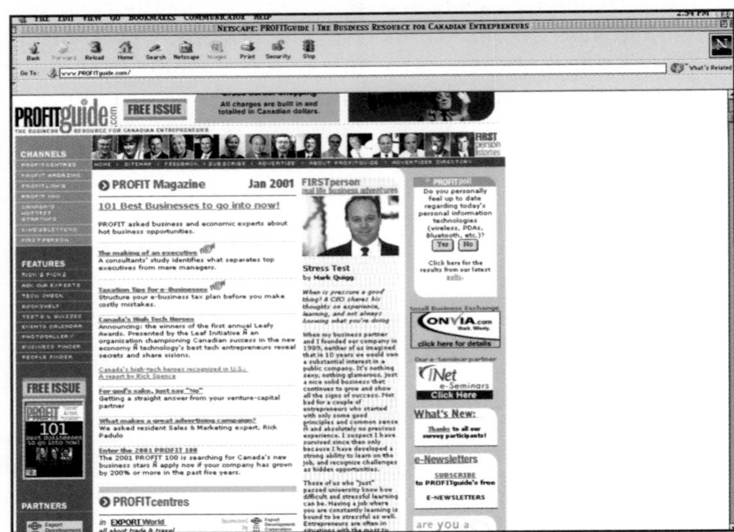

http://www.canadianbusiness.com

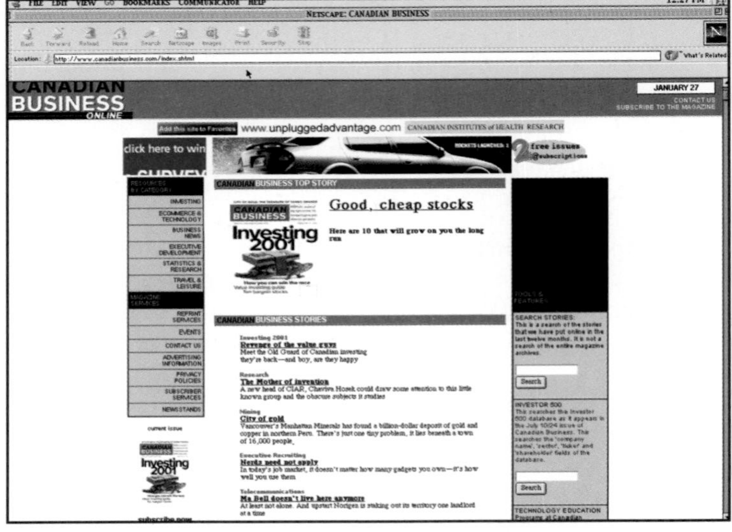

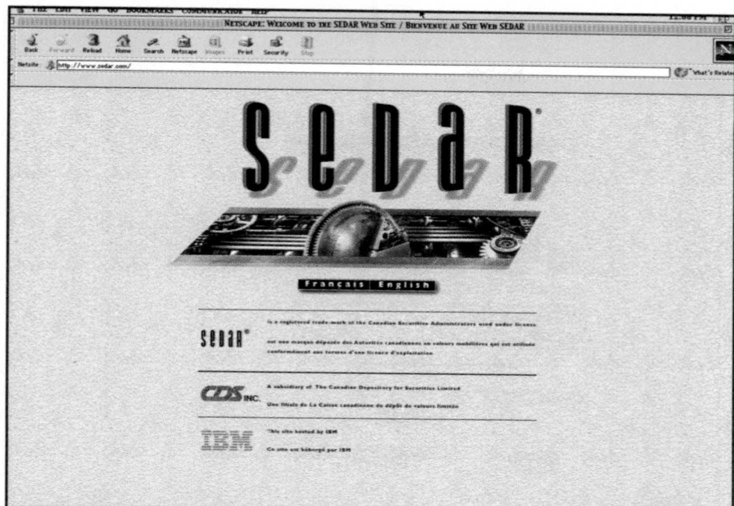

SEDAR is an online database that has accounting information for thousands of public companies that operate in Canada.

http://www.sedar.com

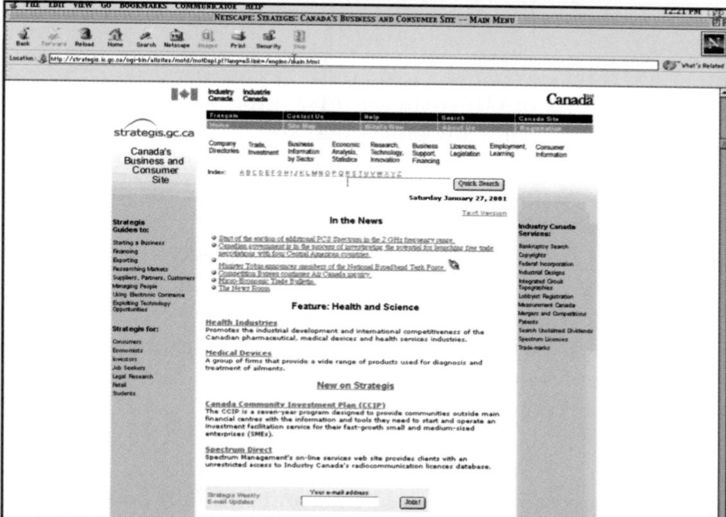

The Canadian Business Map provides access to international, national, provincial, territorial and municipal business information.

http://www.strategis.ic.gc.ca

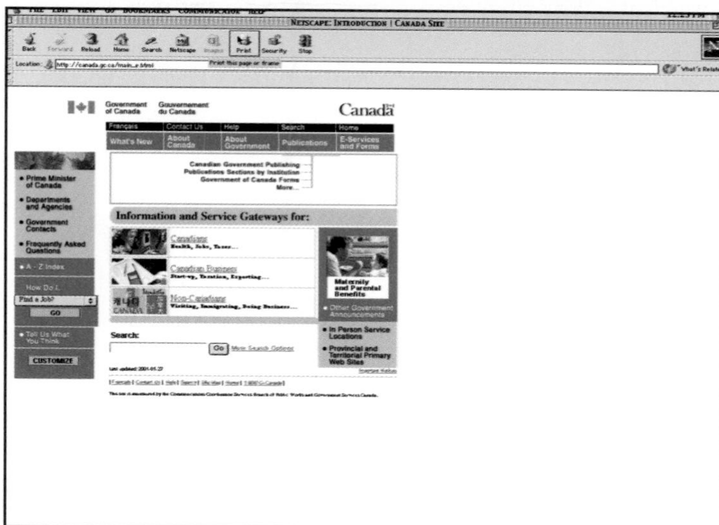

If you need to stay abreast of changes in regulations and legislation that affect your business, The Canada Site is very useful.

http://canada.gc.ca

Canadian Careers provides information as to where the jobs in Canada are.

http://canadiancareers.com

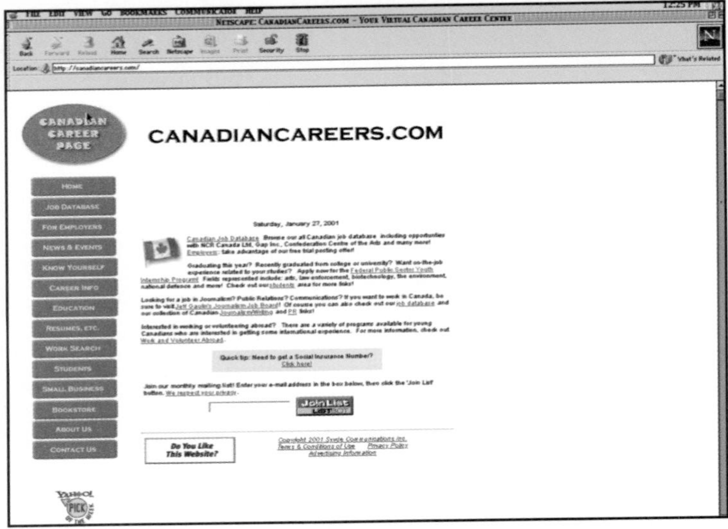

These represent only a handful of Canadian business information sites available on the Internet. Bookmark these and any others that you discover.

In terms of accounting software packages, several exercises and problems throughout the text will have an icon in the margin, like the one shown here. Microsoft Excel® and Simply Accounting® are used to complement your learning.

Why Simply Accounting® when there are more than 250 accounting software applications on the market? Simply Accounting® is one of Canada's top-selling small business accounting software packages and was selected for that reason. Most accounting applications have the same basic operating features, and so by using some of the aspects of Simply Accounting®, you will be able to understand the process involved in a computer software program and transfer that knowledge to other applications.

Technology has created an urgent need for individuals who are able to use their accounting knowledge in a computerized environment. This book launches you on the path to opportunity and success with an introduction to business Web sites and an accounting software application.

Summary of Appendix 1A

LO8 **Explain e-business and identify other technology applications useful to accounting.** e-business, also known as e-commerce, is the operation of a business online. Many businesses conduct sales transactions on the Internet, while others use it for marketing purposes. Difficulties created because of online transactions include unlawful tampering of systems and the inability of tax collection agencies (like CCRA) to track sales. Accounting software applications have made the recording, processing, and storing of accounting information more efficient.

Glossary

Accounting An information system that identifies, measures, records and communicates relevant, reliable, consistent and comparable information about an organization's economic activities. (p. 5)

Audit A check of an organization's accounting systems and records. (p. 18)

Bookkeeping The part of accounting that involves recording economic transactions and events, either electronically or manually; also called recordkeeping. (p. 6)

Budgeting The process of developing formal plans for future activities, which often serve as a basis for evaluating actual performance. (p. 18)

Business One or more individuals selling products or services for profit. (p. 7)

Business entity principle Every business is accounted for separately from its owner's personal activities. (p. 10)

CA Chartered Accountant; an accountant who has met the examination, education and experience requirements of the Institute of Chartered Accountants for an individual professionally competent in accounting. (p. 19)

CCRA Canada Customs and Revenue Agency; the federal government agency responsible for the collection of tax and enforcement of tax laws. (p. 13)

CGA Certified General Accountant; an accountant who has met the examination, education and experience requirements of the Certified General Accountants' Association for an individual professionally competent in accounting. (p. 19)

CMA Certified Management Accountant; an accountant who has met the examination, education and experience requirements of the Society of Management Accountants for an individual professionally competent in accounting. (p. 19)

Common shares The name for a corporation's shares when only one class of share capital is issued. (p. 11)

Controller The chief accounting officer of an organization. (p. 18)

Corporation A business that is a separate legal entity under provincial or federal laws with owners that are called shareholders. (p. 10)

Cost accounting A managerial accounting activity designed to help managers identify, measure and control operating costs. (p. 18)

Costs See *expenses.* (p. 18)

e-business Conducting business online; commonly sales transactions and/or marketing. (p. 22)

e-commerce See *e-business.* (p. 22)

Earnings The amount a business earns after subtracting all expenses necessary to create revenues; also called net income or profit. (p. 7)

Ethics Beliefs that differentiate right from wrong. (p. 15)

Expenses The costs incurred to earn revenues (or sales). (p. 7)

External auditors/auditing Examine and provide assurance that financial statements are prepared according to generally accepted accounting principles (GAAP). (p. 18)

External users Persons using accounting information who are not directly involved in the running of the organization; examples include shareholders, customers, regulators, and suppliers. (p. 13)

Financial accounting The area of accounting aimed at serving external users. (p. 13)

GAAP Generally Accepted Accounting Principles are the rules that indicate acceptable accounting practice. (p. 10)

General accounting The task of recording transactions, processing data, and preparing reports for managers; includes preparing financial statements for disclosure to external users. (p. 18)

Government accountants Accountants who work for local, provincial and federal government agencies. (p. 18)

Internal auditors/auditing Employees within organizations who assess whether managers are following established operating procedures and evaluate the efficiency of operating procedures. (p. 18)

Internal controls Procedures set up to protect assets, ensure reliable accounting reports, promote efficiency, and encourage adherence to company policies. (p. 14)

Internal users Persons using accounting information who are directly involved in managing and operating an organization; examples include managers and officers. (p. 14)

Limited liability The owner's liability is limited to the amount of investment in the business. (p. 11)

Limited liability partnership Restricts partners' liabilities to their own acts and the acts of individuals under their control. (p. 10)

Limited partnership Includes both general partner(s) with unlimited liability and limited partner(s) with liability restricted to the amount invested. (p. 10)

Glossary (continued)

Loss See *net loss.* (p. 7)

Management consulting Activity in which suggestions are offered for improving a company's procedures; the suggestions may concern new accounting and internal control systems, new computer systems, budgeting, and employee benefit plans. (p. 18)

Managerial accounting The area of accounting aimed at serving the decision-making needs of internal users. (p. 14)

Net income The amount a business earns after subtracting all expenses incurred to generate revenues; also called profit or earnings. (p. 7)

Net loss A loss that arises when total expenses are more than revenues (sales). (p. 7)

Partnership A business that is owned by two or more people, which is not organized as a corporation. (p. 10)

Private accountants Accountants who work for a single employer other than the government or a public accounting firm. (p. 18)

Profit The amount a business earns after subtracting all expenses incurred to generate revenues; also called *net income* or *earnings.* (p. 7)

Public accountants Accountants who provide their services to many different clients. (p. 18)

Recordkeeping The recording of financial transactions and events, either manually or electronically; also called *bookkeeping.* (p. 6)

Revenues The amounts earned from selling products or services; also called *sales.* (p. 7)

Sales The amounts earned from selling products or services; also called *revenues.* (p. 7)

Shareholders The owners of a corporation. (p. 11)

Shares A unit of ownership in a corporation. (p. 11)

Single proprietorship A business owned by one individual, which is not organized as a corporation; also called a *sole proprietorship.* (p. 10)

Social responsibility A commitment to considering the impact and being accountable for the effects that actions might have on society. (p. 16)

Sole proprietorship A business owned by one person, which is not organized as a corporation; also called *single proprietorship.* (p. 10)

Tax accounting The field of accounting that includes preparing tax returns and planning future transactions to minimize the amount of tax paid; involves private, public, and government accountants. (p. 18)

Unlimited liability When the debts of a sole proprietorship or partnership are greater than its resources, the owner(s) is (are) financially responsible. (p. 10)

Questions

1. In the chapter's opening article, what does Wynne Powell identify as the key to success in business?
2. Technology is increasingly used to process accounting data. Why, then, should we study accounting?
3. What is the relation between accounting and technology?
4. What is the purpose of accounting in society?
5. What type of accounting information might be useful to those who carry out the marketing activities of a business?
6. Identify three businesses that offer services and three businesses that offer products.
7. Explain business profit and its computation.
8. Identify the total revenues for the year ended December 31, 1999 for WestJet Airlines from its financial statements in Appendix I at the end of the book.

9. Describe three forms of business organizations and their characteristics.
10. Identify three types of organizations that can be formed as either profit-oriented businesses, government units, or not-for-profit establishments.
11. Identify four external users and their uses of accounting information.
12. Describe the internal role of accounting for organizations.
13. Why is accounting described as a service activity?
14. What ethical issues might accounting professionals face in dealing with confidential information?
15. Identify four managerial accounting tasks performed by both private and government accountants.
16. Identify two management-consulting services offered by public accounting professionals.
17. What work do tax accounting professionals perform in addition to preparing tax returns?
18. Identify the auditing firm that audited the financial statements of ClubLink in Appendix I.

CLUBLINK CORPORATION

Quick Study exercises give readers a brief test of many key elements in every chapter.

Quick Study

Explain why accountants need to enhance their knowledge of information technology.

QS 1-1
Impact of technology on accounting
LO1

Identify two possible uses of accounting information.

QS 1-2
Uses of accounting information
LO2

Refer to Appendix I at the end of the book. Did net income increase or decrease from 1998 to 1999 for ClubLink Corporation?

QS 1-3
Identifying net income
LO3

Accounting provides information about an organization's economic transactions and events. Identify examples of economic transactions and events.

QS 1-4
Identifying transactions and events
LO4

An important responsibility of many accounting professionals is to design and implement internal control procedures for organizations. Explain the purpose of internal control procedures.

QS 1-5
Explaining internal control
LO5

Accounting professionals must sometimes choose between two or more acceptable methods of accounting for certain transactions and events. Explain why these situations can involve difficult matters of ethical concern.

QS 1-6
Identifying ethical matters
LO6

Identify at least three main areas of accounting for accounting professionals. For each accounting area, identify at least three accounting-related opportunities in practice.

QS 1-7
Accounting and accounting-related opportunities
LO7

Go to www.canadianbusiness.com and read an article in the *e-commerce & Technology* section. Explain how the article relates to accounting information.

***QS 1-8**
Experience technology
LO8

An asterisk (*) identifies assignment material based on Appendix 1A.

Exercises

Exercise 1-1
Learning the language of business

LO2, 3, 4, 7

Indicate which description best depicts each of the following important terms:

a. Government accountants
b. Internal auditing
c. Canada Customs and Revenue Agency
d. Accounting
e. Recordkeeping
f. Profit
g. Public accountants
h. CGA
i. GAAP
j. Shareholders

______ **1.** Responsibility of an organization's employees involving examining the organization's recordkeeping processes, assessing whether managers are following established operating procedures, and appraising the efficiency of operating procedures.
______ **2.** Revenues less expenses.
______ **3.** Federal department responsible for collecting federal taxes and enforcing tax law.
______ **4.** Accounting professionals who provide services to many different clients
______ **5.** Accounting professionals employed by federal, provincial, or local branches of government.
______ **6.** Accounting rules.

Exercise 1-2
Business profit

LO3

In its most recent year, Jumbo Electronics had total revenues of $850,000. Expenses were $740,000. Did Jumbo earn a profit or a loss?

Exercise 1-3
Business profit

LO3

At the end of its current year, Molly's Maid Services showed a net loss of $18,000. Expenses had totalled $56,000. Calculate total revenues.

Exercise 1-4
Distinguishing business organizations

LO4

Presented below are descriptions of several different business organizations. Determine whether the situation described refers to a sole proprietorship, partnership, or corporation.

a. Ownership of Cola Company is divided into 1,000 shares.
b. Text Tech is owned by Kimberly Fisher, who is personally liable for the debts of the business.
c. Jerry Forrentes and Susan Montgomery own Financial Services, a financial and personal services provider. Neither Forrentes nor Montgomery has personal responsibility for the debts of Financial Services.
d. Nancy Kerr and Frank Levens own Runners, a courier service. Both Kerr and Levens are personally liable for the debts of the business.
e. MRS Consulting Services does not have a separate legal existence apart from the one person who owns it.
f. Biotech Company has one owner and does not pay taxes.
g. Torby Technologies has two owners and pays its own taxes.

Exercise 1-5
Learning the language of business

LO4, 6, 7

Indicate which description best depicts each of the following important terms:

a. Audit
b. Recordkeeping
c. Cost accounting
d. GAAP
e. Ethics
f. General accounting
g. Budgeting
h. Tax accounting

_____ **1.** An accounting area that includes planning future transactions to minimize taxes paid.
_____ **2.** A managerial accounting process designed to help managers identify, measure and control operating costs.
_____ **3.** Principles that determine whether an action is right or wrong.
_____ **4.** An examination of an organization's accounting system and records that adds credibility to financial statements.
_____ **5.** The task of recording transactions, processing recorded data, and preparing reports and financial statements.

Exercise 1-6
Users of accounting information

LO5

Identify the users of TLC Daycare's accounting information as internal (I) or external (E).

	I or E		*I or E*
Bank manager		Parent	
Owner		Canada Customs and Revenue Agency	
Toy supplier		Janitor employed by TLC Daycare	

Exercise 1-7
Identifying accounting users and uses

LO5

Identify at least three external users of accounting information and indicate some questions that they might seek to answer through their use of accounting information.

Exercise 1-8
Identifying ethical decisions

LO6

Assume the following role and describe a situation where ethical considerations play an important part in guiding your action:

a. You are a student in an accounting principles course.
b. You are a manager with responsibility for several employees.
c. You are an accounting professional preparing tax returns for clients.
d. You are an accounting professional with audit clients that are competitors in business.

Exercise 1-9
Describing accounting responsibilities

LO7

Many accounting professionals work in one of the following three areas:

a. Financial accounting
b. Managerial accounting
c. Tax accounting

For each of the following responsibilities, identify the area of accounting that most likely involves that responsibility:

_____ **1.** Auditing financial statements.
_____ **2.** Planning transactions to minimize taxes paid.
_____ **3.** Cost accounting.
_____ **4.** Preparing financial statements.
_____ **5.** Reviewing financial reports for compliance with provincial securities commissions requirements.
_____ **6.** Budgeting.
_____ **7.** Internal auditing.
_____ **8.** Investigating violations of tax laws.

Problems

Problem 1-1A
Determining profits, revenues, and expenses

LO3

Little Lambs Daycare showed daycare revenues totalling $312,000 for the past year. The business also received rental income of $4,800 from its basement tenants. Salaries, utilities, food, and art supplies used by the children for the year were $246,000.

Required
Calculate the net income or net loss.

Problem 1-2A
Identifying type of business organization

LO4

Complete the chart below by placing a checkmark in the appropriate column.

Characteristic	Type of Business Organization		
	Sole Proprietorship	Partnership	Corporation
Limited liability			
Unlimited liability			
Owners are shareholders			
Owners are partners			
Taxed as a separate legal entity			

Alternate Problems

Problem 1-1B
Determining profits, revenues, and expenses

LO3

Roy Rogers Riding Academy provides riding lessons and boards horses. Riding lessons for the past year generated total revenues of $260,000. Boarding revenues were $84,000 for the same period. Salaries, feed, maintenance, and other expenses totalled $350,000.

Required
Calculate the net income or net loss.

Problem 1-2B
Identifying type of business organization

LO4

a. Refer to Appendix I at the end of the book. Determine if WestJet Airlines is a sole proprietorship, partnership, or corporation.

b. Refer to Appendix I at the end of the book. Determine if ClubLink is a sole proprietorship, partnership, or corporation.

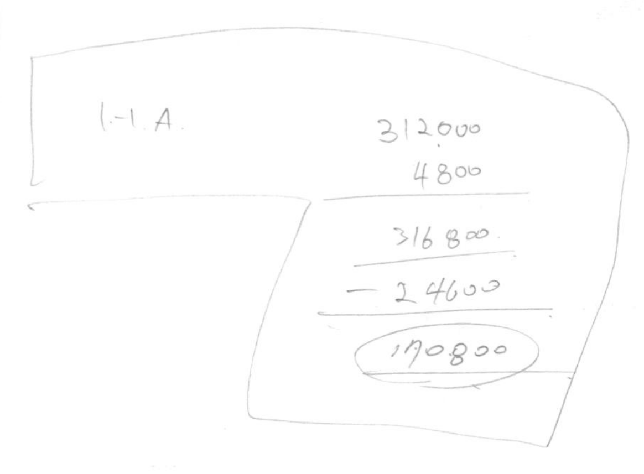

260000 + 8400
− 350000
Rave 84000
Net loss
6000
344000
350000

let loss

6000

CHAPTER

Financial Statements and Accounting Transactions

Shoes on Trial

Tucked along a harbourside street, FastForward could be another trendy sports shop. However, its small back lot, where Chuck Taylor runs up grassy mounds, through sand pits, and in mud, makes clear that this is something far different. These obstacles are product research tools.

FastForward consults on athletic footwear, a potentially exciting, new service. In just one year, Chuck Taylor became a consultant sought after by sports clubs, schools and athletes. In the first six months of operations, the company's profits rose at a 35% rate.

FastForward's story is the envy of every entrepreneur. Taylor, 29, loved sports—but he hated his shoes. He never seemed to have the right shoes for the right conditions. Independent tests of shoe performance were either nonexistent or outdated. So Taylor put an idea into action. He went out and purchased 21 pair of the best basketball shoes on the market. He ran the shoes through a battery of tests under many different court conditions.

Learning Objectives

LO1 Identify and explain the content and reporting aims of financial statements.

LO2 Identify differences in financial statements across forms of business organization.

LO3 Identify, explain and apply accounting principles.

LO4 Explain and interpret the accounting equation.

LO5 Analyze business transactions using the accounting equation.

LO6 Prepare financial statements from business transactions.

The results shocked even him. Many lower-priced, lesser-known shoes performed on par or better than many expensive, better-known shoes. He carried his findings to athletic teams and athletes. He got a welcome reception and payment for his services.

Taylor quit his job to devote himself full-time to his new business. "I instantly needed accounting skills to keep track of receipts, bills, everything," says Taylor. "When I later applied for a loan, the bank couldn't believe my poor accounting records. But what do you expect from a jock!" Taylor eventually got his accounting records in order and got the loan. To boost growth, FastForward is now moving into testing of soccer, track and football shoes. "We are meeting a market need and making people happy," added Taylor. You can count Taylor as one of the happy.

Chapter Preview

Financial statements report on the financial performance and condition of an organization. They are one of the most important products of accounting and are useful to both internal and external decision makers. Chuck Taylor of FastForward recognized the importance of accounting reports when running his own business and in applying for a loan. Financial statements are the means by which businesspeople communicate. Knowledge of their preparation, organization and analysis is important.

In this chapter, we describe the kind of information captured and revealed in financial statements. We also discuss the principles and assumptions guiding their preparation. An important part of this chapter is to illustrate how transactions are reflected in financial statements. The appendix introduces the key organizations that regulate and influence the development and maintenance of accounting standards. This chapter devotes special attention to Finlay Interiors, whose first month's transactions are the focus of our analysis.

Communicating Through Financial Statements

LO1 Identify and explain the content and reporting aims of financial statements.

We discussed in Chapter 1 how accounting provides useful information that helps internal users P. 14 and external users P. 13 to make better decisions. Many organizations report their accounting information in the form of financial statements, which reveal an organization's financial health and performance in an easy-to-read summary format. They are the primary means of financial communication and are the end result of a process, or cycle, which begins with a business transaction like a sale. These transactions are recorded, classified, sorted and summarized in order to produce the statements. In this chapter, we follow this process in an informal manner so that you become familiar with the accounting cycle. In Chapter 3, we present the formal development of the accounting records that are used by businesses.

Previewing Financial Statements

We will begin our study of the four major financial statements—the income statement, balance sheet, statement of owner's equity, and statement of cash flows—with a brief description of each. How these statements are linked is illustrated in Exhibit 2.1.

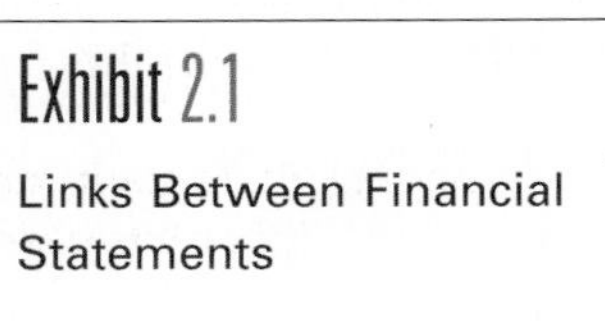

Exhibit 2.1

Links Between Financial Statements

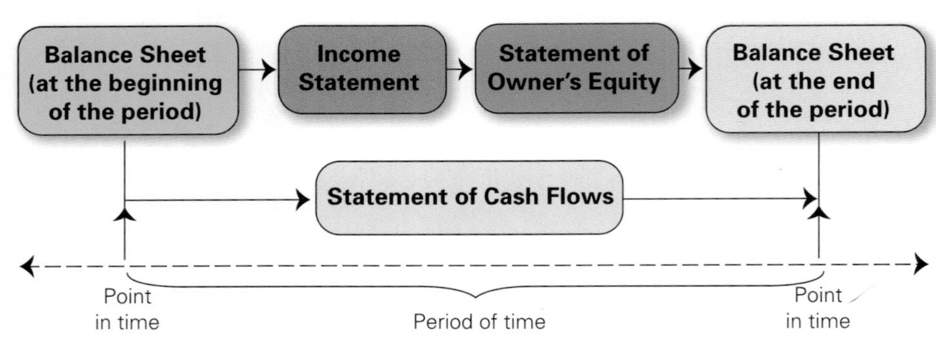

Transactions occur over a period of time, or during the accounting period, and are reported on the income statement, statement of owner's equity, and statement of cash flows. These transactions result in a new balance sheet at the end of the period.

A balance sheet reports on an organization's financial position at a *point in time.* The income statement, statement of owner's equity, and statement of cash flows report on performance over a *period of time.*

Selection of a reporting period is up to preparers and users (including regulatory agencies). A one-year, or annual, reporting period is common, as are semi-annual, quarterly and monthly periods. The one-year reporting period is also known as the accounting or **fiscal year**. Businesses whose reporting period follows the **calendar year** begin on January 1 and end on December 31. Many companies choose a fiscal year based on their **natural business year** that ends when sales and inventories are low. For example, Irwin Toy's fiscal year-end is January 31, after the holiday season.

Income Statement

An **income statement** reports revenues earned less expenses incurred by a business over a period of time. A **net income**, or profit, means that revenues exceed expenses. A **net loss** (or, simply, a loss) means that expenses exceed revenues.

To illustrate financial statements, let's assume that on January 1, 2001, Carol Finlay opened an interior-design business in the name of *Finlay Interiors.* The income statement for Finlay Interiors' first month of operations is shown in Exhibit 2.2. An income statement lists the types and amounts of both revenues and expenses. This is crucial information for users as it helps in understanding and predicting company performance. For example, Laidlaw classifies its revenues and expenses in three categories: passenger services, healthcare transportation services and hazardous waste services. Rogers also separates its revenues into three groups: cable television, wireless communications and multimedia. This information is more useful for making decisions than a simple profit or loss number would be.

Revenues	−	**Expenses**	=	**Net income or Net loss**
For example:				
$100 Revenues	−	$75 Expenses	=	$25 Net income
		OR		
$300 Revenues	−	$360 Expenses	=	$60 Net loss

Revenues

Revenues are inflows of assets in exchange for products and services provided to customers as part of a business's primary operations. Assets include cash, equipment, buildings and land. We can think of assets as economic resources owned by a business, and liabilities as amounts owed. Later in the chapter, we will define these terms more precisely. The income statement in Exhibit 2.2 shows that Finlay Interiors earned total revenues of $4,100 during January from consulting services

Finlay Interiors
Income Statement
For Month Ended January 31, 2001

Revenues:		
Consulting revenue	$3,800	
Rental revenue	300	
Total revenues		$4,100
Operating expenses:		
Rent expense	$1,000	
Salaries expense	700	
Total operating expenses		1,700
Net income		$2,400

Exhibit 2.2

Income Statement for Finlay Interiors

fi Finlay Interiors

and rental revenue. Examples of revenues for other businesses include sales of products and amounts earned from receiving dividends and interest. **Dividends** are distributions of cash or other assets from a corporation to its owners.

Expenses

Expenses are outflows or the using up of assets from providing products and services to customers. The income statement in Exhibit 2.2 shows that Finlay Interiors used up some of its assets in paying for rented office space. The $1,000 expense for office space is reported in the income statement as rent expense. Finlay Interiors also paid for an employee's salary at a cost of $700. This is reported on the income statement as salaries expense. The income statement heading in Exhibit 2.2 identifies the business, the type of statement, and the time period covered. Knowledge of the time period is important for us in judging whether the $2,400 net income earned in January is satisfactory.

Statement of Owner's Equity

The **statement of owner's equity** reports on changes in equity over the reporting period. This statement starts with beginning equity and adjusts it for events that: (1) increase it—investments by the owner and net income; and (2) decrease it—owner withdrawals and net loss. **Owner investments** occur when the owner transfers personal assets, such as cash, into the business. Since owner investments do not result from the sale of a product or service, they are not a revenue and are therefore ***not*** reported on the income statement. **Owner withdrawals**, or **withdrawals**, occur when the owner takes cash or other assets from the business. Withdrawals represent a distribution of net income to the owner. Since withdrawals do not help to create revenue, they are ***not*** expenses and therefore are not reported on the income statement.

The statement of owner's equity for Finlay Interiors' first month of operations is shown in Exhibit 2.3. This statement describes events that changed owner's equity during the month. It shows $30,000 of equity created by Finlay's initial investment. It also shows $2,400 of net income earned during the month. The statement also reports Finlay's $600 withdrawal. Finlay Interiors' equity balance at the end of the month is $31,800.

Balance Sheet

The **balance sheet**, or **statement of financial position**, reports the financial position of a business at a point in time, usually at the end of a month or year. It describes financial position by listing the types and dollar amounts of assets,

Exhibit 2.3

Statement of Owner's Equity for Finlay Interiors

fi Finlay Interiors

Finlay Interiors
Statement of Owner's Equity
For Month Ended January 31, 2001

Carol Finlay, capital, January 1		$ -0-
Add: Investments by owner	$30,000	
Net income	2,400	32,400
Total		$32,400
Less: Withdrawals by owner		600
Carol Finlay, capital, January 31		$31,800

liabilities and equity. Exhibit 2.4 shows the balance sheet for Finlay Interiors as of January 31, 2001. The balance sheet heading lists the business name, the statement, and the specific date on which assets and liabilities are identified and measured. The amounts in the balance sheet are measured as of the close of business on that specific date.

Exhibit 2.4

Balance Sheet for Finlay Interiors

Finlay Interiors
Balance Sheet
January 31, 2001

Assets		**Liabilities**		
Cash	$ 8,400	Accounts payable	$ 200	
Supplies	3,600	Notes payable	6,000	
Furniture	26,000	Total liabilities		$6,200
		Owner's Equity		
		Carol Finlay, capital		31,800
Total assets	$38,000	Total liabilities and owner's equity		$38,000

The balance sheet for Finlay Interiors shows that it owns three different assets at the close of business on January 31, 2001. The assets are cash, supplies and furniture. The total dollar amount for these assets is $38,000. The balance sheet also shows total liabilities of $6,200. Owner's equity is $31,800. Equity is the difference between assets and liabilities. The statement is named a *balance sheet* because: (1) the total amounts on each side of the statement are equal; and (2) the reporting of assets, liabilities and equity are in *balance.*

Assets

Assets are the properties or economic resources owned by a business. A common characteristic of assets is their ability to provide future benefits to the company.[1] Assets are of many types. A familiar asset is *cash.* Another is **accounts receivable,** an asset created by selling products or services on credit. It reflects amounts owed to a business by its credit customers. These customers, and other individuals and organizations who owe amounts to a business, are called its **debtors.** Other common assets owned by businesses include merchandise held for sale, supplies, equipment, buildings and land. Discussed in Chapter 5 are other assets having intangible rights, such as those granted by a patent or copyright.

Liabilities

Liabilities are obligations of a business. They are claims of others against the assets of the business. A common characteristic of liabilities is their capacity to reduce future assets or to require future services or products.[2] Liabilities take many forms. Typical liabilities include *accounts payable* and *notes payable.* An **account payable** is a liability created by buying products or services on credit. It

1 *CICA Handbook,* "Financial Statement Concepts," par. 1000.29
2 *CICA Handbook,* "Financial Statement Concepts," par. 1000.32

reflects amounts owed to others. A **note payable** is a liability expressed by a written promise to make a future payment at a specific time. Other common liabilities are salaries and wages owed to employees, and interest payable.

Individuals and organizations who own the right to receive payments from a business are called its **creditors**. One entity's payable is another entity's receivable. If a business fails to pay its obligations, the law gives creditors a right to force sale of its assets to obtain the money to meet their claims. When assets are sold under these conditions, creditors are paid first but only up to the amount of their claims. Any remaining money, the residual, goes to the owner of the business. Creditors often compare the amounts of liabilities and assets on a balance sheet to help them decide whether to lend money to a business. A loan is less risky if liabilities are small in comparison to assets, because there are more resources than claims on resources. A loan is more risky if liabilities are large compared to assets.

Equity

Equity is the owner's claim on the assets of a business. It is the *residual interest* in the assets of a business that remains after deducting liabilities.[3] Equity is also called **net assets.** Since Finlay Interiors is a sole proprietorship, the equity heading of its balance sheet in Exhibit 2.4 is *owner's equity.*

We explained that net income is the difference between revenues and expenses of a business over a period of time. Net income is also equal to the change in owner's equity due to operating activities over a period of time. In this way, an income statement links balance sheets from the beginning and the end of a reporting period.

The causes of change in owner's equity are highlighted in Exhibit 2.5. Changes in owner's equity are reported in the statement of owner's equity, and give us the ending balance of owner's equity that is reported in the balance sheet.

Exhibit 2.5

The Causes of Change in Owner's Equity

Increases in owner's equity are caused by:	Decreases in owner's equity are caused by
• owner investments	• owner withdrawals
• revenues	• expenses

Statement of Cash Flows

The **statement of cash flows** describes the sources and uses of cash for a reporting period. It also reports the amount of cash at both the beginning and end of a period. The statement of cash flows is organized by a company's major activities: operating, investing and financing. Since a company must carefully manage cash if it is to survive and prosper, cash flow information is important.

To fully appreciate this statement, a solid understanding of some basic accounting concepts is required. Therefore, a detailed discussion has been left to Chapter 19. As an example, the statement of cash flows for Finlay Interiors is shown in Exhibit 2.6.

[3] *CICA Handbook,* "Financial Statement Concepts," par. 1000.35

Finlay Interiors Statement of Cash Flows For Month Ended January 31, 2001		
Cash flows from operating activities:		
Cash received from clients	$ 4,100	
Cash paid for supplies	(2,500)	
Cash paid for rent	(1,000)	
Cash paid to employee	(700)	
Cash paid on account	(900)	
Net cash used by operating activities		$ (1,000)
Cash flows from investing activities:		
Purchase of furniture	$(20,000)	
Net cash used by investing activities		(20,000)
Cash flows from financing activities:		
Investment by owner	$ 30,000	
Withdrawal by owner	(600)	
Net cash provided by financing activities		29,400
Net increase in cash		$ 8,400
Cash balance, January 1		– 0 –
Cash balance, January 31		$ 8,400

Exhibit 2.6

Statement of Cash Flows for Finlay Interiors

Financial Statements and Forms of Organization

Identify differences in financial statements across forms of business organization.

Chapter 1 described three different forms of business organization: sole proprietorships P. 10, partnerships P. 10, and corporations P. 10. Exhibit 2.7 summarizes key differences among these three forms of business ownership. While many differences exist, financial statements for these three types of organizations are very similar.

Difference	Type of Business Organization Sole Proprietorship	Partnership	Corporation
Equity section on the balance sheet is called:	Owner's equity	Partners' equity	Shareholders' equity
Distributions to owners are called:	Withdrawals	Withdrawals	Dividends
When managers are also owners, their salaries are:	Not an expense	Not an expense	An expense

Exhibit 2.7

Financial Statement Differences Based on Type of Business Organization

The emphasis in the early chapters of this book is on sole proprietorships. This allows us to focus on important measurement and reporting issues in accounting without getting caught up in the complexities of additional forms of organization. We do discuss other forms of organization, however, and provide examples when appropriate. Chapters 14, 15 and 16 return to this topic and provide additional detail about the financial statements of partnerships and corporations.

1. What are the four major financial statements?
2. Describe revenues and expenses.
3. Explain assets, liabilities and equity.
4. What are three differences in financial statements for different forms of organization?

Answers—pp. 54–55

Generally Accepted Accounting Principles

The rules that make up acceptable accounting practices are referred to as **Generally Accepted Accounting Principles (GAAP).** The responsibility for setting accounting principles is determined by many individuals and groups, and is discussed in the appendix to this chapter. For us to use and interpret financial statements effectively, we need an understanding of these principles. A primary purpose of GAAP is to make information in financial statements *relevant, reliable, consistent,* and *comparable.* Information that is *relevant* can affect the types of decisions made by users. Information must be *reliable* for decision makers to depend on it. *Consistency* ensures that information is prepared using the same accounting procedures from one accounting period to the next. If companies use similar practices, information is *comparable* and allows users to contrast companies. GAAP impose limits on the range of accounting practices that companies can use. We describe in this section some of the important accounting principles.

Fundamental Principles of Accounting

LO3 Identify, explain and apply accounting principles.

Accounting principles are both general and specific. General principles are the basic assumptions, concepts and guidelines for preparing financial statements; they stem from long-used accounting practices. Specific principles are detailed rules used in reporting on business transactions and events; they arise more often from the rulings of authoritative groups.

We need an understanding of both to effectively use accounting information. Because the general principles (as illustrated in Exhibit 2.8) are especially crucial in using accounting information, we emphasize them in the early chapters of this book. The GAAP described in this chapter include: business entity, objectivity, cost, going-concern, monetary unit, and revenue recognition. General principles described in later chapters (with their relevant chapter in parentheses) include: time period (4), matching (4), materiality (7), full-disclosure (7), consistency (7) and conservatism (7).

Exhibit 2.8

Building Blocks for the House of GAAP

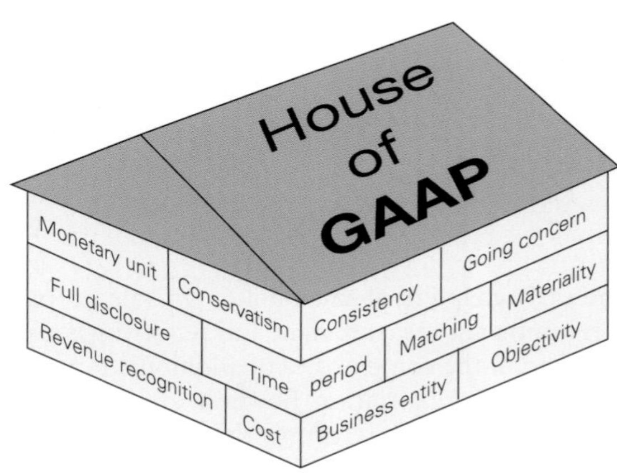

Business Entity Principle or Economic Entity Principle

Each economic entity or business of the owner must keep accounting records and reports that are separate from those of the owner and any other economic entity of the owner.

Example: Looking at Finlay Interiors, Carol Finlay must not include personal expenses, such as clothing and the cost of going to the movies, as expenses of her business.

Objectivity Principle

Financial statement information must be supported by independent, unbiased, and verifiable evidence. The cost principle is also consistent with objectivity because most users consider cost to be objective.

Example: If Carol Finlay purchases new furniture and records the transaction based on an invoice prepared by the store of purchase, the invoice is *independent* and *unbiased* evidence that *verifies* the details of the transaction.

Cost Principle

All transactions are recorded based on the actual cash amount received or paid. In the absence of cash, the cash equivalent amount of the exchange is recorded.[4]

Example: If Finlay Interiors purchased used furniture for $5,000 cash, it is recorded in the accounting records at $5,000. It makes no difference if Carol Finlay thinks that the value of the equipment is $7,000.

Going-concern Principle or Continuing-concern Principle

Financial statement users assume that the statements reflect a business that is going to continue its operations instead of being closed or sold. Therefore, assets are maintained in the accounting records at cost and not reduced to a liquidation value as if the business were being bought or sold. If a company is to be bought or sold, buyers and sellers are advised to obtain additional information, such as estimated market values, from other sources.[5]

Example: It is assumed from a review of Finlay Interiors' financial statements that the business is continuing its operations, because information to the contrary is not included.

Monetary Unit Principle or Stable-dollar Principle

Transactions are expressed using units of money as the common denominator. It is assumed that the monetary unit is stable; therefore, a transaction is left as originally recorded and is not later adjusted for changes in currency value or inflation. The greater the changes in currency value and inflation, the more difficult it is to use and interpret financial statements across time.

Example: Assume that in August 2001 Finlay Interiors purchased furniture from a supplier in the United States at a total cost of $1,000 American, or $1,489 Canadian ($1,000/0.6716 exchange rate). If the exchange rate changes several months later to 0.6412, Finlay Interiors does not restate the value of the furniture to $1,560 ($1,000/0.6412 current exchange rate). The furniture remains in the accounting records at $1,489 Canadian. This is also consistent with the *cost principle.*

---

[4] *CICA Handbook,* "Non-monetary Transactions," par. 3830.05.

[5] *CICA Handbook,* "Financial Instruments" requires that the fair (market) value of financial assets and liabilities be disclosed as supplemental information, par. 3860.78.

✓ **Revenue Recognition Principle or Realization Principle**

Revenue is recorded at the time that it is earned regardless of whether cash or another asset has been exchanged.[6] The amount of revenue to be recorded is measured by the cash plus the cash equivalent value (market value) of any other assets received.

Example: Assume that on April 3, Finlay Interiors performed work for a client in the amount of $600. The client did not pay the $600 until May 15. Revenue is recorded when actually earned on April 3 in the amount of $600, the value of the noncash asset received by Finlay Interiors.

7 matching principle

Answers—p. 55

5. Why is the business entity principle important?
6. How are the objectivity and cost principles related?
7. A customer pays cash today for a product that is to be delivered to her next month. When should revenue be recognized?

The Accounting Equation

Explain and interpret the accounting equation.

Notice in Exhibit 2.4 that there are two main sections of the balance sheet: assets on one side and liabilities and owner's equity on the other side. Observe that the total assets of $38,000 equal the total liabilities and owner's equity of $38,000. This equality is known as the *accounting equation*. This equation is based on relationships fundamental to accounting.

When an organization invests in assets, it is the result of an equal amount of financing. This relationship is expressed in the following equation:

Investing = Financing

Since invested amounts are referred to as *assets*, and financing is made up of owner and non-owner financing, we can also express this equality as:

Assets = Non-owner Financing + Owner Financing

Non-owners are creditors. Creditors and owners hold claims or rights in the assets. Creditors' claims are called *liabilities* and the owner's claim is called *owner's equity*. The equation can be rewritten as shown in Exhibit 2.9.

Exhibit 2.9

The Accounting Equation

The financing side of the equation describes where the assets came from.

Assets = **Liabilities** + **Owner's Equity**

Assets describe what an organization has invested in (such as land, building, machinery, cash).

Liabilities describe non-owner financing (borrowing).

Owner's Equity describes owner financing (what is owned by the owner).

[6] *CICA Handbook*, "Revenue," par. 3400.06-.09

This equation is called the **accounting equation** or **balance sheet equation** because of its link to the balance sheet. It describes the relationship between a company's assets, liabilities, and equity. To demonstrate, assume you want to buy a car that costs $25,000. The bank lends you $15,000 and you pay $10,000 out of your personal savings account.

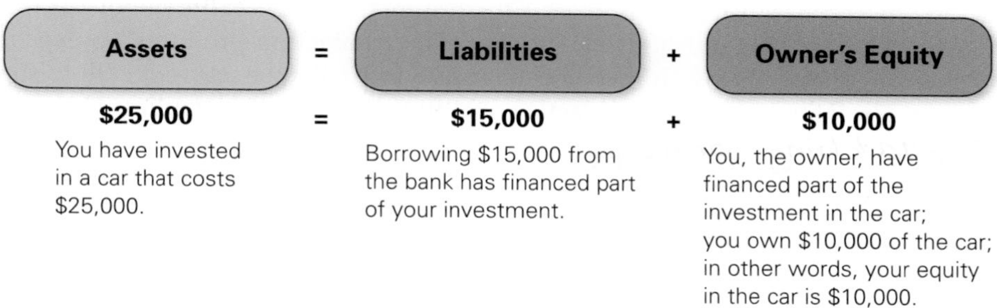

The accounting equation can be changed by moving liabilities to the left side of the equation:

Assets – Liabilities = Owner's Equity

Assets less liabilities equals net assets, another name for equity.

Transactions and the Accounting Equation

LO5 Analyze business transactions using the accounting equation.

To fully reap the benefits of information in financial statements, we need to know how an accounting system captures transactions and reports the data in financial statements. In the next section, we show how to use the accounting equation to keep track of changes in a company's assets, liabilities and owner's equity in a way that provides useful information.

Transaction Analysis

A **business transaction** is an exchange of economic consideration between two parties that causes a change in assets, liabilities or owner's equity. Examples of economic considerations include products, services, money and rights to collect money. Because two different parties exchange assets and liabilities, transactions affect the components of the accounting equation. It is important for us to realize that every transaction leaves the equation in balance. Assets *always* equal the sum of liabilities and equity. We show how this equality is maintained by looking at the assumed transactions of Finlay Interiors in its first month of operations.

Transaction 1: Investment by Owner. On January 1, 2001, Carol Finlay formed her interior-design business and set it up as a sole proprietorship. Finlay is the manager of the business as well as its owner. The marketing plan for the business is to focus primarily on consulting with homebuilders, professionals with offices, and other groups who place a high degree of emphasis on interior design. Finlay invests $30,000 cash in the new company, which she deposits in a bank account opened under the name of Finlay Interiors. After this transaction, the cash (an asset) and the owner's equity (called *Carol Finlay, Capital*) each equal $30,000. The effect of this transaction on the accounting equation is:

	Assets	=	Liabilities	+	Owner's Equity	Explanation
	Cash	=			**Carol Finlay, Capital**	
(1)	+$30,000	=			+$30,000	Investment

The accounting equation is in balance. It reveals that Finlay Interiors has one asset, cash, that is equal to $30,000. It also reveals no liabilities and an owner's equity of $30,000. The source of increase in equity is identified as an investment to distinguish it from revenues.

Transaction 2: Purchase Supplies for Cash. Finlay Interiors uses $2,500 of its cash to purchase various supplies. This transaction is an exchange of cash, an asset, for another kind of asset, supplies. The transaction produces no expense because no value is lost. It merely changes the form of an asset from cash to supplies. The decrease in cash is exactly equal to the increase in supplies. The equation remains in balance.

	Assets		=	Liabilities	+	Owner's Equity	Explanation
	Cash +	**Supplies**	=			**Carol Finlay, Capital**	
Old Bal.	$30,000		=			$30,000	
(2)	−$ 2,500	+$2,500					
New Bal.	$27,500 +	$2,500	=			$30,000	
	$30,000		=	$30,000			

Transaction 3: Purchase Furniture for Cash. Finlay Interiors spends $20,000 of its cash to acquire furniture. In addition to consulting, Finlay Interiors rents furniture to homebuilders to make their houses' interiors appear more attractive and thus make the houses more saleable. Like Transaction 2, Transaction 3 is an exchange of one asset, cash, for another asset, furniture. It is not an expense because no value is lost. This purchase changes the make-up of assets but does not change the asset total. The equation remains in balance.

	Assets			=	Liabilities	+	Owner's Equity	Explanation
	Cash +	**Supplies** +	**Furniture**	=			**Carol Finlay, Capital**	
Old Bal.	$27,500	$2,500		=			$30,000	
(3)	−$20,000		+$20,000					
New Bal.	$ 7,500 +	$2,500 +	$20,000	=			$30,000	
	$30,000			=	$30,000			

Transaction 4: Purchase Furniture and Supplies on Credit. Finlay decides that she needs more furniture and supplies; these purchases total $7,100. As we see from the accounting equation in Transaction 3, however, Finlay Interiors has only $7,500 in cash. Concerned that these purchases would use nearly all of Finlay Interiors' cash, Finlay arranges to purchase them on credit from CanTech Supply Company. This means that Finlay Interiors acquires these items in exchange for a promise to pay for them later. Supplies cost $1,100, and the new furniture costs $6,000. The total liability to CanTech Supply is $7,100. Finlay Interiors will pay for the supplies in 30 days, but has arranged to pay for the furniture by signing a note. The effects of this purchase on the accounting equation are:

	Assets			=	Liabilities		+	Owner's Equity	Explanation
	Cash +	Supplies +	Furniture	=	Accounts + Payable	Notes Payable	+	Carol Finlay, Capital	
Old Bal.	$7,500	$2,500	$20,000	=				$30,000	
(4)		+1,100	+6,000		+$1,100	+6,000			
New Bal.	$7,500 +	$3,600 +	$26,000	=	$1,100 +	$6,000	+	$30,000	
	$37,100				$37,100				

This purchase increases assets by $7,100, while liabilities (called *accounts payable* and *notes payable*) increase by the same amount. Both of these payables are promises by Finlay Interiors to repay its debt, where the note payable reflects a more formal written agreement. We will discuss these liabilities in detail in later chapters.

Transaction 5: Services Rendered for Cash. A primary objective of a business is to increase its owner's wealth. This goal is met when a business produces a profit, also called *net income*. Net income is reflected in the accounting equation as an increase in owner's equity. Finlay Interiors earns revenues by consulting with clients about interior design. We see how the accounting equation is affected by earning consulting revenues in Transaction 5, where Finlay Interiors provides consulting services on January 10 to a dentist opening a dental centre and immediately collects $2,200 cash. This event increases cash by $2,200 and owner's equity by $2,200, identified in the far right column as a revenue because it is earned by providing services. These explanations are useful in preparing and understanding a statement of owner's equity and an income statement.

	Assets			=	Liabilities		+	Owner's Equity	Explanation
	Cash +	Supplies +	Furniture	=	Accounts + Payable	Notes Payable	+	Carol Finlay, Capital	
Old Bal.	$7,500 +	$3,600 +	$26,000	=	$1,100 +	$6,000	+	$30,000	
(5)	+2,200							+2,200	Consulting Revenue
New Bal.	$9,700 +	$3,600 +	$26,000	=	$1,100 +	$6,000	+	$32,200	
	$39,300				$39,300				

Transactions 6 and 7: Payment of Expenses in Cash. On January 10, Finlay Interiors pays the landlord of its office building $1,000 to cover January's rent for office space. The effects of this event on the accounting equation are shown below as Transaction 6. On January 12, Finlay Interiors pays the $700 salary of the business's only employee. This event is reflected in the accounting equation as Transaction 7.

	Assets			=	Liabilities		+	Owner's Equity	Explanation
	Cash +	Supplies +	Furniture	=	Accounts + Payable	Notes Payable	+	Carol Finlay, Capital	
Old Bal.	$9,700 +	$3,600 +	$26,000	=	$1,100 +	$6,000	+	$32,200	
(6)	−1,000							−1,000	Rent Expense
Bal.	$8,700 +	$3,600 +	$26,000	=	$1,100 +	$6,000	+	$31,200	
(7)	−700							−700	Salary Expense
New Bal.	$8,000 +	$3,600 +	$26,000	=	$1,100 +	$6,000	+	$30,500	
	$37,600				$37,600				

Both Transactions 6 and 7 produce expenses for Finlay Interiors as noted in the far right column. They use up cash for the purpose of providing services to clients. Unlike the asset purchases in Transactions 2 and 3, the cash payments in Transactions 6 and 7 acquire services. The benefits of these services do *not* last beyond the end of this month. The accounting equation remains in balance, and shows that both transactions reduce cash and Finlay's equity.

Transaction 8: Services and Rental Revenues Rendered for Credit. On January 15, Finlay Interiors provides consulting services of $1,600 and rented furniture for $300 to a homebuilder, who is billed for $1,900. This transaction results in a new asset: an account receivable from the client. The $1,900 increase in assets produces an equal increase in owner's equity. Notice that the increase in equity is identified as two revenue components in the far right column of the accounting equation:

	Assets				=	Liabilities	+	Owner's Equity	Explanation
	Cash	+ Acounts Receivable	+ Supplies	+ Furniture	=	Accounts Payable	+ Notes Payable	+ Carol Finlay, Capital	
Old Bal.	$8,000		+ $3,600	+ $26,000	=	$1,100	+ $6,000	+ $30,500	
(8)		+1,900						+1,600	Consulting Revenue
								+ 300	Rental Revenue
New Bal.	$8,000	+ $1,900	+ $3,600	+ $26,000	=	$1,100	+ $6,000	+ $32,400	
	$39,500					$39,500			

Transaction 9: Receipt of Cash on Account. The amount of $1,900 is received from the client on January 25, ten days after the billing for consulting services in Transaction 8. Transaction 9 does not change the amount of assets and does not affect liabilities or equity. It converts the receivable to cash and *does not* create new revenue. Revenue was recognized when Finlay Interiors rendered the services on January 15. Therefore, revenue is *not* recorded on January 25 when the cash is collected. This emphasis on the earnings process instead of cash flows is a goal of the revenue recognition principle and provides relevant information to users. The new balances are:

	Assets				=	Liabilities	+	Owner's Equity	Explanation
	Cash	+ Acounts Receivable	+ Supplies	+ Furniture	=	Accounts Payable	+ Notes Payable	+ Carol Finlay, Capital	
Old Bal.	$8,000	+ $1,900	+ $3,600	+ $26,000	=	$1,100	+ $6,000	+ $32,400	
(9)	+1,900	−1,900							
New Bal.	$9,900	+ $ -0-	+ $3,600	+ $26,000	=	$1,100	+ $6,000	+ $32,400	
	$39,500					$39,500			

Transaction 10: Payment of Accounts Payable. Finlay Interiors pays $900 to CanTech Supply on January 25. The $900 payment is for the earlier $1,100 purchase of supplies from CanTech, leaving $200 unpaid. The $6,000 amount due to CanTech for furniture remains unpaid. The accounting equation shows that this transaction decreases Finlay Interiors' cash by $900 and decreases its liability to CanTech Supply by the same amount. As a result, owner's equity does not change. This event does not create an expense, even though cash flows out of Finlay Interiors.

	Assets								=	Liabilities			+	Owner's Equity	Explanation
	Cash	+	Acounts Receivable	+	Supplies	+	Furniture		=	Accounts Payable	+	Notes Payable	+	Carol Finlay, Capital	
Old Bal.	$9,900	+	$ -0-	+	$3,600	+	$26,000		=	$1,100	+	$6,000	+	$32,400	
(10)	−900									−900					
New Bal.	$9,000	+	$ -0-	+	$3,600	+	$26,000		=	$ 200	+	$6,000	+	$32,400	
			$38,600									$38,600			

Transaction 11: Withdrawal of Cash by Owner. Finlay withdraws $600 in cash from Finlay Interiors for personal living expenses. Withdrawals are not expenses because they are not part of the company's earnings process. Therefore, withdrawals are not used in calculating net income.

	Assets								=	Liabilities			+	Owner's Equity	Explanation
	Cash	+	Acounts Receivable	+	Supplies	+	Furniture		=	Accounts Payable	+	Notes Payable	+	Carol Finlay, Capital	
Old Bal.	$9,000	+	$ -0-	+	$3,600	+	$26,000		=	$ 200	+	$6,000	+	$32,400	
(11)	−600													−600	Withdrawal
New Bal.	$8,400	+	$ -0-	+	$3,600	+	$26,000		=	$ 200	+	$6,000	+	$31,800	
			$38,000									$38,000			

Summary of Transactions

Summarized in Exhibit 2.10 are the effects of all of Finlay Interiors' eleven transactions using the accounting equation. Three points should be noted. First, the accounting equation remains in balance after every transaction. Second, transactions can be analyzed by their effects on components of the accounting equation. For example, total assets and equity increase by equal amounts in Transactions 1, 5 and 8. In Transactions 2, 3 and 9, one asset increases while another decreases by an equal amount. For Transaction 4, we see equal increases in assets and liabilities. Both assets and equity decrease by equal amounts in Transactions 6, 7 and 11. In Transaction 10, we see equal decreases in an asset and a liability. Third, the equality of effects in the accounting equation is fundamental to the *double-entry accounting system* that is discussed in the next chapter.

Exhibit 2.10

Summary Analysis of Finlay Interiors' Transactions Using the Accounting Equation

	Assets				=	Liabilities		+ Owner's Equity	Explanation
	Cash	+ Acounts Receivable	+ Supplies	+ Furniture	=	Accounts Payable	+ Notes Payable	+ Carol Finlay, Capital	
(1)	$ 30,000							$30,000	Investment
(2)	– 2,500		+$ 2,500						
Bal.	$ 27,500		$ 2,500					$30,000	
(3)	–20,000			+$20,000					
Bal.	$ 7,500		$ 2,500	$20,000				$30,000	
(4)			+1,100	+ 6,000		+$1,100	+$6,000		
Bal.	$ 7,500		$ 3,600	$26,000		$1,100	$6,000	$30,000	
(5)	+ 2,200							+ 2,200	Consulting Revenue
Bal.	$ 9,700		$ 3,600	$26,000		$1,100	$6,000	$32,200	
(6)	– 1,000							– 1,000	Rent Expense
Bal.	$ 8,700		$ 3,600	$26,000		$1,100	$6,000	$31,200	
(7)	– 700							– 700	Salary Expense
Bal.	$ 8,000		$ 3,600	$26,000		$1,100	$6,000	$30,500	
(8)		+$ 1,900						+ 1,600	Consulting Revenue
								+ 300	Rental Revenue
Bal.	$ 8,000	$ 1,900	$ 3,600	$26,000		$1,100	$6,000	$32,400	
(9)	+ 1,900	–1,900							
Bal.	$ 9,900	$ -0-	$ 3,600	$26,000		$1,100	$6,000	$32,400	
(10)	– 900					– 900			
Bal.	$ 9,000	$ -0-	$ 3,600	$26,000		$ 200	$6,000	$32,400	
(11)	– 600							– 600	Withdrawal
Bal.	$ 8,400	+ $ -0-	+ $ 3,600	+ $26,000	=	$ 200	+ $6,000	+ $31,800	
	$38,000					$38,000			

It is important to recognize that the accounting equation is a representation of the balance sheet. Therefore, we can take the information in Exhibit 2.10 and prepare financial statements for Finlay Interiors. This will be done in the next section.

Flashback

Answers—p. 55

8. How can a transaction not affect liability and equity accounts?
9. Describe a transaction that increases owner's equity and one that decreases it.
10. Identify a transaction that decreases both assets and liabilities.
11. When is the accounting equation in balance, and what does it mean?

Mid-Chapter Demonstration Problem

Bob Delgado founded a new moving firm on May 1. The accounting equation showed the following balances after each of the company's first four transactions. Analyze the equations and describe each of the four transactions with their amounts.

	Assets				= Liabilities	+ Owner's Equity
Transaction	Cash +	Accounts Receivable +	Truck +	Office Furniture =	Accounts Payable +	Bob Delgado, Capital
A	$10,000	$ -0-	$45,000	$ -0-	$ -0-	$55,000
B	10,000	-0-	45,000	5,000	5,000	55,000
C	10,000	4,000	45,000	5,000	5,000	59,000
D	14,000	-0-	45,000	5,000	5,000	59,000

SOLUTION TO Mid-Chapter Demonstration Problem

A Started the business by investing $10,000 cash and a $45,000 truck.

B Purchased office furniture for $5,000 on account.

C Billed a customer $4,000 for services.

D Collected $4,000 from the customer in Transaction C.

Financial Statements

Prepare financial statements from business transactions.

We described financial statements at the beginning of this chapter. These statements are required under GAAP. In this section, we show how financial statements are prepared from business transactions. Recall that the four major financial statements and their purposes are as follows:

1. *Income statement:* describes a company's revenues and expenses along with the resulting net income or loss over a period of time. It helps to explain how owner's equity changes during a period due to earnings activities.
2. *Statement of owner's equity:* explains changes in equity due to items such as net income, and investments and withdrawals by an owner over a period of time.
3. *Balance sheet:* describes a business's financial position (assets, liabilities and equity) at a point in time.
4. *Statement of cash flows:* identifies cash inflows (receipts) and outflows (payments) over a period of time. It explains how the cash balance on the balance sheet changed from the beginning to the end of a period.

We now show how to prepare the first three of these financial statements using the transactions of Finlay Interiors. The statement of cash flows is left to Chapter 19.

Income Statement

Finlay Interiors' income statement is shown at the top of Exhibit 2.11. It is prepared from the January revenue and expense transactions as listed in the owner's equity column of Exhibit 2.10.

Revenues of $4,100 are reported first on the income statement. They include consulting revenues of $3,800 resulting from Transactions 5 and 8, and rental revenue of $300 from Transaction 8. Expenses follow revenues, and can be listed in different ways. For convenience in this chapter, we list larger amounts first. Rent and salaries expenses are from Transactions 6 and 7. Net income is reported at the bottom and is the amount earned during January. Owner's investments and withdrawals are *not* part of measuring income.

Exhibit 2.11

Finlay Interiors Financial Statements

fi Finlay Interiors

Finlay Interiors
Income Statement
For Month Ended January 31, 2001

Revenues:		
Consulting revenue	$3,800	
Rental revenue	300	
Total revenues		$4,100
Operating expenses:		
Rent expense	$1,000	
Salaries expense	700	
Total operating expenses		1,700
Net income		$2,400

Finlay Interiors
Statement of Owner's Equity
For Month Ended January 31, 2001

Carol Finlay, capital, January 1		$ -0-
Add: Investments by owner	$30,000	
Net income	2,400	32,400
Total		$32,400
Less: Withdrawals by owner		600
Carol Finlay, capital, January 31		$31,800

Finlay Interiors
Balance Sheet
January 31, 2001

Assets		**Liabilities**		
Cash	$ 8,400	Accounts payable	$ 200	
Supplies	3,600	Notes payable	6,000	
Furniture	26,000	Total liabilities		$ 6,200
		Owner's Equity		
		Carol Finlay, capital		31,800
Total assets	$38,000	Total liabilities and owner's equity		$38,000

Statement of Owner's Equity

The second report in Exhibit 2.11 is the statement of owner's equity for Finlay Interiors. Its heading lists the month as January 2001 because this statement describes events that happened during that month. The beginning balance of equity is measured as of the start of business on January 1. It is zero because Finlay Interiors did not exist before then. An existing business reports the beginning balance as of the end of the prior reporting period (such as December 31 for a continuing business). Finlay Interiors' statement shows that $30,000 of equity is created by Finlay's initial investment. It also shows the $2,400 of net income earned during the month. This item links the income statement to the statement of owner's equity. The statement also reports Finlay's $600 withdrawal and Finlay Interiors' $31,800 equity balance at the end of the month.

Balance Sheet

Finlay Interiors' balance sheet is the third report listed in Exhibit 2.11. This is the same statement that we described in Exhibit 2.4. Its heading tells us that the statement refers to Finlay Interiors' financial condition at the close of business on January 31, 2001.

The left side of the balance sheet lists Finlay Interiors' assets: cash, supplies and furniture. The right side of the balance sheet shows that Finlay Interiors owes $6,200 to creditors. This is made up of $200 for accounts payable and $6,000 for notes payable. If any other liabilities had existed (such as a bank loan), they would be listed here. The equity section shows an ending balance of $31,800. Note the link between the ending balance from the statement of owner's equity and the equity balance of the capital account. Also, note that the balance sheet equation, Assets = Liabilities + Owner's Equity, is still true ($38,000 = $6,200 + $31,800).

Supplier

You open your own wholesale business, selling home entertainment equipment to small retail outlets. You quickly find that most of your potential customers demand to buy on credit. How can you use the balance sheet in deciding to which customers you wish to extend credit?

Answer—p. 54

12. Explain the link between an income statement and the statement of owner's equity.
13. Describe the link between a balance sheet and the statement of owner's equity.

Answers—p. 55

Summary

LO1 **Identify and explain the content and reporting aims of financial statements.** The major financial statements are: income statement, statement of owner's equity, balance sheet and statement of cash flows. An income statement shows a company's profitability, including revenues, expenses and net income (loss). A balance sheet reports on a company's financial position, including assets, liabilities and owner's equity. A statement of owner's equity explains how owner's equity changes from the beginning to the end of a period, and the statement of cash flows identifies all cash inflows and outflows for the period.

LO2 **Identify differences in financial statements across forms of business organization.** One important difference is in the name of equity section of the balance sheet: Owner's equity for a sole proprietorship, Partner's equity for a partnership, and Shareholders' equity for a corporation. Another difference is in the term used to describe distributions by a business to its owners. When an owner of a proprietorship or a partnership takes cash or other assets from a company, the distributions are called withdrawals. When owners of a corporation receive cash or other assets from a company, the distributions are called dividends. When the owner of a proprietorship or partnership is its manager, no salary expense is reported. Since a corporation is a separate legal entity, however, salaries paid to its employees (including managers who are also shareholders) are always reported as expenses on its income statement.

LO3 **Identify, explain and apply accounting principles.** Accounting principles aid in producing relevant, reliable, consistent, and comparable information. The general principles described in this chapter include:

business entity, objectivity, cost, going-concern, monetary unit, and revenue recognition. We will discuss others in later chapters. The business entity principle means that a business is accounted for separately from its owners. The objectivity principle means that information is supported by independent, objective evidence. The cost principle means that financial statements are based on actual costs incurred in business transactions. The going-concern principle means financial statements reflect an assumption that the business continues to operate. The monetary unit principle assumes that transactions and events can be captured in money terms and that the monetary unit is stable over time. The revenue recognition principle means that revenue is recognized when earned, assets received from selling products and services do not have to be in cash, and revenue recognized is measured by cash received plus the cash equivalent (market) value of other assets received.

LO4 **Explain and interpret the accounting equation.** Investing activities are funded by an organization's financing activities. An organization's assets (investments) must equal its financing (from liabilities and from equity). This basic relation gives us the accounting equation: Assets = Liabilities + Owner's Equity.

LO5 **Analyze business transactions using the accounting equation.** A transaction is an exchange of economic consideration between two parties. Examples of economic considerations include products, services, money and rights to collect money. Because two different parties exchange assets and liabilities, transactions affect the components of the accounting equation. Business transactions always have at least two effects on the components of the accounting equation. The equation is always in balance when business transactions are properly recorded.

LO6 **Prepare financial statements from business transactions.** Using the accounting equation, business transactions can be summarized and organized so that we can readily prepare the financial statements. The balance sheet uses the ending balances in the accounting equation at a point in time. The statement of owner's equity and the income statement use data from the owner's equity account for the period.

GUIDANCE ANSWERS TO Judgement Call

Supplier

We can use the accounting equation to help us identify risky customers to whom we would not want to extend credit. The accounting equation can be written as: Assets – Liabilities = Owner's Equity. A balance sheet provides us with amounts for each of these key components. The lower the owner's equity, the less likely you should be to extend credit. A low owner's equity means that there is little value in the business that other creditors do not already have claims on. Note that any decision to grant credit would normally include an examination of the complete financial statements.

GUIDANCE ANSWERS TO Flashback

1. The four major financial statements are: income statement, balance sheet, statement of owner's equity, and statement of cash flows.
2. Revenues are inflows of assets in exchange for products or services provided to customers as part of the primary operations of a business. Expenses are outflows or the using up of assets that result from providing products or services to customers. Expenses also can arise from increases in liabilities.
3. Assets are the properties or economic resources owned by a business. Liabilities are the obligations of a business, representing the claims of others against the assets of a business. Equity is the owner's claim on the assets of the business. It is the owner's residual interest in the assets of a business after deducting liabilities.
4. Three differences in financial statements for different forms of organization are: (i) A proprietorship's balance sheet titles the equity section as "owner's equity."

Partnerships call equity "partners' equity." A corporation's equity section is named "shareholders' equity." (ii) Distributions of cash or other assets to owners of a proprietorship or partnership are called withdrawals. Distributions of cash or other assets to owners of a corporation are called dividends. (iii) When the owner of a sole proprietorship is also its manager, no salary expense is reported on the income statement. The same is true for a partnership. In a corporation, however, salaries paid to all employees, including managers who are shareholders, are reported as expenses.

5. The business entity principle is important to the usefulness of accounting. Users desire information about the performance of a *specific* entity. If information is mixed between two or more entities, its usefulness decreases. It is imperative that the business entity principle be followed.
6. The objectivity principle means that financial statement information is supported by independent, unbiased evidence. The cost principle means that financial statements are based on actual costs incurred in business transactions. The objectivity and cost principles are related in that most users consider information based on cost to be objective. Information prepared using both principles is considered highly reliable and often relevant.
7. Revenue should be recognized next month when the product is delivered, according to the revenue recognition principle. This principle states that revenue is recognized when the product has been provided and not necessarily when cash has been received. In this case, the business has received the cash from the customer without providing the product. Therefore, the business has not realized a revenue but instead has incurred a liability; it owes the customer the product.
8. A transaction that involves changing the form of one asset for another asset would *not* affect any liability and equity accounts. Both Transactions 2 and 3 offer examples.
9. Performing services for a customer, such as in Transaction 5, increases the owner's equity (and assets). Incurring expenses while servicing clients, such as in Transactions 6 and 7, decrease the owner's equity (and assets). Other examples include owner investments that increase equity, and owner withdrawals that decrease equity.
10. Payment of a liability with an asset reduces both asset and liability totals. An example is Transaction 10, where an account payable is settled by paying cash.
11. The accounting equation is: Assets = Liabilities + Owner's Equity. This equation is always in balance, both before and after every transaction. Balance refers to the equality in this equation, which is always maintained
12. An income statement describes a company's revenues and expenses along with the resulting net income or loss. A statement of owner's equity describes changes in equity that *include* net income. Also, both statements report transactions occurring over a period of time.
13. A balance sheet describes a company's financial position (assets, liabilities and equity) at a point in time. The owner's equity account in the balance sheet is obtained from the statement of owner's equity.

Demonstration Problem

After several months of planning, Barbara Schmidt started a haircutting business called The Cutlery. The following events occurred during its first month, August 2001:

a. On August 1, Schmidt put $3,000 cash into a chequing account in the name of The Cutlery. She also invested $15,000 of equipment that she already owned.

b. On August 2, she paid $600 cash for furniture for the shop.

c. On August 3, she paid $500 cash to rent space in a strip mall for August.

d. On August 4, she furnished the shop by installing the old equipment and some new equipment that she bought on credit for $1,200. This amount is to be repaid in three equal payments at the end of August, September, and October.

e. On August 5, The Cutlery opened for business. Receipts from services provided for cash in the first week and a half of business (ended August 15) were $825.

f. On August 15, Schmidt provided haircutting services on account for $100.

g On August 17, Schmidt received a $100 cheque in the mail for services previously rendered on account.

h. On August 17, Schmidt paid $125 to an assistant for working during the grand opening.

i. Cash receipts from services provided during the second half of August were $930.

j. On August 31, Schmidt paid an instalment on the account payable.

k. On August 31, the August hydro bill for $75 was received. It will be paid on September 14.

l. On August 31, Schmidt withdrew $900 cash for her personal use.

Required

1. Arrange the following asset, liability, and owner's equity titles in a table similar to the one in Exhibit 2.10: Cash, Accounts Receivable, Furniture, Store Equipment, Accounts Payable, and Barbara Schmidt, Capital. Show the effects of each transaction on the equation. Explain each of the changes in owner's equity.
2. Prepare an income statement for August.
3. Prepare a statement of owner's equity for August.
4. Prepare a balance sheet as of August 31.

Planning the Solution

- Set up a table with the appropriate columns, including a final column for describing the events that affect owner's equity.
- Analyze each transaction and show its effects as increases or decreases in the appropriate columns. Be sure that the accounting equation remains in balance after each event.
- To prepare the income statement, find the revenues and expenses in the Explanation of Change column. List those items on the statement, calculate the difference, and label the result as *net income* or *net loss.*
- Use the information in the Explanation of Change column to prepare the statement of owner's equity.
- Use the information in the last row of the table to prepare the balance sheet.

SOLUTION TO Demonstration Problem

1.

	Assets				= Liabilities	+ Owner's Equity	Explanation
	Cash +	**Accounts Receivable** +	**Furniture** +	**Store Equipment** =	**Accounts Payable** +	**Barbara Schmidt, Capital**	
a.	$3,000			$15,000		$18,000	Investment
b.	− 600		+$600				
Bal.	$2,400		$600	$15,000		$18,000	
c.	− 500					− 500	Rent Expense
Bal.	$1,900		$600	$15,000		$17,500	
d.				+ 1,200	+$1,200		
Bal.	$1,900		$600	$16,200	$1,200	$17,500	
e.	+ 825					+ 825	Haircutting Services Revenue
Bal.	$2,725		$600	$16,200	$1,200	$18,325	
f.		+$100				+ $100	Haircutting Services Revenue
Bal.	$2,725	$100	$600	$16,200	$1,200	$18,425	
g.	+ 100	−$100					
Bal.	$2,825	$ -0-	$600	$16,200	$1,200	$18,425	
h.	− 125					− 125	Salaries Expense
Bal.	$2,700		$600	$16,200	$1,200	$18,300	
i.	+ 930					+ 930	Haircutting Services Revenue
Bal.	$3,630		$600	$16,200	$1,200	$19,230	
j.	− 400				− 400		
Bal.	$3,230		$600	$16,200	$800	$19,230	
k.					+ 75	− 75	Hydro Expense
Bal.	$3,230		$600	$16,200	$ 875	$19,155	
l.	− 900					− 900	Withdrawal
Bal.	$2,330 +	$ -0- +	$600 +	$16,200 =	$ 875 +	$18,255	
	= $19,130				= $19,130		

2.

THE CUTLERY
Income Statement
For Month Ended August 31, 2001

Revenues:		
Haircutting services revenue		$1,855
Operating expenses:		
Rent expense	$500	
Salaries expense	125	
Hydro expense	75	
Total operating expenses		700
Net income		$1,155

3.

THE CUTLERY
Statement of Owner's Equity
For Month Ended August 31, 2001

Barbara Schmidt, capital, August 1		$ -0-
Add: Investments by owner	$18,000	
Net income	1,155	19,155
Total		$19,155
Less: Withdrawals by owner		900
Barbara Schmidt, capital, August 31		$18,255

The arrows are imaginary but they emphasize the link between statements.

4.

THE CUTLERY
Balance Sheet
August 31, 2001

Assets		**Liabilities**	
Cash	$ 2,330	Accounts payable	$ 875
Furniture	600		
Store equipment	16,200	**Owner's Equity**	
		Barbara Schmidt, capital	18,255
Total assets	$19,130	Total liabilities and owner's equity	$19,130

Developing Accounting Standards

APPENDIX

Accounting Principles, Auditing Standards, and Financial Accounting

LO7 Describe the process by which generally accepted accounting principles are established.

Generally accepted accounting principles are not natural laws like the laws of physics or other sciences. Instead, GAAP are identified in response to the needs of users and others affected by financial accounting P. 13. Thus, GAAP are subject to change as needs change.

Three groups of people are most directly affected by financial reporting: preparers, auditors, and users. Exhibit 2A.1 shows the relationship between the financial statements and these groups.

Private accountants prepare the financial statements. To give users more confidence in the statements, independent auditors usually examine the financial statements and develop an audit report. The statements and the audit report are then distributed to the users.

Exhibit 2A.1

The Relationship Between Financial Statements and the Three Groups Affected by Them

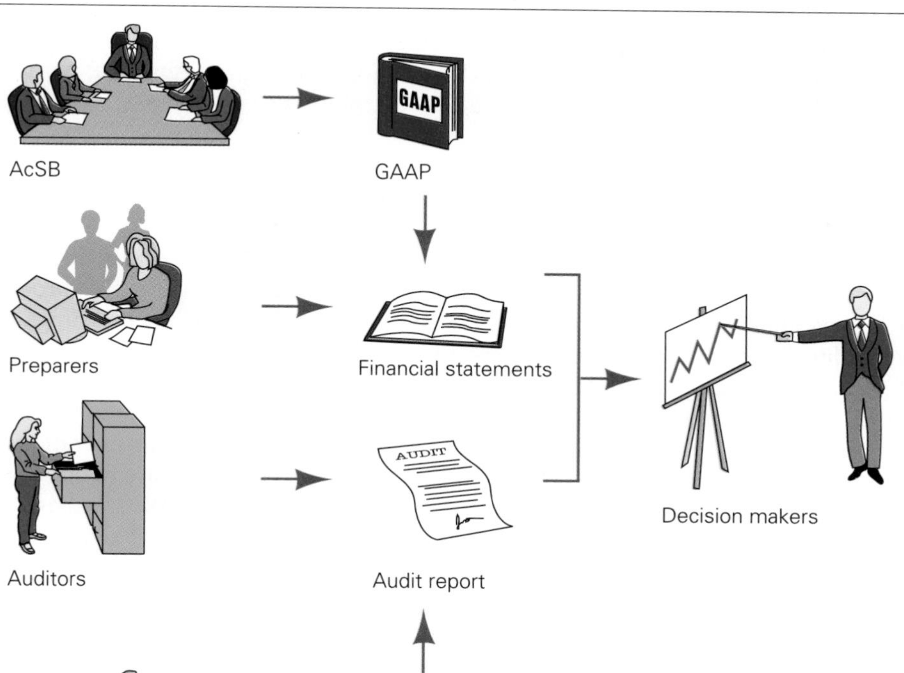

How Accounting Principles Are Established

Exhibit 2A.1 shows that GAAP are applied in preparing the financial statements. Preparers use GAAP to decide what procedures to follow as they account for business transactions and put the statements together.

Exhibit 2A.1 also shows that audits are performed in accordance with **Generally Accepted Auditing Standards (GAAS)** that are developed by the **Auditing Standards Board (ASB).** GAAS are the rules adopted by the accounting profession as guides for conducting audits of financial statements. GAAS tell auditors what they must do in their audits to determine whether the financial statements comply with GAAP.

Applying both GAAP and GAAS assures users that financial statements include relevant, reliable, consistent, and comparable information. The audit does not, however, ensure that they can safely invest in or lend to the company. The audit does not reduce the risk that the company's products and services will not be successfully marketed or that other factors, such as the loss of a key executive, could cause it to fail.

In Exhibit 2A.1, we also identify the two organizations that are the primary authoritative sources of GAAP and GAAS. The primary authoritative source of GAAP is the **Accounting Standards Board (AcSB)**. The board members, supported by a research staff, use their collective knowledge to identify problems in financial accounting and to find ways to solve them. The board also seeks advice from groups and individuals affected by GAAP. The advice comes via comments on the board's "exposure drafts" on specific issues. The finalized recommendations are published as part of the **CICA Handbook**. Under the regulations of the Canada Business Corporations Act, the accounting standards for external reporting set out in the CICA Handbook have the force of law. In summary, the Accounting Standards Board's job is to improve financial reporting while balancing the interests of the affected groups.

International Accounting Standards

In today's world, people in different countries engage in business with each other more easily than in the past. It is common for companies in Canada to sell products all over the world. We see examples of companies in countries such as Singapore selling their products to businesses in Canada and Europe and borrowing from creditors in places such as Saudi Arabia and Germany.

An increasing number of companies have international operations. For example, Four Seasons Hotels, Inc. is a Canadian company with operations in lodging and contract services. Most of the company's operations are in the United States; however, the company also manages properties in the West Indies, New Zealand, Thailand, Hong Kong, Malaysia, England, Australia, Fiji, Singapore, and Taiwan. It also has properties under construction or development in Germany, Hawaii, and the Czech Republic.

Accounting organizations from around the world responded to this challenge of internationalizing accounting standards by creating the **International Accounting Standards Committee (IASC)** in 1973. With headquarters in London, the IASC issues International Accounting Standards that identify preferred accounting practices and then encourages their worldwide acceptance. By narrowing the range of alternative practices, the IASC hopes to create more harmony among the accounting practices of different countries. If standards could be harmonized, a single set of financial statements could be used by one company in all financial markets.

In many countries, the bodies that set accounting standards have encouraged the IASC to reduce the differences. The Accounting Standards Committee has provided this encouragement and technical assistance. However, the IASC does not have the authority to impose its standards on companies. Although progress has been slow, interest is growing in moving Canadian GAAP toward the IASC's preferred practices.

14. Which body currently establishes generally accepted accounting principles in Canada? (a) The Ontario Securities Commission; (b) Parliament; (c) The AcSB; (d) The IASC.
15. What is the difference between GAAP and GAAS?
16. Is it true that Canadian companies with operations in foreign countries are required to prepare their financial statements according to the rules established by the IASC?

Answers—p. 61

Summary of Appendix 2A

LO7 Describe the process by which generally accepted accounting principles are established. Specific accounting principles for financial accounting are established in Canada by the Accounting Standards Board (AcSB), with input from various contributing bodies. Auditing standards are established by the Auditing Standards Board (ASB). The International Accounting Standards Committee (IASC) identifies preferred practices and encourages their adoption throughout the world.

GUIDANCE ANSWERS TO 

14. The AcSB currently establishes generally accepted accounting principles in Canada.
15. GAAP are the Generally Accepted *Accounting* Principles and GAAS are the Generally Accepted *Auditing* Standards.
16. Although companies are not required to adhere to the International Accounting Standards, the AcSB encourages companies to provide financial statements that do comply with IAS.

Glossary

Accounting equation A description of the relationship between a company's assets, liabilities, and equity; expressed as Assets = Liabilities + Owner's Equity; also called the *balance sheet equation.* (p. 45)

Accounts payable A liability created by buying goods or services on credit. (p. 39)

Accounts receivable An asset created by selling products or services on credit. (p. 39)

AcSB: Accounting Standards Board The authoritative committee that identifies generally accepted accounting standards. (p. 60)

ASB: Auditing Standards Board The authoritative committee that identifies generally accepted auditing standards. (p. 60)

Assets Properties or economic resources owned by the business; more precisely, resources with an ability to provide future benefits to the business. (p. 39)

Balance sheet A financial statement that reports the financial position of a business at a point in time; lists the types and dollar amounts of assets, liabilities, and equity as of a specific date; also called the *statement of financial position.* (p. 38)

Balance sheet equation Another name for the *accounting equation.* (p. 45)

Business entity principle The principle that requires every business to be accounted for separately from its owner or owners; based on the goal of providing relevant information about each business to users. (p. 42)

Business transaction An exchange of economic consideration between two parties that causes a change in assets, liabilities, or owner's equity. Examples of economic considerations include products, services, money, and rights to collect money. (p. 45)

Calendar year An accounting year that begins on January 1 and ends on December 31. (p. 37)

CICA Handbook The publication of the Canadian Institute for Chartered Accountants (CICA) that details generally accepted accounting principles in Canada. (p. 60)

Continuing-concern principle See *going-concern principle.* (p. 43)

Cost principle The accounting principle that requires financial statement information to be based on actual costs incurred in business transactions; it requires assets and services to be recorded initially at the cash or cash equivalent amount given in exchange. (p. 43)

Creditors Individuals or organizations entitled to receive payments from a company. (p. 40)

Debtors Individuals or organizations that owe amounts to a business. (p. 39)

Dividends Distributions of assets by a corporation to its owners. (p. 38)

Economic entity principle See *business entity principle.* (p. 42)

Equity The owner's claim on the assets of a business; more precisely, the residual interest in the assets of an entity that remains after deducting its liabilities; also called *net assets.* (p. 40)

Expenses Outflows or the using up of assets as a result of the major or central operations of a business. (p. 38)

Financial statements The most important products of accounting; include the balance sheet, income statement, statement of owner's equity, and the statement of cash flows. (p. 36)

Fiscal year A one-year reporting period. (p. 37)

GAAP See *Generally Accepted Accounting Principles.* (p. 42)

GAAS See *Generally Accepted Auditing Standards.* (p. 60)

Generally Accepted Accounting Principles The rules adopted by the accounting profession that make up acceptable accounting practices for the preparation of financial statements. (p. 42)

Generally Accepted Auditing Standards Rules adopted by the accounting profession as guides for conducting audits of financial statements. (p. 60)

Going-concern principle The rule that requires financial statements to reflect the assumption that the business will continue operating instead of being closed or sold, unless evidence shows that it will not continue; also called *continuing-concern principle.* (p. 43)

IASC: International Accounting Standards Committee A committee that attempts to create more harmony among the accounting practices of different countries by identifying preferred practices and encouraging their worldwide acceptance. (p. 60)

Income statement The financial statement that shows, by subtracting expenses from revenues, whether the business earned a profit; it lists the types and amounts of revenues earned and expenses incurred by a business over a period of time. (p. 37)

Liabilities The obligations of a business; claims by others that will reduce the future assets of a business or require future services or products. (p. 39)

Monetary unit principle The expression of transactions and events in money units; examples include units such as the Canadian dollar, American dollar, peso, and pound sterling. (p. 43)

Natural business year A 12-month period that ends when a company's sales activities are at their lowest point. (p. 37)

Net assets Another name for *equity.* (p. 40)

Net income The excess of revenues over expenses for a period. (p. 37)

Net loss The excess of expenses over revenues for a period. (p. 37)

Note payable A liability expressed by a written promise to make a future payment at a specific time. (p. 40)

Objectivity principle The accounting guideline that requires financial statement information to be supported by independent, unbiased evidence rather than someone's opinion; objectivity adds to the reliability, verifiability, and usefulness of accounting information. (p. 43)

Owner investments The transfer of an owner's personal assets to the business. (p. 38)

Owner withdrawals See *withdrawals.* (p. 38)

Realization principle See *revenue recognition principle.* (p. 44)

Revenue recognition principle Provides guidance on when revenue should be reflected on the income statement; the rule states that revenue is recorded at the time it is earned regardless of whether cash or another asset has been exchanged. (p. 44)

Revenues Inflows of assets received in exchange for goods or services provided to customers as part of the major or primary operations of the business; may occur as inflows of assets or decreases in liabilities. (p. 37)

Stable-dollar principle Another name for the *monetary unit principle.* (p. 43)

Statement of cash flows A financial statement that describes the sources and uses of cash for a reporting period, i.e., where a company's cash came from (receipts) and where it went during the period (payments); the cash flows are arranged by an organization's major activities: operating, investing, and financing activities. (p. 40)

Statement of owner's equity A financial statement that reports the changes in equity over the reporting period; beginning equity is adjusted for increases such as owner investment or net income and for decreases such as owner withdrawals or a net loss. (p. 38)

Statement of financial position See *balance sheet.* (p. 38)

Withdrawals The distributions of cash or other assets from a proprietorship or partnership to its owner or owners. (p. 38)

Questions

1. What information is presented in an income statement?
2. What do accountants mean by the term *revenue*?
3. Why does the user of an income statement need to know the time period that it covers?
4. What information is presented in a balance sheet?
5. Define (a) assets, (b) liabilities, (c) equity, and (d) net assets.
6. Identify two categories of generally accepted accounting principles.
7. What CICA pronouncements identify generally accepted accounting principles?
8. What does the objectivity principle require for information presented in financial statements? Why?
9. A business shows office stationery on the balance sheet at its $430 cost, although it cannot be sold for more than $10 as scrap paper. Which accounting principle justifies this treatment?
10. Why is the revenue recognition principle needed? What does it require?
11. What events or activities change owner's equity?
12. Identify four financial statements that a business presents to its owners and other users.
13. Find the financial statements of ClubLink in Appendix I. To what level of significance are the dollar amounts rounded? What time period does the income statement cover?
14. Review the balance sheet of WestJet Airlines in Appendix I. What is the amount of total assets reported at December 31, 1999? Prove the accounting equation for WestJet at December 31, 1999.
15. Review Finlay Interiors' financial statements presented in the chapter for the year ended January 31, 2001. Review the balance sheet and determine the business form Carol Finlay has chosen to organize her business.

Quick Study

QS 2-1
Identifying financial statement items

LO1

Name the financial statement on which each of the following items appears:

a. Office supplies
b. Service fees earned
c. Accounts receivable
d. Owner, withdrawals
e. Office equipment
f. Accounts payable
g. Notes payable
h. Utilities expense

QS 2-2

Financial statements and forms of organization

LO2

SP - Sole proprietorship
P - Partnership
C - Corporation

Identify the type of business organization based on the following independent financial statement findings:

_____ **1.** The equity section of the balance sheet is called *Owner's Equity.*
_____ **2.** The owners receive distributions of earnings in the form of dividends.
_____ **3.** There are two capital accounts: Tara Davis, Capital and Sheila Kelton, Capital.
_____ **4.** The one owner receives distributions of earnings in the form of withdrawals.
_____ **5.** A manager, also an owner of the business, is paid a salary that is recorded as an expense.
_____ **6.** The equity section of the balance sheet is called *Shareholders' Equity.*

QS 2-3

Identifying accounting principles

LO3

Identify which broad accounting principle describes most directly each of the following practices:

a. Tracy Regis owns two businesses, Second Time Around Clothing and Antique Accents, both of which are sole proprietorships. In having financial statements prepared for the antique store, Regis should be sure that the revenue and expense transactions of Second Time Around are excluded from the statements.

b. In December 2001, Classic Coverings received a customer's order to install carpet and tile in a new house that would not be ready for completion until March 2002. Classic Coverings should record the revenue for the order in March 2002, not in December 2001.

c. If $30,000 cash is paid to buy land, the land should be reported on the purchaser's balance sheet at $30,000 although the purchaser was offered $35,000 the following week.

QS 2-4

Applying the accounting equation

LO4

Determine the missing amount for each of the following equations:

	Assets	=	Liabilities	+	Owner's Equity
a.	$75,000		$40,500		?
b.	$300,000		?		$85,500
c.	?		$187,500		$95,400

QS 2-5

Applying the accounting equation

LO4

Use the accounting equation to determine:

a. The owner's equity in a business that has $374,700 of assets and $252,450 of liabilities.
b. The liabilities of a business having $150,900 of assets and $126,000 of owner's equity.
c. The assets of a business having $37,650 of liabilities and $112,500 of owner's equity.

QS 2-6

Transaction analysis

LO5

For each transaction described, identify which component of the accounting equation increases and/or decreases. The first one is done as an example.

Example: Services were performed for a client on credit.
a. A credit customer paid his account.
b. Supplies were purchased on credit.
c. The balance owing regarding the supplies purchased in (b) was paid.
d. Last month's telephone bill was received today. It will be paid on the due date, which is 10 days from now.
e. Paid the employees their weekly wage.

	Assets	=	Liabilities	+	Owner's Equity
Example:	*Increase*				*Increase*
a.					
b.					
c.					
d.					
e.					

QS 2-7
Financial statements prepared from transaction analysis

LO7

Using the information in QS 2-6, identify which transactions would appear on an income statement.

Exercises

Exercise 2-1
Determining net income

LO1

Net income (net loss), owner withdrawals and owner investment cause equity to change. We also know that revenues less expenses equals net income (loss). Using the following information, calculate net income (loss) for each independent situation.

a. The business earned revenues of $80,000 and had expenses of $65,000.

b. The business showed expenses of $149,000 and revenues of $92,000.

c. The owner's equity at the beginning of the month was $10,000. During the month, the owner made no investments or withdrawals. At the end of the month, owner's equity totalled $86,000.

d. The owner's equity at the beginning of the month was $25,000. During the month, the owner made an investment of $40,000 but made no withdrawals. Owner's equity at the end of the month equalled $52,000.

Exercise 2-2
Information in financial statements

LO1

Match each of these numbered items with the financial statement or statements on which it should be presented. Indicate your answer by writing the letter or letters for the correct statement in the blank space next to each item.

a. Income statement

b. Statement of owner's equity

c. Balance sheet

________	**1.** Net Loss	________	**5.** Accounts payable
________	**2.** Office supplies	________	**6.** Owner's investments
________	**3.** Salaries Expense	________	**7.** Accounts receivable
________	**4.** Net Income	________	**8.** Consulting fees earned

Exercise 2-3
Income statement

LO1

Check figure: Net income = $5,110

On November 1, 2001, Joseph Grayson organized a new consulting firm called The Grayson Group. On November 30, 2001, the company's records showed the following items. Use this information to prepare a November income statement for the business.

Cash	$12,000	Owner's withdrawals	$ 3,360
Accounts receivable	15,000	Consulting fees earned	15,000
Office supplies	2,250	Rent expense	2,550
Automobiles	36,000	Salaries expense	6,000
Office equipment	28,000	Telephone expense	660
Accounts payable	7,500	Miscellaneous expenses	680
Owner's investments	84,000		

Exercise 2-4
Statement of owner's equity

LO1

Use the facts in Exercise 2-3 to prepare a November statement of owner's equity for The Grayson Group.

Exercise 2-5
Balance sheet

LO1

Check figure: Total assets = $93,250

Use the facts in Exercise 2-3 to prepare a November 30 balance sheet for The Grayson Group.

Exercise 2-6
Missing information

LO1

Calculate the amount of the missing item in each of the following independent cases:

	a	b	c	d
Owner's equity, January 1	$ -0-	$ -0-	$ -0-	$ -0-
Owner's investments during the year	120,000	?	63,000	75,000
Owner's withdrawals during the year	?	(54,000)	(30,000)	(31,500)
Net income (loss) for the year	31,500	81,000	(9,000)	?
Owner's equity, December 31	102,000	99,000	?	85,500

49,500 72,000

Exercise 2-7
Differences in business organizations

LO2

Fill in the blanks with the appropriate term(s):

Difference	Type of Business Organization		
	Sole Proprietorship	Partnership	Corporation
Equity section on the balance sheet is called:			
Distributions to owners are called:			
When managers are also owners, their salaries are:			

Exercise 2-8
Accounting principles

LO3

Match each of these numbered descriptions with the term it best describes. Indicate your answer by writing the letter for the correct principle in the blank space next to each description.

a. Cost principle
b. Business entity principle
c. Revenue recognition principle
d. Objectivity principle
e. Going-concern principle

_____ **1.** Requires every business to be accounted for separately from its owner or owners.
_____ **2.** Requires financial statement information to be supported by evidence other than someone's opinion or imagination.
_____ **3.** Requires financial statement information to be based on costs incurred in transactions.
_____ **4.** Requires financial statements to reflect the assumption that the business will continue operating instead of being closed or sold.
_____ **5.** Requires revenue to be recorded only when the earnings process is complete.

Exercise 2-9
Determining net income

LO1, 4

A business had the following amounts of assets and liabilities at the beginning and end of a recent year:

	Assets	Liabilities
Beginning of the year	$ 75,000	$30,000
End of the year	120,000	46,000

Determine the net income earned or net loss incurred by the business during the year under each of the following unrelated assumptions:

a. The owner made no additional investments in the business and withdrew no assets during the year.

b. The owner made no additional investments in the business during the year but withdrew $1,750 per month to pay personal living expenses.
c. The owner withdrew no assets during the year but invested an additional $32,500 cash.
d. The owner withdrew $1,750 per month to pay personal living expenses and invested an additional $25,000 cash in the business.

Exercise 2-10

Effects of transactions on the accounting equation

LO 3, 4, 5

Check figure:
Total assets = $6,100

Northrup Consulting provides support to customers in the area of e-commerce. Using the format provided below, show the effects of the five transactions listed in (a) through (e).

Assets			=	Liabilities +	Owner's Equity
Cash	+ Accounts Receivable	+ Office Supplies	=	Accounts Payable	+ Bonnie Northrup, Capital

a. Bonnie Northrup, the owner, invested cash of $5,000 into the business.
b. The owner purchased office supplies on credit; $400.
c. Northrup Consulting did work for a client and received $1,200 cash.
d. The owner paid her assistant's salary; $3,000 cash.
e. Completed work for a customer on credit; $2,500.

Exercise 2-11

Effects of transactions on the accounting equation

LO 3, 4, 5

Check figure:
Total assets = $10,100

DigiCom repairs computers. Using the format provided below, show the effects of the seven transactions listed in (a) through (g).

Assets				=	Liabilities +	Owner's Equity
Cash	+ Accounts Receivable	+ Parts Supplies	+ Equipment	=	Accounts Payable	+ Janine Commry, Capital

a. Janine, owner of DigiCom, invested cash of $7,000 into her business.
b. DigiCom purchased supplies on credit; $1,200.
c. Janine completed work for a client on credit; $3,400.
d. DigiCom purchased a new piece of equipment by paying cash of $950.
e. Janine paid for the supplies purchased in (b).
f. DigiCom performed work for a client and received cash of $1,400.
g. Janine paid her assistant's salary of $1,700.

Exercise 2-12

Analyzing the accounting equation

LO 5

Check figure:
Total assets = $32,800

Carter Stark founded a new consulting firm on January 3. The accounting equation showed the following balances after each of the company's first five transactions. Analyze the equation and describe each of the five transactions with their amounts. (a) has been done as an example for you.

	Assets				= Liabilities +	Owner's Equity
Transaction	Cash	+ Accounts Receivable	+ Office Supplies	+ Office Furniture	= Accounts Payable	+ Carter Stark, Capital
Beginning Balances	-0-	-0-	-0-	-0-	-0-	-0-
a.	+30,000					+30,000
Totals	30,000					30,000
b.						
Totals	29,000		1,000			30,000
c.						
Totals	21,000		1,000	8,000		30,000
d.						
Totals	21,000	2,000	1,000	8,000		32,000
e.						
Totals	21,000	2,000	1,800	8,000	800	32,000

Description of transaction (a):
a. *The owner invested $30,000 cash into the business.*

Exercise 2-13
Effects of transactions on the accounting equation

LO3, 4, 5

The following equation shows the effects of five transactions on the assets, liabilities, and owner's equity of Pace Design. Answer questions (a) through (e) based on the transactions illustrated below.

	Assets				=	Liabilities +	Owner's Equity
	Cash	+ Accounts Receivable	+ Office Supplies	+ Land	=	Accounts Payable	+ Carol Pace, Capital
	$7,500		$2,500	$14,500			$24,500
a.	−3,000			+3,000			
	$4,500		$ 2,500	$17,500			$24,500
b.			+400			+$400	
	$4,500		$ 2,900	$17,500		$400	$24,500
c.		+$1,050					+1,050
	$4,500	$1,050	$ 2,900	$17,500		$ 400	$25,550
d.	−400					−400	
	$4,100	$1,050	$ 2,900	$17,500		$ -0-	$25,550
e.	+1,050	−1,050					
	$5,150 +	$ -0- +	$ 2,900 +	$17,500	=	$ -0- +	$25,550

For each of the above, describe the transaction that caused:

- **a.** Cash to decrease by $3,000 and land to increase by $3,000.
- **b.** Office supplies and accounts payable each to increase by $400.
- **c.** Accounts receivable and owner's equity to each increase by $1,050.
- **d.** Cash and accounts payable to each decrease by $400.
- **e.** Cash to increase by $1,050 and accounts receivable to decrease by $1,050.

Exercise 2-14
The effects of transactions on the accounting equation

LO3, 4, 5

Check figure:
Total assets = $64,500

Linda Champion began a professional practice on May 1 and plans to prepare financial statements at the end of each month. During May, Champion completed these transactions:

- **a.** Invested $50,000 cash and equipment that had a $10,000 fair market (cash equivalent) value.
- **b.** Paid $1,600 rent for office space for the month.
- **c.** Purchased $12,000 of additional equipment on credit.
- **d.** Completed work for a client and immediately collected $2,000 cash.
- **e.** Completed work for a client and sent a bill for $7,000 to be paid within 30 days.
- **f.** Purchased $8,000 of additional equipment for cash.
- **g.** Paid an assistant $2,400 as wages for the month.
- **h.** Collected $5,000 of the amount owed by the client described in transaction (e).
- **i.** Paid for the equipment purchased in transaction (c).
- **j.** Withdrew $500 for personal use.

Required
Create a table like the one in Exhibit 2.10, using the following headings for the columns: Cash; Accounts Receivable; Equipment; Accounts Payable; and Linda Champion, Capital. Then, use additions and subtractions to show the effects of the transactions on the elements of the equation. Show new totals after each transaction. Also, calculate net income earned during May.

Exercise 2-15
The effects of transactions on the accounting equation

LO3, 4, 5

Following are seven pairs of changes in elements of the accounting equation. Provide an example of a transaction that creates the described effects:

- **a.** Decreases a liability and increases a liability.
- **b.** Increases an asset and decreases an asset.
- **c.** Decreases an asset and decreases equity.
- **d.** Increases a liability and decreases equity.
- **e.** Increases an asset and increases a liability.
- **f.** Increases an asset and increases equity.
- **g.** Decreases an asset and decreases a liability.

Exercise 2-16
The effects of transactions on the accounting equation and financial statement preparation

LO3, 4, 5

Check figure:
Bert Zimm, capital = $7,000

Bert Zimm is a freelance writer who submits articles to various magazines and newspapers. He operates out of a small office where he employs one administrative assistant. The following transactions occurred during March 2001, his first month of business:

a. Bert Zimm invested $5,000 worth of equipment into his business.
b. Submitted a series of articles to *The Globe and Mail* and received $2,500 cash.
c. Purchased supplies on credit; $300.
d. Paid the part-time administrative assistant's salary of $900.
e. Paid the rent for the first month; $600.
f. Submitted an article to *Report on Business*; will receive $1,000 next month.

Using the format provided below, show the effects of the six transactions listed in (a) through (f). For each transaction that affects owner's equity, include a brief description beside it (owner investment, owner withdrawal, revenue, expense).

Assets								=	Liabilities	+	Owner's Equity	
Cash	+	Accounts Receivable	+	Furniture	+	Equipment		=	Accounts Payable	+	Bert Zimm, Capital	Explanation

Exercise 2-17
Financial statements

LO6

Check figure:
Total assets = $7,300

Using your answer from Exercise 2-16, prepare an income statement, statement of owner's equity, and a balance sheet using the formats provided.

Bert Zimm - Freelance Writing
Income Statement
For Month Ended March 31, 2001

Revenues:		
Freelance service revenue		
Operating expenses:		
Salary expense		
Rent expense		
Total operating expenses		
Net income		

Bert Zimm - Freelance Writing
Statement of Owner's Equity
For Month Ended March 31, 2001

Bert Zimm, capital, March 1		
Add: Investments by owner		
Net income		
Bert Zimm, capital, March 31		

Bert Zimm - Freelance Writing
Balance Sheet
March 31, 2001

Assets		**Liabilities**	
Cash		Accounts payable	
Accounts receivable			
Supplies		**Owner's Equity**	
Equipment		Bert Zimm, capital	
		Total liabilities and	
Total assets		owner's equity	

Problems

Problem 2-1A

Financial statements: preparation and analysis of statement of owner's equity

LO[1]

Check figure:
Kent Brennan, capital, December 31, 2002 = $44,000

Required
Calculate the missing amounts.

LDD Services
Statement of Owner's Equity
For Years Ended December 31, 2000-2002

	2002		2001		2000	
Kent Brennan, capital, January 1				$21,000		$0
Add: Investment by owner	$0		$0			
Net income	63,000				2,500	
Total				52,000		26,000
Less: Withdrawals by owner		42,000		29,000		
Kent Brennan, capital, December 31						

Problem 2-2A

Calculating and interpreting net income and preparing a balance sheet

LO[1, 4, 6]

The accounting records of Goodall Delivery Services show the following assets and liabilities as of the end of 2002 and 2001:

	December 31	
	2002	2001
Cash	$ 18,750	$ 52,500
Accounts receivable	22,350	28,500
Office supplies	3,300	4,500
Trucks	54,000	54,000
Office equipment	147,000	138,000
Land	45,000	
Building	180,000	
Accounts payable	37,500	7,500
Notes payable	105,000	

Late in December 2002 (just before the amounts in the first column were calculated), Travis Goodall, the owner, purchased a small office building and moved the business from rented quarters to the new building. The building and the land it occupies cost $225,000. The business paid $120,000 in cash and a note payable was signed for the balance. Goodall had to invest $35,000 cash in the business to enable it to pay the $120,000. The business earned a satisfactory net income during 2002, which enabled Goodall to withdraw $3,000 per month from the business for personal expenses.

Required

1. Prepare balance sheets for the business as of the end of 2001 and the end of 2002. (Remember that owner's equity equals the difference between the assets and the liabilities.)
2. By comparing the owner's equity amounts from the balance sheets and using the additional information presented in the problem, prepare a calculation to show how much net income was earned by the business during 2002.

Problem 2-3A
Missing information

LO4

The following financial statement information is known about five unrelated companies:

	Company A	Company B	Company C	Company D	Company E
December 31, 2001:					
Assets	$45,000	$35,000	$29,000	$80,000	$123,000
Liabilities	23,500	22,500	14,000	38,000	?
December 31, 2002:					
Assets	48,000	41,000	?	125,000	112,500
Liabilities	?	27,500	19,000	64,000	75,000
During 2002:					
Owner investments	5,000	1,500	7,750	?	4,500
Net income	7,500	?	9,000	12,000	18,000
Owner withdrawals	2,500	3,000	3,875	-0-	9,000

Required

1. Answer the following questions about Company A:
   a. What was the owner's equity on December 31, 2001?
   b. What was the owner's equity on December 31, 2002?
   c. What was the amount of liabilities owed on December 31, 2002?
2. Answer the following questions about Company B:
   a. What was the owner's equity on December 31, 2001?
   b. What was the owner's equity on December 31, 2002?
   c. What was the net income for 2002?
3. Calculate the amount of assets owned by Company C on December 31, 2002.
4. Calculate the amount of owner investments in Company D made during 2002.
5. Calculate the amount of liabilities owed by Company E on December 31, 2001.

Problem 2-4A
Analyzing the effects of transactions

LO3, 4, 5

Check figure:
George Hemphill, capital, March 31, 2001 = $106,700

George Hemphill started a new business called Hemphill Enterprises and incurred the following transactions during its first month of operations, March 2001:

a. Hemphill invested $60,000 cash and office equipment valued at $30,000 in the business.
b. Paid $300,000 for a small building to be used as an office. Paid $50,000 in cash and signed a note payable promising to pay the balance over several years.
c. Purchased $4,000 of office supplies for cash.
d. Purchased $36,000 of office equipment on credit.
e. Completed a project on credit and billed the client $4,000 for the work.
f. Paid a local newspaper $1,000 for an announcement that the office had opened.
g. Completed a project for a client and collected $18,000 cash.
h. Made a $2,000 payment on the equipment purchased in transaction (d).
i. Received $3,000 from the client described in transaction (e).
j. Paid $2,500 cash for the office secretary's wages.
k. Hemphill withdrew $1,800 cash from the company bank account to pay personal living expenses.

Required

Preparation component:

1. Create a table like the one in Exhibit 2.10, using the following headings for the columns: Cash; Accounts Receivable; Office Supplies; Office Equipment; Building; Accounts Payable; Notes Payable; and George Hemphill, Capital. Leave space for an Explanation column to the right of the Capital column. Identify revenues and expenses by name in the Explanation column.
2. Use additions and subtractions to show the transactions' effects on the elements of the equation. Show new totals after each transaction. Also, indicate next to each change in the owner's equity whether it was caused by an investment, a revenue, an expense, or a withdrawal.

3. Prepare an income statement, statement of owner's equity, and a balance sheet using the formats provided.

Hemphill Enterprises
Income Statement
For Month Ended March 31, 2001

Revenues:
    Service revenue ....
Operating expenses:
    Wages expense ....
    Advertising expense ....
        Total operating expenses ....
Net income ....

Hemphill Enterprises
Statement of Owner's Equity
For Month Ended March 31, 2001

George Hemphill, capital, March 1 ....
Add: Investments by owner ....
        Net income ....
    Total ....
Less: Withdrawals by owner
George Hemphill, capital, March 31 ....

Hemphill Enterprises
Balance Sheet
March 31, 2001

Assets		Liabilities	
Cash		Accounts payable	
Accounts receivable		Notes payable	
Office supplies		Total liabilities	
Office equipment			
Building		**Owner's Equity**	
		George Hemphill, capital	
Total assets		Total liabilities and owner's equity	

Problem 2-5A

Balance sheet, income statement, and statement of owner's equity

LO 3, 4, 5, 6

Check figure:
Net income = $3,960

Kelly Young started a new business called Resource Consulting Co. and began operations on April 1, 2001. The following transactions were completed during the month:

Apr.	1	Young invested $60,000 cash in the business.
	1	Rented a furnished office and paid $3,200 cash for April's rent.
	3	Purchased office supplies for $1,680 cash.
	5	Paid $800 cash for the month's cleaning services.
	8	Provided consulting services for a client and immediately collected $4,600 cash.
	12	Provided consulting services for a client on credit, $3,000.
	15	Paid $850 cash for an assistant's salary for the first half of the month.
	20	Received payment in full for the services provided on April 12.
	22	Provided consulting services on credit, $2,800.
	23	Purchased additional office supplies on credit, $1,000.
	28	Received full payment for the services provided on April 22.
	29	Paid for the office supplies purchased on April 23.

Apr. 30 Purchased advertising for $60 in the local paper. The payment is due May 1.
30 Paid $200 cash for the month's telephone bill.
30 Paid $480 cash for the month's utilities.
30 Paid $850 cash for an assistant's salary for the second half of the month.
30 Young withdrew $1,200 cash from the business for personal use.

Required

1. Arrange the following asset, liability, and owner's equity titles in an equation like Exhibit 2.10: Cash; Accounts Receivable; Office Supplies; Accounts Payable; and Kelly Young, Capital. Include an Explanation column for changes in owner's equity. Identify revenues and expenses by name in the Explanation column.
2. Show the effects of the transactions on the elements of the equation by recording increases and decreases in the appropriate columns. Do not determine new totals for the items of the equation after each transaction. Next to each change in owner's equity, state whether it was caused by an investment, a revenue, an expense, or a withdrawal. Determine the final total for each item and verify that the equation is in balance.
3. Prepare an income statement, a statement of owner's equity. and a balance sheet.

Problem 2-6A
Analyzing transactions and preparing financial statements

LO3, 4, 5, 6

Check figure:
Cash balance, November 30, 2001 = $49,960

Stan Frey started a new business and incurred these transactions during November, 2001:

Nov. 1 Transferred $56,000 out of a personal savings account to a chequing account in the name of Frey Electrical Co.
1 Rented office space and paid cash for the month's rent of $800.
3 Purchased electrical equipment from an electrician who was going out of business for $14,000 by paying $3,200 in cash and agreeing to pay the balance in six months.
5 Purchased office supplies by paying $900 cash.
6 Completed electrical work and immediately collected $1,000 for doing the work.
8 Purchased $3,800 of office equipment on credit.
15 Completed electrical work on credit in the amount of $4,000.
18 Purchased $500 of office supplies on credit.
20 Paid for the office equipment purchased on November 8.
24 Billed a client $600 for electrical work; the balance is due in 30 days.
28 Received $4,000 for the work completed on November 15.
30 Paid the assistant's salary of $1,200.
30 Paid the monthly utility bills of $440.
30 Withdrew $700 from the business for personal use.

Required

Preparation component:

1. Arrange the following asset, liability, and owner's equity titles in an equation like Exhibit 2.10: Cash; Accounts Receivable; Office Supplies; Office Equipment; Electrical Equipment; Accounts Payable; and Stan Frey, Capital. Leave space for an Explanation column to the right of Stan Frey, Capital. Identify revenues and expenses by name in the Explanation column.
2. Use additions and subtractions to show the effects of each transaction on the items in the equation. Show new totals after each transaction. Next to each change in owner's equity, state whether the change was caused by an investment, a revenue, an expense, or a withdrawal.
3. Use the increases and decreases in the last column of the equation to prepare an income statement and a statement of owner's equity for the month. Also prepare a balance sheet as of the end of the month.

Problem 2-7A
Identifying the effects of transactions on the financial statements

LO5, 6

Identify how each of the following transactions affects the company's financial statements. For the balance sheet, identify how each transaction affects total assets, total liabilities, and owner's equity. For the income statement, identify how each transaction affects net income. If there is an increase, place a "+" in the column or columns. If there is a decrease, place a "−" in the column or columns. If there is both an increase and a decrease, place a "+/−" in the column or columns. The line for the first transaction is completed as an example.

		Balance Sheet			Income Statement
	Transaction	Total Assets	Total Liabilities	Equity	Net Income
1	Owner invests cash	+		+	
2	Sell services for cash				
3	Acquire services on credit				
4	Pay wages with cash				
5	Owner withdraws cash				
6	Borrow cash with note payable				
7	Sell services on credit				
8	Buy office equipment for cash				
9	Collect receivable from (7)				
10	Buy asset with note payable				

Alternate Problems

Problem 2-1B
Financial statements: analysis of statement of owner's equity

LO1

Swan Furnace Cleaners began operations on January 1, 2000. The owner invested $50,000 during the first year and made no withdrawals.

During 2001, the business reported net income of $163,000, owner withdrawals of $52,000 and zero owner investments.

In 2002, Swan Furnace Cleaners earned net income of $183,000. The owner withdrew $69,000 during 2002 and made no investments. Owner's capital at December 31, 2002, was $260,000.

Required
Calculate the net income or loss for the year 2000.

Problem 2-2B
Calculating and interpreting net income and preparing a balance sheet

LO 1, 4, 6

The accounting records of Stiller Co. show the following assets and liabilities as of the end of 2002 and 2001:

	December 31	
	2002	2001
Cash	$ 10,000	$ 14,000
Accounts receivable	30,000	25,000
Office supplies	12,500	10,000
Office equipment	60,000	60,000
Machinery	30,500	30,500
Land	65,000	
Building	260,000	
Accounts payable	15,000	5,000
Notes payable	260,000	

Late in December 2002 (just before the amounts in the first column were calculated), Joseph Stiller, the owner, purchased a small office building and moved the business from rented quarters to the new building. The building and the land it occupies cost $325,000. The business paid $65,000 in cash and a note payable was signed for the balance. Stiller had to invest an additional $25,000 to enable it to pay the $65,000. The business earned a satisfactory net income during 2002, which enabled Stiller to withdraw $1,000 per month from the business for personal use.

Required

1. Prepare balance sheets for the business as of the end of 2001 and the end of 2002. (Remember that owner's equity equals the difference between the assets and the liabilities.)
2. By comparing the owner's equity amounts from the balance sheets and using the additional information presented in the problem, prepare a calculation to show how much net income was earned by the business during 2002.

Problem 2-3B
Missing information

LO 4

The following financial statement information is known about five unrelated companies:

	Company V	Company W	Company X	Company Y	Company Z
December 31, 2001:					
Assets	$45,000	$70,000	$121,500	$82,500	$124,000
Liabilities	30,000	50,000	58,500	61,500	?
December 31, 2002:					
Assets	49,000	90,000	136,500	?	160,000
Liabilities	26,000	?	55,500	72,000	52,000
During 2002:					
Owner investments	6,000	10,000	?	38,100	40,000
Net income	?	30,000	16,500	24,000	32,000
Owner withdrawals	4,500	2,000	-0-	18,000	6,000

Required

1. Answer the following questions about Company V:
   a. What was the owner's equity on December 31, 2001?
   b. What was the owner's equity on December 31, 2002?
   c. What was the net income for 2002?
2. Answer the following questions about Company W:
   a. What was the owner's equity on December 31, 2001?
   b. What was the owner's equity on December 31, 2002?
   c. What was the amount of liabilities owed on December 31, 2002?

3. Calculate the amount of owner investments in Company X made during 2002.
4. Calculate the amount of assets owned by Company Y on December 31, 2002.
5. Calculate the amount of liabilities owed by Company Z on December 31, 2001.

Problem 2-4B

Analyzing the effects of transactions on the accounting equation

LO 3, 4, 5, 6

Check figure:
Cash balance, December 31, 2001 = $30,550

Judith Grimm started a new business on January 1, 2001, called Southwest Consulting and incurred the following transactions during its first year of operations:

a. Grimm invested $50,000 cash and office equipment valued at $5,000 in the business.
b. Paid $120,000 for a small building to be used as an office. Paid $10,000 in cash and signed a note payable promising to pay the balance over several years.
c. Purchased $9,000 of office equipment for cash.
d. Purchased $2,000 of office supplies and $3,200 of office equipment on credit.
e. Paid a local newspaper $1,500 for an announcement that the office had opened.
f. Completed a financial plan on credit and billed the client $3,000 for the service.
g. Designed a financial plan for another client and collected a $5,400 cash fee.
h. Grimm withdrew $2,750 cash from the company bank account to pay personal expenses.
i. Received $1,200 from the client described in transaction (f).
j. Made a $900 payment on the equipment purchased in transaction (d).
k. Paid $1,900 cash for the office secretary's wages.

Required

Preparation component:

1. Create a table like the one presented in Exhibit 2.10, using the following headings for the columns: Cash; Accounts Receivable; Office Supplies; Office Equipment; Building; Accounts Payable; Notes Payable; and Judith Grimm, Capital. Leave space for an Explanation column to the right of the Capital column. Identify revenues and expenses by name in the Explanation column.
2. Use additions and subtractions to show the effects of the above transactions on the elements of the equation. Show new totals after each transaction. Also, indicate next to each change in the owner's equity whether it was caused by an investment, a revenue, an expense, or a withdrawal.
3. Prepare an income statement, statement of owner's equity and a balance sheet using the formats provided.

Southwest Consulting
Income Statement
For Month Ended December 31, 2001

Revenues:		
Consulting services revenue		
Operating expenses:		
Wages expense		
Advertising expense		
Total operating expenses		
Net income		

Southwest Consulting
Statement of Owner's Equity
For Month Ended December 31, 2001

Judith Grimm, capital, January 1		
Add: Investments by owner		
Net income		
Total		
Less: Withdrawals by owner		
Judith Grimm, capital, December 31		

Southwest Consulting
Balance Sheet
December 31, 2001

Assets		**Liabilities**	
Cash		Accounts payable	
Accounts receivable		Notes payable	
Office supplies		Total liabilities	
Office equipment			
Building		**Owner's Equity**	
		Judith Grimm, capital	
Total assets		Total liabilities and owner's equity	

Problem 2-5B
Preparing a balance sheet, income statement, and statement of owner's equity

LO 3, 4, 5, 6

Check figure:
Andrew Martin, capital, June 30, 2001 = $121,305

Andrew Martin began a new business called Universal Maintenance Co. on June 1, 2001. The following transactions were completed during the month:

June 1 Martin invested $120,000 in the business.
1 Rented a furnished office of a maintenance company that was going out of business and paid $4,500 cash for the month's rent.
4 Purchased cleaning supplies for $2,400 cash.
6 Paid $1,125 cash for advertising the opening of the business.
8 Completed maintenance services for a customer and immediately collected $750 cash.
14 Completed maintenance services for First Union Centre on credit, $6,300.
16 Paid $900 cash for an assistant's salary for the first half of the month.
20 Received payment in full for the services completed for First Union Centre on June 14.
21 Completed maintenance services for Skyway Co. on credit, $3,500.
22 Purchased additional cleaning supplies on credit, $750.
24 Completed maintenance services for Comfort Motel on credit, $825.
29 Received full payment from Skyway Co. for the work completed on June 21.
29 Made a partial payment of $375 for the cleaning supplies purchased on June 22.
30 Paid $120 cash for the month's telephone bill.
30 Paid $525 cash for the month's utilities.
30 Paid $900 cash for an assistant's salary for the second half of the month.
30 Martin withdrew $2,000 from the business for personal use.

Required

1. Arrange the following asset, liability, and owner's equity titles in an equation like Exhibit 2.10: Cash; Accounts Receivable; Cleaning Supplies; Accounts Payable; Andrew Martin, Capital. Include an Explanation column for changes in owner's equity. Identify revenues and expenses by name in the Explanation column.
2. Show the effects of the transactions on the elements of the equation by recording increases and decreases in the appropriate columns. Do not determine new totals for the items of the equation after each transaction. Next to each change in owner's equity, state whether it was caused by an investment, a revenue, an expense, or a withdrawal. Determine the final total for each item and verify that the equation is in balance.
3. Prepare an income statement, a statement of owner's equity, and a balance sheet.

Problem 2-6B

Analyzing transactions and preparing financial statements

LO 3, 4, 5, 6

Check figure:
Cash balance, July 31 = $56,280

Cantu Excavating Co., owned by Robert Cantu, began operations July 1, 2001, and incurred these transactions during the month:

July	1	Cantu invested $60,000 cash in the business.
	1	Rented office space and paid the month's rent of $500.
	1	Purchased excavating equipment for $4,000 by paying $800 in cash and agreeing to pay the balance in six months.
	6	Purchased office supplies by paying $500 cash.
	8	Completed work for a customer and immediately collected $2,200 for doing the work.
	10	Purchased $3,800 of office equipment on credit.
	15	Completed work for a customer on credit in the amount of $2,400.
	17	Purchased $1,920 of office supplies on credit.
	23	Paid for the office equipment purchased on July 10.
	25	Billed a customer $5,000 for completed work; the balance is due in 30 days.
	28	Received $2,400 for the work completed on July 15.
	31	Paid an assistant's salary of $1,260.
	31	Paid the monthly utility bills of $260.
	31	Cantu withdrew $1,200 from the business to pay personal expenses.

Required

Preparation component:

1. Arrange the following asset, liability, and shareholders' equity titles in an equation like Exhibit 2.10: Cash; Accounts Receivable; Office Supplies; Office Equipment; Excavating Equipment; Accounts Payable; and Robert Cantu, Capital. Leave space for an Explanation column to the right of Robert Cantu, Capital. Identify revenues and expenses by name in the Explanation column.
2. Use additions and subtractions to show the effects of each transaction on the items in the equation. Show new totals after each transaction. Next to each change in owner's equity, state whether the change was caused by an investment, a revenue, an expense, or a withdrawal.
3. Use the increases and decreases in the last column of the equation to prepare an income statement and a statement of owner's equity for the month. Also, prepare a balance sheet as of the end of the month.

Problem 2-7B

Identifying the effects of transactions on the financial statements

LO 5, 6

You are to identify how each of the following transactions affects the company's financial statements. For the balance sheet, you are to identify how each transaction affects total assets, total liabilities, and owner's equity. For the income statement, you are to identify how each transaction affects net income. If there is an increase, place a "+" in the column or columns. If there is a decrease, place a "−" in the column or columns. If there is both an increase and a decrease, place "+/−" in the column or columns. The line for the first transaction is completed as an example.

	Transaction	Balance Sheet: Total Assets	Balance Sheet: Total Liabilities	Balance Sheet: Equity	Income Statement: Net Income
1	Owner invests cash	+		+	
2	Pay wages with cash				
3	Acquire services on credit				
4	Buy store equipment for cash				
5	Borrow cash with note payable				
6	Sell services for cash				
7	Sell services on credit				
8	Buy rent with cash				
9	Owner withdraws cash				
10	Collect receivable from (7)				

Analytical and Review Problems

A & R Problem 2-1

Check figure:
Total assets = $89,775

Jack Tasker opened his Auto Repair Shop in the first part of this month. The balance sheet, prepared by an inexperienced part-time bookkeeper is shown below.

Required

1. Prepare a correct balance sheet.
2. Explain why the incorrect balance sheet can be in balance.

TASKER AUTO REPAIR SHOP Balance Sheet November 30, 2001			
Assets		**Liabilities and Owner's Equity**	
Cash	$ 6,300	Parts and supplies	$14,175
Accounts payable	34,650	Accounts receivable	47,250
Equipment	22,050	Mortgage payable	28,350
Jack Tasker, capital	26,775		
Total income	$89,775	Total equities	$89,775

A & R Problem 2-2

Check figure:
Total liabilities and owner's equity = $17,430

Susan Huang began the practice of law October 1, 2001, with an initial investment of $10,500 in cash. After completing the first month of practice, the financial statements were prepared by Ryan Player, the secretary/bookkeeper Ms. Huang had hired. Ms. Huang almost burst out laughing when she saw them. She had completed a course in legal accounting in law school and knew the statements prepared by Mr. Player left much to be desired. Consequently, she asks you to revise the statements. The Player version is presented below.

Required
Prepare the corrected financial statements for Susan Huang.

SUSAN HUANG, LAWYER
Balance Sheet
October 31, 2001

Assets		**Liabilities and Owner's Equity**	
Cash	$3,780	Susan Huang, capital	$7,350
Furniture	2,100		
Supplies expense	420		
Accounts payable	1,050		
	$7,350		$7,350

SUSAN HUANG, LAWYER
Income Statement
For Month Ended October 31, 2001

Revenues:		
Legal fees	$11,550	
Accounts receivable	2,100	$13,650
Expenses:		
Salaries expense	$ 2,940	
Telephone expense	210	
Rent expense	2,100	
Supplies	1,050	
Law library	8,400	14,700
Loss		$ 1,050

A & R Problem 2-3

JenStar began operations on January 1, 2000. By the end of its first year, the balance sheet showed assets of $128,000 and liabilities of $30,000.

Early during the second year of business, the owner invested an additional $15,000 of cash. Because of a very profitable year, the owner was able to withdraw a total of $56,000 later in 2001. At December 31, 2001, the balance sheet showed that assets had grown by $102,000 from the previous year and total liabilities were $96,000.

By December 31, 2002, after the third year of operations for JenStar, liabilities had decreased a total of $52,000 from December 31, 2001. During 2002, revenues earned were $894,000 with expenses of $618,000. The owner made no investments during the year but withdrew a total of $65,000.

Required:
Calculate the assets at December 31, 2002.

A & R Problem 2-4

Required:
Calculate all of the missing values.

	Dec 31/2002	Dec 31/2001	Dec 31/2000
Assets		$294,000	
Liabilities			
Owner's equity	$346,000		

Additional Information:	During 2002	During 2001
Net income (loss)		$84,000
Owner investment	$ -0-	32,000
Owner withdrawals	51,000	0
Assets increased	120,000	46,000
Liabilities increased (decreased)	(26,000)	

CHAPTER

3 Analyzing and Recording Transactions

Spinning an Accounting Web

Kitchener, ON—Maria Sanchez's second year on the job was nearly her last. She was working as a staff accountant for a shoe manufacturer where she was assigned to payroll and accounts receivable. In late December of her second year, she was instructed to add 1% to all employees' end-of-year paycheques as a bonus. Instead, she keyed an extra zero and gave everyone a 10% bonus. "The controller was furious," says Sanchez. "To top it off, the employees were so happy that the controller and board couldn't do anything but keep quiet, accept the error and thank everyone."

Today, Sanchez takes the blame for the error. But, it wasn't always that way. "I still partly blame our accounting technology. It was awful," says Sanchez. It was this experience that led Sanchez to add technology to her accounting. While taking evening classes in computing, Sanchez became convinced that accounting packages could be more user friendly. She also foresaw the power of the Web.

Sanchez is today the owner of RecordLink. It is an accounting software firm aimed at recordkeeping services for small business. It is unique in that it relies on the Web. This means there is no

need for software purchases or special computing hardware requirements for small business. Clients link into her Web servers for their computing needs.

The convenience and power of clients having access to their accounting information anytime, anywhere, are attracting new clients. "We offer 24-hour accounting and computing advice, and we are expanding our software options to include strategic planning, budget analyses and other sophisticated programs that few small businesses can individually afford." RecordLink spreads these costs over all its clients.

Sanchez sees recordkeeping services for small business as a lucrative and underserved market. She has plans to expand her business. So far, her creativity has been a hit with clients. RecordLink's revenues are growing rapidly. Adds Sanchez, "Not bad for a high-tech recordkeeper!"

Learning Objectives

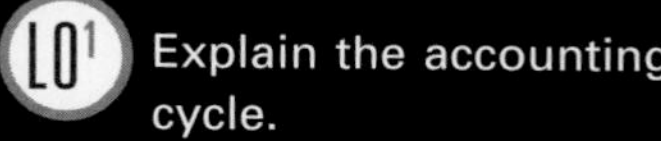

LO1 Explain the accounting cycle.

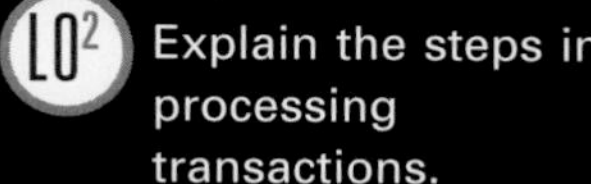

LO2 Explain the steps in processing transactions.

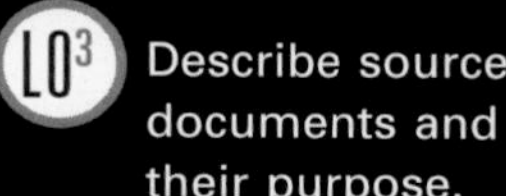

LO3 Describe source documents and their purpose.

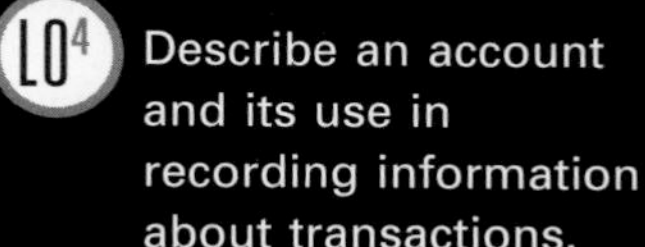

LO4 Describe an account and its use in recording information about transactions.

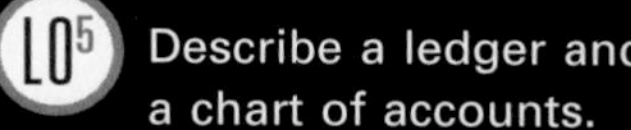

LO5 Describe a ledger and a chart of accounts.

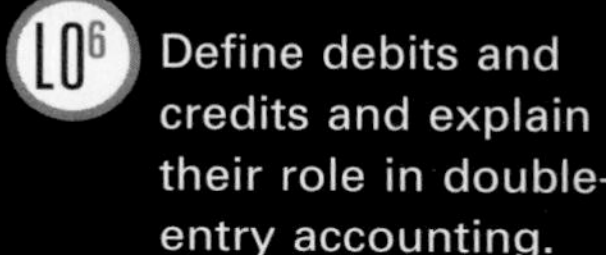

LO6 Define debits and credits and explain their role in double-entry accounting.

LO7 Analyze the impact of transactions on accounts.

LO8 Record transactions in a journal and post entries to a ledger.

LO9 Prepare and explain the use of a trial balance.

Chapter Preview

We explained in Chapter 2 how the accounting equation P. 45 helps us understand and analyze transactions and events. Analyzing financial transactions is the first step in the *accounting cycle*. Chapters 3 through 5 continue to explain and demonstrate each of the steps in the accounting cycle. All accounting systems use steps similar to those described here. These procedures are important because they lead to financial statements P. 36. Maria Sanchez of RecordLink uses a Web-based system, but the steps in the accounting cycle are essentially identical for manual systems.

We begin by providing an overview of the accounting cycle. We then describe how *source documents* provide crucial information about transactions. We describe *accounts* and explain their purpose. *Debits* and *credits* are introduced, which enables us to describe the process of recording events in a *journal* and *posting* them to a *ledger*. We return to transactions of Finlay Interiors, first introduced in Chapter 2, to illustrate many of these procedures.

The Accounting Cycle

LO1 Explain the accounting cycle.

The **accounting cycle** refers to the steps in preparing financial statements for users. It is called a cycle because the steps are repeated each reporting period. Exhibit 3.1 illustrates the accounting cycle. Chapter 3 will focus on the first four steps of the accounting cycle. Step 7, the preparation of financial statements, was introduced in the previous chapters but is reinforced in Chapter 3 and Chapter 4 and expanded upon in Chapter 5.

Exhibit 3.1

Accounting Cycle

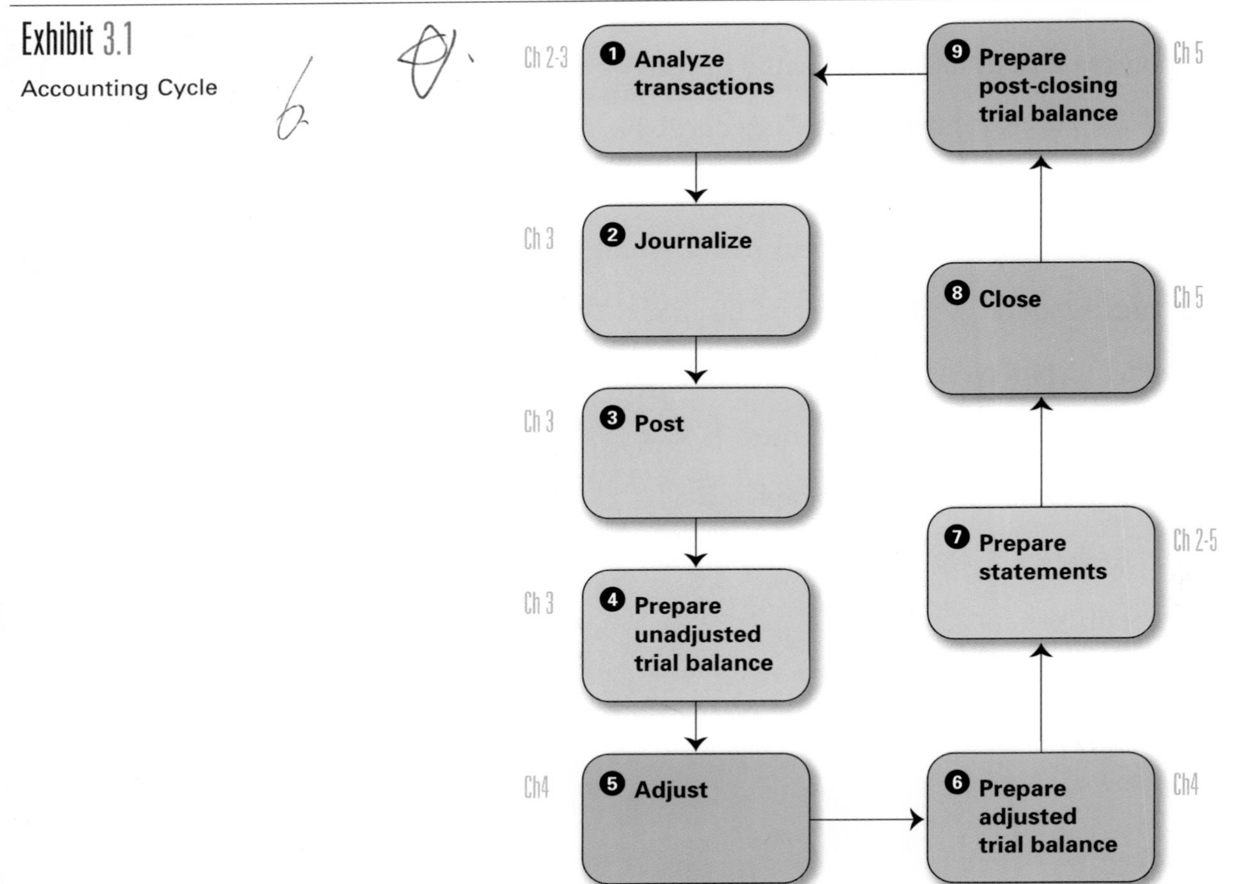

Transactions and Documents

Transactions and events are the starting points in the accounting cycle. Relying on source documents, we analyze transactions and events using the accounting equation to understand how they affect organization performance and financial position. These effects are recorded in accounting records, informally referred to as the accounting books or simply the books. Additional processing steps such as posting and preparing a trial balance help us to summarize and classify the effects of transactions and events. A final step in the accounting process is to provide information in useful reports or financial statements to decision makers.

Explain the steps in processing transactions.

Transactions and Events

Business activities can be described in terms of transactions and events. We know from Chapter 2 that business transactions are exchanges of economic consideration between two parties. We also know that the accounting equation is affected by transactions and events.

External transactions are exchanges between an organization and some other person or organization. These external transactions yield changes in the accounting equation. **Internal transactions** are exchanges within an organization. Internal transactions can also affect the accounting equation. An example is a company using office supplies in its operating activities. As the office supplies are used, its remaining balance decreases. This using up of office supplies is an event that decreases assets and decreases owner's equity.

Many events can affect an organization's performance and financial position. The analysis and record of these events are explained in the next section.

Source Documents

Describe source documents and their purpose.

Organizations use various documents and papers when doing business. **Source documents** identify and describe transactions and events entering the accounting process. They are the source of accounting information, and can be in either paper or electronic form. Examples are sales invoices, cheques, purchase orders, charges to customers, bills from suppliers, employee earnings records, and bank statements.

Both buyers and sellers use sales invoices as source documents. Sellers use them for recording sales and for control purposes. Buyers use them for recording purchases and for monitoring purchasing activity. Source documents, especially if obtained from outside the organization, provide objective evidence about transactions, thus making the information more reliable and useful. Source documents are also part of important procedures used to help prevent mistakes and theft.

Today, computers assist us in recording and processing transaction data, although parts of many small business accounting systems are still manual. Computers are only part of the process and modern technology still demands human insight and understanding of transactions. In our discussion of the steps making up the accounting process, we use a manual system for presentation. The fundamental concepts of the manual system are identical to those of a computerized information system. Our understanding of how information proceeds through an accounting system is made clear through studying a manual system.

Answer—p. 109

Cashier

You are a cashier at a retail convenience store. When you were hired, the assistant manager explained the policy of immediately entering each sale into the cash register. Recently, lunch hour traffic has increased dramatically and the assistant manager asks you to take customers' cash and make change without recording sales in the cash register to avoid delays. The assistant manager says she will add up cash and enter sales equal to the cash amount after lunch. She says that in this way the register will always be accurate when the manager arrives at three o'clock. What do you do?

Answers—p. 109

1. Describe external and internal transactions.
2. Identify examples of accounting source documents.
3. Explain the importance of source documents.

Accounts and Double-Entry Accounting

This section explains an account and its importance to accounting and business. We also describe several crucial elements of an accounting system. These include ledgers, T-accounts, debits and credits, and double-entry accounting.

The Account

LO4 Describe an account and its use in recording information about transactions.

An **account** is a detailed record of increases and decreases in a specific asset, liability, or equity item. Information is taken from accounts, analyzed, summarized, and presented in useful reports and financial statements for users. Separate accounts[1] are kept for each type of asset, liability and equity item. Exhibit 3.2 shows examples of the different types of accounts used by Finlay Interiors.

Exhibit 3.2

Types of Accounts for Finlay Interiors

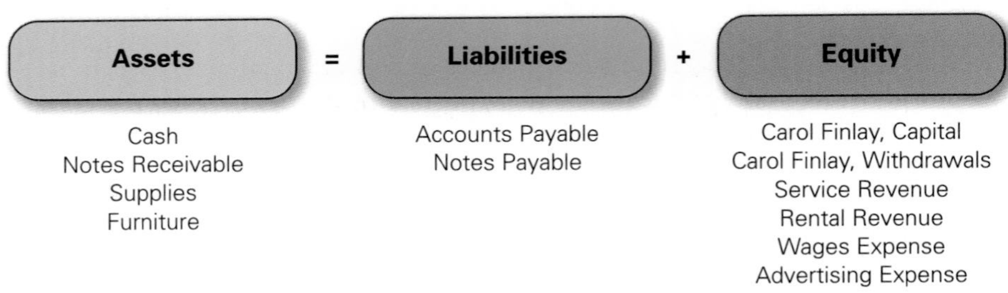

A **ledger** is a record containing all accounts used by a business. This is often in electronic form and is what we mean when we refer to the *books*. While most companies' ledgers contain similar accounts, there are often several accounts that are unique to a company because of its individual type of operation. These accounts directly affect the preparation of financial reports and statements. The remainder of this section introduces accounts that are important to most organizations.

[1] As an example of an account, Exhibit 3.12 shows the Cash account for Finlay Interiors.

Asset Accounts

Assets are resources controlled by an organization that have current and future benefits. They have value and are used in the operations of the business to create revenue. For example, Furniture is an asset held by Finlay Interiors for the purpose of creating rental revenue in current and future periods. Most accounting systems include separate accounts for each asset.

Cash

Increases and decreases in the amount of cash are recorded in a Cash account. A Cash account includes money and any form of exchange that a bank accepts for deposit. Examples are coins, currency, cheques, money orders, and chequing account balances.

Receivables

As the term implies, a receivable is an amount of cash that the business is expecting to receive in the future. There are different kinds of receivables, the most common are *accounts receivable* and *notes receivable.*

- *Accounts Receivable.* When services are performed for or goods are sold to customers in return for promises to pay in the future, an **account receivable** is recorded. These transactions are said to be *on credit* or *on account.* Accounts receivable are *increased* by services performed or goods sold on credit and *decreased* by customer payments.
- *Notes Receivable.* A **note receivable**, or a **promissory note**, is an unconditional written promise to pay a definite sum of money on demand or on a defined future date(s). A company holding a promissory note signed by another party has an asset. This asset is recorded in a Notes Receivable account.

Prepaid Expenses

Prepaid Expenses is an asset account containing payments made for assets that are to be used in the near future. As these assets are used up, the costs of the used assets become expenses. Prepaid expenses that are more crucial to the business are often accounted for in separate asset accounts such as Office Supplies, Store Supplies and Prepaid Insurance, as explained below. Other prepaids include Prepaid Rent and advance payments for legal and accounting services. An asset's cost can be initially recorded as an expense *if* it is used up before the end of the period when statements are prepared. If an asset will not be used before the end of the reporting period, then its cost is recorded in an asset account.

- *Office Supplies.* Companies use office supplies such as stationery, paper and pens. These supplies are assets until they are used. When they are used up, their cost is reported as an expense. The cost of unused supplies is an asset and is recorded in an Office Supplies account.
- *Store Supplies.* Many stores keep supplies for wrapping and packaging purchases for customers. These include plastic and paper bags, gift boxes, cartons and ribbons. The cost of these unused supplies is recorded in a Store Supplies account. Supplies are reported as expenses as they are used.
- *Prepaid Insurance.* Insurance contracts provide us with protection against losses caused by fire, theft, accidents and other events. The insurance policy often requires the fee, called a *premium*, to be paid in advance. Protection can be purchased for almost any time period, including monthly, yearly or even several years. When an insurance

premium is paid in advance, the cost is typically recorded in an asset account called Prepaid Insurance. Over time, the expiring portion of the insurance cost (the amount "used up") is removed from this asset account and reported in expenses on the income statement P. 37. The unexpired portion (the "unused" amount) remains in Prepaid Insurance and is reported on the balance sheet P. 38 as an asset.

Equipment

Most organizations own computers, printers, desks, chairs and other office equipment. Costs incurred to buy this equipment are recorded in an Office Equipment account. The costs of assets used in a store—such as counters, showcases and cash registers—are recorded in a Store Equipment account.

Buildings

A building owned by an organization can provide space for a store, an office, a warehouse or a factory. Buildings are assets because they provide benefits. Their costs are recorded in a Buildings account. When several buildings are owned, separate accounts are sometimes used for each of them.

Land

A Land account records the cost of land owned by a business. The cost of land is separated from the cost of buildings located on the land to provide more useful information in financial statements.

Liability Accounts

Liabilities are obligations to transfer assets or provide services to other entities. An organization often has several different liabilities, each of which is represented by a separate account that shows amounts owed to each creditor. The more common liability accounts are described here.

Payables

Payables are promises by a business to pay later for an asset or service already received. There are different kinds of payables; the most common are accounts payable and notes payable.

- *Accounts Payable.* Purchases of merchandise, supplies, equipment or services made by an oral or implied promise to pay later produce liabilities called Accounts Payable.
- *Notes Payable.* When an organization formally recognizes a promise to pay by signing a promissory note, the resulting liability is a Note Payable. It is recorded in either a Short-Term Notes Payable account or a Long-Term Notes Payable account depending on when it must be repaid. We explain details of account classification in Chapter 5.

Unearned Revenues

Chapter 2 explained that the revenue recognition principle P. 44 requires that revenues be reported on the income statement when earned. This principle means that we must be careful with transactions where customers pay in advance for products or services. Because cash from these transactions is received before revenues are earned, the seller considers them **unearned revenues.** *Unearned revenue* is a liability that is satisfied by delivering products or services in the future. Examples of unearned revenue include magazine subscriptions collected in advance by a publisher, sales of gift certificates by stores, airline tickets sold in advance, and rent collected in advance by a landlord.

WestJet Airlines Ltd. reported *advance ticket sales* of $10,907,000 on December 31, 1999.
See: Appendix I

When cash is received in advance for products and services, the seller records it in a liability account such as Unearned Subscriptions, Unearned Rent, or Unearned Professional Fees. When products and services are delivered, the now earned portion of the unearned revenues is transferred to revenue accounts such as Subscription Fees, Rent Earned or Professional Fees.[2]

Other Liabilities

Other common liabilities include wages payable, taxes payable, and interest payable. Each of these is often recorded in a separate liability account. If they are not large in amount, one or more of them may be added and reported as a single amount on the balance sheet.

The liabilities section of WestJet Airlines Ltd.'s balance sheet at December 31, 1999 included income taxes payable of $7,410,000.
See: Appendix I

Equity Accounts

We described in the previous chapter four types of transactions that affect owner's equity. They are (1) investments by the owner, (2) withdrawals by the owner, (3) revenues and (4) expenses. In Chapter 2, we entered all equity transactions in a single column under the owner's name. When we later prepared the income statement and the statement of owner's equity P. 38, we had to review the items in that column to properly classify them in financial statements.

A preferred approach is to use separate accounts, as illustrated under the Equity heading in Exhibit 3.2.

Owner Capital

Owner investments P. 38 are recorded in an account identified by the owner's name and the title *Capital.*

Owner Withdrawals

Most accounting systems use an account with the name of the owner and the word *Withdrawals* in recording owner withdrawals P. 38. The owner withdrawals account also is sometimes called the owner's *Personal* account or *Drawing* account.

Revenues and Expenses

Decision makers often want information about revenues earned and expenses incurred for a period. Businesses use a variety of revenue and expense accounts to report this information on income statements. Different companies have different

[2] There are variations in account titles in practice. As one example, Subscription Fees is sometimes called: Subscription Fees Revenue, Subscription Fees Earned, or Earned Subscription Fees. As another example, Rent Earned is sometimes called Rent Revenue, Rental Revenue, or Earned Rent Revenue. We must use our good judgement when reading financial statements since titles can differ even within the same industry. Revenue or Sales are the most commonly used terms.

kinds of revenue and expense accounts reflecting their own important activities. Examples of revenue accounts are Sales, Commissions Earned, Professional Fees Earned, Rent Earned and Interest Earned. Examples of expense accounts are Advertising Expense, Store Supplies Expense, Office Salaries Expense, Office Supplies Expense, Rent Expense, Utilities Expense and Insurance Expense.

We can get an idea of the variety of revenues by looking at the chart of accounts in Appendix III. It lists accounts needed to solve some of the exercises and problems in this book.[3]

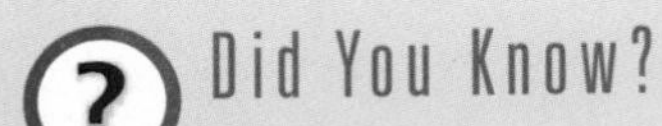

NHL Accounting

The Vancouver Canucks report the following major revenue and expense accounts:

Revenues:
Game ticket sales
Radio and television
Merchandise and programs
Advertising and promotions

Expenses:
Hockey operations
Merchandise and programs
Administrative and marketing

SOURCE: Orca Bay Hockey Holdings' Financial Statements.

Ledger and Chart of Accounts

LO5 Describe a ledger and a chart of accounts.

The actual recording of accounts can differ depending on the system. Computerized systems store accounts in files on electronic storage devices. Manual systems often record accounts on separate pages in a special booklet. The collection of all accounts for an electronic or manual information system is called a *ledger*.

A company's size and diversity of operations affect the number of accounts needed in its accounting system. A small company may get by with as few as 20 or 30 accounts, while a large company may need several thousand. The **chart of accounts** is a list of all accounts used by a company. The chart includes an identification number assigned to each account. A typical small business might use the following numbering system for its accounts:

101 – 199	Asset accounts
201 – 299	Liability accounts
301 – 399	Owner capital and withdrawals accounts
401 – 499	Revenue accounts
501 – 599	Expense accounts

While this particular system provides for 99 asset accounts, a company may not use all of them. The numbers provide a three-digit code that is useful in recordkeeping. In this case the first digit assigned to asset accounts is 1, while the first digit assigned to liability accounts is 2, and so on. The first digit of an account's number also shows whether the account appears on the balance sheet or the income statement. The second and subsequent digits may also relate to the accounts' categories. A partial chart of accounts for Finlay Interiors follows.

[3] Different companies can use different account titles than those in the list. For example, a company might use Interest Revenue instead of Interest Earned, or Rental Expense instead of Rent Expense. It is only important that an account title describes the item it represents.

Account Number	Account Name	Account Number	Account Name
101	Cash	301	Carol Finlay, Capital
106	Accounts Receivable	302	Carol Finlay, Withdrawals
125	Supplies	403	Consulting Revenue
128	Prepaid Insurance	406	Rental Revenue
167	Furniture	641	Rent Expense
201	Accounts Payable	622	Salaries Expense
236	Unearned Consulting Revenue	690	Utilities Expense
240	Notes Payable		

4. Classify the following accounts as either assets, liabilities or equity: (1) Prepaid Rent, (2) Unearned Fees, (3) Buildings, (4) Owner Capital, (5) Wages Payable and (6) Office Supplies.
5. What is an account? What is a ledger?
6. What determines the quantity and types of accounts used by a company?

Answers—p. 109

T-Account

A **T-account** is a helpful tool in showing the effects of transactions and events on specific accounts. The T-account gets its name from its shape. Its shape looks like the letter T and is shown in Exhibit 3.3 below:

Exhibit 3.3

The T-Account

Account Title	
(Left side) *Debit*	(Right side) *Credit*

The format of a T-account includes (1) the account title on top, (2) a left or debit side, and (3) a right or credit side. A T-account provides one side for recording increases in the item and the other side for decreases. As an example, the T-account for Finlay Interiors' Cash account after recording the transactions in Chapter 2 is in Exhibit 3.4:

Exhibit 3.4

Cash T-Account for Finlay Interiors

Cash			
Investment by owner	30,000	Purchase of supplies	2,500
Consulting services revenue received	2,200	Purchase of furniture	20,000
Collection of account receivable	1,900	Payment of rent	1,000
		Payment of salary	700
		Payment of account payable	900
		Withdrawal by owner	600

Finlay Interiors

T-accounts are used throughout this text to help illustrate debits and credits and to solve accounting problems. This form of account is not used in the real business world.

Balance of an Account

An **account balance** is the difference between the increases and decreases recorded in an account. To determine the balance, we (1) compute the total increases shown on one side (including the beginning balance), (2) compute the total decreases shown on the other side, and (3) subtract the sum of the decreases from the sum of the increases. The total increases in Finlay Interiors' Cash account are $34,100, the total decreases are $25,700, and the account balance is $8,400. The T-account in Exhibit 3.5 shows how we calculate the $8,400 balance:

Exhibit 3.5

Computing the Balance of a T-Account

Cash			
Investment by owner	30,000	Purchase of supplies	2,500
Consulting services revenue earned	2,200	Purchase of furniture	20,000
Collection of account receivable	1,900	Payment of rent	1,000
		Payment of salary	700
		Payment of account payable	900
		Withdrawal by owner	600
Total increases	34,100	Total decreases	25,700
Less decreases	−25,700		
Balance	8,400		

Debits and Credits

LO6 Define debits and credits and explain their role in double-entry accounting.

The left side of a T-account is called the **debit** side, often abbreviated Dr. The right side is called the **credit** side, abbreviated Cr.[4] To enter amounts on the left side of an account is to *debit* the account. To enter amounts on the right side is to *credit* the account. The difference between total debits and total credits for an account is the account balance. When the sum of debits exceeds the sum of credits, the account has a *debit balance.* It has a *credit balance* when the sum of credits exceeds the sum of debits. When the sum of debits equals the sum of credits, the account has a zero balance. This dual method of recording transactions as debits and credits is an essential feature of *double-entry accounting,* and is the topic of the next section.

Double-Entry Accounting

Debits = Credits

Double-entry accounting means every transaction affects and is recorded in at least two accounts. *The total amount debited must equal the total amount credited* for each transaction. Therefore, the sum of the debits for all entries must equal the sum of the credits for all entries. As well, the sum of debit account balances in the ledger must equal the sum of credit account balances. The only reason that the sum of debit balances would not equal the sum of credit balances is if an error has

[4] These abbreviations are remnants of 18th-century English recordkeeping practices where the terms *Debitor* and *Creditor* were used instead of *debit* and *credit.* The abbreviations use the first and last letters of these terms, just as we still do for *Saint* (St.) and *Doctor* (Dr.).

occurred. Double-entry accounting helps to prevent errors by assuring that debits and credits for each transaction are equal.

The system for recording debits and credits follows from the accounting equation in Exhibit 3.6.

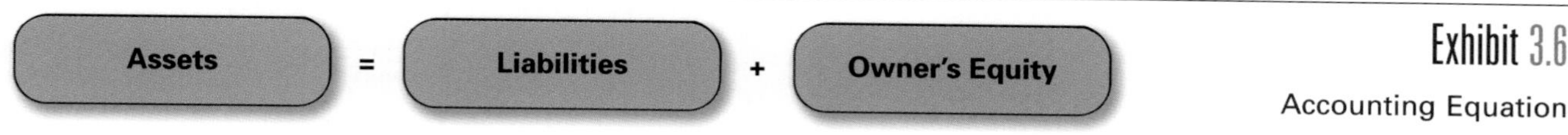

Exhibit 3.6

Accounting Equation

Assets are on the left side of this equation. Liabilities and equity are on the right side. Like any mathematical equation, increases or decreases on one side have equal effects on the other side. For example, the net increase in assets must be accompanied by an identical net increase in the liabilities and equity side. Some transactions only affect one side of the equation. This means that two or more accounts on one side are affected, but their net effect on this one side is zero.

The debit and credit effects for asset, liability and owner's equity accounts are captured in Exhibit 3.7.

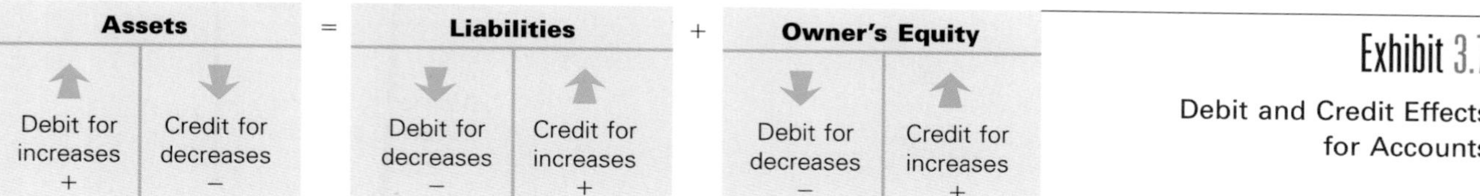

Exhibit 3.7

Debit and Credit Effects for Accounts

Three important rules for recording transactions in a double-entry accounting system follow from Exhibit 3.7:

1. Increases in assets are debited to asset accounts. Decreases in assets are credited to asset accounts.
2. Increases in liabilities are credited to liability accounts. Decreases in liabilities are debited to liability accounts.
3. Increases in owner's equity are credited to owner's equity accounts. Decreases in owner's equity are debited to owner's equity accounts.

CAUTION: We must guard against the error of thinking that the terms debit and credit mean increase or decrease. In an account where a *debit is an increase*, such as an asset, a credit is a decrease. *But* notice that in an account where a debit is a decrease, such as a liability, a *credit is an increase.*

We explained in Chapter 2 how owner's equity increases with owner investments and revenues and decreases with expenses and owner withdrawals. We can therefore expand the accounting equation and debit and credit effects as shown in Exhibit 3.8.

Exhibit 3.8

Debit and Credit Effects for Accounts

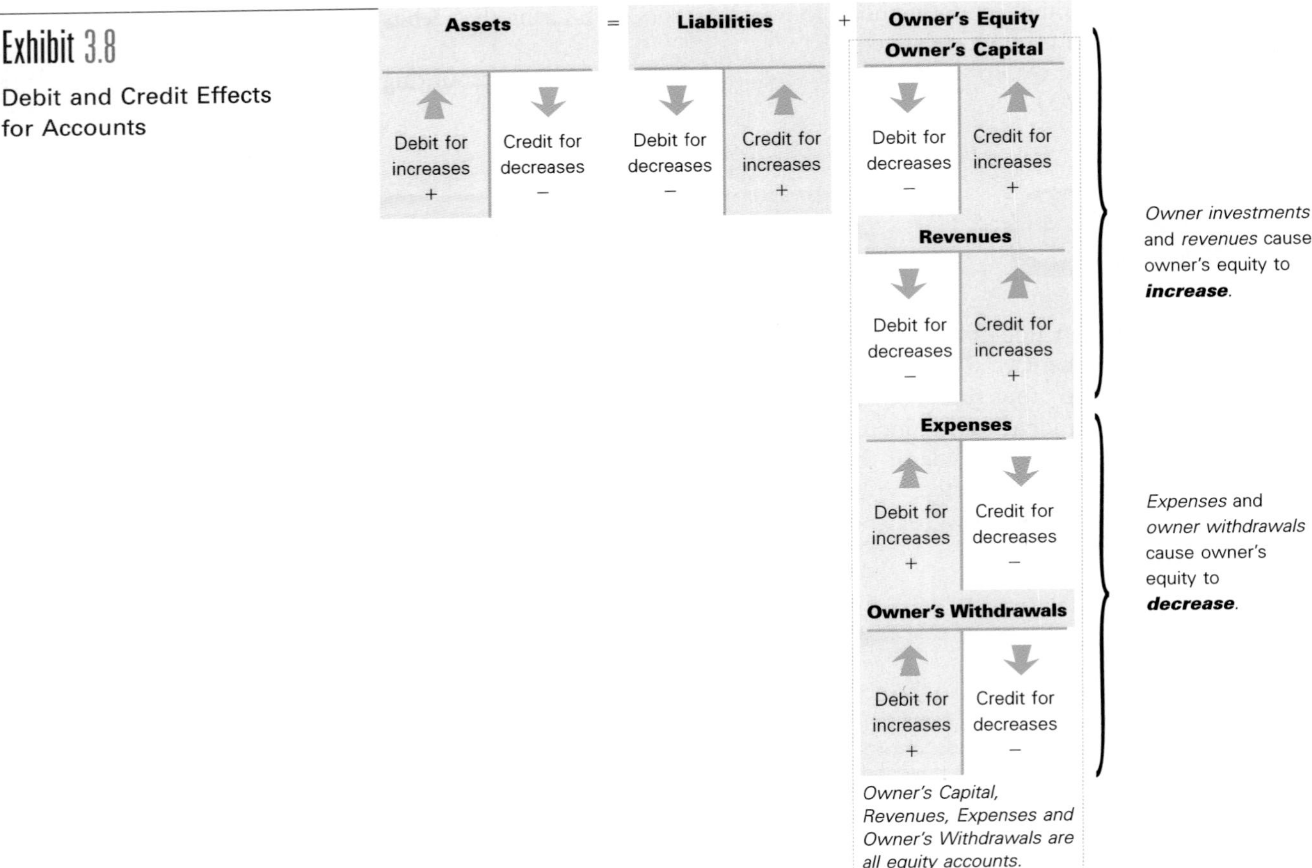

Increases in owner's capital or revenues *increase* owner's equity. Increases in owner's withdrawals or expenses *decrease* owner's equity. These relations are reflected in the following important rules:

4. Investments by the owner are credited to owner's capital because they increase equity.
5. Revenues are credited to revenue accounts because they increase equity.
6. Expenses are debited to expense accounts because they decrease equity.
7. Withdrawals made by the owner are debited to owner's withdrawals because they decrease equity.

Our understanding of these diagrams and rules is crucial to analyzing and recording transactions. This also helps us to prepare and analyze financial statements.[5]

Notice in Exhibit 3.8 that the debit or credit side of each T-account is shaded. The shaded areas highlight the *normal balance* of each type of account. The **normal balance** of each account refers to the debit or credit side where increases are recorded. For example, the normal balance for an asset account would be a debit because debits cause assets to increase. The normal balance for a revenue account would be a credit because revenues are increased by credits.

[5] We can use good judgement to our advantage in applying double-entry accounting. For example, revenues and expenses normally (but not always) accumulate in business. This means they increase and rarely decrease during an accounting period. Accordingly, we should be alert to decreases in these accounts (debit revenues or credit expenses) to be certain that this is our intent.

Mid-Chapter Demonstration Problem

Indicate whether the following transactions increase or decrease the relevant account.

a. A liability account is debited for $500.
b. A revenue account is credited for $1,000.
c. An asset account is debited for $300.
d. An expense account is credited for $75.
e. Owner's capital is credited for $1,000.

SOLUTION TO Mid-Chapter Demonstration Problem

a. decrease; b. increase; c. increase; d. decrease; e. increase

Analyzing Transactions

LO7 Analyze the impact of transactions on accounts.

We return to the activities of Finlay Interiors to show how debit and credit rules and double-entry accounting are useful in analyzing and processing transactions. We analyze Finlay Interiors' transactions in two steps. *Step One* analyzes a transaction and its source document(s). *Step Two* applies double-entry accounting to identify the effect of a transaction on account balances.

We should study each transaction thoroughly before proceeding to the next transaction. The first 11 transactions are familiar to us from Chapter 2. We expand our analysis of these transactions and consider four new transactions (numbered 12 through 15) of Finlay Interiors that were omitted earlier.

1. Investment by owner.

Cash			
(1)	30,000		

Carol Finlay, Capital			
		(1)	30,000

Transaction. Carol Finlay invested $30,000 in Finlay Interiors on January 1, 2001.
Analysis. Assets increase. Owner's equity increases.
Double-entry. Debit the Cash asset account for $30,000. Credit the Carol Finlay, Capital account in owner's equity for $30,000.

2. Purchase supplies for cash.

Supplies			
(2)	2,500		

Cash			
(1)	30,000	(2)	2,500

Transaction. Finlay Interiors purchases supplies by paying $2,500 cash.
Analysis. Assets increase. Assets decrease. This changes the composition of assets, but does not change the total amount of assets.
Double-entry. Debit the Supplies asset account for $2,500. Credit the Cash asset account for $2,500.

3. Purchase furniture for cash.

Furniture			
(3)	20,000		

Cash			
(1)	30,000	(2)	2,500
		(3)	20,000

Transaction. Finlay Interiors purchases furniture by paying $20,000 cash.
Analysis. Assets increase. Assets decrease. This changes the composition of assets, but does not change the total amount of assets.
Double-entry. Debit the Furniture asset account for $20,000. Credit the Cash asset account for $20,000.

4. Purchase furniture and supplies on credit.

Supplies

(2)	2,500		
(4)	**1,100**		

Furniture

(3)	20,000		
(4)	**6,000**		

Accounts Payable

		(4)	**1,100**

Notes Payable

		(4)	**6,000**

Transaction. Finlay Interiors purchases $1,100 of supplies and $6,000 of furniture on credit. Finlay Interiors signs a promissory note for the $6,000 of furniture.

Analysis. Assets increase. Liabilities increase.

Double-entry. Debit two asset accounts: Supplies for $1,100 and Furniture for $6,000. Credit two liability accounts: Accounts Payable for $1,100 and Notes Payable for $6,000.

5. Services rendered for cash.

Cash

(1)	30,000	(2)	2,500
(5)	**2,200**	(3)	20,000

Consulting Revenue

		(5)	**2,200**

Transaction. Finlay Interiors provided consulting services to a customer and immediately collected $2,200 cash.

Analysis. Assets increase. Owner's equity increases from Revenue.

Double-entry. Debit the Cash asset account for $2,200. Credit the Consulting Revenue account for $2,200 (this increases owner's equity).

6. Payment of expense in cash.

Rent Expense

(6)	**1,000**		

Cash

(1)	30,000	(2)	2,500
(5)	2,200	(3)	20,000
		(6)	**1,000**

Transaction. Finlay Interiors pays $1,000 cash for January rent.

Analysis. Assets decrease. Owner's equity decreases from Expense.

Double-entry. Debit the Rent Expense account for $1,000 (this decreases owner's equity). Credit the Cash asset account for $1,000.

7. Payment of expense in cash.

Salaries Expense

(7)	**700**		

Cash

(1)	30,000	(2)	2,500
(5)	2,200	(3)	20,000
		(6)	1,000
		(7)	**700**

Transaction. Finlay Interiors pays $700 cash for employee's salary for the pay period ending on January 12.

Analysis. Assets decrease. Owner's equity decreases from Expense.

Double-entry. Debit the Salaries Expense account for $700 (this decreases owner's equity). Credit the Cash asset account for $700.

8. Services and rental revenues rendered on credit.

Accounts Receivable			
(8)	1,900		

Consulting Revenue			
		(5)	2,200
		(8)	1,600

Rental Revenue			
		(8)	300

Transaction. Finlay Interiors provided consulting services of $1,600 and rented furniture for $300 to a customer. The customer is billed $1,900 for the services and Finlay Interiors expects to collect this money in the near future.

Analysis. Assets increase. Owner's equity increases from Revenue.

Double-entry. Debit the Accounts Receivable asset account for $1,900. Credit two revenue accounts: Consulting Revenue for $1,600 (this increases owner's equity) and Rental Revenue for $300 (this increases owner's equity).

9. Receipt of cash on account.

Cash			
(1)	30,000	(2)	2,500
(5)	2,200	(3)	20,000
(9)	1,900	(6)	1,000
		(7)	700

Accounts Receivable			
(8)	1,900	(9)	1,900

Transaction. On January 25, an amount of $1,900 is received from the client in Transaction 8.

Analysis. Assets increase. Assets decrease. This changes the composition of assets, but does not change the total amount of assets.

Double-entry. Debit the Cash asset account for $1,900. Credit Accounts Receivable asset account for $1,900.

10. Partial payment of accounts payable.

Accounts Payable			
(10)	900	(4)	1,100

Cash			
(1)	30,000	(2)	2,500
(5)	2,200	(3)	20,000
(9)	1,900	(6)	1,000
		(7)	700
		(10)	900

Transaction. Finlay Interiors pays CanTech Supply $900 cash toward the account payable of $1,100 owed from the purchase of supplies in Transaction 4.

Analysis. Assets decrease. Liabilities decrease.

Double-entry. Debit the Accounts Payable liability account for $900. Credit the Cash asset account for $900.

11. Withdrawal of cash by owner.

Carol Finlay, Withdrawals			
(11)	600		

Cash			
(1)	30,000	(2)	2,500
(5)	2,200	(3)	20,000
(9)	1,900	(6)	1,000
		(7)	700
		(10)	900
		(11)	600

Transaction. Carol Finlay withdraws $600 from Finlay Interiors for personal living expenses.

Analysis. Assets decrease. Owner's equity decreases.

Double-entry. Debit the Carol Finlay, Withdrawals account in owner's equity for $600. Credit the Cash asset account for $600.

12. Receipt of cash for future services.

Cash

(1)	30,000	(2)	2,500
(5)	2,200	(3)	20,000
(9)	1,900	(6)	1,000
(12)	**3,000**	(7)	700
		(10)	900
		(11)	600

Unearned Consulting Revenue

		(12)	**3,000**

Transaction. Finlay Interiors enters into (signs) a contract with a customer to provide future consulting. Finlay Interiors receives $3,000 cash in advance of providing these consulting services.

Analysis. Assets increase. Liabilities increase. Accepting the $3,000 cash obligates Finlay Interiors to perform future services, and is a liability. No revenue is earned until services are provided.

Double-entry. Debit the Cash asset account for $3,000. Credit the Unearned Consulting Revenue liability account for $3,000.

13. Payment of cash for future insurance coverage.

Prepaid Insurance

(13)	**2,400**		

Cash

(1)	30,000	(2)	2,500
(5)	2,200	(3)	20,000
(9)	1,900	(6)	1,000
(12)	3,000	(7)	700
		(10)	900
		(11)	600
		(13)	**2,400**

Transaction. Finlay Interiors pays $2,400 cash (premium) for a two-year insurance policy. Coverage begins on January 1.

Analysis. Assets increase. Assets decrease. This changes the composition of assets from cash to a "right" of insurance coverage. This does not change the total amount of assets. Expense will be incurred as insurance coverage is provided.

Double-entry. Debit the Prepaid Insurance asset account for $2,400. Credit the Cash asset account for $2,400.

14. Payment of expense in cash.

Utilities Expense

(14)	**230**		

Cash

(1)	30,000	(2)	2,500
(5)	2,200	(3)	20,000
(9)	1,900	(6)	1,000
(12)	3,000	(7)	700
		(10)	900
		(11)	600
		(13)	2,400
		(14)	**230**

Transaction. Finlay Interiors pays $230 cash for January utilities.

Analysis. Assets decrease. Owner's equity decreases from Expense.

Double-entry. Debit the Utilities Expense account for $230 (this decreases owner's equity). Credit the Cash asset account for $230.

15. Payment of expense in cash.

Salaries Expense

(7)	700		
(15)	**700**		

Cash

(1)	30,000	(2)	2,500
(5)	2,200	(3)	20,000
(9)	1,900	(6)	1,000
(12)	3,000	(7)	700
		(10)	900
		(11)	600
		(13)	2,400
		(14)	230
		(15)	**700**

Transaction. Finlay Interiors pays $700 cash for employee's salary for the two-week pay period ending on January 26.

Analysis. Assets decrease. Owner's equity decreases from Expense.

Double-entry. Debit the Salaries Expense account for $700 (this decreases owner's equity). Credit the Cash asset account for $700.

Accounting Equation Analysis

Exhibit 3.9 shows the accounts of Finlay Interiors after all 15 transactions are recorded and the balances computed. The accounts are grouped into three major columns. These columns represent the terms in the accounting equation: assets, liabilities and owner's equity.

Exhibit 3.9 highlights several important points. First, as with each transaction, the totals for the three columns show that the accounting equation is in balance:

Assets	=	Liabilities	+	Owner's Equity
$40,070	=	$9,200	+	$30,870

Second, the owner's investment is recorded in the capital account and the withdrawals, revenue and expense accounts reflect the events that change owner's equity. Their ending balances make up the statement of owner's equity. Third, the revenue and expense account balances are summarized and reported in the income statement.

Exhibit 3.9

Ledger for Finlay Interiors

fi Finlay Interiors

Assets

Cash

	Debit		Credit
(1)	30,000	(2)	2,500
(5)	2,200	(3)	20,000
(9)	1,900	(6)	1,000
(12)	3,000	(7)	700
		(10)	900
		(11)	600
		(13)	2,400
		(14)	230
		(15)	700
Total	37,100	Total	29,030
	−29,030		
Balance	**8,070**		

Accounts Receivable

	Debit		Credit
(8)	1,900	(9)	1,900
Balance	0		

Prepaid Insurance

	Debit		Credit
(13)	2,400		
Balance	**2,400**		

Supplies

	Debit		Credit
(2)	2,500		
(4)	1,100		
Balance	**3,600**		

Furniture

	Debit		Credit
(3)	20,000		
(4)	6,000		
Balance	**26,000**		

Liabilities

Accounts Payable

	Debit		Credit
(10)	900	(4)	1,100
		Balance	**200**

Unearned Consulting Revenue

	Debit		Credit
		(12)	3,000
		Balance	**3,000**

Notes Payable

	Debit		Credit
		(4)	6,000
		Balance	**6,000**

Accounts in the white area reflect increases and decreases in owner's equity. Their balances are reported on the income statement or the statement of owner's equity.

Owner's Equity

Carol Finlay, Capital

	Debit		Credit
		(1)	30,000
		Balance	**30,000**

Carol Finlay, Withdrawals

	Debit		Credit
(11)	600		
Balance	**600**		

Consulting Revenue

	Debit		Credit
		(5)	2,200
		(8)	1,600
		Balance	**3,800**

Rental Revenue

	Debit		Credit
		(8)	300
		Balance	**300**

Rent Expense

	Debit		Credit
(6)	1,000		
Balance	**1,000**		

Salaries Expense

	Debit		Credit
(7)	700		
(15)	700		
Balance	**1,400**		

Utilities Expense

	Debit		Credit
(14)	230		
Balance	**230**		

TOTALS:	Assets	=	Liabilities	+	Owner's Equity
	$40,070[1]	=	**$9,200[2]**	+	**$30,870[3]**

[1] $8,070 + $0 + $2,400 + $3,600 + $26,000 = $40,070

[2] $200 + $3,000 + 6,000 = $9,200

[3] $30,000 − $600 + $3,800 + $300 − $1,000 − $1,400 − $230 = $30,870

Answers—p. 110

7. Does debit always mean increase and credit always mean decrease?
8. What kinds of transactions increase owner's equity? What kinds decrease owner's equity?
9. Why are most accounting systems called *double-entry*?
10. Double-entry accounting requires that:
    a. All transactions that create debits to asset accounts must create credits to liability or owner's equity accounts.
    b. A transaction that requires a debit to a liability account also requires a credit to an asset account.
    c. Every transaction must be recorded with total debits equal to total credits.

Recording and Posting Transactions

LO8 Record transactions in a journal and post entries to a ledger.

In the previous section, we analyzed transactions, *Step One* of the accounting cycle, and recorded their effects directly in T-accounts to help you understand the double-entry accounting system. Yet accounting systems rarely record transactions directly in accounts. Instead, *Step Two* of the accounting cycle requires that we record transactions in a record called a **journal** before recording them in accounts. This is to avoid the potential for error and the difficulty in tracking mistakes. A journal gives us a complete record of each transaction in one place. It also directly links the debits and credits for each transaction. The process of recording transactions in a journal is called **journalizing.**

Step Three of the accounting cycle is to **post**, or transfer, entries from the journal to the ledger. ***Posting occurs after debits and credits for each transaction are entered into a journal.*** This process leaves a helpful trail in checking for accuracy. It also helps us avoid errors. This section describes both journalizing and posting of transactions. *Step Four* of the accounting cycle, preparing a *trial balance*, is explained in the next section. Each of these steps in processing transactions is shown in Exhibit 3.10.

Exhibit 3.10

First Four Steps of the Accounting Cycle

Step 1: Analyze transactions and source documents.

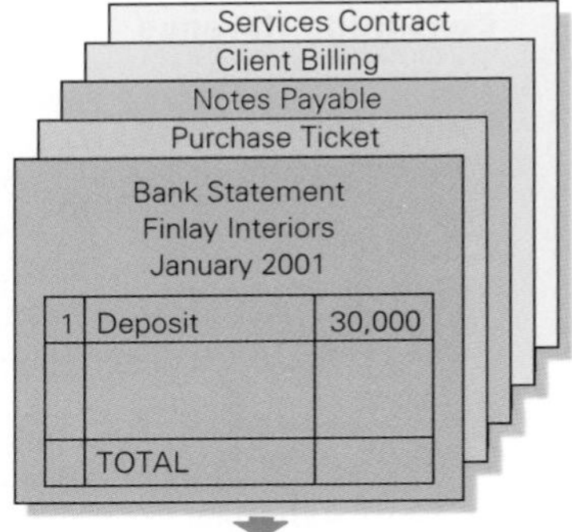

Step 2: Record journal entry.

2001	General Journal		
Jan. 1	Cash	30,000	
	Carol Finlay, Capital		30,000
2	Supplies	2,500	
	Cash		2,500

Step 3: Post entry to ledger.

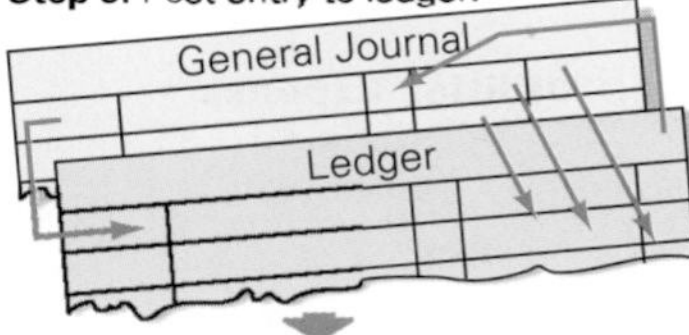

Step 4: Prepare trial balance.

Finlay Interiors Trial Balance January 31, 2001	Debit	Credit
Cash	$8,070	
Accounts receivable	-0-	
Prepaid insurance	$2,400	

The Journal Entry

The **General Journal** is flexible in that it can be used to record any economic transaction. A General Journal entry includes the following information about each transaction:

1. Date of transaction.
2. Titles of affected accounts.
3. Dollar amount of each debit and credit.
4. Explanation of transaction.

Exhibit 3.11 shows how the first four transactions of Finlay Interiors are recorded in a General Journal. A journal is often referred to as the *book of original entry.* The accounting process is similar for manual and computerized systems. Many computer programs even copy the look of a paper journal.

The January 4 entry in Exhibit 3.11 uses four accounts. There are debits to the two assets purchased, Supplies and Furniture. There are also credits to the two sources of payment, Accounts Payable and Notes Payable. A transaction affecting three or more accounts is called a **compound journal entry**.

Exhibit 3.11

Partial General Journal for Finlay Interiors

Date	General Journal Account Titles and Explanation	PR	Debit	Page 1 Credit
2001				
Jan. 1	Cash		30,000	
	Carol Finlay, Capital			30,000
	Investment by owner.			
2	Supplies		2,500	
	Cash			2,500
	Purchased store supplies for cash.			
3	Furniture		20,000	
	Cash			20,000
	Purchased furniture for cash.			
4	Supplies		1,100	
	Furniture		6,000	
	Accounts Payable			1,100
	Notes Payable			6,000
	Purchased supplies and furniture on credit.			

Journalizing Transactions

There are standard procedures for recording entries in a General Journal. We can identify nine steps in journalizing the entries in Exhibit 3.11. It is helpful to review the entries when studying these steps.

1. Enter the year on the first line at the top of the first column.
2. Enter the month in Column One on the first line of the journal entry. Later entries for the same month and year on the same page of the journal do not require re-entering the same month and year.
3. Enter the day of the transaction in Column Two on the first line of each entry. Transactions are journalized in chronological order (by date).
4. Enter the titles of accounts debited. Account titles are taken from the chart of accounts and are aligned with the left margin of the Account Titles and Explanation column.
5. Enter the debit amounts in the Debit column on the same line as the accounts to be debited.
6. Enter the titles of accounts credited. Account titles are taken from the chart of accounts and are indented from the left margin of the Account Titles and Explanation column to distinguish them from debited accounts (an indent of 1 cm is common).
7. Enter the credit amounts in the Credit column on the same line as the accounts to be credited.
8. Enter a brief explanation of the transaction on the line below the entry. This explanation is indented about half as far as the credited account titles to avoid confusing an explanation with accounts. For illustrative purposes, we italicize explanations so they stand out. This is not normally done.
9. Skip a line after each journal entry for clarity.

A complete journal entry gives us a useful description of the transaction and its effects on the organization.

The **posting reference (PR) column** is left blank when a transaction is initially recorded. Individual account numbers are later entered into the PR column when entries are posted to the ledger. The PR column is also called the *folio column*. This follows from past recordkeeping procedures where each account took up a page in a book, and an old word for page is *folio*.

Computerized Journals

Journals in computerized and manual systems serve the same purposes. Computerized journals are often designed to look like a manual journal page (as in Exhibit 3.11). Computerized systems typically include error-checking routines that ensure that debits equal credits for each entry. Shortcuts often allow recordkeepers to enter account numbers instead of names, and to enter account names and numbers with pull-down menus.

Balance Column Ledger

T-accounts are a simple and direct tool to show how the accounting process works. They allow us to omit less relevant details and concentrate on main ideas. Accounting systems in practice need more structure and use **balance column ledger accounts**. Exhibit 3.12 is an example.

Exhibit 3.12

Cash Account in Balance Column Ledger

Cash						Account No. 101
Date		Explanation	PR	Debit	Credit	Balance
2001						
Jan.	1		G1	30,000		30,000
	2		G1		2,500	27,500
	3		G1		20,000	7,500
	10		G1	2,200		9,700

The T-account was derived from the balance column ledger account format and it too has a column for debits and a column for credits. Look at the imaginary T-account superimposed over Exhibit 3.12. The balance column ledger account is different from a T-account because it includes a transaction's date and explanation and has a third column with the balance of the account after each entry is posted. This means that the amount on the last line in this column is the account's current balance. For example, Finlay Interiors' Cash account in Exhibit 3.12 is debited on January 1 for the $30,000 investment by Finlay. The account then shows a $30,000 debit balance. The account is credited on January 2 for $2,500, and its new $27,500 balance is shown in the third column. On January 3, it is credited again, this time for $20,000, and its balance is reduced to $7,500. The Cash account is debited for $2,200 on January 10, and its balance increases to $9,700.

When a balance column ledger is used, the heading of the Balance column does not show whether it is a debit or credit balance. This omission is no problem because every account has a normal balance, as previously highlighted in Exhibit 3.8.

Abnormal Balance

Unusual events can sometimes give an abnormal balance for an account. An *abnormal balance* refers to a balance on the side where decreases are recorded. For example, a customer might mistakenly overpay a bill. This gives that customer's account receivable an abnormal credit balance.

Zero Balance

A zero balance for an account is usually shown by writing zeros or a dash in the Balance column. This practice avoids confusion between a zero balance and one omitted in error.

Posting Journal Entries

To ensure that the ledger is up to date, entries are posted as soon as possible. This might be daily, weekly or when time permits. All entries must be posted to the ledger by the end of a reporting period. This is so that account balances are current when financial statements are prepared. Because the ledger is the final destination for individual transactions, it is referred to as the *book of final entry.*

When posting entries to the ledger, the debits in journal entries are copied into ledger accounts as debits, and credits are copied into the ledger as credits. Exhibit 3.13 lists six steps of manual systems to post each debit and credit from a journal entry.

Exhibit 3.13

Posting an Entry to the Ledger

Finlay Interiors

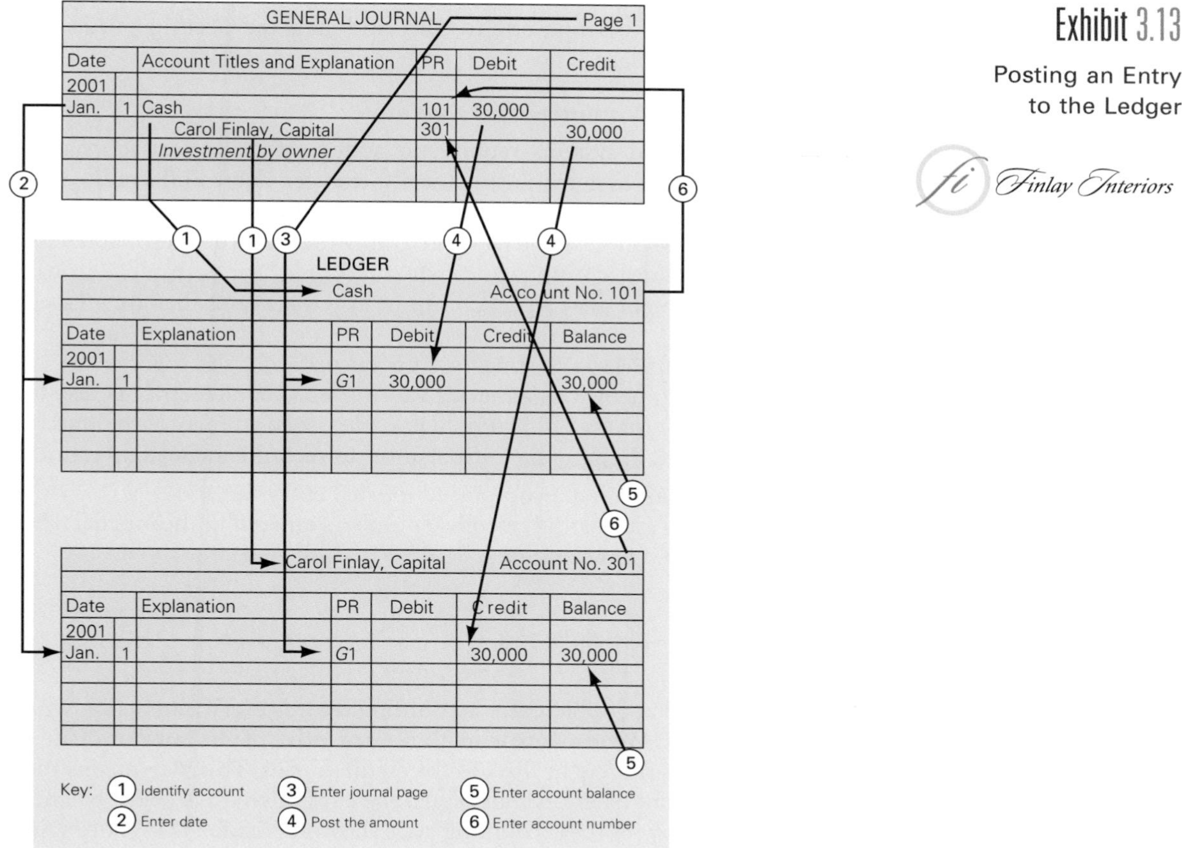

For each journal entry, the usual process is to post debit(s) and then credit(s). The steps in posting are:

1. Identify the ledger account that was debited in the journal entry.
2. Enter the date of the journal entry in this ledger account.
3. Enter the source of the debit in the PR column, both the journal and page. The letter *G* shows it came from the General Journal.[6]
4. Enter the amount debited from the journal entry into the Debit column of the ledger account.
5. Compute and enter the account's new balance in the Balance column.
6. Enter the ledger account number in the PR column of the journal entry.

Repeat the six steps for credit amounts and Credit columns. Notice that posting does not create new information; posting simply transfers (or copies) information from the General Journal to the appropriate account in the ledger.

Step Six in the posting process for both debit and credit amounts of an entry inserts the account number in the journal's PR column. This creates a cross-reference between the ledger and the journal entry for tracing an amount from one record to another. It also readily shows the stage of completion in the posting process. This permits one to start and stop the posting process easily without losing one's place.

Posting in Computerized Systems

Computerized systems require no added effort to post journal entries to the ledger. These systems automatically transfer debit and credit entries from the journal to the ledger database. Journal entries are posted directly to ledger accounts. Many systems have programs that test the reasonableness of a journal entry and the account balance when recorded. For example, RecordLink's payroll program might alert a preparer to hourly wage rates that are greater than $100.

Flashback

Answers—p. 110

11. When Maria Sanchez set up RecordLink, she invested $15,000 cash and equipment with a market value of $23,000. RecordLink also took responsibility for an $18,000 note payable issued to finance the purchase of equipment. Prepare the journal entry to record Sanchez's investment.
12. Explain what a compound journal entry is.
13. Why are posting reference numbers entered in the journal when entries are posted to accounts?

Trial Balance

LO9 Prepare and explain the use of a trial balance.

We know that double-entry accounting records every transaction with equal debits and credits. We also know that an error exists if the sum of debit entries in the ledger does not equal the sum of credit entries. This also means that the sum of debit account balances must equal the sum of credit account balances.

Step Four of the accounting cycle shown in Exhibit 3.1 requires the preparation of a trial balance to check whether debit and credit account balances are equal. A **trial balance** is a list of accounts and their balances at a point in time. Account balances are reported in the debit or credit column of the trial balance. Exhibit 3.14 shows the trial balance for Finlay Interiors after the fifteen entries described earlier in the chapter are posted to the ledger.

[6] Other journals are identified by their own letters. We discuss other journals later in the book.

Another use of the trial balance is as an internal report for preparing financial statements. Preparing statements is easier when we can take account balances from a trial balance instead of searching the ledger. The preparation of financial statements using a trial balance is illustrated in the demonstration problem at the end of the chapter. We expand on this process in Chapter 4.

Exhibit 3.14

Trial Balance

FINLAY INTERIORS
Trial Balance
January 31, 2001

	Debit	Credit
Cash	$ 8,070	
Accounts receivable	-0-	
Prepaid insurance	2,400	
Supplies	3,600	
Furniture	26,000	
Accounts payable		$ 200
Unearned consulting revenue		3,000
Notes payable		6,000
Carol Finlay, capital		30,000
Carol Finlay, withdrawals	600	
Consulting revenue		3,800
Rental revenue		300
Rent expense	1,000	
Salaries expense	1,400	
Utilities expense	230	
Totals	$43,300	$43,300

Preparing a Trial Balance

Preparing a trial balance involves five steps:

1. Identify each account balance from the ledger.
2. List each account and its balance (in the same order as the Chart of Accounts). Debit balances are entered in the Debit column and credit balances in the Credit column.[7]
3. Compute the total of debit balances.
4. Compute the total of credit balances.
5. Verify that total debit balances equal total credit balances.

Notice that the total debit balance equals the total credit balance for the trial balance in Exhibit 3.14. If these two totals were not equal, we would know that one or more errors exist. Equality of these two totals does ***not*** guarantee the absence of errors.

Using a Trial Balance

We know that one or more errors exist when a trial balance does not *balance* (when its columns are not equal). When one or more errors exist, they often arise from one of the following steps in the accounting process:

[7] If an account has a zero balance, it can be listed in the trial balance with a zero in the column for its normal balance.

1. Preparing journal entries.
2. Posting entries to the ledger.
3. Computing account balances.
4. Copying account balances to the trial balance.
5. Totalling the trial balance columns.

When a trial balance does balance, the accounts are likely free of the kinds of errors that create unequal debits and credits. Yet errors can still exist. One example is when a debit or credit of a correct amount is made to a wrong account. This can occur when either journalizing or posting. The error would produce incorrect balances in two accounts but the trial balance would balance. Another error is to record equal debits and credits of an incorrect amount. This error produces incorrect balances in two accounts but again the debits and credits are equal. We give these examples to show that when a trial balance does balance, it does not prove that all journal entries are recorded and posted correctly.

In a computerized accounting system, the trial balance would always balance. Accounting software is such that unbalanced entries would not be accepted by the system. However, errors as described in the last paragraph can still exist in a computerized system.

Searching for Errors

At least one error exists if the trial balance does not balance. The error (or errors) must be found and corrected ***before*** preparing financial statements. Searching for the error is more efficient if we check the journalizing, posting and trial balance preparation process in *reverse order.* Otherwise we would need to look at every transaction until the error is found.

Several steps are involved. Step One is to verify that the trial balance columns are correctly added.

If Step One fails to find the error, then Step Two is to verify that account balances are accurately copied from the ledger.

Step Three in identifying the error is to see if a debit or credit balance is mistakenly listed in the trial balance as a credit or debit. A clue pointing to this kind of error is when the difference between total debits and total credits in the trial balance equals twice the amount of the incorrect account balance.

If the error is still undiscovered, Step Four is to recalculate each account balance.

Step Five if the error remains is to verify that each journal entry is properly posted to ledger accounts.

Step Six is to verify that the original journal entry has equal debits and credits.

One frequent error is called a *transposition.* This error is when two digits are switched or transposed within a number. If transposition is the only error, then it yields a difference between two trial balance columns that is *evenly divisible by nine.* For example, assume that a $691 debit in a journal entry is incorrectly posted to the ledger as $619 instead of the correct $691. Total credits in the trial balance are then larger than total debits by $72 ($691–$619). The $72 error is evenly divisible by 9 ($72/9=8). Also, the quotient (in our example, it is 8) equals the difference between the two transposed numbers (91 vs. 19). The number of digits in the quotient also tells the location of the transposition. Because the quotient in our example had only one digit (8), it tells us that the transposition is in the first digit of the transposed numbers, starting from the right.[8]

[8] Consider another example where a transposition error involves posting $961 instead of the correct $691. The difference in these numbers is $270, and its quotient is $30 ($270/9). Because the quotient has two digits, it tells us to check the second digits from the right for a transposition of two numbers that have a difference of 3.

Correcting Errors

If errors are discovered in either the journal or the ledger, they must be corrected. Our approach to correcting errors depends on the kind of error and when it is discovered.

If an error in a journal entry is discovered before the error is posted, it can be corrected in a manual system by drawing a line through the incorrect information. The correct information is written above it to create a record of change for the auditor. Many computerized systems allow the operator to replace the incorrect information directly. If a correct amount in the journal is posted incorrectly to the ledger, we can correct it the same way.

Another case is when an error in a journal entry is not discovered until after it is posted. We usually do not erase incorrect entries in the journal and ledger. Instead, the usual practice is to correct the error in the original journal entry by creating *another* journal entry. This *correcting entry* removes the amount from the wrong account and records it to the correct account. As an example, suppose we recorded a purchase of office supplies in the journal with an incorrect debit to Office Equipment as follows:

Oct. 14	Office Equipment	1,600	
	Cash		1,600
	To record the purchase of office supplies.		

We then post this entry to the ledger. The Office Supplies ledger account balance is understated by $1,600 and the Office Equipment ledger account balance is overstated by the same amount. When we discover the error three days later, the following correcting entry is made:

17	Office Supplies	1,600	
	Office Equipment		1,600
	To correct the entry of October 14 that incorrectly debited Office Equipment instead of Office Supplies.		

The credit in the correcting entry removes the error from the first entry. The debit correctly records the supplies. The explanation reports exactly what happened.

An alternative approach to correcting the entry would be to reverse the incorrect entry and then journalize the entry as it should have been recorded in the first place.

17	Cash	1,600	
	Office Equipment		1,600
	To reverse the incorrect entry.		
	Office Supplies	1,600	
	Cash		1,600
	To correctly journalize the purchase of office supplies.		

Both methods achieve the same final results.

Computerized systems often use similar correcting entries. The exact procedure depends on the system used and management policy. Yet nearly all systems include controls to show when and where a correction is made.

Formatting Conventions

Dollar signs are *not* used in journals and ledgers. They *do* appear in financial statements and other reports, including trial balances to identify the kind of currency being used. This book follows the usual practice of putting a dollar sign beside the first amount in each column of numbers and the first amount appearing after a ruled line that indicates that an addition or subtraction has been performed. The financial statements in Exhibit 2.11 on page 52 demonstrate how dollar signs are used in this book. Different companies use various conventions for dollar signs. For example, dollar signs are usually printed beside only the first and last numbers in columns of the financial statements for ClubLink.

When amounts are entered manually in a journal, ledger or trial balance, commas are not needed to indicate thousands, millions and so forth. Also, decimal points are not needed to separate dollars and cents. If an amount consists of even dollars without cents, a convenient shortcut uses a dash in the cents column instead of two zeros. However, commas and decimal points are used in financial statements and other reports. An exception is when this detail is not important to users.

It is common for companies to round amounts to the nearest dollar, and to an even higher level for certain accounts. ClubLink is typical of many companies in that it rounds its financial statement amounts to the nearest thousand dollars.

Answers—p. 110

14. Explain a chart of accounts.
15. When are dollar signs typically used in accounting reports?
16. If a $4,000 debit to Equipment in a journal entry is incorrectly posted to the ledger as a $4,000 credit, and the ledger account has a resulting debit balance of $20,000, what is the effect of this error on the trial balance column totals?

Summary

LO1 Explain the accounting cycle. The accounting cycle includes the steps in preparing financial statements for users that are repeated each reporting period.

LO2 Explain the steps in processing transactions. The accounting cycle captures business transactions and events, analyzes and records their effects, and summarizes and prepares information useful in making decisions. Transactions and events are the starting points in the accounting cycle. Source documents help in analyzing them. The effects of transactions and events are recorded in the accounting books. Postings and the trial balance help to summarize and classify these effects. The final step is to provide this information in useful reports or financial statements to decision makers.

LO3 Describe source documents and their purpose. Source documents are business papers that identify and describe transactions and events. Examples are sales invoices, cheques, purchase orders, bills, and bank statements. Source documents help to ensure that accounting records include all transactions. They also help to prevent mistakes and theft, and are important to internal control. Source documents provide objective evidence that makes information more reliable and useful.

LO4 Describe an account and its use in recording information about transactions. An account is a detailed record of increases and decreases in a specific asset, liability or equity item. Information is taken from accounts, analyzed, summarized, and presented in useful reports and financial statements for users.

LO5 Describe a ledger and a chart of accounts. A ledger is a record that contains all accounts used by a company. This is what is referred to as *the books*. The chart of accounts is a listing of all accounts and usually includes an identification number that is assigned to each account.

LO6 Define debits and credits and explain their role in double-entry accounting. Debit refers to left, and credit refers to right. The following table summarizes debit and credit effects by account type:

Increase/ Decrease	Assets =	Liabil- ities +	Owner's Equity			
			Owner's Capital	Owner's Withdrawals	Revenues	Expenses
Increases	Debits	Credits	Credits	Debits	Credits	Debits
Decreases	Credits	Debits	Debits	Credits	Debits	Credits

Double-entry accounting means that every transaction affects at least two accounts. The total amount debited must equal the total amount credited for each transaction. The system for recording debits and credits follows from the accounting equation. The debit side is the normal balance for assets, owner's withdrawals, and expenses, and the credit side is the normal balance for liabilities, owner's capital, and revenues.

LO7 **Analyze the impact of transactions on accounts.** We analyze transactions using the concepts of double-entry accounting. This analysis is performed by determining a transaction's effects on accounts. These effects are recorded in journals and posted to accounts in the ledger.

LO8 **Record transactions in a journal and post entries to a ledger.** We record transactions in a journal to give a record of their effects. Each entry in a journal is posted to the accounts in the ledger. This provides information in accounts that is used to produce financial statements. Balance column ledger accounts are widely used and include columns for debits, credits and the account balance after each entry.

LO9 **Prepare and explain the use of a trial balance.** A trial balance is a list of accounts in the ledger showing their debit and credit balances in separate columns. The trial balance is a convenient summary of the ledger's contents and is useful in preparing financial statements. It reveals errors of the kind that produce unequal debit and credit account balances.

GUIDANCE ANSWER TO Judgement Call

Cashier

There are advantages to the process proposed by the assistant manager. They include improved customer service, fewer delays, and less work for you. However, you should have serious concerns about control and the potential for fraud. In particular, there is no control over the possibility of embezzlement by the assistant manager. The assistant manager could steal cash and simply enter fewer sales in the cash register to match the remaining cash. You should reject her suggestion without approval by the manager. Moreover, you should have an ethical concern about the assistant manager's suggestion to ignore store policy.

GUIDANCE ANSWERS TO

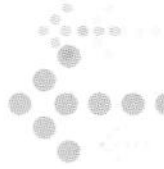

Flashback

1. External transactions are exchanges between an organization and some other person or organization. Internal transactions are exchanges within an organization; for example, a company that is using supplies in its operating activities.
2. Examples of source documents are sales invoices, cheques, purchase orders, charges to customers, bills from suppliers, employee earnings records, and bank statements.
3. Source documents serve many purposes, including recordkeeping and internal control. Source documents, especially if obtained from outside the organization, provide objective evidence about transactions and their amounts for recording. Objective evidence is important because it makes information more reliable and useful.
4. | Assets | Liabilities | Equity |
   |---|---|---|
   | 1, 3, 6 | 2, 5 | 4 |
5. An account is a record in an accounting system where increases and decreases in a specific asset, liability, or equity item are recorded and stored. A ledger is a collection of all accounts used by a business.
6. A company's size and diversity affect the number of accounts needed in its accounting system. The types of accounts used by a business depend on information that the business needs to both effectively operate and report its activities in financial statements.

7. No. Debit and credit both can mean increase or decrease. The particular meaning depends on the type of account.

8. Owner's equity is increased by revenues and owner's investments in the company. Owner's equity is decreased by expenses and owner's withdrawals.

9. The name double-entry is used because all transactions affect and are recorded in at least two accounts. There must be at least one debit in one account and at least one credit in another.

10. Answer is (c).

11. The entry is:

Account	Debit	Credit
Cash	15,000	
Equipment	23,000	
Notes Payable		18,000
Maria Sanchez, Capital		20,000

12. A compound journal entry is one that affects three or more accounts.

13. Posting reference numbers are entered in the journal when posting to the ledger as a control over the posting process. They provide a cross-reference that allows the bookkeeper or auditor to trace debits and credits from journals to ledgers and vice versa. They also create a marker in case the posting process is interrupted.

14. A chart of accounts is a listing of all of a company's accounts and their identifying numbers.

15. Dollar signs are used in financial statements and other reports to identify the kind of currency being used in the reports. At a minimum, they are placed beside the first and last numbers in each column. Some companies place dollar signs beside any amount that appears after a ruled line to indicate that an addition or subtraction has taken place.

16. The effect of this error is to understate the trial balance's debit column total by $8,000 and overstate the credit column total by $4,000. This results in a $4,000 difference between the two totals.

Demonstration Problem

This demonstration problem is based on the same facts as the demonstration problem at the end of Chapter 2 except for two additional items: (b) August 1 and (j) August 18. The following events occurred during the first month of Barbara Schmidt's new haircutting business called The Cutlery:

a. On August 1, Schmidt put $3,000 cash into a chequing account in the name of The Cutlery. She also invested $15,000 of equipment that she already owned.

b. On August 1, Barbara paid $600 for six months of insurance effective immediately.

c. On August 2, she paid $600 cash for furniture for the shop.

d. On August 3, she paid $500 cash to rent space in a strip mall for August.

e. On August 4, she furnished the shop by installing the old equipment and some new equipment that she bought on credit for $1,200. This amount is to be repaid in three equal payments at the end of August, September, and October.

f. On August 5, The Cutlery opened for business. Cash receipts from haircutting services provided in the first week and a half of business (ended August 15) were $825.

g. On August 15, Schmidt provided haircutting services on account for $100.

h. On August 17, Schmidt received a $100 cheque in the mail for services previously rendered on account.

i. On August 17, Schmidt paid $125 to an assistant for working during the grand opening.

j. On August 18, a regular customer paid $500 for services to be provided over the next three months.

k. Cash receipts from haircutting services provided during the second half of August were $930.

l. On August 31, Schmidt paid an instalment on the accounts payable.

m. On August 31, the August hydro bill for $75 was received. It will be paid on September 14.

n. On August 31, she withdrew $900 cash for her personal use.

Required

1. Prepare General Journal entries for the preceding transactions.
2. Open the following accounts: Cash, 101; Accounts Receivable 102; Prepaid Insurance, 128; Furniture, 161; Store Equipment, 165; Accounts Payable, 201; Unearned Haircutting Services Revenue, 236; Barbara Schmidt, Capital, 301; Barbara Schmidt, Withdrawals, 302; Haircutting Services Revenue, 403; Wages Expense, 623; Rent Expense, 640; and Hydro Expense, 690.
3. Post the journal entries to the ledger accounts.
4. Prepare a trial balance as of August 31, 2001.

Review of Financial Statement Preparation Component:

5. Prepare an income statement and a statement of owner's equity for the month ended August 31, 2001 and a balance sheet at August 31, 2001.

Planning the Solution

- Analyze each transaction to identify the accounts affected by the transaction and the amount of each effect.
- Use the debit and credit rules to prepare a journal entry for each transaction.
- Post each debit and each credit in the journal entries to the appropriate ledger accounts and cross-reference each amount in the Posting Reference columns in the journal and account.
- Calculate each account balance and list the accounts with their balances on a trial balance.
- Verify that the total debits in the trial balance equal total credits.
- Prepare an income statement, statement of owner's equity and a balance sheet using the information in the trial balance.

SOLUTION TO Demonstration Problem

1. General Journal entries:

Date	General Journal Account Titles and Explanations	PR	Debit	Page G1 Credit
2001				
Aug. 1	Cash	101	3,000	
1	Store Equipment	165	15,000	
	Barbara Schmidt, Capital	301		18,000
	Owner's initial investment.			
1	Prepaid Insurance	128	600	
	Cash	101		600
	Purchased six months of insurance.			
2	Furniture	161	600	
	Cash	101		600
	Purchased furniture for cash.			
3	Rent Expense	640	500	
	Cash	101		500
	Paid rent for August.			
4	Store Equipment	165	1,200	
	Accounts Payable	201		1,200
	Purchased additional equipment on credit.			
15	Cash	101	825	
	Haircutting Services Revenue	403		825
	Cash receipts from 10 days of operations.			
15	Accounts Receivable	102	100	
	Haircutting Services Revenue	403		100
	To record revenue for services provided on account.			
17	Cash	101	100	
	Accounts Receivable	102		100
	To record cash received as payment on account.			
17	Wages Expense	623	125	
	Cash	101		125
	Paid wages to assistant.			
18	Cash	101	500	
	Unearned Haircutting Services Revenue	236		500
	To record payment in advance.			
31	Cash	101	930	
	Haircutting Services Revenue	403		930
	Cash receipts from second half of August.			
31	Accounts Payable	201	400	
	Cash	101		400
	Paid an instalment on accounts payable.			
31	Hydro Expense	690	75	
	Accounts Payable	201		75
	August hydro to be paid by Sept. 14.			
31	Barbara Schmidt, Withdrawals	302	900	
	Cash	101		900
	Owner withdrew cash from the business.			

2. & 3.
Accounts in the ledger:

Cash						Account No. 101
Date		Explanation	PR	Debit	Credit	Balance
2001						
Aug.	1		G1	3,000		3,000
	1		G1		600	2,400
	2		G1		600	1,800
	3		G1		500	1,300
	15		G1	825		2,125
	17		G1	100		2,225
	17		G1		125	2,100
	18		G1	500		2,600
	31		G1	930		3.530
	31		G1		400	3,130
	31		G1		900	2,230

Accounts Receivable						Account No. 102
Date		Explanation	PR	Debit	Credit	Balance
2001						
Aug.	15		G1	100		100
	17		G1		100	-0-

Prepaid Insurance						Account No. 128
Date		Explanation	PR	Debit	Credit	Balance
2001						
Aug.	1		G1	600		600

Furniture						Account No. 161
Date		Explanation	PR	Debit	Credit	Balance
2001						
Aug.	2		G1	600		600

Store Equipment						Account No. 165
Date		Explanation	PR	Debit	Credit	Balance
2001						
Aug.	1		G1	15,000		15,000
	4		G1	1,200		16,200

Accounts Payable						Account No. 201
Date		Explanation	PR	Debit	Credit	Balance
2001						
Aug.	4		G1		1,200	1,200
	31		G1	400		800
	31		G1		75	875

Unearned Haircutting Services Revenue						Account No. 236
Date		Explanation	PR	Debit	Credit	Balance
2001						
Aug.	18		G1		500	500

Barbara Schmidt, Capital						Account No. 301
Date		Explanation	PR	Debit	Credit	Balance
2001						
Aug.	1		G1		18,000	18,000

Barbara Schmidt, Withdrawals						Account No. 302
Date		Explanation	PR	Debit	Credit	Balance
2001						
Aug.	31		G1	900		900

Haircutting Services Revenue						Account No. 403
Date		Explanation	PR	Debit	Credit	Balance
2001						
Aug.	15		G1		825	825
	15		G1		100	925
	31		G1		930	1,855

Wages Expense						Account No. 623
Date		Explanation	PR	Debit	Credit	Balance
2001						
Aug.	17		G1	125		125

Rent Expense						Account No. 640
Date		Explanation	PR	Debit	Credit	Balance
2001						
Aug.	3		G1	500		500

Hydro Expense						Account No. 690
Date		Explanation	PR	Debit	Credit	Balance
2001						
Aug.	31		G1	75		75

4.

THE CUTLERY
Trial Balance
August 31, 2001

Account Title	Debit	Credit
Cash	$ 2,230	
Accounts receivable	-0-	
Prepaid insurance	600	
Furniture	600	
Store equipment	16,200	
Accounts payable		$ 875
Unearned haircutting services revenue		500
Barbara Schmidt, capital		18,000
Barbara Schmidt, withdrawals	900	
Haircutting services revenue		1,855
Wages expenses	125	
Rent expense	500	
Hydro expense	75	
Totals	$ 21,230	$ 21,230

5.

THE CUTLERY
Income Statement
For Month Ended August 31, 2001

Revenues:		
Haircutting services revenue		$1,855
Operating expenses:		
Rent expense	$500	
Wages expense	125	
Hydro expense	75	
Total operating expenses		700
Net income		$1,155

THE CUTLERY
Statement of Owner's Equity
For Month Ended August 31, 2001

Barbara Schmidt, capital August 1		$ -0-
Add: Investments by owner	$18,000	
Net income	1,155	19,155
Total		$19,155
Less: Withdrawals by owner		900
Barbara Schmidt, capital, August 31		$ 18,255

THE CUTLERY
Balance Sheet
August 31, 2001

Assets		
Cash		$ 2,230
Prepaid insurance		600
Furniture		600
Store equipment		16,200
Total assets		$ 19,630
Liabilities		
Accounts payable	$ 875	
Unearned haircutting services revenue	500	
Total liabilities		$ 1,375
Owner's Equity		
Barbara Schmidt, capital		$ 18,255
Total liabilities and owner's equity		$ 19,630

Glossary

Account A place or location within an accounting system in which the increases and decreases in a specific asset, liability, or equity are recorded and stored. (p. 86)

Account balance The difference between the increases (including the beginning balance) and decreases recorded in an account. (p. 92)

Accounting cycle The steps repeated each reporting period for the purpose of preparing financial statements for users. (p. 84)

Accounts receivable When services are performed for or goods are sold to customers in return for promises to pay in the future, an *account receivable* is recorded. These transactions are said to be *on credit* or *on account.* Accounts receivable are *increased* by services performed or goods sold on credit and *decreased* by customer payments. (p. 87)

Balance column ledger account An account with debit and credit columns for recording entries and a third column for showing the balance of the account after each entry is posted. (p. 102)

Chart of accounts A list of all accounts used by a company; includes the identification number assigned to each account. (p. 90)

Compound journal entry A journal entry that affects at least three accounts. (p. 100)

Credit An entry that decreases asset, expense, and owner's withdrawals accounts or increases liability, owner's capital, and revenue accounts; recorded on the right side of a T-account. (p. 92)

Debit An entry that increases asset, expense, and owner's withdrawals accounts or decreases liability, owner's capital, and revenue accounts; recorded on the left side of a T-account. (p. 92)

Double-entry accounting An accounting system where every transaction affects and is recorded in at least two accounts; the sum of the debits for all entries must equal the sum of the credits for all entries. (p. 92)

External transactions Exchanges between the entity and some other person or organization. (p. 85)

General Journal The most flexible type of journal; can be used to record any kind of transaction. (p. 100)

Internal transactions Exchanges within an organization that can also affect the accounting equation. (p. 85)

Journal A record where transactions are recorded before they are recorded in accounts; amounts are posted from the journal to the ledger; also called the *book of original entry.* (p. 100)

Journalizing The process of recording transactions in a journal. (p. 100)

Normal balance The debit or credit side on which an account increases. For example, assets increase with debits, therefore the normal balance for an asset is a debit. Revenues increase with credits, therefore a credit is the normal balance for a revenue account. (p. 94)

Ledger A record containing all accounts used by a business. (p. 86)

Note receivable An unconditional written promise to pay a definite sum of money on demand or on a defined future date(s); also called a *promissory note.* (p. 87)

Post(ing) Transfer journal entry information to ledger accounts. (p. 100)

Posting reference (PR) column A column in *journals* where individual account numbers are entered when entries are posted to the ledger. A column in *ledgers* where journal page numbers are entered when entries are posted. (p. 102)

Prepaid Expenses An asset account containing payments made for assets that are not to be used until later. (p. 87)

Promissory note An unconditional written promise to pay a definite sum of money on demand or on a defined future date(s); also called a *note receivable.* (p. 87)

Source documents Documents that are the source of information recorded with accounting entries; can be in either paper or electronic form. (p. 85)

T-account A simple characterization of an account form used as a helpful tool in showing the effects of transactions and events on specific accounts. (p. 91)

Trial balance A list of accounts and their balances at a point in time; the total debit balances should equal the total credit balances. (p. 104)

Unearned revenues Liabilities created when customers pay in advance for products or services; created when cash is received before revenues are earned; satisfied by delivering the products or services in the future. (p. 88)

Questions

1. Describe the fundamental steps in the accounting process.
2. What is the difference between a note receivable and an account receivable?
3. If assets are valuable resources and asset accounts have debit balances, why do expense accounts have debit balances?
4. Why does the bookkeeper prepare a trial balance?
5. Should a transaction be recorded first in a journal or the ledger? Why?
6. Are debits or credits listed first in general journal entries? Are the debits or the credits indented?
7. What kinds of transactions can be recorded in a General Journal?
8. If an incorrect amount was journalized and posted to the accounts, how should the error be corrected?
9. Review the WestJet balance sheet for fiscal year-end December 31, 1999 in Appendix I. Identify three accounts on the balance sheet that would carry debit balances and three accounts on the balance sheet that would carry credit balances.

WEST JET

10. Review the ClubLink balance sheet for fiscal year-end December 31, 1999 in Appendix I. Identify four different asset accounts that include the word "receivable" in the account title.

CLUBLINK CORPORATION

11. Reread the chapter's opening scenario describing Maria Sanchez's company, RecordLink. Last year, RecordLink's revenues exceeded $850,000. Suggest an appropriate account title for RecordLink's revenue account.

Quick Study

QS 3-1

Identifying source documents

LO3

Select the items from the following list that are likely to serve as source documents:

- **a.** Income statement.
- **b.** Trial balance.
- **c.** Telephone bill.
- **d.** Invoice from supplier.
- **e.** Owner's withdrawals account.
- **f.** Balance sheet.
- **g.** Bank statement.
- **h.** Sales invoice.

QS 3-2

Developing a chart of accounts

LO5

Using the numbering system on page 90, develop a chart of accounts that assigns an account number to each of the following accounts:

- **a.** Buildings.
- **b.** Interest Revenue.
- **c.** Bob Norton, Withdrawals.
- **d.** Bob Norton, Capital.
- **e.** Prepaid Insurance.
- **f.** Interest Payable.
- **g.** Accounts Receivable.
- **h.** Salaries Expense.
- **i.** Office Supplies.
- **j.** Repair Services Revenue.

QS 3-3

Identifying normal balance as a debit or credit

LO6

Indicate whether the normal balance of each of the following accounts is a debit or a credit:

- **a.** Equipment.
- **b.** Land.
- **c.** Al Tait, Withdrawals.
- **d.** Rent Expense.
- **e.** Interest Revenue.
- **f.** Prepaid Rent.
- **g.** Accounts Receivable.
- **h.** Office Supplies.
- **i.** Notes Receivable.
- **j.** Notes Payable.

QS 3-4

Linking credit or debit with normal balance

LO6

Indicate whether a debit or credit is necessary to *decrease* the normal balance of each of the following accounts:

- **a.** Buildings.
- **b.** Interest Revenue.
- **c.** Bob Norton, Withdrawals.
- **d.** Bob Norton, Capital.
- **e.** Prepaid Insurance.
- **f.** Interest Payable.
- **g.** Accounts Receivable.
- **h.** Salaries Expense.
- **i.** Office Supplies.
- **j.** Repair Services Revenue.

QS 3-5

Analyzing debit or credit by account

LO6

Identify whether a debit or credit entry would be made to record the indicated change in each of the following accounts:

- **a.** To increase Notes Payable.
- **b.** To decrease Accounts Receivable.
- **c.** To increase Owner, Capital.
- **d.** To decrease Unearned Fees.
- **e.** To decrease Prepaid Insurance.
- **f.** To decrease Cash.
- **g.** To increase Utilities Expense.
- **h.** To increase Fees Earned.
- **i.** To increase Store Equipment.
- **j.** To increase Owner, Withdrawals.

QS 3-6

Preparing journal entries

LO8

Prepare journal entries for the following transactions that occurred during January 2001:

- **a.** On January 15, Stan Adams opened a landscaping business by investing $60,000 cash and equipment having a $40,000 fair value.
- **b.** On January 20, purchased office supplies on credit for $340.
- **c.** On January 28, received $5,200 in return for providing landscaping services to a customer.

QS 3-7
Recording in T-accounts
LO7

Post the journal entries from QS 3-6 into the following T-accounts:

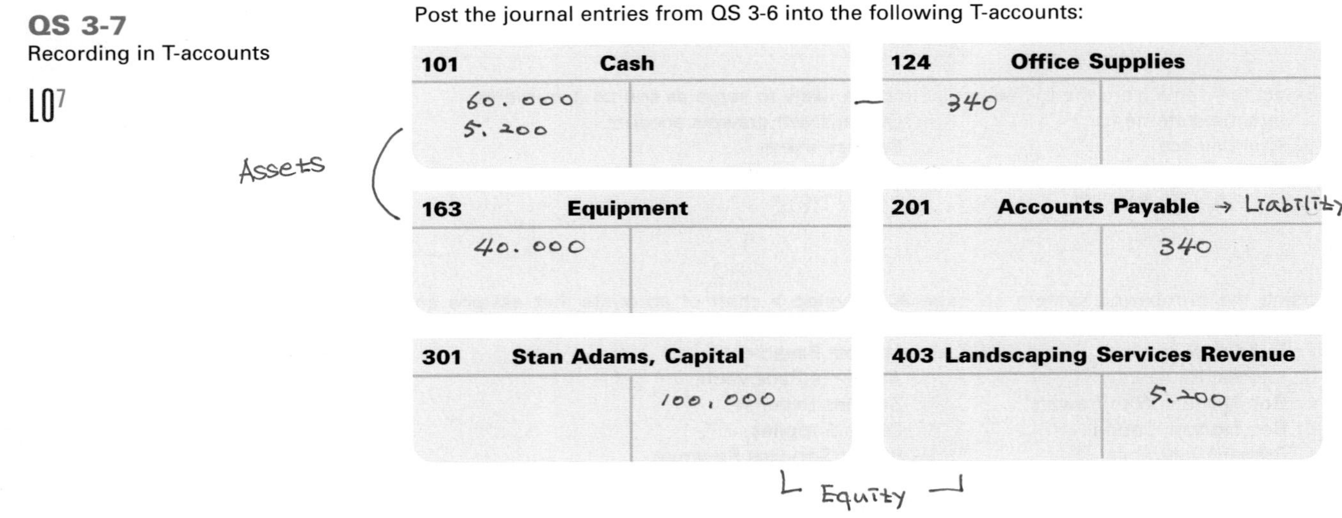

QS 3-8
Preparing a trial balance
LO7

Using your account balances from QS 3-7, prepare a trial balance at January 31, 2001.

QS 3-9
Identifying a posting error
LO9

A trial balance has total debits of $21,000 and total credits of $25,500. Which one of the following errors would create this imbalance? Explain.

a. A $4,500 debit to Salaries Expense in a journal entry was incorrectly posted to the ledger as a $4,500 credit, leaving the Salaries Expense account with a $750 debit balance.
b. A $2,250 credit to Consulting Fees Earned in a journal entry was incorrectly posted to the ledger as a $2,250 debit, leaving the Consulting Fees Earned account with a $6,300 credit balance.
c. A $2,250 debit to Rent Expense in a journal entry was incorrectly posted to the ledger as a $2,250 credit, leaving the Rent Expense account with a $3,000 debit balance.

Exercises

Exercise 3-1
Increases, decreases, and normal balances of accounts
LO4, 6

Complete the following table by: 1. Identifying the type of account listed on each line. 2. Entering *debit* or *credit* in the blank spaces to identify the kind of entry that would increase or decrease the account balance. 3. Identifying the normal balance of the account.

	Account	Type of Account	Increase	Decrease	Normal Balance
a.	Land				
b.	Harold Cooper, Capital				
c.	Accounts Receivable				
d.	Harold Cooper, Withdrawals				
e.	Cash				
f.	Equipment				
g.	Unearned Revenue				
h.	Accounts Payable				
i.	Postage Expense				
j.	Prepaid Insurance				
k.	Wages Expense				
l.	Fees Earned				

Exercise 3-2
Chart of accounts

LO5

You have been given the following guide regarding the chart of accounts for NorthCo:

100 – 199	Assets	400 – 499	Revenues
200 – 299	Liabilities	500 – 599	Expenses
300 – 399	Owner's Equity		

Using the account information from Exercise 3-3 (found in requirement 1), develop a chart of accounts for NorthCo.

Exercise 3-3
Journalizing, posting, preparing a trial balance, and financial statements

LO7, 8, 9

Check figure
Total assets = $30,500

NorthCo incurred the following transactions during July 2001, its first month of operations:

July	1	The owner, Greg Duggan, invested $10,000 cash.
	10	Purchased $5,000 worth of equipment on credit.
	12	Performed services for a client and received $20,000 cash.
	14	Paid for expenses; $7,000.
	15	Completed services for a client and sent a bill for $3,000.
	31	The owner withdrew $500 cash.

Required

1. Create a General Ledger by opening the following accounts: Cash; Accounts Receivable; Equipment; Accounts Payable; Greg Duggan, Capital; Greg Duggan, Withdrawals; Revenue; Expenses.
2. Journalize the July transactions in the General Journal.
3. Post the July transactions from your General Journal into your General Ledger accounts.
4. Prepare a trial balance based on the balances in your General Ledger accounts.
5. Prepare an income statement, statement of owner's equity and a balance sheet based on your trial balance.

Exercise 3-4
Chart of accounts

LO5

You have been given the following guide regarding the chart of accounts for EastCo:

100 – 199	Assets	400 – 499	Revenues
200 – 299	Liabilities	500 – 599	Expenses
300 – 399	Owner's Equity		

Using the account information from Exercise 3-5, develop a chart of accounts for EastCo.

Exercise 3-5
Journalizing, posting, preparing a trial balance and financial statements

LO7, 8, 9

Check figure:
Total assets = $57,000

EastCo showed the following account balances in its General Ledger accounts as at January 31, 2001.

Account	Debit	Credit
Cash	23,000	
Accounts Receivable	12,000	
Office Equipment	25,000	
Accounts Payable		6,000
Unearned Revenue		1,000
Bill Evans, Capital		19,000
Bill Evans, Withdrawals	4,000	
Consulting Revenues		75,000
Salaries Expense	20,000	
Rent Expense	15,000	
Utilities Expense	2,000	

During February, the following transactions occurred:

Feb.	1	Performed work for a client and received cash of $17,000.
	5	Paid $4,000 regarding outstanding accounts payable.
	10	Received cash of $5,000 for work to be done in March.
	17	The owner withdrew cash of $1,000.
	27	Paid salaries of $20,000.

Required

1. Journalize the February transactions in the General Journal.
2. Post the transactions from your General Journal to the General Ledger (T-accounts above).
3. Prepare a trial balance based on the balances in your General Ledger.
4. Prepare the balance sheet as at February 27, 2001.

Exercise 3-6

Recording the effects of transactions directly in T-accounts

Check figure:
Total cash = $6,425

Open the following T-accounts: Cash; Accounts Receivable; Office Supplies; Office Equipment; Accounts Payable; Steve Moore, Capital; Steve Moore, Withdrawals; Fees Earned; and Rent Expense. Next, record these transactions of the Moore Company by recording the debit and credit entries directly in the T-accounts. Use the letters beside each transaction to identify the entries. Finally, determine the balance of each account.

a. Steve Moore invested $12,750 cash in the business.
b. Purchased $375 of office supplies for cash.
c. Purchased $7,050 of office equipment on credit.
d. Received $1,500 cash as fees for services provided to a customer.
e. Paid for the office equipment purchased in transaction (c).
f. Billed a customer $2,700 as fees for services.
g. Paid the monthly rent with $525 cash.
h. Collected $1,125 of the account receivable created in transaction (f).
i. Steve Moore withdrew $1,000 cash from the business.

Exercise 3-7

Preparing a trial balance

LO9

Check figure:
Total Dr = $16,950

After recording the transactions of Exercise 3-6 in T-accounts and calculating the balance of each account, prepare the trial balance for the ledger. Use May 31, 2001, as the date.

Exercise 3-8

Analyzing transactions from T-accounts

Cash

(a)	7,000	(b)	3,600
(e)	2,500	(c)	600
		(f)	2,400
		(g)	700

Automobiles

(a)	11,000		

Accounts Payable

(f)	2,400	(d)	9,600

Office Supplies

(c)	600		
(d)	200		

Jerry Steiner, Capital

		(a)	23,600

Delivery Services Revenue

		(e)	2,500

Prepaid Insurance

(b)	3,600		

Gas and Oil Expense

(g)	700		

Equipment

(a)	5,600		
(d)	9,400		

Seven transactions were posted to these T-accounts. Provide a short description of each transaction. Include the amounts in your descriptions. The first one is done as an example.

(a) *The owner invested a total of $23,600, including cash of $7,000, an automobile valued at $11,000 and equipment worth $5,600.*

Exercise 3-9
General Journal entries

LO8

Use the information in the T-accounts in Exercise 3-8 to prepare General Journal entries for the seven transactions.

Exercise 3-10
General Journal entries

LO8

TLC Laser Eye Centres showed the following selected transactions during the month of April 2002. Journalize the transactions in your General Journal.

April 5	Performed surgery on a customer today and collected $1,500 cash.
8	Purchased surgical supplies on credit; $3,000.
15	Paid salaries; $57,000.
20	Paid for the surgical supplies purchased on April 8.
27	Performed six surgeries today, all on credit; $1,500 each.
30	Paid the April utilities bill today; $1,800.

Exercise 3-11
Analyzing and journalizing revenue transactions

LO8

Examine the following transactions and identify those that created revenues for Jarrell Services, a sole proprietorship owned by John Jarrell. Prepare General Journal entries to record those transactions and explain why the other transactions did not create revenues.

a. John Jarrell invested $38,250 cash in the business.
b. Provided $1,350 of services on credit.
c. Received $1,575 cash for services provided to a client.
d. Received $9,150 from a client in payment for services to be provided next year.
e. Received $4,500 from a client in partial payment of an account receivable.
f. Borrowed $150,000 from the bank by signing a promissory note.

Exercise 3-12
Analyzing and journalizing expense transactions

LO8

Examine the following transactions and identify those that created expenses for Jarrell Services. Prepare General Journal entries to record those transactions and explain why the other transactions did not create expenses.

a. Paid $14,100 cash for office supplies purchased 30 days previously.
b. Paid the $1,125 salary of the receptionist.
c. Paid $45,000 cash for equipment.
d. Paid utility bill with $930 cash.
e. John Jarrell withdrew $5,000 from the business account for personal use.

Exercise 3-13
Posting from the General Journal to the ledger

LO8

Hay's Landscape Consultants is in its second month of operations. You have been given the following journal entries regarding its January 2001 transactions.

Required

a. Open the following accounts (use the balance column format) entering the opening balances brought forward from the end of last month, December 31, 2000: Cash (101) $1,700; Accounts Receivable (106) $600; Equipment (167) $3,000; Accounts Payable (201) $650; Alice Hay, Capital (301) $4,650; Alice Hay, Withdrawals (302) $600; Fees Earned (401) $3,600; and Salaries Expense (622) $3,000.
b. Post the journal entries to the accounts and enter the balance after each posting.

General Journal — Page 1

Date	Account Titles and Explanation	PR	Debit	Credit
2001				
Jan. 1	Cash		7,000	
	Alice Hay, Capital			7,000
	Additional owner investment.			
12	Accounts Receivable		18,000	
	Fees Earned			18,000
	Performed work for a customer on account.			
20	Equipment		24,000	
	Accounts Payable			20,000
	Cash			4,000
	Purchased equipment by paying cash and the balance on credit.			
31	Cash		10,000	
	Accounts Receivable			10,000
	Collected cash from credit customer.			
31	Salaries Expense		6,000	
	Cash			6,000
	Paid month-end salaries.			
31	Alice Hay, Withdrawals		1,500	
	Cash			1,500
	Alice Hay withdrew cash for personal use.			

Exercise 3-14
Preparing a trial balance

LO9

Check figure:
Total Dr = $53,900

Required
Using the information in Exercise 3-13, prepare a trial balance.

Exercise 3-15
General Journal entries

LO8

Prepare General Journal entries to record the following August 2001 transactions of a new business called PhotoFinish Co.

Aug.	1	Hannah Young, the owner, invested $7,500 cash and photography equipment with a fair value of $32,500.
	1	Rented a studio, paying $3,000 for the next three months in advance.
	5	Purchased office supplies for $1,400 cash.
	20	Received $2,650 in photography fees.
	31	Paid $875 for August utilities.

Exercise 3-16
Ledger accounts and the trial balance

LO8, 9

Check figure:
Total Dr = $42,650

Open the following accounts (use the balance column format): Cash; Office Supplies; Prepaid Rent; Photography Equipment; Hannah Young, Capital; Photography Fees Earned; and Utilities Expense. Then, using your General Journal entries from Exercise 3-15, post to the T-accounts. Finally, prepare the August 31, 2001 trial balance.

Exercise 3-17
Effects of posting errors on the trial balance

LO[7, 9]

Complete the following table by filling in the blanks. For each of the listed posting errors:

1. Enter in column (1) the amount of the difference that the error would create between the two trial balance columns (show a zero if the columns would balance).
2. Identify if there would be a difference between the two columns, identify in column (2) the trial balance column that would be larger.
3. Identify the account(s) affected in column (3).
4. Identify the amount by which the account(s) is under- or overstated in column (4). The answer for the first error is provided as an example.

	Description	(1) Difference between Debit and Credit Columns	(2) Column with the Larger Total	(3) Identify Account(s) Incorrectly Stated	(4) Amount That Account(s) Is Over- or Understated
a.	*A $2,400 debit to Rent Expense was posted as a $1,590 debit.*	*$810*	*Credit*	*Rent Expense*	*Rent Expense is understated by $810*
b.	A $42,000 debit to Machinery was posted as a debit to Accounts Payable.				
c.	A $4,950 credit to Services Revenue was posted as a $495 credit.				
d.	A $1,440 debit to Store Supplies was not posted at all.				
e.	A $2,250 debit to Prepaid Insurance was posted as a debit to Insurance Expense.				
f.	A $4,050 credit to Cash was posted twice as two credits to the Cash account.				
g.	A $9,900 debit to the owner's withdrawals account was debited to the owner's capital account.				

Exercise 3-18
Preparation of financial statements from a trial balance

LO[9]

Check figure: Total assets = $2,950

JenCo showed the following trial balance information (in alphabetical order) for its first month just ended March 31, 2001:

Account	Debit	Credit
Accounts payable		$ 260
Accounts receivable	$ 950	
Cash	1,000	
Equipment	700	
Interest expense	10	
Marie Jensen, capital		2,050
Marie Jensen, withdrawals	1,500	
Notes payable		800
Prepaid insurance	300	
Salaries expense	800	
Service revenue		1,900
Unearned service revenue		250
Totals	$5,260	$5,260

Required

Use the format provided to complete an income statement, statement of owner's equity, and a balance sheet.

Jenco
Income Statement
For Month Ended March 31, 2001

Revenues:		
Service revenue		
Operating expenses:		
Salaries expense		
Interest expense		
Total operating expenses		
Net income		

JenCo
Statement of Owner's Equity
For Month Ended March 31, 2001

Marie Jensen, capital, March 1		
Add: Investments by owner		
Net income		
Total		
Less: Withdrawal by owner		
Marie Jensen, capital, March 31		

Jenco
Balance Sheet
March 31, 2001

Assets		Liabilities	
Cash		Accounts payable	
Accounts receivable		Unearned service revenue	
Prepaid insurance		Notes payable	
Equipment		Total liabilities	
		Owner's Equity	
		Marie Jensen, capital	
Total assets	$38,000	Total liabilities and owner's equity	$38,000

Exercise 3-19
Preparation of financial statements from a trial balance

LO9

XYZ Co. showed the following trial balance information (in alphabetical order) for its first month just ended March 31, 2001:

Account	Debit	Credit
Accounts payable		$ 23,000
Accounts receivable	$ 7,000	
Building	40,000	
Cash	15,000	
Fees earned		85,000
John Biggs, capital		61,000
John Biggs, withdrawals	9,000	
Land	58,000	
Machinery	25,000	
Notes payable		73,000
Office supplies	1,500	
Office supplies expense	3,500	
Wages expense	83,000	
Totals	$242,000	$242,000

Required
Using the information provided, prepare an income statement, a statement of owner's equity, and a balance sheet.

XYZ Co. Income Statement For Month Ended March 31, 2001		
Revenues:		
Operating expenses:		
Total operating expenses		
Net loss		

XYZ Co. Statement of Owner's Equity For Month Ended March 31, 2001		
John Biggs, capital, March 1		
John Biggs, capital, March 31		

XYZ Co. Balance Sheet March 31, 2001			
Assets		**Liabilities**	
		Total liabilities	
		Owner's Equity	
		John Biggs, capital	
		Total liabilities and	
Total assets		owner's equity	

Check figure: Total assets = $146,500

Exercise 3-20
Journalizing correcting entries

LO[9]

For each of the following incorrect entries, journalize the appropriate correcting entry(ies).

a. The purchase of office supplies on credit for $1,800 was recorded as:

Office Supplies	1,800	
Cash		1,800

b. A credit customer paid her account in full: $4,500. This was recorded as:

Cash	4,500	
Revenue		4,500

c. The owner withdrew cash of $1,500. This was recorded as:

Salaries Expense	1,500	
Cash		1,500

d. Work was performed for a customer today and cash of $750 was received. This was recorded as:

Cash	750	
Accounts Receivable		750

Exercise 3-21
Preparing a corrected trial balance

LO9

On January 1, 2001, Jan Taylor started a new business called The Party Place. Near the end of the year, she hired a new bookkeeper without making a careful reference check. As a result, a number of mistakes have been made in preparing the following trial balance:

THE PARTY PLACE Trial Balance December 31		
	Debit	**Credit**
Cash	$ 5,500	
Accounts receivable		$ 7,900
Office supplies	2,650	
Office equipment	20,500	
Accounts payable		9,465
Jan Taylor, capital	16,745	
Services revenue		22,350
Wages expense		6,000
Rent expense		4,800
Advertising expense		1,250
Totals	$45,395	$52,340

Taylor's analysis of the situation has uncovered these errors:

a. The sum of the debits in the Cash account is $37,175 and the sum of the credits is $30,540.
b. A $275 payment from a credit customer was posted to Cash but was not posted to Accounts Receivable.
c. A credit purchase of office supplies for $400 was completely unrecorded.
d. A transposition error occurred in copying the balance of the Services Revenue account to the trial balance. The correct amount was $23,250.

Other errors were made in placing account balances in the trial balance columns and in taking the totals of the columns. Use all of this information to prepare a correct trial balance.

Check figure:
Total Dr = $49,860

Problems

Problem 3-1A
Recording transactions in T-accounts

LO7

Check figure:
Cash balance = $18,600

Following are business transactions completed by Kevin Smith during the month of November 2001:

a. Kevin Smith invested $80,000 cash and office equipment with a $30,000 fair value in a new sole proprietorship named Apex Consulting.
b. Purchased land and a small office building. The land was worth $30,000, and the building was worth $170,000. The purchase price was paid with $40,000 cash and a long-term note payable for $160,000.
c. Purchased $2,400 of office supplies on credit.
d. Kevin Smith transferred title of his personal automobile to the business. The automobile had a value of $18,000 and was to be used exclusively in the business.
e. Purchased $6,000 of additional office equipment on credit.
f. Paid $1,500 salary to an assistant.
g. Provided services to a client and collected $6,000 cash.
h. Paid $800 for the month's utilities.
i. Paid account payable created in transaction (c).
j. Purchased $20,000 of new office equipment by paying $18,600 cash and trading in old equipment with a recorded cost of $1,400.
k. Completed $5,200 of services for a client. This amount is to be paid within 30 days.
l. Paid $1,500 salary to an assistant.
m. Received $3,800 payment on the receivable created in transaction (k).
n. Kevin Smith withdrew $6,400 cash from the business for personal use.

Required

1. Open the following T-accounts: Cash; Accounts Receivable; Office Supplies; Automobiles; Office Equipment; Building; Land; Accounts Payable; Long-Term Notes Payable; Kevin Smith, Capital; Kevin Smith, Withdrawals; Fees Earned; Salaries Expense; and Utilities Expense.
2. Record the effects of the listed transactions by entering debits and credits directly in the T-accounts. Use the transaction letters to identify each debit and credit entry.

Problem 3-2A
Preparing General Journal entries

LO8

Carrie Ford opened a new accounting practice called Carrie Ford, Public Accountant, and completed these transactions during March 2001:

Mar. 1	Invested $25,000 in cash and office equipment that had a fair value of $6,000.
1	Prepaid $1,800 cash for three months' rent for an office.
3	Made credit purchases of office equipment for $3,000 and office supplies for $600.
5	Completed work for a client and immediately received $500 cash.
9	Completed a $2,000 project for a client, who will pay within 30 days.
11	Paid the account payable created on March 3.
15	Paid $1,500 cash for the annual premium on an insurance policy.
20	Received $1,600 as partial payment for the work completed on March 9.
23	Completed work for another client for $660 on credit.
27	Carrie Ford withdrew $1,800 cash from the business to pay some personal expenses.
30	Purchased $200 of additional office supplies on credit.
31	Paid $175 for the month's utility bill.

Required
Prepare General Journal entries to record the transactions.

Problem 3-3A
Posting, preparing a trial balance

LO8, 9

Check figure:
Total Dr = $34,360

Required
Using the General Journal entries prepared in Problem 3-2A, complete the following:

1. Open the following accounts (use the balance column format): Cash (101); Accounts Receivable (106); Office Supplies (124); Prepaid Insurance (128); Prepaid Rent (131); Office Equipment (163); Accounts Payable (201); Carrie Ford, Capital (301); Carrie Ford, Withdrawals (302); Accounting Fees Earned (401); and Utilities Expense (690).
2. Post the entries to the accounts and enter the balance after each posting.
3. Prepare a trial balance as of the end of the month.

Problem 3-4A
Preparing journal entries

LO8

Spin Master Toys showed the following selected transactions for the month ended May 31, 2002:

May 1	Purchased new equipment, paying cash of $50,000 and signing a 90-day note payable for the balance of $175,000.
2	Purchased 12 months of insurance to begin May 2; paid $3,600.
3	Completed a toy design for a customer today and received $12,000.
4	Purchased office supplies on account; $7,500.
6	Returned to the supplier $1,000 of defective office supplies purchased on May 4.
10	Provided services to a client today on account; $23,000.
15	Paid for the May 4 purchase less the return of May 6.
20	Received payment from the client of May 10.
25	Received cash of $1,200 from a client for work to be done in June.
30	Paid month-end salaries of $94,000
30	Paid the May telephone bill today; $4,500.
30	Received the May electrical bill today; $1,800. It will be paid on June 15.

Required
Prepare journal entries for each of the above transactions.

Problem 3-5A
Analyzing accounting errors

LO 7, 8, 9

Check figure:
Total Dr = $59,200

During January, Dallas Glynn, the owner of Glynn's Window Washing Services, had difficulty getting the debits to equal credits on the January 31, 2000 trial balance.

The following errors were discovered:

a. Glynn omitted a $2,000 purchase of Equipment on credit.
b. In posting a $700 collection from a credit customer, Glynn debited Accounts Receivable and credited Cash.
c. In journalizing a cash receipt, Glynn correctly debited Cash for $350 but incorrectly credited Accounts Receivable for $530.
d. In posting a $2,200 payment on account, Glynn debited Accounts Payable but forgot to post the credit to Cash.
e. In journalizing services of $1,800 performed for a customer on credit, Glynn debited Accounts Receivable but credited Maintenance Expense.

Glynn's Window Washing Services
Trial Balance
January 31, 2000

	Debit	Credit
Cash	$ 5,800	
Accounts receivable	4,620	
Prepaid insurance	1,200	
Equipment	12,000	
Accounts payable		$ 2,700
Dallas Glynn, capital		22,500
Dallas Glynn, withdrawals	4,100	
Service revenues		30,200
Salaries expense	18,000	
Insurance expense	2,600	
Maintenance expense	6,500	
Utilities expense	2,600	
Totals	$57,420	$55,400

Required
Prepare a corrected trial balance.

Problem 3-6A
Preparing and posting General Journal entries and preparing a trial balance

LO 8, 9

Check figure:
Total Dr = $137,440

Hector Mendez opened a computer consulting business called Capital Consultants and completed the following transactions during May 2001:

May 1	Mendez invested $100,000 in cash and office equipment that had a fair value of $24,000 in the business.
1	Prepaid $7,200 cash for three months' rent for an office.
2	Made credit purchases of office equipment for $12,000 and office supplies for $2,400.
6	Completed services for a client and immediately received $2,000 cash.
9	Completed an $8,000 project for a client, who will pay within 30 days.
10	Paid the account payable created on May 2.
19	Paid $6,000 cash for the annual premium on an insurance policy.
22	Received $6,400 as partial payment for the work completed on May 9.
25	Completed work for another client for $2,640 on credit.
31	Mendez withdrew $6,200 cash from the business for personal use.
31	Purchased $800 of additional office supplies on credit.
31	Paid $700 for the month's utility bill.

Required

1. Prepare General Journal entries to record the transactions. Use page 1 for the journal.
2. Open the following accounts (use the balance column format): Cash (101); Accounts Receivable (106); Office Supplies (124); Prepaid Insurance (128); Prepaid Rent (131); Office Equipment (163); Accounts Payable (201); Hector Mendez, Capital (301); Hector Mendez, Withdrawals (302); Services Revenue (403); and Utilities Expense (690).
3. Post the entries to the accounts and enter the balance after each posting.
4. Prepare a trial balance as of the end of the month.

Problem 3-7A

Journalizing, posting, preparing a trial balance

LO8, 9

Jamil Engineering, a sole proprietorship, completed the following transactions during July 2001, the second month of operations:

July	1	Jamil Alsuwaidi, the owner, invested $105,000 cash, office equipment with a value of $6,000, and $45,000 of drafting equipment in the business.
	2	Purchased land for an office. The land was worth $54,000, which was paid with $5,400 cash and a long-term note payable for $48,600.
	3	Purchased a portable building with $75,000 cash and moved it onto the land.
	5	Paid $6,000 cash for the premiums on two one-year insurance policies.
	7	Completed and delivered a set of plans for a client and collected $5,700 cash.
	9	Purchased additional drafting equipment for $22,500. Paid $10,500 cash and signed a long-term note payable for the $12,000 balance.
	10	Completed $12,000 of engineering services for a client. This amount is to be paid within 30 days.
	12	Purchased $2,250 of additional office equipment on credit.
	15	Completed engineering services for $18,000 on credit.
	16	Received a bill for rent on equipment that was used on a completed job. The $1,200 rent must be paid within 30 days.
	17	Collected $7,200 from the client of July 10.
	19	Paid $1,500 wages to a drafting assistant.
	22	Paid the account payable created on July 12.
	25	Paid $675 cash for some repairs to an item of drafting equipment.
	26	Jamil Alsuwaidi withdrew $9,360 cash from the business for personal use.
	30	Paid $1,500 wages to a drafting assistant.
	31	Paid $3,000 cash to advertise in the local newspaper.

Required

1. Prepare General Journal entries to record the transactions. Use page 1 for the journal.
2. Open the following accounts (use the balance column format) entering the balances brought forward from June 30, 2001: Cash (101) $3,000; Accounts Receivable (106) $1,500; Prepaid Insurance (128) $250; Office Equipment (163) $850; Drafting Equipment (167) $600; Building (173) $21,000; Land (183) $14,000; Accounts Payable (201) $870; Long-Term Notes Payable (251) $12,000; Jamil Alsuwaidi, Capital (301) $17,000; Jamil Alsuwaidi, Withdrawals (302) $500; Engineering Fees Earned (401) $14,800; Wages Expense (623) $2,000; Equipment Rental Expense (645) $500; Advertising Expense (655) $320; and Repairs Expense (684) $150.
3. Post the entries to the accounts and enter the balance after each posting.
4. Prepare a trial balance as of the end of the month.

Check figure:
Total Dr = $298,170

Alternate Problems

Problem 3-1B

Recording transactions in T-accounts

West Consulting completed these transactions during June 2001:

a. Susan West, the sole proprietor, invested $23,000 cash and office equipment with a $12,000 fair value in the business.
b. Purchased land and a small office building. The land was worth $8,000 and the building was worth $33,000. The purchase price was paid with $15,000 cash and a long-term note payable for $26,000.
c. Purchased $600 of office supplies on credit.
d. Susan West transferred title of her personal automobile to the business. The automobile had a value of $7,000 and was to be used exclusively in the business.
e. Purchased $1,100 of additional office equipment on credit.
f. Paid $800 salary to an assistant.
g. Provided services to a client and collected $2,700 cash.
h. Paid $430 for the month's utilities.
i. Paid account payable created in transaction (c).
j. Purchased $4,000 of new office equipment by paying $2,400 cash and trading in old equipment with a recorded cost of $1,600.
k. Completed $2,400 of services for a client. This amount is to be paid within 30 days.

l. Paid $800 salary to an assistant.
m. Received $1,000 payment on the receivable created in transaction (k).
n. Susan West withdrew $1,050 cash from the business for personal use.

Required

1. Open the following T-accounts: Cash; Accounts Receivable; Office Supplies; Automobiles; Office Equipment; Building; Land; Accounts Payable; Long-Term Notes Payable; Susan West, Capital; Susan West, Withdrawals; Fees Earned; Salaries Expense; and Utilities Expense.
2. Record the effects of the listed transactions by entering debits and credits directly in the T-accounts. Use the transaction letters to identify each debit and credit entry.

Problem 3-2B
Preparing General Journal entries

LO8

Adam Uppe, Public Accountant, completed these transactions during September 2001, the first month of operations:

Sept. 1	Began a public accounting practice by investing $4,200 in cash and office equipment having a $4,800 fair value.
1	Prepaid two months' rent in advance on suitable office space, $1,800.
2	Purchased on credit office equipment, $420, and office supplies, $75.
4	Completed accounting work for a client and immediately received payment of $180 cash.
8	Completed accounting work on credit for Frontier Bank, $700.
10	Paid for the items purchased on credit on September 2.
14	Paid the annual $750 premium on an insurance policy.
18	Received payment in full from Frontier Bank for the work completed on September 8.
24	Completed accounting work on credit for Travis Realty, $500.
28	Adam Uppe withdrew $300 cash from the practice to pay personal expenses.
29	Purchased additional office supplies on credit, $45.
30	Paid the September utility bills, $165.

Required
Prepare General Journal entries to record the transactions.

Problem 3-3B
Posting, preparing a trial balance.

LO8, 9

Check figure:
Total Dr = $10,425

Required
Using the General Journal entries prepared in Problem 3-2B, complete the following:

1. Open the following accounts (use the balance column format): Cash (101); Accounts Receivable (106); Office Supplies (124); Prepaid Insurance (128); Prepaid Rent (131); Office Equipment (163); Accounts Payable (210); Adam Uppe, Capital (301); Adam Uppe, Withdrawals (302); Accounting Fees Earned (401); and Utilities Expense (690).
2. Post the entries to the accounts and enter the balance after each posting.
3. Prepare a trial balance as of the end of the month.

Problem 3-4B
Preparing journal entries

LO8

SunBlush Technologies showed the following selected transactions for the month ended March 31, 2002:

Mar.	1	Purchased a new building, paying cash of $250,000 and signing a note payable for the balance of $500,000.
	1	Purchased six months of insurance to begin March 1; paid $7,200.
	3	Provided consulting services to the local botanical garden society; collected $5,000.
	4	Purchased cleaning supplies on account; $750.
	10	Performed work for a client today on account; $55,000.
	15	Paid for the March 4 purchase.
	20	Collected cash of $10,000 from a customer. The consulting work will be done in April.
	30	Paid month-end salaries of $49,000.
	30	Received the March telephone bill today; $1,300. It will be paid April 14.
	30	Collected half of the amount owed by the customer of March 10.

Required

Prepare journal entries for each of the above transactions.

Problem 3-5B
Analyzing accounting errors

LO7, 8, 9

During March, Shawna Cameron, the owner of Cameron Cleaning Services, had trouble keeping her debits and credits equal.

Required

For each of the errors described below, indicate:

1. Whether debits equal credits on the trial balance, and
2. Which account(s) have incorrect balances.
   a. Shawna omitted the entry to record $7,000 of services performed on account.
   b. In posting a $600 payment on account, Shawna debited Cash and credited Accounts Payable.
   c. In journalizing a cash payment, Shawna correctly debited Accounts Payable for $850 but incorrectly credited Cash for $580.
   d. In posting a cash receipt, Shawna debited Cash but forgot to post the credit to Accounts Receivable.
   e. In journalizing the purchase of $2,000 of equipment on credit, Shawna debited Accounts Payable and credited Equipment.

Problem 3-6B
Preparing and posting General Journal entries; preparing a trial balance

LO8, 9

Leonard Management Services completed these transactions during November 2001:

Nov.	1	Arthur Leonard, the owner, invested $28,000 cash and office equipment that had a fair value of $25,000 in the business.
	2	Prepaid $10,500 cash for three months' rent for an office.
	4	Made credit purchases of office equipment for $9,000 and office supplies for $1,200.
	8	Completed work for a client and immediately received $2,600 cash.
	12	Completed a $13,400 project for a client, who will pay within 30 days.
	13	Paid the account payable created on November 4.
	19	Paid $5,200 cash as the annual premium on an insurance policy.
	22	Received $7,800 as partial payment for the work completed on November 12.
	24	Completed work for another client for $1,900 on credit.
	28	Arthur Leonard withdrew $5,300 from the business for personal use.
	29	Purchased $1,700 of additional office supplies on credit.
	30	Paid $460 for the month's utility bill.

Required

1. Prepare general journal entries to record the transactions. Use General Journal, page 1.
2. Open the following accounts (use the balance column format): Cash (101); Accounts Receivable (106); Office Supplies (124); Prepaid Insurance (128); Prepaid Rent (131); Office Equipment (163); Accounts Payable (201); Arthur Leonard, Capital (301); Arthur Leonard, Withdrawals (302); Service Fees Earned (401); and Utilities Expense (690).
3. Post the entries to the accounts, and enter the balance after each posting.
4. Prepare a trial balance as of the end of the month.

Check figure:
Total Dr = $72,600

Problem 3-7B
Journalizing, posting, preparing a trial balance

LO8, 9

At the beginning of June 2001, Avery Wilson created a custom computer programming company called Softouch Co. The company had the following transactions during July, its second month of operations:

July	1	Avery Wilson purchased on credit office equipment for $4,500 and computer equipment for $28,000.
	2	Purchased land for an office. The land was worth $24,000, which was paid with $4,800 cash and a long-term note payable for $19,200.
	3	Purchased a portable building with $21,000 cash and moved it onto the land.
	5	Paid $6,600 cash for the premiums on two one-year insurance policies.
	9	Provided services to a client and collected $3,200 cash.
	12	Purchased additional computer equipment for $3,500. Paid $700 cash and signed a long-term note payable for the $2,800 balance.
	15	Completed $3,750 of services for a client. This amount is to be paid within 30 days.
	16	Purchased $750 of additional office equipment on credit.
	20	Completed another software job for $9,200 on credit.
	21	Received a bill for rent on a computer that was used on the completed job. The $320 rent must be paid within 30 days.
	22	Collected $4,600 from the client described in the transaction on July 20.
	23	Paid $1,600 wages to an assistant.
	24	Paid the account payable created in the transaction of July 16.
	25	Paid $425 cash for some repairs to an item of computer equipment.
	26	Avery Wilson withdrew $3,875 in cash from the business for personal use.
	27	Paid $1,600 wages to an assistant.
	28	Paid $800 cash to advertise in the local newspaper.
	29	Received $1,400 from a client for services to be performed in August.

Check figure:
Total Dr = $148,495

Required

1. Prepare General Journal entries to record the transactions. Use page 1 for the journal.
2. Open the following accounts (use the balance column format) entering the balances brought forward from June 30, 2001: Cash (101) $51,175; Accounts Receivable (106) $950; Prepaid Insurance (128) $275; Office Equipment (163) $1,200; Computer Equipment (167) $800; Building (173) $14,000; Land (183) $6,000; Accounts Payable (201) $725; Unearned Fees (233) $ -0-; Long-Term Notes Payable (251) $7,000; Avery Wilson, Capital (301) $60,000; Avery Wilson, Withdrawals (302) $600; Fees Earned (401) $8,400; Wages Expense (623) $780; Computer Rental Expense (645) $230; Advertising Expense (655) $75; and Repairs Expense (684) $40.
3. Post the entries to the accounts and enter the balance after each posting.
4. Prepare a trial balance as of the end of the month.

Analytical and Review Problems

A & R Problem 3-1
Analyzing account balances

Carlos Young started an engineering firm called Young Engineering. He began operations in March 2001 and completed seven transactions, including his initial investment of $17,000 cash. After these transactions, the ledger included the following accounts with their normal balances:

Cash	$26,660
Office Supplies	660
Prepaid Insurance	3,200
Office Equipment	16,500
Accounts Payable	16,500
Carlos Young, Capital	17,000
Carlos Young, Withdrawals	3,740
Engineering Fees Earned	24,000
Rent Expense	6,740

Required

Preparation component:
Prepare a trial balance for the business.

Analysis component:
Analyze the accounts and balances and prepare narratives that describe each of the seven most likely transactions and their amounts.

A & R Problem 3-2
Analyzing financial statement errors

Travis McAllister operates a surveying company. For the first few months of the company's life (through April), the accounting records were maintained by an outside bookkeeping service. According to those records, McAllister's owner's equity balance was $75,000 as of April 30. To save on expenses, McAllister decided to keep the records himself. He managed to record May's transactions properly, but was a bit rusty when the time came to prepare the financial statements. His first versions of the balance sheet and income statement follow. McAllister is bothered that the company apparently operated at a loss during the month, even though he had been very busy.

McALLISTER SURVEYING
Income Statement
For Month Ended May 31, 2001

Revenue:		
Investments by owner		$ 3,000
Unearned surveying fees		6,000
Total revenues		$ 9,000
Operating expenses:		
Rent expense	$3,100	
Telephone expense	600	
Surveying equipment	5,400	
Advertising expense	3,200	
Utilities expense	300	
Insurance expense	900	
Withdrawals by owner	6,000	
Total operating expenses		19,500
Net income (loss)		$(10,500)

McALLISTER SURVEYING
Balance Sheet
May 31, 2001

Assets		**Liabilities**	
Cash	$ 3,900	Accounts payable	$ 2,400
Accounts receivable	2,700	Surveying fees earned	18,000
Prepaid insurance	1,800	Short-term notes payable	48,000
Prepaid rent	4,200	Total liabilities	$ 68,400
Office supplies	300		
Buildings	81,000	**Owner's Equity**	
Land	36,000	Travis McAllister, capital	64,500
Salaries expense	3,000	Total liabilities and	
Total assets	$132,900	owner's equity	$132,900

Required
Using the information contained in the original financial statements, prepare revised statements, including a statement of owner's equity, for the month of May.

A & R Problem 3-3

Sandra Castell started a computer consulting business called Aribas Computer Services. She invested $25,000 and her automobile, which had a market value of $23,000. The business was an instant success; however she could not say the same about her bookkeeper, who prepared the following trial balance:

ARIBAS COMPUTER SERVICES Trial Balance September 30, 2001		
Cash	$26,200	
Accounts receivable	4,000	
Supplies	4,800	
Automobiles	26,000	
Accounts payable		$ -0-
Sandra Castell, capital		61,000
Totals	$61,000	$61,000

The following information was obtained from the accounting records:

a. Consulting fees earned and billed during September amounted to $16,000, of which $9,000 was collected.
b. Office equipment purchased but not as yet paid for, $3,000.
c. Supplies purchased for cash, $1,800.
d. Paid $1,800 for two months' office rent.
e. Wages paid for September, $2,200.
f. Castell withdrew $3,000 for living expenses.

Required

1. List the errors the bookkeeper made.
2. Prepare a corrected trial balance.
3. Explain why the original trial balance balanced.

Serial Problem

Echo Systems

(This comprehensive problem starts in this chapter and continues in Chapters 4, 5, and 6. Because of its length, this problem is most easily solved if you use the Working Papers that accompany this text.)

On October 1, 2001, Mary Graham organized a computer service company called Echo Systems. Echo is organized as a sole proprietorship and will provide consulting services, computer system installations, and custom program development. Graham has adopted the calendar year for reporting, and expects to prepare the company's first set of financial statements as of December 31, 2001. The initial chart of accounts for the accounting system includes these items:

Account Number	Account Name	Account Number	Account Name
101	Cash	301	Mary Graham, Capital
106	Accounts Receivable	302	Mary Graham, Withdrawals
126	Computer Supplies	403	Computer Services Revenue
128	Prepaid Insurance	623	Wages Expense
131	Prepaid Rent	655	Advertising Expense
163	Office Equipment	676	Mileage Expense
167	Computer Equipment	677	Miscellaneous Expense
201	Accounts Payable	684	Repairs Expense, Computer

Required

1. Prepare journal entries to record each of the following transactions for Echo Systems.
2. Open balance column accounts for the company and post the journal entries to them.

Oct.	1	Mary Graham invested $45,000 cash, an $18,000 computer system, and $9,000 of office equipment in the business.
	2	Paid rent in advance of $4,500.
	3	Purchased computer supplies on credit for $1,320 from Abbott Office Products.
	5	Paid $2,160 cash for one year's premium on a property and liability insurance policy.
	6	Billed Capital Leasing $3,300 for installing a new computer.
	8	Paid for the computer supplies purchased from Abbott Office Products.
	10	Hired Carly Smith as a part-time assistant for $100 per day, as needed.
	12	Billed Capital Leasing another $1,200 for computer services rendered.
	15	Received $3,300 from Capital Leasing on its account.
	17	Paid $705 to repair computer equipment damaged when moving into the new office.
	20	Paid $1,860 for an advertisement in the local newspaper.
	22	Received $1,200 from Capital Leasing on its account.
	28	Billed Decker Company $3,225 for services.
	31	Paid Carly Smith for seven days' work.
	31	Mary Graham withdrew $3,600 cash from the business for personal use.
Nov.	1	Reimbursed Mary Graham's business automobile expense for 1,000 kilometres at $0.50 per kilometre.
	2	Received $4,650 cash from Elite Corporation for computer services rendered.
	5	Purchased $960 of computer supplies from Abbott Office Products.
	8	Billed Fostek Co. $4,350 for computer services rendered.
	13	Notified by Alamo Engineering Co. that Echo's bid of $3,750 for an upcoming project was accepted.
	18	Received $1,875 from Decker Company against the bill dated October 28.
	22	Donated $750 to the United Way in the company's name.
	24	Completed work for Alamo Engineering Co. and sent a bill for $3,750.
	25	Sent another bill to Decker Company for the past due amount of $1,350.
	28	Reimbursed Mary Graham's business automobile expense for 1,200 kilometres at $0.50 per kilometre.
	30	Paid Carly Smith for 14 days' work.
	30	Mary Graham withdrew $1,800 cash from the business for personal use.

CHAPTER

Adjusting Accounts for Financial Statements

Creative Accountant

Edmonton, AB—Larisa Sembaliuk is living her dream. She is an artist, and after years of working for an employer and painting only part-time, she has turned her talent into a business. Larisa operates out of her home selling her paintings, lithographs, greeting cards, and bookmarks—but she's still not painting full-time. Her business demands that she market her products, which involves extensive travelling locally and internationally.

Larisa's paintings are based on themes. Her first, 'Flowers of the Americas,' required a year and a half of research, followed by a year of painting to produce 25 originals that sold out almost immediately. Her second theme was 'Flowers of the Bible' and currently 'Shakespeare's Garden,' each involving about a three-year cycle of research and painting. Her revenue materials, such

Learning Objectives

- **LO1** Describe the purpose of adjusting accounts at the end of a period.
- **LO2** Explain the importance of periodic reporting and the time period principle.
- **LO3** Explain accrual accounting and how it adds to the usefulness of financial statements.
- **LO4** Identify the types of adjustments and their purpose.
- **LO5** Prepare and explain adjusting entries for prepaid expenses, amortization and unearned revenues.
- **LO6** Prepare and describe adjusting entries for accrued expenses and accrued revenues.
- **LO7** Explain how accounting adjustments link to financial statements.
- **LO8** Explain and prepare an adjusted trial balance.
- **LO9** Prepare financial statements from an adjusted trial balance.
- **LO10** Prepare and describe accrual adjustments in later periods.

as the lithographs, provide her with a livelihood between shows, but more importantly she depends on sponsors to cover her travel, insurance, framing, and other expenses. She notes that accounting is essential. "I've tried Simply Accounting and it worked well but I don't have the time to keep it up properly. Sponsors expect accurate recording and matching of revenues and expenses to the project they are supporting. I need accounting information to satisfy my current sponsor and solicit new ones, but I'm finding it a challenge to do it myself." Larisa would rather use a paintbrush than a calculator! However, she understands the value of accurate financial statements.

artby Larisa .com

Chapter Preview

Financial statements P. 36 reflect revenues when earned and expenses when incurred. This is known as *accrual basis accounting.* Accrual basis accounting is achieved by following the steps of the accounting cycle P. 84. We described the first four of these steps in Chapter 3.

An important part of the accounting cycle is the adjustment of account balances. The adjusted account balances are what is reported in financial statements that are prepared according to generally accepted accounting principles P. 42. Adjustment of accounts is necessary so that financial statements at the end of a reporting period reflect the effects of all transactions. This chapter emphasizes Steps Five and Six of the accounting cycle as highlighted in Exhibit 4.1. Preparation of financial statements, Step Seven of the accounting cycle, is reinforced in this chapter, with an emphasis on how *adjusting entries* impact the financial statements. To illustrate the adjusting process, we continue with the example of Finlay Interiors used in previous chapters.

Purpose of Adjusting

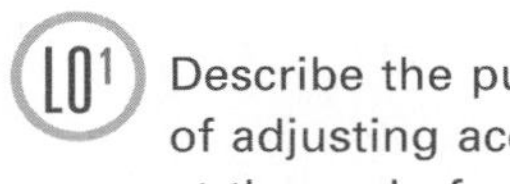

Describe the purpose of adjusting accounts at the end of a period.

The usual process during an accounting period is to record external transactions and events. After external transactions are recorded, several accounts in the ledger need adjustment for their balances to appear in financial statements. This need arises because internal transactions and events remain unrecorded.

An example is the cost of certain assets that expire or are used up as time passes. The Prepaid Insurance account of Finlay Interiors is one of these. Finlay Interiors' trial balance (Exhibit 4.2) shows Prepaid Insurance with a balance of $2,400. This amount is the premium for two years of insurance protection beginning on January 1, 2001. By January 31, 2001, because one month's coverage is used up, the $2,400 is no longer the correct account balance for Prepaid Insurance. The Prepaid Insurance account balance must be reduced by one month's cost, or $100 ($2,400/24 months). The income statement P. 37 must report this $100 cost as insurance expense for January.

Exhibit 4.1

Steps in the Accounting Cycle Introduced in Chapter 4

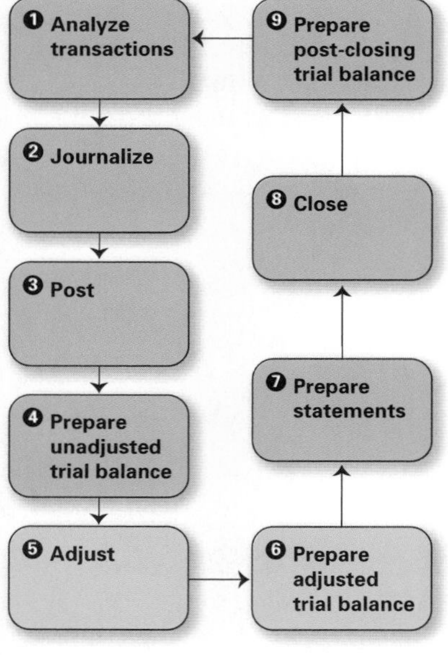

Exhibit 4.2

Trial Balance

FINLAY INTERIORS
Trial Balance
January 31, 2001

	Debit	Credit
Cash	$ 8,070	
Accounts receivable	-0-	
Prepaid insurance	2,400	
Supplies	3,600	
Furniture	26,000	
Accounts payable		$ 200
Unearned consulting revenue		3,000
Notes payable		6,000
Carol Finlay, capital		30,000
Carol Finlay, withdrawals	600	
Consulting revenue		3,800
Rental revenue		300
Rent expense	1,000	
Salaries expense	1,400	
Utilities expense	230	
Totals	$43,300	$43,300

Another example is the $3,600 balance in Supplies. Part of this balance includes the cost of supplies that were used in January. The cost of the supplies used must be reported as an expense in January. The balances of both the Prepaid Insurance and Supplies accounts must be *adjusted* before they are reported on the January 31 balance sheet P. 38.

Another adjustment necessary for Finlay Interiors relates to one month's usage of furniture. The balances of the Unearned Consulting Revenue, Consulting Revenue, and Salaries Expense accounts often also need adjusting before they appear on the statements. We explain *why* this adjusting process is carried out in the next section.

The Accounting Period

LO2 Explain the importance of periodic reporting and the time period principle.

The adjusting process is often linked to timeliness of information. Information must reach decision makers frequently and promptly, therefore accounting systems need to prepare periodic reports at regular intervals. This results in an accounting process impacted by the *time period (or periodicity) principle.* The **time period principle** assumes that an organization's activities can be divided into specific time periods such as a month, a three-month quarter, or a year as illustrated in Exhibit 4.3.

Time periods covered by statements are called **accounting** (or *reporting*) **periods.** Reports covering a one-year period are known as *annual financial statements.* Recall that a company can adopt a *fiscal year* P. 37 based on the *calendar year* P. 37 or its *natural business year* P. 37.

On November 30, 2000 Dia Met Minerals announced a change in its fiscal year-end to May 31 from January 31, effective in 2001 for the purpose of improved reporting efficiencies and administrative cost savings.
SOURCE: www.diamet.com

Many organizations also prepare **interim financial reports** covering one, three (quarterly) or six (semi-annual) months of activity.

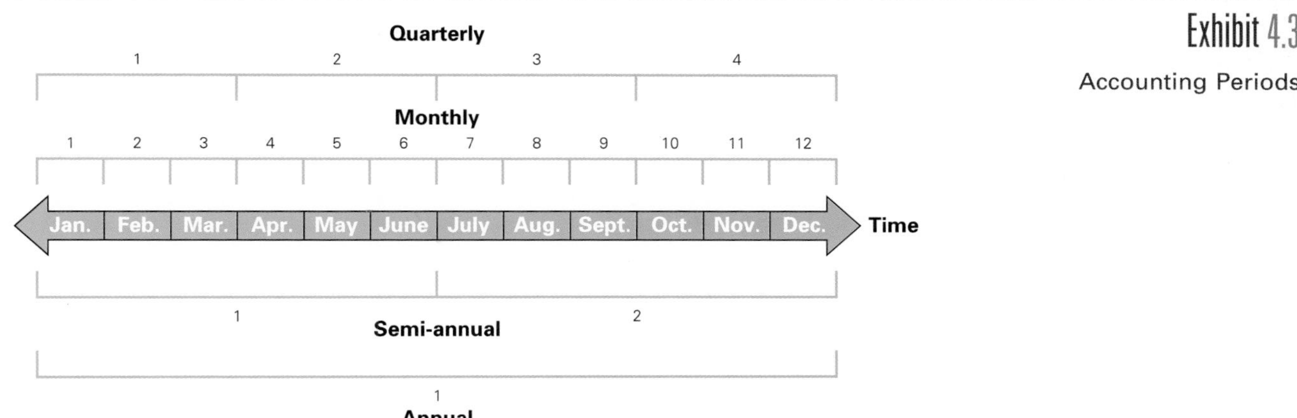

Exhibit 4.3
Accounting Periods

Recognizing Revenues and Expenses

LO3 Explain accrual accounting and how it adds to the usefulness of financial statements.

Because of the need for regular reporting of information, activities are often reported on or before their completion so as not to mislead decision makers.

These activities are recorded through the adjusting process. Two main generally accepted accounting principles are used in the adjusting process: the *revenue recognition principle* P. 44 and the *matching principle*. To illustrate revenue recognition, if Finlay Interiors provides consulting services to a client in January, the revenue is earned in January. This means that it must be reported on the January income statement, even if the client pays for the services in some other month than January. A major goal of the adjusting process is to have revenue recognized (reported) in the time period when it is earned.

The **matching principle** aims to report expenses in the same accounting period as the revenues that are earned as a result of these expenses. This matching of expenses with revenues is a major part of the adjusting process. A common example is a business like Finlay Interiors that earns monthly revenues while operating out of rented office space. To earn revenues, office space had to be rented. The matching principle tells us that rent must be reported on the income statement for January, even if rent is paid in a month before or after January. This ensures that the rent expense for January is matched with January's revenues.

Accrual Basis Compared to Cash Basis

Accrual basis accounting is founded on the revenue recognition principle, where revenues and expenses are recorded when earned or incurred regardless of when cash is received or paid. Accrual accounting also demands that revenues and expenses be *matched* to the *time period* in which they were actually earned or incurred. Accrual basis accounting then, is based on the three GAAP of *revenue recognition, matching,* and *time period.*

In contrast, **cash basis accounting** recognizes revenues and expenses when *cash* is received or paid. Cash basis accounting for the income statement, balance sheet, and statement of owner's equity P. 38 is *not* consistent with generally accepted accounting principles. It is commonly held that accrual basis accounting provides a better indication of business performance than information about current cash receipts and payments. Accrual basis accounting also increases the comparability of financial statements from one period to another. Yet information about cash flows is also useful. This is why companies also include a statement of cash flows, discussed in Chapter 19.

Answers—p. 158

1. Describe a company's annual reporting period.
2. Why do companies prepare interim financial statements?
3. What accounting principles most directly lead to the adjusting process?
4. Is cash basis accounting consistent with generally accepted accounting principles?

Adjusting Accounts

The process of adjusting accounts is similar to our process of analyzing and recording transactions in Chapter 3. We must analyze each account balance and the transactions and events that affect it to determine any needed adjustments. An **adjusting entry** is recorded to bring an asset or liability account balance to its proper amount when an adjustment is needed. This entry also updates the related expense or revenue account and is necessary to prepare the financial statements. Adjusting entries are posted to accounts in the ledger like any other entry. This next section shows the mechanics of adjusting entries and their links to financial statements.

Framework for Adjustments

It is helpful to group adjustments by their timing of cash receipt or payment in comparison to when they are recognized as revenues or expenses. Exhibit 4.4 identifies the five main adjustments, each of which is detailed in the following sections.

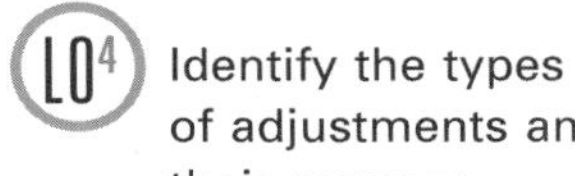

LO4 Identify the types of adjustments and their purpose.

Exhibit 4.4

Framework for Adjustments

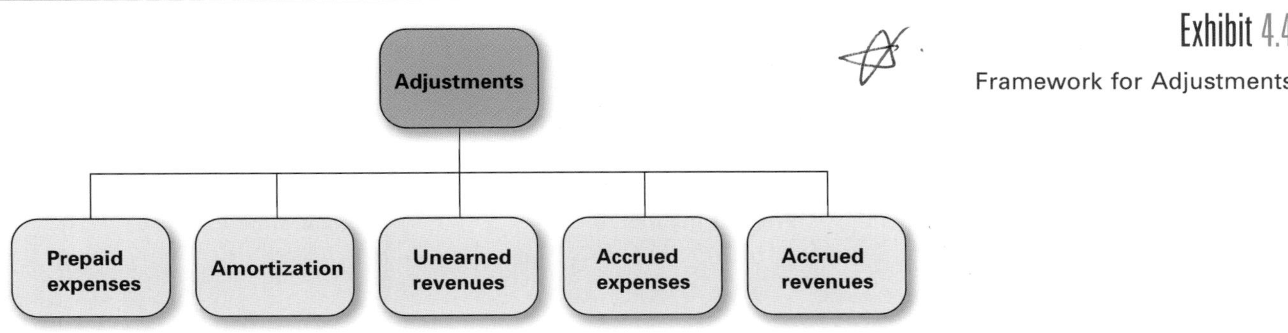

Adjusting Prepaid Expenses

Prepaid expenses[1] refer to items *paid for* in advance of receiving their benefits. Prepaid expenses are assets. As these assets are used, their costs become expenses. Adjusting entries for prepaids involve increasing (debiting) expenses and decreasing (crediting) assets as shown in Exhibit 4.5.

LO5 Prepare and explain adjusting entries for prepaid expenses, amortization and unearned revenues.

Exhibit 4.5

Adjusting for Prepaid Expenses

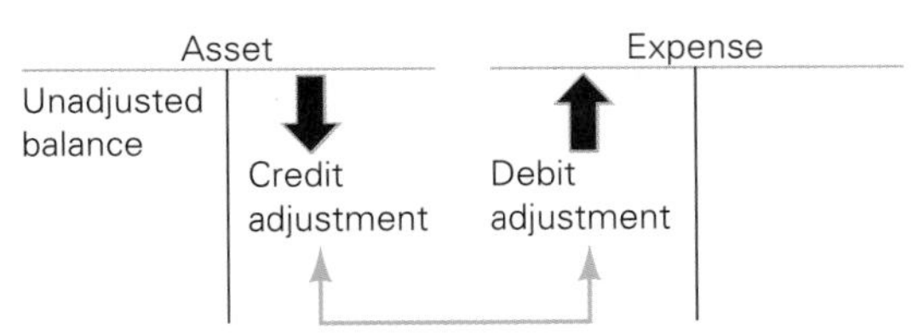

The three common prepaid expenses are insurance, supplies, and amortization.

Prepaid Insurance

We illustrate prepaid insurance using Finlay Interiors' payment of $2,400 for two years of insurance protection beginning on January 1, 2001. The following entry records the purchase of the insurance:

Jan. 1	Prepaid Insurance	2,400	
	Cash		2,400
	To record purchase of insurance for 24 months.		

[1] Prepaids are also called *deferrals* because the recognition of an expense or revenue is deferred.

By January 31, one month's insurance coverage is used, causing a portion of the asset Prepaid Insurance to become an expense. This expense is $100 ($2,400 × 1/24). Our adjusting entry to record this expense and reduce the asset is:

Adjustment (a)

Jan. 31	Insurance Expense	100	
	Prepaid Insurance		100
	To record expired insurance.		

Posting this adjusting entry affects the accounts shown in Exhibit 4.6:

Exhibit 4.6

Insurance Accounts after Adjusting for Prepaids

Prepaid Insurance			
Jan. 1	2,400	**Jan. 31**	**100**
Balance	2,300		

Insurance Expense		
Jan. 31	**100**	

After posting, the $100 balance in Insurance Expense and the $2,300 balance in Prepaid Insurance are ready for reporting in the financial statements. If the adjustment is *not* made at January 31, then (a) expenses are understated by $100 and net income is overstated by $100 for the January income statement, and (b) both Prepaid Insurance and owner's equity are overstated by $100 in the January 31 balance sheet.

Supplies

Finlay Interiors purchased $3,600 of supplies in January and used some of them during this month. Daily usage of supplies was not recorded in Finlay Interiors' accounts because this information was not needed. When we report account balances in financial statements only at the end of a month, recordkeeping costs can be reduced by making only one adjusting entry at that time. This entry needs to record the total cost of all supplies used in the month.

The cost of supplies used during January must be recognized as an expense. Finlay Interiors computes ("takes inventory of") the remaining unused supplies. The cost of the remaining supplies is then deducted from the cost of the purchased supplies to compute the amount used. Finlay Interiors has $2,550 of supplies remaining out of the $3,600 purchased in January. The $1,050 difference between these two amounts is the cost of the supplies used. This amount is January's Supplies Expense. Our adjusting entry to record this expense and reduce the Supplies asset account is:

Adjustment (b)

Jan. 31	Supplies Expense	1,050	
	Supplies		1,050
	To record supplies used.		

Posting this adjusting entry affects the accounts shown in Exhibit 4.7:

Exhibit 4.7

Supplies Accounts after Adjusting for Prepaids

Supplies			
Jan. 2	2,500	**Jan. 31**	**1,050**
6	1,100		
Total	3,600	Total	1,050
	−1,050		
Balance	2,550		

Supplies Expense		
Jan. 31	**1,050**	

The balance of the Supplies account is $2,550 after posting and equals the cost of remaining unused supplies. If the adjustment is *not* made at January 31, then (a) expenses are understated by $1,050 and net income overstated by $1,050 for the January income statement, and (b) both Supplies and owner's equity are overstated by $1,050 in the January 31 balance sheet.

Other Prepaid Expenses

There are other prepaid expenses (including Prepaid Rent), which are accounted for in exactly the same manner as Insurance and Supplies above. We should also note that some prepaid expenses are both paid for and fully used up within a single accounting period. One example is when a company pays monthly rent on the first day of each month. The payment creates a prepaid expense on the first day of each month that fully expires by the end of the month. In these special cases, we can record the cash paid with a debit to the expense account instead of an asset account.

Adjusting for Amortization[2]

Capital assets include long-term tangible assets (such as **plant and equipment**) that are used to produce and sell products and services, and **intangible assets** (such as patents) that convey the right to use a product or process. These assets are expected to provide benefits for more than one period. Examples of plant and equipment are land, buildings, machines, vehicles and fixtures. Because plant and equipment assets (except for land) wear out or decline in usefulness as they are used, an expense must be recorded to match the cost of the asset over the periods benefited. **Amortization** is the process of computing expense from matching (or allocating) the cost of capital assets over their expected useful lives.

Finlay Interiors uses furniture in earning revenue. This furniture's cost must be amortized. Recall that Finlay Interiors made two purchases of furniture—one for $20,000 and the other for $6,000—in early January. Carol Finlay expects the furniture to have a useful life (benefit period) of four years. Carol expects to sell the furniture for about $8,000 at the end of four years. This means that the *net cost* expected to expire over the estimated useful life is $18,000 (=$26,000 − $8,000).

There are several methods that we can use to allocate this $18,000 net cost to expense. Finlay Interiors uses *straight-line amortization.*[3] The **straight-line amortization method** allocates equal amounts of an asset's net cost over its estimated useful life. When the $18,000 net cost is divided by the asset's useful life of 48 months (4 years × 12 months per year), we get an average monthly cost of $375 ($18,000/48). Our adjusting entry to record monthly amortization expense is:

Straight-line Amortization

Calculated as:

$$= \frac{\text{Cost of asset} - \text{Estimated value at end of estimated useful life}}{\text{Estimated Useful Life}}$$

$$= \frac{\$26{,}000 - \$8{,}000}{48 \text{ months}}$$

$$= \$375 \text{ per month}$$

Adjustment (c)

Jan. 31	Amortization Expense, Furniture	375	
	Accumulated Amortization, Furniture		375
	To record monthly amortization on furniture.		

[2] In 1990, the revised *CICA Handbook*, section 3600, recommended the use of the term *amortization* instead of *depreciation*, but the use of *depreciation* was not ruled out. Also, *fixed assets* was replaced by *capital assets*. Despite these recommendations, the new terminology has not yet been adopted by all users. Thus, *depreciation* continues to be a common term.

[3] We explain the details of *amortization* methods in Chapter 12. We briefly describe the straight-line method here to help you understand the adjusting process.

Posting this adjusting entry affects the accounts shown in Exhibit 4.8:

Exhibit 4.8

Accounts after Amortization Adjustments

Furniture		
Jan. 3	20,000	
6	6,000	
Bal.	26,000	

Accumulated Amortization, Furniture		
	Jan. 31	375

Amortization Expense, Furniture		
Jan. 31	375	

Amortization is recorded in a *contra account.* A **contra account** is an account that is linked with another account and has an opposite normal balance P. 94 to its counterpart. It is reported as a subtraction from the other account's balance. On Finlay Interiors' balance sheet, the balance in the contra account, *Accumulated Amortization, Furniture,* will be subtracted from the Furniture account balance as shown in Exhibit 4.10.

The cost of the asset less its accumulated amortization is the **book value** of the asset. The **market value** of an asset is the amount it can be sold for. Market value is not tied to the book value of an asset.

The use of contra accounts allows balance sheet readers to know both the cost of assets and the total amount of amortization charged to expense. Notice that the title of the contra account is *accumulated amortization.* This means that the account includes *total* amortization expense for all prior periods when the assets were being used. Finlay Interiors' Furniture and Accumulated Amortization, Furniture accounts would appear on March 31, 2001 after three monthly adjusting entries as shown in Exhibit 4.9.

Exhibit 4.9

Accounts after Three Months of Amortization Adjustments

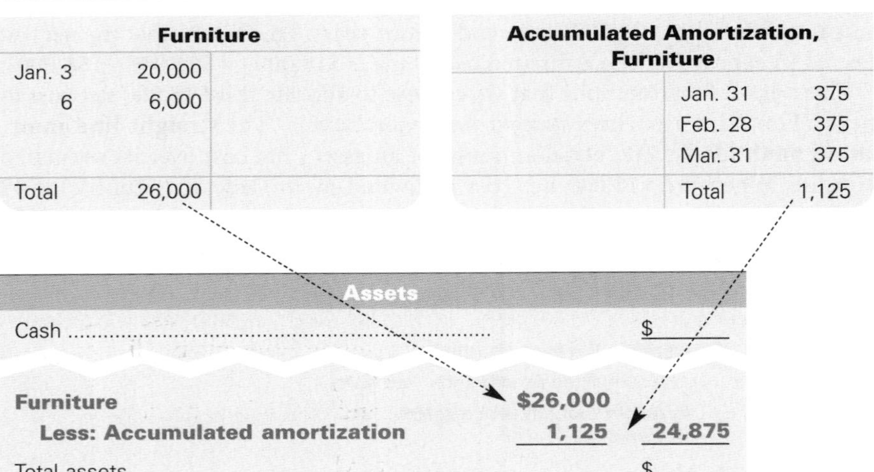

Furniture		
Jan. 3	20,000	
6	6,000	
Total	26,000	

Accumulated Amortization, Furniture		
	Jan. 31	375
	Feb. 28	375
	Mar. 31	375
	Total	1,125

Exhibit 4.10

Accumulated Amortization Contra Account in the Balance Sheet

Assets		
Cash		$
Furniture	**$26,000**	
Less: Accumulated amortization	**1,125**	**24,875**
Total assets		$

After posting the adjustment, the *Furniture* account less its *Accumulated Amortization, Furniture* account equals the January 31 balance sheet amount for this asset. The balance in the Amortization Expense, Furniture account is the expense reported in the January income statement. If the adjustment is *not* made at January 31, then (a) expenses are understated by $375 and net income is overstated by $375 for the January income statement, and (b) both assets and owner's equity are overstated by $375 in the January 31 balance sheet.

Small Business Owner

You are preparing to make an offer to purchase a small family-run restaurant. The manager gives you a copy of her amortization schedule for the restaurant's building and equipment. It shows costs of $75,000 and accumulated amortization of $55,000. This leaves a net total for building and equipment of $20,000. Is this information valuable in deciding on a purchase offer for the restaurant?

Answers—p. 157

Adjusting Unearned Revenues

Unearned revenues refer to cash received in advance of providing products and services. Unearned revenues, also known as *deferred revenues*, are a *liability*. When cash is accepted, an obligation to provide products and services is also accepted. As products and services are provided, the amount of unearned revenues becomes *earned* revenues. Adjusting entries for unearned revenues involve increasing (crediting) revenues and decreasing (debiting) unearned revenues as shown in Exhibit 4.11. These adjustments reflect economic events (including passage of time) that impact unearned revenues.

Exhibit 4.11

Adjusting for Unearned Revenues

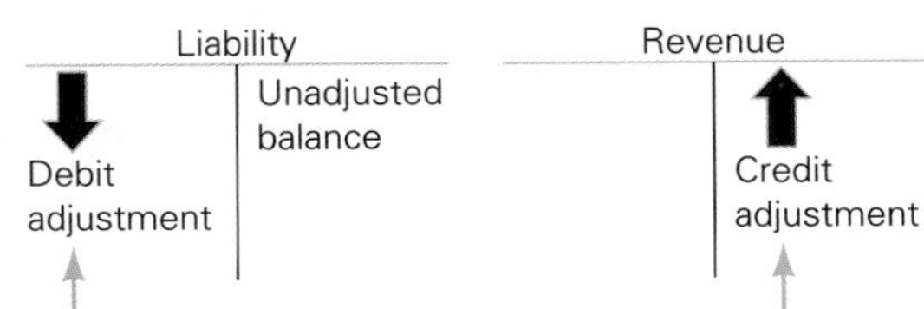

We see an example of unearned revenues in Rogers Communications' 1999 annual report. Rogers reports unearned revenue of $117.3 million on its balance sheet. Another example is Air Canada, which reports advance (unearned) ticket sales at June 30, 2000 of $945 million.

Finlay Interiors also has unearned revenues. On January 26, Finlay Interiors agreed to provide consulting services to a client for a fixed fee of $1,500 per month. On that same day, this client paid the first two months' fees in advance, covering the period from January 27 to March 27. The entry to record the cash received in advance is:

Jan. 26	Cash	3,000	
	Unearned Consulting Revenue		3,000
	Received advance payment for services over the next two months.		

This advance payment increases cash and creates an obligation to do consulting work over the next two months. As time passes, Finlay Interiors will earn this payment. No external transactions are linked with this earnings process. By January 31, Finlay Interiors provides five days' service that amounts to consulting revenue of $250 (=$1,500 × 5/30). The revenue recognition principle implies that $250 of unearned revenue is reported as revenue on the January income statement. The adjusting entry to reduce the liability account and recognize earned revenue is:

Adjustment (d)

Jan. 31	Unearned Consulting Revenue	250	
	Consulting Revenue		250
	To record the earned portion of revenue received in advance calculated as $1,500 × 5/30.		

The accounts look as shown in Exhibit 4.12 after posting the adjusting entry.

Exhibit 4.12

Unearned Revenue and Revenue Accounts after Adjustments

Unearned Consulting Revenue			
Jan. 31	**250**	Jan. 26	3,000
		Balance	2,750

Consulting Revenue			
		Jan. 10	2,200
		12	1,900
		31	**250**
		Total	4,350

The adjusting entry transfers $250 out of Unearned Consulting Revenue (a liability account) to a revenue account. If the adjustment is *not* made, then (a) revenue and net income are understated by $250 in the January income statement, and (b) Unearned Consulting Revenue is overstated and owner's equity understated by $250 on the January 31 balance sheet.

Adjusting Accrued Expenses

LO6 Prepare and describe adjusting entries for accrued expenses and accrued revenues.

Accrued expenses refer to costs incurred in a period that are both unpaid and unrecorded. Accrued expenses are part of expenses and reported on the income statement. Adjusting entries for recording accrued expenses involve increasing (debiting) expenses and increasing (crediting) liabilities as shown in Exhibit 4.13.

Common examples of accrued expenses are salaries, interest, rent and taxes. We use salaries and interest to show how to adjust accounts for accrued expenses.

Exhibit 4.13

Adjusting for Accrued Expenses

Accrued Salaries Expense

Finlay Interiors' only employee earns $70 per day or $350 for a five-day workweek beginning on Monday and ending on Friday. This employee gets paid every two weeks on Friday. On the 12th and the 26th of January, the wages are paid, recorded in the journal, and posted to the ledger. The *unadjusted* Salaries Expense and Cash paid for salaries appear as shown in Exhibit 4.14.

Exhibit 4.14

Salary and Cash Accounts Before Adjusting

Cash			
		Jan. 12	700
		26	700

Salaries Expense			
Jan. 12	700		
26	700		

Exhibit 4.15

Salary Accrual Period and Paydays

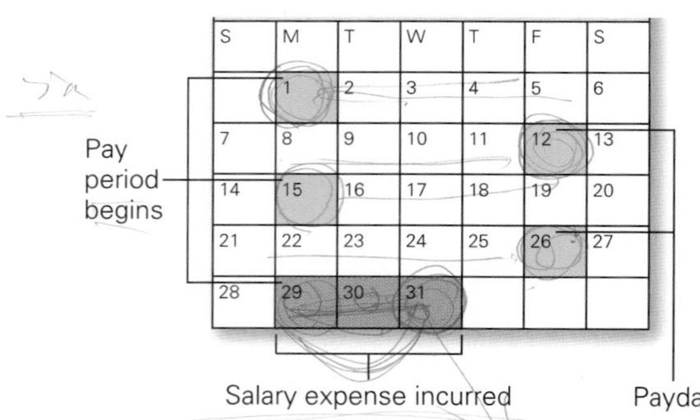

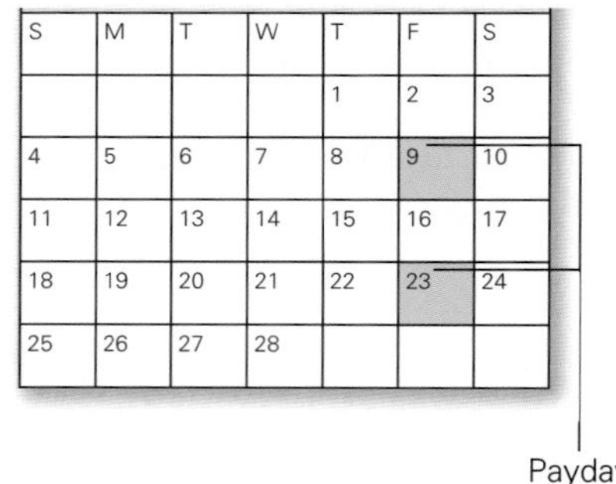

The calendar in Exhibit 4.15 shows three working days after the January 26 payday (January 29, 30, and 31). This means that the employee earns three days' salary by the close of business on Wednesday, January 31. While this salary cost is incurred, it is not yet paid or recorded. The period-end adjusting entry to account for accrued salaries is:

Adjustment (e)

Jan. 31	Salaries Expense	210	
	Salaries Payable		210
	To record three days' accrued salary; 3 × $70.		

After the adjusting entry is posted, the expense and liability accounts appear as shown in Exhibit 4.16.

Exhibit 4.16

Salary Accounts After Accrual Adjustments

Salaries Expense			Salaries Payable		
Jan. 12	700			Jan. 31	210
26	700				
31	**210**				
Total	1,610				

This means that $1,610 of salaries expense is reported on the income statement and that $210 in salaries payable (liability) is reported in the balance sheet. If the adjustment is *not* made, then (a) Salaries Expense is understated and net income overstated by $210 in the January income statement, and (b) Salaries Payable is understated and owner's equity overstated by $210 on the January 31 balance sheet.

Accrued Interest Expense

It is common for companies to have accrued interest expense on notes payable and certain accounts payable at the end of a period. Interest expense is incurred with the passage of time. Unless interest is paid on the last day of an accounting period, we need to adjust accounts for interest expense incurred but not yet paid. This means that we must accrue interest cost from the most recent payment date up to the end of the period.[4] We fully describe computation of interest expense later in the book.

Interest of $32 has accrued on Finlay Interiors' $6,000 note payable for the month of January. The journal entry is:

Adjustment (f)

Jan. 31	Interest Expense	32	
	Interest Payable		32
	To record accrued interest.		

After the adjusting entry is posted, the expense and liability accounts appear as shown in Exhibit 4.17.

[4] The formula for computing accrued interest is: *[Payable amount]* × *[Annual interest rate]* × *[Fraction of year since last payment date]*.

Exhibit 4.17

Notes Payable and Interest Accounts after Accrual Adjustments

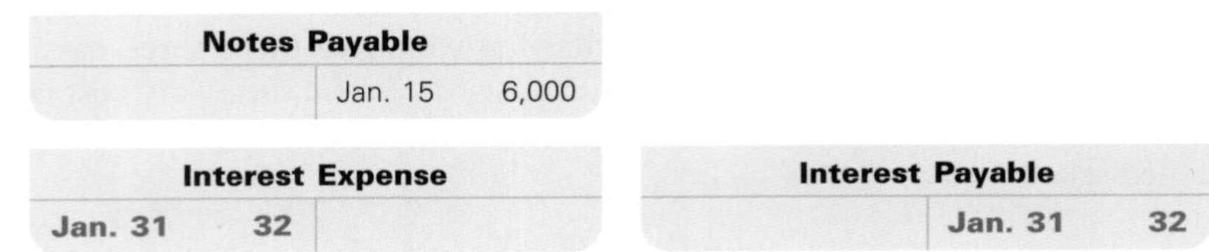

This means that $32 of interest expense is reported on the income statement and that $32 interest payable is reported on the balance sheet. Notice that the Notes Payable account is *not* affected by recording interest. If the interest adjustment is not made, then (a) Interest Expense is understated and net income overstated by $32 in the January income statement, and (b) Interest Payable is understated and owner's equity overstated by $32 on the January 31 balance sheet.

Adjusting Accrued Revenues

When products and services are delivered, we expect to receive payment for them. **Accrued revenues** refer to revenues earned in a period that are both unrecorded and not yet received in cash (or other assets). Accrued revenues are part of revenues and must be reported on the income statement. The adjusting entries increase (debit) assets and increase (credit) revenues as shown in Exhibit 4.18.

Common examples of accrued revenues are fees for services and products, interest and rent. We use service fees and interest to show how to adjust accounts for accrued revenues.

Exhibit 4.18

Adjusting for Accrued Revenues

Accrued Services Revenue

Accrued revenues are earned but unrecorded because either the customer has not paid for them or the seller has not yet billed the customer. Finlay Interiors provides us with an example of an accrued revenue. In the second week of January, Finlay Interiors agreed to provide consulting services to a client for a fixed fee of $2,700 per month from January 11 to February 10, or 30 days of service. The client agrees to pay $2,700 cash to Finlay Interiors on February 10, 2001 when the service period is complete.

At January 31, 2001, 20 days of services are already provided to the client. Since the contracted services are not yet entirely provided, the client is not yet billed nor has Finlay Interiors recorded the services already provided. Finlay Interiors has earned $1,800 (=$2,700 × 20/30). The *revenue recognition principle* implies that we must report the $1,800 on the January income statement because it is earned in January. The balance sheet also must report that this client owes Finlay Interiors $1,800. The year-end adjusting entry to account for accrued consulting services revenue is:

Adjustment (g)

Jan. 31	Accounts Receivable	1,800	
	Consulting Revenue		1,800
	To record 20 days' accrued revenue.		

After the adjusting entry is posted, the affected accounts look as shown in Exhibit 4.19.

Accounts Receivable			
Jan. 12	1,900	Jan. 22	1,900
31	**1,800**		
Total	3,700 −1,900	Total	1,900
Balance	1,800		

Consulting Revenue			
		Jan. 10	2,200
		12	1,600
		31	250
		31	**1,800**
		Total	5,850

Exhibit 4.19

Receivable and Revenue Accounts After Accrual Adjustments

Accounts receivable are reported on the balance sheet at $1,800, and $5,850 of revenues are reported on the income statement. If the adjustment is *not* made, then (a) both Consulting Revenue and net income are understated by $1,800 in the January income statement, and (b) both Accounts Receivable and owner's equity are understated by $1,800 on the January 31 balance sheet.

Accrued Interest Revenue

In addition to the accrued interest expense we described earlier, interest can yield an accrued revenue when a company is owed money (or other assets) from a debtor. If a company is holding notes or accounts receivable that produce interest revenue, we must adjust the accounts to record any earned and yet uncollected interest revenue. The adjusting entry is similar to the one for accruing services revenue, with a debit to Interest Receivable (asset) and a credit to Interest Revenue (equity).

Adjustments and Financial Statements

Exhibit 4.20 lists the five major types of transactions requiring adjustment. Adjusting entries are necessary for each. Understanding this exhibit is important to understanding the adjusting process and its link to financial statements. Remember that each adjusting entry affects one or more income statement accounts and one or more balance sheet accounts.

Explain how accounting adjustments link to financial statements.

Type	Before Adjusting: Balance Sheet Account	Before Adjusting: Income Statement Account	Adjusting Entry
Prepaid Expense	Asset Overstated	Expense Understated	Dr. Expense Cr. Asset
Amortization	Asset Overstated	Expense Understated	Dr. Expense Cr. Contra Asset
Unearned Revenues	Liability Overstated	Revenue Understated	Dr. Liability Cr. Revenue
Accrued Expenses	Liability Understated	Expense Understated	Dr. Expense Cr. Liability
Accrued Revenues	Asset Understated	Revenue Understated	Dr. Asset Cr. Revenue

Exhibit 4.20

Summary of Adjustments and Financial Statement Links

Note that adjusting entries related to the framework in Exhibit 4.20 never affect cash.[5] A common error made by students learning to prepare adjusting entries is to either debit or credit cash. In the case of prepaids and unearned revenues, cash has already been correctly recorded; it is the prepaids and unearned revenues account balances that need to be *fixed* or adjusted. In the case of accrued revenues and expenses, cash will be received or paid in the future and is not to be accounted for until that time; it is the revenue or expense account balance that needs to be fixed or adjusted. Amortization is a non-cash transaction and therefore does not affect cash; a more detailed explanation will be provided in Chapter 12.

Exhibit 4.21 summarizes the adjusting entries of Finlay Interiors on January 31. The posting of adjusting entries to individual ledger accounts was shown when we described the transactions above and is not repeated here. Adjusting entries are often set apart from other journal entries with the caption Adjusting Entries.

Exhibit 4.21

Journalizing Adjusting Entries of Finlay Interiors

Date	GENERAL JOURNAL Account Titles and Explanation	PR	Page #2 Debit	Credit
2001	**Adjusting Entries**			
Jan. 31	Insurance Expense		100	
	Prepaid Insurance			100
	To record expired insurance; $2,400/24.			
31	Supplies Expense		1,050	
	Supplies			1,050
	To record supplies used; $3,600 − $2,550.			
31	Amortization Expense, Furniture		375	
	Accumulated Amortization, Furniture			375
	To record monthly amortization on furniture; $26,000 − $8,000 = $18,000/48.			
31	Unearned Consulting Revenue		250	
	Consulting Revenue			250
	To record earned revenue received in advance; $1,500 × 5/30.			
31	Salaries Expense		210	
	Salaries Payable			210
	To record three days' accrued salary; 3 × $70.			
31	Interest Expense		32	
	Interest Payable			32
	To record one month of accrued interest.			
31	Accounts Receivable		1,800	
	Consulting Revenue			1,800
	To record 20 days of accrued revenue; $2,700 × 20/30.			

Answers—p. 158

5. If you omit an adjusting entry for accrued service revenues of $200 at year-end, what is the effect of this error on the income statement and balance sheet?
6. Explain what a contra account is.
7. What is an accrued expense? Give an example.
8. Describe how an unearned revenue arises. Give an example.

[5] Adjusting entries related to bank reconciliations affect cash but these adjustments are excluded from the framework in Exhibit 4.20 and will be discussed in Chapter 9.

Mid-Chapter Demonstration Problem

The owner of a lawn service company prepares ***monthly*** financial statements. The following information is available at the end of July. Prepare the appropriate adjusting entries for July 31.

a. The annual insurance amounting to $1,200 went into effect on July 1. The prepaid insurance account was debited and cash credited on the same date.

b. The lawn service company's lawn tractor was purchased for $3,200 last year. The value of the lawn tractor at the end of its estimated four-year useful life was determined to be $800. This information was made available to record amortization for July.

c. A customer paid for the entire summer's service in April. The journal entry credited the Unearned Service Fees account when the payment was received. The monthly fee is $500.

d. The last weekly salary of $1,400 was paid to employees on Friday, July 27. Employees are paid based on a five-day workweek. Salaries for July 30 and 31 have accrued.

e. Revenues of $1,800 were earned by July 31 but not recorded.

SOLUTION TO Mid-Chapter Demonstration Problem

		Debit	Credit
a.	Insurance Expense	100	
	Prepaid Insurance		100
	To record insurance for July.		
b.	Amortization Expense, Lawn Tractor	50	
	Accumulated Amortization, Lawn Tractor		50
	Amortization for July, calculated as $3,200 – $800 = $2,400/48 months = $50/month.		
c.	Unearned Service Fees	500	
	Service Fees Earned		500
	To record service fees earned for July.		
d.	Salaries Expense	560	
	Salaries Payable		560
	To record salaries for the last two days of July, calculated as $1,400/5 = $280/day × 2 days = $560		
e.	Accounts Receivable	1,800	
	Service Revenue		1,800
	To record accrued service revenue for July.		

Adjusted Trial Balance

Explain and prepare an adjusted trial balance.

An **unadjusted trial balance** is a listing of accounts and balances prepared *before* adjustments are recorded. An **adjusted trial balance** is a list of accounts and balances prepared *after* adjusting entries are recorded and posted to the ledger. Exhibit 4.22 shows the unadjusted and adjusted trial balances for Finlay Interiors at January 31, 2001. Notice several new accounts arising from the adjusting entries. The listing of accounts is also slightly changed to match the order listed in the Chart of Accounts in Appendix III at the end of the book.

We show in the next chapter how to prepare an adjusted trial balance and financial statements from a *work sheet*. To focus on the important aspects of the adjusting process in this chapter, we did not introduce the work sheet format. Yet some users prefer this format in introducing the adjusted trial balance, and we present it in Exhibit 4.22.

Exhibit 4.22

Unadjusted and Adjusted Trial Balances for Finlay Interiors

Finlay Interiors
Trial Balances
January 31, 2001

	Unadjusted Trial Balance		Adjustments		Adjusted Trial Balance	
	Dr.	**Cr.**	**Dr.**	**Cr.**	**Dr.**	**Cr.**
Cash	$ 8,070				$ 8,070	
Accounts receivable			(g)1,800		1,800	
Supplies	3,600			(b)1,050	2,550	
Prepaid insurance	2,400			(a) 100	2,300	
Furniture	26,000				26,000	
Accumulated amortization, furniture				(c) 375		$ 375
Accounts payable		$ 200				200
Interest payable				(f) 32		32
Salaries payable				(e) 210		210
Unearned consulting revenue		3,000	(d) 250			2,750
Notes payable		6,000				6,000
Carol Finlay, capital		30,000				30,000
Carol Finlay, withdrawals	600				600	
Consulting revenue		3,800		(d) 250 (g)1,800		5,850
Rental revenue		300				300
Amortization expense, furniture			(c) 375		375	
Salaries expense	1,400		(e) 210		1,610	
Interest expense			(f) 32		32	
Insurance expense			(a) 100		100	
Rent expense	1,000				1,000	
Supplies expense			(b)1,050		1,050	
Utilities expense	230				230	
Totals	$43,300	$43,300	$3,817	$3,817	$45,717	$45,717

Preparing Financial Statements

 Prepare financial statements from an adjusted trial balance.

We can prepare financial statements directly from information in the *adjusted* trial balance. An adjusted trial balance includes all balances appearing in financial statements. We know that a trial balance summarizes information in the ledger by listing accounts and their balances. This summary is easier to work from than the entire ledger when preparing financial statements.

Exhibit 4.23 shows how Finlay Interiors' revenue and expense balances are transferred from the adjusted trial balance to the (1) income statement, and (2) statement of owner's equity. Note how we use the net income and withdrawals account to prepare the statement of owner's equity.

Exhibit 4.24 shows how Finlay Interiors' asset and liability balances on the adjusted trial balance are transferred to the balance sheet. The ending owner's equity is determined on the statement of owner's equity and transferred to the balance sheet. There are different formats for the balance sheet. The **account form**, used in previous chapters, lists assets on the left and liabilities and owner's equity on the right side of the balance sheet. Its name comes from its link to the accounting equation, *Assets = Liabilities + Equity.* The balance sheet in Exhibit 2.11 (on P. 52) is in account form. The **report form** balance sheet lists items vertically as shown in Exhibit 4.24. Both forms are widely used and are considered equally helpful to users. For consistency, we will use the report form in the preparation of financial statements from this point forward.

We usually prepare financial statements in the order shown: income statement, statement of owner's equity, and balance sheet. This order makes sense since the balance sheet uses information from the statement of owner's equity, which in turn uses information from the income statement.

Exhibit 4.23

Preparing the Income Statement and Statement of Owner's Equity from the Adjusted Trial Balance

Finlay Interiors
Adjusted Trial Balance
January 31, 2001

Acct. No.	Account Title	Debit	Credit
101	Cash	$ 8,070	
106	Accounts receivable	1,800	
125	Supplies	2,550	
128	Prepaid insurance	2,300	
167	Furniture	26,000	
168	Accumulated amortization, furniture		$ 375
201	Accounts payable		200
203	Interest payable		32
209	Salaries payable		210
236	Unearned consulting revenue		2,750
240	Notes payable		6,000
301	Carol Finlay, capital		30,000*
302	Carol Finlay, withdrawals	600	
403	Consulting revenue		5,850
406	Rental revenue		300
614	Amortization expense, furniture	375	
622	Salaries expense	1,610	
633	Interest expense	32	
637	Insurance expense	100	
641	Rent expense	1,000	
651	Supplies expense	1,050	
690	Utilities expense	230	
	Totals	$45,717	$45,717

*Recall that this balance is the result of a $30,000 investment by Carol Finlay during January 2001.

Step One Prepare income statement

Finlay Interiors
Income Statement
For Month Ended January 31, 2001

Revenues:		
Consulting revenue	$5,850	
Rental revenue	300	
Total revenues		$6,150
Operating expenses:		
Amortization expense, furniture	$ 375	
Salaries expense	1,610	
Interest expense	32	
Insurance expense	100	
Rent expense	1,000	
Supplies expense	1,050	
Utilities expense	230	
Total operating expenses		4,397
Net income		$1,753

Step Two Prepare statement of owner's equity

Finlay Interiors
Statement of Owner's Equity
For Month Ended January 31, 2001

Carol Finlay, capital, January 1		$ -0-
Add: Investments by owner	$30,000	
Net income	1,753	31,753
Total		$31,753
Less: Withdrawal by owner		600
Carol Finlay, capital, January 31		$31,153

Exhibit 4.24

Preparing the Balance Sheet from the Adjusted Trial Balance

Finlay Interiors
Adjusted Trial Balance
January 31, 2001

Acct. No.	Account Title	Debit	Credit
101	Cash	$ 8,070	
106	Accounts receivable	1,800	
125	Supplies	2,550	
128	Prepaid insurance	2,300	
167	Furniture	26,000	
168	Accumulated amortization, furniture		$ 375
201	Accounts payable		200
203	Interest payable		32
209	Salaries payable		210
236	Unearned consulting revenue		2,750
240	Notes payable		6,000
301	Carol Finlay, capital		30,000
302	Carol Finlay, withdrawals	600	
403	Consulting revenue		5,850
406	Rental revenue		300
614	Amortization expense, furniture	375	
622	Salaries expense	1,610	
633	Interest expense	32	
637	Insurance expense	100	
641	Rent expense	1,000	
651	Supplies expense	1,050	
690	Utilities expense	230	
	Totals	$45,717	$45,717

Step Three Prepare balance sheet

Finlay Interiors
Balance Sheet
January 31, 2001

Assets		
Cash		$ 8,070
Accounts receivable		1,800
Supplies		2,550
Prepaid insurance		2,300
Furniture	$ 26,000	
Less: Accumulated amortization	375	25,625
Total assets		$ 40,345
Liabilities		
Accounts payable	$ 200	
Interest payable	32	
Salaries payable	210	
Unearned consulting revenue	2,750	
Notes payable	6,000	
Total liabilities		$ 9,192
Owner's Equity		
Carol Finlay, capital		$ 31,153
Total liabilities and owner's equity		$ 40,345

From statement of owner's equity in Exhibit 4.23

Answers—p. 158

9. Jordan Air Company has the following information in its unadjusted and adjusted trial balances:

	Unadjusted Debit	Unadjusted Credit	Adjusted Debit	Adjusted Credit
Prepaid insurance	$6,200		$5,900	
Salaries payable		$ -0-		$1,400

What are the adjusting entries that Jordan Air likely recorded?

10. What types of accounts are taken from the adjusted trial balance to prepare an income statement?

11. In preparing financial statements from an adjusted trial balance, what statement is usually prepared second?

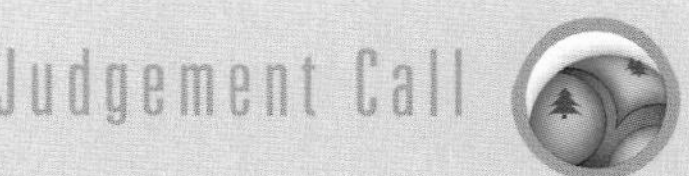

Financial Officer

You are the financial officer for a retail outlet company. At the calendar year-end when you are reviewing adjusting entries to record accruals, you are called into the president's office. The president asks about accrued expenses and instructs you not to record these expenses until next year because they will not be paid until January or later. The president also asks how much the current year's revenues increased because of the recent purchase order from a new customer. You state that there is no effect on sales until next year because the purchase order says merchandise is to be delivered after January 15 and that is when your company plans to make delivery. The president points out that the order is already received, and your company is ready to make delivery, and tells you to record this sale in the current year. Your company would report a net income instead of a net loss if you carried out the president's orders for adjusting accruals. What do you do?

Answer—p. 157

Accrual Adjustments in Later Periods

Prepare and describe accrual adjustments in later periods.

Accrued revenues at the end of one accounting period often result in cash *receipts* from customers in the next period. Also, accrued expenses at the end of one accounting period often result in cash *payments* in the next period. This section explains how we account for these cash receipts or payments in these later periods.

Paying Accrued Expenses

Finlay Interiors recorded three days of accrued salaries for its employee with this adjusting entry:

Jan. 31	Salaries Expense	210	
	Salaries Payable		210
	To record three days' accrued salary; 3 × $70.		

When the first payday of the next bi-weekly period occurs on Friday, February 9, the following entry settles the accrued liability (salaries payable) and records added salaries expense for work in February:

Feb. 9	Salaries Payable (3 days at $70)	210	
	Salaries Expense (7 days at $70)	490	
	Cash		700
	Paid two weeks salary including three days accrued in January.		

The first debit in the February 9 entry records the payment of the liability for the three days' salary accrued on January 31. The second debit records the salary for February's first seven working days as an expense of the new accounting period. The credit records the total amount of cash paid to the employee.

Receiving Accrued Revenues

Finlay Interiors made the following adjusting entry to record 20 days' accrued revenue earned from its consulting contract with a client:

Jan. 31	Accounts Receivable	1,800	
	Consulting Revenue		1,800
	To record 20 days' accrued revenue.		

When the first month's fee is received on February 10, Finlay Interiors makes the following entry to remove the accrued asset (accounts receivable) and recognize the added revenue earned in February:

Feb. 10	Cash	2,700	
	Accounts Receivable		1,800
	Consulting Revenue		900
	Received cash for accrued asset, and earned consulting revenue.		

The debit reflects the cash received. The first credit reflects the removal of the receivable, and the second credit records the earned revenue.

Answer—p. 158

12. Music-Mart records $1,000 of accrued salaries on December 31. Five days later on January 5 (the next payday), salaries of $7,000 are paid. What is the January 5 entry?

Summary

LO1 Describe the purpose of adjusting accounts at the end of a period. After external transactions are recorded, several accounts in the ledger often need adjusting for their balances to appear correctly in financial statements. This need arises because internal transactions and events remain unrecorded. The purpose of adjusting accounts at the end of a period is to recognize unrecorded revenues and expenses.

LO2 Explain the importance of periodic reporting and the time period principle. The value of information is often linked to its timeliness. Useful information must reach decision makers frequently and promptly. To provide timely information, accounting systems prepare periodic reports at regular intervals. The time period principle assumes that an organization's activities can be divided into specific time periods such as a month, a three-month quarter, or a year for periodic reporting.

LO3 Explain accrual accounting and how it adds to the usefulness of financial statements. Accrual accounting recognizes revenue when earned and expenses when incurred. Accrual accounting reports the economic effects of events when they occur, not necessarily when cash inflows and outflows occur. This information is viewed as valuable in assessing a company's financial position and performance.

LO4 Identify the types of adjustments and their purpose. Adjustments can be grouped according to their timing of cash receipts or payments relative to when they are recognized as revenues or expenses. There are two major groups, prepaids/unearned and accruals. Both of these can be subdivided into expenses and revenues. Adjusting entries are necessary for each of these groups so that revenues, expenses, assets and liabilities are correctly reported for each period.

LO5 Prepare and explain adjusting entries for prepaid expenses, amortization and unearned revenues. Prepaid expenses, an asset, refer to items paid for in advance of receiving their benefits. As this asset is used, its cost becomes an expense. Amortization is the expense created by spreading the cost of capital assets over the periods these assets are used. Accumulated Amortization, a contra asset account, is credited to track the total amount of the capital asset used. Unearned (or prepaid) revenues, a liability, refer to cash received in advance of providing products and services. As products and services are provided, the amount of unearned revenues becomes earned revenues. The adjustments for prepaids, amortization and unearned revenues are:

Type	Adjusting Entry
Prepaid Expense	Dr. Expense Cr. Prepaid
Amortization	Dr. Amortization Expense Cr. Accumulated Amortization
Unearned Revenues	Dr. Unearned Revenue Cr. Revenue

LO6 Prepare and describe adjusting entries for accrued expenses and accrued revenues. Accrued expenses, part of expenses reported on the income statement, refer to costs incurred in a period that are both unpaid and unrecorded. Accrued revenues, part of revenues reported on the income statement, refer to revenues earned in a period that are both unrecorded and not yet received in cash. The adjustments for accrued expenses and accrued revenues are:

Type	Adjusting Entry
Accrued Expenses	Dr. Expense Cr. Liability
Accrued Revenues	Dr. Accounts Receivable (or other type of receivable) Cr. Revenue

LO7 Explain how accounting adjustments link to financial statements. Accounting adjustments bring an asset or liability account balance to its correct amount. They also update related expense or revenue accounts. Every adjusting entry affects one or more income statement accounts and one or more balance sheet accounts. An adjusting entry never affects cash. Adjustments are necessary for transactions and events that extend over more than one period. Exhibit 4.20 summarizes financial statement links by type of adjustment.

LO8 Explain and prepare an adjusted trial balance. An adjusted trial balance is a list of accounts and balances prepared after adjusting entries are recorded and posted to the ledger. Financial statements are often prepared from the adjusted trial balance.

LO9 Prepare financial statements from an adjusted trial balance. We can prepare financial statements directly from the adjusted trial balance that includes all account balances. Revenue and expense balances are transferred to the income statement and statement of owner's equity. Asset, liability and owner's equity balances are transferred to the balance sheet. We usually prepare statements in the following order: income statement, statement of owner's equity, and balance sheet.

LO10 Prepare and describe accrual adjustments in later periods. Accrued revenues at the end of one accounting period usually result in cash receipts from customers in later periods. Accrued expenses at the end of one accounting period usually result in cash payments in later periods. When cash is received or paid in these later periods, the entries must account for the accrued assets or liabilities initially recorded.

GUIDANCE ANSWERS TO Judgement Call

Small Business Owner

We know amortization is a process of cost allocation, not asset valuation. Knowing the amortization schedule of the restaurant is not especially useful in your estimation of what the restaurant's building and equipment are currently worth. Your assessment of the age, quality and usefulness of the building and equipment is much more important. Also, you would use the current market values of similar assets in estimating the value of this restaurant's building and equipment.

Financial Officer

It appears you must make a choice between following the president's orders or not. The requirements of acceptable practice are clear. Omitting adjustments and early recognition of revenue can mislead users of financial statements (including managers, owners and lenders). One action is to request a second meeting with the president where you explain that accruing expenses and recognizing revenue when earned are required practices. You should also mention the ethical implications of not complying with accepted practice. Point out that the president's orders involve intentional falsification of the statements. If the president persists, you might discuss the situation with legal counsel and any auditors involved. Your ethical action might cost you this job. But the potential pitfalls of falsification of statements, reputation loss, personal integrity, and other costs are too great.

GUIDANCE ANSWERS TO 

1. An annual reporting (or accounting) period covers one year and refers to the preparation of annual financial statements. The annual reporting period can follow the calendar year or a fiscal year. The fiscal year can follow the business's natural business year.
2. Interim (less than one year) financial statements are prepared to provide decision makers with information frequently and promptly.
3. The revenue recognition principle, time period principle and the matching principle lead most directly to the adjusting process.
4. No. Cash basis accounting is not consistent with generally accepted accounting principles.
5. If the accrued services revenue adjustment of $200 is not made, then both revenue and net income are understated by $200 on the current year's income statement. Assets and equity are also understated on the balance sheet.
6. A contra account is an account that is subtracted from the balance of a related account. Use of a contra account often provides more complete information than simply reporting a net amount.
7. An accrued expense refers to costs incurred in a period that are both unpaid and unrecorded prior to adjusting entries. One example is salaries earned by employees but not yet paid at the end of a period.
8. An unearned revenue arises when cash (or other assets) is received from a customer before the services and products are delivered to the customer. Magazine subscription receipts in advance are one example.
9. The probable adjusting entries of Jordan Air are:

	Debit	Credit
Insurance Expense	300	
Prepaid Insurance		300
To record insurance expired.		

	Debit	Credit
Salaries Expense	1,400	
Salaries Payable		1,400
To record accrued salaries.		

10. Revenue accounts and expense accounts.
11. Statement of owner's equity is usually prepared second.
12. The January 5 entry to settle the accrued salaries and pay for added salaries is:

		Debit	Credit
Jan. 5	Salaries Payable	1,000	
	Salaries Expense	6,000	
	Cash		7,000
	Paid salary including accrual from December.		

Demonstration Problem

The following information continues with The Cutlery, featured in the Chapter 3 Demonstration Problem. After the first month of business, The Cutlery's August 31, 2001 unadjusted trial balance appeared as follows:

THE CUTLERY
Trial Balance
August 31, 2001

Account	Debit	Credit
Cash	$ 2,230	
Accounts receivable	-0-	
Prepaid insurance	600	
Furniture	600	
Store equipment	16,200	
Accounts payable		$ 875
Unearned haircutting services revenue		500
Barbara Schmidt, capital		18,000
Barbara Schmidt, withdrawals	900	
Haircutting services revenue		1,855
Rent expense	500	
Wages expense	125	
Hydro expense	75	
Totals	$21,230	$21,230

The following additional information is available for the month just ended:

a. Amortization of $50 per month will be taken on the furniture.

b. It is estimated that the store equipment will have no value at the end of its estimated five-year (or 60-month) useful life. Barbara Schmidt will record a full month of amortization for August.

c. It was determined that the balance in unearned revenue at August 31 was $420.

d. The prepaid insurance represents six months of insurance beginning August 1.

e. Accrued revenues at August 31 totalled $65.

Required

1. Prepare the adjusting entries needed on August 31 2001 to record the previously unrecorded effects of the events.
2. Prepare T-accounts for accounts affected by the adjusting entries. Post the adjusting entries to the T-accounts.
3. Complete the following table describing the effects of your adjusting entries on the 2001 income statement and the August 31, 2001 balance sheet. Use arrows to indicate an increase ↑ or decrease ↓.

Entry	Amount in the Entry	Effect on Net Income	Effect on Total Assets	Effect on Total Liabilities	Effect on Owner's Equity
a					
b					
c					
d					
e					

4. Prepare an adjusted trial balance.
5. Prepare an income statement, statement of owner's equity, and a balance sheet.

Planning the Solution

- Analyze the information for each situation to determine which accounts need to be updated with an adjustment.
- Calculate the size of each adjustment and prepare the necessary journal entries.
- Show the amount entered by each adjustment in the designated accounts and determine the adjusted balance.
- Determine each entry's effect on net income for the year and on total assets, total liabilities, and owner's equity at the end of the year.
- Using the adjusted balances, prepare an adjusted trial balance.
- Using the adjusted trial balance, prepare the income statement, statement of owner's equity, and balance sheet.

SOLUTION TO Demonstration Problem

1. Adjusting journal entries.

a. Aug. 31	Amortization Expense, Furniture	50	
	Accumulated Amortization, Furniture		50
	To record amortization expense for the month of August for the furniture.		
b. 31	Amortization Expense, Store Equipment	270	
	Accumulated Amortization, Store Equipment		270
	To record amortization expense for the month; $16,200/60 months = $270/month.		
c. 31	Unearned Haircutting Services Revenue	80	
	Haircutting Services Revenue		80
	To recognize haircutting services revenues earned; $500 − $420 = $80.		
d. 31	Insurance Expense	100	
	Prepaid Insurance		100
	To adjust for the expired portion of prepaid insurance; $600/6 months = $100/month.		
e. 31	Accounts Receivable	65	
	Haircutting Services Revenue		65
	To record revenues earned.		

2.

Amortization Expense, Furniture

(a)	50		

Amortization Expense, Store Equipment

(b)	270		

Unearned Haircutting Services Revenue

(c)	80	Balance	500
		Balance	420

Insurance Expense

(d)	100		

Accounts Receivable

(e)	65		

Accumulated Amortization, Furniture

		(a)	50

Accumulated Amortization, Store Equipment

		(b)	270

Haircutting Services Revenue

		Balance	1,855
		(c)	80
		(e)	65
		Balance	2,000

Prepaid Insurance

Balance	600	(d)	100
Balance	500		

3.

Entry	Amount in the Entry	Effect on Net Income	Effect on Total Assets	Effect on Total Liabilities	Effect on Owner's Equity
a	$50	$50 ↓	$50 ↓	No effect	$50 ↓
b	$270	$270 ↓	$270 ↓	No effect	$270 ↓
c	$80	$80 ↑	No effect	$80 ↓	$80 ↑
d	$100	$100 ↓	$100 ↓	No effect	$100 ↓
e	$65	$65 ↑	$65 ↑	No effect	$65 ↑

4.

THE CUTLERY
Adjusted Trial Balance
August 31, 2001

Account	Debit	Credit
Cash	$ 2,230	
Accounts receivable	65	
Prepaid insurance	500	
Furniture	600	
Accumulated amortization, furniture		$ 50
Store equipment	16,200	
Accumulated amortization, store equipment		270
Accounts payable		875
Unearned haircutting services revenue		420
Barbara Schmidt, capital		18,000
Barbara Schmidt, withdrawals	900	
Haircutting services revenue		2,000
Amortization expense, furniture	50	
Amortization expense, store equipment	270	
Insurance expense	100	
Rent expense	500	
Wages expense	125	
Hydro expense	75	
Totals	$21,615	$21,615

5.

THE CUTLERY
Income Statement
For Month Ended August 31, 2001

Revenues:		
Haircutting services revenue		$2,000
Operating expenses:		
Amortization expense, furniture	$ 50	
Amortization expense, store equipment	270	
Insurance expense	100	
Rent expense	500	
Salaries expense	125	
Hydro expense	75	
Total operating expenses		1,120
Net income		$ 880

THE CUTLERY
Statement of Owner's Equity
For Month Ended August 31, 2001

Barbara Schmidt, capital, August 1		$ -0-
Add: Investment by owner	$18,000	
Net income	880	18,880
Total		$18,880
Less: Withdrawal by owner		900
Barbara Schmidt, capital, August 31		$17,980

THE CUTLERY
Balance Sheet
August 31, 2001

Assets

Cash		$ 2,230
Accounts receivable		65
Prepaid insurance		500
Furniture	$ 600	
Less: Accumulated amortization	50	550
Store equipment	$16,200	
Less: Accumulated amortization	270	15,930
Total assets		$19,275

Liabilities

Accounts payable	$ 875	
Unearned haircutting services revenue	420	
Total liabilities		$ 1,295

Owner's Equity

Barbara Schmidt, capital		$17,980
Total liabilities and owner's equity		$19,275

Alternatives in Accounting for Prepaids and Unearned Revenues

APPENDIX

This section explains two alternatives in accounting for prepaid expenses and unearned revenues. We show the accounting for both alternatives.

LO11 Identify and explain two alternatives in accounting for prepaids and unearned revenues.

Recording Prepaid Expenses in Expense Accounts

We explained that prepaid expenses are assets when they are purchased and are recorded with debits to asset accounts. Adjusting entries transfer the costs that expire to expense accounts at the end of an accounting period.

There is an acceptable alternative practice of recording *all* prepaid expenses with debits to expense accounts. If any prepaids remain unused or unexpired at the end of an accounting period, then adjusting entries must transfer the cost of the unused portions from expense accounts to prepaid expense (asset) accounts. The financial statements are identical under either procedure, but the adjusting entries are different.

To illustrate the accounting differences between these two practices, let's look at Finlay Interiors' cash payment for 24 months of insurance coverage beginning on January 1. Finlay Interiors recorded that payment with a debit to an asset account, but it could have been recorded as a debit to an expense account. These alternatives are:

Exhibit 4A.1 Initial Entry for Prepaid Expenses for Two Alternatives

		Payment Recorded as Asset		Payment Recorded as Expense	
Jan. 1	Prepaid Insurance	2,400			
	Cash		2,400		
1	Insurance Expense			2,400	
	Cash				2,400

On January 31, insurance protection for one month is used up. This means $100 ($2,400/24) of the asset expires and becomes an expense for January. The adjusting entry depends on how the original payment is recorded:

Exhibit 4A.2 Adjusting Entry for Prepaid Expenses for Two Alternatives

		Payment Recorded as Asset		Payment Recorded as Expense	
Jan. 31	Insurance Expense	100			
	Prepaid Insurance		100		
31	Prepaid Insurance			2,300	
	Insurance Expense				2,300

When these entries are posted to the accounts, we can see that these two alternative practices give identical results. The January 31 adjusted account balances show prepaid insurance of $2,300 and insurance expense of $100 for both methods.

Exhibit 4A.3

Account Balances Under Two Alternatives for Recording Prepaid Expenses

Payment Recorded as Asset

Prepaid Insurance			
Jan. 1	2,400 −100	Jan. 31	100
Balance	2,300		

Insurance Expense			
Jan. 31	100		

Payment Recorded as Expense

Prepaid Insurance			
Jan. 31	2,300		

Insurance Expense			
Jan. 1	2,400 −2,300	Jan. 31	2,300
Balance	100		

Recording Unearned Revenues in Revenue Accounts

Unearned revenues are liabilities requiring delivery of products and services. We explained how unearned revenues are recorded as credits to liability accounts when cash and other assets are received. Adjusting entries at the end of an accounting period transfer to revenue accounts the earned portion of unearned revenues.

An acceptable alternative is to record *all* unearned revenues with credits to revenue accounts. If any revenues are unearned at the end of an accounting period, then adjusting entries must transfer the unearned portions from revenue accounts to unearned revenue (liability) accounts. While the adjusting entries are different for these two alternatives, the financial statements are identical.

To illustrate the accounting differences between these two practices, let's look at Finlay Interiors' January 26 receipt of $3,000 for consulting services covering the period January 27 to March 27. Finlay Interiors recorded this transaction with a credit to a liability account. The alternative is to record it with a credit to a revenue account as follows:

Exhibit 4A.4

Initial Entry for Unearned Revenues for Two Alternatives

		Receipt Recorded as Liability		Receipt Recorded as Revenue	
Jan. 26	Cash	3,000			
	Unearned Consulting Revenue		3,000		
26	Cash			3,000	
	Consulting Revenue				3,000

By the end of the accounting period (January 31), Finlay Interiors earns $250 of this revenue. This means that $250 of the liability is satisfied. Depending on how the initial receipt is recorded, the adjusting entry is:

Exhibit 4A.5

Adjusting Entry for Unearned Revenues for Two Alternatives

		Receipt Recorded as Liability		Receipt Recorded as Revenue	
Jan. 31	Unearned Consulting Revenue	250			
	Consulting Revenue		250		
31	Consulting Revenue			2,750	
	Unearned Consulting Revenue				2,750

After adjusting entries are posted, the two alternatives give identical results. The January 31 adjusted account balances show unearned consulting revenue of $2,750 and consulting revenue of $250 for both methods.

Exhibit 4A.6

Account Balances Under Two Alternatives for Recording Unearned Revenues

Receipt Recorded as Liability

Unearned Consulting Revenue			
Jan. 31	250	Jan. 26	3,000 −250
		Balance	2,750

Consulting Revenue			
		Jan. 31	250

Receipt Recorded as Revenue

Unearned Consulting Revenue			
		Jan. 31	2,750

Consulting Revenue			
Jan. 31	2,750	Jan. 26	3,000 −2,750
		Balance	250

13. Miller Company records cash receipts of unearned revenues and cash payments of prepaid expenses in balance sheet accounts. Bud Company records these items in income statement accounts. Explain any difference in the financial statements of these two companies from their alternative accounting for prepaids.

Answer—p. 165

Summary of Appendix 4A

LO11 Identify and explain two alternatives in accounting for prepaids and unearned revenues. It is acceptable to charge all prepaid expenses to expense accounts when they are purchased. When this is done, adjusting entries must transfer any unexpired amounts from expense accounts to asset accounts. It is also acceptable to credit all unearned revenues to revenue accounts when cash is received. In this case the adjusting entries must transfer any unearned amounts from revenue accounts to unearned revenue accounts.

GUIDANCE ANSWER TO 

13. When adjusting entries are correctly prepared, the financial statements of these companies will be identical under both methods.

Glossary

Account form balance sheet A balance sheet that lists assets on the left and liabilities and owner's equity on the right side of the balance sheet. (p. 153)

Accounting period The length of time covered by financial statements and other reports; also called *reporting periods.* (p. 139)

Accrual basis accounting The approach to preparing financial statements that uses the adjusting process to recognize revenues when earned and expenses when incurred, not when cash is paid or received; the basis for generally accepted accounting principles. (p. 140)

Accrued expenses Costs incurred in a period that are both unpaid and unrecorded; adjusting entries for recording accrued expenses involve increasing (debiting) expenses and increasing (crediting) liabilities. (p. 146)

Accrued revenues Revenues earned in a period that are both unrecorded and not yet received in cash (or other assets); adjusting entries for recording accrued revenues involve increasing (debiting) assets and increasing (crediting) revenues. (p. 148)

Adjusted trial balance A listing of accounts and balances prepared after adjustments are recorded and posted to the ledger. (p. 152)

Adjusting entry A journal entry at the end of an accounting period to bring an asset or liability account balance to its proper amount while also updating the related expense or revenue account. (p. 140)

Amortization The expense created by allocating the cost of plant and equipment to the periods in which they are used; represents the expense of using the assets. (p. 143)

Book value of an asset The cost of the asset less its accumulated amortization. (p. 144)

Capital assets Include long-term tangible assets, such as plant and equipment, and intangible assets, such as patents. Capital assets are expected to provide benefits for more than one period. (p. 143)

Cash basis accounting Revenues are recognized when cash is received, and expenses are recorded when cash is paid. (p. 140)

Contra account An account linked with another account and having an opposite normal balance; reported as a subtraction from the other account's balance so that more complete information than simply the net amount is provided. (p. 144)

Depreciation See *amortization.* (p. 143)

Intangible assets Long-lived (capital) assets that have no physical substance but convey a right to use a product or process. (p. 143)

Interim financial reports Financial reports covering less than one year; usually based on one-, three- or six-month periods. (p. 139)

Market value of an asset The amount that an asset can be sold for. Market value is not tied to the book value of an asset. (p. 144)

Matching principle The broad principle that requires expenses to be reported in the same period as the revenues that were earned as a result of the expenses. (p. 140)

Plant and equipment Tangible long-lived assets used to produce goods or services. See *capital assets.* (p. 143)

Prepaid expenses Items that are paid for in advance of receiving their benefits. These are assets. (p. 141)

Report form balance sheet A balance sheet that lists items vertically with assets above the liabilities and owner's equity. (p. 153)

Reporting period See *accounting period.*

Straight-line amortization method Allocates equal amounts of an asset's cost to amortization expense during its useful life. (p. 143)

Time period principle A broad principle that assumes that an organization's activities can be divided into specific time periods such as months, quarters, or years. (p. 139)

Unadjusted trial balance A listing of accounts and balances prepared before adjustments are recorded and posted to the ledger. (p. 152)

Unearned revenues Cash received in advance of providing products and services. (p. 145)

Questions

1. What type of business is most likely to select a fiscal year that corresponds to the natural business year instead of the calendar year?
2. What kind of assets require adjusting entries to record amortization?
3. What contra account is used when recording and reporting the effects of amortization? Why is it used?
4. Where is an unearned revenue reported in the financial statements?
5. What is an accrued revenue? Give an example.
6. What is the difference between the cash and accrual bases of accounting?
7. Where is a prepaid expense reported in the financial statements?
8. Why is the accrual basis of accounting preferred over the cash basis?

9. If a company initially records prepaid expenses with debits to expense accounts, what type of account is debited in the adjusting entries for prepaid expenses?

10. Review the consolidated balance sheet of ClubLink Corporation in Appendix I. Identify two asset accounts that require adjustment before annual financial statements can be prepared. What would be the effect on the income statement if these two asset accounts were not adjusted?

11. Review the income statement of WestJet in Appendix I. How much amortization was recorded in the adjusting entry for amortization at the end of 1999?

Quick Study

QS 4-1
Accrual and cash accounting
LO3

In its first year of operations, Harris Co. earned $39,000 in revenues and received $33,000 cash from customers. The company incurred expenses of $22,500, but had not paid for $2,250 of them at year-end. In addition, Harris prepaid $3,750 for expenses that would be incurred the next year. Calculate the first year's net income under a cash basis and calculate the first year's net income under an accrual basis.

QS 4-2
Preparing adjusting entries
LO4

In recording its transactions during the year, Stark Company records prepayments of expenses in asset accounts and receipts of unearned revenues in liability accounts. At the end of its annual accounting period, the company must make three adjusting entries. They are: (a) to accrue salaries expense, (b) to adjust the Unearned Services Revenue account to recognize earned revenue, and (c) to record the earning of services revenue for which cash will be received the following period. For each of these adjusting entries, use the numbers assigned to the following accounts to indicate the correct account to be debited and the correct account to be credited.

1. Prepaid Salaries Expense
2. Cash
3. Salaries Payable
4. Accounts Receivable
5. Salaries Expense
6. Services Revenue Earned
7. Unearned Services Revenue

QS 4-3
Identifying accounting adjustments
LO4

Classify the following adjusting entries as involving prepaid expenses (P), amortization (A), unearned revenues (U), accrued expenses (E), or accrued revenues (R).

____ a. Entry to record annual amortization expense.
____ b. Entry to show wages earned but not yet paid.
____ c. Entry to show revenue earned but not yet billed.
____ d. Entry to show expiration of prepaid insurance.
____ e. Entry to show revenue earned that was previously received as cash in advance.

QS 4-4
Preparing adjusting entries – prepaid expense
LO5

Fargo's Detective Agency purchased a two-year insurance policy on April 1, 2001, paying cash of $7,680. Its year-end is December 31. Record the following:

a. Journal entry on April 1, 2001.
b. Adjusting entry on December 31, 2001.
c. Adjusting entry on December 31, 2002.
d. How much of the insurance policy purchased on April 1, 2001 was actually used during the year 2003?

QS 4-5
Preparing adjusting journal entries – amortization expense
LO5

Softrock Minerals purchased a vehicle on March 1, 2001 for cash of $32,000. It will be used by the president for four years and then sold for about $8,000. Softrock's year-end is December 31. Record the adjusting entry required at the end of 2001 and 2002.

QS 4-6
Preparing adjusting journal entries – unearned revenues

LO 5

On November 1, 2001, Fastfoot Industries collected $12,000 from a customer for services to be provided in the future. On December 31, 2001, Fastfoot's year-end, it was determined that $3,000 of this amount remained unearned. Prepare the entries for November 1 and December 31.

QS 4-7
Interpreting adjusting entries

LO 5, 6

The following information has been taken from Shank Company's unadjusted and adjusted trial balances at October 31, 2001.

	Unadjusted		Adjusted	
	Debit	Credit	Debit	Credit
Prepaid insurance	$3,100		$2,350	
Interest payable		$ -0-		$ 150
Insurance expense		-0-	750	
Interest expense		-0-	150	

Given this trial balance information, prepare the adjusting journal entries.

QS 4-8
Preparing adjusting entries – accrued expenses

LO 6, 10

On October 31, 2001, Offsite Data Services recorded three days of unpaid salaries of $46,800. The total salaries of $78,000 for the five-day workweek will be paid on November 2, 2001. Prepare the entries for October 31 and November 2.

QS 4-9
Preparing adjusting journal entries – accrued revenues

LO 6,10

TigrSoft recorded unbilled and uncollected revenues of $17,000 on March 31, 2001. On April 16, $12,000 of these were collected. Prepare the entries for March 31 and April 16.

QS 4-10
Recording and analyzing adjusting entries

LO 7

Adjusting entries affect one balance sheet account and one income statement account. For the entries listed below, identify the account to be debited and the account to be credited. Indicate which of the two accounts is the income statement account and which is the balance sheet account.

a. Entry to record annual amortization expense.
b. Entry to show wages earned but not yet paid.
c. Entry to show revenue earned that was previously received as cash in advance.
d. Entry to show expiration of prepaid insurance.
e. Entry to show revenue earned but not yet billed.

***QS 4-11**
Recording prepaids and unearned events as expenses and revenues

LO 11

Foster Company initially records prepaid and unearned items in income statement accounts. Given Foster Company's practices, what is the appropriate adjusting entry for each of the following at November 30, 2001, the end of the company's first accounting period?

a. There are unpaid salaries of $3,000.
b. Unused office supplies of $800 were counted at year-end. There was no beginning balance in office supplies.
c. Earned but unbilled consulting fees of $2,300 were discovered.
d. It was determined that there were unearned fees of $4,200.

* The asterisk refers to the topic having been discussed in the appendix to this chapter.

Exercises

Exercise 4-1
Identifying adjusting entries

LO4

In the blank space beside each of these adjusting entries, enter the letter of the explanation that most closely describes the entry:

a. To record the year's amortization expense.
b. To record accrued salaries expense.
c. To record the year's use of a prepaid expense.
d. To record accrued income.
e. To record accrued interest expense.
f. To record the earning of previously unearned income.

_____ 1.	Unearned Professional Fees	18,450	
	Professional Fees Earned		18,450
_____ 2.	Interest Receivable	2,700	
	Interest Earned		2,700
_____ 3.	Amortization Expense	49,500	
	Accumulated Amortization		49,500
_____ 4.	Salaries Expense	16,400	
	Salaries Payable		16,400
_____ 5.	Interest Expense	3,800	
	Interest Payable		3,800
_____ 6.	Insurance Expense	4,200	
	Prepaid Insurance		4,200

Exercise 4-2
Identifying adjusting entries

LO4, 5, 6

Selected information in T-account format is presented below. Journalize the most likely adjustments that caused the balances to change.

a) Accounts Receivable

Debit	Credit
Unadjusted Bal. 6,000 Dec. 31/01	
Adjusted Bal. 7,000 Dec. 31/01	

b) Prepaid Rent

Debit	Credit
Unadjusted Bal. 14,000 Dec. 31/01	
Adjusted Bal. 10,000 Dec. 31/01	

c) Accumulated Amortization, Machinery

Debit	Credit
	2,400 Unadjusted Bal. Dec. 31/01
	2,600 Adjusted Bal. Dec. 31/01

d) Unearned Fees

Debit	Credit
	1,700 Unadjusted Bal. Dec. 31/01
	300 Adjusted Bal. Dec. 31/01

e) Salaries Expense

Debit	Credit
Unadjusted Bal. 35,000 Dec. 31/01	
Adjusted Bal. 37,500 Dec. 31/01	

Exercise 4-3
Missing data in supplies expense calculations

LO5

Determine the missing amounts in each of these four independent situations:

	a	b	c	d
Supplies on hand, January 1	$ 300	$1,600	$1,360	?
Supplies purchased during the year	2,100	5,400	?	$6,000
Supplies on hand, December 31	750	?	1,840	800
Supplies expense for the year	?	1,300	9,600	6,575

Exercise 4-4
Adjusting entries

LO5

Prepare adjusting journal entries for the financial statements for the year ended December 31, 2001, for each of these independent situations. Assume that prepaid expenses are initially recorded in asset accounts. Assume that fees collected in advance of work are initially recorded as liabilities.

a. Amortization on the company's equipment for 2001 was estimated to be $16,000.
b. The Prepaid Insurance account had a $7,000 debit balance at December 31, 2001, before adjusting for the costs of any expired coverage. An analysis of the company's insurance policies showed $1,040 of unexpired insurance remaining.
c. The Office Supplies account had a $300 debit balance on January 1, 2001; $2,680 of office supplies were purchased during the year; and the December 31, 2001, count showed that $354 of supplies are on hand.
d. One-half of the work for a $10,000 fee received in advance has now been performed.
e. The Prepaid Insurance account had a $5,600 debit balance at December 31, 2001, before adjusting for the costs of any expired coverage. An analysis of the company's insurance policies showed that $4,600 of coverage had expired.
f. Wages of $4,000 have been earned by workers but not paid as of December 31, 2001.

Exercise 4-5
Adjusting entries

LO5, 6

Enviro Waste's year-end is December 31. The following information is available at year-end for the preparation of adjusting entries:

a. Of the $37,000 balance in Unearned Revenue, $5,000 remains unearned.
b. The annual building amortization is $21,000.
c. The Spare Parts Inventory account shows an unadjusted balance of $900. A physical count reveals a balance on hand of $200.
d. Unbilled and uncollected services provided to customers totalled $7,100.
e. The utility bill for the month of December was received but is unpaid; $2,600.

Required
Prepare the required adjusting entries at December 31, 2001.

Exercise 4-6
Adjusting entries

LO5, 6

Valu-Net's year-end is September 30. The following information is available at year-end for the preparation of adjusting entries:

a. Of the $9,000 balance in Unearned Revenue, $6,000 has been earned.
b. Furniture costing $3,600 was purchased on September 1 of this accounting period. It will be used for four years and donated to charity after that time.
c. The Office Supplies account shows an unadjusted balance of $3,000. A physical count reveals that $2,500 has been used.
d. Services provided to customers today (year-end) but unbilled total $14,000.
e. Rent of $3,500 for the month of September is unpaid and unrecorded.

Required
Prepare the required adjusting entries at September 30, 2001.

Exercise 4-7
Unearned and accrued revenues

LO5, 6, 10

Landmark Properties owns and operates an apartment building and prepares annual financial statements based on a March 31 fiscal year.

a. The tenants of one of the apartments paid five months' rent in advance on November 1, 2000. The monthly rental is $1,500 per month. The journal entry credited the Unearned Rent account when the payment was received. No other entry had been recorded prior to March 31, 2001. Give the adjusting journal entry that should be recorded on March 31, 2001.
b. On January 1, 2001, the tenants of another apartment moved in and paid the first month's rent. The $1,350 payment was recorded with a credit to the Rent Earned account. However, the tenants have not paid the rent for February or March. They have agreed to pay it as soon as possible. Give the adjusting journal entry that should be recorded on March 31, 2001.
c. On April 2, 2001, the tenants described in part (b) paid $4,050 rent for February, March, and April. Give the journal entry to record the cash collection.

Exercise 4-8
Identifying the effects of adjusting entries

LO 5, 6, 10

Following are two income statements for Pemberton Company for the year ended December 31, 2001. The left column was prepared before any adjusting entries were recorded and the right column includes the effects of adjusting entries. The company records cash receipts and disbursements related to unearned and prepaid items in balance sheet accounts. Analyze the statements and prepare the adjusting entries that must have been recorded. (Note: Of the $6,000 increase in *Fees earned*, 30% represent additional fees earned but not billed. The other 70% were earned by performing services that the customers had paid for in advance.)

PEMBERTON COMPANY
Income Statements
For Year Ended December 31, 2001

	Before Adjustments		After Adjustments	
Revenues:				
Fees earned	$24,000		$30,000	
Commissions earned	42,500		42,500	
Total revenues		$66,500		$72,500
Operating expenses:				
Amortization expense, computers			$ 1,500	
Amortization expense, office furniture			1,750	
Salaries expense	$12,500		14,950	
Insurance expense			1,300	
Rent expense	4,500		4,500	
Office supplies expense			480	
Advertising expense	3,000		3,000	
Utilities expense	1,250		1,320	
Total operating expenses		$21,250		$28,800
Net income		$45,250		$43,700

Exercise 4-9
Adjusting and subsequent entries for accrued expenses

LO 6, 10

Resource Management has five part-time employees, each of whom earns $100 per day. They are normally paid on Fridays for work completed on Monday through Friday of the same week. They were all paid in full on Friday, December 28, 2001. The next week, all five of the employees worked only four days because New Year's Day was an unpaid holiday. Show the adjusting entry that would be recorded on Monday, December 31, 2001, and the journal entry that would be made to record paying the employees' wages on Friday, January 4, 2002.

Exercise 4-10
Adjustments and payments of accrued items

LO 6, 10

The following three situations require adjusting journal entries to prepare financial statements as of April 30, 2001. For each situation, present the adjusting entry and the entry that would be made to record the payment of the accrued liability during May, 2001.

a. The company has a $780,000 note payable that requires 0.8% interest to be paid each month on the 20th of the month. The interest was last paid on April 20 and the next payment is due on May 20.

b. The total weekly salaries expense for all employees is $9,000. This amount is paid at the end of the day on Friday of each week with five working days. April 30 falls on Tuesday of this year, which means that the employees had worked two days since the last payday. The next payday is May 3.

c. On April 1, the company retained a lawyer at a flat monthly fee of $2,500. This amount is payable on the 12th of the following month.

Exercise 4-11
Adjusting entries

LO8

Check figure:
Adjusted trial balance, debits = $65,000

Ayotte Music Trial Balances February 28, 2001	Unadjusted Trial Balance		Adjustments		Adjusted Trial Balance	
	Dr.	Cr.	Dr.	Cr.	Dr.	Cr.
Cash	$ 5,000					
Accounts receivable	4,500					
Prepaid insurance	700					
Equipment	12,000					
Accumulated amortization, equipment		$ 6,000				
Accounts payable		1,200				
Jane Adams, capital		9,000				
Jane Adams, withdrawals	3,000					
Revenues		45,000				
Amortization expense, equipment	-0-					
Salaries expense	29,000					
Insurance expense	7,000					
Totals	$61,200	$61,200				

Additional information:

a. Annual amortization of the equipment; $2,400.
b. $250 of the Prepaid Insurance balance has expired.
c. Unbilled and unrecorded revenues at year-end totalled $1,400.

Required
Referring to Exhibit 4.22, use the information provided to complete the above.

Exercise 4-12
Preparing financial statements

LO9

Check figure:
Total assets = $14,950

Using the completed adjusted trial balance columns from Exercise 4-11, prepare an income statement, statement of owner's equity and a balance sheet. Assume that the owner made no investments during the year.

*Exercise 4-13
Adjustments for prepaid items recorded in expense and revenue accounts

LO11

Classic Customs began operations on December 1, 2001. In setting up the bookkeeping procedures, the company decided to debit expense accounts when the company prepays its expenses and to credit revenue accounts when customers pay for services in advance. Prepare journal entries for items (a) through (d) and adjusting entries as of December 31, 2001 for items (e) through (g):

a. Supplies were purchased on December 1 for $3,000.
b. The company prepaid insurance premiums of $1,440 on December 2.
c. On December 15, the company received an advance payment of $12,000 from one customer for remodeling work.
d. On December 28, the company received $3,600 from a second customer for remodelling work to be performed in January.
e. By counting them on December 31, Classic Customs determined that $1,920 of supplies were on hand.
f. An analysis of the insurance policies in effect on December 31 showed that $240 of insurance coverage had expired.
g. As of December 31, only one project had been completed. The $6,300 fee for this particular project had been received in advance.

* The asterisk refers to the topic having been discussed in the appendix to this chapter.

***Exercise 4-14**
Alternative procedures for revenues received in advance
LO11

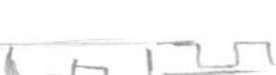

Pavillion Company experienced the following events and transactions during July:

July	1	Received $2,000 in advance of performing work for Andrew Renking.
	6	Received $8,400 in advance of performing work for Matt Swarbuck.
	12	Completed the job for Andrew Renking.
	18	Received $7,500 in advance of performing work for Drew Sayer.
	27	Completed the job for Matt Swarbuck.
	31	The job for Drew Sayer is still unfinished.

a. Give journal entries (including any adjusting entry as of the end of the month) to record these events using the procedure of initially crediting the Unearned Fees account when a payment is received from a customer in advance of performing services.
b. Give journal entries (including any adjusting entry as of the end of the month) to record these events using the procedure of initially crediting the Fees Earned account when a payment is received from a customer in advance of performing services.
c. Under each method, determine the amount of earned fees that should be reported on the income statement for July and the amount of unearned fees that should appear on the balance sheet as of July 31.

Problems

Problem 4-1A
Preparing adjusting entries – prepaid expenses
LO5

Lister Window Washing Services shows the following selected accounts on its December 31, 2001 unadjusted trial balance:

Account	Debit	Credit
Prepaid equipment rental...............	$18,000	
Prepaid insurance..........................	6,000	
Prepaid office rent	36,000	
Prepaid subscriptions.....................	450	

Required
Prepare the required adjusting entries at December 31, 2001 based on the following additional information:
a. The balance in Prepaid Insurance was for a six-month insurance policy purchased and in effect on September 1, 2001.
b. $3,000 of the balance in Prepaid Office Rent had not been used as at December 31, 2001.
c. $120 of the balance in Prepaid Subscriptions had been used as at December 31, 2001.
d. The company paid $18,000 to rent equipment for a three-year period beginning April 1, 2001.

Problem 4-2A
Preparing adjusting journal entries – amortization expense
LO5

Details regarding ComJet's purchases of plant and equipment items during 2001 follow:

Date of Purchase	Plant and Equipment Item	Cost	Estimated Useful Life	Estimated Sales Value at End of Estimated Useful Life
a. Jan. 1	Machine A	$14,000	5 years	$ -0-
b. Apr. 1	Machine B	28,000	4 years	4,000
c. Nov. 1	Machine C	4,200	2 years	600

Required
Prepare the adjusting entry at December 31, 2001, ComJet's year-end, for each plant and equipment item.

* The asterisk refers to the topic having been discussed in the appendix to this chapter.

Problem 4-3A

Preparing adjusting journal entries – unearned revenues

LO5

Outdoor's Best pre-sells yard maintenance packages for the gardening season. During October, the company collects cash from clients for Christmas trees to be delivered in December. Snow removal services are also provided. The following selected accounts appear on the November 30, 2001 year-end unadjusted trial balance:

Account	Debit	Credit
Unearned Christmas tree sales........		$ 87,000
Unearned lawn services		225,000
Unearned garden services................		41,000
Unearned snow removal services....		18,000

Required

Prepare adjusting journal entries at November 30, 2001 using the following additional information.

a. $132,000 of the Unearned Lawn Services account represents payments received from customers for the 2002 season. The remainder represents services actually performed during the 2001 season.

b. $39,000 of the Unearned Garden Services account had been earned by November 30, 2001.

c. $17,500 of the Unearned Snow Removal Services account remained unearned at November 30, 2001.

d. Outdoor's arranges with its customers to deliver trees prior to December 20. As a result, the Unearned Christmas Tree Sales account will be earned in total by that date.

Problem 4-4A

Preparing adjusting entries – accrued expenses

LO6

In reviewing the accounts on March 31 for the month just ended, DigiTech discovered the following accrued expenses:

a. Interest of $1,125 had accrued on the note payable.

b. Unpaid and unrecorded salaries at month-end totalled $9,800.

c. The March telephone bill for $480 is unpaid and unrecorded at March 31.

d. DigiTech normally pays rent in three-month instalments. Rent of $2,500 per month has not been paid for February, March, and April.

e. DigiTech pays commissions to the technicians at the rate of 4% of services performed. During March, total services performed were $480,000. Commissions are unrecorded and unpaid at March 31.

Required

Prepare adjusting journal entries at March 31 based on the information provided.

Problem 4-5A

Preparing adjusting entries – accrued revenues

LO6

In reviewing the accounts on March 31 for the month just ended, DigiTech discovered the following accrued revenues:

a. DigiTech owns the building that it occupies. Part of the building is rented to E-Quip Company for $1,600 per month. E-Quip has not paid the March rent.

b. Services performed but unrecorded at March 31 totalled $5,400.

c. Interest for the month of March had accrued on the note receivable in the amount of $350.

d. On February 1, DigiTech signed a $12,000 six-month contract to perform services for a client. DigiTech has been providing the services but as of March 31 no cash had been received.

Required

Prepare adjusting journal entries at March 31 based on the information provided.

Problem 4-6A
Adjusting entries

LO5, 6

Southwest Careers, a school owned by Sheila Carr, provides training to individuals who pay tuition directly to the business. The business also offers extension training to groups in off-site locations. The school's unadjusted trial balance as of December 31, 2001 follows. Southwest Careers follows the practice of initially recording prepaid expenses and unearned revenues in balance sheet accounts. Facts that require eight adjusting entries on December 31, 2001 are presented after the trial balance:

SOUTHWEST CAREERS
Unadjusted Trial Balance
December 31, 2001

Account	Debit	Credit
Cash	$ 26,000	
Accounts receivable	-0-	
Teaching supplies	10,000	
Prepaid insurance	15,000	
Prepaid rent	2,000	
Professional library	30,000	
Accumulated amortization, professional library		$ 9,000
Equipment	70,000	
Accumulated amortization, equipment		16,000
Accounts payable		36,000
Salaries payable		-0-
Unearned extension fees		11,000
Sheila Carr, capital		63,600
Sheila Carr, withdrawals	40,000	
Tuition fees earned		102,000
Extension fees earned		38,000
Amortization expense, equipment	-0-	
Amortization expense, professional library	-0-	
Salaries expense	48,000	
Insurance expense	-0-	
Rent expense	22,000	
Teaching supplies expense	-0-	
Advertising expense	7,000	
Utilities expense	5,600	
Totals	$275,600	$275,600

Additional facts:

a. An analysis of the company's policies shows that $3,000 of insurance coverage has expired.

b. An inventory shows that teaching supplies costing $2,600 are on hand at the end of the year.

c. The estimated annual amortization on the equipment is $12,000.

d. The estimated annual amortization on the professional library is $6,000.

e. The school offers off-campus services for specific employers. On November 1, the company agreed to do a special six-month course for a client. The contract calls for a monthly fee of $2,200, and the client paid the first five months' fees in advance. When the cash was received, the Unearned Extension Fees account was credited.

f. On October 15, the school agreed to teach a four-month class for an individual for $3,000 tuition per month payable at the end of the class. The services to date have been provided as agreed, but no payment has been received.

g. The school's two employees are paid weekly. As of the end of the year, two days' wages have accrued at the rate of $100 per day for each employee.

h. The balance in the Prepaid Rent account represents the rent for December.

Required

Prepare the eight necessary adjusting journal entries.

Problem 4-7A
Adjusting entries

LO5, 6

DataMirror's year-end is January 31. Based on an analysis of the unadjusted trial balance at January 31, 2001, the following information was available for the preparation of adjusting entries:

a. Equipment purchased on November 1 of this accounting period for $72,000 is estimated to have a useful life of three years. After three years of use, it is expected that the equipment will be scrapped due to technological obsolescence.
b. Of the $18,000 balance in Unearned Consulting Fees, $6,000 had been earned.
c. The Prepaid Rent account showed a balance of $45,000. This was paid on October 1 of this accounting period and represents six months of rent commencing on the same date.
d. Accrued wages at January 31 totalled $19,000.
e. Three months of interest had accrued at the rate of 7% on the $84,000 note payable.
f. Unrecorded and uncollected consulting fees at year-end were $9,500.
g. A $2,700 insurance policy was purchased on April 1 of the current accounting period and debited to the Prepaid Insurance account. Coverage began April 1 for 18 months.
h. The annual amortization on the office furniture was $900.
i. Repair revenues accrued at year-end totalled $4,100.
j. The Store Supplies Inventory account had a balance of $1,600 at the beginning of the accounting period. During the year, $3,000 of supplies were purchased and debited to the Store Supplies Inventory account. At year-end, a count of the supplies revealed a balance of $300.

Required

Prepare adjusting journal entries on January 31, 2001 based on the above.

Problem 4-8A
Adjusting entries

LO5, 6

ATC Environmental Consultants is just finishing its second year of operations. The company's unadjusted trial balance at October 31, 2001 follows:

ATC Environmental Consultants
Unadjusted Trial Balance
October 31, 2001

Acct. No.	Account	Debit	Credit
101	Cash	$ 14,000	
106	Accounts receivable	28,000	
109	Interest receivable	-0-	
111	Notes receivable	15,000	
126	Supplies	2,300	
128	Prepaid insurance	4,675	
131	Prepaid rent	10,500	
161	Office furniture	30,720	
162	Accumulated amortization, office furniture		$ 10,240
201	Accounts payable		17,500
210	Wages payable		-0-
233	Unearned consulting fees		6,580
301	Jeff Moore, capital		30,000
302	Jeff Moore, withdrawals	8,225	
401	Consulting fees earned		157,300
409	Interest revenue		700
601	Amortization expense, office furniture	-0-	
622	Wages expense	73,500	
637	Insurance expense	-0-	
640	Rent expense	32,000	
650	Supplies expense	3,400	
	Totals	$222,320	$222,320

The following additional information is available on October 31 for the year just ended:

a. It was determined that $6,000 of the unearned consulting fees had not yet been earned.
b. It was discovered that $3,000 of the balance in the Consulting Fees Earned account was for services to be performed in November.
c. The balance in the Prepaid Rent account represents three months of rent beginning September 1, 2001.
d. Accrued wages at October 31 totalled $3,400.
e. The office furniture was purchased on February 1, 2000 and has an estimated useful life of two years. After two years of use, it is expected that the furniture will be worthless.
f. Accrued consulting fees at year-end totalled $2,100.
g. Interest of $100 had accrued on the note receivable for the month of October.
h. The balance in the Prepaid Insurance account represents the remaining balance of a two-year policy purchased on April 1, 2000.
i. A count of the supplies on October 31 revealed a balance remaining of $450.

Required

Prepare adjusting journal entries for October 31, 2001 based on the above.

Problem 4-9A

Posting, adjusted trial balance, and preparing financial statements

LO 8, 9

Check figure:
Adjusted trial balance, debits = $243,280

Required

Using the information in Problem 4-8A, complete the following:

1. Open balance column accounts for ATC Environmental Consultants and enter the balances listed in the unadjusted trial balance.
2. Post the adjusting entries prepared in Problem 4-8A to the balance column accounts.
3. Prepare an adjusted trial balance.
4. Use the adjusted trial balance to prepare an income statement, statement of owner's equity and a balance sheet. Assume that the owner, Jeff Moore, made no owner investments during the year.

Problem 4-10A

Adjusting entries

LO 5, 6

Service Plus Hospitality showed the following:

Service Plus Hospitality
Unadjusted Trial Balance
September 30, 2001

Account	Debit	Credit
Cash	$ 3,000	
Accounts receivable	5,600	
Repair supplies inventory	1,100	
Prepaid rent	7,000	
Office furniture	13,000	
Accounts payable		$ 4,000
Notes payable		10,800
Al Zink, capital		3,879
Al Zink, withdrawals	9,500	
Hospitality revenues		94,000
Salaries expense	71,100	
Repair supplies expense	750	
Interest expense	729	
Other expenses	900	
Totals	$112,679	$112,679

Additional information available at year-end:

a. Interest of $81 had accrued on the notes payable for the month of September.
b. The office furniture was acquired on February 1, 2001 and has an estimated four-year life. The furniture will be sold for about $1,000 at the end of its four-year life.
c. A count of the Repair Supplies Inventory revealed a balance on hand of $350.
d. A review of the Prepaid Rent account showed that $5,000 had been used.

e. Accrued salaries of $1,400 had not been recorded at year-end.
f. The September Internet bill for $50 had been received and must be paid by October 14.
g. Accrued revenues of $3,100 were not recorded at year-end.

Required
Prepare adjusting entries for (a) through (g) using the information provided.

Problem 4-11A
Preparation of financial statements

 7, 8

Check figures:
Adjustments columns = $12,381
Adjusted trial balance columns = $119,310

Required
1. Refer to the format presented in Exhibit 4.22 and prepare an adjusted trial balance using the information in Problem 4-10A.
2. Prepare an income statement, statement of owner's equity and a balance sheet based on the adjusted trial balance completed in Part 1. Assume that the owner, Al Zink, made an investment during the year of $1,800.

Problem 4-12A
Preparing financial statements from the adjusted trial balance

LO 9

This adjusted trial balance is for Conquest Company as of December 31, 2001:

	Debit	Credit
Cash	$ 22,000	
Accounts receivable	44,000	
Interest receivable	10,000	
Notes receivable (due in 90 days)	160,000	
Office supplies	8,000	
Automobiles	160,000	
Accumulated amortization, automobiles		$ 42,000
Equipment	130,000	
Accumulated amortization, equipment		10,000
Land	70,000	
Accounts payable		88,000
Interest payable		12,000
Salaries payable		11,000
Unearned fees		22,000
Long-term notes payable		130,000
John Conroe, capital		247,800
John Conroe, withdrawals	38,000	
Fees earned		420,000
Interest earned		16,000
Amortization expense, automobiles	18,000	
Amortization expense, equipment	10,000	
Salaries expense	180,000	
Wages expense	32,000	
Interest expense	24,000	
Office supplies expense	26,000	
Advertising expense	50,000	
Repairs expense, automobiles	16,800	
Totals	$998,800	$998,800

Check figures:
Net income = $79,200
Total assets = $552,000

Required
Use the information in the trial balance to prepare:
a. The income statement for the year ended December 31, 2001.
b. The statement of owner's equity for the year ended December 31, 2001.
c. The balance sheet as of December 31, 2001.
Assume the owner, John Conroe, to have made no additional investments during the year.

Problem 4-13A
Identifying adjusting and subsequent entries

LO4, 10

For these adjusting and transaction entries, enter the letter of the explanation that most closely describes the adjustment or transaction in the blank space beside each entry. (You can use some letters more than once.)

a. To record collection of an unearned revenue.
b. To record the earning of previously unearned income.
c. To record payment of an accrued expense.
d. To record collection of an accrued revenue.
e. To record an accrued expense.
f. To record accrued income.
g. To record the year's use of a prepaid expense.
h. To record payment of a prepaid expense.
i. To record the year's amortization expense.

		Account	Debit	Credit
____	1.	Amortization Expense	3,000	
		Accumulated Amortization		3,000
____	2.	Unearned Professional Fees	2,000	
		Professional Fees Earned		2,000
____	3.	Rent Expense	1,000	
		Prepaid Rent		1,000
____	4.	Interest Expense	4,000	
		Interest Payable		4,000
____	5.	Prepaid Rent	3,500	
		Cash		3,500
____	6.	Salaries Expense	5,000	
		Salaries Payable		5,000
____	7.	Insurance Expense	6,000	
		Prepaid Insurance		6,000
____	8.	Salaries Payable	1,500	
		Cash		1,500
____	9.	Cash	6,500	
		Unearned Professional Fees		6,500
____	10.	Cash	9,000	
		Interest Receivable		9,000
____	11.	Interest Receivable	7,000	
		Interest Earned		7,000
____	12.	Cash	8,000	
		Accounts Receivable		8,000

Problem 4-14A
Adjusting and subsequent journal entries

LO5, 6, 10

Garza Company's annual accounting period ends on December 31, 2001. Garza follows the practice of recording prepaid expenses and unearned revenues in balance sheet accounts. The following information concerns the adjusting entries to be recorded as of that date:

a. The Office Supplies account started the year with a $3,000 balance. During 2001, the company purchased supplies at a cost of $12,400, which was added to the Office Supplies account. The inventory of supplies on hand at December 31 had a cost of $2,640.
b. An analysis of the company's insurance policies provided these facts:

Policy	Date of Purchase	Years of Coverage	Total Cost
1	April 1, 2000	2	$15,840
2	April 1, 2001	3	13,068
3	August 1, 2001	1	2,700

The total premium for each policy was paid in full at the purchase date, and the Prepaid Insurance account was debited for the full cost. Appropriate adjusting entries have been made to December 31, 2000.

c. The company has 15 employees who earn a total of $2,100 in salaries for every working day. They are paid each Monday for their work in the five-day workweek ending on the preceding Friday. December 31, 2001, falls on Monday, and all 15 employees worked the first day of the week. They will be paid salaries for five full days on Monday, January 7, 2002.

d. The company purchased a building on August 1, 2001. The building cost $855,000 and is expected to have a $45,000 salvage value at the end of its predicted 30-year life.

e. Because the company is not large enough to occupy the entire building, it arranged to rent some space to a tenant at $2,400 per month, starting on November 1, 2001. The rent was paid on time on November 1, and the amount received was credited to the Rent Earned account. However, the tenant has not paid the December rent. The company has worked out an agreement with the tenant, who has promised to pay both December's and January's rent in full on January 15. The tenant has agreed not to fall behind again.

f. On November 1, the company also rented space to another tenant for $2,175 per month. The tenant paid five months' rent in advance on that date. The payment was recorded with a credit to the Unearned Rent account.

Required

1. Use the information to prepare adjusting entries as of December 31, 2001.
2. Prepare journal entries to record the subsequent cash transactions in January 2001 described in parts (c) and (e).

*Problem 4-15A

Recording prepaid expenses and unearned revenues

LO5, 6, 11

The following events occurred for a company during the last two months of its fiscal year ended December 31:

Nov.	1	Paid $1,500 for future newspaper advertising.
	1	Paid $2,160 for insurance through October 31 of the following year.
	30	Received $3,300 for future services to be provided to a customer.
Dec.	1	Paid $2,700 for the services of a consultant, to be received over the next three months.
	15	Received $7,650 for future services to be provided to a customer.
	31	Of the advertising paid for on November 1, $900 worth had not yet been published by the newspaper.
	31	Part of the insurance paid for on November 1 had expired.
	31	Services worth $1,200 had not yet been provided to the customer who paid on November 30.
	31	One-third of the consulting services paid for on December 1 had been received.
	31	The company had performed $3,000 of the services that the customer had paid for on December 15.

Required

Preparation component:

1. Prepare entries for the above events under the approach that records prepaid expenses as assets and records unearned revenues as liabilities. Also, prepare adjusting entries at the end of the year.
2. Prepare entries under the approach that records prepaid expenses as expenses and records unearned revenues as revenues. Also, prepare adjusting entries at the end of the year.

Analysis component:

3. Explain why the alternative sets of entries in requirements 1 and 2 do not result in different financial statement amounts.

* The asterisk refers to the topic having been discussed in the appendix to this chapter.

Alternate Problems

Problem 4-1B
Preparing adjusting entries – prepaid expenses
LO5

Welsh's Cleaning Services is gathering information for its year-end, April 30, 2001. Selected accounts on the April 30, 2001 unadjusted trial balance are reproduced below:

Account	Debit	Credit
Prepaid equipment rental..............	$9,000	
Prepaid warehouse rental.............	7,800	
Prepaid insurance..........................	3,600	
Cleaning supplies..........................	1,450	

Required
Prepare the required adjusting entries at April 30, 2001 based on the following additional information:

a. The balance in the Prepaid Equipment Rental account is for 18 months of equipment rental that began December 1, 2000.
b. $3,000 of the balance in the Prepaid Warehouse Rental account had been used as of April 30, 2001.
c. The balance in the Prepaid Insurance account represents six months of insurance effective February 1, 2001.
d. A count of the cleaning supplies revealed that $1,200 had been used.

Problem 4-2B
Preparing adjusting journal entries – amortization expense
LO5

Details regarding Hornby Bay Consulting's plant and equipment items follow:

Date of Purchase	Plant and Equipment Item	Cost	Estimated Useful Life	Estimated Sales Value at End of Estimated Useful Life
a. Dec. 1, 2000	Furniture	$ 30,600	3 years	$ -0-
b. Mar. 1, 2001	Equipment	210,000	10 years	12,000
c. Nov. 1, 2001	Building	307,600	15 years	70,000

Required
Prepare the adjusting entry to record amortization for each capital asset item at November 30, 2001, Hornby Bay Consulting's year-end.

Problem 4-3B
Preparing adjusting journal entries – unearned revenues
LO5

Ocean Tours sells scuba diving and kayaking excursions, along with a number of unique sightseeing packages. The company requires a 50% payment from the customer at the time of booking. The following selected accounts appear on Ocean Tours' January 31, 2002 year-end unadjusted trial balance:

Account	Debit	Credit
Unearned kayaking tour revenue		$ 64,000
Unearned tour package revenue......		480,000
Unearned scuba diving revenue.......		133,000
Unearned heli-tour revenue.............		26,000

Required
Prepare adjusting journal entries at January 31, 2002 using the following additional information:

a. Ocean Tours has custom helicopter packages in which groups are flown in and out of island retreats. The balance in this unearned account is for a group scheduled for early March 2002.
b. $397,000 of the Unearned Tour Package Revenue account had been earned by January 31, 2002.
c. $36,000 of the Unearned Scuba Diving Revenue account remained unearned at January 31, 2002.
d. $8,350 of the Unearned Kayaking Tour Revenue account represents payments received from customers for February and March 2002.

Problem 4-4B
Preparing adjusting entries – accrued expenses

LO6

In reviewing the accounts on September 30, 2001 for the month just ended, WonderWeb Designers discovered the following accrued expenses:

a. Interest of $3,800 had accrued on the bank loan.
b. Accrued wages at month-end totalled $27,000.
c. The September cell phone bill for $180 is unpaid and unrecorded.
d. In error, WonderWeb did not record or pay cable charges totalling $390 for the past two months.
e. $1,950 of property taxes covering the last six months have not been paid or recorded.

Required
Prepare adjusting journal entries at September 30, 2001 based on the information provided.

Problem 4-5B
Preparing adjusting entries – accrued revenues

LO6

In reviewing the accounts on March 31, 2001 for the month just ended, WonderWeb discovered the following accrued revenues:

a. Interest of $650 had accrued on the note receivable.
b. Accrued consulting fees totalled $5,400 at March 31.
c. Web design work totalling $6,800 was just completed but not recorded.
d. WonderWeb rents the basement of its building to a student. The student has not paid rent of $350 per month for the past four months.

Required
Prepare adjusting journal entries at March 31, 2001 based on the information provided.

Problem 4-6B
Adjusting entries; financial statements; profit margin

LO5, 6

Presented below is the unadjusted trial balance for Design Institute as of December 31, 2001. Design Institute follows the practice of initially recording prepaid expenses and unearned revenues in balance sheet accounts. The institute provides one-on-one training to individuals who pay tuition directly to the business and also offers extension training to groups in off-site locations. Presented after the trial balance are facts that will lead to eight adjusting entries as of December 31, 2001.

DESIGN INSTITUTE
Unadjusted Trial Balance
December 31, 2001

	Debit	Credit
Cash	$ 50,000	
Accounts receivable	-0-	
Teaching supplies	60,000	
Prepaid insurance	18,000	
Prepaid rent	2,600	
Professional library	10,000	
Accumulated amortization, professional library		$ 1,500
Equipment	30,000	
Accumulated amortization, equipment		16,000
Accounts payable		12,200
Salaries payable		-0-
Unearned extension fees		27,600
Jay Stevens, capital		68,500
Jay Stevens, withdrawals	20,000	
Tuition fees earned		105,000
Extension fees earned		62,000
Amortization expense, equipment	-0-	
Amortization expense, professional library	-0-	
Salaries expense	43,200	
Insurance expense	-0-	
Rent expense	28,600	
Teaching supplies expense	-0-	
Advertising expense	18,000	
Utilities expense	12,400	
Totals	$292,800	$292,800

Additional facts:

a. An analysis of the company's policies shows that $6,400 of insurance coverage has expired.
b. An inventory shows that teaching supplies costing $2,500 are on hand at the end of the year.
c. The estimated annual amortization on the equipment is $4,000.
d. The estimated annual amortization on the professional library is $2,000.
e. The school offers off-campus services for specific operators. On November 1, the company agreed to do a special four-month course for a client. The contract calls for a $4,600 monthly fee, and the client paid the first two months' fees in advance. When the cash was received, the Unearned Extension Fees account was credited.
f. On October 15, the school agreed to teach a four-month class to an individual for $2,200 tuition per month payable at the end of the class. The services have been provided as agreed, and no payment has been received.
g. The school's only employee is paid weekly. As of the end of the year, wages of $540 have accrued.
h. The balance in the Prepaid Rent account represents the rent for December.

Required

Prepare the eight necessary adjusting journal entries.

Problem 4-7B
Adjusting entries

LO5, 6

Boardwalk Equities' year-end is May 31. Based on an analysis of the unadjusted trial balance at May 31, 2001, the following information was available:

a. Machinery costing $21,000 was acquired on September 1 of this accounting period. It is estimated to have a useful life of six years. The machinery will have no value at the end of its six-year life.
b. It was determined that $3,000 of completed work was included in the $8,000 Unearned Revenue account balance at year-end.
c. The Prepaid Insurance account showed a balance of $90,000. This was paid and takes effect on March 1 of this accounting period and represents a two-year policy.
d. Accrued salaries at year-end were $5,000.
e. $2,520 of interest had accrued on the $72,000 note payable.
f. Accrued revenues at year-end totalled $1,700.
g. $12,000 worth of advertising was prepaid on January 1 of the current accounting period and debited to the Prepaid Advertising account. This covered four months of advertising beginning on the same date.
h. The annual amortization on the office equipment was $1,800.
i. Interest revenue accrued at year-end totalled $350.
j. The Office Supplies account had a balance of $2,000 at the beginning of the accounting period. During the year, $5,000 of supplies were purchased and debited to the Office Supplies account. At year-end, a count of the supplies revealed that $1,500 had been used.

Required

Prepare adjusting journal entries based on the above.

Problem 4-8B
Adjusting entries

LO5, 6

Alissa Kay, the owner of Colt Surveying Services, has been in business for two years. The unadjusted trial balance at December 31, regarding the month just ended, follows:

Colt Surveying Services Unadjusted Trial Balance December 31, 2001			
Acct. No.	**Account**	**Debit**	**Credit**
101	Cash	$ 2,800	
106	Accounts receivable	3,955	
126	Supplies	320	
128	Prepaid advertising	2,800	
131	Prepaid rent	13,500	
167	Surveying equipment	29,000	
168	Accumulated amortization, surveying equipment		$ 3,674
201	Accounts payable		1,900
203	Interest payable		-0-
210	Wages payable		-0-
233	Unearned surveying fees		2,400
251	Notes payable		18,000
301	Alissa Kay, capital		14,326
302	Alissa Kay, withdrawals	2,150	
401	Surveying fees earned		67,049
601	Amortization expense, surveying equipment	1,837	
622	Wages expense	19,863	
633	Interest expense	945	
640	Rent expense	22,000	
650	Supplies expense	1,479	
655	Advertising expense	500	
690	Utilities expense	6,200	
	Totals	$107,349	$107,349

The following additional information is available on December 31, 2001:

a. Amortization on the equipment for the month was $167.
b. $2,000 of the balance in Unearned Revenue is unearned at December 31.
c. The balance in Prepaid Rent is for six months of rent beginning December 1.
d. Accrued wages at month-end were $5,000.
e. December's interest in the amount of $105 had accrued on the notes payable.
f. Accrued surveying fees at month-end totalled $790.
g. The balance in Prepaid Advertising covers four months of advertising beginning December 15.
h. A count of the supplies on December 31 showed $150 had been used.
i. The December electricity bill for $540 was received on December 31. It is unrecorded and unpaid.

Required

Prepare adjusting journal entries based on the above.

Problem 4-9B

Posting, adjusted trial balance, and preparing financial statements

LO 8, 9

Check figure:
Adjusted trial balance, debits = $113,951

Required

Using the information in Problem 4-8B, complete the following:

1. Open balance column accounts for Colt Surveying Services and enter the balances listed in the unadjusted trial balance.
2. Post the adjusting entries prepared in Problem 4-8B to the balance column accounts.
3. Prepare an adjusted trial balance.
4. Use the adjusted trial balance to prepare an income statement, statement of owner's equity and a balance sheet. Assume that the owner, Alissa Kay, made owner investments of $2,000 during the year.

Problem 4-10B
Adjusting entries

LO5, 6

Orca Bay Hockey Holdings showed the following:

Orca Bay Hockey Holdings
Unadjusted Trial Balance
June 30, 2001

Account	Debit	Credit
Cash	$ 56,000	
Accounts receivable	14,000	
Repair supplies inventory	1,400	
Prepaid arena rental	91,000	
Hockey equipment	214,000	
Accumulated amortization, hockey equipment		$ 82,000
Accounts payable		2,700
Unearned ticket revenue		9,800
Notes payable		80,000
Ben Gibson, capital		225,700
Ben Gibson, withdrawals	36,000	
Ticket revenue		275,000
Salaries expense	175,000	
Arena rental expense	84,000	
Other expenses	3,800	
Totals	$675,200	$675,200

Additional information available at year-end:

a. The Prepaid Arena Rental of $91,000 was paid on February 1, 2001. It represents seven months of rent on the arena.
b. A count of the Repair Supplies Inventory at year-end revealed that $950 had been used.
c. Annual amortization of the hockey equipment was $41,000.
d. A review of the Unearned Ticket Revenue account at year-end showed that included in the balance was $6,300 that had not yet been earned.
e. Accrued salaries of $29,000 had not been recorded at year-end.
f. Interest of $900 had accrued regarding the Notes Payable.
g. On June 5, 2001, cash of $46,000 was received for 2001/2002 Season Tickets. This amount is included in the Ticket Revenue balance.

Required

Prepare adjusting entries on June 30, 2001 for (a) through (g) using the information provided.

Problem 4-11B
Preparation of financial statements

LO7, 8

Required

1. Refer to the format presented in Exhibit 4.22 and prepare an adjusted trial balance using the information in Problem 4-10B.
2. Prepare an income statement, statement of owner's equity and a balance sheet based on the adjusted trial balance completed in Part 1. Assume that the owner, Ben Gibson, made an investment during the year of $10,000.

Check figures:
Adjustments columns = $186,350;
Adjusted trial balance columns = $746,100

Problem 4-12B

Preparing financial statements from the adjusted trial balance

LO9

This adjusted trial balance is for Horizon Courier as of December 31, 2001:

	Debit	Credit
Cash	$ 48,000	
Accounts receivable	110,000	
Interest receivable	6,000	
Notes receivable (due in 90 days)	200,000	
Office supplies	12,000	
Trucks	124,000	
Accumulated amortization, trucks		$ 48,000
Equipment	260,000	
Accumulated amortization, equipment		190,000
Land	90,000	
Accounts payable		124,000
Interest payable		22,000
Salaries payable		30,000
Unearned delivery fees		110,000
Long-term notes payable		190,000
Kim Ainesworth, capital		115,000
Kim Ainesworth, withdrawals	40,000	
Delivery fees earned		580,000
Interest earned		24,000
Amortization expense, trucks	24,000	
Amortization expense, equipment	46,000	
Salaries expense	64,000	
Wages expense	290,000	
Interest expense	25,000	
Office supplies expense	33,000	
Advertising expense	26,400	
Repairs expense, trucks	34,600	
Totals	$1,433,000	$1,433,000

Check figures:
Net income = $61,000
Total assets = $612,000

Required

Use the information in the trial balance to prepare:

a. The income statement for the year ended December 31, 2001.
b. The statement of owner's equity for the year ended December 31, 2001.
c. The balance sheet as of December 31, 2001.

Problem 4-13B

Identifying adjusting and subsequent entries

LO4, 10

For these adjusting and transaction entries, enter the letter of the explanation that most closely describes the adjustment or transaction in the blank space beside each entry. (You can use some letters more than once.)

a. To record collection of an accrued revenue.
b. To record payment of an accrued expense.
c. To record payment of a prepaid expense.
d. To record the year's amortization expense.
e. To record the earning of previously unearned income.
f. To record the year's use of a prepaid expense.
g. To record accrued income.
h. To record collection of an unearned revenue.
i. To record an accrued expense.

_____	1.	Salaries Payable Cash	8,000	 8,000
_____	2.	Amortization Expense Accumulated Amortization	6,000	 6,000
_____	3.	Unearned Professional Fees Professional Fees Earned	3,500	 3,500
_____	4.	Interest Receivable Interest Earned	1,500	 1,500
_____	5.	Cash Accounts Receivable	5,000	 5,000
_____	6.	Interest Expense Interest Payable	9,000	 9,000
_____	7.	Cash Unearned Professional Fees	4,000	 4,000
_____	8.	Insurance Expense Prepaid Insurance	3,000	 3,000
_____	9.	Rent Expense Prepaid Rent	6,500	 6,500
_____	10.	Prepaid Rent Cash	7,000	 7,000
_____	11.	Salaries Expense Salaries Payable	1,000	 1,000
_____	12.	Cash Interest Receivable	2,000	 2,000

Problem 4-14B

Adjusting and subsequent journal entries

LO5, 6, 10

The Perfecto Company's annual accounting period ends on October 31, 2001. Perfecto follows the practice of recording prepaid expenses and unearned revenues in balance sheet accounts. The following information concerns the adjusting entries that need to be recorded as of that date:

a. The Office Supplies account started the fiscal year with a $500 balance. During the fiscal year, the company purchased supplies at a cost of $3,650, which was added to the Office Supplies account. The inventory of supplies on hand at October 31 had a cost of $700.

b. An analysis of the company's insurance policies provided these facts:

Policy	Date of Purchase	Years of Coverage	Total Cost
1	April 1, 2000	2	$3,000
2	April 1, 2001	3	3,600
3	August 1, 2001	1	660

The total premium for each policy was paid in full at the purchase date, and the Prepaid Insurance account was debited for the full cost.

c. The company has 10 employees who earn a total of $800 for every working day. They are paid each Monday for their work in the five-day workweek ending on the preceding Friday. October 31, 2001 falls on Wednesday, and all 10 employees worked the first three days of the week. They will be paid salaries for five full days on Monday, November 5, 2001.

d. The company purchased a building on August 1, 2001. The building cost $155,000, and is expected to have a $20,000 salvage value at the end of its predicted 25-year life.

e. Because the company is not large enough to occupy the entire building, it arranged to rent some space to a tenant at $600 per month, starting on September 1, 2001. The rent was paid on time on September 1, and the amount received was credited to the Rent Earned account. However, the tenant has not paid the October rent. The company has worked out an agreement with the tenant, who has promised to pay both October's and November's rent in full on November 15. The tenant has agreed not to fall behind again.

f. On September 1, the company also rented space to another tenant for $525 per month. The tenant paid five months' rent in advance on that date. The payment was recorded with a credit to the Unearned Rent account.

Required

1. Use the information to prepare adjusting entries as of October 31, 2001.
2. Prepare journal entries to record the subsequent cash transactions described in items (c) and (e).

***Problem 4-15B**
Recording prepaid expenses and unearned revenues

LO5, 6, 11

The following events occurred for a company during the last two months of its fiscal year ended May 31:

Apr.	1	Paid $3,450 for future consulting services.
	1	Paid $2,700 for insurance through March 31 of the following year.
	30	Received $7,500 for future services to be provided to a customer.
May	1	Paid $3,450 for future newspaper advertising.
	23	Received $9,450 for future services to be provided to a customer.
	31	Of the consulting services paid for on April 1, $1,500 worth had been received.
	31	Part of the insurance paid for on April 1 had expired.
	31	Services worth $3,600 had not yet been provided to the customer who paid on April 30.
	31	Of the advertising paid for on May 1, $1,050 worth had not been published yet.
	31	The company had performed $4,500 of the services that the customer had paid for on May 23.

Required

Preparation component:

1. Prepare entries for the above events under the approach that records prepaid expenses and unearned revenues in balance sheet accounts. Also, prepare adjusting entries at the end of the year.
2. Prepare journal entries under the approach that records prepaid expenses and unearned revenues in income statement accounts. Also, prepare adjusting entries at the end of the year.

Analysis component:

3. Explain why the alternative sets of entries in requirements 1 and 2 do not result in different financial statement amounts.

Analytical and Review Problems

A&R Problem 4-1

The Salaries Payable account of James Bay Company Limited appears below:

Salaries Payable			
Entries during 2002		22,520	Bal. Jan. 1, 2002
	398,120	388,400	Entries during 2002

The company records the salary expense and related liability at the end of each week and pays the employees on the last Friday of the month.

Required

Calculate:

1. Salary expense for 2002.
2. How much was paid to employees in 2002 for work done in 2001?
3. How much was paid to employees in 2002 for work done in 2002?
4. How much will be paid to employees in 2003 for work done in 2002?

* The asterisk refers to the topic having been discussed in the appendix to this chapter.

Serial Problem

Echo Systems

(This comprehensive problem was introduced in Chapter 3 and continues in Chapters 5 and 6. If the Chapter 3 segment has not been completed, the assignment can begin at this point. You need to use the facts presented on PP. 134–135 *in Chapter 3. Because of its length, this problem is most easily solved if you use the Working Papers that accompany this book.)*

After the success of its first two months, Mary Graham has decided to continue operating Echo Systems. (The transactions that occurred in these months are described in Chapter 3.) Before proceeding in December, Graham adds these new accounts to the chart of accounts for the ledger:

Account	No.
Accumulated Amortization, Office Equipment	164
Accumulated Amortization, Computer Equipment	168
Wages Payable	210
Unearned Computer Services Revenue	236
Amortization Expense, Office Equipment	612
Amortization Expense, Computer Equipment	613
Insurance Expense	637
Rent Expense	640
Computer Supplies Expense	652

Required

1. Prepare journal entries to record each of the following transactions for Echo Systems. Post the entries to the accounts in the ledger.
2. Prepare adjusting entries to record the events described on December 31. Post the entries to the accounts in the ledger.
3. Prepare an adjusted trial balance as of December 31, 2001.
4. Prepare an income statement for the three months ended December 31, 2001.
5. Prepare a statement of owner's equity for the three months ended December 31, 2001.
6. Prepare a balance sheet as of December 31, 2001.

Transactions and other data:

Dec.	3	Paid $1,050 to the Lakeshore Mall for the company's share of mall advertising costs.
	3	Paid $600 to repair the company's computer.
	4	Received $3,750 from Alamo Engineering Co. for the receivable from the prior month.
	10	Paid Carly Smith for six days' work at the rate of $100 per day.
	14	Notified by Alamo Engineering Co. that Echo's bid of $6,000 on a proposed project was accepted. Alamo paid an advance of $1,500.
	17	Purchased $1,155 of computer supplies on credit from Abbott Office Products.
	18	Sent a reminder to Fostek Co. to pay the fee for services originally recorded on November 8.
	20	Completed project for Elite Corporation and received $5,625 cash.
	24-28	Took the week off for the holidays.
	31	Received $2,850 from Fostek Co. on their receivable.
	31	Reimbursed Mary Graham's business automobile expenses of 600 kilometres at $0.50 per kilometre.
	31	Mary Graham withdrew $1,800 cash from the business
	31	The following information was collected to be used in adjusting entries prior to preparing financial statements for the company's first three months: a. The December 31 inventory of computer supplies was $720. b. Three months have passed since the annual insurance premium was paid. c. As of the end of the year, Carly Smith has not been paid for four days of work at the rate of $100 per day. d. The computer is expected to have a four-year life with no salvage value. e. The office equipment is expected to have a three-year life with no salvage value. f. Prepaid rent for three of the four months has expired.

CHAPTER

Completing the Accounting Cycle and Classifying Accounts

Accounting Edge

Montreal, PQ—Marie Nguyen wasn't trying to jump on the latest management bandwagon, but when she founded **Statistics Analysis** to analyze marketing survey data, her son did her company's accounting. When demand for her services grew—and her son went off to become a correspondent—Nguyen knew she needed outside accounting help. She lacked the knowledge to prepare work sheets and financial reports and to use other tools needed for business decisions. "I realized how little I knew—like not even knowing how to bill clients or set salaries," said Nguyen.

For support, Nguyen turned her books over to a local firm called **Accounting Assistance**. The firm took care of her basic accounting needs, but it also told her something that shocked her: she was consistently underestimating her expenses—sometimes by as much as 75%. Today, Accounting Assistance is not only keeping Nguyen's books, but it is helping with strategic analyses. Nguyen says her profits have doubled since she started using accounting information.

Nguyen relies on outsourcing, contracting out services she once did in-house. More business owners are using outsourcing as a strategic tool. Instead of simply looking for cost savings, they seek services at a higher quality than they can provide themselves. Providers review every part of the accounting cycle using work

Learning Objectives

- LO[1] Prepare a work sheet and explain its usefulness.
- LO[2] Describe the closing process.
- LO[3] Explain why temporary accounts are closed each period.
- LO[4] Describe and prepare closing entries.
- LO[5] Explain and prepare a post-closing trial balance.
- LO[6] Review the steps in the accounting cycle.
- LO[7] Explain and prepare a classified balance sheet.

sheets and other tools such as what-if and ratio analyses. A recent survey of executives showed the top two reasons to outsource to be improving company focus and reaching company potential. Effectively managing data and preparing classified financial reports are important steps in achieving these goals. A study by a large accounting firm found that companies who effectively used these services had 22% more revenues than those who didn't, including greater profit margins and cash flows.

Accounting is the gold mine of outsourcers. They look for ways companies can better manage and analyze financial data. The surprise is that they tackle tasks with tools readily available to us. The tasks include payroll, recordkeeping, statement preparation and computing. They now are experimenting with inventory, pensions and sales—even customer service. This creates enormous accounting-related opportunities in managing and analyzing data. As one consultant said, "I have data everywhere but not a drop of information." Work sheets and other analysis tools are one remedy.

SOURCE: Adapted from *Business Week*, May 13, 1996.

Chapter Preview

Financial statement preparation is a major purpose of accounting. Many of the important steps in the accounting cycle P. 84 leading to financial statements P. 36 are explained in earlier chapters. We described how transactions and events are analyzed, journalized, and posted. We also described important adjusting entries P. 140 that are often necessary to properly reflect revenues when earned and expenses when incurred.

This chapter begins with the introduction of the work sheet, a useful tool in preparing financial statements. Chapter 5 also describes the final steps in the accounting cycle (Exhibit 5.1), Steps 8 and 9, involving the closing process that prepares revenue, expense, and withdrawals accounts for the next reporting period and updates the owner's capital account. We explain how accounts are classified on a balance sheet P. 38 to give more useful information to decision makers. These tools for managing data are the kind Marie Nguyen refers to in the opening article; such tools improve decision making.

Work Sheet as a Tool

Prepare a work sheet and explain its usefulness.

When organizing the information presented in formal reports to internal P. 14 and external users P. 13, accountants prepare numerous analyses and informal documents. These informal documents, called **working papers**, are important tools for accountants. The **work sheet** is an *optional* working paper that can simplify the accountant's efforts in preparing financial statements. It is not distributed to decision makers. The work sheet is prepared before making adjusting entries at the end of a reporting period. It gathers information about the accounts, the needed adjustments, and the financial statements. When it is finished, the work sheet contains information that is recorded in the journal and then presented in the statements.

Exhibit 5.1

Steps in the Accounting Cycle Introduced in Chapter 5

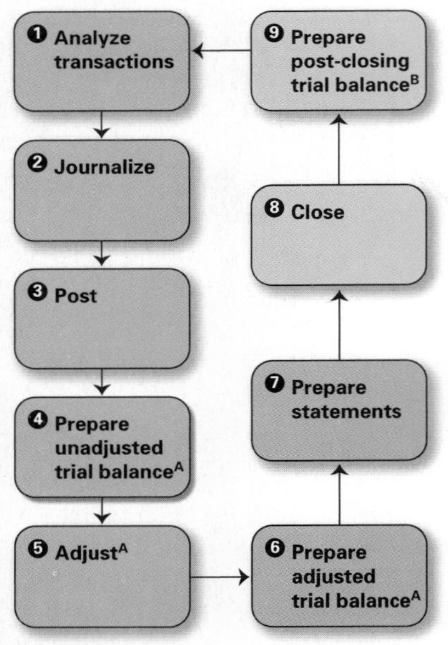

^A Steps 4, 5, and 6 can be done on a *work sheet*.
^B *Reversing entries* are optional and, if prepared, are done between Steps 9 and 1. Reversing entries are covered in Appendix 5A.

Benefits of a Work Sheet

When a business has only a few accounts and adjustments, preparing a work sheet is unnecessary. Computerized accounting systems give financial statements without the need for a work sheet. Yet there are several potential benefits to using a manual or electronic work sheet:

1. It is useful in preparing interim (monthly or quarterly) financial statements when journalizing and posting of adjusting entries are postponed until the year-end.
2. It captures the entire accounting process, linking economic transactions and events to their effects in financial statements.
3. Auditors of financial statements often use a work sheet for planning and organizing the audit. It can also be used to reflect any additional adjustments necessary as a result of the audit.
4. It helps preparers to avoid errors when working with a lot of information in accounting systems involving many accounts and adjustments.

Using a Work Sheet

Exhibit 5.2 shows a blank work sheet. Notice that it has five sets of double columns for the:

1. Unadjusted trial balance.
2. Adjustments.
3. Adjusted trial balance.
4. Income statement.
5. Balance sheet and statement of owner's equity.

The purpose of double columns is to accommodate both debits and credits. Note that a separate set of double columns is not provided for the statement of owner's equity. Because that statement includes only a few items, they are simply listed with the balance sheet items. A work sheet can be completed manually or with a computer.

The work sheet can be completed by following five steps.

Step One

Enter Unadjusted Trial Balance

Turn the first transparency over to create Exhibit 5.3. To begin the work sheet, we list the number and title of each account from the ledger along with the account's unadjusted debit or credit balance.[1] We use the information of Finlay Interiors to describe and interpret the work sheet.

Step Two

Enter Adjustments

Turn the second transparency over to create Exhibit 5.4. The work sheet now appears as it would after Step 2 is completed. Step 2 begins with the entry of adjustments in the adjustment columns. The adjustments shown are the same as those discussed in Chapter 4. They are as follows:

a. Expiration of $100 of prepaid insurance.
b. Used $1,050 of supplies.
c. Amortization on furniture of $375.
d. Earned $250 of revenue received in advance.
e. Accrued $210 of salaries owed to an employee.
f. Accrued interest of $32 on the note payable.
g. Accrued $1,800 of revenue owed by a customer.

To help you correctly match the debit and credit of each adjusting entry, notice that an identifying letter is used for each adjustment. In entering adjustments, we sometimes find additional accounts that need to be inserted on the work sheet. The additional accounts can be inserted below the initial list. ***After preparing a work sheet, we still must enter adjusting entries in the journal and post them to the ledger.***

[1] In practice, accounts with a zero balance that are likely to require an adjusting entry would also be listed.

Step Three

Prepare Adjusted Trial Balance

Turn the third transparency over to create Exhibit 5.5. The adjusted trial balance is prepared by combining the adjustments with the unadjusted balances for each account. As an example, in Exhibit 5.5, the Supplies account has a $3,600 debit balance in the Unadjusted Trial Balance columns. This $3,600 debit is combined with the $1,050 credit in the Adjustments columns to give Supplies a $2,550 debit in the Adjusted Trial Balance columns. The totals of the Adjusted Trial Balance columns confirm the equality of debits and credits.

Step Four

Extend Adjusted Trial Balance Amounts to Financial Statement Columns

Turn the fourth transparency over to create Exhibit 5.6. This step involves sorting adjusted amounts to their proper financial statement columns. Expense items go to the Income Statement Debit column, and revenues to the Income Statement Credit column. Assets and withdrawals go to the Balance Sheet and Statement of Owner's Equity Debit column. Liabilities and owner's capital go to the Balance Sheet and Statement of Owner's Equity Credit column. Recall that accumulated amortization P. 143 is a contra asset account P. 144, so it also goes to the Balance Sheet and Statement of Owner's Equity Credit column. Each statement column is totalled. Notice that the debits do not equal the credits (explained in Step Five).

Step Five

Enter Net Income (or Loss) and Balance the Financial Statement Columns

To see the completed work sheet, turn the fifth transparency over to create Exhibit 5.7. The difference between the debit and credit totals of the Income Statement columns is net income or net loss. If the Credit total exceeds the Debit total, there is a net income. If the Debit total exceeds the Credit total, there is a net loss. In Exhibit 5.7, Finlay Interiors' work sheet shows the Credit total to exceed the Debit total, resulting in net income of $1,753. The difference is added to the *Income Statement* and *Balance Sheet & Statement of Owner's Equity* columns for balancing. In the case of Finlay Interiors where a net income of $1,753 has been calculated, the $1,753 is listed as a *debit* in the Income Statement columns. It is also listed in the Balance Sheet & Statement of Owner's Equity columns, but as a *credit*. The new totals are entered for both sets of columns, showing that the Income Statement columns and Balance Sheet & Statement of Owner's Equity columns now balance. If they do not balance, an error has occurred in the completion of the work sheet.[2] The term *Net income* (or *Net loss*) is listed in the Account column to label the $1,753.

Adding net income to the last Credit column implies that it is to be added to owner's capital. If a loss occurs, it is listed in the last Debit column, implying that it is to be subtracted from owner's capital.

---

[2] If the columns balance, an error(s) could still be present. For example, the columns would still balance if Accounts Payable were listed as a credit, but in the Income Statement columns. Net income would be incorrect, but the columns would still balance.

Step Six — Prepare Financial Statements from Work Sheet Information

A work sheet is not a substitute for financial statements. The completed work sheet is used to prepare the financial statements. The Income Statement columns are used to prepare the income statement. The statement of owner's equity and balance sheet are prepared using the information in the Balance Sheet & Statement of Owner's Equity columns. While the ending balance of owner's capital does not appear in the last two columns as a single amount, it is computed as the owner's capital account balance plus net income (or minus net loss) minus the withdrawals account balance. The opening capital balance for the period would be determined by subtracting any owner investments made during the period from the owner's capital account balance, as shown in the last credit column on the work sheet. Exhibit 5.8 shows the statements for Finlay Interiors as prepared from the work sheet.[3]

Work sheets are also useful in analyzing the effects of proposed or *what-if* transactions. This is done by entering their adjusted financial statement amounts in the first two columns, arranging them in the form of financial statements. Proposed transactions are entered in the second two columns. Extended amounts in the last columns show the effects of these proposed transactions on financial statements. These final columns are called **pro forma statements** because they show the statements *as if* the proposed transactions had occurred.

1. Where do we get the amounts entered in the Unadjusted Trial Balance columns of a work sheet?
2. What are the advantages of using a work sheet to prepare adjusting entries?
3. What are the benefits of a work sheet?

Answers—p. 212

[3] Notice that the $41,320 balance of the last two columns in the work sheet in Exhibit 5.7 does not agree with the balance of $40,345 on the balance sheet; there is a difference of $975 (= $41,320 − $40,345). *This is not an error!* Notice that accumulated amortization of $375 is subtracted on the balance sheet to arrive at total assets; it is *added* in the last Credit column on the work sheet. Also, withdrawals of $600 are *subtracted* on the statement of owner's equity to arrive at ending capital; on the work sheet, they are *added* in the last Debit column. These two items account for the difference of $975 (= $375 + $600).

Exhibit 5.2

Preparing the Work Sheet at the End of the Accounting Period

Finlay Interiors
Work Sheet
For Month Ended January 31, 2001

The heading should identify the entity, the document, and the time period.

Account	Unadjusted Trial Balance		Adjustments		Adjusted Trial Balance		Income Statement		Balance Sheet & Statement of Owner's Equity	
	Debit	Credit	Debit	Credit	Debit	Credit	Debit	Credit	Debit	Credit

The work sheet can be prepared manually or with a computer spreadsheet program.

The work sheet collects and summarizes the information used to prepare financial statements, adjusting entries, and closing entries.

NOTE: Exhibits 5.3 – 5.7 are colour coded to illustrate each step in preparing a work sheet.

Exhibit 5.8

Step Six—Prepare Financial Statements from Work Sheet Information

Finlay Interiors
Income Statement
For Month Ended January 31, 2001

Revenues:		
Consulting revenue	$5,850	
Rental revenue	300	
Total revenues		$6,150
Operating expenses:		
Amortization expense, furniture	$ 375	
Salaries expense	1,610	
Interest expense	32	
Insurance expense	100	
Rent expense	1,000	
Supplies expense	1,050	
Utilities expense	230	
Total operating expenses		4,397
Net income		$1,753

Finlay Interiors
Statement of Owner's Equity
For Month Ended January 31, 2001

Carol Finlay, capital, January 1		$ -0-
Add: Investments by owner	$30,000	
Net income	1,753	31,753
Total		$31,753
Less: Withdrawals by owner		600
Carol Finlay, capital, January 31		$31,153

Finlay Interiors
Balance Sheet
January 31, 2001

Assets		
Cash		$ 8,070
Accounts receivable		1,800
Supplies		2,550
Prepaid insurance		2,300
Furniture	$26,000	
Less: Accumulated amortization	375	25,625
Total assets		$40,345
Liabilities		
Accounts payable	$ 200	
Interest payable	32	
Salaries payable	210	
Unearned consulting revenue	2,750	
Notes payable	6,000	
Total liabilities		$ 9,192
Owner's Equity		
Carol Finlay, capital		31,153
Total liabilities and owner's equity		$40,345

Closing Process

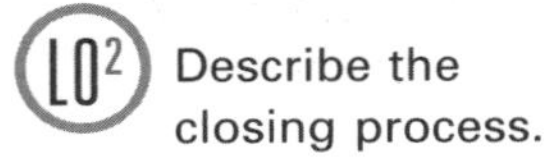
LO2 Describe the closing process.

The **closing process** is an important step of the accounting cycle; it prepares accounts for recording the transactions of the next period. The closing process is performed at the end of an accounting period after financial statements are prepared.

An income statement aims to report revenues earned and expenses incurred during one accounting period. We know that the net income (or loss) from the income statement is shown on the statement of owner's equity, along with withdrawals, to show the change caused to the owner's capital account during one period. Because revenues, expenses, and withdrawals are a part of owner's equity, their balances need to be transferred to the owner's capital account at the end of the period. This transfer of account balances is accomplished by using closing entries.

Therefore, closing entries are a necessary step because we want the:

1. Revenue, expense and withdrawals accounts:
   a. To be reflected in owner's equity.
   b. To begin with zero balances to measure the results from the period just ending.
2. Owner's capital account to reflect:
   a. Increases from net income.
   b. Decreases from net losses and withdrawals from the period just ending.

In the closing process, we must:

1. Identify accounts for closing.
2. Record and post the closing entries.
3. Prepare the post-closing trial balance.

Identify Accounts for Closing—Temporary and Permanent Accounts

LO3 Explain why temporary accounts are closed each period.

Temporary (or nominal) accounts accumulate data related to one accounting period. They include all income statement accounts, withdrawals accounts, and the *Income Summary*. They are temporary because the accounts are opened at the beginning of a period, used to record events for that period, and then closed at the end of the period. They are *temporary* because the accounts describe events or changes that have occurred rather than the financial position that exists at the end of the period. ***The closing process applies only to temporary accounts.***

Temporary Accounts	**Permanent Accounts**
Revenues	Assets
Expenses	Liabilities
Withdrawals	Owner's Capital
Income Summary	

Permanent (or real) accounts report on activities related to one or more future accounting periods. They carry their ending balances into the next period, and include all balance sheet accounts. ***Asset, liability, and owner's capital accounts are not closed*** as long as a company continues to own the assets, owe the liabilities and have owner's equity. They are permanent because they describe the existing financial position.

Recording and Posting Closing Entries

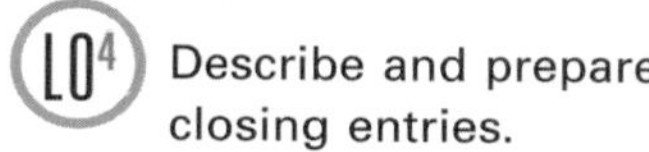

Recording and posting **closing entries** transfer the end-of-period balances in the revenue, expense, and withdrawals accounts to the permanent owner's capital account.

To close revenue and expense accounts, we transfer their balances first to an account called *Income Summary.* **Income Summary** is a temporary account that contains a credit for the sum of all revenues and a debit for the sum of all expenses. Its balance equals net income or net loss, and is transferred to the owner's capital account. Next, we transfer the withdrawals account balance to the owner's capital account. After these closing entries are posted, the revenue, expense, Income Summary, and withdrawals accounts have zero balances. These accounts are then said to be closed or cleared. The four-step closing process is illustrated in Exhibit 5.9.

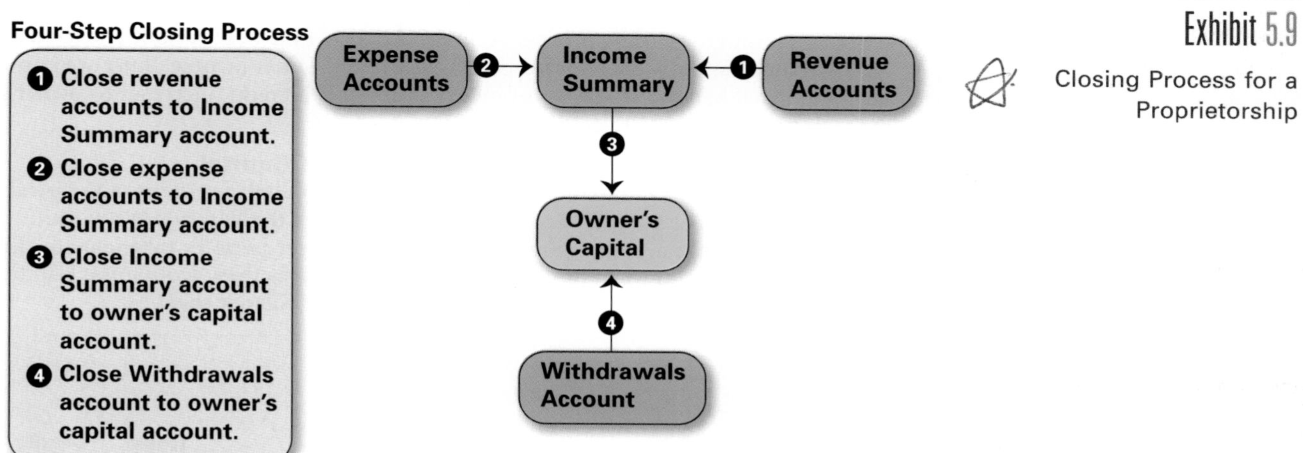

Exhibit 5.9
Closing Process for a Proprietorship

Finlay Interiors' adjusted trial balance on January 31, 2001, is shown in Exhibit 5.10. Exhibit 5.11 shows the four closing entries necessary to close Finlay Interiors' revenue, expense, Income Summary, and withdrawals accounts. We explain each of these four entries.

Entry 1: Close Credit Balances in Revenue Accounts to Income Summary
The first closing entry in Exhibit 5.11 transfers credit balances in revenue accounts to the Income Summary account. We get accounts with credit balances to zero by debiting them. This clearing of accounts prepares them to record new revenues for the next period. The Income Summary account is created and used only for the closing process. The $6,150 credit balance in Income Summary equals the total revenues for the year.

Entry 2: Close Debit Balances in Expense Accounts to Income Summary
The second closing entry in Exhibit 5.11 transfers debit balances in expense accounts to the Income Summary account. We get the debit balances in the expense accounts to zero by crediting them as shown in Exhibit 5.12. This prepares each account for expense entries for the next period. The entry makes the balance of Income Summary equal to January's net income of $1,753. All debit and credit balances related to expense and revenue accounts have now been collected in the Income Summary account.

Entry 3: Close Income Summary to Owner's Capital
The third closing entry in Exhibit 5.11 transfers the balance of the Income Summary account to the owner's capital account. As illustrated in Exhibit 5.12, the Income Summary account has a zero balance after posting this entry. It continues to have a zero balance until the closing process occurs at the end of the next period. The owner's capital account has now been increased by the amount of net income. Since we know that the normal balance P. 94 of owner's capital is a credit, increases to owner's capital from net income are credits.

Entry 4: Close Withdrawals Account to Owner's Capital
The fourth closing entry in Exhibit 5.11 transfers any debit balance in the withdrawals account to the owner's capital account. This entry gives the withdrawals account a zero balance, and the account is ready to accumulate next period's payments to the owner. As illustrated in Exhibit 5.12, this entry also reduces the Carol Finlay, Capital account balance to $31,153, the amount reported on the balance sheet.

Exhibit 5.10

Adjusted Trial Balance

Finlay Interiors
Adjusted Trial Balance
January 31, 2001

	Debit	Credit
Cash	$ 8,070	
Accounts receivable	1,800	
Supplies	2,550	
Prepaid insurance	2,300	
Furniture	26,000	
Accumulated amortization, furniture		$ 375
Accounts payable		200
Interest payable		32
Notes payable		6,000
Salaries payable		210
Unearned consulting revenue		2,750
Carol Finlay, capital		30,000
Carol Finlay, withdrawals	600	
Consulting revenue		5,850
Rental revenue		300
Amortization expense, furniture	375	
Salaries expense	1,610	
Interest expense	32	
Insurance expense	100	
Rent expense	1,000	
Supplies expense	1,050	
Utilities expense	230	
Totals	$45,717	$45,717

Exhibit 5.11

Closing Entries for Finlay Interiors

Finlay Interiors

Entry 1:	**Close revenue accounts**		
Jan. 31	Consulting Revenue	5,850	
	Rental Revenue	300	
	Income Summary		6,150
	To close the revenue accounts and create the Income Summary account.		
Entry 2:	**Close expense accounts**		
31	Income Summary	4,397	
	Amortization Expense, Furniture		375
	Salaries Expense		1,610
	Interest Expense		32
	Insurance Expense		100
	Rent Expense		1,000
	Supplies Expense		1,050
	Utilities Expense		230
	To close expense accounts.		
Entry 3:	**Close Income Summary to owner's capital**		
31	Income Summary	1,753	
	Carol Finlay, Capital		1,753
	To close the Income Summary account.		
Entry 4:	**Close withdrawals account to owner's capital**		
31	Carol Finlay, Capital	600	
	Carol Finlay, Withdrawals		600
	To close the withdrawals account.		

Exhibit 5.12

Closing Entries of Finlay Interiors

Finlay Interiors

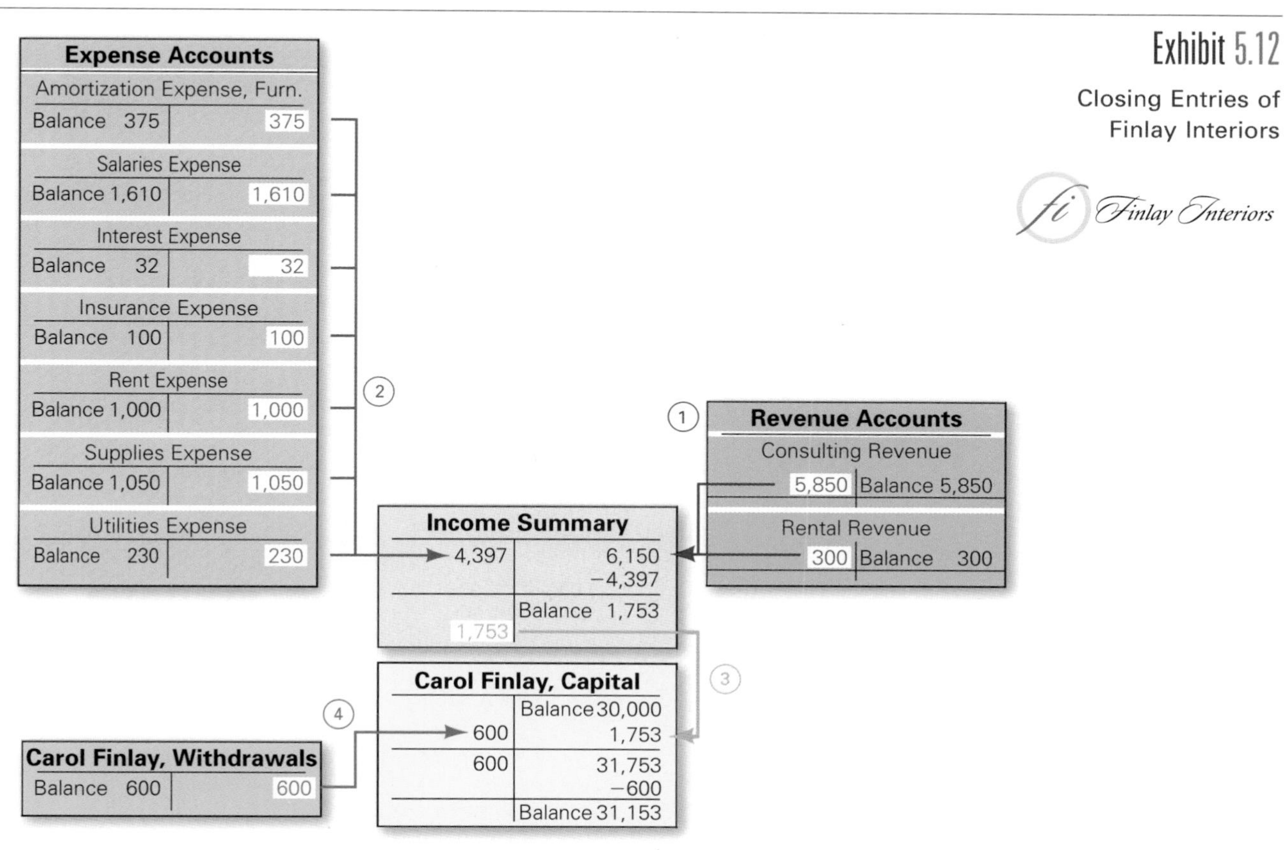

Sources of Closing Entry Information

We can identify the accounts that need to be closed and the amounts in the closing entries by looking to individual revenue, expense and withdrawals accounts in the ledger. If we prepare an adjusted trial balance after the adjusting process, the information for closing entries is available on the trial balance as illustrated in Exhibit 5.10.

Exhibit 5.13

Ledger after the Closing Process for Finlay Interiors

Ledger

Asset Accounts

Cash #101

Date	Debit	Credit	Balance
2001			
Jan. 1	30,000		30,000
2		2,500	27,500
3		20,000	7,500
10	2,200		9,700
12		1,000	8,700
12		700	8,000
22	1,900		9,900
24		900	9,000
24		600	8,400
26	3,000		11,400
26		2,400	9,000
26		230	8,770
26		700	8,070

Accounts Receivable #106

Date	Debit	Credit	Balance
2001			
Jan. 12	1,900		1,900
22		1,900	-0-
31	1,800		1,800

Supplies #125

Date	Debit	Credit	Balance
2001			
Jan. 2	2,500		2,500
6	1,100		3,600
31		1,050	2,550

Prepaid Insurance #128

Date	Debit	Credit	Balance
2001			
Jan. 26	2,400		2,400
31		100	2,300

Furniture #167

Date	Debit	Credit	Balance
2001			
Jan. 3	20,000		20,000
6	6,000		26,000

Accumulated Amortization, Furniture #168

Date	Debit	Credit	Balance
2001			
Jan. 31		375	375

Liability and Equity Accounts

Accounts Payable #201

Date	Debit	Credit	Balance
2001			
Jan. 6		1,100	1,100
24	900		200

Interest Payable #203

Date	Debit	Credit	Balance
2001			
Jan. 31		32	32

Salaries Payable #209

Date	Debit	Credit	Balance
2001			
Jan. 31		210	210

Unearned Consulting Revenue #236

Date	Debit	Credit	Balance
2001			
Jan. 26		3,000	3,000
31	250		2,750

Notes Payable #240

Date	Debit	Credit	Balance
2001			
Jan. 6		6,000	6,000

Carol Finlay, Capital #301

Date	Debit	Credit	Balance
2001			
Jan. 1		30,000	30,000
31		1,753	31,753
31	600		31,153

Carol Finlay, Withdrawals #302

Date	Debit	Credit	Balance
2001			
Jan. 24	600		600
31		600	-0-

Exhibit 5.13 (continued)

Ledger after the Closing Process for Finlay Interiors

Revenue and Expense Accounts (including Income Summary)

Consulting Revenue #403

Date	Debit	Credit	Balance
2001			
Jan. 10		2,200	2,200
12		1,600	3,800
31		250	4,050
31		1,800	5,850
31	5,850		-0-

Rental Revenue #406

Date	Debit	Credit	Balance
2001			
Jan. 12		300	300
31	300		-0-

Amortization Expense, Furniture #614

Date	Debit	Credit	Balance
2001			
Jan. 31	375		375
31		375	-0-

Salaries Expense #622

Date	Debit	Credit	Balance
2001			
Jan. 12	700		700
26	700		1,400
31	210		1,610
31		1,610	-0-

Interest Expense #633

Date	Debit	Credit	Balance
2001			
Jan. 31	32		32
31		32	-0-

Insurance Expense #637

Date	Debit	Credit	Balance
2001			
Jan. 31	100		100
31		100	-0-

Rent Expense #641

Date	Debit	Credit	Balance
2001			
Jan. 12	1,000		1,000
31		1,000	-0-

Supplies Expense #651

Date	Debit	Credit	Balance
2001			
Jan. 31	1,050		1,050
31		1,050	-0-

Utilities Expense #690

Date	Debit	Credit	Balance
2001			
Jan. 26	230		230
31		230	-0-

Income Summary #901

Date	Debit	Credit	Balance
2001			
Jan. 31		6,150	6,150
31	4,397		1,753
31	1,753		-0-

Exhibit 5.13 illustrates the ledger accounts for Finlay Interiors as they would appear after posting the closing entries of Exhibit 5.11. Notice that all of the temporary accounts (revenues, expenses, and withdrawals) have a zero balance. The closing process transferred the balances of the temporary accounts to the Carol Finlay, Capital account. The capital account balance of $31,153 includes owner investment of $30,000 and net income of $1,753, less withdrawals of $600.

4. What are the four major closing entries?
5. Why are revenue and expense accounts called temporary? Are there other temporary accounts?

Answers—p. 212

Preparing a Post-Closing Trial Balance

Explain and prepare a post-closing trial balance.

A **post-closing trial balance** is a list of permanent accounts and their balances from the ledger after all closing entries are journalized and posted. It is a list of balances for accounts not closed. These accounts are a company's assets, liabilities and owner's equity at the end of a period. They are identical to those in the balance sheet. The aim of a post-closing trial balance is to verify that (1) total debits equal total credits for permanent accounts, and (2) all temporary accounts have zero balances.

Finlay Interiors' post-closing trial balance is shown in Exhibit 5.14 and is the last step in the accounting process. The post-closing trial balance in Exhibit 5.14 was created by listing the account balances found in Exhibit 5.13. Like the trial balance, the post-closing trial balance does not prove that all transactions are recorded or that the ledger is correct.

Exhibit 5.14

Post-Closing Trial Balance

Finlay Interiors
Post-Closing Trial Balance
January 31, 2001

	Debit	Credit
Cash	$ 8,070	
Accounts receivable	1,800	
Supplies	2,550	
Prepaid insurance	2,300	
Furniture	26,000	
Accumulated amortization, furniture		$ 375
Accounts payable		200
Interest payable		32
Salaries payable		210
Notes payable		6,000
Unearned consulting revenue		2,750
Carol Finlay, capital		31,153
Totals	$40,720	$40,720

Closing Entries After Period-End Date

We are not usually able to make closing entries on the last day of each period. This is because information about certain transactions and events that require *adjusting* is not always available until several days or even weeks later. Because some adjusting entries are recorded later, closing entries are recorded later, but both are dated as of the last day of the period. Financial statements therefore reflect what is known on the date they are prepared instead of what was known as of the last day of the period.

One example is a company that receives a utility bill on February 14 for costs incurred for the month of January. When the bill is received, the company records the expense and the payable as of January 31. The income statement for January then reflects expenses incurred and the January 31 balance sheet includes the payable, even though the amounts are not actually known on January 31.

Answer—p. 212

6. What accounts are listed on the post-closing trial balance?

Reviewing the Accounting Cycle

LO6 Review the steps in the accounting cycle.

The steps in the accounting cycle have been the focus in this and the previous chapters. We now briefly review these steps in Exhibit 5.15 to emphasize their importance in providing users with information for decision making.

1. Analyze transaction	Analyze transactions in preparation for journalizing.
2. Journalize	Record debits and credits with explanations in a journal.
3. Post	Transfer debits and credits from journal entries to the ledger accounts.
4. Unadjusted trial balance [A]	Summarize ledger accounts and amounts.
5. Adjust [A]	Record adjustments to bring account balances up to date; journalize and post adjusting entries to the accounts.
6. Adjusted trial balance [A]	Summarize adjusted ledger accounts and amounts.
7. Prepare statements	Use adjusted trial balance to prepare: income statement, statement owner's equity, balance sheet, and statement of cash flows (details in preparing the statement of cash flows are in Chapter 19).
8. Close	Journalize and post entries to close temporary (revenue, expense and withdrawals) accounts and update the owner's capital account.
9. Post-closing trial balance [B]	Tests clerical accuracy of adjusting and closing steps.

[A] Steps 4, 5, and 6 can be done on a *work sheet.*

[B] *Reversing entries* are optional and, if prepared, are done between Steps 9 and 1. Reversing entries are covered in Appendix 5A.

Exhibit 5.15

Summary of Steps in the Accounting Cycle

7. What steps in the accounting cycle are optional?

Answer—p. 212

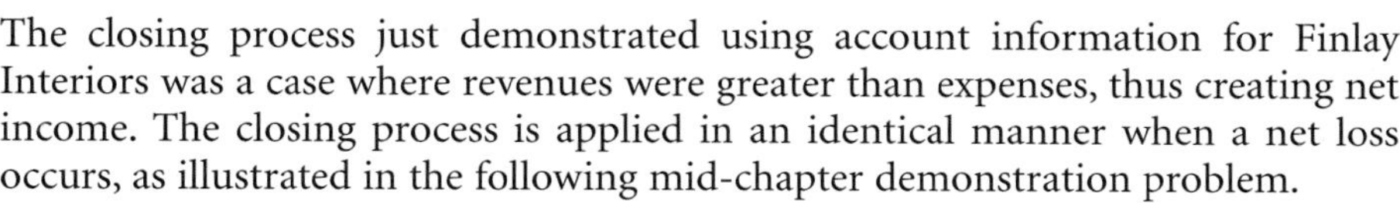

The closing process just demonstrated using account information for Finlay Interiors was a case where revenues were greater than expenses, thus creating net income. The closing process is applied in an identical manner when a net loss occurs, as illustrated in the following mid-chapter demonstration problem.

Mid-Chapter Demonstration Problem

Using the account information in the following adjusted trial balance for Booster's Towing Service:

1. Prepare the closing entries for December 31, 2001.
2. Post the closing entries.
3. Prepare the post-closing trial balance at December 31, 2001.

Booster's Towing Service
Adjusted Trial Balance
December 31, 2001

	Debit	Credit
Cash	$ 7,000	
Accounts receivable	3,000	
Tow truck	31,000	
Accumulated amortization, tow truck		$27,000
Salaries payable		700
Terry Booster, capital		17,200
Terry Booster, withdrawals	2,300	
Towing revenue		38,000
Salaries expense	30,000	
Amortization expense, tow truck	5,000	
Utilities expense	4,600	
Totals	$82,900	$82,900

Planning the solution:

1. Identify accounts for closing.
2. Journalize and post the four types of closing entries.
3. Prepare the post-closing trial balance.

SOLUTION TO Mid-Chapter Demonstration Problem

Part 1

		Debit	Credit
Entry 1:	**Close the revenue account:**		
	Towing Revenue	38,000	
	Income Summary		38,000
	To close the revenue account and create the Income Summary account.		
Entry 2:	**Close the expense accounts:**		
	Income Summary	39,600	
	Salaries Expense		30,000
	Amortization Expense, Truck		5,000
	Utilities Expense		4,600
	To close the expense accounts.		
Entry 3:	**Close Income Summary to owner's capital:**		
	Terry Booster, Capital	1,600	
	Income Summary		1,600
	To close the net loss in the Income Summary account to capital.		
Entry 4:	**Close withdrawals account to owner's capital:**		
	Terry Booster, Capital	2,300	
	Terry Booster, Withdrawals		2,300
	To close the withdrawals account.		

Part 2

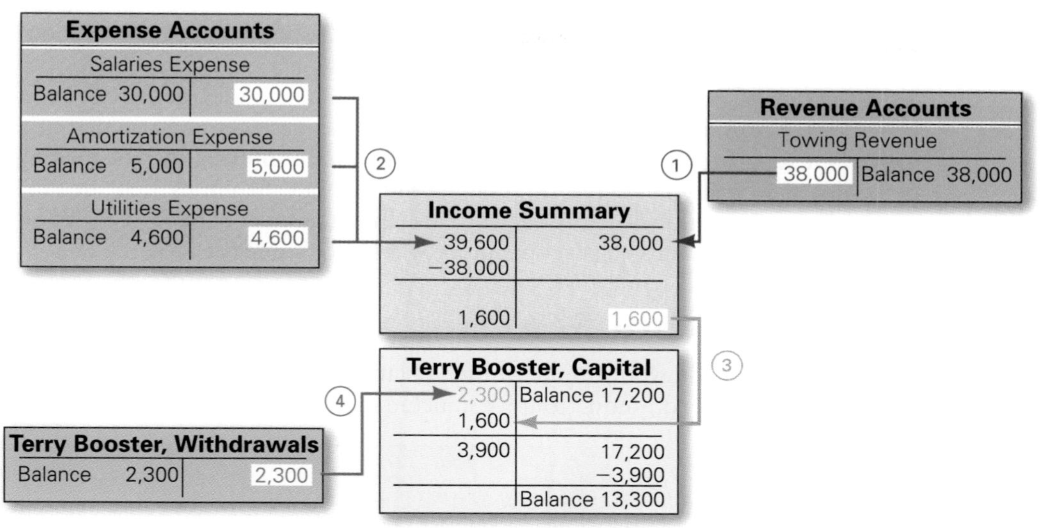

Part 3

Booster's Towing Service
Post-Closing Trial Balance
December 31, 2001

	Debit	Credit
Cash	$ 7,000	
Accounts receivable	3,000	
Tow truck	31,000	
Accumulated amortization, tow truck		$27,000
Salaries payable		700
Terry Booster, capital		13,300
Totals	$41,000	$41,000

Classified Balance Sheet

LO7 Explain and prepare a classified balance sheet.

Our discussion to this point has been limited to unclassified financial statements. An **unclassified balance sheet** is one where its items are broadly grouped into assets, liabilities and owner's equity. One example is Finlay Interiors' balance sheet in Exhibit 5.8. A **classified balance sheet** organizes assets and liabilities into important subgroups to provide users with more useful information for making decisions. One example is information to differentiate liabilities that are due shortly from those not due for several years. Information in this case helps us assess a company's ability to meet liabilities when they come due.

Classification Scheme

There is no required layout for a classified balance sheet. Yet a classified balance sheet often contains common groupings, including those shown in Exhibit 5.16:

Exhibit 5.16

Sections of a Classified Balance Sheet

Assets	Liabilities and Owner's Equity
Current Assets	Current Liabilities
Long-Term Investments	Long-Term Liabilities
Capital Assets: Plant and Equipment	Owner's Equity
Intangible Assets	

One of the more important classifications is the separation between current and noncurrent items for both assets and liabilities. Current items are those that are expected to come due within the longer of one year or the company's normal operating cycle. An **operating cycle** is the length of time between (1) paying employees who perform services and receiving cash from customers for a service company and (2) paying for merchandise and receiving cash from customers for a company that sells goods.

Exhibit 5.17 shows the steps of an operating cycle for both service and merchandising companies. For a company that sells services, the operating cycle is the average time between (1) paying employees who do the services and (2) receiving cash from customers. For a company that sells products, the operating cycle is the average time between (1) paying suppliers for merchandise and (2) receiving cash from customers.

Exhibit 5.17

Operating Cycles for a Service Company and a Merchandising Company

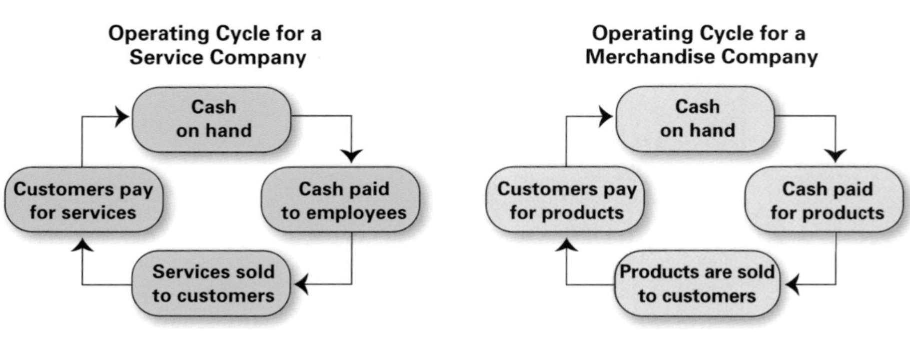

Most operating cycles are less than one year. This means that most companies use a one-year period in deciding which assets and liabilities are current. Yet there are companies with an operating cycle that is longer than one year. One example is a company that routinely allows customers to take more than one year to pay for purchases. Another example is a producer of beverages and other products that require aging for several years. These companies use their operating cycle in deciding which balance sheet items are current.[4]

[4] In these uncommon situations, companies provide supplemental information about their current assets and liabilities to allow users to compare them with other companies.

A balance sheet usually lists current assets before long-term assets, and current liabilities before long-term liabilities. This highlights assets that are most easily converted to cash, and liabilities that are shortly coming due. Items in the current group are usually listed in the order of how quickly they will be converted to or paid in cash.

Classification Example

The balance sheet for Music Components is shown in Exhibit 5.18. It shows the most commonly used groupings. Its assets are classified into (1) current assets, (2) long-term investments, (3) plant and equipment, and (4) intangible assets. Its liabilities are classified as either current or long-term. Not all companies use the same categories of assets and liabilities on their balance sheets. Cominco's 1999 balance sheet lists only three asset classes: current assets; capital assets; and other assets.

Exhibit 5.18

A Classified Balance Sheet

Music Components Balance Sheet January 31, 2001			
Assets			
Current assets:			
Cash		$ 6,500	
Temporary investments		2,100	
Accounts receivable		4,400	
Notes receivable		1,500	
Merchandise inventory		27,500	
Prepaid expenses		2,400	
Total current assets			$ 44,400
Long-term investments:			
WestJet common shares		$ 18,000	
Land held for future expansion		48,000	
Total investments			66,000
Capital assets:			
Plant and equipment:			
Store equipment	$ 33,200		
Less: Accumulated amortization	8,000	$ 25,200	
Buildings	$170,000		
Less: Accumulated amortization	45,000	125,000	
Land		73,200	
Total plant and equipment			223,400
Intangible assets:			
Trademark			10,000
Total assets			$343,800
Liabilities			
Current liabilities:			
Accounts payable	$ 15,300		
Wages payable	3,200		
Notes payable	3,000		
Current portion of long-term liabilities	7,500		
Total current liabilities		$ 29,000	
Long-term liabilities:			
Notes payable (less current portion)		150,000	
Total liabilities			$179,000
Owner's Equity			
Donald Bowie, capital			164,800
Total liabilities and owner's equity			$343,800

Classification Groups

Current Assets

Current assets are cash and other resources that are expected to be sold, collected or used within the longer of one year or the company's operating cycle.[5] Examples are cash, temporary investments in marketable securities, accounts receivable, notes receivable, goods for sale to customers (called *merchandise inventory* or *inventory*), and prepaid expenses. As of June 30, 2000, Maple Leaf Foods' current assets were reported as shown in Exhibit 5.19.

Exhibit 5.19

Current Assets Section

Maple Leaf Foods	
Current assets (in thousands)	
Cash and cash equivalents	$ 63,005
Accounts receivable	212,312
Inventories	203,634
Prepaid expenses	15,077
Total current assets	$494,028

A company's prepaid expenses are usually small compared to other assets, and are often combined and shown as a single item. It is likely that Prepaid Expenses in Exhibits 5.18 and 5.19 include such items as prepaid insurance, prepaid rent, office supplies and store supplies. Prepaid expenses are usually listed last because they will not be converted to cash.

Long-Term Investments

Long-term investments are held for more than one year or the operating cycle. Notes receivable and investments in shares and bonds are in many cases long-term assets. Note that the *temporary* investments in Exhibit 5.18 are current assets and not shown as long-term investments. We explain the differences between short- and long-term investments later in this book. Long-term investments also often include land that is not being used in operations but is held for future expansion.

Capital Assets

Plant and equipment

Plant and equipment, also called plant assets, are tangible long-lived assets used to produce or sell products and services. Examples are equipment, vehicles, buildings and land. Land held for future expansion is *not* a plant and equipment asset because it is not used to produce or sell products and services. Plant and equipment assets are also called "*property, plant and equipment*" or "*land, buildings and equipment*." The order of listing plant assets within this category varies.

Intangible assets

Intangible assets are long-term resources used to produce or sell products and services; they lack physical form and their benefits are uncertain. Examples are patents, trademarks, copyrights, franchises and goodwill. Their value comes from the privileges or rights granted to or held by the owner. Second Cup lists an intangible asset for 1999 as shown in Exhibit 5.20.

[5] *CICA Handbook*, "Current Assets and Current Liabilities," par. 1510.01

Second Cup	
Goodwill, net *(in thousands)*................................	$8,749

Exhibit 5.20

Intangible Assets Section

Current Liabilities

Current liabilities are obligations due to be paid or settled within the longer of one year or the operating cycle. They are usually settled by paying out current assets. Current liabilities include accounts payable, notes payable, wages payable, taxes payable, interest payable, and unearned revenues. Any portion of a long-term liability due to be paid within the longer of one year or the operating cycle is a current liability. Exhibit 5.18 shows how the current portion of long-term liabilities is usually reported. Unearned revenues are current liabilities when they will be settled by delivering products or services within the longer of the year or the operating cycle. While practice varies, current liabilities are often reported in the order of those to be settled first.

Long-Term Liabilities

Long-term liabilities are obligations not due within the longer of one year or the operating cycle. Notes payable, mortgages payable, bonds payable, and lease obligations are often long-term liabilities. If a company has both short- and long-term items in one of these accounts, it is common to separate them in the ledger for reporting.

Owner's Equity

Owner's equity is the owner's claim on the assets of a company. It is reported in the equity section with an owner's capital account for a sole proprietorship P. 10. For a partnership P. 10, the equity section reports a capital account for each partner. For a corporation P. 10, the equity section is called Shareholders' Equity. Partnership equity and shareholders' equity are discussed in detail in later chapters.

8. Identify which of the following assets are classified as (1) current assets or (2) capital assets: (a) land used in operations; (b) office supplies; (c) receivables from customers due in 10 months; (d) insurance protection for the next nine months; (e) trucks used to provide services to customers; (f) trademarks used in advertising the company's services.
9. Name two examples of assets classified as investments on the balance sheet.
10. Explain an operating cycle for a service company.

Answers—p. 212

Summary

LO1 Prepare a work sheet and explain its usefulness. A work sheet can be a useful tool when preparing and analyzing financial statements. It is helpful at the end of a period for preparing adjusting entries, an adjusted trial balance, and financial statements. A work sheet often contains five pairs of columns for an unadjusted trial balance, the adjustments, an adjusted trial balance, an income statement, and the balance sheet (including the statement of owner's equity).

LO2 Describe the closing process. The closing process is the final step of the accounting cycle; it prepares accounts for recording the transactions of the next period.

LO3 Explain why temporary accounts are closed each period. Temporary accounts are closed at the end of each accounting period for two main reasons: (1) to update the owner's capital account to include the effects of all revenue, expense, and withdrawals transactions and events recorded for the period; and (2) to prepare revenue, expense and withdrawals accounts for the next reporting period by giving them zero balances.

LO4 **Describe and prepare closing entries.** Recording and posting closing entries transfer the end-of-period balances in revenue, expense and withdrawals accounts to the owner's capital account. Closing entries involve four steps: (1) close credit balances in revenue accounts to income summary, (2) close debit balances in expense accounts to income summary, (3) close income summary to owner's capital, and (4) close withdrawals account to owner's capital.

LO5 **Explain and prepare a post-closing trial balance.** A post-closing trial balance is a list of permanent accounts and their balances after all closing entries are journalized and posted. Permanent accounts are asset, liability and owner's equity accounts. The purpose of a post-closing trial balance is to verify that (1) total debits equal total credits for permanent accounts and (2) all temporary accounts have zero balances.

LO6 **Review the steps in the accounting cycle.** The accounting cycle consists of nine steps: (1) analyze transactions, (2) journalize, (3) post, (4) prepare unadjusted trial balance, (5) adjust, (6) prepare adjusted trial balance, (7) prepare statements, (8) close, and (9) prepare post-closing trial balance. If a work sheet is prepared, it covers Steps 4 to 6. Reversing entries is an optional step that is done between Steps 9 and 1.

LO7 **Explain and prepare a classified balance sheet.** Classified balance sheets usually report four groups of assets: current assets, long-term investments, plant and equipment, and intangible assets. Also, they include at least two groups of liabilities: current and long-term. Owner's equity for proprietorships reports the capital account balance.

GUIDANCE ANSWERS TO  Flashback

1. Amounts in the Unadjusted Trial Balance columns are taken from account balances in the ledger.
2. A work sheet offers the advantage of listing on one page all of the necessary information to make adjusting entries.
3. A work sheet can help in: (a) preparing interim financial statements, (b) linking transactions and events to their effects in financial statements, (c) showing adjustments for audit purposes, (d) avoiding errors, and (e) showing effects of proposed or "what-if" transactions.
4. The four major closing entries consist of closing: (1) credit balances in revenue accounts to Income Summary, (2) debit balances in expense accounts to Income Summary, (3) Income Summary to owner's capital, and (4) withdrawals account to owner's capital.
5. Revenue and expense accounts are called temporary because they are opened and closed every reporting period. The Income Summary and owner's withdrawals accounts are also temporary accounts.
6. Permanent accounts are listed on the post-closing trial balance. These accounts are the asset, liability and owner's equity accounts.
7. Making reversing entries is an optional step in the accounting cycle. Also, a work sheet is an optional tool for completing Steps 4 to 6.
8. Current assets: *b, c, d.* Capital assets: *a, e, f.*
9. Investment in common shares, investment in bonds, land held for future expansion.
10. An operating cycle for a company is the length of time between (1) purchases of services and products from suppliers to carry out a company's plans and (2) the sale of services and products to customers. The length of a company's operating cycle depends on its activities. For a service company, the operating cycle is the average time between (1) paying employees who do the services and (2) receiving cash from customers.

Demonstration Problem

This work sheet shows the December 31, 2001, unadjusted trial balance of Westside Appliance Repair Company:

Westside Appliance Repair Company
Work Sheet
For Year Ended December 31, 2001

Account	Unadjusted Trial Balance		Adjustments		Adjusted Trial Balance		Income Statement		Balance Sheet & Statement of Owner's Equity	
	Debit	Credit	Debit	Credit	Debit	Credit	Debit	Credit	Debit	Credit
Cash	83,300									
Notes receivable	60,000									
Prepaid insurance	19,000									
Prepaid rent	17,000									
Equipment	165,000									
Accumulated amortization, equipment		26,000								
Accounts payable		37,000								
Long-term notes payable		58,000								
Brian Westside, capital		173,500								
Brian Westside, withdrawals	25,000									
Repair services revenue		294,000								
Interest revenue		6,500								
Amortization expense, equipment	-0-									
Wages expense	179,000									
Rent expense	35,000									
Insurance expense	7,000									
Interest expense	4,700									
Totals	595,000	595,000								

Required

1. Using the information provided above, complete the work sheet.
2. Prepare closing entries for Westside Appliance Repair Co.
3. Set up Income Summary and Brian Westside, Capital accounts and post the closing entries to these accounts.
4. Determine the balance of the Brian Westside, Capital account to be reported on the December 31, 2001 balance sheet.
5. Prepare a classified balance sheet at December 31, 2001 for Westside Appliance Repair Co.

Planning the Solution

- Using the additional information provided, enter the adjustments into the adjustment columns of the work sheet. Combine the adjustments with the unadjusted balances for each account to determine the adjusted trial balance amounts.
- Extend the adjusted trial balance account balances to the appropriate financial statement columns.
- Prepare entries to close the revenue accounts to Income Summary, close the expense accounts to Income Summary, close Income Summary to the capital account, and close the withdrawals account to the capital account.
- Post the first and second closing entries to the Income Summary account. Examine the balance of Income Summary and verify that it agrees with the net income shown on the work sheet.

- Post the third and fourth closing entries to the capital account.
- Prepare a classified balance sheet.

SOLUTION TO Demonstration Problem

1. Completing the work sheet:

Westside Appliance Repair Company
Work Sheet
For Year Ended December 31, 2001

Account	Unadjusted Trial Balance		Adjustments		Adjusted Trial Balance		Income Statement		Balance Sheet & Statement of Owner's Equity	
	Debit	Credit	Debit	Credit	Debit	Credit	Debit	Credit	Debit	Credit
Cash	83,300				83,300				83,300	
Notes receivable	60,000				60,000				60,000	
Prepaid insurance	19,000				19,000				19,000	
Prepaid rent	17,000			b) 12,000	5,000				5,000	
Equipment	165,000				165,000				165,000	
Accumulated amortization, equipment	26,000			a) 26,000	52,000				52,000	
Accounts payable		37,000				37,000				37,000
Long-term notes payable		58,000				58,000				58,000
Brian Westside, capital		173,500				173,500				173,500
Brian Westside, withdrawals	25,000				25,000				25,000	
Repair services revenue		294,000				294,000		294,000		
Interest revenue		6,500				6,500		6,500		
Amortization expense, equipment	-0-		a) 26,000		26,000		26,000			
Wages expense	179,000				179,000		179,000			
Rent expense	35,000		b) 12,000		47,000		47,000			
Insurance expense	7,000				7,000		7,000			
Interest expense	4,700				4,700		4,700			
Totals	595,000	595,000	38,000	38,000	621,000	621,000	263,700	300,500	357,300	320,500
Net income							36,800			36,800
							300,500	300,500	357,300	357,300

2. Closing Entries:

Date	Account	Debit	Credit
Dec. 31	Repair Services Revenue	294,000	
	Interest Revenue	6,500	
	Income Summary		300,500
	To close the revenue accounts and create the income summary account.		
31	Income Summary	263,700	
	Amortization Expense, Equipment		26,000
	Wages Expense		179,000
	Rent Expense		47,000
	Insurance Expense		7,000
	Interest Expense		4,700
	To close the expense accounts and debit the income summary account.		
31	Income Summary	36,800	
	Brian Westside, Capital		36,800
	To close the Income Summary account.		
31	Brian Westside, Capital	25,000	
	Brian Westside, Withdrawals		25,000
	To close the withdrawals account.		

3.

Income Summary					Account No. 999
Date	**Explanation**	**PR**	**Debit**	**Credit**	**Balance**
2001					
Jan. 1	Beginning balance				-0-
Dec. 31	Close revenue accounts			300,500	300,500
31	Close expense accounts		263,700		36,800
31	Close Income Summary		36,800		-0-

Brian Westside, Capital					Account No. 301
Date	**Explanation**	**PR**	**Debit**	**Credit**	**Balance**
2001					
Jan. 1	Beginning balance				173,500
Dec. 31	Close Income Summary			36,800	210,300
31	Close Brian Westside, Withdrawals		25,000		185,300

4. The final capital balance of $185,300 will be reported on the December 31, 2001 balance sheet. Note that the final capital balance reflects the increase due to the net income earned during the year and the decrease for the owner's withdrawals during the year.

5.

Westside Appliance Repair Company
Balance Sheet
December 31, 2001

Assets		
Current assets:		
Cash	$ 83,300	
Notes receivable	60,000	
Prepaid insurance	19,000	
Prepaid rent	5,000	
Total current assets		$167,300
Capital assets:		
Plant and equipment:		
Equipment	$165,000	
Less: Accumulated amortization	52,000	113,000
Total assets		$280,300
Liabilities		
Current liabilities:		
Accounts payable	$ 37,000	
Long-term liabilities:		
Long-term notes payable	58,000	
Total liabilities		$ 95,000
Owner's Equity		
Brian Westside, capital		185,300
Total liabilities and owner's equity		$280,300

APPENDIX

5A Reversing Entries and Account Numbering

Reversing Entries

LO8 Prepare reversing entries and explain their purpose.

Reversing entries are optional entries. They are linked to accrued assets and liabilities that were created by adjusting entries at the end of a reporting period. Reversing entries are used to simplify a company's recordkeeping.

Exhibit 5A.1 shows how reversing entries work for Finlay Interiors. The top of the exhibit shows the adjusting entry recorded by Finlay Interiors on January 31, 2001, for earned but unpaid salary. The entry recorded three days' salary to increase January's total salary expense to $1,610. The entry also recognized a liability of $210. The expense is reported on January's income statement and the expense account is closed. As a result, the ledger on February 1, 2001 reflects a $210 liability and a zero balance in the Salaries Expense account. At this point, the choice is made to use reversing entries or not.

Accounting *Without* Reversing Entries

The path down the left side of Exhibit 5A.1 is described in Chapter 4. That is, when the next payday occurs on February 9, we record payment with a compound entry that debits both the expense and liability accounts. Posting that entry creates a $490 balance in the expense account and reduces the liability account balance to zero because the debt has been settled.

The disadvantage of this approach is the complex entry required on February 9. Paying the accrued liability means that this entry differs from the routine entries made on all other paydays. To construct the proper entry on February 9, we must recall the effect of the adjusting entry. Reversing entries overcome this disadvantage.

Accounting *With* Reversing Entries

The right side of Exhibit 5A.1 shows how a reversing entry on February 1 overcomes the disadvantage of the complex February 9 entry. The reversing entry is the exact opposite of the adjusting entry recorded on January 31. The Salaries Payable liability is debited for $210, meaning that this account now has a zero balance after the entry is posted. Technically, the Salaries Payable account now understates the liability, but this is not a problem since financial statements are not prepared before the liability is settled on February 9. The credit to the Salaries Expense account is unusual because it gives the account an *abnormal credit balance.*

Exhibit 5A.1

Reversing Entries for Accrued Expenses

Finlay Interiors

Accrue salaries expense on December 31, 2000

Salaries Expense 210
Salaries Payable 210

Salaries Expense

Date	Expl.	Debit	Credit	Balance
2000				
Dec. 12	(7)	700		700
26	(16)	700		1,400
31	(*e*)	210		1,610

Salaries Payable

Date	Expl.	Debit	Credit	Balance
2000				
Dec. 31	(*e*)		210	210

No reversing entry recorded on January 1, 2001

NO ENTRY

Salaries Expense

Date	Expl.	Debit	Credit	Balance
2001				

Salaries Payable

Date	Expl.	Debit	Credit	Balance
2000				
Dec. 31	(*e*)		210	210
2001				

Reversing entry recorded on January 1, 2001

Salaries Payable 210
Salaries Expense 210

Salaries Expense

Date	Expl.	Debit	Credit	Balance
2001				
Jan. 1			**210**	**(210)**

Salaries Payable

Date	Expl.	Debit	Credit	Balance
2000				
Dec. 31	(*e*)		210	
2001				-0-
Jan. 1		**210**		**210**

Pay the accrued and current salaries on January 9, the first payday in 2001.

Salaries Expense 490
Salaries Payable 210
Cash 700

Salaries Expense

Date	Expl.	Debit	Credit	Balance
2001				
Jan. 9		**490**		**490**

Salaries Payable

Date	Expl.	Debit	Credit	Balance
2000				
Dec. 31	(*e*)		210	210
2001				
Jan. 9		**210**		**-0-**

Salaries Expense 700
Cash 700

Salaries Expense

Date	Expl.	Debit	Credit	Balance
2001				
Jan. 1			210	(210)
Jan. 9		**700**		**490**

Salaries Payable

Date	Expl.	Debit	Credit	Balance
2000				
Dec. 31	(*e*)		210	210
2001				
Jan. 1		210		-0-

Under both approaches, the expense and liability accounts have the same balances after the subsequent payment on January 9:

Salaries Expense	$490
Salaries Payable	$ 0

Because of the reversing entry, the February 9 entry to record payment is simple. This entry debits the Salaries Expense account for the full $700 paid. It is the same as all other entries made to record 10 days' salary for the employee.

We should also look at the accounts on the lower right side of Exhibit 5A.1. After the payment entry is posted, the Salaries Expense account has a $490 balance that reflects seven days' salary of $70 per day. The zero balance in the Salaries Payable account is now correct. The lower section of Exhibit 5A.1 shows that the expense and liability accounts have exactly the same balances whether reversing occurs or not.

As a general rule, adjusting entries that create new asset or new liability accounts are likely candidates for reversing.

Answer—p. 221

11. How are financial statements affected by a decision to make reversing entries?

Account Numbering System

We described a three-digit account numbering system in Chapter 3. In such a system, the code number assigned to an account both identifies the account and gives information about the account's financial statement category.

In this section, we describe a more detailed system, although we see many different systems in practice. The first digit in an account's number identifies its primary balance sheet or income statement category. For example, account numbers beginning with "1" are assigned to asset accounts, and account numbers beginning with "2" are assigned to liability accounts. The numbers shown in Exhibit 5A.2 could be assigned to the accounts of a company that buys and sells merchandise:

Exhibit 5A.2

Account Numbering for a Merchandiser

101 – 199	Asset accounts
201 – 299	Liability accounts
301 – 399	Owner's equity (including withdrawals)
401 – 499	Sales or revenue accounts
501 – 599	Cost of goods sold accounts (These are discussed in Chapter 6.)
601 – 699	Operating expense accounts
701 – 799	Accounts that reflect unusual and/or infrequent gains
801 – 899	Accounts that reflect unusual and/or infrequent losses

The second digit of each account number identifies its classification within the primary category, as shown in Exhibit 5A.3.

Exhibit 5A.3

Second Digit Account Numbering

101 – 199	**Assets**
101 – 139	Current assets (second digit is 0, 1, 2, or 3)
141 – 149	Long-term investments (second digit is 4)
151 – 179	Plant assets (second digit is 5, 6, or 7)
181 – 189	Natural resources (second digit is 8)
191 – 199	Intangible assets (second digit is 9)
201 – 299	**Liabilities**
201 – 249	Current liabilities (second digit is 0, 1, 2, 3, or 4)
251 – 299	Long-term liabilities (second digit is 5, 6, 7, 8, or 9)

The third digit completes the unique code for each account. For example, specific current asset accounts might be assigned the numbers shown in Exhibit 5A.4:

101 - 199	Assets
101 - 139	Current assets
101	Cash
106	Accounts receivable
110	Rent receivable
128	Prepaid insurance

Exhibit 5A.4

Three-digit Account Numbering

A three-digit account numbering system is often adequate for smaller businesses. An extensive list of accounts using this code is provided in Appendix III to this book. A numbering system for more complex businesses might use four, five or even more digits.

APPENDIX

5B Using the Information

Current Ratio

LO9 Compute the current ratio and describe what it reveals about a company's financial condition.

Financial statements are important tools for helping decision makers to determine a company's ability to pay its debts in the near future.

The **current ratio** is one important measure used to evaluate a company's ability to pay its short-term obligations. The *ability to pay* day-to-day obligations (current liabilities) with existing *liquid assets* is commonly referred to as **liquidity**. **Liquid assets** are those that can be easily converted to cash or used to pay for services or obligations. Cash is the most liquid asset. The current ratio helps us to make decisions like whether or not to lend money to a company or allow a customer to buy on credit, or how to use cash to pay existing debts when they come due.

The current ratio is computed as follows in Exhibit 5B.1:

Exhibit 5B.1

Current Ratio

$$\text{Current ratio} = \frac{\text{Current assets}}{\text{Current liabilities}}$$

Using information from the financial statements of WestJet and ClubLink from Appendix I, we compute their current ratios at December 31, 1999:

	WestJet	ClubLink
Current assets	$60,493,000	$68,143,000
Current liabilities	$49,926,000	$29,431,000
	= 1.21	= 2.32

Another way to express the result is to say, for example, that WestJet has a current ratio of **1.21:1**. This means that WestJet has current assets of $1.21 to cover each $1.00 of current liability. ClubLink has current assets available of $2.32 to cover each $1.00 of current debt. This tells us that both companies are in a good position to pay their day-to-day obligations. A current ratio greater than or equal to 1 is favourable (or good). When the current ratio is less than 1, a company would likely face problems in covering current liabilities with current assets.

Flashback

Answer—p. 221

12. If a company misclassifies a portion of liabilities as long-term when they are short-term, how does this affect its current ratio?

Summary of Appendices 5A and 5B

LO8 **Prepare reversing entries and explain their purpose.** Reversing entries are an optional step. They are applied to accrued assets and liabilities. The purpose of reversing entries is to simplify subsequent journal entries. Financial statements are unaffected by the choice to use reversing entries or not.

LO9 **Compute the current ratio and describe what it reveals about a company's financial condition.** A company's current ratio is defined as current assets divided by current liabilities. We use it to evaluate a company's ability to pay its current liabilities out of current assets.

GUIDANCE ANSWERS TO  Flashback

11. Financial statements are unchanged by the choice between using reversing entries or not.

12. Since the current ratio is defined as current assets divided by current liabilities, then ignoring a portion of current liabilities (1) decreases the reported amount of current liabilities and (2) increases the current ratio because current assets are now divided by a smaller number.

Glossary

Classified balance sheet A balance sheet that presents the assets and liabilities in relevant subgroups. (p. 208)

Closing entries Journal entries recorded at the end of each accounting period that transfer the end-of-period balances in revenue, expense, and withdrawals accounts to the permanent owner's capital account in order to prepare for the upcoming period and update the owner's capital account for the events of the period just finished. (p. 199)

Closing process A step at the end of the accounting period that prepares accounts for recording the transactions of the next period. (p. 198)

Current assets Cash or other assets that are expected to be sold, collected, or used within the longer of one year or the company's operating cycle. (p. 210)

Current ratio A ratio that is used to evaluate a company's ability to pay its short-term obligations, calculated by dividing current assets by current liabilities. (p. 220)

Current liabilities Obligations due to be paid or settled within the longer of one year or the operating cycle. (p. 211)

Income Summary A temporary account used only in the closing process to which the balances of revenue and expense accounts are transferred; its balance equals net income or net loss and is transferred to the owner's capital account. (p. 199)

Intangible assets Long-term assets (resources) used to produce or sell products or services; these assets lack physical form. (p. 210)

Liquidity The ability to pay day-to-day obligations (current liabilities) with existing liquid assets. (p. 220)

Liquid assets Assets that can be easily converted to cash or used to pay for services or obligations; cash is the most liquid asset. (p. 220)

Long-term investments Assets such as notes receivable or investments in shares and bonds that are held for more than one year or the operating cycle. (p. 210)

Long-term liabilities Obligations that are not due to be paid within the longer of one year or the operating cycle. (p. 211)

Nominal accounts See *temporary accounts.* (p. 198)

Operating cycle For a business, the average time between paying cash for employee salaries or merchandise and receiving cash from customers. (p. 208)

Owner's equity The owner's claim on the assets of a company. (p. 211)

Permanent accounts Accounts that are used to report on activities related to one or more future accounting periods; their balances are carried into the next period, and include all balance sheet accounts; permanent account balances are not closed as long as the company continues to own the assets, owe the liabilities, and have owner's equity; also called *real accounts.* (p. 198)

Post-closing trial balance A list of permanent accounts and their balances from the ledger after all closing entries are journalized and posted; a list of balances for all accounts not closed. (p. 203)

Pro forma statements Statements that show the effects of the proposed transactions as if the transactions had already occurred. (p. 195)

Real accounts See *permanent accounts.* (p. 198)

Reversing entries Optional entries recorded at the beginning of a new period that prepare the accounts for simplified journal entries subsequent to accrual adjusting entries. (p. 216)

Temporary accounts Accounts that are used to describe revenues, expenses, and owner's withdrawals for one accounting period; they are closed at the end of the reporting period; also called *nominal accounts.* (p. 198)

Unclassified balance sheet A balance sheet that broadly groups the assets, liabilities and owner's equity. (p. 208)

Work sheet A 10-column spreadsheet used to draft a company's unadjusted trial balance, adjusting entries, adjusted trial balance, and financial statements; an optional step in the accounting process. (p. 192)

Working papers Internal documents that are used to assist the preparers in doing the analyses and organizing the information for reports to be presented to internal and external decision makers. (p. 192)

Questions

1. What two purposes are accomplished by recording closing entries?
2. What are the four closing entries?
3. What accounts are affected by closing entries? What accounts are not affected?
4. Describe the similarities and differences between adjusting and closing entries.
5. What is the purpose of the Income Summary account?
6. Explain whether an error has occurred if a post-closing trial balance includes an Amortization Expense, Building account.
7. How is an unearned revenue classified on the balance sheet?
8. What classes of assets and liabilities are shown on a typical classified balance sheet?
9. What is a company's operating cycle?

10. What are the characteristics of plant and equipment?
*11. What tasks are performed with the work sheet?
*12. Why are the debit and credit entries in the Adjustments columns of the work sheet identified with letters?
*13. How do reversing entries simplify a company's book-keeping efforts?
*14. If a company had accrued unpaid salaries expense of $500 at the end of a fiscal year, what reversing entry could be made? When would it be made?
15. Refer to WestJet's income statement in Appendix I at the end of the book. What journal entry was recorded as of December 31, 1999 to close the Interest Expense account?
16. Refer to the December 31, 1999 balance sheet for ClubLink in Appendix I at the end of the book. What amount of ClubLink's long-term debt is coming due before December 31, 2000?

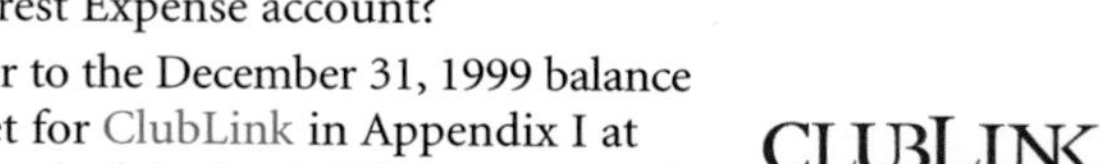

Quick Study

QS 5-1
Work sheet information

LO[1]

The following information is from the work sheet for Pursley Company as of December 31, 2001. Using this information, determine the amount that should be reported for Alice Pursley, Capital on the December 31, 2001 balance sheet.

	Income Statement		Balance Sheet and Statement of Owner's Equity	
	Debit	Credit	Debit	Credit
Alice Pursley, capital				50,000
Alice Pursley, withdrawals			32,000	
Totals	125,000	184,000		

QS 5-2
Interpreting a work sheet

LO[1]

The following information is from the work sheet for Hascal Company as of December 31, 2001. Using this information, determine the amount for Sam Hascal, Capital that should be reported on the December 31, 2001 balance sheet.

	Income Statement		Balance Sheet and Statement of Owner's Equity	
	Debit	Credit	Debit	Credit
Sam Hascal, capital				165,000
Sam Hascal, withdrawals			32,000	
Totals	115,000	74,000		

An asterisk (*) identifies assignment material based on Appendix 5A or Appendix 5B.

QS 5-3
Applying a work sheet
LO 4

In preparing a work sheet, indicate the financial statement debit column to which a normal balance of each of the following accounts should be extended. Use *IS* for the Income Statement Debit column and *BS* for the Balance Sheet or Statement of Owner's Equity Debit column.

1. Equipment
2. Owner, withdrawals
3. Insurance expense
4. Prepaid insurance
5. Accounts receivable
6. Amortization expense, equipment

QS 5-4
Effects of closing entries
LO 2, 3, 4, 5

Jontil Co. began the current period with a $14,000 balance in the Peter Jontil, Capital account. At the end of the period, the company's adjusted account balances include the following temporary accounts with normal balances:

Service fee earned	$35,000
Salaries expense	19,000
Amortization expense.............	4,000
Interest earned........................	3,500
Peter Jontil, withdrawals.........	6,000
Utilities expense......................	2,300

After closing the revenue and expense accounts, what will be the balance of the Income Summary account?

After all of the closing entries are journalized and posted, what will be the balance of the Peter Jontil, Capital account?

QS 5-5
Explaining the accounting cycle
LO 6

List the following steps of the accounting cycle in the proper order:

a. Preparing the unadjusted trial balance.
b. Preparing the post-closing trial balance.
c. Journalizing and posting adjusting entries.
d. Journalizing and posting closing entries.
e. Preparing the financial statements.
f. Journalizing transactions.
g. Posting the transaction entries.
h. Completing the work sheet.

QS 5-6
Classifying balance sheet items
LO 7

The following are categories on a classified balance sheet:

a. Current assets
b. Long-term investments
c. Property, plant, and equipment
d. Intangible assets
e. Current liabilities
f. Long-term liabilities

For each of the following items, select the letter that identifies the balance sheet category in which the item should appear.

_____ **1.** Store equipment
_____ **2.** Wages payable
_____ **3.** Cash
_____ **4.** Notes payable (due in three years)
_____ **5.** Land not currently used in business operations
_____ **6.** Accounts receivable
_____ **7.** Trademarks

***QS 5-7**
Reversing entries
LO 8

On December 31, 2001, Ace Management Co. prepared an adjusting entry for $9,800 of earned but unrecorded rent revenue. On January 20, 2002, Ace received rent payments in the amount of $15,500. Assuming Ace uses reversing entries, prepare the 2002 entries pertaining to the rent transactions.

An asterisk (*) identifies assignment material based on Appendix 5A or Appendix 5B.

***QS 5-8**
Computing current ratio
LO9

Calculate Tucker Company's current ratio, given the following information about its assets and liabilities:

Accounts receivable	$15,000
Accounts payable	10,000
Buildings	42,000
Cash	6,000
Long-term notes payable	20,000
Office supplies	1,800
Prepaid insurance	2,500
Unearned services revenue	4,000

Exercises

Exercise 5-1
Preparing a work sheet
LO11

Check figure:
Adjusted trial balance columns = $452,950

The unadjusted trial balance for Musical Sensations after its second year of operations follows:

Musical Sensations
Work Sheet
For Year Ended December 31, 2001

Account	Unadjusted Trial Balance Debit	Unadjusted Trial Balance Credit
Cash	14,000	
Accounts receivable	26,000	
Office supplies	950	
Musical equipment	212,000	
Accumulated amortization, musical equipment		16,200
Accounts payable		3,350
Unearned performance revenue		12,400
Jim Daley, capital		272,000
Jim Daley, withdrawals	52,000	
Performance revenue		119,000
Salaries expense	76,000	
Travelling expense	42,000	
Totals	422,950	422,950

Required

1. Enter the unadjusted trial balance onto a work sheet.
2. Using the following additional information, enter the adjustments into the work sheet:
   a. A review of the Unearned Performance Revenue account revealed a balance remaining of $1,800.
   b. Annual amortization on the musical equipment is $16,200.
   c. Accrued salaries at December 31 totalled $13,800.
   d. It was determined that $430 of the balance in the Office Supplies account had been used.
3. Complete the work sheet.
4. Calculate the balance in the capital account as it would appear on the December 1, 2001 balance sheet.

Exercise 5-2
Extending accounts in the work sheet
LO1

Check figure:
Net income = $30,300

The Adjusted Trial Balance columns of a 10-column work sheet for Plummer Co. follow. Complete the work sheet by extending the account balances into the appropriate financial statement columns and by entering the amount of net income for the reporting period.

An asterisk (*) identifies assignment material based on Appendix 5A or Appendix 5B.

No.	Title	Adjusted Trial Balance	
		Credit	**Debit**
101	Cash	6,000	
106	Accounts receivable	26,200	
153	Trucks	82,000	
154	Accumulated amortization, trucks		33,000
193	Franchise	30,000	
201	Accounts payable		14,000
209	Salaries payable		3,200
233	Unearned fees		2,600
301	Farley Plummer, capital		75,500
302	Farley Plummer, withdrawals	14,400	
401	Plumbing fees earned		98,000
611	Amortization expense, trucks	11,000	
622	Salaries expense	37,000	
640	Rent expense	12,000	
677	Miscellaneous expense	7,700	
	Totals	226,300	226,300

Exercise 5-3

Preparing adjusting entries from work sheet information

LO1

Use the following information from the Adjustments columns of a 10-column work sheet to prepare adjusting journal entries:

No.	Title	Adjustments	
		Debit	**Credit**
109	Interest receivable	(d) 580	
124	Office supplies		(b) 1,650
128	Prepaid insurance		(a) 900
164	Accumulated amortization, office equipment		(c) 3,300
209	Salaries payable		(e) 660
409	Interest revenue		(d) 580
612	Amortization expense, office equipment	(c) 3,300	
620	Office salaries expense	(e) 660	
636	Insurance expense, office equipment	(a) 432	
637	Insurance expense, store equipment	(a) 468	
650	Office supplies expense	(b) 1,650	
	Totals	7,090	7,090

Exercise 5-4

Extending adjusted account balances on a work sheet

LO1

These accounts are from the Adjusted Trial Balance columns in a company's 10-column work sheet. In the blank space beside each account, write the letter of the appropriate financial statement column to which a normal account balance should be extended.

a. Debit column for the income statement.
b. Credit column for the income statement.
c. Debit column for the balance sheet and statement of owner's equity.
d. Credit column for the balance sheet and statement of owner's equity.

____	**1.** Roberta Jefferson, withdrawals	____	**9.** Cash
____	**2.** Interest earned	____	**10.** Office supplies
____	**3.** Accumulated amortization, machinery	____	**11.** Roberta Jefferson, capital
____	**4.** Service fees revenue	____	**12.** Wages payable
____	**5.** Accounts receivable	____	**13.** Machinery
____	**6.** Rent expense	____	**14.** Insurance expense
____	**7.** Amortization expense, machinery	____	**15.** Interest expense
____	**8.** Accounts payable	____	**16.** Interest receivable

Exercise 5-5
Work sheet interpretation and closing entries

LO 1, 2, 3, 4, 5

The following is an excerpt from the work sheet of Foxglove Interiors as at March 31, 2002. It shows those rows that calculate totals at the bottom of the last two sets of columns.

Income Statement		Balance Sheet and Statement of Owner's Equity	
Debit	Credit	Debit	Credit
263,700	300,500	357,300	320,500
36,800			36,800
300,500	300,500	357,300	357,300

Required

Answer the following questions:

1. Identify the net income or net loss for the year ended March 31, 2002.
2. Prepare the entry to close the Income Summary account to Pat Beck, Capital.
3. Assuming the adjusted balances for withdrawals and capital were $17,000 and $63,000 respectively, calculate the post-closing balance in Pat Beck, Capital at March 31, 2002.

Exercise 5-6
Work sheet interpretation and closing entries

LO 1, 2, 3, 4, 5

The following is an excerpt from the work sheet of Dreamweavers at June 30, 2002. It shows those rows that calculate totals at the bottom of the last two sets of columns.

Income Statement		Balance Sheet and Statement of Owner's Equity	
Debit	Credit	Debit	Credit
540,000	480,000	945,000	1,005,000
	60,000	60,000	
540,000	540,000	1,005,000	1,005,000

Required

Answer the following questions:

1. Identify the net income or net loss for the year ended June 30, 2002.
2. Prepare the entry to close the Income Summary account to Jon Nissen, Capital.
3. Assuming the adjusted balances for withdrawals and capital were 0 and $114,000 respectively, calculate the post-closing balance in Jon Nissen, Capital at June 30, 2002.

Exercise 5-7

Completing the income statement columns and preparing closing entries

LO1, 3, 4

These partially completed Income Statement columns from a 10-column work sheet are for the Winston Sail'em Boat Rental Company. Use the information to determine the amount that should be entered on the Net income line of the work sheet. In addition, draft closing entries for the company. The owner's name is Carl Winston, and the preclosing balance of the withdrawals account is $18,000.

	Debit	Credit
Rent earned		99,000
Salaries expense	35,300	
Insurance expense	4,400	
Dock rental expense	12,000	
Boat supplies expense	6,220	
Amortization expense, boats	21,500	
Totals		
Net income		
Totals		

Exercise 5-8

Preparing closing entries and the post-closing trial balance

LO2, 3, 4, 5

Check figure:
Post-closing trial balance columns = $103,200

The adjusted trial balance at April 30, 2001 for West Plumbing Co. follows. Prepare the four closing entries and the post-closing trial balance.

No.	Title	Adjusted Trial Balance	
		Credit	**Debit**
101	Cash	$ 8,200	
106	Accounts receivable	24,000	
153	Trucks	41,000	
154	Accumulated amortization, trucks		$ 16,500
193	Franchise	30,000	
201	Accounts payable		14,000
209	Salaries payable		3,200
233	Unearned fees		2,600
301	Francis West, capital		64,500
302	Francis West, withdrawals	14,400	
401	Plumbing fees earned		79,000
611	Amortization expense, trucks	11,000	
622	Salaries expense	31,500	
640	Rent expense	12,000	
677	Miscellaneous expenses	7,700	
901	Income summary		
	Totals	$179,800	$179,800

Exercise 5-9
Post-closing trial balance

LO 2, 3, 4, 5

Jay's Moving Services showed the following post-closing trial balance after the posting of the closing entries on June 30, 2002:

Jay's Moving Services Post-Closing Trial Balance June 30, 2002	Debit	Credit
Cash	$21,000	
Accounts receivable	6,500	
Equipment	18,000	
Accumulated amortization, equipment		$6,000
Trucks	69,000	
Accumulated amortization, trucks		33,000
Accounts payable		2,900
Jay Moore, capital		108,100
Jay Moore, withdrawals	36,000	
Interest revenue		575
Other expenses	75	
Totals	$150,575	$150,575

Required

1. Identify the error(s) in the post-closing trial balance.
2. What entry is required to correct the error?
3. Calculate the correct balance at June 30, 2002 for Jay Moore, Capital.

Exercise 5-10
Closing entries

LO 3, 4

The following adjusted trial balance contains the accounts and balances of Painters Co. as of December 31, 2001, the end of its fiscal year:

No.	Title	Debit	Credit
101	Cash	$18,000	
126	Supplies	12,000	
128	Prepaid insurance	2,000	
167	Equipment	23,000	
168	Accumulated amortization, equipment		$ 6,500
301	Richard Tanner, capital		46,600
302	Richard Tanner, withdrawals	6,000	
404	Services revenue		36,000
612	Amortization expense, equipment	2,000	
622	Salaries expense	21,000	
637	Insurance expense	1,500	
640	Rent expense	2,400	
652	Supplies expense	1,200	
	Totals	$89,100	$89,100

Required

Journalize closing entries for the company.

Exercise 5-11
Closing entries

LO3, 4

Following is the adjusted trial balance, with accounts in alphabetical order, for eSOFT as at September 30, 2002:

eSoft Adjusted Trial Balance September 30, 2002		
	Debit	**Credit**
Accounts payable		$ 9,000
Accumulated amortization, office equipment		21,000
Amortization expense, office equipment	$ 7,000	
Cash	49,000	
Consulting fees earned		136,000
Office equipment	63,000	
Prepaid rent	28,000	
Sandra Sloley, capital		46,000
Sandra Sloley, withdrawals	38,000	
Unearned consulting fees		3,500
Rent expense	3,500	
Wages expense,	27,000	
Totals	$215,500	$215,500

Required
Prepare the closing entries.

Exercise 5-12
Closing entries

LO3, 4

Following is the adjusted trial balance, with accounts in alphabetical order, for KRG Television as at January 31, 2002:

KRG Television Adjusted Trial Balance January 31, 2002		
	Debit	**Credit**
Accounts receivable	$ 13,000	
Accumulated amortization, equipment		$ 12,000
Amortization expense, equipment	2,000	
Cash	9,000	
Equipment	22,000	
Interest revenue		450
Kate Goldberg, capital		19,950
Kate Goldberg, withdrawals	4,000	
Rent expense	7,400	
Salaries expense,	56,000	
Subscription revenues		62,000
Unearned subscription revenue		19,000
Totals	$113,400	$113,400

Required
Prepare the closing entries.

Exercise 5-13
Preparing and posting closing entries

LO4

Check figure:
Post-closing capital balance = $41,900

Open the following T-accounts with the balances provided. Prepare closing journal entries at December 31, 2001 and post them to the accounts.

Marcy Jones, Capital			
		Dec. 31	41,000

Rent Expense			
Dec. 31	8,600		

Marcy Jones, Withdrawals			
Dec. 31	24,000		

Salaries Expense			
Dec. 31	20,000		

Income Summary			

Insurance Expense			
Dec. 31	3,500		

Services Revenue			
		Dec. 31	73,000

Amortization Expense			
Dec. 31	16,000		

Exercise 5-14
Preparing a classified balance sheet

LO7

Check figure:
Total assets = $235,500

Use the following adjusted trial balance of Hanson Trucking Company to prepare a classified balance sheet as of December 31, 2001.

Account Title	Debit	Credit
Cash	$ 7,000	
Accounts receivable	16,500	
Office supplies	2,000	
Trucks	170,000	
Accumulated amortization, trucks		$ 35,000
Land	75,000	
Accounts payable		11,000
Interest payable		3,000
Long-term notes payable		52,000
Stanley Hanson, capital		161,000
Stanley Hanson, withdrawals	19,000	
Trucking fees earned		128,000
Amortization expense, trucks	22,500	
Salaries expense	60,000	
Office supplies expense	7,000	
Repairs expense, trucks	11,000	
Total	$390,000	$390,000

***Exercise 5-15**
Reversing entries

LO8

Breaker Corporation records the prepaid assets and unearned revenues in balance sheet accounts. The following information was used to prepare adjusting entries for Breaker Corporation as of August 31, 2001, the end of the company's fiscal year:

a. The company has earned $5,000 of unrecorded service fees.
b. The expired portion of prepaid insurance is $2,700.
c. The earned portion of the Unearned Fees account balance is $1,900.
d. Amortization expense for the office equipment is $2,300.
e. Employees have earned but have not been paid salaries of $2,400.

Required

Prepare the appropriate reversing entries that would simplify the bookkeeping effort for recording subsequent events related to these adjustments.

An asterisk (*) identifies assignment material based on Appendix 5A or Appendix 5B.

***Exercise 5-16**
Reversing entries

LO8

The following two conditions existed for Maxit Co. on October 31, 2001, the end of its fiscal year:

a. Maxit rents a building from its owner for $3,200 per month. By a prearrangement, the company delayed paying October's rent until November 5. On this date, the company paid the rent for both October and November.

b. Maxit rents space in a building it owns to a tenant for $750 per month. By prearrangement, the tenant delayed paying the October rent until November 8. On this date, the tenant paid the rent for both October and November.

Required

1. Prepare the adjusting entries that Maxit should record for these situations as of October 31.
2. Assuming that Maxit does not use reversing entries, prepare journal entries to record Maxit's payment of rent on November 5 and the collection of rent on November 8 from Maxit's tenant.
3. Assuming that Maxit does use reversing entries, prepare those entries and the journal entries to record Maxit's payment of rent on November 5 and the collection of rent on November 8 from Maxit's tenant.

***Exercise 5-17**
Calculating the current ratio

LO9

Calculate the current ratio in each of the following cases and indicate whether it is *Favourable* (F) or *Unfavourable* (U):

	Current Assets	Current Liabilities
Case 1	$ 78,000	$31,000
Case 2	104,000	75,000
Case 3	44,000	48,000
Case 4	84,500	80,600
Case 5	60,000	99,000

Problems

Problem 5-1A
Completing a work sheet

LO1

Check figure:
Adjusted trial balance columns = $32,575

The unadjusted trial balance for Maverick Consulting after its first year of operations follows:

Maverick Consulting
Work Sheet
June 30, 2001

Account	Unadjusted Trial Balance Debit	Unadjusted Trial Balance Credit
Cash	1,720	
Accounts receivable	1,495	
Prepaid rent	3,300	
Equipment	3,200	
Accounts payable		720
Jean Maverick, capital		13,325
Jean Maverick, withdrawals	400	
Consulting fees earned		15,100
Wages expense	14,060	
Insurance expense	810	
Rent expense	4,160	
Totals	29,145	29,145

An asterisk (*) identifies assignment material based on Appendix 5A or Appendix 5B.

Required

1. Enter the unadjusted trial balance onto a work sheet.
2. Using the following additional information, enter the adjustments into the work sheet:
   a. Annual amortization on the equipment is $1,270.
   b. The balance in the Prepaid Rent account is for six months of rent commencing March 1, 2001.
   c. Unpaid and unrecorded wages at June 30 totalled $1,250.
   d. Accrued revenues at June 30 totalled $910.
3. Complete the work sheet.
4. Calaculate the balance in the capital account as it would appear on the June 30, 2001 balance sheet.

Problem 5-2A
Closing entries

LO4

The adjusted trial balance for Graw Construction as of December 31, 2002, follows:

Graw Construction Adjusted Trial Balance December 31, 2002			
No.	**Account**	**Debit**	**Credit**
101	Cash	$ 4,000	
104	Temporary investments	22,000	
126	Supplies	7,100	
167	Equipment	39,000	
168	Accumulated amortization, equipment		$ 20,000
173	Building	130,000	
174	Accumulated amortization, building		55,000
183	Land	45,000	
201	Accounts payable		15,500
203	Interest payable		1,500
233	Unearned professional fees		6,500
251	Long-term notes payable		66,000
301	Tracy Graw, capital		56,900
302	Tracy Graw, withdrawals	12,000	
401	Professional fees earned		96,000
406	Rent earned		13,000
606	Amortization expense, building	10,000	
612	Amortization expense, equipment	5,000	
623	Wages expense	31,000	
633	Interest expense	4,100	
637	Insurance expense	9,000	
652	Supplies expense	6,400	
688	Telephone expense	2,200	
690	Utilities expense	3,600	
	Totals	$330,400	$330,400

An analysis of other information reveals that Graw Construction is required to make a $6,600 payment on the long-term note payable during 2003. Also, Tracy Graw invested $50,000 cash early in 2002.

Required

Prepare the closing entries made at the end of the year.

***Problem 5-3A**
Financial statements

LO7

Check figure:
Total assets = $172,100

Using the adjusted trial balance in Problem 5-2A, prepare the income statement, statement of owner's equity, and classified balance sheet.

Problem 5-4A
Closing entries

LO4, 5

Check figure:
Post-closing trial balance = $64,150

T & D Autobody's adjusted trial balance on December 31, 2002 appears in the work sheet as follows:

		Adjusted Trial Balance	
No.	**Account**	**Debit**	**Credit**
101	Cash	$ 13,000	
124	Shop supplies	1,200	
128	Prepaid insurance	1,950	
167	Equipment	48,000	
168	Accumulated amortization, equipment		$ 4,000
201	Accounts payable		12,000
210	Wages payable		500
301	Ted Dunwood, capital		40,000
302	Ted Dunwood, withdrawals	15,000	
401	Repair fees earned		77,750
612	Amortization expense, equipment	4,000	
623	Wages expense	36,500	
637	Insurance expense	700	
640	Rent expense	9,600	
650	Office supplies expense	2,600	
690	Utilities expense	1,700	
999	Income summary		-0-
	Totals	$134,250	$134,250

Required

1. Prepare closing entries.
2. Prepare the post-closing trial balance at December 31, 2002.

Problem 5-5A
Financial statements

LO7

Check figure:
Total assets = $60,150

Using the information from Problem 5-4A, prepare an income statement and a statement of owner's equity for the year ended December 31, 2002, and a classified balance sheet at the end of the year. There were no investments by the owner during the year.

Problem 5-6A
Financial statements

LO5

The adjusted trial balance for Alpine Climbing Adventures has been alphabetized as follows:

Alpine Climbing Adventures
Adjusted Trial Balance
March 31, 2002

No.	Account	Debit	Credit
251	Amy Rooniak, capital		$ 36,700
301	Amy Rooniak, withdrawals	$ 47,000	
201	Accounts payable		2,400
103	Accounts receivable	6,000	
168	Accumulated amortization, equipment		14,000
406	Amortization expense, equipment	1,400	
101	Cash	15,000	
167	Equipment	41,000	
633	Insurance expense	3,900	
623	Interest expense	660	
233	Long-term notes payable		11,000
410	Rent expense	15,000	
302	Revenues		122,000
126	Supplies	540	
637	Supplies expense	3,600	
652	Telephone expense	4,200	
203	Unearned revenues		22,000
688	Utilities expense	1,800	
612	Wages expense	68,000	
	Totals	$208,100	$208,100

Required
Journalize the closing entries.

Problem 5-7A
Financial statements

LO7

Using the information in Problem 5-6A, prepare an income statement and statement of owner's equity for the year ended March 31, 2002 and a classified balance sheet at March 31, 2002. The owner made an additional investment during the year of $5,000. A $6,000 payment on the long-term notes payable will be made during the year ended March 31, 2003.

Check figure:
Total assets = $48,540

Problem 5-8A
Analyzing closing entries

LO5

The following closing entries were prepared for Superior Architectural Designs regarding its year just ended June 30, 2001:

Date	Account	Debit	Credit
Mar. 31	Design Fees Earned	248,000	
	Income Summary		248,000
	To close the revenue account.		
31	Income Summary	146,040	
	Amortization Expense, Office Equipment		3,500
	Amortization Expense, Office Furniture		1,900
	Insurance Expense		1,200
	Interest Expense		1,440
	Supplies Expense		4,300
	Telephone Expense		3,200
	Utilities Expense		1,500
	Salaries Expense		129,000
	To close expense accounts.		
31	Income Summary	101,960	
	Al Rusnak, Capital		101,960
	To close the Income Summary to capital.		
31	Al Rusnak, Capital	70,000	
	Al Rusnak, Withdrawals		70,000
	To close withdrawals to capital.		

Check figure:
Net income = $101,960

Required

1. Prepare an income statement based on the information provided.
2. Calculate the post-closing balance in the capital account at June 30, 2001 given that the adjusted balance on June 30, 2000 was $86,000.

Problem 5-9A
Balance sheet classifications

LO7

In the blank space beside each numbered balance sheet item, enter the letter of its balance sheet classification. If the item should not appear on the balance sheet, enter a *z* in the blank.

a. Current assets
b. Long-term investments
c. Plant and equipment
d. Intangible assets
e. Current liabilities
f. Long-term liabilities
g. Owner's equity

_____ 1. Amortization expense, trucks
_____ 2. Lee Hale, capital
_____ 3. Interest receivable
_____ 4. Lee Hale, withdrawals
_____ 5. Automobiles
_____ 6. Notes payable–due in three years
_____ 7. Accounts payable
_____ 8. Prepaid insurance
_____ 9. Land held for future expansion
_____ 10. Unearned services revenue
_____ 11. Accumulated amortization, trucks
_____ 12. Cash
_____ 13. Building
_____ 14. Patent
_____ 15. Office equipment
_____ 16. Land (used in operations)
_____ 17. Repairs expense
_____ 18. Prepaid property taxes
_____ 19. Current portion of long-term notes payable
_____ 20. Investment in Magna common shares (long-term holding)

Problem 5-10A
Work sheet, journal entries and financial statements

LO 1, 4, 5, 7

This unadjusted trial balance is for Blue Max construction as of the end of its fiscal year. The beginning balance of the owner's capital account was $12,660 and the owner invested another $15,000 cash in the company during the year.

Blue Max Construction Unadjusted Trial Balance September 30, 2001			
No.	**Account**	**Debit**	**Credit**
101	Cash	$ 18,000	
126	Supplies	9,400	
128	Prepaid insurance	6,200	
167	Equipment	81,000	
168	Accumulated amortization, equipment		$ 20,250
201	Accounts payable		4,800
203	Interest payable		
208	Rent payable		
210	Wages payable		
213	Estimated business taxes payable		
251	Long-term notes payable		25,000
301	Tony Morrison, capital		27,660
302	Tony Morrison, withdrawals	36,000	
401	Construction fees earned		140,000
612	Amortization expense, equipment		
623	Wages expense	41,000	
633	Interest expense	1,500	
637	Insurance expense		
640	Rent expense	13,200	
652	Supplies expense		
683	Business taxes expense	5,000	
684	Repairs expense	2,510	
690	Utilities expense	3,900	
	Totals	$217,710	$217,710

Required

1. Prepare a 10-column work sheet for 2001, starting with the unadjusted trial balance and including these additional facts:
   a. The inventory of supplies at the end of the year had a cost of $2,500.
   b. The cost of expired insurance for the year is $4,000.
   c. Annual amortization of the equipment is $9,000.
   d. The September utilities expense was not included in the trial balance because the bill arrived after it was prepared. Its $400 amount needs to be recorded.
   e. The company's employees have earned $1,500 of accrued wages.
   f. The lease for the office requires the company to pay total rent for the year equal to 10% of the company's annual revenues. The rent is paid to the building owner with monthly payments of $1,100. If the annual rent exceeds the total monthly payments, the company must pay the excess before October 31. If the total is less than the amount previously paid, the building owner will refund the difference by October 31.
   g. Additional business taxes of $800 have been assessed on the company but have not been paid or recorded in the accounts.
   h. The interest of $250 for September has not yet been paid or recorded. In addition, the company is required to make a $5,000 payment on the note on November 30, 2001.
2. Use the work sheet to prepare the adjusting and closing entries.
3. Prepare an income statement, a statement of owner's equity, and a classified balance sheet.

Check figures:
Adjusted trial balance columns = $230,460;
Total assets = $74,450

Analysis component:

4. Analyze the following potential errors and describe how each would affect the 10-column work sheet. Explain whether the error is likely to be discovered in completing the work sheet and, if not, the effect of the error on the financial statements.
   a. The adjustment to record used supplies was credited to Supplies for $2,500 and debited the same amount to Supplies Expense.
   b. When completing the adjusted trial balance in the work sheet, the $18,000 cash balance was incorrectly entered in the Credit column.

Problem 5-11A
Completing a partial work sheet, preparing a classified balance sheet

LO[1, 7]

A partial work sheet for Northern Lights Dance School has been provided. In error, the new bookkeeper alphabetized the accounts.

Northern Lights Dance School
Partial Work Sheet
For Year Ended September 30, 2001

	Unadjusted Trial Balance		Income Statement		Balance Sheet & Statement of Owners Equity	
Account	**Debit**	**Credit**	**Debit**	**Credit**	**Debit**	**Credit**
Accounts payable		3,660				
Accounts receivable	3,290					
Accumulated amortization, automobiles		19,680				
Accumulated amortization, building		72,000				
Amortization expense, automobiles	3,280					
Amortization expense, building	4,800					
Automobiles	32,800					
Building	120,000					
Cash	5,060					
Copyright	2,180					
Fees earned		127,340				
Gas, oil, and repairs expense	14,800					
Land	14,000					
Land for future expansion	25,000					
Natalie Urovsky, capital		24,480				
Natalie Urovsky, withdrawals	45,000					
Notes payable*		45,000				
Patents	4,300					
Rent earned		59,000				
Salaries expense	87,000					
Store supplies	1,400					
Unearned fees		11,750				
Totals	362,910	362,910				

* *The notes payable plus interest are due in 18 months.*

Check figures:
Net income = $76,460;
Total assets = $116,350

Required

1. Complete the work sheet.
2. Calculate the balance in the capital account as it would appear on the September 30, 2001 balance sheet.
3. Prepare a classified balance sheet.

Problem 5-12A
Completing a work sheet

LO1

The unadjusted trial balance for Prestige Rentals after its first year of operations is shown below:

Prestige Rentals
Work Sheet
For Year Ended March 31, 2001

No.	Account	Unadjusted Trial Balance Debit	Unadjusted Trial Balance Credit
101	Cash	34,000	
110	Rent receivable	126,000	
124	Office supplies	13,600	
141	Investment in ClubLink shares	286,000	
161	Furniture	92,000	
173	Building	1,250,000	
183	Land	220,000	
201	Accounts payable		11,600
252	Long-term notes payable		750,000
301	Chris Jenson, capital		999,050
302	Chris Jenson, withdrawals	56,000	
406	Rent earned		812,400
620	Office salaries expense	248,000	
633	Interest expense	41,250	
655	Advertising expense	56,000	
673	Janitorial expense	82,000	
690	Utilities expense	68,200	
	Totals	2,573,050	2,573,050

Required

1. Enter the unadjusted trial balance onto a work sheet.
2. Using the following additional information, enter the adjustments into the work sheet (the Chart of Accounts at the back of the text may be useful when additional accounts are required):
   a. It was determined that the balance in the Rent Receivable account at March 31 should be $142,000.
   b. A count of the office supplies showed $12,200 of the balance had been used.
   c. Annual amortization on the building is $50,000 and $7,000 on the furniture.
   d. The five office staff members each get paid $2,100 bi-weekly. The last bi-weekly pay period ended Friday, March 23. At March 31, five days' salary had accrued.
   e. A review of the balance in Advertising Expense showed that $800 was for advertisements to appear in the April issue of *Canadian Business* magazine.
   f. Accrued utilities at March 31 totalled $5,240.
   g. March interest of $3,750 on the long-term note payable is unrecorded and unpaid as of March 31.
3. Complete the work sheet.

Check figure:
Adjusted trial balance columns = $2,660,290

Problem 5-13A

Preparing a classified balance sheet

Check figure:
Total assets = $1,969,200

Use your completed work sheet from Problem 5-12A to solve this question.

Required

1. Calculate the capital balance as it would appear on the March 31, 2001 balance sheet.
2. Prepare a classified balance sheet. Assume that $150,000 of the Long-Term Notes Payable will be paid during the year ended March 31, 2002.

Problem 5-14A

Performing the steps in the accounting cycle

On June 1, 2001, Jack Farr created a new travel agency called International Tours. These events occurred during the company's first month:

June 1	Farr created the new company by investing $20,000 cash and computer equipment worth $30,000.
2	The company rented furnished office space by paying $1,600 rent for the first month.
3	The company purchased $1,200 of office supplies for cash.
10	The company paid $3,600 for the premium on a one-year insurance policy.
14	The owner's assistant was paid $800 for two weeks' salary.
24	The company collected $6,800 of commissions from airlines on tickets obtained for customers.
28	The assistant was paid another $800 for two weeks' salary.
29	The company paid the month's $750 phone bill.
30	The company paid $350 cash to repair the company's computer.
30	The owner withdrew $1,425 cash from the business.

The company's chart of accounts included these accounts:

101	Cash	405	Commissions Earned
106	Accounts Receivable	612	Amortization Expense, Computer Equipment
124	Office Supplies	622	Salaries Expense
128	Prepaid Insurance	637	Insurance Expense
167	Computer Equipment	640	Rent Expense
168	Accumulated Amortization, Computer Equipment	650	Office Supplies Expense
209	Salaries Payable	684	Repairs Expense
301	Jack Farr, Capital	688	Telephone Expense
302	Jack Farr, Withdrawals	901	Income Summary

Required

1. Use the balance-column format to create each of the listed accounts.
2. Prepare journal entries to record the transactions for June and post them to the accounts.
3. Prepare a 10-column work sheet that starts with the unadjusted trial balance as of June 30. Use the following information to draft the adjustments for the month:
   a. Two-thirds of one month's insurance coverage was consumed.
   b. There were $800 of office supplies on hand at the end of the month.
   c. Amortization on the computer equipment was estimated to be $825.
   d. The assistant had earned $160 of unpaid and unrecorded salary.
   e. The company had earned $1,750 of commissions that had not yet been billed.

   Complete the remaining columns of the work sheet.

4. Prepare journal entries to record the adjustments drafted on the work sheet and post them to the accounts.
5. Prepare an income statement, a statement of owner's equity, and a classified balance sheet.
6. Prepare journal entries to close the temporary accounts and post them to the accounts.
7. Prepare a separate post-closing trial balance.

Check figures:
Adjusted trial balance columns = $59,535;
Total assets = $51,400;
Post-closing trial balance = $52,225

***Problem 5-15A**
Adjusting, reversing, and subsequent entries

LO8

The unadjusted trial balance for Milton's Pool Parlor as of December 31, 2001 follows:

Milton's Pool Parlor December 31, 2001		
	Unadjusted Trial Balance	
Account	**Debit**	**Credit**
Cash	$ 11,000	
Accounts receivable	-0-	
Supplies	4,500	
Equipment	150,000	
Accumulated amortization, equipment		$ 15,000
Interest payable		-0-
Salaries payable		-0-
Unearned membership fees		24,000
Notes payable		50,000
Unger Milton, capital		58,250
Unger Milton, withdrawals	30,000	
Membership fees earned		90,000
Amortization expense, equipment	-0-	
Salaries expense	38,000	
Interest expense	3,750	
Supplies expense	-0-	
Totals	$237,250	$237,250

Required

Information necessary to prepare adjusting entries is as follows:

a. As of December 31, employees have earned $800 of unpaid and unrecorded wages. The next payday is January 4, and the total wages to be paid will be $1,200.
b. The cost of supplies on hand at December 31 is $1,800.
c. The note payable requires an interest payment to be made every three months. The amount of unrecorded accrued interest at December 31 is $1,250, and the next payment is due on January 15. This payment will be $1,500.
d. An analysis of the unearned membership fees shows that $16,000 remains unearned at December 31.
e. In addition to the membership fees included in the revenue account,the company has earned another $12,000 in fees that will be collected on January 21. The company is also expected to collect $7,000 on the same day for new fees earned during January.
f. Amortization expense for the year is $15,000.

An asterisk (*) identifies assignment material based on Appendix 5A or Appendix 5B.

1. Prepare adjusting journal entries.
2. Prepare journal entries to reverse the effects of the adjusting entries that involve accruals.
3. Prepare journal entries to record the cash payments and collections that are described for January.

Alternate Problems

Problem 5-1B
Completing a worksheet—net income

LO[1]

The unadjusted trial balance for Family Photographers after the first month of operations is shown below:

Family Photographers
Work Sheet
For Month Ended December 31, 2001

Account	Unadjusted Trial Balance	
	Debit	**Credit**
Cash	14,000	
Accounts receivable	3,100	
Prepaid equipment rental	1,930	
Automobile	26,000	
Accumulated amortization, automobile		-0-
Accounts payable		960
Unearned fees		2,870
Jim Tucker, capital		39,400
Jim Tucker, withdrawals	700	
Fees earned		4,200
Amortization expense, automobile	-0-	
Equipment rental expense	1,700	
Totals	47,430	47,430

Required

1. Enter the unadjusted trial balance onto a work sheet.
2. Using the following additional information, enter the adjustments into the work sheet.
   a. It was determined that $1,240 of the balance in the Prepaid Equipment Rental account had been used during December.
   b. Amortization on the automobile for the month of December was $275.
   c. Accrued utilities expense of $980 was unrecorded at December 31.
   d. $250 of the Unearned Fees account had been earned by December 31.
3. Complete the work sheet.
4. Calculate the balance in the capital account as it would appear on the December 31, 2001 balance sheet.

Check figures:
Adjusted trial balance columns = $48,685

Problem 5-2B
Closing entries

LO4

The adjusted trial balance for Bea's Photo Studio as of December 31, 2002 follows:

Bea's Photo Studio
Adjusted Trial Balance
December 31, 2002

No.	Account	Debit	Credit
101	Cash	$ 6,400	
104	Temporary investments	10,200	
126	Supplies	3,600	
167	Equipment	18,000	
168	Accumulated amortization, equipment		$ 3,000
173	Building	60,000	
174	Accumulated amortization, building		29,000
183	Land	28,500	
201	Accounts payable		2,500
203	Unearned professional fees		650
233	Long-term notes payable		32,000
251	Bea Jones, capital		44,316
301	Bea Jones, withdrawals	6,000	
302	Photography fees earned		47,000
401	Dividends earned		500
406	Amortization expense, building	2,000	
606	Amortization expense, equipment	1,000	
612	Wages expense	17,500	
623	Interest expense	1,200	
633	Insurance expense	1,425	
637	Supplies expense	900	
652	Telephone expense	421	
688	Utilities expense	1,820	
	Totals	$158,966	$158,966

An analysis of other information reveals that Bea's Photo Studio is required to make a $6,400 payment on the long-term notes payable during 2003. Also, Bea Jones invested $20,000 cash early in the year.

Required
Prepare the closing entries made at the end of the year.

Problem 5-3B
Financial statements

LO7

Check figure:
Total assets = $94,700

Using the adjusted trial balance in Problem 5-2B, prepare the income statement, statement of owner's equity, and classified balance sheet.

Problem 5-4B
Closing entries

LO4, 5

Anne's Tailoring Services' adjusted trial balance on December 31, 2002 appears in the work sheet as follows:

Anne's Tailoring Services
Work Sheet
For Year Ended December 31, 2002

No.	Account	Adjusted Trial Balance Debit	Adjusted Trial Balance Credit
101	Cash	$ 13,450	
125	Store supplies	4,140	
128	Prepaid insurance	2,200	
167	Equipment	33,000	
168	Accumulated amortization, equipment		$ 9,000
201	Accounts payable		1,000
210	Wages payable		3,200
301	Anne Taylor, capital		31,650
302	Anne Taylor, withdrawals	16,000	
401	Sewing fees earned		62,000
612	Amortization expense, equipment	3,000	
623	Wages expense	28,400	
637	Insurance expense	1,100	
640	Rent expense	2,400	
651	Store supplies expense	1,300	
690	Utilities expense	1,860	
999	Income summary		
	Totals	$106,850	$106,850

Check figure:
Post-closing trial balance = $52,790

Required

1. Prepare closing entries.
2. Prepare a post-closing trial balance.

Problem 5-5B
Financial statements

Using the information from Problem 5-4B, prepare an income statement and a statement of owner's equity for the year ended December 31, 2002, and a classified balance sheet at December 31, 2002. The owner made no investments during the year.

Check figure:
Total assets = $43,790

Problem 5-6B
Financial statements

LO5

The adjusted trial balance for Wellness Consulting Services has been alphabetized as follows:

Wellness Consulting Services
Adjusted Trial Balance
December 31, 2002

No.	Account	Debit	Credit
251	Abby Dehara, capital		$ 11,360
301	Abby Dehara, withdrawals	$ 38,000	
201	Accounts payable		1,200
168	Accumulated amortization, equipment		17,000
184	Accumulated amortization, office furniture		6,900
406	Amortization expense, equipment	2,000	
606	Amortization expense, office furniture	900	
101	Cash	4,000	
302	Consulting fees earned		127,000
401	Dividends earned		2,300
167	Equipment	49,000	
633	Insurance expense	1,200	
623	Interest expense	720	
233	Long-term notes payable		8,000
183	Office furniture	10,200	
126	Supplies	1,500	
637	Supplies expense	4,300	
652	Telephone expense	940	
104	Temporary investments	14,000	
203	Unearned professional fees		750
688	Utilities expense	1,750	
612	Wages expense	46,000	
	Totals	$174,510	$174,510

Required
Journalize the closing entries.

Problem 5-7B
Financial statements

LO7

Check figure:
Total assets = $54,800

Using the information in Problem 5-6B, prepare an income statement and statement of owner's equity for the year ended December 31, 2002 and a classified balance at December 31, 2002. The owner made no additional investments during the year. A $5,000 payment on the long-term notes payable will be made during 2003.

Problem 5-8B
Analyzing closing entries

LO5

The following closing entries were prepared for Enviro Gardening Services regarding the year just ended October 31, 2001:

2001			
Oct. 31	Service Revenue	74,000	
	Income Summary		74,000
	To close the revenue account.		
31	Income Summary	89,130	
	Amortization Expense, Gardening Equipment		4,800
	Amortization Expense, Vehicles		5,300
	Insurance Expense		3,600
	Interest Expense		680
	Supplies Expense		12,400
	Telephone Expense		850
	Utilities Expense		900
	Fuel Expense		4,600
	Wages Expense		56,000
	To close expense accounts.		
31	Grant Craig, Capital	15,130	
	Income Summary		15,130
	To close the Income Summary to capital.		
31	Grant Craig, Capital	5,000	
	Grant Craig, Withdrawals		5,000
	To close withdrawals to capital.		

Check figure:
Total operating expenses = $89,130

Required
1. Prepare an income statement based on the information provided.
2. Calculate the post-closing balance in the capital account at October 31, 2001 given that the adjusted balance on October 31, 2000 was $38,000.

Problem 5-9B
Balance sheet classifications

LO6

In the blank space beside each numbered item, enter the letter of its balance sheet classification. If the item should not appear on the balance sheet, enter a *z* in the blank.

a. Current assets
b. Long-term investments
c. Plant and equipment
d. Intangible assets
e. Current liabilities
f. Long-term liabilities
g. Owner's equity

_____ 1. Office supplies
_____ 2. Owner, capital
_____ 3. Goodwill
_____ 4. Notes receivable–due in 120 days
_____ 5. Accumulated amortization, trucks
_____ 6. Salaries payable
_____ 7. Commissions earned
_____ 8. Notes Receivable (due in 18 months)
_____ 9. Office equipment
_____ 10. Notes payable–due in three years
_____ 11. Building
_____ 12. Prepaid insurance
_____ 13. Current portion of long-term notes payable
_____ 14. Interest receivable
_____ 15. Short-term investments
_____ 16. Land (used in operations)
_____ 17. Copyrights
_____ 18. Owner, withdrawals
_____ 19. Trademark
_____ 20. Investment in Ford common shares (long-term holding)

Problem 5-10B
Work sheet, journal entries, financial statements

LO 1, 4, 5, 7

Presented below is the unadjusted trial balance of Boomer Demolition Company as of June 30, the end of its fiscal year. The beginning balance of the owner's capital account was $36,900 and the owner invested another $30,000 cash in the company during the year.

Boomer Demolition Company
Unadjusted Trial Balance
June 30, 2002

		Debit	Credit
101	Cash	$ 9,000	
126	Supplies	18,000	
128	Prepaid insurance	14,600	
167	Equipment	140,000	
168	Accumulated amortization, equipment		$ 10,000
201	Accounts payable		16,000
203	Interest Payable		
208	Rent payable		
210	Wages payable		
213	Business tax payable		
251	Long-term notes payable		20,000
301	Rusty Boomer, capital		66,900
302	Rusty Boomer, withdrawals	24,000	
401	Demolition fees earned		177,000
612	Amortization expense, equipment		
623	Wages expense	51,400	
633	Interest expense	2,200	
637	Insurance expense		
640	Rent expense	8,800	
652	Supplies expense		
683	Business tax expense	8,400	
684	Repairs expense	6,700	
690	Utilities expense	6,800	
	Totals	$289,900	$289,900

Required

Preparation component:

1. Prepare a 10-column work sheet for 2002, starting with the unadjusted trial balance and including these additional facts:
   a. The inventory of supplies at the end of the year had a cost of $8,100.
   b. The cost of expired insurance for the year is $11,500.
   c. Annual amortization on the equipment is $18,000.
   d. The June utilities expense of $700 was not included in the trial balance because the bill arrived after it was prepared. The $700 amount owed needs to be recorded.
   e. The company's employees have earned $2,200 of accrued wages.
   f. The lease for the office requires the company to pay total rent for each fiscal year equal to 8% of the company's annual revenues. The rent is paid to the building owner with monthly payments of $800. If the annual rent exceeds the total monthly payments, the company must pay the excess before July 31. If the total is less than the amount previously paid, the building owner will refund the difference by July 31.
   g. Additional business tax of $450 has been assessed but has not been paid or recorded in the accounts.

Check figures:
Adjusted trial balance columns = $316,810;
Total assets = $132,200

h. Interest of $200 for June has not yet been paid or recorded. In addition, the company is required to make a $4,000 payment on the note on August 30, 2002.

2. Use the work sheet to journalize the adjusting and closing entries.
3. Prepare an income statement, a statement of owner's equity and a classified balance sheet.

Analysis component:

4. Analyze the following independent errors and describe how each would affect the 10-column work sheet. Explain whether the error is likely to be discovered in completing the work sheet and, if not, the effect of the error on the financial statements.
   a. The adjustment for consumption of the insurance coverage credited the Prepaid Insurance account for $3,100 and debited the same amount to the Insurance Expense account.
   b. When completing the adjusted trial balance in the work sheet, the $6,700 Repairs Expense account balance was extended to the Debit column for the balance sheet.

Problem 5-11B
Completing a partial work sheet; classified balance sheet

LO[1, 7]

Check figures:
Net income = $25,300
Total assets = $90,560

The following partial work sheet is available for TelsCo Drill Servicing for the month just ended August 21, 2001:

TelsCo Drill Servicing
Partial Work Sheet
For Year Ended August 30, 2001

		Unadjusted Trial Balance		Income Statement		Balance Sheet & Statement of Owner's Equity	
No.	**Account**	**Debit**	**Credit**	**Debit**	**Credit**	**Debit**	**Credit**
101	Cash	10,000					
106	Accounts receivable	28,000					
124	Office supplies	850					
141	Investment in Nortel shares	29,000					
161	Furniture	38,000					
162	Accumulated amortization, furniture		21,750				
193	Franchise	6,320					
201	Accounts payable		14,950				
205	Short-term notes payable		1,600				
230	Unearned servicing revenue		2,500				
251	Long-term notes payable*		14,000				
301	Angela Telsco, capital		49,210				
302	Angela Telsco, withdrawals	17,000					
403	Drill servicing revenue		106,000				
409	Interest earned		1,300				
623	Wages expense	71,000					
637	Insurance expense	8,340					
688	Telephone expense	1,400					
	Totals						
109	Interest receivable	140					
690	Utilities expense	230					
601	Amortization expense, furniture	1,030					
	Totals	211,310	211,310				

* *A $9,000 payment will be made on the long-term notes payable during the year ended August 31, 2002.*

Required

1. Complete the partial work sheet.
2. Calculate the August 31, 2001 balance in the capital account.
3. Prepare a classified balance sheet.

Analysis component:

4. Why are the accounts Interest Receivable, Utilities Expense, and Amortization Expense listed below the first Totals heading?

Problem 5-12B
Completing a work sheet

LO1

The unadjusted trial balance for Landmark Tours after its first month of operations is shown below:

Landmark Tours
Work Sheet
For Month Ended July 31, 2001

No.	Account	Unadjusted Trial Balance Debit	Unadjusted Trial Balance Credit
101	Cash	17,800	
106	Accounts receivable	42,500	
111	Notes receivable	28,000	
128	Prepaid insurance	21,000	
161	Furniture	13,500	
201	Accounts payable		13,850
230	Unearned tour revenue		28,000
301	Jan Rider, capital		66,950
302	Jan Rider, withdrawals	-0-	
403	Tour revenue		86,000
623	Wages expense	72,000	
	Totals	194,800	194,800

Check figure:
Adjusted trial balance columns = $221,008

Required

1. Enter the unadjusted trial balance onto a work sheet.
2. Using the following additional information, enter the adjustments into the work sheet (the Chart of Accounts at the back of the text may be useful when additional accounts are required):
   a. Interest of $400 had accrued on the note receivable by month end.
   b. The July utility bill for $650 was received in the mail on July 31. It is unpaid and unrecorded.
   c. Amortization on the furniture for the month of July is $350.
   d. The balance in prepaid insurance is from an eight-month policy that went into effect on July 1, 2001.
   e. The company has four employees who each get paid $630 every Friday for a five-day workweek. July 31 falls on a Tuesday, therefore, two days of accrued wages need to be recorded.
   f. At July 31, it was determined that $9,800 of the balance in unearned tour revenue was not yet earned.
   g. Landmark Tours signed a contract with a school effective July 9 for four weeks. From Monday through Friday each week, Landmark Tours will be taking a total of 40 children camping. The charge is $35 per day per child. The school will pay Landmark Tours at the end of the four-week period, on Friday, August 3. No entries have been recorded to date regarding this contract.
3. Complete the work sheet.

Problem 5-13B
Preparing a classified balance sheet

LO7

Check figure:
Total assets = $144,025

Use your completed work sheet from Problem 5-12B to solve the following questions.

Required

1. Calculate the balance in the capital account as it would appear on the July 31, 2001 balance sheet.
2. Prepare a classified balance sheet.

Problem 5-14B
Performing the steps in the accounting cycle

LO6

On July 1, 2001, Cindy Tucker created a new self-storage business called Lockit Co. These events occurred during the company's first month:

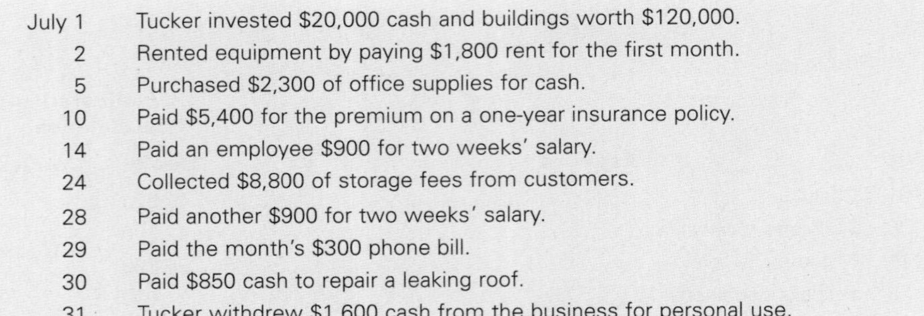

July	1	Tucker invested $20,000 cash and buildings worth $120,000.
	2	Rented equipment by paying $1,800 rent for the first month.
	5	Purchased $2,300 of office supplies for cash.
	10	Paid $5,400 for the premium on a one-year insurance policy.
	14	Paid an employee $900 for two weeks' salary.
	24	Collected $8,800 of storage fees from customers.
	28	Paid another $900 for two weeks' salary.
	29	Paid the month's $300 phone bill.
	30	Paid $850 cash to repair a leaking roof.
	31	Tucker withdrew $1,600 cash from the business for personal use.

The company's chart of accounts included these accounts:

101	Cash	401	Storage Fees Earned
106	Accounts Receivable	606	Amortization Expense, Buildings
124	Office Supplies	622	Salaries Expense
128	Prepaid Insurance	637	Insurance Expense
173	Buildings	640	Equipment Rental Expense
174	Accumulated Amortization, Buildings	650	Office Supplies Expense
209	Salaries Payable	684	Repairs Expense
301	Cindy Tucker, Capital	688	Telephone Expense
302	Cindy Tucker, Withdrawals	901	Income Summary

Required

1. Use the balance-column format to create each of the listed accounts.
2. Prepare journal entries to record the transactions for July and post them to the accounts. Record prepaid and unearned items in balance sheet accounts.
3. Prepare a 10-column work sheet that starts with the unadjusted trial balance as of July 31. Use the following information to draft the adjustments for the month:
   a. Two-thirds of one month's insurance coverage was consumed.
   b. There was $1,550 of office supplies on hand at the end of the month.
   c. Amortization on the buildings was estimated to be $1,200.
   d. The employee had earned $180 of unpaid and unrecorded salary.
   e. The company had earned $950 of storage fees that had not yet been billed.
   Complete the remaining columns of the work sheet.
4. Prepare journal entries to record the adjustments drafted on the work sheet and post them to the accounts.
5. Prepare an income statement, a statement of owner's equity, and a classified balance sheet.
6. Prepare journal entries to close the temporary accounts and post them to the accounts.
7. Prepare a separate post-closing trial balance.

Check figures:
Unadjusted trial balance = $148,800;
Total assets = $141,150;
Post-closing trial balance = $142,350

***Problem 5-15B**
Adjusting, closing, and reversing entries

LO8

Leeward Service Company's unadjusted trial balance on December 31, 2000, the end of its annual accounting period, is as follows:

Leeward Service Company Unadjusted Trial Balance December 31, 2000		
Account	**Debit**	**Credit**
Cash	$ 73,725	
Notes receivable	37,500	
Office supplies	4,200	
Land	45,000	
Unearned service fees		$ 18,000
Notes payable		90,000
Jean Boat, capital		37,500
Jean Boat, withdrawals	60,000	
Service fees earned		267,000
Interest revenue		2,550
Rent revenue		12,375
Salaries expense	193,500	
Insurance expense	4,950	
Interest expense	8,550	
Totals	$427,425	$427,425

Information necessary to prepare adjusting entries is as follows:

a. Employees, who are paid $7,500 every two weeks, have earned $5,250 since the last payment. The next payment of $7,500 will be on January 4.
b. Leeward rents office space to a tenant who has paid only $450 of the $1,125 rent for December. On January 12, the tenant will pay the remainder along with the rent for January.
c. An inventory of office supplies discloses $675 of unused supplies.
d. Premiums for insurance against injuries to employees are paid monthly. The $450 premium for December will be paid January 12.
e. Leeward owes $90,000 on a note payable that requires quarterly payments of accrued interest. The quarterly payments of $2,700 each are made on the 15th of January, April, July, and October.
f. An analysis of Leeward's service contracts with customers shows that $6,300 of the amount customers have prepaid remains unearned.
g. Leeward has a $37,500 note receivable on which interest of $175 has accrued. On January 22, the note and the total accrued interest of $575 will be repaid to Leeward.
h. Leeward has earned but unrecorded revenue for $8,250 for services provided to a customer who will pay for the work on January 24. At that time, the customer will also pay $3,100 for services Leeward will perform in early January.

Required

1. Prepare adjusting journal entries.
2. Prepare reversing entries.
3. Prepare journal entries to record the January 2001 cash receipts and cash payments identified in the above information.

An asterisk (*) identifies assignment material based on Appendix 5A or Appendix 5B.

Analytical and Review Problems

A & R Problem 5-1

The owner of Dynamo Stores has come to you for assistance because his bookkeeper has just moved to another city. The following is the only information his bookkeeper left him.

1. Balance sheets as of December 31, 2001 and 2002.

	2002	2001
Assets	$168,000	$210,000
Liabilities	$ 42,000	$ 63,000
Capital	126,000	147,000
	$168,000	$210,000

2. The owner withdrew $105,000 in 2002 for his personal use.
3. The business incurred total expenses of $168,000 for 2002, of which $126,000 was for wages and $42,000 was for advertising.

Required

1. Compute the total revenue and net income for 2002.
2. Prepare closing or clearing entries for 2002 (omit narratives).

A & R Problem 5-2

The partially completed work sheet for the current fiscal year of Sandy's Delivery Service appears below:

Sandy's Delivery Service
Work Sheet
For the Year Ended December 31, 2002

Account	Unadjusted Trial Balance		Adjustments		Adjusted Trial Balance		Income Statement		Balance Sheet & Statement of Owner's Equity	
	Debit	Credit	Debit	Credit	Debit	Credit	Debit	Credit	Debit	Credit
Cash	10,650									
Accounts receivable	7,000				9,000					
Supplies	4,200								1,600	
Prepaid insurance	2,400									
Prepaid rent	1,800									
Delivery trucks	40,000				40,000					
Accounts payable		3,130				3,130				
Unearned delivery fees		4,500								2,000
Sandra Berlasty, capital		50,000								
Sandra Berlasty, withdrawals	3,000									
Delivery service revenue		18,500								
Advertising expense	600									
Gas and oil expense	680									
Salaries expense	5,600									
Utilities expense	200									
Totals	76,130	76,130								
Insurance expense					800					
Rent expense					900					
Supplies expense										
Amortization expense, delivery trucks										
Accumulated amortization, delivery trucks										2,000
Accrued salaries payable										400
Net Income										

Required

1. Complete the work sheet.
2. Journalize the adjusting and closing entries (omit narratives).

Serial Problem

Echo Systems

Check figure:
Total credits in post-closing trial balance = $77,860

(The first two segments of this comprehensive problem were in Chapters 3 and 4, and the final segment is presented in Chapter 6. If the Chapter 3 and 4 segments have not been completed, the assignment can begin at this point. It is recommended that you use the Working Papers that accompany this book because they reflect the account balances that resulted from posting the entries required in Chapters 3 and 4.)

The transactions of Echo Systems for October through December 2001 have been recorded in the problem segments in Chapters 3 and 4, as well as the year-end adjusting entries. Prior to closing the revenue and expense accounts for 2001, the accounting system is modified to include the Income Summary account, which is given the number 901.

Required

1. Record and post the appropriate closing entries.
2. Prepare a post-closing trial balance.

CHAPTER 6

Accounting for Merchandising Activities

Fizzling Inventory

Toronto, ON—With the opening of Liquid Nectar, a small retail outlet devoted to serving the quirky tastes of young and old alike, Rob Stavos was living his dreams. But within months, this young entrepreneur's dream had become a nightmare.

Liquid Nectar started out with a bang. Customers raved about its stock of exotic and unique beverage products. Profit margins on successful drinks far outweighed the costs of unsold products. "We were ready to take on the large producers," boasts Rob. Within two months, however, Rob lost control of inventory and margins were being squeezed. What happened? Was Liquid Nectar soon to be another flash-in-the pan?

Two problems emerged. One was Rob's installation of what's called a periodic inventory system. This system reports inventory levels at periodic intervals such as once a month. This means the inventory system couldn't give Rob up-to-date information on sales and inventory he'd need for stocking and ordering.

"Our popular brands were being sold out and nothing was in inventory," says Rob. "We were turning away too many customers." Hardly a ticket for success. The second problem was that Rob did not skillfully negotiate purchase contracts. Purchase discounts and returns left too much power and too many decisions with suppliers.

But Rob fought back. With the help of a consultant, Rob installed a perpetual inventory system and renegotiated purchase contracts. His new inventory system gives up-to-date details on sales and inventory. "We now know what's hot and what's not," says Rob, "and we don't turn customers away." Also, his new contracts allow Rob to return unsold inventories and to deeply discount others. "This time," claims Rob, "we'll not disappoint!" And the future of Liquid Nectar looks downright bubbly.

Learning Objectives

- LO1 Describe merchandising activities and identify business examples.
- LO2 Identify and explain the important components of income for a merchandising company.
- LO3 Identify and explain the inventory asset of a merchandising company.
- LO4 Describe both periodic and perpetual inventory systems.
- LO5 Analyze and record transactions for merchandise purchases using a perpetual system.
- LO6 Analyze and record transactions for sales of merchandise using a perpetual system.
- LO7 Prepare adjustments for a merchandising company.
- LO8 Analyze and interpret cost flows and operating activities of a merchandising company.
- LO9 Define and prepare multiple-step and single-step income statements.
- LO10 Prepare closing entries for a merchandising company.

Chapter Preview

Our emphasis in previous chapters was on the accounting and reporting activities of companies providing services. Chapter 6 emphasizes merchandising, a major part of modern business. Consumers expect a wealth of products, discount prices, inventory on demand, and high quality. This chapter introduces us to the business and accounting practices used by companies engaged in merchandising activities. These companies buy products and then resell them to customers. We show how financial statements capture these merchandising activities. The new financial statement elements created by merchandising activities are explained. We also analyze and record merchandise purchases and sales of these companies. Adjusting entries and the closing process for merchandising companies are explained. An understanding of these important topics is what Rob Stavos of Liquid Nectar needed in order to avoid the problems he encountered.

Merchandising Activities

LO[1] Describe merchandising activities and identify business examples.

A merchandising company's activities are different from those of a service company. A **merchandiser** earns net income by buying and selling merchandise. **Merchandise** consists of products, also called *goods*, that a company acquires for the purpose of reselling them to customers. The cost of these goods is an expense called **cost of goods sold**. Merchandisers are often identified as either *wholesalers* or *retailers*.

A **wholesaler** is a company that buys products from manufacturers or other wholesalers and sells them to retailers or other wholesalers. Wholesalers include companies such as Provigo, Cassidy's, The Oshawa Group and Westfair Foods. A **retailer** is a *middleman* that buys products from manufacturers or wholesalers and sells them to consumers. Examples of retailers include The Bay, Loblaw, Zellers, The Gap, and Sam the Record Man. Some retailers, such as Bell Canada, often sell both products and services.

Reporting Financial Performance

LO[2] Identify and explain the important components of income for a merchandising company.

Net income to a merchandiser results when revenue from selling merchandise exceeds both the cost of merchandise sold to customers and the cost of other operating expenses for the period (see Exhibit 6.1). The usual accounting term for revenues from selling merchandise is *sales* and the term used for the cost of buying and preparing the merchandise is an expense called *cost of goods sold.*[1] A merchandiser's other expenses are often called *operating expenses.*

Exhibit 6.1 Computing Income for Both a Merchandising Company and a Service Company

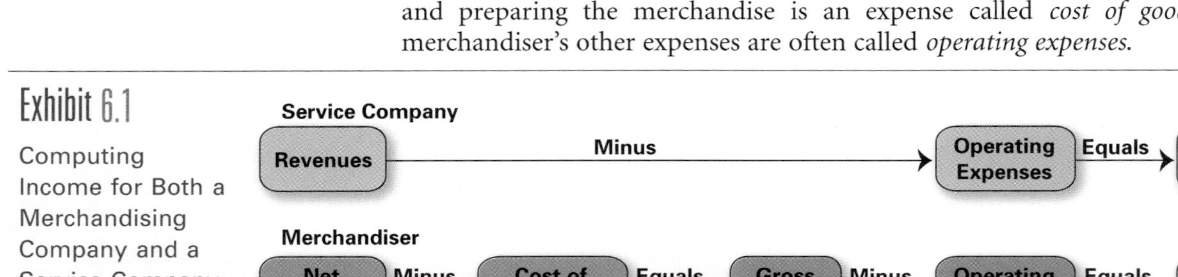

[1] Cost of goods sold is often described as an operating expense. Also, many companies use the term *sales* in their income statements to describe revenues. Loblaw is one example. Because the *CICA Handbook* does not specifically require the separate disclosure of cost of goods sold, most Canadian companies combine their cost of goods sold and operating expenses into one amount.

Exhibit 6.2

Condensed Income Statement for a Merchandiser

Z-Mart Condensed Income Statement For Year Ended December 31, 2001	
Net sales	$314,700
Cost of goods sold	230,400
Gross profit from sales	$ 84,300
Total operating expenses and other revenues and expenses	68,960
Net income	$ 15,340

The condensed income statement for Z-Mart in Exhibit 6.2 shows us how these three elements of net income are related. This statement shows that Z-Mart sold products to customers for $314,700. Z-Mart acquired these goods at a cost of $230,400. This yields an $84,300 gross profit. **Gross profit**, also called **gross margin**, equals net sales less cost of goods sold. Changes in gross profit often greatly impact a merchandiser's operations since gross profit must cover all other expenses and yield a return for the owner. Z-Mart, for instance, used gross profit to cover $68,960 of operating and other revenues and expenses. This left $15,340 in net income for the year 2001.

Reporting Financial Condition

Identify and explain the inventory asset of a merchandising company.

A merchandising company's balance sheet includes an item not on the balance sheet of a service company. This item is a current asset called *merchandise inventory*. **Merchandise inventory** refers to products a company owns for the purpose of selling to customers. Exhibit 6.3 shows the classified balance sheet P. 211 for Z-Mart, including merchandise inventory of $21,000. The cost of this asset

Exhibit 6.3

Classified Balance Sheet for a Merchandiser

Z-Mart Balance Sheet December 31, 2001			
Assets			
Current assets:			
Cash		$ 8,200	
Accounts receivable		11,200	
Merchandise inventory		**21,000**	
Prepaid expenses		1,100	
Total current assets			$41,500
Capital assets:			
Office equipment	$ 4,200		
Less: Accumulated amortization	1,400	$ 2,800	
Store equipment	$30,000		
Less: Accumulated amortization	6,000	24,000	
Total capital assets			26,800
Total assets			$68,300
Liabilities			
Current liabilities:			
Accounts payable		$ 16,000	
Salaries payable		800	
Total liabilities			$16,800
Owner's Equity			
Kent Marty, capital			51,500
Total liabilities and owner's equity			$68,300

includes the cost incurred to buy the goods, ship them to the store, and other costs necessary to make them ready for sale. Although companies usually hold inventories of other items such as supplies, *most companies simply refer to merchandise inventory as inventory*. We will use both terms in reference to merchandise inventory.

Operating Cycle

A merchandising company's operating cycle begins with the purchase of merchandise and ends with the collection of cash from the sale of merchandise. An example is a merchandiser who buys products at wholesale and distributes and sells them to consumers at retail. The length of an operating cycle differs across the types of businesses. Department stores such as The Bay and Sears commonly have operating cycles of three to five months, but operating cycles for grocery merchants such as Loblaw and Safeway usually range from one to two months.

Exhibit 6.4 graphically shows an operating cycle for a merchandiser with (1) cash sales and (2) credit sales. Credit sales delay the receipt of cash until the account receivable is paid by the customer. Companies try to shorten their operating cycles to increase income. Assets tied up in the form of merchandise inventory or receivables are not productive assets. Merchandise inventory is not productive (earning income) until it is sold. Receivables need to be collected so that the resulting cash can be used to earn income.

Exhibit 6.4

Operating Cycle of a Merchandiser

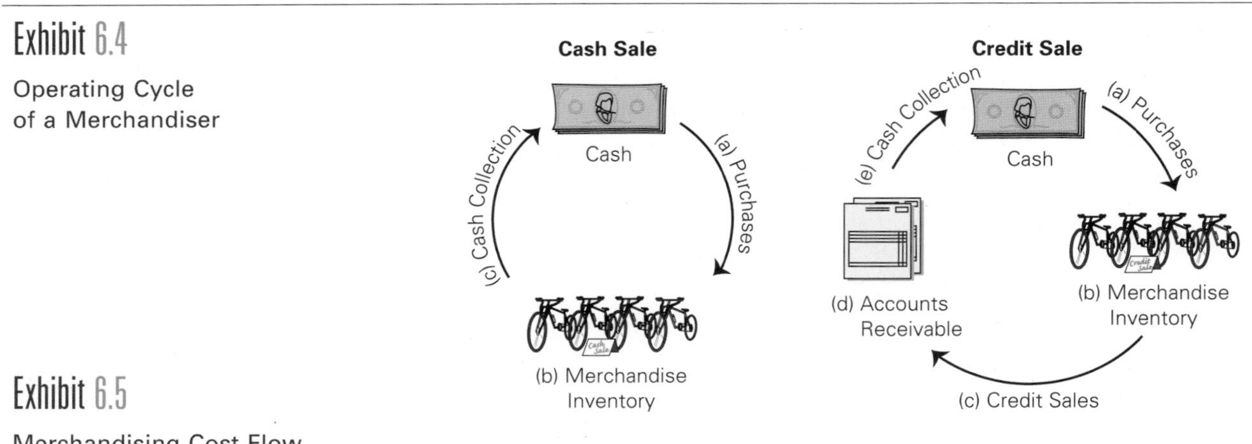

Exhibit 6.5

Merchandising Cost Flow

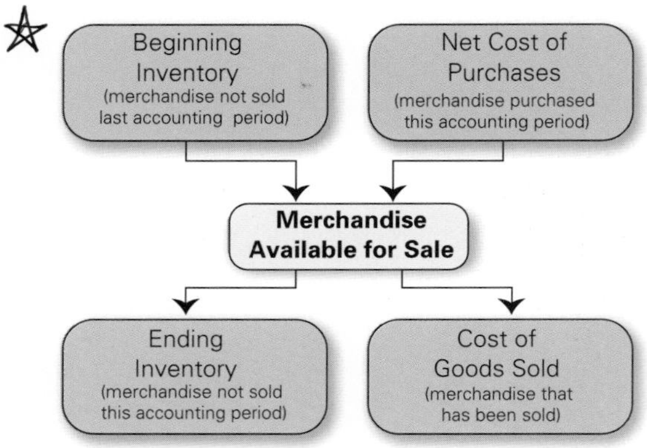

Inventory Systems

Cost of goods sold is the cost of merchandise sold to customers during a period and is reported on the income statement. It is often the largest single deduction on the income statement of a merchandiser. Merchandise inventory is reported as a current asset on the balance sheet. Cost of goods sold and merchandise inventory are part of merchandising activities captured in Exhibit 6.5. This exhibit shows that a company's merchandise available for sale is a combination of what it begins with (beginning inventory) and what it purchases (net cost of purchases). The merchandise available is either sold (cost of goods sold) or kept for future sales (ending inventory).

Two inventory accounting systems are used to collect information about cost of goods sold and cost of inventory on hand. The two systems are called *periodic* and *perpetual.* Both inventory systems are generally accepted, therefore, companies have a choice. We introduce these systems in this section.

Perpetual Inventory System

Describe both periodic and perpetual inventory systems.

A **perpetual inventory system** gives a continuous record of the amount of inventory on hand. A perpetual system accumulates the net cost of merchandise purchases in the inventory account and transfers the cost of each sale from the same inventory account to the Cost of Goods Sold account when an item is sold. With a perpetual system, we can find out the cost of merchandise on hand at any time by looking at the balance of the inventory account. We can also find out the cost of goods sold to date during a period by looking at the balance in the Cost of Goods Sold account.

Before advancements in computing technology, a perpetual system was often limited to businesses making a small number of daily sales, such as automobile dealers and major appliance stores. Because there were relatively few transactions, a perpetual system was feasible. Today, with widespread use of computing technology, the use of a perpetual system has dramatically grown to include merchandisers with high-volume sales as well, such as Canadian Tire, Superstore, Staples, and London Drugs. The number of companies that use a perpetual system continues to increase.[2]

Because perpetual inventory systems give users more timely information and are widely used in practice, our discussion in this chapter emphasizes a perpetual system. Many companies provide their suppliers with point-of-sale data that allow the suppliers to know how quickly items are being sold so that replacement merchandise can be shipped on a timely basis.

Periodic Inventory System

A **periodic inventory system** requires updating the inventory account only at the *end of a period* to reflect the quantity and cost of both goods on hand and goods sold. It does not require continual updating of the inventory account. The company records the cost of new merchandise in a temporary expense account called *Purchases.* When merchandise is sold, revenue is recorded but the cost of the merchandise sold is *not* yet recorded as a cost. When financial statements are prepared, the company takes a *physical count of inventory* by counting the quantities of merchandise on hand. Cost of merchandise on hand is determined by relating the quantities on hand to records showing each item's original cost. This cost of merchandise on hand is used to compute cost of goods sold. The inventory account is then adjusted to reflect the amount computed from the physical count of inventory.

Periodic systems were historically used by companies such as hardware, drug, and department stores that sold large quantities of low-value items. Without today's computers and scanners, it was not feasible for accounting systems to track such small items as pencils, toothpaste, paper clips, socks, and toothpicks through inventory and into customers' hands. *We analyze and record merchandising transactions using both periodic and perpetual inventory systems in Appendix 6A.*

---

[2] During December 2000, the authors conducted a brief survey of seven businesses (five large, one medium, and one small). Each of these businesses has a perpetual inventory system in place (six computerized and one manual). Statistics on the number of Canadian businesses that use a perpetual inventory system were not available at the time of writing.

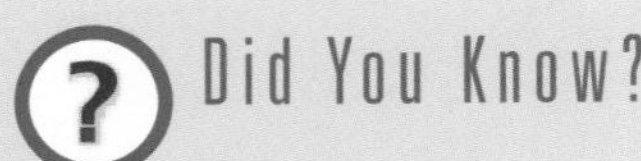

From Periodic to Perpetual to Virtual Inventory Systems

"Traditional models ... are going away," according to Keyur Patel, a KPMG partner. Web businesses are changing the way inventory is managed and accounted for. Rather than risk having too little or too much in inventory along with all of the related costs, e-businesses are turning to the manufacturers to package and ship products direct to consumers. The result is that these merchants maintain zero inventory. Instead, they take customer orders and transmit that information directly to the respective manufacturer, who fulfills the distribution obligation to the customer. Therefore, for these merchants, discussion of an inventory costing system has become redundant.

SOURCE: www.planetit.com; December 5, 1999.

Answers—p. 282

1. Describe a company's cost of goods sold.
2. What is gross profit for a merchandising company?
3. Explain why use of the perpetual inventory system has grown dramatically.

Accounting for Merchandise Purchases — Perpetual Inventory System

LO5 Analyze and record transactions for merchandise purchases using a perpetual system.

We explained that with a perpetual inventory system, the cost of merchandise bought for resale is recorded in the Merchandise Inventory account. Z-Mart records a $1,200 credit purchase of merchandise on November 2 with this entry:

Nov. 2	Merchandise Inventory	1,200	
	Accounts Payable		1,200
	Purchased merchandise on credit.		

Note that neither GST (Goods and Services Tax) nor PST (Provincial Sales Tax) has been considered in this transaction. The accounting for GST and PST is deferred until Chapter 8. Although GST and PST affect merchandising transactions, they are specifically a tax issue. To include discussion of GST and PST at this point would complicate merchandising transactions for the introductory student.

The invoice for this merchandise is shown in Exhibit 6.6. The buyer usually receives the original, while the seller keeps a copy. Notice that this single source document serves as the purchase invoice of Z-Mart (buyer) and the sales invoice for Trex (seller). The amount recorded for merchandise inventory includes its purchase cost, shipping fees, taxes, and any other costs necessary to make it ready for sale.

Exhibit 6.6

Invoice

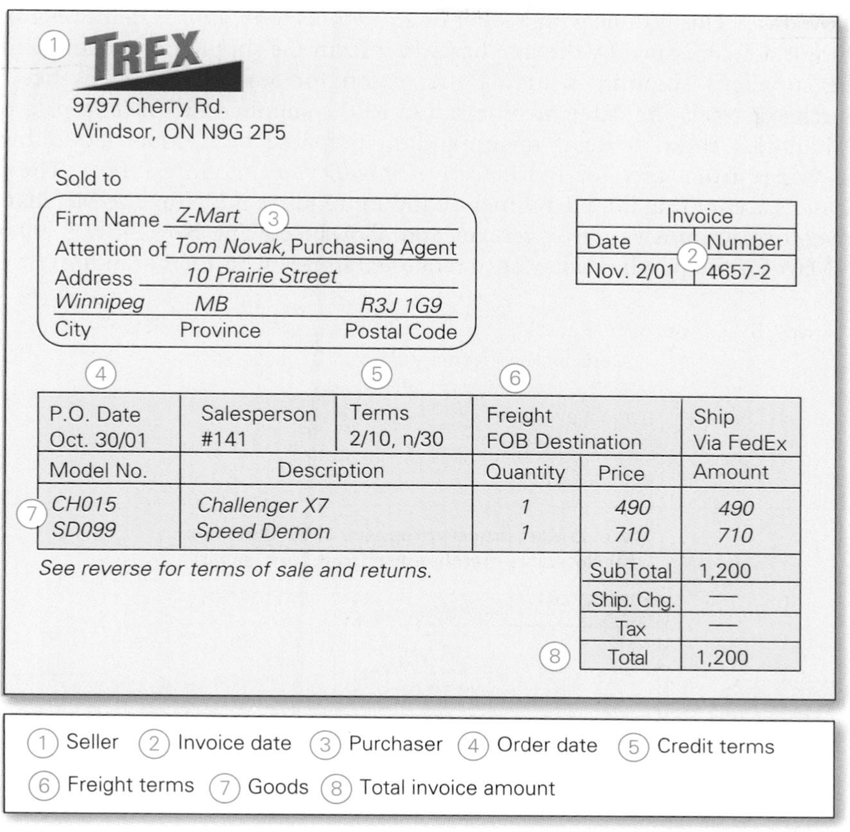
TREX
9797 Cherry Rd.
Windsor, ON N9G 2P5

Sold to

Firm Name *Z-Mart*
Attention of *Tom Novak,* Purchasing Agent
Address *10 Prairie Street*
Winnipeg *MB* *R3J 1G9*
City Province Postal Code

Invoice Date	Number
Nov. 2/01	4657-2

P.O. Date Oct. 30/01	Salesperson #141	Terms 2/10, n/30	Freight FOB Destination		Ship Via FedEx
Model No.	Description		Quantity	Price	Amount
CH015	*Challenger X7*		*1*	*490*	*490*
SD099	*Speed Demon*		*1*	*710*	*710*

See reverse for terms of sale and returns.

SubTotal	1,200
Ship. Chg.	—
Tax	—
Total	1,200

(1) Seller (2) Invoice date (3) Purchaser (4) Order date (5) Credit terms (6) Freight terms (7) Goods (8) Total invoice amount

To compute the total cost of merchandise purchases, we must adjust the invoice cost for:

(1) Any returns and allowances for unsatisfactory items received from a supplier;

(2) Any discounts given to a purchaser by a supplier for early payment; and

(3) Any required freight costs paid by a purchaser.

This section explains these items in more detail.

Purchase Returns and Allowances

Purchase returns are merchandise received by a purchaser but returned to the supplier. Reasons for returns vary. Perhaps the merchandise received was the incorrect colour or wrong size. A *purchase allowance* is a reduction in the cost of defective merchandise received by a purchaser from a supplier. Purchasers will often keep defective merchandise that is still marketable if the supplier grants an acceptable allowance. For example, assume that the merchandise received by the purchaser was furniture scratched during shipment. The purchaser may repair the furniture if the supplier provides an allowance.

To illustrate how a buyer accounts for an allowance, we assume that Z-Mart's purchase of merchandise for $1,200 was on credit. Z-Mart's entry to record this credit purchase is:

Nov. 2	Merchandise Inventory	1,200	
	Accounts Payable		1,200
	Purchased merchandise on credit, invoice dated November 2.		

The purchaser usually informs the supplier in writing of any returns and allowances. This is done with a letter or a *debit memorandum.* A **debit memorandum** is a form issued by the purchaser to inform the supplier of a debit made to the supplier's account, including the reason for a return or allowance. The purchaser sends the debit memorandum to the supplier and also keeps a copy. Exhibit 6.7 shows a debit memorandum prepared by Z-Mart requesting an allowance from Trex for the defective *SpeedDemon* mountain bike. The purchaser's accounting for a debit memorandum requires updating the Merchandise Inventory account to reflect returns and allowances. The November 5 entry by Z-Mart for the purchase allowance requested in the debit memorandum is:

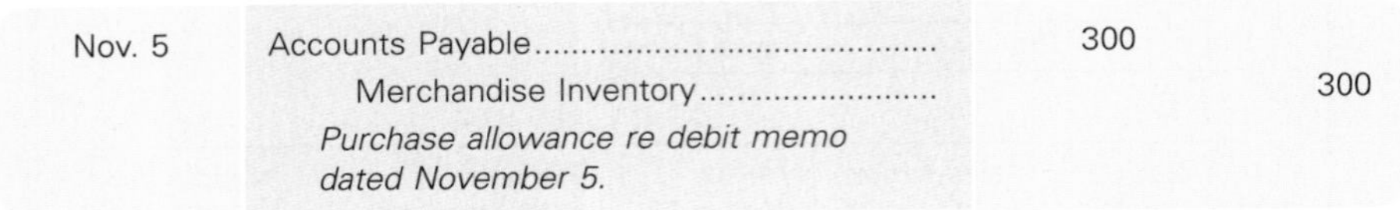

Nov. 5	Accounts Payable..	300	
	Merchandise Inventory.........................		300
	Purchase allowance re debit memo dated November 5.		

Exhibit 6.7

Debit Memorandum

Case: Z-Mart (buyer) proposes $300 allowance for defective merchandise from Trex (seller)

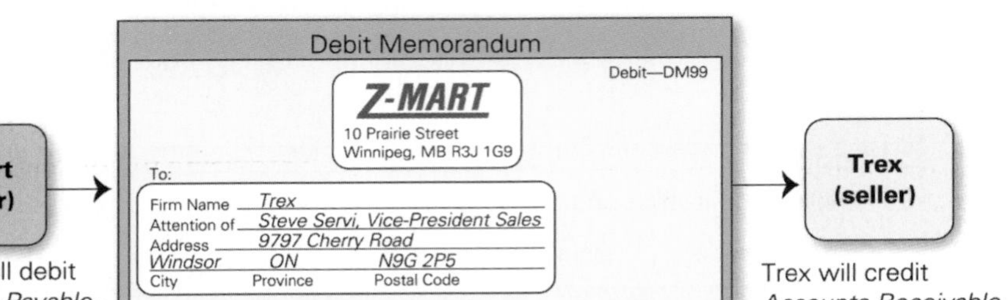

Debit Memorandum

Debit—DM99

Z-MART
10 Prairie Street
Winnipeg, MB R3J 1G9

To:
Firm Name *Trex*
Attention of *Steve Servi, Vice-President Sales*
Address *9797 Cherry Road*
Windsor *ON* *N9G 2P5*
City Province Postal Code

Date	Contact:	Invoice	Invoice	Type:
Nov. 5/01	T. Novak	No. 4657-2	Date: Nov. 2/01	Allowance

Catalogue No.	Description	Quantity	Price	Amount
SD 099	*Speed Demon: Allowance to cover defective frame: kept for parts*	1	300	300
☑ Debit Account ☐ Cash Refund ☐ Other (see reverse)			Total	300

If this had been a return, then the recorded cost[3] of the defective merchandise would be entered. Z-Mart's agreement with this supplier says that the cost of returned and defective merchandise is offset against Z-Mart's next purchase or its current account payable balance. Some agreements with suppliers involve refunding the cost to a buyer. If there is a refund of cash, then the Cash account is debited for $300 instead of Accounts Payable as follows:

Nov. 5	Cash	300	
	Merchandise Inventory.........................		300
	Cash refund for return of defective merchandise.		

[3] Recorded cost is the cost reported in a merchandise inventory account minus any discounts.

Trade Discounts

When a manufacturer or wholesaler prepares a catalogue of items it has for sale, each item is usually given a **list price**, also called a *catalogue price*. List price often is not the intended selling price of an item. Instead, the intended selling price equals list price minus a given percentage called a **trade discount**.

The amount of trade discount usually depends on whether a buyer is a wholesaler, retailer, or final consumer. A wholesaler buying in large quantities is often granted a larger discount than a retailer buying in smaller quantities.

Trade discounts are commonly used by manufacturers and wholesalers to change selling prices without republishing their catalogues. When a seller wants to change selling prices, it can notify its customers merely by sending them a new table of trade discounts that they can apply to catalogue prices.

Because a list price is not intended to reflect actual selling price of merchandise, a buyer records the net amount of list price minus trade discount. In the November 2 purchase of merchandise by Z-Mart, it received a 40% trade discount for the items that were listed in the seller's catalogue at $2,000. Z-Mart's purchase price is $1,200, computed as [$2,000 − (40% × $2,000)].

Purchase Discounts

The purchase of goods on credit requires a clear statement of expected amounts and dates of future payments to avoid misunderstandings. **Credit terms** for a purchase are a listing of the amounts and timing of payments between a buyer and seller. In some industries, purchasers expect terms requiring full or "net" payment within 10 days after the end of a month in which purchases occur. These credit terms are entered on sales invoices or tickets as "n/10 EOM." The **EOM** refers to "end of month." In some other industries, invoices are often due and payable 30 calendar days after the invoice date. These credit terms are entered as "n/30," meaning "net amount due in 30 days." The 30-day period is called the **credit period**. Referring to Exhibit 6.6, notice that Z-Mart's November 2 credit purchase was on terms of 2/10, n/30. Exhibit 6.8 portrays these credit terms.

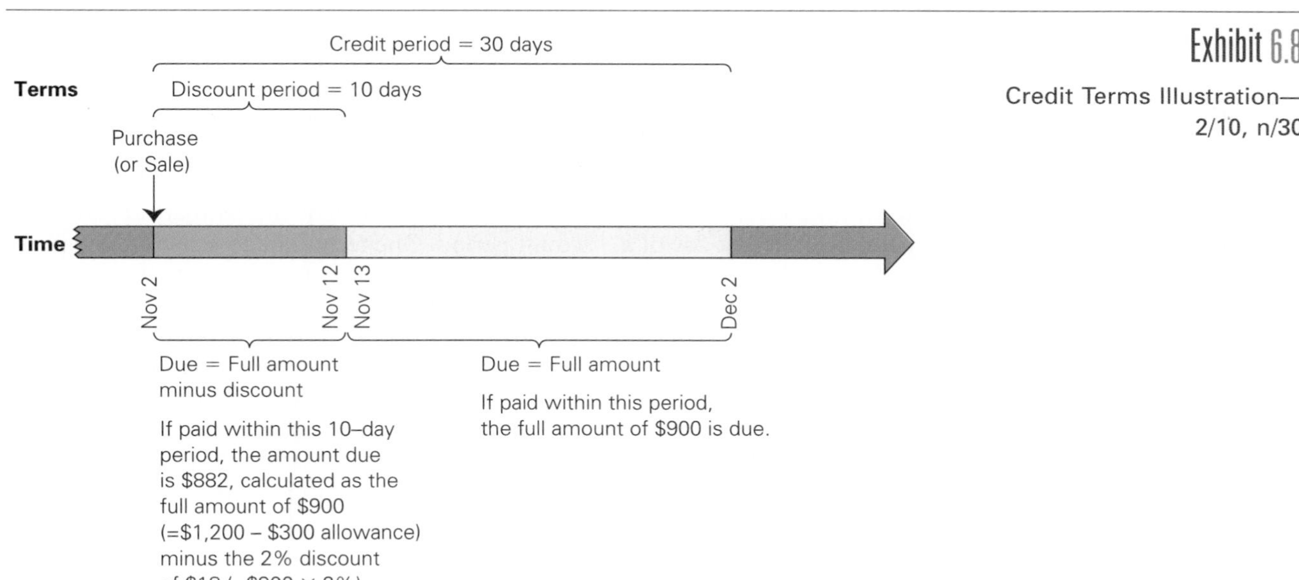

Exhibit 6.8

Credit Terms Illustration—2/10, n/30

Sellers often grant a **cash discount** when the credit period is long and buyers pay promptly. A buyer views a cash discount as a **purchase discount.** A seller views a cash discount as a **sales discount.** If cash discounts for early payment exist, they are described in the credit terms on an invoice. The credit terms of "2/10, n/30" mean there is a 30-day credit period before full payment is due. The seller allows a buyer to deduct 2% of the invoice amount from the payment if it is paid within 10 days of the invoice date, however. Sellers do this to encourage early payment. A **discount period** is the period where the reduced payment can be made.

When Z-Mart takes advantage of the discount and pays the amount due on November 12, the entry to record payment is:

Nov. 12	Accounts Payable	900	
	Merchandise Inventory........................		18
	Cash..		882
	Paid for the purchase of November 2 less the allowance of November 5 and the discount; $1,200 − $300 = $900; 2% × $900 = $18; $900 − $18 = $882.		

Notice that this entry shows that when goods are returned within the discount period, a buyer will take the discount only on the remaining balance of the invoice.

Z-Mart's Merchandise Inventory account now reflects the net cost of merchandise purchased. Its Accounts Payable account also shows the debt to be satisfied.

Merchandise Inventory			
Nov. 2	1,200	Nov. 5	300
		Nov. 12	18
Balance	882		

Accounts Payable			
Nov. 5	300	Nov. 2	1,200
Nov. 12	900		
		Balance	-0-

Managing Discounts

A buyer's failure to pay within a discount period is often quite expensive. If Z-Mart does not pay within the 10-day discount period, it delays the payment by 20 more days. This delay costs Z-Mart an added 2%. Most buyers try to take advantage of purchase discounts. For Z-Mart's terms of 2/10, n/30, missing the 2% discount for an additional 20 days is equal to an annual interest rate of 36.5%, computed as (365 days ÷ 20 days × 2%).

Most companies set up a system to pay invoices with favourable discounts within the discount period. Careful cash management means that no invoice is paid until the last day of a discount period. One technique to achieve these goals is to file each invoice so that it automatically comes up for payment on the last day of its discount period. A simple manual system uses 31 folders, one for each day in a month. After an invoice is recorded, it is placed in the folder matching the last day of its discount period. If the last day of an invoice's discount period is November 12, it is filed in folder number 12. This invoice and other invoices in the same folder are removed and paid on November 12. Computerized systems achieve the same result by using a code that identifies the last date in the discount period. When that date occurs, the system automatically identifies accounts to be paid.

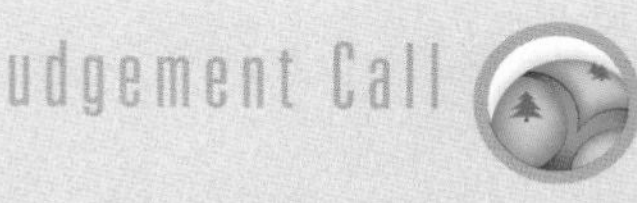

Credit Manager

You are the new credit manager for a merchandising company that purchases its merchandise on credit. You are trained for your new job by the outgoing employee. You are to oversee payment of payables to maintain the company's credit standing with suppliers and to take advantage of favourable cash discounts. The outgoing employee explains that the computer system is programmed to prepare cheques for amounts net of favourable cash discounts, and cheques are dated the last day of the discount period. You are told cheques are not mailed until five days later, however. "It's simple," this employee explains. "Our company gets free use of cash for an extra five days, and our department looks better. When a supplier complains, we blame the computer system and the mail room." Your first invoice arrives with a 10-day discount period for a $10,000 purchase. This transaction occurs on April 9 with credit terms of 2/10, n/30. Do you mail the $9,800 cheque on April 19 or April 24?

Answer—p. 282

Transfer of Ownership

The buyer and seller must reach agreement on who is responsible for paying any freight costs and who bears the risk of loss during transit for merchandising transactions. This is essentially the same as asking, "At what point does ownership transfer from the buyer to the seller?" The point of transfer is called the **FOB** point, where FOB stands for *free on board.* The point when ownership transfers from the seller to the buyer is a very important consideration because it determines who pays transportation costs and other incidental costs of transit such as insurance. The party responsible for paying shipping costs is also responsible for insuring the merchandise during transport.

Exhibit 6.9 identifies two alternative points of transfer. *FOB shipping point,* also called *FOB factory,* means the buyer accepts ownership at the seller's place of business. The buyer is then responsible for paying shipping costs and bears the risk of damage or loss when goods are in transit. The goods are part of the buyer's inventory when they are in transit since ownership has transferred to the buyer.

Exhibit 6.9

Identifying Transfer of Ownership

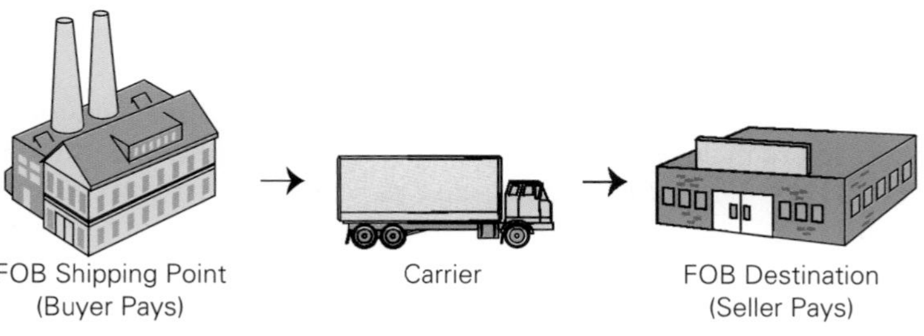

	Ownership transfers when goods passed to	Transportation costs paid by
FOB Shipping Point	**Carrier**	**Buyer**
FOB Destination	**Buyer**	**Seller**

FOB destination means ownership of the goods transfers to the buyer at the buyer's place of business. The seller is responsible for paying shipping charges and bears the risk of damage or loss in transit. The seller does not record revenue from this sale until the goods arrive at the destination because this transaction is not complete before that point.

Compaq Computer used to ship its products FOB shipping point. Compaq found customers' delivery firms to be undependable in picking up shipments at scheduled times, causing backups at the plant, missed deliveries, and unhappy consumers. Compaq then changed its agreements to FOB destination and its problems were eliminated.

There are situations when the party not responsible for shipping costs pays the carrier. In these cases, the party paying these costs either bills the party responsible or, more commonly, adjusts its account payable or receivable with the other party.

Transportation Costs

Shipping costs on purchases are called *transportation-in* or *freight-in* costs. Z-Mart's $1,200 purchase on November 2 is on terms of FOB destination. This means Z-Mart is not responsible for paying transportation costs.

A different situation arises when a company is responsible for paying transportation costs. The cost principle P.43 requires these transportation costs to be included as part of the cost of merchandise inventory. This means that a separate entry is necessary when they are not listed on the invoice. For example, Z-Mart's entry to record a $75 freight charge to an independent carrier for merchandise purchased FOB shipping point is:

Nov. 24	Merchandise Inventory	75	
	Cash		75
	Paid freight charges on purchased merchandise.		

The costs of shipping goods to customers are different from transportation-in costs. Transportation-out or freight-out costs regarding the shipping of goods to customers are recorded in a Delivery Expense account when the seller is responsible for these costs, and are reported as a selling expense in the income statement.

Recording Purchases Information

We explained how purchase returns and allowances, purchase discounts, and transportation-in are included in computing the total cost of merchandise inventory. Z-Mart's 2001 total cost of merchandise purchases is made up of the items listed in Exhibit 6.10.

Exhibit 6.10

Net Cost of Merchandise Purchases Computation

Z-Mart Net Cost of Merchandise Purchases For Year Ended December 31, 2001	
Invoice cost of merchandise purchases	$ 235,800
Less: Purchase discounts received	4,200
Purchase returns and allowances received	1,500
Add: Cost of transportation-in	2,300
Net cost of merchandise purchases	$232,400

Combining these costs in the Merchandise Inventory account means this account reflects the net cost of purchased merchandise according to the cost principle. Recall that the Merchandise Inventory account is updated after each transaction affecting the cost of goods purchased. We later explain how this account is updated each time merchandise is sold. These timely updates of the Merchandise Inventory account reflect a perpetual inventory system.

The accounting system described here does not provide separate records for total purchases, total purchase discounts, total purchase returns and allowances, and total transportation-in. Yet managers usually need this information to evaluate and control each of these cost elements. Many companies collect this information in *supplementary records.* **Supplementary records** are a register of information outside the usual accounting records and accounts. We explain in Chapter 8 a process where supplementary records can be maintained.

4. How long are the credit and discount periods when credit terms are 2/10, n/60?
5. Identify items subtracted from the list amount when computing purchase price: (a) freight-in, (b) trade discount, (c) purchase discount, (d) purchase return and/or allowance.
6. Explain the meaning of *FOB.* What does *FOB destination* mean?

Answers—p. 282

Accounting for Merchandise Sales — Perpetual Inventory System

Analyze and record transactions for sales of merchandise using a perpetual system.

Merchandising companies also must account for sales, sales discounts, sales returns and allowances, and cost of goods sold. A merchandising company such as Z-Mart reports these items in an income statement as shown in Exhibit 6.11.

Exhibit 6.11

Gross Profit Section of Income Statement

Z-Mart Computation of Gross Profit For Year Ended December 31, 2001		
Sales		$321,000
Less: Sales discounts	$4,300	
Sales returns and allowances	2,000	6,300
Net sales		$314,700
Cost of goods sold		230,400
Gross profit from sales		$ 84,300

This section explains how information in this computation is derived from transactions involving sales, sales discounts, and sales returns and allowances.

Sales Transactions

Accounting for a sales transaction for a seller of merchandise involves capturing information about two related parts:

1. Revenue received in the form of an asset from a customer, and
2. Recognizing the cost of merchandise sold to a customer.

As an example, Z-Mart sold $2,400 of merchandise on credit on November 3. The revenue part of this transaction is recorded as:

Nov. 3	Accounts Receivable	2,400	
	Sales		2,400
	Sold merchandise on credit.		

This entry reflects an increase in Z-Mart's assets in the form of an account receivable. It also shows the revenue from the credit sale.[4] If the sale is for cash, the debit is to Cash instead of Accounts Receivable.

The expense or cost of the merchandise sold by Z-Mart on November 3 is $1,600. We explain in Chapter 7 how the cost of this merchandise is computed. The entry to record the cost part of this sales transaction (under a perpetual inventory system) is:

Nov. 3	Cost of Goods Sold	1,600	
	Merchandise Inventory		1,600
	To record the cost of Nov. 3 sale and reduce inventory.		

This entry records the cost of the merchandise sold as an expense and reduces the Merchandise Inventory account to reflect the remaining balance of inventory on hand.

Sales Discounts

Companies granting cash discounts to customers refer to these as *sales discounts.* Sales discounts can benefit a seller by decreasing the delay in receiving cash. Prompt payments also reduce future efforts and costs of billing customers.

A seller does not know whether a customer will pay within the discount period and take advantage of a cash discount at the time of a credit sale, so a sales discount is usually not recorded until a customer pays within the discount period. As an example, Z-Mart completed a credit sale for $1,000 on November 12, subject to terms of 2/10, n/60 (the cost of the inventory sold was $600). The entry to record this sale is:

Nov. 12	Accounts Receivable	1,000	
	Sales		1,000
	Sold merchandise under terms of 2/10, n/60.		
12	Cost of Goods Sold	600	
	Merchandise Inventory		600
	To record cost of goods actually sold.		

This entry records the receivable and the revenue as if the full amount will be paid by the customer.

[4] We describe in Chapter 9 how companies account for sales to customers who use third-party credit cards such as those issued by banks.

The customer has two options, however. One option is to wait 60 days until January 11 and pay the full $1,000. In this case, Z-Mart records the payment as:

Jan. 11	Cash	1,000	
	Accounts Receivable		1,000
	Received payment for November 12 sale.		

The customer's second option is to pay $980 within a 10-day period that runs through November 22. If the customer pays on or before November 22, Z-Mart records the payment as:

Nov. 22	Cash	980	
	Sales Discounts	20	
	Accounts Receivable		1,000
	Received payment for November 12 sale less the discount.		

Sales discounts are recorded in a *contra-revenue* account called Sales Discounts. This is so management can monitor sales discounts to assess their effectiveness and cost. The Sales Discounts account is deducted from the Sales account when computing a company's net sales (refer to Exhibit 6.11). While information about sales discounts is useful, it is seldom reported on income statements distributed to external users P.13.

Sales Returns and Allowances

Sales returns refer to merchandise that customers return to the seller after a sale. Customers return merchandise for a variety of reasons, such as having received an incorrect item or one of poor quality. Many companies allow customers to return merchandise for a full refund. *Sales allowances* refer to reductions in the selling price of merchandise sold to customers. This can occur with damaged merchandise that a customer is willing to purchase if the selling price is decreased. Sales returns and allowances involve dissatisfied customers and the possibility of lost future sales. Managers need information about returns and allowances to monitor these problems. Many accounting systems record returns and allowances in a separate contra-revenue account for this purpose.

Recall Z-Mart's sale of merchandise on November 3. As already recorded, the merchandise is sold for $2,400 and cost $1,600, but what if the customer returns part of the merchandise on November 6, when returned items sell for $800 and cost $600? The revenue part of this transaction must reflect the decrease in sales from the customer's return:

Nov. 6	Sales Returns and Allowances	800	
	Accounts Receivable		800
	Customer returned merchandise.		

Z-Mart can record this return with a debit to the Sales account instead of Sales Returns and Allowances. This method provides the same net sales, but does not provide information needed by managers to monitor returns and allowances. By using the Sales Returns and Allowances contra account, this information is available. Published income statements usually omit this detail and show only net sales.

If the merchandise returned to Z-Mart is not defective and can be resold to another customer, then Z-Mart returns these goods to its inventory. The entry necessary to restore the cost of these goods to the Merchandise Inventory account is:

Nov. 6	Merchandise Inventory	600	
	Cost of Goods Sold		600
	Returned goods to inventory.		

If the merchandise returned is defective, however, the seller may discard the returned items. In this case, the cost of returned merchandise is not restored to the Merchandise Inventory account. Instead, most companies leave the cost of defective merchandise in the Cost of Goods Sold account.[5]

Another possibility is that $800 of the merchandise sold by Z-Mart on November 3 is defective but the customer decides to keep it because Z-Mart grants the customer a price reduction of $500. The only entry that Z-Mart must make in this case is one to reflect the decrease in revenue:

Nov. 6	Sales Returns and Allowances	500	
	Accounts Receivable		500
	To record sales allowance.		

The seller usually prepares a **credit memorandum** to confirm a customer's return or allowance. A credit memorandum informs a customer of a credit to his or her Accounts Receivable account from a sales return or allowance. The information in a credit memorandum is similar to that of a debit memorandum. Z-Mart's credit memorandum issued to the customer for the return of $800 of merchandise on November 6 is shown in Exhibit 6.12.

Exhibit 6.12

Credit Memorandum

Case: Z-Mart (seller) accepts $800 of returned merchandise from Bricks (buyer)

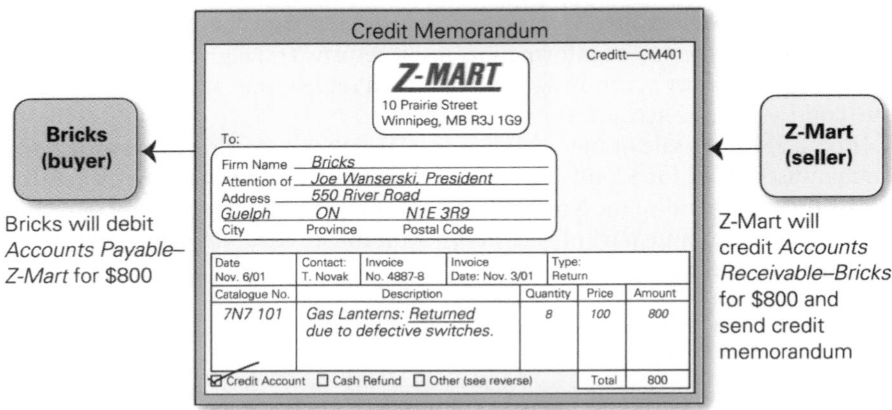

The following table summarizes what debit and credit memoranda (memos) are and why they arise:

[5] When managers want to monitor the cost of defective merchandise, a better method is to remove the cost from Cost of Goods Sold and charge it to a *Loss from Defective Merchandise* account.

Debit Memos	Credit Memos
What is a Debit Memo? • A document prepared by the purchaser to "debit" or reduce the purchaser's account payable	What is a Credit Memo? • A document prepared by the seller to "credit" or reduce the customer's account receivable
Why is a Debit Memo issued? • To reduce the purchaser's account payable because of: 1. Return of unsatisfactory goods 2. Allowance 3. Error	Why is a Credit Memo issued? • To reduce the seller's account receivable because of: 1. Return of unsatisfactory goods 2. Allowance 3. Error

Mid-Chapter Demonstration Problem

Beta Company, a retail store, had the following transactions in March:

March 2	Purchased merchandise from Alfa Company under the following terms: $1,800 invoice price, 2/15, n/60, FOB factory. (The cost of the merchandise to Alfa Company was $990.)
3	Paid CanPar Shipping $125 for shipping charges on the purchase of March 2.
4	Returned to Alfa Company unacceptable merchandise that had an invoice price of $300 (and a cost to Alfa of $165). Alfa returned the merchandise to inventory.
17	Sent a cheque to Alfa Company for the March 2 purchase, net of the discount and the returned merchandise.

Required

Assuming both Beta and Alfa use a perpetual inventory system:

a. Present the journal entries Beta Company should record for these transactions.

b. Present the journal entries Alfa Company should record for these transactions.

SOLUTION TO Mid-Chapter Demonstration Problem

a.

	Beta Company (the buyer)		
March 2	Merchandise Inventory	1,800	
	Accounts Payable–Alfa Company		1,800
	Purchased merchandise on credit.		
3	Merchandise Inventory	125	
	Cash		125
	Paid shipping charges on purchased merchandise.		
4	Accounts Payable–Alfa Company	300	
	Merchandise Inventory		300
	Returned unacceptable merchandise.		
17	Accounts Payable–Alfa Company	1,500	
	Merchandise Inventory		30
	Cash		1,470
	Paid balance within the discount period and took a 2% discount.		

b.

Alfa Company (the seller)		
Accounts Receivable–Beta Company	1,800	
Sales		1,800
Sold merchandise under terms 2/15, n/60.		
Cost of Goods Sold	990	
Merchandise Inventory		990
Recorded cost of sales.		
No entry		
Sales Returns and Allowances	300	
Accounts Receivable–Beta Company		300
Customer returned merchandise.		
Merchandise Inventory	165	
Cost of Goods Sold		165
Merchandise returned to inventory.		
Cash	1,470	
Sales Discounts	30	
Accounts Receivable–Beta Company		1,500
Received payment for March 2 sale less the return and discount.		

Additional Merchandising Issues—Perpetual Inventory System

This section identifies and explains how merchandising activities affect other accounting processes. We address cost and price adjustments, preparing adjusting entries, and relations between important accounts.

Cost and Price Adjustments

Buyers and sellers often find they need to adjust the amount owed between them. Examples include a situation where purchased merchandise does not meet specifications, unordered goods are received, different quantities are received than were ordered and billed, and errors occur in billing. The original balance can sometimes be adjusted by the buyer without negotiation. An example would be if the buyer discovers an error made by the seller on the invoice. The buyer can make an adjustment and notify the seller by sending a debit memorandum or a credit memorandum. Sometimes adjustments can be made only after negotiations between the buyer and seller. An example is when a buyer claims that some merchandise does not meet specifications. In these cases, the amount of allowance given by the seller is usually arrived at only after discussion.

Adjusting Entries

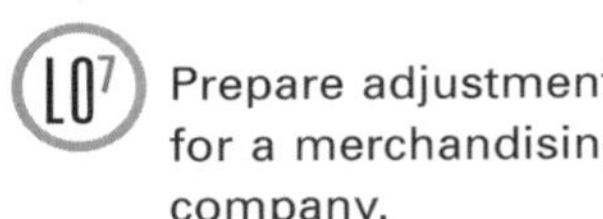
Prepare adjustments for a merchandising company.

Most adjusting entries are the same for merchandising companies and service companies and involve prepaid expenses, amortization, accrued expenses, unearned revenues, and accrued revenues.

A merchandising company using a perpetual inventory system is often required to make one additional adjustment. This adjustment updates the Merchandise Inventory account to reflect any losses of merchandise. Merchandising companies can lose merchandise in several ways, including theft and deterioration. **Shrinkage** refers to the loss of inventory for merchandising companies.

While a perpetual inventory system tracks all goods as they move in and out of the company, a perpetual system is unable to measure shrinkage directly. Yet we can compute shrinkage by comparing a physical count of the inventory with recorded quantities. A physical count is usually performed at least once annually to verify the Merchandise Inventory account. Most companies record any necessary adjustment due to shrinkage by charging it to Cost of Goods Sold, assuming that shrinkage is not abnormally large.

As an example, Z-Mart's Merchandise Inventory account at the end of 2001 had an unadjusted balance of $21,250, but a physical count of inventory revealed only $21,000 of inventory on hand. The adjusting entry to record this $250 shrinkage is:

Date	Account	Debit	Credit
Dec. 31	Cost of Goods Sold	250	
	Merchandise Inventory		250
	To adjust for $250 shrinkage disclosed by physical count of inventory.		

A new study by GPI Atlantic reports that businesses have to build the cost of security systems, guards, shoplifting and employee theft — all sources of shrinkage — into their product pricing. The average Nova Scotian household, according to the study, pays $800 more per year because of such shrinkage.

SOURCE: eda.gov.ns.ca/press/1999/0414.

Did You Know?

7. Why are sales discounts and sales returns and allowances recorded in contra-revenue accounts instead of directly in the Sales account?
8. Under what conditions are two entries necessary to record a sales return?
9. When merchandise is sold on credit and the seller notifies the buyer of a price reduction, does the seller send a credit memorandum or a debit memorandum?
10. When a merchandising company uses a perpetual inventory system, why is it often necessary to adjust the Merchandise Inventory balance with an adjusting entry?

Answers—p. 282

Summary of Merchandising Cost Flows

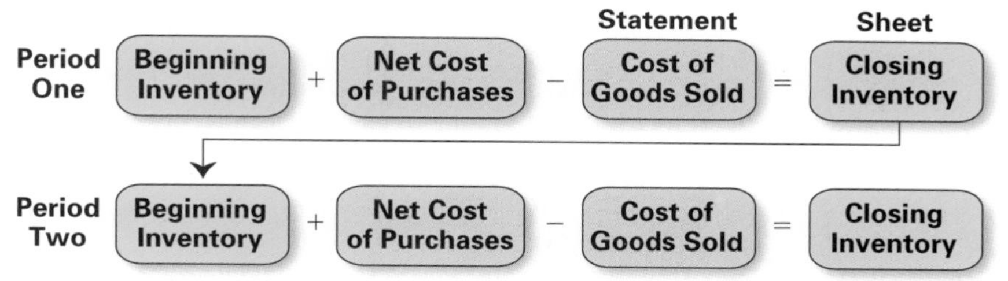

Exhibit 6.13

Merchandising Cost Flows Across Periods

LO8 Analyze and interpret cost flows and operating activities of a merchandising company.

Exhibit 6.13 shows the relation between merchandise inventory, purchases, and cost of goods sold across periods. We already explained how the net cost of purchases captures trade discounts, purchase discounts granted, transportation-in, and purchase returns and allowances. These items comprising the cost of purchases are recorded in the Merchandise Inventory account when using a perpetual system as shown in Exhibit 6.14. When each sale occurs the cost of items sold is transferred from Merchandise Inventory to the Cost of Goods Sold account as shown in Exhibit 6.14.

Notice in Exhibit 6.13 that the Merchandise Inventory account balance at the end of Period One is the amount of beginning inventory in Period Two. The sequence of events during Period Two (and every period) is the same as during Period One.

To summarize the effects of merchandising transactions on the Merchandise Inventory and Cost of Goods Sold accounts, Z-Mart's merchandising activities during 2001 are illustrated in Exhibit 6.14. Most amounts in these T-accounts are summary representations of several entries during the year 2001. Notice that the Cost of Goods Sold balance of $230,400 is the amount reported on the income statement in Exhibit 6.2. The Merchandise Inventory balance of $21,000 is the amount reported as a current asset on the balance sheet in Exhibit 6.3. These amounts also appear on Z-Mart's adjusted trial balance in Exhibit 6.19.

Exhibit 6.14

Summary of Z-Mart's Merchandising Activities for 2001 Reflected in T-accounts.

Merchandise Inventory

Debit		Credit	
Dec. 31, 2000, balance	19,000		
Reflects entries to record **purchases of merchandise** during 2001	235,800	Reflects entries to record **purchase discounts** during 2001	4,200
Reflects **transportation-in** costs incurred during 2001	2,300	Reflects entries to record **purchase returns and allowances** during 2001	1,500
Reflects entries to record **merchandise returned by customers** and restored to inventory during 2001	1,400	Reflects **cost of sales** transactions during 2001	231,550
Total	258,500	Total	237,250
	−237,250		
Dec. 31, 2001, unadjusted balance	21,250	Dec. 31 **Shrinkage**......................	250
	−250		
Dec. 31, 2001, adjusted balance	21,000		

Net Cost of Purchases (purchases of merchandise, transportation-in, and merchandise returned by customers)

Cost of goods sold transferred from inventory account.

Cost of Goods Sold

Debit		Credit	
Reflects entries to record the cost of sales	231,550	Reflects entries to record **merchandise returned** by customers and restored to inventory during 2001	1,400
Total	231,550	Total	1,400
	−1,400		
Dec. 31, 2001, unadjusted balance	230,150		
Inventory **shrinkage** recorded in Dec. 31, 2001 adjusting entry..............................	250		
Dec. 31, 2001 adjusted balance	230,400		

Income Statement Formats—Perpetual Inventory System

LO9 Define and prepare multiple-step and single-step income statements.

Generally accepted accounting principles do not require companies to use a specific format for financial statements. We see many different formats in practice. The first part of this section looks at formulating a draft income statement through the preparation of a work sheet. The second part of this section describes two common income statement formats using Z-Mart's data: multiple-step and single-step.

A Work Sheet For A Merchandising Company

Exhibit 6.15 presents a version of the work sheet that the accountant for Z-Mart could prepare in the process of developing its 2001 financial statements. It differs from the 10-column work sheet described in Chapter 5.

The difference is the deletion of the adjusted trial balance columns to reduce the size of the work sheet. The omission of the columns causes the accountants to first compute the adjusted balances and then extend them directly into the financial statement columns.

Exhibit 6.15

Work Sheet (Perpetual) for Z-Mart for Year Ended December 31, 2001

No.	Account	Unadjusted Trial Balance		Adjustments		Income Statement		Balance Sheet & Statement of Owner's Equity	
		Debit	Credit	Debit	Credit	Debit	Credit	Debit	Credit
101	Cash	8,200						8,200	
106	Accounts receivable	11,200						11,200	
119	Merchandise inventory	21,250			(g) 250			21,000	
124	Office supplies	2,350			(c) 1,800			550	
125	Store supplies	1,450			(b) 1,200			250	
128	Prepaid insurance	900			(a) 600			300	
163	Office equipment	4,200						4,200	
164	Accum. amort., office equipment		700		(e) 700				1,400
165	Store equipment	30,000						30,000	
166	Accum. amort., store equipment		3,000		(d) 3,000				6,000
201	Accounts payable		16,000						16,000
209	Salaries payable				(f) 800				800
301	Kent Marty, capital		40,160						40,160
302	Kent Marty, withdrawals	4,000						4,000	
406	Rent revenue		2,800				2,800		
413	Sales		321,000				321,000		
414	Sales returns and allowances	2,000				2,000			
415	Sales discounts	4,300				4,300			
502	Cost of goods sold	230,150		(g) 250		230,400			
612	Amort. expense, store equipment			(d) 3,000		3,000			
613	Amort. expense, office equipment			(e) 700		700			
620	Office salaries expense	25,000		(f) 300		25,300			
621	Sales salaries expense	18,000		(f) 500		18,500			
633	Interest expense	360				360			
637	Insurance expense			(a) 600		600			
641	Rent expense, office space	900				900			
642	Rent expense, selling space	8,100				8,100			
650	Office supplies expense			(c) 1,800		1,800			
651	Store supplies expense			(b) 1,200		1,200			
655	Advertising expense	11,300				11,300			
	Totals	383,660	383,660	8,350	8,350	308,460	323,800	79,700	64,360
	Net income					15,340			15,340
	Totals					323,800	323,800	79,700	79,700

The adjustments in the work sheet reflect the following economic events:

a. Expiration of $600 of prepaid insurance.
b. Use of $1,200 of store supplies.
c. Use of $1,800 of office supplies.
d. Amortization of the store equipment for $3,000.
e. Amortization of the office equipment for $700.
f. Accrual of $300 of unpaid office salaries and $500 of unpaid store salaries.
g. Physical count of merchandise inventory revealed $21,000 on hand.

Once the adjusted amounts are extended into the financial statement columns, the accountant uses the information to develop the company's financial statements.

Multiple-step Income Statement

Multiple-step income statements often contain more detail than simply a listing of revenues and expenses. There are two general types of multiple-step income statement. The usual format we see in external reports is what people commonly call the *multiple-step* format. A more detailed format is also available, but, usually seen only in internal documents. It is called the *classified, multiple-step* format. Both formats can be used in either a perpetual or periodic inventory system.

Classified, Multiple-step Format

Exhibit 6.16 shows a **classified, multiple-step income statement** for Z-Mart. This format shows a detailed computation of net sales. Operating expenses are classified separately as selling expenses or general and administrative expenses. This format reports subtotals between sales and net income. This is why it is called a *classified* format.

Z-Mart's sales section is the same as shown earlier in the chapter. The difference between net sales and cost of goods sold is Z-Mart's gross profit. Its operating expenses are classified into two categories. **Selling expenses** include the expenses of promoting sales through displaying and advertising merchandise, making sales, and delivering goods to customers. **General and administrative expenses** support the overall operations of a company and include expenses related to accounting, human resource management, and financial management.

Expenses are often divided between categories when they contribute to more than one activity. Exhibit 6.16 shows that Z-Mart allocates rent expense of $9,000 for its store building between two categories. Selling expense includes $8,100 of it while $900 is listed as general and administrative expense.[6] Any cost allocation should reflect an economic relation between the amounts assigned and the activities. Allocation of Z-Mart's rent is based on relative rental values.

[6] These expenses can be recorded in a single ledger account or in two separate accounts. If they are recorded in one account, we allocate its balance between the two expenses when preparing statements.

Revenues and expenses that are ***not*** part of normal operating activities are reported in the *Other revenues and expenses* section of the income statement. Z-Mart's main operating activity is merchandising, therefore rent revenue — not a merchandising activity — is shown under *Other revenues and expenses.* Another example, interest expense, arises because of a financing (or borrowing) activity and not because of Z-Mart's merchandising (or operating) activities. Other examples of Other revenues and expenses include dividend income and gains and losses on the sale of capital assets.

Exhibit 6.16

Classified, Multiple-step Income Statement—Perpetual Inventory System

Z-Mart Income Statement For Year Ended December 31, 2001			
Sales			$321,000
Less: Sales discounts		$ 4,300	
Sales returns and allowances		2,000	6,300
Net sales			$314,700
Cost of goods sold			230,400
Gross profit from sales			$ 84,300
Operating expenses:			
Selling expenses:			
Amortization expense, store equipment	$ 3,000		
Sales salaries expense	18,500		
Rent expense, selling space	8,100		
Store supplies expense	1,200		
Advertising expense	11,300		
Total selling expenses		$42,100	
General and administrative expenses:			
Amortization expense, office equipment	$ 700		
Office salaries expense	25,300		
Insurance expense	600		
Rent expense, office space	900		
Office supplies expense	1,800		
Total general and administrative expenses		29,300	
Total operating expenses			71,400
Income from operations			$ 12,900
Other revenues and expenses:			
Rent revenue		$ 2,800	
Interest expense		360	2,440
Net income			$ 15,340

Multiple-step Format

Exhibit 6.17 shows a multiple-step income statement format common in external reports. In comparison to Exhibit 6.16, a multiple-step statement leaves out the detailed computation of net sales. Selling expenses are also combined with general and administrative expenses.

Exhibit 6.17

Multiple-step Income Statement—Perpetual Inventory System

Z-Mart Income Statement For Year Ended December 31, 2001		
Net sales		$314,700
Cost of goods sold		230,400
Gross profit from sales		$ 84,300
Operating expenses:		
Amortization expense	$ 3,700	
Salaries expense	43,800	
Rent expense	9,000	
Insurance expense	600	
Supplies expense	3,000	
Advertising expense	11,300	
Total operating expenses		71,400
Income from operations		$ 12,900
Other revenues and expenses:		
Rent revenue	$ 2,800	
Interest expense	360	2,440
Net income		$ 15,340

Single-step Income Statement

A **single-step income statement** is another widely used format; it is shown in Exhibit 6.18 for Z-Mart. This simple format includes cost of goods sold as an operating expense and shows only one subtotal for total expenses. Operating expenses are highly summarized.

Exhibit 6.18

Single-step Income Statement—Perpetual Inventory System

Z-Mart Income Statement For Year Ended December 31, 2001		
Revenues:		
Net sales	$314,700	
Rent revenue	2,800	
Total revenues		$317,500
Expenses:		
Cost of goods sold	$230,400	
Selling expenses	42,100	
General and administrative expense	29,300	
Interest expense	360	
Total expenses		302,160
Net income		$ 15,340

Many companies use formats that combine features of both the single- and multiple-step statements. As long as income statement items are shown sensibly, management can choose the format it wants.[7]

[7] We describe certain items in later chapters, such as extraordinary gains and losses, that must be shown in certain locations on the income statement.

Closing Entries for a Merchandising Company —Perpetual Inventory System

Prepare closing entries for a merchandising company.

Closing entries are similar for merchandising companies and service companies when using a perpetual system. Both use an adjusted trial balance to prepare closing entries. The one difference is that we must close temporary accounts related to merchandising activities.

These accounts are bolded in the adjusted trial balance in Exhibit 6.19 and include: Sales, Sales Discounts, Sales Returns and Allowances, and Cost of Goods Sold. Therefore, the four closing entries for a merchandiser are slightly different from the ones described in Chapter 5 for a service company. These differences are highlighted in the closing entries in Exhibit 6.20.

Exhibit 6.19

Adjusted Trial Balance

Z-Mart
Adjusted Trial Balance
December 31, 2001

	Debit	Credit
Cash	$ 8,200	
Accounts receivable	11,200	
Merchandise inventory	21,000	
Office supplies	550	
Store supplies	250	
Prepaid insurance	300	
Office equipment	4,200	
Accumulated amortization, office equipment		$ 1,400
Store equipment	30,000	
Accumulated amortization, store equipment		6,000
Accounts payable		16,000
Salaries payable		800
Kent Marty, capital		40,160
Kent Marty, withdrawals	4,000	
Rent revenue		2,800
Sales		**321,000**
Sales returns and allowances	**2,000**	
Sales discounts	**4,300**	
Cost of goods sold	**230,400**	
Amortization expense, store equipment	3,000	
Amortization expense, office equipment	700	
Office salaries expense	25,300	
Sales salaries expense	18,500	
Interest expense	360	
Insurance expense	600	
Rent expense, office space	900	
Rent expense, selling space	8,100	
Office supplies expense	1,800	
Store supplies expense	1,200	
Advertising expense	11,300	
Totals	$388,160	$388,160

Exhibit 6.20

Closing Entries for Z-Mart

Entry 1: **Close Credit Balances in Temporary Accounts to Income Summary.** The first entry closes temporary accounts having credit balances. Z-Mart has two temporary accounts with a credit balance and they are closed with the entry:

Date	Account	Debit	Credit
Dec. 31	Rent Revenue	2,800	
	Sales	**321,000**	
	Income Summary		323,800
	To close temporary accounts having credit balances.		

Posting this entry to the ledger gives a zero balance to the Rent Revenue and Sales accounts and opens the Income Summary account.

Entry 2: **Close Debit Balances in Temporary Accounts to Income Summary.** The second entry closes temporary accounts having debit balances. These include Cost of Goods Sold, Sales Discounts, and Sales Returns and Allowances. This entry also yields the amount of net income as the balance in the Income Summary account. Z-Mart's second closing entry is:

As contra-revenue accounts, these are income statement accounts and must be closed.

Date	Account	Debit	Credit
Dec. 31	Income Summary	308,460	
	Sales Discounts		**4,300**
	Sales Returns and Allowances		**2,000**
	Cost of Goods Sold		**230,400**
	Amortization Expense, Store Equipment		3,000
	Amortization Expense, Office Equipment		700
	Office Salaries Expense		25,300
	Sales Salaries Expense		18,500
	Interest Expense		360
	Insurance Expense		600
	Rent Expense, Office Space		900
	Rent Expense, Selling Space		8,100
	Office Supplies Expense		1,800
	Store Supplies Expense		1,200
	Advertising Expense		11,300
	To close temporary accounts having debit balances.		

Entry 3: **Close Income Summary to Owner's Capital.** The third closing entry is the same for a merchandising company and a service company. It closes the Income Summary account and updates the owner's capital account for income or loss. Z-Mart's third closing entry is:

Date	Account	Debit	Credit
Dec. 31	Income Summary	15,340	
	Kent Marty, Capital		15,340
	To close the income summary account.		

Notice that the $15,340 amount in the entry is net income reported on the income statement in Exhibit 6.2.

Entry 4: **Close Withdrawals Account to Owner's Capital.** The fourth closing entry for a merchandising company is the same as the fourth closing entry for a service company. It closes the withdrawals account and reduces the owner's capital account balance to the amount shown on the balance sheet. The fourth closing entry for Z-Mart is:

Date	Account	Debit	Credit
Dec. 31	Kent Marty, Capital	4,000	
	Kent Marty, Withdrawals		4,000
	To close the withdrawals account.		

When this entry is posted, all temporary accounts are closed and ready to record events for the year 2002. The owner's capital account is also updated and reflects transactions of 2001.

11. What temporary accounts do you expect to find in a merchandising business but not in a service business?
12. Describe the closing entries normally made by a merchandising company.
13. What income statement format shows detailed computations for net sales? What format gives no subtotals except total expenses?

Answers—p. 282

Summary

LO1 Describe merchandising activities and identify business examples. Operations of merchandising companies involve buying products and reselling them.

LO2 Identify and explain the important components of income for a merchandising company. A merchandiser's costs on an income statement include an amount for cost of goods sold. Gross profit, or gross margin, equals net sales minus cost of goods sold.

LO3 Identify and explain the inventory asset of a merchandising company. The current asset section of a merchandising company's balance sheet includes merchandise inventory. Merchandise inventory refers to the products a merchandiser sells and are on hand at the balance sheet date.

LO4 Describe both periodic and perpetual inventory systems. A perpetual inventory system continuously tracks the cost of goods on hand and the cost of goods sold. A periodic system accumulates the cost of goods purchased during the period and does not compute the amount of inventory on hand or the cost of goods sold until the end of a period.

LO5 Analyze and record transactions for merchandise purchases using a perpetual system. For a perpetual inventory system, purchases net of trade discounts are added (debited) to the Merchandise Inventory account. Purchase discounts and purchase returns and allowances are subtracted (credited) from Merchandise Inventory, and transportation-in costs are added (debited) to Merchandise Inventory. Many companies keep supplementary records to accumulate information about the total amounts of purchases, purchase discounts, purchase returns and allowances, and transportation-in.

LO6 Analyze and record transactions for sales of merchandise using a perpetual system. A merchandiser records sales at list price less any trade discounts. The cost of items sold is transferred from Merchandise Inventory to Cost of Goods Sold. Refunds or credits given to customers for unsatisfactory merchandise are recorded (debited) in Sales Returns and Allowances, a contra account to Sales. If merchandise is returned and restored to inventory, the cost of this merchandise is removed from Cost of Goods Sold and transferred back to Merchandise Inventory. When cash discounts from the sales price are offered and customers pay within the discount period, the seller records (debits) discounts in Sales Discounts, a contra account to Sales. Debit and credit memoranda are documents sent between buyers and sellers to communicate that the sender is either debiting or crediting an account of the recipient.

LO7 Prepare adjustments for a merchandising company. With a perpetual inventory system, it is often necessary to make an adjustment for inventory shrinkage. This is computed by comparing a physical count of inventory with the Merchandise Inventory account balance. Shrinkage is normally charged to Cost of Goods Sold.

LO8 Analyze and interpret cost flows and operating activities of a merchandising company. Net costs of merchandise purchases flows into Merchandise Inventory and from there to Cost of Goods Sold on the income statement. Any remaining Merchandise Inventory balance is reported as a current asset on the balance sheet. This is the beginning inventory for the next period.

LO9 **Define and prepare multiple-step and single-step income statements.** Multiple-step income statements include greater detail for sales and expenses than do single-step income statements. Classified multiple-step income statements are usually limited to internal use. They show more details, including the computation of net sales, and reporting of expenses in categories reflecting different activities. Income statements published for external parties can be either multiple-step or single-step.

LO10 **Prepare closing entries for a merchandising company.** Temporary accounts of merchandising companies include Sales, Sales Discounts, Sales Returns and Allowances, and Cost of Goods Sold. Each is closed to Income Summary.

GUIDANCE ANSWER TO Judgement Call

Credit Manager

Your decision is whether to comply with prior policy or create new policy not to abuse discounts offered by suppliers. Your first step should be to meet with your superior to find out if the automatic late payment policy is the actual policy and, if so, its rationale. It is possible that the prior employee was reprimanded because of this behaviour. If it is the policy to pay late, then you must apply your own sense of right and wrong. One point of view is that the late payment policy is unethical. A deliberate plan to make late payments means that the company lies when it pretends to make purchases within the credit terms. There is the potential that your company could lose its ability to get future credit. Another view is that the late payment policy is acceptable. There may exist markets where attempts to take discounts through late payments are accepted as a continued phase of price negotiation. Also, your company's suppliers can respond by billing your company for the discounts not accepted because of late payments. This is a dubious viewpoint, especially given the old employee's proposal to cover up late payments as computer or mail problems, and given that some suppliers have previously complained.

GUIDANCE ANSWERS TO  Flashback

1. Cost of goods sold is the cost of merchandise sold to customers during a period.
2. Gross profit is the difference between net sales and cost of goods sold.
3. Widespread use of computing and related technology has dramatically increased use of the perpetual inventory system in practice.
4. Under credit terms of 2/10, n/60, the credit period is 60 days and the discount period is 10 days.
5. *b*
6. *FOB* means free on board. It is used in identifying the point where ownership transfers from seller to buyer. *FOB destination* means that the seller does not transfer ownership of goods to the buyer until they arrive at the buyer's place of business. The seller is responsible for paying shipping charges and bears the risk of damage or loss during shipment.
7. Recording sales discounts and sales returns and allowances separately from sales gives useful information to managers for internal monitoring and decision making.
8. When a customer returns merchandise and the seller restores the merchandise to inventory, two entries are necessary. One entry records the decrease in revenue and credits the customer's account. The second entry debits inventory and reduces cost of goods sold.
9. A credit memorandum.
10. Merchandise Inventory balance may need adjusting to reflect shrinkage.
11. Sales, Sales Discounts, Sales Returns and Allowances, and Cost of Goods Sold.
12. Four closing entries: (1) close credit balances in temporary accounts to income summary, (2) close debit balances in temporary accounts to income summary, (3) close income summary to owner's capital, and (4) close withdrawals account to owner's capital.
13. Classified, multiple-step income statement. Single-step income statement.

Demonstration Problem

Use the following adjusted trial balance and additional information to complete the requirements:

Ingersoll Antiques Adjusted Trial Balance December 31, 2002		
Cash	$ 19,300	
Merchandise inventory	50,000	
Store supplies	1,000	
Equipment	44,600	
Accumulated amortization, equipment		$ 16,500
Accounts payable		8,000
Salaries payable		1,000
Dee Rizzo, capital		69,000
Dee Rizzo, withdrawals	8,000	
Interest revenue		300
Sales		325,000
Sales discounts	6,000	
Sales returns and allowances	5,000	
Cost of goods sold	148,000	
Amortization expense, store equipment	4,000	
Amortization expense, office equipment	1,500	
Sales salaries expense	28,000	
Office salaries expense	32,000	
Insurance expense	12,000	
Rent expense (70% is store, 30% is office)	24,000	
Store supplies expense	6,000	
Advertising expense	30,400	
Totals	$419,800	$419,800

Ingersoll Antiques' *supplementary records* for 2002 reveal the following merchandising activities:

Invoice cost of merchandise purchases	$140,000
Purchase discounts received	3,500
Purchase returns and allowances received	2,600
Cost of transportation-in	4,000

Required

1. Use the supplementary records to compute the total cost of merchandise purchases.
2. Prepare a 2002 classified, multiple-step income statement for internal use.
3. Present a single-step income statement for 2002 similar to the one in Exhibit 6.18.
4. Prepare closing entries.

Planning the Solution

- Compute the total cost of merchandise purchases.
- Compute net sales. Subtract cost of goods sold from net sales to get gross profit. Then, classify the operating expenses as selling expenses and general administrative expenses.

- To prepare the single-step income statement, begin with the net sales and interest earned. Then, subtract the cost of goods sold and operating expenses.
- The first closing entry debits all temporary accounts with credit balances and opens the Income Summary account. The second closing entry credits all temporary accounts with debit balances. The third entry closes the Income Summary account to the owner's capital account, and the fourth closing entry closes the withdrawals account to the capital account.

SOLUTION TO Demonstration Problem

1.

Invoice cost of merchandise purchases	$140,000
Less: Purchase discounts received	3,500
Purchase returns and allowances received	2,600
Add: Cost of transportation-in	4,000
Total cost of merchandise purchases	$137,900

2. Classified, multiple-step income statement

Ingersoll Antiques Income Statement For Year Ended December 31, 2002			
Sales			$325,000
Less: Sales discounts		$ 6,000	
Sales returns and allowances		5,000	11,000
Net sales			$314,000
Cost of goods sold			148,000
Gross profit from sales			$166,000
Operating expenses:			
Selling expenses:			
Amortization expense, store equipment	$ 4,000		
Sales salaries expense	28,000		
Rent expense, selling space	16,800		
Store supplies expense	6,000		
Advertising expense	30,400		
Total selling expenses		$85,200	
General and administrative expenses:			
Amortization expense, office equipment	$ 1,500		
Office salaries expense	32,000		
Insurance expense	12,000		
Rent expense, office space	7,200		
Total general and administrative expenses		52,700	
Total operating expenses			137,900
Income from operations			$ 28,100
Other revenues and expenses:			
Interest revenue			300
Net income			$ 28,400

3. Single-step income statement

Ingersoll Antiques Income Statement For Year Ended December 31, 2002		
Revenues:		
Net sales		$314,000
Interest revenue		300
Total revenues		$314,300
Expenses:		
Cost of goods sold	$148,000	
Selling expenses	85,200	
General and administrative expense	52,700	
Total expenses		285,900
Net income		$ 28,400

4.

Date	Account	Debit	Credit
Dec. 31	Sales	325,000	
	Interest Revenue	300	
	Income Summary		325,300
	To close temporary accounts with credit balances.		
31	Income Summary	296,900	
	Sales Discounts		6,000
	Sales Returns and Allowances		5,000
	Cost of Goods Sold		148,000
	Amortization Expense, Store Equipment		4,000
	Amortization Expense, Office Equipment		1,500
	Sales Salaries Expense		28,000
	Office Salaries Expense		32,000
	Insurance Expense		12,000
	Rent Expense		24,000
	Store Supplies Expense		6,000
	Advertising Expense		30,400
	To close temporary accounts with debit balances.		
31	Income Summary	28,400	
	Dee Rizzo, Capital		28,400
	To close the income summary account.		
31	Dee Rizzo, Capital	8,000	
	Dee Rizzo, Withdrawals		8,000
	To close the withdrawals account.		

APPENDIX

6A Periodic and Perpetual Inventory Systems

Accounting Comparisons

LO11 Record and compare merchandising transactions using both periodic and perpetual inventory systems.

Recall that under a perpetual system, the Merchandise Inventory account is updated after each purchase and each sale. The Cost of Goods Sold account is also updated after each sale so that during the period the account balance reflects the period's total cost of goods sold to date.

Under a periodic inventory system, the Merchandise Inventory account is updated only once each accounting period. This update occurs at the *end* of the period. During the next period, the Merchandise Inventory balance remains unchanged. It reflects the beginning inventory balance until it is updated again at the end of the period. Similarly, in a periodic inventory system, cost of goods sold is not recorded as each sale occurs. Instead, the total cost of goods sold during the period is computed at the end of the period.

Recording Merchandise Transactions

Under a perpetual system, each purchase, purchase return and allowance, purchase discount, and transportation-in transaction is recorded in the Merchandise Inventory account. Under a periodic system, a separate temporary account is set up for each of these items. At the end of a period, each of these temporary accounts is closed and the Merchandise Inventory account is updated. To illustrate the differences, we use parallel columns to show journal entries for the most common transactions using both periodic and perpetual inventory systems (we drop explanations for simplicity).

Purchases

Z-Mart purchases merchandise for $1,200 on credit with terms of 2/10, n/30 and records this purchase as:

Periodic			Perpetual		
Purchases	1,200		Merchandise Inventory	1,200	
Accounts Payable		1,200	Accounts Payable		1,200

The periodic system uses a temporary *Purchases* account that accumulates the cost of all purchase transactions during the period.

Purchase Returns and Allowances

Z-Mart returns merchandise purchased on November 2 because of defects. If the recorded cost[8] of the defective merchandise is $300, Z-Mart records the return with this entry:

Periodic			Perpetual		
Accounts Payable	300		Accounts Payable	300	
Purchase Returns and Allowances		300	Merchandise Inventory		300

This entry is the same if Z-Mart is granted a price reduction (allowance) instead of returning the merchandise. In the periodic system, the temporary *Purchase Returns and Allowances* account accumulates the cost of all returns and allowances transactions during a period.

Purchase Discount

When Z-Mart pays the supplier for the previous purchase within the discount period, the required payment is $882 (= 1,200 − 300 = 900 × 98% = 882) and is recorded as:

Periodic			Perpetual		
Accounts Payable	900		Accounts Payable	900	
Purchase Discounts		18	Merchandise Inventory		18
Cash		882	Cash		882

The periodic system uses a temporary *Purchase Discounts* account that accumulates discounts taken on purchase transactions during the period. If payment is delayed until after the discount period expires, the entry under both methods is to debit Accounts Payable and credit Cash for $900 each.

Transportation-in

Z-Mart paid a $75 freight charge to haul merchandise to its store. In the periodic system, this cost is charged to a temporary *Transportation-in* account.

Periodic			Perpetual		
Transportation-in	75		Merchandise Inventory	75	
Cash		75	Cash		75

[8] Recorded cost is the cost recorded in the account after any discounts.

Sales

Z-Mart sold $2,400 of merchandise on credit and Z-Mart's cost of this merchandise is $1,600:

Periodic			Perpetual		
Accounts Receivable	2,400		Accounts Receivable	2,400	
Sales		2,400	Sales		2,400
			Cost of Goods Sold	1,600	
			Merchandise Inventory		1,600

Under the periodic system, the cost of goods sold is not recorded at the time of sale. We later show how the periodic system computes total cost of goods sold at the end of a period.

Sales Returns

A customer returns part of the merchandise from the previous transaction, where returned items sell for $800 and cost $600. Z-Mart restores the merchandise to inventory and records the return as:

Periodic			Perpetual		
Sales Returns and Allowances	800		Sales Returns and Allowances	800	
Accounts Receivable		800	Accounts Receivable		800
			Merchandise Inventory	600	
			Cost of Goods Sold		600

The periodic system records only the revenue reduction.

Inventory Shrinkage

The Merchandise Inventory balance is $19,000 under the periodic system and $21,250 under the perpetual system. Because the periodic system does not revise the Merchandise Inventory balance during the period, the $19,000 amount is the beginning inventory. The $21,250 balance under the perpetual system is the recorded ending inventory before adjusting for any inventory shrinkage.

A physical count of inventory taken at the end of the period disclosed $21,000 of merchandise on hand. We then know inventory shrinkage is $21,250 − $21,000 = $250. The adjusting entry for shrinkage is:

Periodic			Perpetual		
No entry			Cost of Goods Sold	250	
			Merchandise Inventory		250

The periodic system does not require an adjusting entry to record inventory shrinkage. Instead, the periodic system puts the ending inventory of $21,000 in the Merchandise Inventory account in the first closing entry, and removes the $19,000 beginning inventory balance from the account in the second closing entry.

Z-Mart's unadjusted trial balances at the end of 2001 under each system are shown in Exhibit 6A.1.

Exhibit 6A.1

Comparison of Unadjusted Trial Balances—Periodic and Perpetual

Z-Mart
Unadjusted Trial Balance
December 31, 2001
Periodic

Account	Debit	Credit
Cash	$ 8,200	
Accounts receivable	11,200	
Merchandise inventory	**19,000**	
Office supplies	2,350	
Store supplies	1,450	
Prepaid insurance	900	
Office equipment	4,200	
Accumulated amortization, office equipment		700
Store equipment	30,000	
Accumulated amortization, store equipment		3,000
Accounts payable		16,000
Kent Marty, capital		40,160
Kent Marty, withdrawals	4,000	
Rent revenue		2,800
Sales		321,000
Sales discounts	4,300	
Sales returns and allowances	2,000	
Purchases	**235,800**	
Purchase discounts		**4,200**
Purchase returns and allowances		**1,500**
Transportation-in	**2,300**	
Office salaries expense	25,000	
Sales salaries expense	18,000	
Interest expense	360	
Rent expense, office space	900	
Rent expense, selling space	8,100	
Advertising expense	11,300	
Totals	$389,360	$389,360

Z-Mart
Unadjusted Trial Balance
December 31, 2001
Perpetual

Account	Debit	Credit
Cash	$ 8,200	
Accounts receivable	11,200	
Merchandise inventory	**21,250**	
Office supplies	2,350	
Store supplies	1,450	
Prepaid insurance	900	
Office equipment	4,200	
Accumulated amortization, office equipment		700
Store equipment	30,000	
Accumulated amortization, store equipment		3,000
Accounts payable		16,000
Kent Marty, capital		40,160
Kent Marty, withdrawals	4,000	
Rent revenue		2,800
Sales		321,000
Sales discounts	4,300	
Sales returns and allowances	2,000	
Cost of goods sold	**230,150**	
Office salaries expense	25,000	
Sales salaries expense	18,000	
Interest expense	360	
Rent expense, office space	900	
Rent expense, selling space	8,100	
Advertising expense	11,300	
Totals	$383,660	$383,660

14. Why does the *Merchandise inventory* account on the periodic unadjusted trial balance differ from the *Merchandise inventory* balance on the perpetual unadjusted trial balance?
15. Identify those accounts that are included on the periodic unadjusted trial balance which are not on the perpetual unadjusted trial balance.
16. The perpetual unadjusted trial balance has a *Cost of goods sold* account. Explain why the periodic unadjusted trial balance does not have a *Cost of goods sold* account.

Answers—p. 296

Adjusting Entries

The periodic and perpetual inventory systems show differences in the adjusting entries. Compare the adjusting entries in Exhibit 6A.2 for a periodic system to adjustments under a perpetual system shown in Exhibit 6.15. Closing entries for both a periodic and perpetual system are contrasted in Exhibit 6A.4.

A Work Sheet and Income Statement for a Merchandising Company—Periodic Inventory

Exhibit 6A.2 presents a version of the work sheet that the accountant for Z-Mart could prepare in the process of developing its financial statements. It differs from the work sheet described earlier in the chapter in Exhibit 6.15.

The differences appear on the line for the Merchandise Inventory account and the addition of lines for Purchases, Purchase Discounts, Purchase Returns and Allowances, and Transportation-in. The unadjusted trial balance includes the beginning inventory balance of $19,000. This amount, along with Purchases and Transportation-in, is extended into the Debit column for the income statement. The other two amounts are entered in the Credit column for the income statement. Then, the ending inventory balance is entered in the Credit column for the income statement ***and*** the Debit column for the balance sheet. This step allows the calculation of cost of goods sold to be included in net income while the correct ending inventory balance is included on the balance sheet.

The adjustments in the work sheet reflect the following economic events:

- **a.** Expiration of $600 of prepaid insurance.
- **b.** Use of $1,200 of store supplies.
- **c.** Use of $1,800 of office supplies.
- **d.** Amortization of the store equipment for $3,000.
- **e.** Amortization of the office equipment for $700.
- **f.** Accrual of $300 of unpaid office salaries and $500 of unpaid store salaries.

Once the adjusted amounts are extended into the financial statement columns, the accountant uses the information to develop the company's financial statements.

The classified, multiple-step income statement under a periodic inventory system is shown in Exhibit 6A.3.

Exhibit 6A.2

Work Sheet for Z-Mart for the Year Ended December 31, 2001

No.	Account	Unadjusted Trial Balance		Adjustments		Income Statement		Balance Sheet & Statement of Owner's Equity	
		Debit	Credit	Debit	Credit	Debit	Credit	Debit	Credit
101	Cash	8,200						8,200	
106	Accounts receivable	11,200						11,200	
119	Merchandise inventory	19,000				19,000	21,000	21,000	
124	Office supplies	2,350			(c) 1,800			550	
125	Store supplies	1,450			(b) 1,200			250	
128	Prepaid insurance	900			(a) 600			300	
163	Office equipment	4,200						4,200	
164	Accum. amort., office equipment		700		(e) 700				1,400
165	Store equipment	30,000						30,000	
166	Accum. amort., store equipment		3,000		(d) 3,000				6,000
201	Accounts payable		16,000						16,000
209	Salaries payable				(f) 800				800
301	Kent Marty, capital		40,160						40,160
302	Kent Marty, withdrawals	4,000						4,000	
406	Rent revenue		2,800				2,800		
413	Sales		321,000				321,000		
414	Sales returns and allowances	2,000				2,000			
415	Sales discounts	4,300				4,300			
505	Purchases	235,800				235,800			
506	Purchases returns and allowances		1,500				1,500		
507	Purchases discounts		4,200				4,200		
508	Transportation-in	2,300				2,300			
612	Amort. expense, store equipment			(d) 3,000		3,000			
613	Amort. expense, office equipment			(e) 700		700			
620	Office salaries expense	25,000		(f) 300		25,300			
621	Sales salaries expense	18,000		(f) 500		18,500			
633	Interest expense	360				360			
637	Insurance expense			(a) 600		600			
641	Rent expense, office space	900				900			
642	Rent expense, selling space	8,100				8,100			
650	Office supplies expense			(c) 1,800		1,800			
651	Store supplies expense			(b) 1,200		1,200			
655	Advertising expense	11,300				11,300			
	Totals	389,360	389,360	8,100	8,100	335,160	350,500	79,700	64,360
	Net Income					15,340			15,340
	Totals					350,500	350,500	79,700	79,700

Exhibit 6A.3

Classified, Multiple-step Income Statement — Periodic

Z-Mart Income Statement For Year Ended December 31, 2001				
Sales				$321,000
Less: Sales discounts			$ 4,300	
Sales returns and allowances			2,000	6,300
Net sales				$314,700
Cost of goods sold				
Merchandise inventory, Dec. 31, 2000			$ 19,000	
Purchases		$235,800		
Less: Purchase returns and allowances	$1,500			
Purchase discounts	4,200	5,700		
Net purchases		$230,100		
Add: Transportation-in		2,300		
Cost of goods purchased			232,400	
Goods available for sale			$251,400	
Merchandise inventory, Dec. 31, 2001			21,000	
Cost of goods sold				230,400
Gross profit from sales				$ 84,300
Operating expenses:				
Selling expenses:				
Amortization expense, store equipment		$ 3,000		
Sales salaries expense		18,500		
Rent expense, selling space		8,100		
Store supplies expense		1,200		
Advertising expense		11,300		
Total selling expenses			$ 42,100	
General and administrative expenses				
Amortization expense, office equipment		$ 700		
Office salaries expense		25,300		
Insurance expense		600		
Rent expense, office space		900		
Office supplies expense		1,800		
Total general and administrative expense			29,300	
Total operating expenses				71,400
Income from operations				$ 12,900
Other revenues and expenses:				
Rent revenue			$2,800	
Interest expense			360	2,440
Net income				$ 15,340

Exhibit 6A.4

Comparison of Closing Entries—Periodic and Perpetual

Periodic			Perpetual		
Closing Entries			**Closing Entries**		
(1)			**(1)**		
Rent Revenue	2,800		Rent Revenue	2,800	
Sales	321,000		Sales	321,000	
Merchandise Inventory	**21,000**		Income Summary		323,800
Purchase Discounts	**4,200**				
Purchase Returns and Allowances	**1,500**				
Income Summary		350,500			
(2)			**(2)**		
Income Summary	335,160		Income Summary	308,460	
Sales Discounts		4,300	Sales Discounts		4,300
Sales Returns and Allowances		2,000	Sales Returns and Allowances		2,000
Merchandise Inventory		**19,000**	**Cost of Goods Sold**		**230,400**
Purchases		**235,800**			
Transportation-in		**2,300**			
Amortization Expense, Store Equipment		3,000	Amortization Expense, Store Equipment		3,000
Amortization Expense, Office Equipment		700	Amortization Expense, Office Equipment		700
Office Salaries Expense		25,300	Office Salaries Expense		25,300
Sales Salaries Expense		18,500	Sales Salaries Expense		18,500
Interest Expense		360	Interest Expense		360
Insurance Expense		600	Insurance Expense		600
Rent Expense, Office Space		900	Rent Expense, Office Space		900
Rent Expense, Selling Space		8,100	Rent Expense, Selling Space		8,100
Office Supplies Expense		1,800	Office Supplies Expense		1,800
Store Supplies Expense		1,200	Store Supplies Expense		1,200
Advertising Expense		11,300	Advertising Expense		11,300
(3)			**(3)**		
Income Summary	15,340		Income Summary	15,340	
Kent Marty, Capital		15,340	Kent Marty, Capital		15,340
(4)			**(4)**		
Kent Marty, Capital	4,000		Kent Marty, Capital	4,000	
Kent Marty, Withdrawals		4,000	Kent Marty, Withdrawals		4,000

Closing Entries

By updating Merchandise Inventory and closing Purchases, Purchase Discounts, Purchase Returns and Allowances, and Transportation-In, the periodic system transfers the cost of goods sold amount to Income Summary. Review the periodic side of Exhibit 6A.4 and notice that the boldface items affect Income Summary as follows:

Exhibit 6A.5

Merchandising Cost Flows Across Periods*

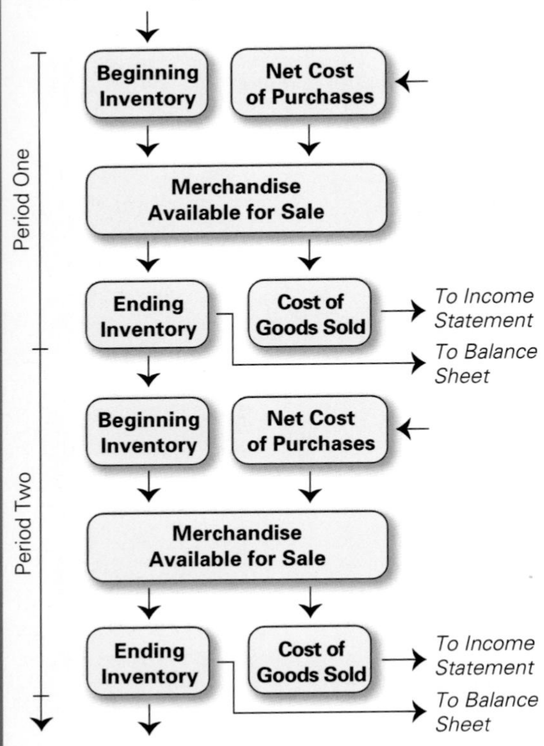

* Cost of goods sold is reported on the income statement. Ending inventory is reported on the balance sheet. One period's ending inventory is the next period's beginning inventory.

Credited to Income Summary in the first closing entry:	
Merchandise Inventory	$ 21,000
Purchase Discounts	4,200
Purchase Returns and Allowances	1,500
Debited to Income Summary in the second closing entry:	
Merchandise Inventory	(19,000)
Purchases	(235,800)
Transportation-in	(2,300)
Net effect on Income Summary	($230,400)

This $230,400 effect on Income Summary is the cost of goods sold amount. This figure is confirmed as follows:

Beginning inventory		$ 19,000
Purchases	$235,800	
Less: Purchase discounts	4,200	
Less: Purchase returns and allowances	1,500	
Add: Transportation-in	2,300	
Net cost of goods purchased		232,400
Cost of goods available for sale		$251,400
Less: Ending inventory		21,000
Cost of goods sold		$230,400

The periodic system transfers cost of goods sold to the Income Summary account but does not use a Cost of Goods Sold account. Exhibit 6A.5 shows the relation between inventory, purchases, and cost of goods sold across periods.

The periodic system does not measure shrinkage. Instead it computes cost of goods available for sale, subtracts the cost of ending inventory, and defines the difference as cost of goods sold. This difference, called the cost of goods sold, includes shrinkage.

Flashback

Answers—p. 296

17. What account is used in a perpetual inventory system but not in a periodic system?
18. Which of the following accounts are temporary accounts? (a) Merchandise Inventory, (b) Purchases, (c) Transportation-in.
19. How is cost of goods sold computed under a periodic inventory accounting system?

Using the Information

APPENDIX

Gross Margin Ratio

LO12 Compute the gross margin ratio and explain its use as an indicator of profitability.

Gross profit, also called gross margin, is the relation between sales and cost of goods sold and is a major part of profit for merchandising companies. A merchandising company needs sufficient gross profit to cover operating expenses or it will likely fail. To help us focus on gross profit, users often compute a *gross margin ratio*. The **gross margin ratio** is defined as shown in Exhibit 6B.1.

Exhibit 6B.1

Gross Margin Ratio

$$\text{Gross margin ratio} = \frac{\text{Gross Margin}}{\text{Net Sales}}$$

Exhibit 6B.2 shows the gross margin ratios of Mitel Corporation for 1999 and 2000.

Exhibit 6B.2

Mitel's Gross Margin Ratio

(in millions)	2000	1999
Gross margin	$ 645.1	$ 645.6
Net sales	$1,396.5	$1,310.4
Gross margin ratio	**46.2%**	**49.3%**

This ratio represents the gross margin in each dollar of sales. For example, Exhibit 6B.2 shows that Mitel's gross margin ratio in 2000 is 46.2%. This means that each $1 of sales yields about 46.2¢ in gross margin to cover all other expenses. Results in Exhibit 6B.2 show Mitel's gross margin ratio decreased from 1999 to 2000. This decrease is an important development. Success for companies such as Mitel depends on maintaining an adequate gross margin to cover operating expenses.

Summary of Appendices 6A and 6B

LO11 **Record and compare merchandising transactions using both periodic and perpetual inventory systems.** Transactions involving the sale and purchase of merchandise are recorded and analyzed under both inventory systems. Adjusting and closing entries for both inventory systems are also illustrated and explained.

LO12 **Compute the gross margin ratio and explain its use as an indicator of profitability.** The gross margin (or gross profit) ratio is computed as gross margin (net sales minus cost of goods sold) divided by net sales. It is an indicator of a company's profitability before deducting operating expenses. A gross margin ratio must be large enough to cover operating expenses and give an adequate net income.

GUIDANCE ANSWERS TO  Flashback

14. The Merchandise inventory account on the periodic unadjusted trial balance represents the balance at the beginning of the period. The Merchandise inventory account on the perpetual unadjusted trial balance has been adjusted regularly during the accounting period for all transactions affecting inventory, such as purchases, returns, discounts, transportation-in, and cost of sales.
15. The beginning Merchandise inventory balance of $19,000 is included on the periodic unadjusted trial balance and not the perpetual along with Purchases, Purchase discounts, Purchase returns and allowances, and Transportation-in.
16. Cost of goods sold is calculated under periodic using the account balances of Merchandise inventory (beginning inventory balance), Purchases, Purchase discounts, Purchase returns and allowances, Transportation-in, and subtracting the ending inventory amount determined through a physical count.
17. Cost of Goods Sold.
18. (b) Purchases and (c) Transportation-in.
19. Under a periodic inventory system, the cost of goods sold is determined at the end of an accounting period by adding the net cost of goods purchased to the beginning inventory and subtracting the ending inventory.

Glossary

Cash discount A reduction in the price of merchandise that is granted by a seller to a purchaser in exchange for the purchaser paying within a specified period of time called the discount period. (p. 264)

Classified, multiple-step income statement An income statement format that shows intermediate totals between sales and net income and detailed computations of net sales and costs of goods sold. (p. 276)

Cost of goods sold The cost of merchandise sold to customers during a period. (p. 256)

Credit memorandum A notification that the sender has entered a credit in the recipient's account maintained by the sender. (p. 270)

Credit period The time period that can pass before a customer's payment is due. (p. 263)

Credit terms The description of the amounts and timing of payments that a buyer agrees to make in the future. (p. 263)

Debit memorandum A notification that the sender has entered a debit in the recipient's account maintained by the sender. (p. 262)

Discount period The time period in which a cash discount is available and a reduced payment can be made by the buyer. (p. 264)

EOM The abbreviation for *end of month*, used to describe credit terms for some transactions. (p. 263)

FOB The abbreviation for *free on board*, the designated point at which ownership of goods passes to the buyer; FOB shipping point (or factory) means that the buyer pays the shipping costs and accepts ownership of the goods at the seller's place of business; FOB destination means that the seller pays the shipping costs and the ownership of the goods transfers to the buyer at the buyer's place of business. (p. 265)

General and administrative expenses Expenses that support the overall operations of a business and include the expenses of such activities as providing accounting services, human resource management, and financial management. (p. 276)

Gross margin The difference between net sales and the cost of goods sold; also called *gross profit*. (p. 257)

Gross margin ratio Gross margin (net sales minus cost of goods sold) divided by net sales; also called *gross profit ratio*. (p. 295)

Gross profit The difference between net sales and the cost of goods sold; also called *gross margin*. (p. 257)

Gross profit ratio See *gross margin ratio*. (p. 295)

Inventory See *Merchandise inventory*. (p. 257)

List price The catalogue price of an item before any trade discount is deducted. (p. 263)

Merchandise Products, also called *goods*, that a company acquires for the purpose of reselling them to customers. (p. 256)

Merchandiser Earns net income by buying and selling merchandise. (p. 256)

Merchandise inventory Products that a company owns for the purpose of selling them to customers. (p. 257)

Periodic inventory system A method of accounting that records the cost of inventory purchased but does not track the quantity on hand or sold to customers; the records are updated at the end of each period to reflect the results of physical counts of the items on hand. (p. 259)

Perpetual inventory system A method of accounting that maintains continuous records of the cost of inventory on hand and the cost of goods sold. (p. 259)

Purchase discount A term used by a purchaser to describe a cash discount granted to the purchaser for paying within the discount period. (p. 264)

Retailer A middleman that buys products from manufacturers or wholesalers and sells them to consumers. (p. 256)

Sales discount A term used by a seller to describe a cash discount granted to customers for paying within the discount period. (p. 264)

Selling expenses The expenses of promoting sales by displaying and advertising the merchandise, making sales, and delivering goods to customers. (p. 276)

Shrinkage Inventory losses that occur as a result of shoplifting or deterioration. (p. 272)

Single-step income statement An income statement format that includes cost of goods sold as an operating expense and shows only one subtotal for total expenses. (p. 278)

Supplementary records A register of information outside the usual accounting records and accounts; also called *supplemental records*. (p. 267)

Trade discount A reduction below a list or catalogue price that may vary in amount for wholesalers, retailers, and final consumers. (p. 263)

Wholesaler A middleman that buys products from manufacturers or other wholesalers and sells them to retailers or other wholesalers. (p. 256)

Questions

1. What items appear in the financial statements of merchandising companies but not in the statements of service companies?
2. Explain how a business can earn a gross profit on its sales and still have a net loss.
3. Why would a company offer a cash discount?
4. What is the difference between a sales discount and a purchase discount?
5. Distinguish between cash discounts and trade discounts. Is the amount of a trade discount on purchased merchandise recorded in the accounts?
6. How does a company that uses a perpetual inventory system determine the amount of inventory shrinkage?
7. Why would a company's manager be concerned about the quantity of its purchase returns if its suppliers allow unlimited returns?
8. Does the sender of a debit memorandum record a debit or a credit in the account of the recipient? Which does the recipient record?
9. What is the difference between single-step and multiple-step income statement formats?
10. In comparing the accounts of a merchandising company with those of a service company, what additional accounts would the merchandising company be likely to use, assuming it employs a perpetual inventory system?
11. Refer to the income statement for ClubLink in Appendix I at the end of the book. Does the company present a detailed calculation of the cost of goods sold?

12. Refer to the balance sheet for ClubLink in Appendix I. What would be the equivalent for merchandise inventory in ClubLink's balance sheet?
13. Rob Stavos talks about the need to be skillful in negotiating purchase contracts with suppliers. What type of shipping terms should Rob Stavos attempt to negotiate to minimize his freight-in costs?

Quick Study

QS 6-1

Profitability

LO2

Compute net sales and gross profit from sales in each of the following situations:

	a	b	c	d
Sales	$130,000	$512,000	$35,700	$245,700
Sales discounts	4,200	16,500	400	3,500
Sales returns and allowances	17,000	5,000	5,000	700
Cost of goods sold	76,600	326,700	21,300	125,900

QS 6-2

Contrast periodic and perpetual systems

LO4

For each description below, identify whether the reference is to a periodic or perpetual inventory system.

a. Requires a physical count of inventory to determine the amount of inventory to report on the balance sheet.
b. Records the cost of goods sold each time a sales transaction occurs.
c. Provides more timely information to managers.
d. Was traditionally used by companies such as drug and department stores that sold large quantities of low-valued items.
e. Requires an adjusting entry to record inventory shrinkage.

QS 6-3

Journal entries—perpetual system

LO5

Prepare journal entries to record each of the following transactions of a merchandising company. Show any supporting calculations. Assume a perpetual inventory system.

Mar. 5	Purchased 500 units of product with a list price of $5 per unit. The purchaser was granted a trade discount of 20% and the terms of the sale were 2/10, n/60.
7	Returned 50 defective units from the March 5 purchase and received full credit.
15	Paid the amount due resulting from the March 5 purchase, less the return and applicable discount, on March 7.

QS 6-4
Journal entries—perpetual system
LO6

Prepare journal entries to record each of the following transactions of a merchandising company. Show any supporting calculations. Assume a perpetual inventory system.

Apr. 1	Sold merchandise for $2,000, granting the customer terms of 2/10, EOM. The cost of the merchandise was $1,400.
4	The customer in the April 1 sale returned merchandise and received credit for $500. The merchandise, which had cost $350, was returned to inventory.
11	Received payment for the amount due resulting from the April 1 sale, less the return and applicable discount, on April 4.

QS 6-5
Shrinkage
LO7

Beamer Company's ledger on July 31, the end of the fiscal year, includes the following accounts which have normal balances:

Merchandise inventory	$ 34,800
Joy Beamer, capital	115,300
Joy Beamer, withdrawals	4,000
Sales	157,200
Sales discounts	1,700
Sales returns and allowances	3,500
Cost of goods sold	102,000
Amortization expense	7,300
Salaries expense	29,500
Miscellaneous expenses	2,000

A physical count of the inventory discloses that the cost of the merchandise on hand is $32,900. Prepare the entry to record this information.

QS 6-6
Closing entries
LO10

Refer to QS 6-5 and prepare the entries to close the income statement accounts. Do not forget to take into consideration the entry that was made to solve QS 6-5.

***QS 6-7**
Journal entries—periodic system
LO11

Using the information in QS 6-3, prepare journal entries to record each of the transactions of the merchandising company assuming a periodic inventory system.

***QS 6-8**
Journal entries—periodic system
LO11

Using the information in QS 6-4, prepare journal entries to record each of the transactions of the merchandising company assuming a periodic inventory system.

An asterisk (*) identifies assignment material based on Appendix 6A or Appendix 6B.

Closing entries—periodic

LO[11]

Prepare the entries to close the following income statement accounts.

Merchandise inventory (January 1, 2001)	$ 40,000
Kay Bondar, capital	102,000
Kay Bondar, withdrawals	65,000
Sales	450,000
Sales returns and allowances	27,000
Purchases	180,000
Purchase discounts	1,400
Transportation-in	14,000
Merchandise inventory (December 31, 2001)	22,000
Salaries expense	120,000
Amortization expense	31,000

***QS 6-10**

Profitability—periodic

LO[11]

Compute net sales, cost of goods sold, and gross profit in each of the following situations.

	a	b	c	d
Sales	$130,000	$512,000	$35,700	$245,700
Sales discounts	4,200	16,500	400	3,500
Merchandise inventory, Jan. 1, 2001	8,000	21,000	1,500	4,300
Purchases	120,000	350,000	29,000	131,000
Purchase returns and allowances	4,000	14,000	750	3,100
Merchandise inventory, Dec. 1, 2001	7,500	22,000	900	4,100

***QS 6-11**

Gross margin ratio

LO[12]

Willaby Company had net sales of $248,000 and cost of goods sold of $114,080. Calculate and interpret the gross margin ratio.

Exercises

Exercise 6-1

Merchandising terms

LO[1,2]

Insert the letter for each term in the blank space beside the definition that it most closely matches:

a. Cash discount
b. Credit period
c. Discount period
d. FOB destination
e. FOB shipping point
f. Gross profit
g. Merchandise inventory
h. Purchase discount
i. Sales discount
j. Trade discount

d **1.** An agreement that ownership of goods is transferred at the buyer's place of business.
c **2.** The time period in which a cash discount is available.
f **3.** The difference between net sales and the cost of goods sold.
a **4.** A reduction in a receivable or payable that is granted if it is paid within the discount period.
h **5.** A purchaser's description of a cash discount received from a supplier of goods.
e **6.** An agreement that ownership of goods is transferred at the seller's place of business.
j **7.** A reduction below a list or catalogue price that is negotiated in setting the selling price of goods.
i **8.** A seller's description of a cash discount granted to customers in return for early payment.
b **9.** The time period that can pass before a customer's payment is due.
g **10.** The goods that a company owns and expects to sell to its customers.

An asterisk (*) identifies assignment material based on Appendix 6A or Appendix 6B.

Exercise 6-2
Calculating cost of goods sold

LO2

Determine each of the missing numbers in the following situations:

	a	b	c
Purchases	$45,000	$80,000	$61,000
Purchases discounts	2,000	?	1,300
Purchase returns and allowances	1,500	3,000	2,200
Transportation-in	?	7,000	8,000
Beginning inventory	3,500	?	18,000
Cost of goods purchased	44,700	79,000	?
Ending inventory	2,200	15,000	?
Cost of goods sold	?	83,200	68,260

Exercise 6-3
Recording journal entries for merchandise purchase transactions—perpetual

LO5

Prepare journal entries for March 2001 to record the following transactions for a retail store. Assume a perpetual inventory system.

Mar.	2	Purchased merchandise from Blanton Company under the following terms: $3,600 invoice price, 2/15, n/60, FOB factory.
	3	Paid $200 for shipping charges on the purchase of March 2.
	4	Returned to Blanton Company unacceptable merchandise that had an invoice price of $600.
	17	Sent a cheque to Blanton Company for the March 2 purchase, net of the returned merchandise and applicable discount.
	18	Purchased merchandise from Fleming Corp. under the following terms: $7,500 invoice price, 2/10, n/30, FOB destination.
	21	After brief negotiations, received from Fleming Corp. a $2,100 allowance on the purchase of March 18.
	28	Sent a cheque to Fleming Corp. paying for the March 18 purchase, net of the discount and the allowance.

Exercise 6-4
Analyzing and recording merchandise transactions—perpetual

LO5, 6

On May 11, 2001, Wilson Sales accepted delivery of $30,000 of merchandise it purchased for resale. With the merchandise was an invoice dated May 11, with terms of 3/10, n/90, FOB Hostel Corporation's factory. The cost of the goods to Hostel was $20,000. When the goods were delivered, Wilson paid $335 to Express Shipping Service for the delivery charges on the merchandise. The next day, Wilson returned $1,200 of goods to the seller, who received them one day later and restored them to inventory. The returned goods had cost Hostel $800. On May 20, Wilson mailed a cheque to Hostel Corporation for the amount owed on that date. It was received the following day.

Required

a. Present the journal entries that Wilson Sales should record for these transactions. Assume that Wilson Sales uses a perpetual inventory system.

b. Present the journal entries that Hostel Corporation should record for these transactions. Assume that Hostel uses a perpetual inventory system.

Exercise 6-5
Analyzing and recording merchandise transactions—perpetual

LO5, 6

Sundown Company purchased merchandise for resale from Raintree with an invoice price of $22,000 and credit terms of 3/10, n/60. The merchandise had cost Raintree $15,000. Sundown paid within the discount period. Assume that both the buyer and seller use perpetual inventory systems.

Required

a. Prepare the entries that the purchaser should record for the purchase and payment.

b. Prepare the entries that the seller should record for the sale and collection.

c. Assume that the buyer borrowed enough cash to pay the balance on the last day of the discount period at an annual interest rate of 8% and paid it back on the last day of the credit period. Compute how much the buyer saved by following this strategy. *Use a 365-day year and round all calculations to the nearest whole cent.*

Exercise 6-6
Purchase returns and allowances—perpetual

LO5

Refer to Exercise 6-7 and prepare the appropriate journal entries on the books of Decker Co. to record the purchase and each of the three independent alternatives presented. Assume that Decker is a retailer that uses a perpetual inventory system and purchased the units for resale.

Exercise 6-7
Sales returns and allowances—perpetual

LO6

Travis Parts was organized on June 1, 2001, and made its first purchase of merchandise on June 3. The purchase was for 1,000 units of Product X at a price of $10 per unit. On June 5, Travis sold 600 of the units for $14 per unit to Decker Co. Terms of the sale were 2/10, n/60.

Required
Prepare entries to record the sale and each of the following independent alternatives on the books of Travis Parts under a perpetual inventory system.

a. On June 7, Decker returned 100 units because they did not fit the customer's needs. Travis restored the units to its inventory.

b. Decker discovered that 100 units were damaged but of some use. Therefore, Decker kept the units. Travis sent Decker a credit memorandum for $600 to compensate for the damage.

c. Decker returned 100 defective units and Travis concluded that the units could not be resold. As a result, Travis discarded the units.

Exercise 6-8
Sales returns and allowances

LO6

Briefly explain why a company's manager would want the accounting system to record a customer's return of unsatisfactory goods in the Sales Returns and Allowances account instead of the Sales account. In addition, explain whether the information would be useful for external decision makers.

Exercise 6-9
Calculating expenses and income

LO2, 8

Fill in the following blanks. Identify any losses by putting the amount in brackets.

	a	b	c	d	e
Sales	$60,000	$42,500	$36,000	$?	$23,600
Cost of goods sold:					
Merchandise inventory (beginning)	$ 6,000	$17,050	$ 7,500	$ 7,000	$ 2,560
Total cost of merchandise purchases	36,000	?	?	32,000	5,600
Merchandise inventory (ending)	?	(2,700)	(9,000)	(6,600)	?
Cost of goods sold	$34,050	$15,900	$?	$?	$ 5,600
Gross profit	$?	$?	$ 3,750	$45,600	$?
Expenses	9,000	10,650	12,150	2,600	6,000
Net income (loss)	$?	$15,950	$(8,400)	$43,000	$?

Exercise 6-10
Components of cost of goods sold

LO8

Using the data provided, determine each of the missing numbers in the following situations:

	a	b	c
Invoice cost of merchandise purchases	$90,000	$40,000	$30,500
Purchase discounts received	4,000	?	650
Purchase returns and allowances received	3,000	1,500	1,100
Cost of transportation-in	?	3,500	4,000
Merchandise inventory (beginning of period)	7,000	?	9,000
Total cost of merchandise purchases	89,400	39,500	?
Merchandise inventory (end of period)	4,400	7,500	?
Cost of goods sold	?	41,600	34,130

Exercise 6-11
Calculating income statement components
LO 2, 9

Calculate the missing amounts.

	a	b	c	d
Sales	$240,000	$75,000	?	?
Cost of goods sold	?	42,000	268,000	46,000
Gross profit	114,000	?	?	39,000
Operating expenses	95,000	?	146,000	?
Net income (loss)	?	($8,000)	$ 48,000	($14,000)

Exercise 6-12
Calculating income statement components
LO 2, 9

Calculate the missing amounts.

	a	b	c	d
Sales	$95,200	$150,400	?	$33,900
Sales discounts	1,100	?	2,900	950
Sales returns and allowances	?	14,000	4,000	?
Net sales	?	134,700	?	32,950
Cost of goods sold	37,000	?	260,000	?
Gross profit	53,600	?	238,900	12,450
Selling expenses	26,000	12,000	92,000	?
Administrative expenses	34,000	?	105,000	28,000
Total operating expenses	?	40,000	?	?
Net income (loss)	?	$ 2,700	?	($31,550)

Exercise 6-13
Effects of merchandising activities on the accounts—perpetual
LO 8

The following amounts taken from supplementary and accounting records summarize Transeer Company's merchandising activities during 2002. Set up T-accounts for Merchandise Inventory and Cost of Goods Sold (see Exhibit 6.14). Then record the summarized activities directly in the accounts and compute the account balances.

Cost of merchandise sold to customers in sales transactions	$186,000
Merchandise inventory balance, Dec. 31, 2001	27,000
Invoice cost of merchandise purchases	190,500
Shrinkage determined on Dec. 31, 2002	700
Cost of transportation-in	1,900
Cost of merchandise returned by customers and restored to inventory	2,200
Purchase discounts received	1,600
Purchase returns and allowances received	4,100

Exercise 6-14
Calculating expenses and cost of goods sold—perpetual
LO 2, 9

Westlawn Company's ledger and supplementary records at the end of the period disclose the following information:

Sales	$500,000
Sales discounts	17,000
Sales returns	3,000
Gross profit	124,000
Net loss	28,000

Required
Compute the (a) net sales, (b) total operating expenses, and (c) cost of goods sold.

Exercise 6-15
Preparing reports from closing entries—perpetual

LO9, 10

The following closing entries for Sabba Co. were made on January 31, 2001 the end of its annual accounting period:

1.	Sales	531,000	
	Income Summary		531,000
	To close temporary accounts with credit balances.		
2.	Income Summary	548,750	
	Cost of Goods Sold		301,000
	Sales Returns and Allowances		14,000
	Sales Discounts		7,000
	Selling Expenses		117,000
	General and Administrative Expenses		109,000
	Interest Expense		750
	To close temporary accounts with debit balances.		

Check figure:
Net loss = $17,750

Required
Use the information in the closing entries to prepare:
a. A calculation of net sales.
b. A multiple-step income statement for the year.

Exercise 6-16
Preparing an income statement and closing entries—perpetual

LO9, 10

The following account information, in alphabetical order, was taken from the work sheet of Compu-Soft for the month ended November 30, 2001.

Required
a. Prepare a multiple-step income statement for the month ended November 30, 2001.
b. Prepare closing entries.
c. Calculate the post-closing balance in the capital account at November 30, 2001.

		Adjusted Trial Balance	
	Account	**Debit**	**Credit**
201	Accounts payable		600
106	Accounts receivable	850	
166	Accumulated amortization, store equipment		4,550
612	Amortization expense, store equipment	120	
101	Cash	1,800	
502	Cost of goods sold	14,800	
301	Peter Delta, capital		1,635
302	Peter Delta, withdrawals	3,500	
413	Sales		27,700
415	Sales discounts	45	
414	Sales returns and allowances	720	
165	Store equipment	7,200	
690	Utilities expense	2,100	
406	Rent revenue		850
623	Wages expense	4,200	
	Totals	35,335	35,335

Exercise 6-17
Adjusting and closing entries, preparing a work sheet and income statement—perpetual

LO 9, 10

Check figure:
Balance sheet columns = $37,800

The following list of accounts is taken from the December 31, 2002, unadjusted trial balance of Perry Sales, a business that is owned by Deborah Perry. Assuming a perpetual inventory system:

a. Prepare a work sheet.
b. Prepare a multiple-step income statement for the year ended December 31, 2002.
c. Journalize the closing entries.

	Debit	Credit
Cash	$ 13,000	
Merchandise inventory	1,000	
Prepaid selling expense	4,000	
Equipment	20,000	
Accumulated amortization, equipment		$ 4,500
Accounts payable		6,000
Salaries payable		-0-
Deborah Perry, capital		22,800
Deborah Perry, withdrawals	1,800	
Sales		429,000
Sales returns and allowances	16,500	
Sales discounts	4,000	
Cost of goods sold	211,000	
Sales salaries expense	47,000	
Utilities expense, store	14,000	
Other selling expenses	35,000	
Other administrative expenses	95,000	

Additional information:
Accrued sales salaries amount to $1,600. Prepaid selling expenses of $2,000 have expired.

***Exercise 6-18**
Journal entries to contrast the periodic and perpetual systems

LO 5, 6, 11

Journalize the following merchandising transactions for Scout Systems assuming (a) a periodic system and (b) perpetual system.

Nov. 1	Scout Systems purchases merchandise for $1,400 on credit with terms of 2/10, n/30.
5	Scout Systems pays for the previous purchase.
7	Scout Systems receives payment for returned defective merchandise of $100 that was purchased on November 1.
10	Scout Systems pays $80 to haul merchandise to its store.
13	Scout Systems sells merchandise for $1,500 on account. The cost of the merchandise was $750.
16	A customer returns merchandise from the November 13th transaction. The returned item sold for $200 and cost $100. The item will be returned to inventory.

***Exercise 6-19**
Recording journal entries for merchandise transactions—periodic

LO 11

Using the information in Exercise 6-3, prepare journal entries to record the March transactions assuming a periodic inventory system.

An asterisk (*) identifies assignment material based on Appendix 6A or Appendix 6B.

***Exercise 6-20**
Analyzing and recording merchandise transactions and returns—periodic

LO 11

Using the information in Exercise 6-4:

a. Present the journal entries that Wilson Sales should record for these transactions. Assume that Wilson Sales uses a periodic inventory system.

b. Present the journal entries that Hostel Corporation should record for these transactions. Assume that Hostel uses a periodic inventory system.

***Exercise 6-21**
Analyzing and recording merchandise transactions and discounts—periodic

LO 11

Using the information in Exercise 6-5, and assuming instead a periodic inventory system:

a. Prepare the entries that the purchaser should record for the purchase and payment.

b. Prepare the entries that the seller should record for the sale and collection.

***Exercise 6-22**
Calculating expenses and cost of goods sold—periodic

LO 11

Friar Company's ledger and supplementary records at the end of the period disclose the following information:

Sales	$340,000
Sales discounts	5,500
Sales returns	14,000
Merchandise inventory (beginning of period)	30,000
Invoice cost of merchandise purchases	175,000
Purchase discounts received	3,600
Purchase returns and allowances received	6,000
Cost of transportation-in	11,000
Gross profit from sales	145,000
Net income	65,000

Check figure:
c. $30,900

Required
Compute the (a) total operating expenses, (b) cost of goods sold, and (c) merchandise inventory (end of period).

***Exercise 6-23**
Sales returns and allowances—periodic

LO 11

Using the information from Exercise 6-7, assume a periodic inventory system, and prepare the entries to record (a), (b), and (c).

***Exercise 6-24**
Purchase returns and allowances—periodic

LO 11

Refer to Exercise 6-7 and prepare the appropriate journal entries on the books of Decker Co. to record the purchase and each of the three independent alternatives presented. Assume that Decker is a retailer that uses a *periodic* inventory system and purchased the units for resale.

An asterisk (*) identifies assignment material based on Appendix 6A or Appendix 6B.

***Exercise 6-25**
Preparing a work sheet — periodic

LO 11

The following unadjusted trial balance was taken from the ledger of Johnson's Newsstand at the end of its fiscal year. (To reduce your effort, the account balances are relatively small.)

Johnson's Newsstand
Unadjusted Trial Balance
December 31, 2001

No.	Title	Debit	Credit
101	Cash	$ 3,700	
106	Accounts receivable	1,800	
119	Merchandise inventory	1,200	
125	Store supplies	600	
201	Accounts payable		$ 140
209	Salaries payable		
301	Tod Johnson, capital		5,785
302	Tod Johnson, withdrawals	375	
413	Sales		6,000
414	Sales returns and allowances	145	
505	Purchases	3,200	
506	Purchases discounts		125
507	Transportation-in	80	
622	Salaries expense	700	
640	Rent expense	250	
651	Store supplies expense		
	Totals	$12,050	$12,050

Required

Use the preceding information and the following additional facts to complete an eight-column work sheet for the company (do not include columns for the adjusted trial balance).

a. The ending inventory of store supplies was $450.
b. Accrued salaries at the end of the year were $60.
c. The ending merchandise inventory was $1,360.

Check figure:
Income statement columns = 7,485

An asterisk (*) identifies assignment material based on Appendix 6A or Appendix 6B.

***Exercise 6-26**
Preparing reports from closing entries—periodic

LO11

Check figure:
d. Net income = $37,300

The following closing entries for Fox Fixtures Co. were made on March 31, 2001, the end of its annual accounting period:

1.	Interest Revenue	1,200	
	Merchandise Inventory	11,000	
	Sales	445,000	
	Purchases Returns and Allowances	22,000	
	Purchases Discounts	11,400	
	Income Summary		490,600
	To close temporary accounts with credit balances and record the ending inventory.		
2.	Income Summary	453,300	
	Merchandise Inventory		15,000
	Sales Returns and Allowances		25,000
	Sales Discounts		16,000
	Purchases		286,000
	Transportation-in		8,800
	Selling Expenses		69,000
	General and Administrative Expenses		33,500
	To close temporary accounts with debit balances and to remove the beginning inventory balance.		

Required

Use the information in the closing entries to prepare:

a. A calculation of net sales.
b. A calculation of cost of goods purchased.
c. A calculation of cost of goods sold.
d. A multiple-step income statement for the year.

***Exercise 6-27**
Preparing an income statement and closing entries—periodic

LO11

Check figure:
Income from operations = $4,686

The following account information, in alphabetical order, was taken from the work sheet of the Music Masters for the month ended April 30, 2001, and revealed a balance actually on hand of $1,230.

Required

a. Calculate net sales.
b. Calculate cost of goods sold.
c. Prepare a multiple-step income statement for the month ended April 30, 2001.
d. Prepare closing entries.
e. Calculate the post-closing balance in the capital account at April 30, 2001.

An asterisk (*) identifies assignment material based on Appendix 6A or Appendix 6B.

	Account	Adjusted Trial Balance Debit	Adjusted Trial Balance Credit
201	Accounts payable		$ 1,050
154	Accumulated amortization, trucks		7,100
611	Amortization expense, trucks	$ 320	
101	Cash	2,300	
633	Interest expense	65	
119	Merchandise inventory	3,100	
505	Purchases	8,338	
507	Purchases discounts		14
506	Purchases returns and allowances		55
413	Sales		21,850
414	Sales returns and allowances	870	
688	Telephone expense	245	
301	Tod Whitten, capital		10,159
302	Tod Whitten, withdrawals	4,600	
508	Transportation-in	190	
153	Trucks	14,800	
623	Wages expense	5,400	
	Totals	$40,228	$40,228

***Exercise 6-28**
Gross margin ratio

LO12

Compute net sales, gross profit, and gross margin ratio in each of the following situations:

	a	b	c	d
Sales	$130,000	$512,000	$35,700	$245,700
Sales discounts	4,200	16,500	400	3,500
Sales returns and allowances	17,000	5,000	5,000	700
Cost of goods sold	76,600	326,700	21,300	125,900

a. Which situation has the highest net sales?
b. Which situation has the highest gross margin ratio?

Problems

Problem 6-1A

Journal entries for merchandising activities—perpetual

LO5, 6

Prepare General Journal entries to record the following perpetual system merchandising transactions of Belton Company. *Use a separate account for each receivable and payable; for example, record the purchase on July 1 in Accounts Payable—Jones Company.*

An asterisk (*) identifies assignment material based on Appendix 6A or Appendix 6B.

July	1	Purchased merchandise from Jones Company for $6,000 under credit terms of 1/15, n/30, FOB factory.
	2	Sold merchandise to Terra Co. for $800 under credit terms of 2/10, n/60, FOB shipping point. The merchandise had cost $500.
	3	Paid $100 for freight charges on the purchase of July 1.
	8	Sold merchandise that cost $1,200 for $1,600 cash.
	9	Purchased merchandise from Keene Co. for $2,300 under credit terms of 2/15, n/60, FOB destination.
	12	Received a $200 credit memorandum acknowledging the return of merchandise purchased on July 9.
	12	Received the balance due from Terra Co. for the credit sale dated July 2.
	13	Purchased office supplies from EastCo on credit, $480, n/30.
	16	Paid the balance due to Jones Company.
	19	Sold merchandise that cost $900 to Urban Co. for $1,250 under credit terms of 2/15, n/60, FOB shipping point.
	21	Issued a $150 credit memorandum to Urban Co. for an allowance on goods sold on July 19.
	22	Received a debit memorandum from Urban Co. for an error that overstated the total invoice by $50.
	24	Paid Keene Co. the balance due.
	30	Received the balance due from Urban Co. for the credit sale dated July 19.
	31	Sold merchandise that cost $3,200 to Terra Co. for $5,000 under credit terms of 2/10, n/60, FOB shipping point.

Problem 6-2A

Journal entries for merchandising activities—perpetual

LO5, 6

Prepare General Journal entries to record the following perpetual system merchandising transactions of Hanifin Company. *Use a separate account for each receivable and payable; for example, record the purchase on August 1 in Accounts Payable—Dickson Company.*

Aug.	1	Purchased merchandise from Dickson Company for $6,000 under credit terms of 1/10, n/30, FOB destination.
	4	At Dickson's request, paid $100 for freight charges on the August 1 purchase, reducing the amount owed to Dickson.
	5	Sold merchandise to Griften Corp. for $4,200 under credit terms of 2/10, n/60, FOB destination. The merchandise had cost $3,000.
	8	Purchased merchandise from Kendall Corporation for $5,300 under credit terms of 1/10, n/45, FOB shipping point, plus $240 shipping charges. The invoice showed that at Hanifin's request, Kendall had paid $240 shipping charges and added that amount to the bill.
	9	Paid $120 shipping charges related to the August 5 sale to Griften Corp.
	10	Griften returned merchandise from the August 5 sale that had cost $500 and been sold for $700. The merchandise was restored to inventory.
	12	After negotiations with Kendall Corporation concerning problems with the merchandise purchased on August 8, received a credit memorandum from Kendall granting a price reduction of $800.
	15	Received balance due from Griften Corp. for the August 5 sale.
	17	Purchased office equipment from WestCo on credit, $1,200, n/45.
	18	Paid the amount due Kendall Corporation for the August 8 purchase.
	19	Sold merchandise to Farley for $3,600 under credit terms of 1/10, n/30, FOB shipping point. The merchandise had cost $2,500.
	22	Farley requested a price reduction on the August 19 sale because the merchandise did not meet specifications. Sent Farley a credit memorandum for $600 to resolve the issue.
	29	Received Farley's payment of the amount due from the August 19 purchase.
	30	Paid Dickson Company the amount due from the August 1 purchase.

Problem 6-3A
Proprietorship work sheet, income statement, and closing entries—perpetual

LO9

The unadjusted trial balance of Classic Threads on December 31, 2001, the end of the annual accounting period, is as follows:

Classic Threads Unadjusted Trial Balance December 31, 2001	Debit	Credit
Cash	$ 10,275	
Accounts receivable	22,665	
Merchandise inventory	54,365	
Store supplies	2,415	
Office supplies	775	
Prepaid insurance	3,255	
Store equipment	61,980	
Accumulated amortization, store equipment		$ 10,830
Office equipment	12,510	
Accumulated amortization, office equipment		2,825
Accounts payable		8,000
Salaries payable		-0-
Sally Fowler, capital		106,015
Sally Fowler, withdrawals	15,000	
Interest revenue		310
Sales		562,140
Sales returns and allowances	5,070	
Cost of goods sold	381,160	
Sales salaries expense	43,220	
Rent expense, selling space	20,250	
Store supplies expense	-0-	
Amortization expense, store equipment	-0-	
Office salaries expense	48,330	
Rent expense, office space	8,850	
Office supplies expense	-0-	
Insurance expense	-0-	
Amortization expense, office equipment	-0-	
Totals	$690,120	$690,120

Required

1. Copy the unadjusted trial balance on a work sheet form and complete the work sheet using the information that follows:
   a. Ending store supplies inventory, $445.
   b. Ending office supplies inventory, $225.
   c. Expired insurance, $2,805.
   d. Amortization on the store equipment, $5,415.
   e. Amortization on the office equipment, $1,485.
   f. Accrued sales salaries payable, $445, and accrued office salaries payable, $210.
   g. A count of the merchandise inventory revealed a balance on hand December 31, 2001 of $53,800.
2. Prepare a multiple-step income statement showing in detail the expenses.

Check figure:
Income statement columns = $562,450

Problem 6-4A

Income statement computations and formats—perpetual

LO9

The following amounts appeared on Davison Company's adjusted trial balance as of October 31, 2002, the end of its fiscal year:

	Debit	Credit
Merchandise inventory	$ 31,000	
Other assets	128,400	
Liabilities		$ 35,000
Brenda Davison, capital		117,090
Brenda Davison, withdrawals	16,000	
Interest revenue		560
Sales		212,000
Sales discounts	3,250	
Sales returns and allowances	14,000	
Cost of goods sold	82,600	
Sales salaries expense	29,000	
Rent expense, selling space	10,000	
Store supplies expense	2,500	
Advertising expense	18,000	
Office salaries expense	26,500	
Rent expense, office space	2,600	
Office supplies expense	800	
Totals	$364,650	$364,650

Check figure:
Income from operations = $22,750

Required

1. Compute the company's net sales for the year.
2. Prepare a classified, multiple-step income statement for internal use (see Exhibit 6.17) that lists the company's net sales, cost of goods sold, and gross profit, as well as the components and amounts of selling expenses and general and administrative expenses.
3. Present a condensed single-step income statement that lists these costs: cost of goods sold, selling expenses, and general and administrative expenses.

Problem 6-5A

Closing entries and interpreting information about discounts and returns—perpetual

LO10

Use the data for Davison Company in Problem 6-4A to prepare closing entries for the company as of October 31.

Problem 6-6A
Income statements—perpetual

LO[9]

On December 31, 2001, the end of Seaside Sales' annual accounting period, the financial statement columns of its work sheet appeared as follows:

	Income Statement		Balance Sheet and Statement of Owner's Equity	
	Debit	**Credit**	**Debit**	**Credit**
Merchandise inventory			66,545	
Other assets			487,785	
Debra Kelso, capital				200,000
Liabilities				312,370
Debra Kelso, withdrawals			50,000	
Dividend revenue		720		
Sales		963,000		
Sales returns and allowances	5,715			
Sales discounts	14,580			
Cost of goods sold	652,025			
Sales salaries expense	80,080			
Rent expense, selling space	33,000			
Store supplies expense	1,620			
Amortization expense, store equipment	8,910			
Office salaries expense	65,945			
Rent expense, office space	3,000			
Office supplies expense	735			
Insurance expense	3,390			
Amortization expense, office equipment	2,760			
Totals	871,760	963,720	604,330	512,370
Net income	91,960			91,960
Totals	963,720	963,720	604,330	604,330

Required

1. Prepare a 2001 classified, multiple-step income statement for Seaside, showing in detail the expenses.
2. Prepare a single-step income statement. Condense each revenue and expense category into a single item.

Check figure:
Income from operations = $91,240

Problem 6-7A
Closing entries—perpetual

LO[10]

Using the information in Problem 6-6A, prepare compound closing entries for Seaside.

Problem 6-8A
Proprietorship work sheet, income statement, and closing entries—perpetual

LO 9, 10

The following unadjusted trial balance was prepared at the end of the fiscal year for Ruth's Place:

Ruth's Place
Unadjusted Trial Balance
December 31, 2001

		Debit	Credit
101	Cash	$ 4,000	
119	Merchandise inventory	11,500	
125	Store supplies	5,000	
128	Prepaid insurance	2,000	
165	Store equipment	45,000	
166	Accumulated amortization, equipment		$ 6,000
201	Accounts payable		8,000
301	Ruth Helm, capital		35,200
302	Ruth Helm, withdrawals	3,500	
413	Sales		90,000
415	Sales discounts	1,000	
505	Cost of goods sold	37,400	
612	Amortization expense, equipment		
622	Salaries expense	16,000	
637	Insurance expense		
640	Rent expense	5,000	
651	Supplies expense		
655	Advertising expense	8,800	
	Totals	$139,200	$139,200

Check figure:
Part 1: Income statement columns = $90,000

Required

1. Use the unadjusted trial balance and the following information to prepare a work sheet for the company:
   a. The ending inventory of supplies is $650.
   b. Expired insurance for the year is $1,200.
   c. Amortization expense for the year is $9,000.
   d. The ending merchandise inventory is $11,250.
2. Prepare a detailed multiple-step income statement that would be used by the store's owner.
3. Prepare a single-step income statement that would be provided to decision makers outside the company. Assume 80% of operating expenses are selling and 20% are general and administrative.

***Problem 6-9A**
Journal entries for merchandising transactions—periodic

LO11

Prepare General Journal entries to record the following transactions of Schafer Merchandising, assuming a periodic system (omit narratives):

Oct.	1	Purchased merchandise from Zeon Company on credit, terms 2/10, n/30, $7,200.
	2	Sold merchandise for cash, $750.
	7	Purchased merchandise on credit from Billings Co., terms 2/10, n/30, $5,250, FOB the seller's factory.
	7	Paid $225 cash for freight charges on the merchandise shipment of the previous transaction.
	8	Purchased delivery equipment from Finlay Supplies on credit, $12,000.
	12	Sold merchandise on credit to Comry Holdings, terms 2/15, 1/30, n/60, $3,000.
	13	Received a $750 credit memorandum for merchandise purchased on October 7 and returned for credit.
	13	Purchased office supplies on credit from Staples, $240, n/30.
	15	Sold merchandise on credit to Tom Willis, terms 2/10, 1/30, n/60, $2,100.
	15	Paid for the merchandise purchased on October 7.
	16	Received a credit memorandum for unsatisfactory office supplies purchased on October 13 and returned, $60.
	19	Issued a $210 credit memorandum to the customer who purchased merchandise on October 15 and returned a portion for credit.
	25	Received payment for the merchandise sold on October 15.
	27	The customer of October 12 paid for the purchase of that date.
	31	Paid for the merchandise purchased on October 1.

***Problem 6-10A**
Income statement computations and formats—periodic

LO11

The following amounts appeared on the Gershwin Company's adjusted trial balance as of October 31, 2001 the end of its fiscal year:

	Debit	Credit
Merchandise inventory	$ 25,000	
Other assets	140,000	
Liabilities		$ 37,000
George Gershwin, capital		117,350
George Gershwin, withdrawals	17,000	
Interest revenue		300
Sales		210,000
Sales returns and allowances	15,000	
Sales discounts	2,250	
Purchases	90,000	
Purchases returns and allowances		4,300
Purchases discounts		1,800
Transportation-in	3,100	
Sales salaries expense	28,000	
Rent expense, selling space	10,000	
Store supplies expense	3,000	
Advertising expense	18,000	
Office salaries expense	16,000	
Rent expense, office space	2,500	
Office supplies expense	900	
Totals	$370,750	$370,750

A physical count shows that the cost of the ending inventory is $27,000.

An asterisk (*) identifies assignment material based on Appendix 6A or Appendix 6B.

Check figures:
3. $85,000
4. Income from operations = $29,350

Required

1. Calculate the company's net sales for the year.
2. Calculate the company's cost of goods purchased for the year.
3. Calculate the company's cost of goods sold for the year.
4. Present a classified multiple-step income statement that lists the company's net sales, cost of goods sold, and gross profit, as well as the components and amounts of selling expenses and general and administrative expenses.
5. Present a condensed single-step income statement that lists these expenses: cost of goods sold, selling expenses, and general and administrative expenses.

*Problem 6-11A
Closing entries—periodic

LO[11]

Use the data for the Gershwin Company in *Problem 6-10A to prepare closing entries for the company as of October 31.

*Problem 6-12A
Proprietorship work sheet, income statement and closing entries—periodic

LO[11]

The December 31, 2001 year-end, unadjusted trial balance of the ledger of Eastman Store, a sole proprietorship business, is as follows:

Eastman Store
Unadjusted Trial Balance
December 31, 2001

	Debit	Credit
Cash	$ 7,305	
Merchandise inventory	47,000	
Store supplies	1,715	
Office supplies	645	
Prepaid insurance	3,840	
Store equipment	57,735	
Accumulated amortization, store equipment		$ 9,575
Office equipment	14,130	
Accumulated amortization, office equipment		3,670
Accounts payable		4,000
Bob Eastman, capital		93,585
Bob Eastman, withdrawals	31,500	
Rental revenue		680
Sales		478,850
Sales returns and allowances	3,185	
Sales discounts	5,190	
Purchases	331,315	
Purchases returns and allowances		1,845
Purchases discounts		4,725
Transportation-in	2,810	
Sales salaries expense	34,710	
Rent expense, selling space	24,000	
Advertising expense	1,220	
Store supplies expense	-0-	
Amortization expense, store equipment	-0-	
Office supplies expense	27,630	
Rent expense, office space	3,000	
Office supplies expense	-0-	
Insurance expense	-0-	
Amortization expense, office equipment	-0-	
Totals	$596,930	$596,930

An asterisk (*) identifies assignment material based on Appendix 6A or Appendix 6B.

Required

1. Copy the unadjusted trial balance on an 8-column work sheet form and complete the work sheet using the following information:
   a. Store supplies inventory, $385.
   b. Office supplies inventory, $180.
   c. Expired insurance, $2,765.
   d. Amortization on the store equipment, $5,865.
   e. Amortization on the office equipment, $1,755.
   f. Ending merchandise inventory, $48,980.
2. Journalize closing entries for the store. Use page 10 for your journal.
3. Open a balance column Merchandise Inventory account (110) and enter a December 31, 2000 balance of $47,000. Then post those portions of the closing entries that affect the account.

Check figure:
1. Balance sheet columns = $161,290

Alternate Problems

Problem 6-1B
Journal entries for merchandising activities—perpetual

LO5, 6

Prepare General Journal entries to record the following perpetual system merchandising transactions of Minchew Company. (Use a separate account for each receivable and payable; for example, record the purchase on May 2 in Accounts Payable—Mobley Co.) Minchew Company does not use supplemental records for inventory accounting.

May	2	Purchased merchandise from Mobley Co. for $9,000 under credit terms of 1/15, n/30, FOB factory.
	4	Sold merchandise to Cornerstone Co. for $1,200 under credit terms of 2/10, n/60, FOB shipping point. The merchandise had cost $750.
	4	Paid $150 for freight charges on the purchase of May 2.
	9	Sold merchandise that cost $1,800 for $2,400 cash.
	10	Purchased merchandise from Richter Co. for $3,450 under credit terms of 2/15, n/60, FOB destination.
	12	Received a $300 credit memorandum acknowledging the return of merchandise purchased on May 10.
	14	Received the balance due from Cornerstone Co. for the credit sale dated May 4.
	15	Sold for cash a piece of office equipment for its original cost, $500.
	17	Paid the balance due to Mobley Co.
	18	Purchased $820 of cleaning supplies from A & Z Suppliers; terms n/15.
	20	Sold merchandise that cost $1,350 to Harrill Co. for $1,875 under credit terms of 2/15, n/60, FOB shipping point.
	22	Issued a $225 credit memorandum to Harrill Co. for an allowance on goods sold on May 20.
	23	Received a debit memorandum from Harrill Co. for an error that overstated the total invoice by $75.
	25	Paid Richter Co. the balance due.
	31	Received the balance due from Harrill Co. for the credit sale dated May 20.
	31	Sold merchandise that cost $4,800 to Cornerstone Co. for $7,500 under credit terms of 2/10, n/60, FOB shipping point.

Problem 6-2B

Journal entries for merchandising activities—perpetual

LO5, 6

Prepare General Journal entries to record the following perpetual system merchandising transactions of Treadwell Company. (Use a separate account for each receivable and payable; for example, record the purchase on July 3 in Accounts Payable—CMP Corp.) Treadwell Company does not use supplemental records for inventory accounting.

July 3	Purchased merchandise from CMP Corp. for $15,000 under credit terms of 1/10, n/30, FOB destination.
4	At CMP's request, paid $250 for freight charges on the July 3 purchase, reducing the amount owed to CMP.
7	Sold merchandise to Harbison Co. for $10,500 under credit terms of 2/10, n/60, FOB destination. The merchandise had cost $7,500.
10	Purchased merchandise from Cimarron Corporation for $13,250 under credit terms of 1/10, n/45, FOB shipping point, plus $600 shipping charges. The invoice showed that at Treadwell's request, Cimarron had paid the $600 shipping charges and added that amount to the bill.
11	Paid $300 shipping charges related to the July 7 sale to Harbison Co.
12	Harbison returned merchandise from the July 7 sale that had cost $1,250 and been sold for $1,750. The merchandise was restored to inventory.
14	After negotiations with Cimarron Corporation concerning problems with the merchandise purchased on July 10, received a credit memorandum from Cimarron granting a price reduction of $2,000.
17	Received balance due from Harbison Co. for the July 7 sale.
18	Sold for cash a piece of vacant land for its original cost of $15,000.
19	Purchased a used van for the business, $18,000; paid cash of $5,000 and borrowed the balance from the bank.
20	Paid the amount due Cimarron Corporation for the July 10 purchase.
21	Sold merchandise to Hess for $9,000 under credit terms of 1/10, n/30, FOB shipping point. The merchandise had cost $6,250.
24	Hess requested a price reduction on the July 21 sale because the merchandise did not meet specifications. Sent Hess a credit memorandum for $1,500 to resolve the issue.
31	Received Hess' payment of the amount due from the July 21 purchase.
31	Paid CMP Corp. the amount due from the July 3 purchase.

Problem 6-3B

Adjusting and closing entries, income statements—perpetual

LO9

The following unadjusted trial balance was prepared at the end of the fiscal year for Resource Products Company:

Resource Products Company
Unadjusted Trial Balance
October 31, 2001

	Debit	Credit
Cash	$ 6,400	
Merchandise inventory	23,000	
Store supplies	9,600	
Prepaid insurance	4,600	
Store equipment	83,800	
Accumulated amortization, store equipment		$ 30,000
Accounts payable		16,000
Jan Smithers, capital		70,400
Jan Smithers, withdrawals	6,000	
Sales		208,000
Sales discounts	2,000	
Sales returns and allowances	4,000	
Cost of goods sold	74,800	
Amortization expense, store equipment		
Salaries expense	62,000	
Interest expense	400	
Insurance expense		
Rent expense	28,000	
Store supplies expense		
Advertising expense	19,800	
Totals	$324,400	$324,400

Rent and salaries expense are equally divided between the selling and administrative functions. Resource Products Company uses a perpetual inventory system.

Required

1. Copy the unadjusted trial balance on a work sheet form and complete the work sheet using the following information:
   a. Store supplies on hand at year-end amount to $3,300.
   b. Expired insurance, an administrative expense, for the year is $3,000.
   c. Amortization expense, a selling expense, is $2,800 for the year.
   d. A physical count of the ending merchandise inventory shows $22,200 of goods on hand.
2. Prepare a multiple-step income statement.

Check figure: Income statement columns = $208,000

Problem 6-4B

Income statement calculations and formats—perpetual

LO[9]

The following amounts appeared on Reyna Company's adjusted trial balance as of May 31, 2001 the end of its fiscal year:

	Debit	Credit
Merchandise inventory	$ 46,500	
Other assets	192,600	
Liabilities		$ 52,500
Paul Reyna, capital		176,475
Paul Reyna, withdrawals	24,000	
Sales		318,000
Sales discounts	4,875	
Sales returns and allowances	21,000	
Cost of goods sold	123,900	
Sales salaries expense	43,500	
Rent expense, selling space	15,000	
Store supplies expense	3,750	
Advertising expense	27,000	
Office salaries expense	39,750	
Rent expense, office space	3,900	
Office supplies expense	1,200	
Totals	$546,975	$546,975

Check figure:
Net income = $34,125

Required

1. Compute the company's net sales for the year.
2. Present a classified multiple-step income statement for internal users that lists the company's net sales, cost of goods sold, and gross profit, as well the components and amounts of selling expenses and general and administrative expenses.
3. Present a condensed single-step income statement that lists these costs: cost of goods sold, selling expenses, and general and administrative expenses.

Problem 6-5B

Closing entries and interpreting information about discounts and returns—perpetual

LO[10]

Use the data for Reyna Company in Problem 6-4B to prepare closing entries for the company as of May 31.

Problem 6-6B
Income statements—perpetual

LO[9]

On December 31, 2001, the end of Bandara Sales' annual accounting period, the financial statement columns of its work sheet appeared as follows in alphabetical order:

	Income Statement		Balance Sheet and Statement of Owner's Equity	
	Debit	**Credit**	**Debit**	**Credit**
Amortization expense, office equipment	3,450			
Amortization expense, store equipment	16,020			
Cost of goods sold	649,820			
Diego Amara, capital				232,735
Diego Amara, withdrawals			102,500	
Insurance expense	6,200			
Liabilities				420,000
Merchandise inventory			17,000	
Other assets			520,000	
Rent expense (80% sales)	49,760			
Salaries expense (70% sales)	213,550			
Sales		946,300		
Sales discounts	1,390			
Sales returns and allowances	7,345			
Supplies expense (35% sales)	12,000			
Totals	959,535	946,300	639,500	652,735
Net loss		13,235	13,235	
Totals	959,535	959,535	652,735	652,735

Required

1. Prepare a classified, multiple-step income statement for Bandara Sales, showing in detail the expenses.
2. Prepare a single-step income statement. Condense each revenue and expense category into a single item.

Check figure:
1. Total operating expenses = $300,980

Problem 6-7B
Closing entries—perpetual

LO[10]

Using the information in Problem 6-6B, prepare compound closing entries for Bandara Sales.

Problem 6-8B
Adjusting entries, income statements—perpetual

LO 9, 10

The following unadjusted trial balance was prepared at the end of the fiscal year for Tinker Sales Company:

Tinker Sales Company
Unadjusted Trial Balance
July 31, 2001

	Debit	Credit
Cash	$ 4,200	
Merchandise inventory	11,500	
Store supplies	4,800	
Prepaid insurance	2,300	
Store equipment	41,900	
Accumulated amortization, equipment		$ 15,000
Accounts payable		9,000
Betsey Tinker, capital		35,200
Betsey Tinker, withdrawals	3,200	
Sales		104,000
Sales discounts	1,000	
Sales returns and allowances	2,000	
Cost of goods sold	37,400	
Amortization expense, equipment		
Salaries expense	31,000	
Insurance expense		
Rent expense	14,000	
Supplies expense		
Advertising expense	9,900	
Totals	$163,200	$163,200

Rent and salaries expense are equally divided between the selling and general and administrative functions. Tinker Sales Company uses a perpetual inventory system.

Check figures:
Part 1: Income statement columns = 104,000
Part 3: Total expenses = 98,750

Required

1. Copy the unadjusted trial balance on a work sheet form and complete the work sheet using the following information:
   a. Supplies on hand at year-end amount to $1,650.
   b. Expired insurance for the year is $1,500.
   c. Amortization expense for the year is $1,400.
   d. A physical count of the ending merchandise inventory shows $11,100 of goods on hand.
2. Prepare a multiple-step income statement for external users.
3. Prepare a single-step income statement. Assume 50% of operating expenses are selling and 50% are general and administrative.

***Problem 6-9B**
Journal entries for merchandising transactions—periodic

LO11

Prepare General Journal entries to record the following transactions of Schafer Merchandising, assuming a periodic system:

March	1	Purchased merchandise on credit terms form Zender Holdings, terms 1/10, n/15, $20,000.
	2	Sold merchandise for cash, $1,800.
	7	Purchased merchandise on credit from Red River Co., terms 2/10, n/30, $16,000, FOB the seller's factory.
	8	Incurred freight charges for $350 on credit to Dan's Shipping regarding the merchandise shipment of the previous transaction.
	12	Sold merchandise on credit to Bev Dole, terms 2/10, n/45, $9,000.
	13	Received a $500 credit memorandum for merchandise purchased on March 7 and returned for credit.
	14	Purchased furniture for the office on credit from Wilson Supplies, $1,600.
	15	Sold merchandise on credit to Ted Smith, terms 2/10, n/45, $17,000.
	16	Paid for the merchandise purchased on March 7.
	17	Issued a credit memorandum to the customer of March 15 granting an allowance of $1,000 due to damage during shipment.
	19	The supplier issued a credit memorandum for $750 regarding unsatisfactory furniture purchased on March 14 and returned.
	24	Received payment for the merchandise sold on March 15.
	27	The customer of March 12 paid for the purchase of that date.
	31	Paid for the merchandise purchased on March 1.

***Problem 6-10B**
Income statement computations and formats—periodic

LO11

The following amounts appeared on the Garneau Company's adjusted trial balance in alphabetical order as of November 30, 2001, the end of its fiscal year:

	Debit	Credit
Advertising expense	$ 6,000	
Interest expense	700	
Liabilities		$ 62,000
Merchandise inventory	50,000	
Other assets	289,300	
Purchase discounts		2,300
Purchase returns and allowances		8,100
Purchases	240,000	
Rent expense (70% selling space; 30% office space)	72,000	
Salaries expense (60% sales salaries; 40% office salaries)	120,000	
Sales		540,000
Sales discounts	4,700	
Sales returns and allowances	57,000	
Supplies expense (35% selling supplies; 65% office supplies)	10,000	
Teresa Garneau, capital		267,000
Teresa Garneau, withdrawals	20,000	
Transportation-in	9,700	
Totals	$879,400	$879,400

A physical count shows that the cost of the ending inventory is $32,000.

An asterisk (*) identifies assignment material based on Appendix 6A or Appendix 6B.

Check figures:
3. $257,300
4. Income from operations = $13,000

Required

1. Calculate the company's net sales for the year.
2. Calculate the company's cost of goods purchased for the year.
3. Calculate the company's cost of goods sold for the year.
4. Present a classified multiple-step income statement that lists the company's net sales, cost of goods sold, and gross profit, as well as the components and amounts of selling expenses and general and administrative expenses.
5. Present a modified single-step income statement that lists these expenses: cost of goods sold, selling expenses, general and administrative expenses, and interest expense.

*Problem 6-11B

Closing entries

LO11

Use the data for the Garneau Company in *Problem 6-10B to prepare closing entries for the company as of November 30, 2001.

*Problem 6-12B

Proprietorship work sheet, income statement, and closing entries—periodic

LO11

The March 31, 2001 year-end, unadjusted trial balance of The Downtown Store, a sole proprietorship business, is as follows:

The Downtown Store
Unadjusted Trial Balance
July 31, 2001

	Debit	Credit
Cash	$ 14,000	
Merchandise inventory	96,000	
Supplies	1,200	
Prepaid rent	14,000	
Store equipment	120,000	
Accumulated amortization, store equipment		$ 28,000
Office equipment	46,000	
Accumulated amortization, office equipment		13,000
Accounts payable		32,000
Lucy Baker, capital		269,200
Lucy Baker, withdrawals	68,000	
Sales		998,000
Sales returns and allowances	23,000	
Sales discounts	12,000	
Purchases	692,000	
Purchase returns and allowances		5,700
Purchase discounts		14,300
Transportation-in	32,000	
Sales salaries expense	120,000	
Rent expense (80% selling space; 20% office space)	84,000	
Advertising expense	14,000	
Supplies expense (30% selling supplies; 70% office supplies)	17,000	
Rent expense	7,000	
Amortization expense, store equipment	-0-	
Amortization expense, office equipment	-0-	
Totals	$1,360,200	$1,360,200

An asterisk (*) identifies assignment material based on Appendix 6A or Appendix 6B.

Required

1. Copy the unadjusted trial balance on an 8-column work sheet form and complete the work sheet using the following information:
   a. Supplies inventory at year-end, $900.
   b. Expired rent, $4,300.
   c. Amortization on the store equipment, $3,200.
   d. Amortization on the office equipment, $2,900.
   e. Ending merchandise inventory, $18,000.
2. Journalize closing entries for the store. Use page 14 for your journal.
3. Open a balance column Merchandise Inventory account (110) and enter the March 31, 2000 balance of $96,000. Then post those portions of the closing entries that affect the account.

Check figure:
1. Balance sheet columns = $348,300

Analytical and Review Problems

A & R Problem 6-1 —Perpetual

The partially completed work sheet of Missing Information Company appears below:

Missing Information Company
Work Sheet
For Year Ended October 31, 2001

Account	Unadjusted Trial Balance		Adjustments		Adjusted Trial Balance		Income Statement		Balance Sheet & Statement of Owner's Equity	
	Debit	Credit	Debit	Credit	Debit	Credit	Debit	Credit	Debit	Credit
Cash									14,000	
Merchandise inventory				300					2,800	
Trucks	28,000									
Accumulated amortization, trucks				730						11,650
Accounts payable				450		3,100				
Wages payable		-0-								
Brian Westside, capital										
Brian Westside, withdrawals					36,000					
Sales						141,000				
Sales returns and allowances	1,950									
Sales discounts							675			
Cost of goods sold	62,000									
Amortization expense, trucks										
Wages expense	38,200		1,250							
Interest expense			-0-		185					
Telephone expense	4,800									
Totals										

Required

Complete the work sheet for the year ended October 31, 2001.

A & R Problem 6-2 —Perpetual

The following are the selected data for the Allen Sales Company for the year ended December 31, 2001.

1. Selected closing entries:

Dec. 31	Income Summary	304,000	
	Cost of Goods Sold		212,700
	Sales Salaries Expense		40,000
	Advertising Expense		10,000
	Rent Expense, Office Space		8,000
	Delivery Expense		4,800
	Office Salaries Expense		26,000
	Amortization, Office Equipment		2,000
	Miscellaneous Expense		500
	To close expense and other nominal accounts.		
31	Greg Allen, Capital	28,000	
	Greg Allen, Withdrawals		28,000
	To close the withdrawals account.		

2. Greg Allen follows the practice of withdrawing half of the annual net income from the business.
3. There were no sales returns and allowances for the year. However, sales discounts amounted to $2,000.

Required

For the year ended December 31, 2001:

1. Compute the amount of net income.
2. Compute sales.
3. Prepare a classified, multiple-step income statement.

*A & R Problem 6-3 —Periodic

Required

Using the following chart to organize your answer, prepare journal entries for each of the transactions listed below under both the perpetual and periodic inventory systems.

Transaction	Perpetual	Periodic

a. Sold merchandise for $2,000 granting the customer terms of 2/10, EOM. The cost of the merchandise was $1,400.
b. Purchased 500 units of product with a list price of $5 per unit. The terms of the sale were 1/10, n/60.
c. The customer in (a) above returned merchandise and received credit for $600. The merchandise, which had a cost of $240, was returned to inventory.
d. Received payment within 10 days of sale for the amount due regarding transaction (a) above.
e. After brief negotiations, received a $75 allowance on the purchase of (b).
f. Paid within the discount period the amount owed regarding the purchase of (b) above.

An asterisk (*) identifies assignment material based on Appendix 6A or Appendix 6B.

The partially completed work sheet of Incomplete Data Company appears below:

***A & R Problem 6-4 —Periodic**

Incomplete Data Company
Work Sheet
For the Year Ended December 31, 2001

	Unadjusted Trial Balance		Adjustments		Income Statement		Balance Sheet & Statement of Owner's Equity	
Account	**Debit**	**Credit**	**Debit**	**Credit**	**Debit**	**Credit**	**Debit**	**Credit**
Cash	36,780							
Accounts receivable							4,600	
Merchandise inventory					31,400	26,400		
Prepaid fire insurance	720						480	
Prepaid rent	4,800							
Office equipment							12,000	
Accum. amortization, office equipment		4,500						
Accounts payable		8,000						
Clay Camp, capital		24,000						
Clay Camp, withdrawals							20,000	
Sales		320,000						
Sales returns and allowances					1,000			
Purchases	219,200							
Purchases returns and allowances						1,400		
Advertising expense	1,000							
Supplies expense	1,800							
Salaries expense	23,200							
Utilities expense	1,400							
Fire insurance expense								
Rent expense					2,400			
Amortization expense, office equipment					1,600			
Salaries payable								660

Required
Complete the work sheet for the year ended December 31, 2001.

An asterisk (*) identifies assignment material based on Appendix 6A or Appendix 6B.

Serial Problem

Echo Systems — perpetual or *periodic

Note: Solutions are available for both perpetual and *periodic.

(The first three segments of this comprehensive problem were presented in Chapters 3, 4, and 5. If those segments have not been completed, the assignment can begin at this point. However, you should use the Working Papers that accompany this text because they reflect the account balances that resulted from posting the entries required in Chapters 3, 4, and 5.)

Earlier segments of this problem have described how Mary Graham created Echo Systems on October 1, 2001. The company has been successful, and its list of customers has started to grow. To accommodate the growth, the accounting system is ready to be modified to set up separate accounts for each customer. The following list of customers includes the account number used for each account and any balance as of the end of 2001. Graham decided to add a fourth digit with a decimal point to the 106 account number that had been used for the single Accounts Receivable account. This modification allows the existing chart of accounts to continue being used. The list also shows the balances that two customers owed as of December 31, 2001:

Customer Account	No.	Dec. 31 Balance
Alamo Engineering Co.	106.1	-0-
Buckman Services	106.2	-0-
Capital Leasing	106.3	-0-
Decker Co.	106.4	$1,350
Elite Corporation	106.5	-0-
Fostek Co.	106.6	$1,500
Grandview Co.	106.7	-0-
Hacienda, Inc.	106.8	-0-
Images, Inc.	106.9	-0-

In response to frequent requests from customers, Graham has decided to begin selling computer software. The company will extend credit terms of 1/10, n/30 to customers who purchase merchandise. No cash discount will be available on consulting fees. The following additional accounts were added to the General Ledger to allow the system to account for the company's new merchandising activities:

Account	No.
Merchandise Inventory	119
Sales	413
Sales Discounts	414
Sales Returns and Allowances	415
Cost of Goods Sold	502

Because the accounting system does not use reversing entries, all revenue and expense accounts have zero balances as of January 1, 2002.

Required

1. Prepare journal entries to record each of the following transactions for Echo Systems, assuming either a perpetual system or a periodic system.
2. Post the journal entries to the accounts in the company's General Ledger. (Use asset, liability, and equity accounts that start with balances as of December 31, 2001.)
3. Prepare a partial work sheet consisting of the first six columns showing the unadjusted trial balance, the March 31 adjustments, and the adjusted trial balance. Do not prepare closing entries and do not journalize the adjusting entries or post them to the ledger.
4. Prepare an interim multiple-step income statement for the three months ended March 31, 2002. Use a single-step format. List all expenses without differentiating between selling expenses and general and administrative expenses.
5. Prepare an interim statement in owner's equity for the three months ended March 31, 2002.
6. Prepare an interim balance sheet as of March 31, 2002.

Transactions:

Jan.	4	Paid Carly Smith for five days at the rate of $100 per day, including one day in addition to the four unpaid days from the prior year.
	5	Mary Graham invested an additional $24,000 cash in the business.
	7	Purchased $5,600 of merchandise from Shephard Corp. with terms of 1/10, n/30, FOB shipping point.
	9	Received $1,500 from Fostek Co. as final payment on its account.
	11	Completed five-day project for Alamo Engineering Co. and billed them $4,500, which is the total price of $6,000 less the advance payment of $1,500.
	13	Sold merchandise with a retail value of $4,200 and a cost of $3,360 to Elite Corporation with terms of 1/10, n/30, FOB shipping point.
	15	Paid $700 for freight charges on the merchandise purchased on January 7.
	16	Received $3,000 cash from Grandview Co. for computer services.
	17	Paid Shephard Corp. for the purchase on January 7.
	20	Elite Corporation returned $400 of defective merchandise from its purchase on January 13. The returned merchandise, which had a cost of $320, was scrapped.
	22	Received the balance due from Elite Corporation.
	24	Returned defective merchandise to Shephard Corp. and accepted credit against future purchases. Its cost, net of the discount, was $396.
	26	Purchased $8,000 of merchandise from Shephard Corp. with terms of 1/10, n/30, FOB destination.
	26	Sold merchandise with a cost of $4,640 for $5,800 on credit to Hacienda, Inc.
	29	Received a $396 credit memo from Shephard Corp. concerning the merchandise returned on January 24.
	31	Paid Carly Smith for 10 days' work at $100 per day.
Feb.	1	Paid $3,375 to the Lakeshore Mall for another three months' rent in advance.
	3	Paid Shephard Corp. for the balance due.
	5	Paid $800 to the local newspaper for advertising.
	11	Received the balance due from Alamo Engineering Co. for fees billed on January 11.
	15	Mary Graham withdrew $4,800 cash for personal use.
	23	Sold merchandise with a cost of $2,560 for $3,200 on credit to Grandview Co.
	26	Paid Carly Smith for eight days' work at $100 per day.
	27	Reimbursed Mary Graham's business automobile expenses for 600 kilometres at $0.50 per kilometre.
Mar.	8	Purchased $2,400 of computer supplies from Abbott Office Products on credit.
	9	Received the balance due from Grandview Co. for merchandise sold on February 23.
	11	Repaired the company's computer at the cost of $860.
	16	Received $4,260 cash from Images, Inc. for computing services.
	19	Paid the full amount due to Abbott Office Products, including amounts created on December 15 and March 8.
	24	Billed Capital Leasing for $5,900 of computing services.
	25	Sold merchandise with a cost of $1,002 for $1,800 on credit to Buckman Services.
	30	Sold merchandise with a cost of $1,100 for $2,220 on credit to Decker Company.
	31	Reimbursed Mary Graham's business automobile expenses for 400 kilometres at $0.50 per kilometre.

Information for the March 31 adjustments and financial statements:

a. The March 31 inventory of computer supplies is $2,115.
b. Three more months have passed since the company purchased the annual insurance policy at the cost of $2,160.
c. Carly Smith has not been paid for seven days of work.
d. Three months have passed since any prepaid rent cost has been transferred to expense. The monthly rent is $1,125.
e. Amortization on the computer for January through March is $1,125.
f. Amortization on the office equipment for January through March is $750.
g. The March 31 inventory of merchandise is $980.

CHAPTER

Merchandise Inventory and Cost of Sales

High Turnover

Inventory management is a priority for today's merchandiser, especially if it is in the computer business like Macrotronics. Operating out of locations in Edmonton, Vancouver, Calgary, and Cold Lake, Macrotronics offers custom-built computers to its many satisfied corporate and homeowner clients. Macrotronics' owner, Wilson Mak, is dedicated to his family-run business that focuses on service, leading-edge hardware, and competitive pricing.

With sales last year of more than $6 million, you may be surprised to find that the company's back room does not have shelves full of inventory. "Inventory has a shelf life of less than two weeks in this business," says Mak. "It is not unusual for the value of

Learning Objectives

LO1 Identify the items making up merchandise inventory.

LO2 Identify the costs of merchandise inventory.

LO3 Compute inventory in a perpetual system using the methods of specific identification, weighted average, FIFO, and LIFO.

LO4 Analyze the effects of inventory methods for financial reporting.

LO5 Analyze the effects of inventory errors on current and future financial statements.

LO6 Compute the lower of cost or market value of inventory.

LO7 Apply both the gross profit and retail inventory methods to estimate inventory.

inventory to drop 10% on average per month or even 30% on some items because computer technology is changing so fast. If I buy $100,000 of inventory that does not sell for a month, it is probable that at the end of the month it is worth less than $90,000. That means we've lost more than $10,000 in just a month. So the faster we sell, the less the impact of price changes."

To keep inventory levels down to a minimum, Wilson depends on three things: the ability of his sales personnel to communicate sales requirements, a good relationship with suppliers, and a perpetual inventory system that provides up-to-date information. "Inventory management is critical in my business."

www.macrotronics.com

Chapter Preview

Activities of merchandising companies involve the purchase and resale of products. We explained accounting for merchandisers in the last chapter and explained how perpetual and periodic inventory systems P. 259 account for merchandise inventory. In this chapter, we extend our study and analysis of inventory by identifying the items that make up inventory and how they are computed. We also explain methods used to assign costs to merchandise inventory and to cost of goods sold. These methods include those that differ from historical cost. The principles and methods we describe are used in department stores, grocery stores, and many other merchandising companies that purchase products for resale. These principles and methods affect reported amounts of income, assets, and equity. Understanding these fundamental concepts of inventory accounting increases our ability to analyze and interpret financial statements. As Wilson Mak says in the opening article, an understanding of these topics also helps in running one's own business.

Accounting for inventory affects both the balance sheet and income statement. A major goal in accounting for inventory is matching P. 140 relevant costs against revenues. This is important to properly compute income.[1] We use the matching principle when accounting for inventory to decide how much of the cost of the goods available for sale is deducted from sales and how much is carried forward as inventory and matched against future sales. Management must make this decision and several others when accounting for inventory. These decisions include selecting the:

- Items included and their costs.
- Costing method (specific identification, weighted average, FIFO, or LIFO)
- Inventory system (perpetual or periodic)
- Use of market or other estimates.

These selections affect the reported amounts for inventory, cost of goods sold, gross profit P. 257, income, current assets, and other accounts. This chapter discusses all of these important issues and their reporting effects.

Inventory Items and Costs

Items in Merchandise Inventory

LO1 Identify the items making up merchandise inventory.

Merchandise inventory includes all goods owned by a company and held for sale. This rule holds regardless of where goods are located at the time inventory is counted. Most inventory items are no problem when applying this rule, but certain items require special attention. These include goods in transit, goods on consignment, and goods damaged or obsolete.

Goods in Transit

Do we include in a purchaser's inventory the goods in transit from a supplier? Our answer depends on whether the rights and risks of ownership have passed from the supplier to the purchaser: whether the goods are FOB shipping point P. 265 or FOB destination P. 265. If ownership has passed to the purchaser, they are included in the purchaser's inventory.

[1] *CICA Handbook*, section 3030, "Inventories," par. 09.

Goods on Consignment

Goods on consignment are goods shipped by their owner, called the **consignor**, to another party called the **consignee**. A consignee is to sell goods for the owner. Consigned goods are owned by the consignor and are reported in the consignor's inventory.

Goods Damaged or Obsolete

Damaged goods and obsolete (or deteriorated) goods are not counted in inventory if they are unsalable. If these goods are salable at a reduced price, they are included in inventory at a conservative estimate of their *net realizable value (NRV)*. **Net realizable value** is sales price minus the cost of making the sale. The period when damage or obsolescence (or deterioration) occurs is the period where the loss is reported.

Costs of Merchandise Inventory

Identify the costs of merchandise inventory.

Costs included in merchandise inventory are those expenditures necessary, directly or indirectly, in bringing an item to a salable condition and location.[2] This means the cost of an inventory item includes its invoice price minus any discount, plus any added or incidental costs necessary to put it in a place and condition for sale. Added or incidental costs can include import duties, transportation-in, storage, insurance, and costs incurred in an aging process (for example, aging of wine and cheese).

Accounting principles imply that incidental costs are assigned to every unit purchased. This is so that all inventory costs are properly matched against revenue in the period when inventory is sold. The **materiality principle** states that an amount may not be ignored if its effect on the financial statements is important to their users. The *materiality principle* or the *cost-to-benefit constraint* is used by some companies to not assign incidental costs of acquiring merchandise to inventory. These companies argue either that incidental costs are immaterial or that the effort in assigning these costs to inventory outweighs the benefits. Such companies price inventory using invoice prices only. When this is done, the incidental costs are allocated to cost of goods sold in the period when they are incurred.

Physical Count of Merchandise Inventory

To help determine the value of inventory included on financial statements, units on hand need to be confirmed through a **physical count** (also known as **taking an inventory**). This often occurs at the end of the fiscal year P. 37 or when inventory amounts are low. The physical count is used to adjust the Merchandise Inventory account balance to the actual inventory on hand. Differences occur because of events including theft, loss, damage and errors. This means that nearly all companies take a physical count of inventory at least once each year regardless of whether a perpetual or periodic inventory system is in place.

---

[2] Ibid., par. 3030.02.

Exhibit 7.1

Inventory Ticket

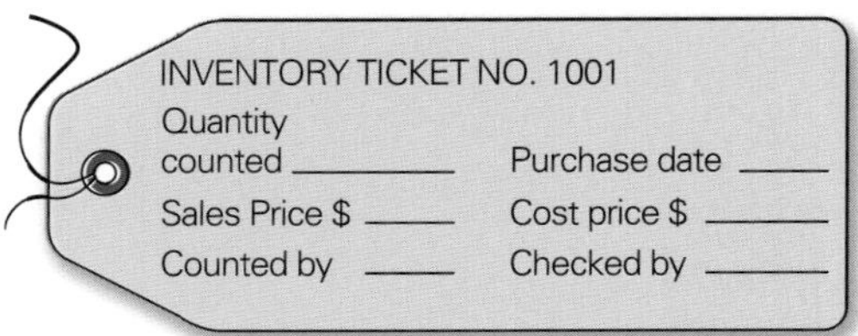

When performing a physical count of inventory, *internal controls* should be followed to minimize errors. **Internal controls**, discussed in more detail in Chapter 9, are the policies and procedures used to protect assets, ensure reliable accounting, promote efficient operations, and urge adherence to company policies. An example of an internal control technique is the use of prenumbered inventory tickets, one for each product on hand, to reduce the risk of items being counted more than once or omitted. We show a typical inventory ticket in Exhibit 7.1. By multiplying the number of units counted for each product by its unit cost, we get the dollar amount for each product in inventory. The sum total of all products is the dollar amount reported for inventory on the balance sheet.

In lieu of inventory tickets, the merchandise inventory items of many businesses are labelled with UPC (Universal Product Code) bar codes. The UPC bar codes are not only used for the pricing and costing of sales, but can also be used to make physical counts easier.

If you look at any grocery product, you will find a UPC bar code printed on the package. Universal Product Codes were created in 1973 to assist in the checkout and inventory process of grocery stores, and UPC bar codes have since spread to nearly every item in the retail world. The Uniform Code Council (UCC) is responsible for issuing the manufacturer's portion of the code. The manufacturer's UPC coordinator assigns the next digits as the item number. The retailer can then assign a price to each individual UPC code along with costing information. In this way, inventory and sales records can be updated instantly when the bar code is scanned.

Answers—p. 352

1. If Irwin Toy sells goods to The Bay with terms FOB Irwin Toy's factory, does Irwin Toy or The Bay report these goods in its inventory when they are in transit?
2. An art gallery purchases a painting for $11,400. Additional costs in obtaining and offering the artwork for sale include $130 for transportation-in, $150 for import duties, $100 for insurance during shipment, $180 for advertising, $400 for framing, and $800 for sales salaries. For computing inventory cost, what is assigned to the painting?

Assigning Costs to Inventory

LO3 Compute inventory in a perpetual system using the methods of specific identification, weighted average, FIFO, and LIFO.

One of the most important decisions in accounting for inventory is determining the per unit costs assigned to inventory items. When all units are purchased at the same unit cost, this process is simple, but when identical items are purchased at different costs, a question arises as to what amounts are recorded in cost of goods sold when sales occur and what amounts remain in inventory. When using a perpetual inventory system, we must record cost of goods sold and reductions in inventory as sales occur. A periodic inventory system determines cost of goods sold and inventory amounts at the end of a period. How we assign these costs to inventory and cost of goods sold affects the reported amounts for both systems.

There are four methods often used in assigning costs to inventory and cost of goods sold:

- specific identification
- weighted average
- first-in, first-out (FIFO)
- last-in, first-out (LIFO).

Each method assumes a particular pattern for how costs flow through inventory. All four methods are accepted under GAAP P. 42 and are described in this section.

The inventory cost flow assumption does not necessarily match the actual physical flow of inventory.[3] In reality, companies will choose the inventory cost flow method that satisfies their financial reporting objectives. Some companies will use a method that is acceptable for tax purposes; this excludes LIFO, which is not permitted by the Canada Customs and Revenue Agency P. 13. For simplicity, other companies may want to average the cost of their product. Loblaw Companies Limited chose to use FIFO as per its 1999 annual report. Canadian Tire and Maple Leaf Foods Inc. also use FIFO. Some companies use different methods for different types of inventory. Perlite Canada Inc. uses FIFO for one type of inventory and weighted average for another, while Bombardier Inc. uses three methods: specific identification, weighted average, and FIFO depending on the inventory item. Exhibit 7.2 categorizes 5% of companies as users of 'other methods' including specific identification. Finning International Inc. uses specific identification to account for its inventory while Suzy Shier Limited, a clothing retailer, uses a method for financial reporting purposes other than one of the four already noted.

We use information from Trekking, a sporting goods store, to describe the four methods. Among its many products, Trekking carries one type of mountain bike. Its mountain bike ("unit") inventory at the beginning of August 2001 and its purchases during August are shown in Exhibit 7.3

Exhibit 7.2

Frequency in Use of Inventory Methods in Practice

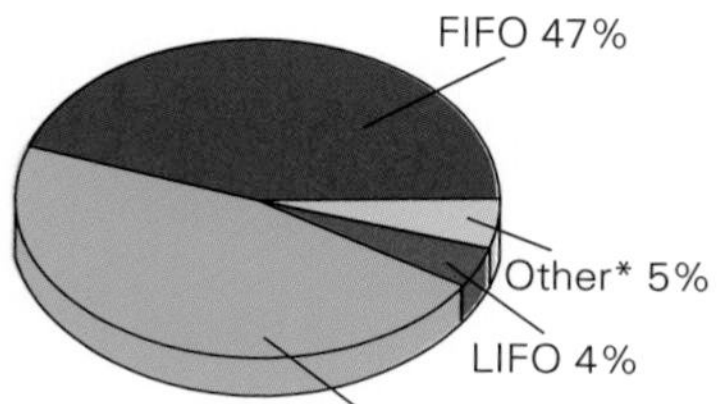

*Includes Specific Identification.

Exhibit 7.3

Cost of Goods Available for Sale

		Units		Cost of Unit		Total Cost
Aug. 1	Beginning inventory	10	@	$ 91	=	$ 910
3	Purchased	15	@	$106	=	1,590
17	Purchased	20	@	$115	=	2,300
28	Purchased	10	@	$119	=	1,190
Total goods available for sale		55 units available for sale				$5,990 total cost of goods that were available for sale

[3] Physical flow of goods depends on the type of product and the way it is stored. Perishable goods such as fresh fruit demand that a business attempts to sell them in a first-in, first-out pattern. Other products such as lanterns or grills can often be sold in a last-in, first-out pattern. Physical flow and cost flow need not be the same.

Exhibit 7.4

Retail Sales of Goods

		Units		Selling Price per Unit		Total Sales
Aug. 14	Sales	20	@	$130	=	$2,600
31	Sales	23	@	$150	=	3,450
Total sales		43 units				$6,050

Trekking had two sales of mountain bikes to two different biking clubs in August as shown in Exhibit 7.4. Trekking ends August with 12 bikes on hand in inventory (55 units available for sale less 43 units sold).

In this section, we will determine how much of the cost of goods available for sale is to be assigned to cost of goods sold and to ending merchandise inventory using the four different cost flow assumptions.

We explained in the last chapter how use of a perpetual inventory system is increasing dramatically due to advances in information and computing technology. Widespread use of electronic scanners and product bar codes further encourages its use. Accordingly, we discuss the assignment of costs to cost of goods sold and merchandise inventory in a perpetual system. The assignment of costs to inventory using a periodic system is discussed in Appendix 7A.

Specific Identification

When each item sold and remaining in inventory can be directly identified with a specific purchase and its invoice, we can use **specific identification** (also called **specific invoice inventory pricing**) to assign costs. Trekking's internal documents reveal that on August 14, 20 units were sold; specifically, these were eight units from beginning inventory and 12 units from the August 3 purchase. Specific identification assigns costs to the goods sold and to ending inventory based on specific items identified, as shown in Exhibit 7.5.

Exhibit 7.5

Specific Identification Computations—Perpetual

Date	Purchases			Sales (at cost)			Inventory Balance		
	Units	Unit Cost	Total Cost	Units	Unit Cost	Cost of Goods Sold	Units	Unit Cost	Total Cost
Aug. 1	Beginning inventory								
	10 @	$ 91	= $ 910				10 @	$ 91 =	$ 910
							10 @	$ 91 =	$ 910
3	15 @	$106	= $1,590				15 @	106 =	1,590
							25		$2,500
14				8 @	$ 91	= $ 728	2 @	$ 91 =	$ 182
				12 @	$106	= 1,272	3 @	106 =	318
				20		$2,000	5		$ 500
							2 @	$ 91 =	$ 182
							3 @	106 =	318
17	20 @	$115	= $2,300				20 @	115 =	2,300
							25		$2,800
							2 @	$ 91 =	$ 182
							3 @	106 =	318
							20 @	115 =	2,300
28	10 @	$119	= $1,190				10 @	119 =	1,190
							35		$3,990
31				2 @	$ 91	= $ 182			
				3 @	106	= 318			
				14 @	115	= 1,610	6 @	$115 =	$ 690
				4 @	119	= 476	6 @	119 =	714
				23		$2,586	12		$1,404
Totals	**55**		**$5,990**	**43**		**$4,586**	**12**		**$1,404**

Cost of goods available for sale = *Cost of goods sold* + *Ending inventory*

① Eight of the 10 units from beginning inventory were specifically identified as being sold.

② Two of the 10 units from beginning inventory remain in ending inventory.

③ Twelve of the 15 units purchased on August 3 were specifically identified as being sold.

④ Three of the 15 units purchased on August 3 remain in ending inventory

When using specific identification, Trekking's cost of goods sold reported on the income statement is $4,586 (= $2,000 + $2,586) and its ending inventory reported on the balance sheet is $1,404.

The specific identification method works best when each item of inventory is unique or different as in an antique store, art gallery, or a custom furniture manufacturer. For example, a car dealership would use specific identification because each car has a unique cost. That cost is tied to a specific car by using the vehicle identification number. In all cases where specific identification is used, each inventory item needs to be identified separately.

When inventory items are homogeneous (or similar), quantities are often purchased at different times, possibly with different costs. In these situations, using the specific identification method may cause difficulties such as management manipulation of the cost of goods sold. This can happen by management choosing to deliver a unit with a lower (or higher) cost. It is of no concern to the customer since all the units are identical, but it will affect the cost of goods sold. Another difficulty might be the cost versus benefit of tracking the sale of individual units that are similar. Therefore, when the inventory items are homogeneous, one of the following methods may be better conceptually and more efficient to use.

Weighted Average

The **weighted average method** (also called **average cost method**) of assigning cost requires computing the average cost per unit of merchandise inventory at the time of each purchase by dividing the cost of goods available for sale by the units on hand. Using weighted average for Trekking means the costs of mountain bikes are assigned to inventory and goods sold as shown in Exhibit 7.6.

Exhibit 7.6

Weighted Average Computations—Perpetual

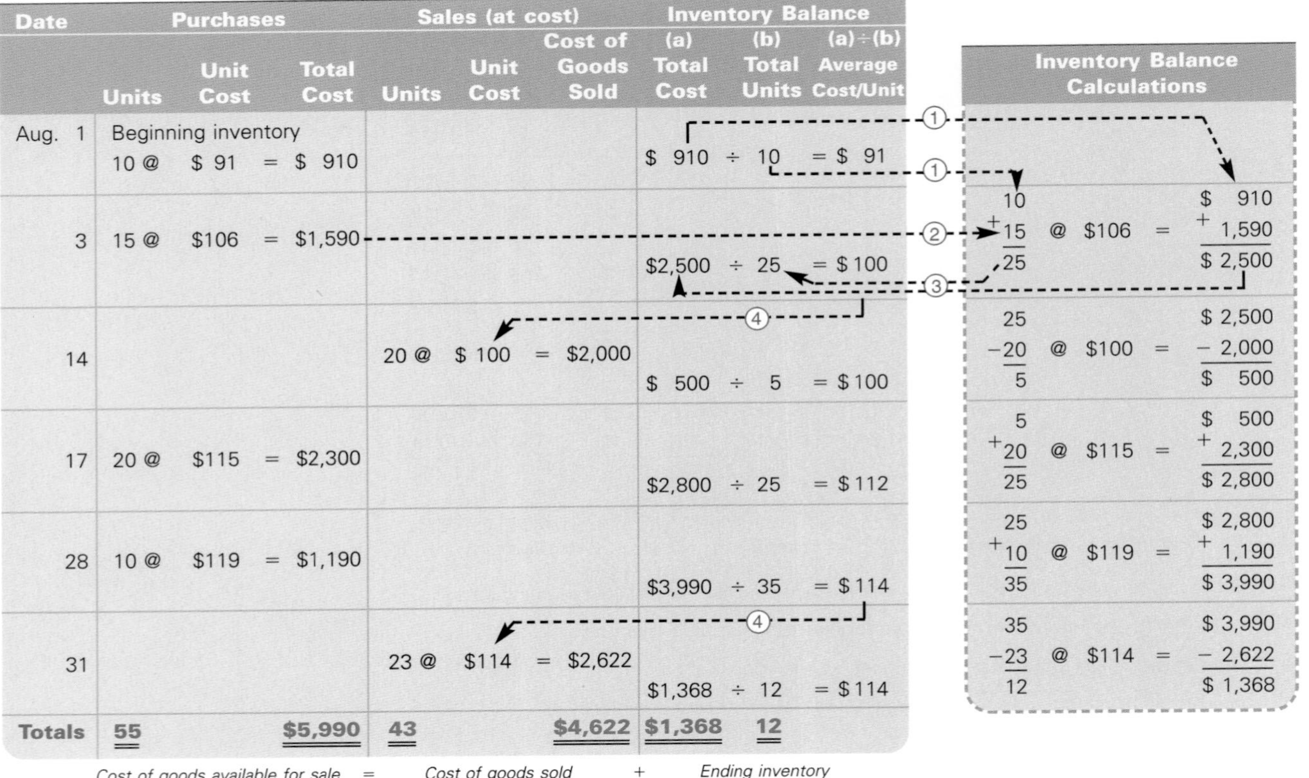

Date	Purchases: Units	Purchases: Unit Cost	Purchases: Total Cost	Sales (at cost): Units	Sales (at cost): Unit Cost	Sales (at cost): Cost of Goods Sold	Inventory Balance: (a) Total Cost	Inventory Balance: (b) Total Units	Inventory Balance: (a)÷(b) Average Cost/Unit	Inventory Balance Calculations
Aug. 1	Beginning inventory 10 @	$ 91 =	$ 910				$ 910 ÷	10	= $ 91	
3	15 @	$106 =	$1,590				$2,500 ÷	25	= $100	10 + 15 @ $106 = 25; $ 910 + 1,590 = $ 2,500
14				20 @	$ 100 =	$2,000	$ 500 ÷	5	= $100	25 − 20 @ $100 = 5; $ 2,500 − 2,000 = $ 500
17	20 @	$115 =	$2,300				$2,800 ÷	25	= $112	5 + 20 @ $115 = 25; $ 500 + 2,300 = $ 2,800
28	10 @	$119 =	$1,190				$3,990 ÷	35	= $114	25 + 10 @ $119 = 35; $ 2,800 + 1,190 = $ 3,990
31				23 @	$114 =	$2,622	$1,368 ÷	12	= $114	35 − 23 @ $114 = 12; $ 3,990 − 2,622 = $ 1,368
Totals	55		$5,990	43		$4,622	$1,368	12		

Cost of goods available for sale = Cost of goods sold + Ending inventory

(1) August 1 beginning inventory in units and dollars.

(2) August 1 beginning inventory is added to the purchase of August 3 to determine the total cost of the units in inventory on August 3.

(3) The total cost of all units is divided by the total number of units to get the average cost per unit of $100 on August 3.

(4) The most current average cost is assigned as the cost per unit sold.

Trekking's cost of goods sold reported on the income statement is $4,622 (=$2,000 + $2,622) and its ending inventory reported on the balance sheet is $1,368. The weighted average perpetual system often raises a rounding problem in the computations because the currency figures are limited to two decimal places. The typical solution is to adjust or "plug" the cost of goods sold figure after calculating the closing inventory amount at the weighted average cost.

First-in, First-out

The **first-in, first-out (FIFO)** method of assigning cost to inventory and the goods sold assumes that inventory items are sold in the order acquired. When sales occur, costs of the earliest units purchased are charged to cost of goods sold. This leaves the costs from the most recent purchases in inventory. Use of FIFO for Trekking means the costs of mountain bikes are assigned to inventory and goods sold as shown in Exhibit 7.7.

Exhibit 7.7

FIFO Computations—Perpetual

Date	Purchases			Sales (at cost)			Inventory Balance		
	Units	Unit Cost	Total Cost	Units	Unit Cost	Cost of Goods Sold	Units	Unit Cost	Total Cost
Aug. 1	Beginning inventory								
	10 @	$ 91	= $ 910				10 @	$ 91	= $ 910
3	15 @	$106	= $1,590				10 @ ①	$ 91	= $ 910
							15 @ ②	106	= 1,590
							25 ③		$2,500
14				10 @	$ 91	= $ 910			
				10 @	106	= 1,060	5 @	$106	= $ 530
				20		$1,970			
17							5 @	$106	= $ 530
	20 @	$115	= $2,300				20 @	115	= 2,300
							25		$2,830
28							5 @	$106	= $ 530
							20 @	115	= 2,300
	10 @	$119	= $1,190				10 @	119	= 1,190
							35		$4,020
31				5 @	$106	= $ 530			
				18 @	115	= 2,070	2 @	$115	= $ 230
							10 @	119	= 1,190
				23		$2,600	12		$1,420
Totals	55		$5,990	43		$4,570	12		$1,420
	Cost of goods available for sale		=	Cost of goods sold		+	Ending inventory		

① Under FIFO, units are assumed to be sold in the order acquired; therefore, of the 20 units sold on August 14, the first 10 units come from beginning inventory.

② The remaining 10 units sold on August 14 come from the next purchase, August 3.

③ All of the units from beginning inventory have been sold but five units remain from the August 3 purchase.

Trekking's cost of goods sold reported on the income statement is $4,570 (= $1,970 + $2,600) and its ending inventory reported on the balance sheet is $1,420.

Last-in, First-out

The **last-in, first-out (LIFO)** method assumes that the most recently purchased units are sold first and their costs charged to cost of goods sold. The earliest purchases are assigned to inventory.

One appeal of LIFO is that companies purchase new inventory to replace items that have been sold. The costs of the new purchases are close approximations (and sometimes equal) to replacement costs. Because LIFO assigns the most recent purchase costs to cost of goods sold, LIFO comes closest to matching replacement costs with revenues (compared to FIFO or weighted average).[4]

Use of LIFO for Trekking means costs of mountain bikes are assigned to inventory and goods sold as shown in Exhibit 7.8.

Exhibit 7.8

LIFO Computations—Perpetual

Date	Purchases			Sales (at cost)			Inventory Balance		
	Units	Unit Cost	Total Cost	Units	Unit Cost	Cost of Goods Sold	Units	Unit Cost	Total Cost
Aug. 1	Beginning inventory 10 @	$ 91 =	$ 910				10 @	$ 91 =	$ 910
3	15 @	$106 =	$1,590				10 @ ② 15 @ ① 25 ③	$ 91 = 106 =	$ 910 1,590 $2,500
14				15 @ ① 5 @ ② 20	$106 = 91 =	$1,590 455 $2,045	5 @ ③	$ 91 =	$ 455
17	20 @	$115 =	$2,300				5 @ 20 @ 25	$ 91 = 115 =	$ 455 2,300 $2,755
28	10 @	$119 =	$1,190				5 @ 20 @ 10 @ 35	$ 91 = 115 = 119 =	$ 455 2,300 1,190 $3,945
31				10 @ 13 @ 23	$119 = 115 =	$1,190 1,495 $2,685	5 @ 7 @ 12	$ 91 = 115 =	$ 455 805 $1,260
Totals	**55**		**$5,990**	**43**		**$4,730**	**12**		**$1,260**

Cost of goods available for sale = Cost of goods sold + Ending inventory

① Under LIFO, the most recently purchased units are assumed to be sold first. Therefore, of the 20 units sold on August 14, the 15 units purchased on August 3 are assumed to be sold first.

② The remaining five units sold on August 14 come from the next most recent purchase, which is the August 1 beginning inventory.

③ All of the August 3 purchase has been sold, but five units from the August 1 beginning inventory remain.

Trekking's cost of goods sold reported on the income statement is $4,730 (=$2,045 + $2,685) and its ending inventory reported on the balance sheet is $1,260.

[4] Although LIFO is allowed for financial reporting purposes, it is not commonly used in Canada because CCRA does not permit it for tax purposes. LIFO is commonly used in the United States and Japan and is gradually gaining acceptance in Germany and Italy.

Exhibit 7.9

Comparison of Inventory Methods

	Specific Identification		Weighted Average		FIFO		LIFO	
	Units	$	Units	$	Units	$	Units	$
Cost of Goods Sold (or Cost of Sales)...................	43	$4,586	43	$4,622	43	$4,570	43	$4,730
Ending Inventory	12	1,404	12	1,368	12	1,420	12	1,260
Goods Available for Sale	55	$5,990	55	$5,990	55	$5,990	55	$5,990

Notice in Exhibit 7.9 that the total units and cost of the goods available for sale are the same regardless of the method used. What is different is the *dollar amount* assigned to the ending inventory and the cost of goods sold.

Inventory Costing and Technology

A perpetual inventory system can be kept in either electronic or manual form. A manual form is often too costly for businesses, especially those with many purchases and sales or many units in inventory. Advances in information and computing technology have greatly reduced the cost of an electronic perpetual inventory system, and many companies are now asking whether they can afford not to have one. This is because timely access to information is being used strategically by companies to gain a competitive advantage. Scanned sales data, for instance, can reveal crucial information on buying patterns, and can also help companies target promotional and advertising activities. These and other applications have greatly increased the use of the perpetual system. Maintaining inventory records is discussed in detail in Chapter 8.

3. What accounting principle most governs allocations of cost of goods available for sale between ending inventory and cost of goods sold?

Answer—p. 352

Inventory Analysis and Effects

This section analyzes and compares the effects of using alternative inventory costing methods. We also analyze the income effects of inventory methods, examine managers' preferences for an inventory method, and look at the effects of inventory errors.

Financial Reporting

Analyze the effects of inventory methods for financial reporting.

In our analysis of financial statements, it is important to know and understand inventory costing methods because the method used can have a material impact on the income statement and balance sheet as illustrated in Exhibit 7.10. For this reason, the inventory costing method used must be disclosed in the notes to the financial statements.

The **full disclosure principle**[5] is the generally accepted accounting principle that requires financial statements to report all relevant information about the operations and financial position of the entry. Financial statements are normally accompanied by notes such as those for WestJet in Appendix I of the text.

When purchase prices do not change, the choice of an inventory costing method is unimportant. All methods assign the same cost amounts when prices remain constant. When purchase prices are rising or falling, however, the methods are likely to assign different cost amounts.

[5] *CICA Handbook*, section 1506, par. 16.

Exhibit 7.10

Income Statement Effects of Inventory Costing Methods

Trekking Company Segment Income Statement—Mountain Bikes For Month Ended August 31, 2001	Specific Identification	Weighted Average	FIFO	LIFO
Sales	$6,050	$6,050	$6,050	$6,050
Cost of goods sold	4,586*	4,622*	4,570*	4,730*
Gross profit	$1,464	$1,428	$1,480	$1,320
Operating expenses	450	450	450	450
Income from operations	$1,014	$ 978	$1,030	$ 870

* from Exhibit 7.9

Trekking Company Partial Balance Sheet August 31, 2001	Specific Identification	Weighted Average	FIFO	LIFO
Assets				
Current assets:				
Merchandise inventory	$1,404*	$1,368*	$1,420*	$1,260*

* from Exhibit 7.9

Because Trekking's purchase prices rose in August, FIFO assigned the least amount to cost of goods sold. This led to the highest gross profit and the highest income. This result will always occur in times of rising prices because the most recent and therefore most costly units are in ending inventory, leaving the least expensive units in cost of goods sold. LIFO assigned the highest amount to cost of goods sold. This yielded the lowest gross profit and the lowest net income. As expected, amounts from using the weighted average method fall between FIFO and LIFO.[6] The amounts from using specific identification depend on what units are actually sold.

Exhibit 7.11 summarizes advantages and disadvantages for the cost flow assumptions discussed.

Exhibit 7.11

Advantages and Disadvantages of Cost Flow Assumptions

	Specific Identification	Weighted Average	FIFO	LIFO
Advantages:	Exactly matches costs and revenues	Smooths out purchase price changes	Most current values are on the balance sheet as ending inventory	Places the most most current cost on the income statement as cost of goods sold
Disadvantages:	Relatively more costly to implement and maintain	Averaging does not accurately match expenses to revenues	Cost of goods sold does not reflect current costs, therefore violates matching principle	LIFO is not accepted for tax purposes Ending inventory on the balance sheet is stated at the oldest costs

6 The weighted average amount can be outside the FIFO or LIFO amounts if prices do not steadily increase or decrease but exhibit a cyclical pattern.

4. Describe one advantage for each inventory costing method: specific identification, weighted average, FIFO, and LIFO.
5. When costs and prices are rising, does LIFO or FIFO report higher net income?
6. When costs and prices are rising, what effect does weighted average have on a balance sheet compared to FIFO?

Answers—p. 352

Consistency in Reporting

The last section illustrated that inventory costing methods can materially affect amounts on financial statements: cost of goods sold on the income statement and inventory on the balance sheet. Therefore, some managers might be inclined to choose a method most consistent with their hoped-for results each period. These managers' objective might be to pick the method that gave the most favourable financial statement amounts. Managers might also be inclined to pick the method that gave them the highest bonus since many management bonus plans are based on net income. If managers were allowed to pick the method each period, it would be more difficult for users of financial statements to compare a company's financial statements from one period to the next. If income increased, for instance, a user would need to decide whether it resulted from successful operations or from the accounting method change. The *consistency principle* is used to avoid this problem.

The **consistency principle** requires a company to use the same accounting methods period after period so that the financial statements are comparable across periods.[7] The consistency principle applies to all accounting methods.

The consistency principle *does not* require a company to use one method exclusively. It can use different methods to value different categories of inventory. As mentioned earlier, Bombardier Inc. uses three methods (specific identification, weighted average, and FIFO) to assign costs to various types of inventory. Also, the consistency principle does not mean that a company can never change from one accounting method to another. Instead, it means a company must argue that the method it is changing to will improve its financial reporting. Under this circumstance, a change is acceptable; yet, when such a change is made, the full disclosure principle requires that the notes to the statements report the type of change, its justification, and its effect on net income.[8]

Inventory Manager

You are the inventory manager for a merchandiser. Your compensation includes a bonus plan based on the amount of gross profit reported in the financial statements. Your superior comes to you and asks your opinion about changing the inventory costing method from weighted average to FIFO. Since costs have been rising and are expected to continue to rise, your superior predicts the company will be more attractive to investors because of the reported higher income using FIFO. You realize this proposed change will likely increase your bonus as well. What do you recommend?

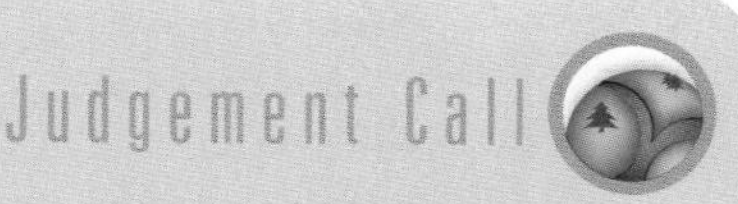

Answer—p. 351

[7] *CICA Handbook*, section 1000, par. 23.

[8] Ibid., par. 1506.16.

Errors in Reporting Inventory

Analyze the effects of inventory errors on current and future financial statements.

Companies must take care in computing and taking a physical count of inventory. If inventory is reported in error, it causes misstatements of cost of goods sold, gross profit, net income, current assets, and owner's equity. It also means misstatements will exist in the next period's statements. This is because ending inventory of one period is the beginning inventory of the next. An error carried forward causes misstatements of the next period's cost of goods sold, gross profit, and net income. Since the inventory amount often is large, misstatements can reduce the usefulness of financial statements.

Income Statement Effects

The income statement effects of an inventory error are evident when looking at the components of cost of goods sold in Exhibit 7.12.

Exhibit 7.12

Cost of Goods Sold Components

The effect of an inventory error on cost of goods sold is determined by computing it with the correct amount and comparing the result to the result of the calculation when using the incorrect amount, as in Exhibit 7.13.

Exhibit 7.13

Effects of $2,000 Overstatement in Ending Inventory for 2001 on Three Periods' Income Statement Information

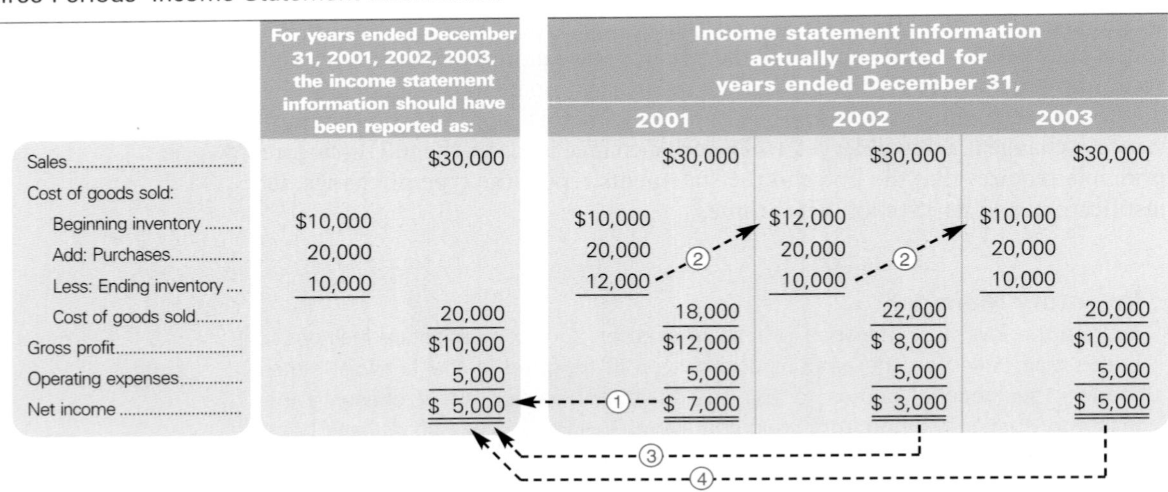

	For years ended December 31, 2001, 2002, 2003, the income statement information should have been reported as:		Income statement information actually reported for years ended December 31, 2001		2002		2003	
Sales		$30,000		$30,000		$30,000		$30,000
Cost of goods sold:								
Beginning inventory	$10,000		$10,000		$12,000		$10,000	
Add: Purchases	20,000		20,000		20,000		20,000	
Less: Ending inventory	10,000		12,000		10,000		10,000	
Cost of goods sold		20,000		18,000		22,000		20,000
Gross profit		$10,000		$12,000		$ 8,000		$10,000
Operating expenses		5,000		5,000		5,000		5,000
Net income		$ 5,000		$ 7,000		$ 3,000		$ 5,000

① 2001 net income and gross profit are overstated (too high) and cost of goods sold is understated (too low) when ending inventory is overstated (too high).

② Ending inventory for one period becomes the beginning inventory for the next period, carrying forward any errors that existed.

③ 2002 net income and gross profit are understated (too low) and cost of goods sold is overstated (too high) when beginning inventory is overstated (too high). Notice that the error has reversed itself in 2002, the second year.

④ An inventory error in the year 2001 does not affect 2003.

Exhibit 7.13 assumes that $2,000 of merchandise out on consignment was incorrectly excluded from ending inventory on December 31, 2001. This ending inventory error carries over to the next period as a beginning inventory error yielding a reverse effect. We can see that overstating ending inventory will understate cost of goods sold. An understatement of cost of goods sold yields an overstatement of net income. We can do the same analysis with understating ending inventory and for an error in beginning inventory. Exhibit 7.14 shows the effects of inventory errors on the current period's income statement amounts.

Inventory Error	Cost of Goods Sold	Net Income
Understate ending inventory	Overstated	Understated
Understate beginning inventory	Understated	Overstated
Overstate ending inventory	Understated	Overstated
Overstate beginning inventory	Overstated	Understated

Exhibit 7.14

Effect of Inventory Errors on This Period's Income Statement

Notice that inventory errors yield opposite effects in cost of goods sold and net income.

Because an inventory error causes an offsetting error in the next period, it is sometimes said to be *self-correcting*. Do not think, however, that this makes inventory errors less serious. Managers, lenders, owners and other users make important decisions on changes in net income and cost of goods sold. Imagine how a lender's decision would be affected by each of the graphs presented in Exhibit 7.15. Inventory errors must be avoided.

Exhibit 7.15

Graphing the Effects of Inventory Errors on Net Income

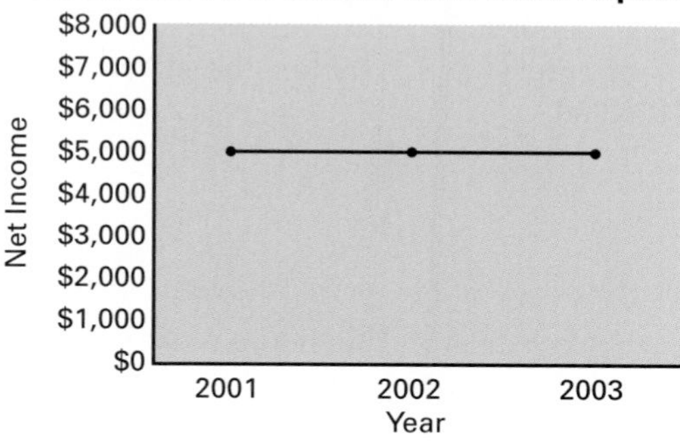

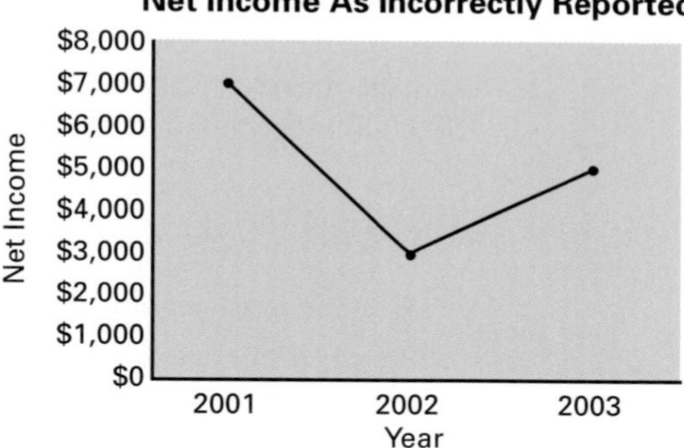

Balance Sheet Effects

Balance sheet effects of an inventory error are made evident by looking at the components of the accounting equation in Exhibit 7.16.

Assets = Liabilities + Owner's Equity

Exhibit 7.16

Accounting Equation

We can see, for example, that understating ending inventory will understate both current and total assets. An understatement of ending inventory also yields an understatement in owner's equity because of the understatement of net income. We can do the same analysis with overstating ending inventory. Exhibit 7.17 shows the effects of inventory errors on the current period's balance sheet amounts.

Exhibit 7.17

Effects of Inventory Errors on This Period's Balance Sheet

Inventory Error	Assets	Owner's Equity
Understate ending inventory	Understated	Understated
Overstate ending inventory	Overstated	Overstated

Errors in beginning inventory do not yield misstatements in the balance sheet, but they do affect the income statement.

Answer—p. 352

7. A company takes a physical count of inventory at the end of 2001 and finds ending inventory to be overstated by $10,000. Does this error cause cost of goods sold to be overstated or understated in 2001? In 2002? By how much?

Mid-Chapter Demonstration Problem

Coe Company had $435,000 of sales during each of three consecutive years, and it purchased merchandise costing $300,000 during each of the years. It also maintained a $105,000 inventory from the beginning to the end of the three-year period. However, $15,000 of merchandise inventory shipped FOB shipping point was accidentally excluded from the December 31, 2001 inventory. This error caused the company's ending 2001 inventory to appear on the statements at $90,000 rather than at the correct $105,000.

Required

1. State the actual amount of the company's gross profit in each of the years.
2. Prepare a comparative income statement like Exhibit 7.13 to show the effect of this error on the company's cost of goods sold and gross profit in 2001, 2002, and 2003.

SOLUTION TO Mid-Chapter Demonstration Problem

1. $435,000 – ($105,000 + $300,000 – $105,000) = $135,000

2.

	For years ended December 31, 2001, 2002, 2003, the income statement information should have been reported as:		Income statement information actually reported for years ended December 31, 2001		2002		2003	
Sales		$435,000		$435,000		$435,000		$435,000
Cost of goods sold:								
Beginning inventory	$105,000		$105,000		$90,000		$105,000	
Add: Purchases	300,000		300,000		300,000		300,000	
Less: Ending inventory	105,000		90,000		105,000		105,000	
Cost of goods sold		300,000		315,000		285,000		300,000
Gross profit		$135,000		$120,000		$150,000		$135,000

Other Inventory Valuations

This section describes other methods to value inventory. Knowledge of these methods is important for users in understanding and analyzing financial statements.

LO6 Compute the lower of cost or market value of inventory.

Lower of Cost or Market

We explained how costs are assigned to ending inventory and cost of goods sold using one of four costing methods (specific identification, weighted average, FIFO, or LIFO). Yet the cost of inventory is not necessarily the amount always reported on a balance sheet. The *conservatism principle* (or, simply, *conservatism*) requires that inventory be reported at market value when market is lower than cost. Merchandise inventory is then said to be reported on the balance sheet at the lower of cost or market (LCM).

The **conservatism principle** says that when faced with a choice of two or more equally likely amounts, the least optimistic value should be selected. Why? If, for example, the December 31, 2001 inventory of a music store included eight-track cassettes that cost the merchandiser a total of $100,000 but had a market value on that date of $500, which value is the *most realistic*? Because we know that cassettes are essentially obsolete, the least optimistic or most realistic value is $500. We do ***not*** write inventory up if the market value is greater than cost because market, in that situation, is not the least optimistic value: cost is.

Computing the Lower of Cost or Market

In applying LCM, **market** can be defined as either net realizable value (selling price less any costs of making the sale) or current **replacement cost** (current purchasing cost). Most Canadian companies tend to use NRV as their definition of market value.[9]

The decline in merchandise inventory from cost to market is recorded at the end of the period. LCM is applied in one of three ways:

(1) Separately to each individual item;
(2) To major categories of items; or
(3) To the whole inventory.

The less similar the items in inventory are, the more likely companies are to apply LCM to individual items. Advances in technology further encourage the individual item application.

We show in Exhibit 7.18 how LCM is applied to the ending inventory of a motorsports retailer.

Exhibit 7.18

Lower of Cost or Market Computations

Inventory Items	Total Cost	Total Market	LCM applied to: Items	Categories	Whole
Cycles:					
Roadster	$160,000	$140,000	$140,000		
Sprint	50,000	60,000	50,000		
Category subtotal	$210,000	$200,000		$200,000	
Off-road:					
Trax-4	40,000	52,000	40,000		
Blaz'm	45,000	35,000	35,000		
Category subtotal	$ 85,000	87,000		85,000	
Totals	$295,000	$287,000	$265,000	$285,000	$287,000

[9] C. Byrd and Ida Chen, *Financial Reporting in Canada 1997* (Toronto: CICA, 1997), p. 169.

Using the information in Exhibit 7.18, if LCM is applied to *individual items* of inventory, market of $265,000 is lower than cost of $295,000; therefore market of $265,000 would be reported on the balance sheet. The entry to accomplish this result is:

Cost of Goods Sold	30,000	
Merchandise Inventory		30,000
To write inventory down to market value.		

After posting this entry, merchandise inventory would appear on the balance sheet as:

Current assets:	
Cash	$ x,xxx
Accounts receivable	x,xxx
Merchandise inventory, at market	**265,000**

Any one of the three applications of LCM is acceptable in practice. ClubLink reports that its inventories are stated at the lower of cost and net realizable value.

Answer—p. 352

8. A company's ending inventory includes the following items:

Product	Units on Hand	Unit Cost	Market Value per Unit
A	20	$ 6	$ 5
B	40	9	8
C	10	12	15

Using LCM applied separately to individual items, compute the reported amount for inventory.

Gross Profit Method

Gross Profit Ratio

$$= \frac{\text{Gross Profit}}{\text{Net Sales}}$$

E.g.

		%
Net sales	$10	100
COGS*	6	60
Gross Profit	$ 4	40

**COGS = Cost of goods sold*

The **gross profit method** estimates the cost of ending inventory by applying the *gross profit ratio* to net sales (at *retail*). The **gross profit ratio**, also commonly known as the gross margin ratio, measures how much of each sales dollar is gross profit. A need for the gross profit estimate can arise when inventory is destroyed, lost, or stolen. These cases need an estimate of inventory so a company can file a claim with its insurer. Users also apply this method to see if inventory amounts from either management or a physical count are reasonable. This method uses the historical relation between cost of goods sold and net sales to estimate the proportion of cost of goods sold making up current sales. This cost of goods sold estimate is then subtracted from cost of goods available for sale to give us an estimate of ending inventory at cost.

To illustrate, assume the following in March of 2001 when the company's inventory is destroyed by fire:

Sales	$31,500
Sales returns	1,500
Inventory, January 1, 2001	12,000
Net cost of goods purchased	20,500
Gross profit ratio	30%

To estimate the inventory loss, we first need to recognize that each dollar of net sales is made up of gross profit and cost of goods sold. If this company's gross profit ratio is 30% as given, then 30% of each net sales dollar is gross profit and 70% is cost of goods sold. We show in Exhibit 7.19 how this 70% is used to estimate lost inventory.

Exhibit 7.19

Computing Inventory Using the Gross Profit Method

Goods available for sale:		
Inventory, January 1, 2001		$12,000
Net cost of goods purchased		20,500
Goods available for sale		$32,500
Less: Estimated cost of goods sold:		
Sales	$31,500	
Less: Sales returns	1,500	
Net sales	$30,000	
Estimated cost of goods sold (70% × $30,000)		21,000
Estimated March inventory loss		$11,500

Retail Inventory Method

LO7 Apply both the gross profit and retail inventory methods to estimate inventory.

Many companies prepare financial statements on a quarterly or monthly basis. The cost of goods sold information needed to prepare these interim financial reports P.7 is readily available if a perpetual inventory system is used. A periodic system, however, requires a physical inventory to determine cost of goods sold. To avoid the time-consuming and expensive process of taking a physical inventory each month or quarter, some companies use the **retail inventory method** to estimate cost of goods sold and ending inventory. Some companies even use the retail inventory method to prepare the annual statements. Reitman's (Canada) Limited, for instance, reports in its January 29, 2000 annual report that:

> Merchandise inventories are accounted for by the retail method.

All companies should take a physical inventory at least once each year to identify any errors or shortages.

Computing the Retail Inventory Estimate

When the retail inventory method is used to estimate inventory, we need to know the amount of inventory a company had at the beginning of the period in both *cost* and *retail* amounts. The **retail** amount of inventory refers to its dollar amount measured using selling prices of inventory items. We also need the net amount of goods purchased (minus returns, allowances and discounts) during the period, both at cost and at retail. The amount of net sales at retail is also needed.

A three-step process is used to estimate ending inventory after we compute the amount of goods available for sale during the period both at cost and at retail. This process is shown in Exhibit 7.20.

The reasoning behind the retail inventory method is that if we can get a good estimate of the cost to retail ratio, then we can multiply ending inventory at retail by this ratio to estimate ending inventory at cost. We show in Exhibit 7.21 how these steps are applied to estimate ending inventory.

Exhibit 7.20

Inventory Estimation Using Retail Inventory Method

Exhibit 7.21

Computing Ending Inventory Using the Retail Inventory Method

		At Cost	At Retail
	Goods available for sale:		
	Beginning inventory	$20,500	$ 34,500
	Cost of goods purchased	39,500	65,500
	Goods available for sale	$60,000	$100,000
Step 1:	Less: Net sales at retail		70,000
	Ending inventory at retail		$ 30,000
Step 2:	Cost to retail ratio: ($60,000 ÷ $100,000)		× 60%
Step 3:	Estimated ending inventory at cost		$ 18,000

Estimating Physical Inventory at Cost

Items for sale by retailers usually carry price tags listing selling prices. When a retailer takes a physical inventory, it commonly totals inventory using selling prices of items on hand. It then reduces the dollar total of this inventory to a cost basis by applying the cost to retail ratio. This is done because selling prices are readily available and using the cost to retail ratio eliminates the need to look up invoice prices of items on hand.

Let's assume that the company in Exhibit 7.21 estimates its inventory by the retail method and takes a physical inventory using selling prices. If the retail value of this physical inventory is $29,600, then we can compute the cost of this inventory by applying its cost to retail ratio as follows: $29,600 × 60% = $17,760. The $17,760 cost figure for ending physical inventory is an acceptable number for annual financial statements. It is also acceptable to CCRA for tax reporting.

Estimating Inventory Shortage at Cost

The inventory estimate in Exhibit 7.21 is an estimate of the amount of goods on hand (at cost). Since it is computed by deducting sales from goods available for sale (at retail), it does not reveal any shrinkage due to breakage, loss, or theft. However, we can estimate the amount of shrinkage by comparing the inventory computed in Exhibit 7.21 with the amount from taking a physical inventory. In Exhibit 7.21, for example, we estimated ending inventory at retail as $30,000, but a physical inventory revealed only $29,600 of inventory on hand (at retail). The company has an inventory shortage (at retail) of $400, computed as $30,000 − $29,600. The inventory shortage (at cost) is $240, computed as $400 × 60%.

Answer—p. 352

9. The following data pertain to a company's inventory during 2001:

	Cost	Retail
Beginning inventory	$324,000	$530,000
Cost of goods purchased	195,000	335,000
Net sales		320,000

Using the retail method, estimate the cost of ending inventory.

Summary

LO1 Identify the items making up merchandise inventory. Merchandise inventory comprises goods owned by a company and held for resale. Three special cases merit our attention. Goods in transit are reported in inventory of the company that holds ownership rights. Goods out on consignment are reported in inventory of the consignor. Goods damaged or obsolete are reported in inventory at a conservative estimate of their net realizable value, computed as sales price minus the selling costs.

LO2 Identify the costs of merchandise inventory. Costs of merchandise inventory comprise expenditures necessary, directly or indirectly, in bringing an item to a salable condition and location. This means the cost of an inventory item includes its invoice price minus any discount, plus any added or incidental costs necessary to put it in a place and condition for sale.

LO3 Compute inventory in a perpetual system using the methods of specific identification, weighted average, FIFO, and LIFO. Costs are assigned to the cost of goods sold account *each time* that a sale occurs in a perpetual system. Specific identification assigns a cost to each item sold by referring to its actual cost (for example, its net invoice cost). Weighted average assigns a cost to items sold by taking the current balance in the merchandise inventory account and dividing it by the total items available for sale to determine the weighted average cost per unit. We then multiply the number of units sold by this cost per unit to get the cost of each sale. FIFO assigns cost to items sold assuming earliest units purchased are the first units sold. LIFO assigns cost to items sold assuming the most recent units purchased are the first units sold.

LO4 Analyze the effects of inventory methods for financial reporting. When purchase prices do not change, the choice of an inventory method is unimportant. When purchase prices are rising or falling, however, the methods are likely to assign different cost amounts. Specific identification exactly matches costs and revenues. Weighted average smooths out price changes. FIFO assigns an amount to inventory closely approximating current replacement cost. LIFO assigns the most recent costs incurred to cost of goods sold, and likely better matches current costs with revenues.

LO5 Analyze the effects of inventory errors on current and future financial statements. An error in the amount of ending inventory affects assets (inventory), net income (cost of goods sold), and owner's equity of that period. Since ending inventory is next period's beginning inventory, an error in ending inventory affects next period's cost of goods sold and net income. The financial statement effects of errors in one period are offset (reversed) in the next.

LO6 Compute the lower of cost or market value of inventory. Inventory is reported at market value when market is lower than cost. This is called the lower of cost or market (LCM) value of inventory. Market may be measured as net realizable value or replacement cost. Lower of cost or market can be applied separately to each item, to major categories of items, or to the whole of inventory.

LO7 Apply both the gross profit and retail inventory methods to estimate inventory. The gross profit method involves two computations: (1) net sales at retail multiplied by the gross profit ratio gives estimated cost of goods sold; and (2) goods available at cost minus estimated cost of goods sold gives estimated ending inventory at cost. The retail inventory method involves three computations: (1) goods available at retail minus net sales at retail gives ending inventory at retail; (2) goods available at cost divided by goods available at retail gives the cost to retail ratio; and (3) ending inventory at retail is multiplied by the cost to retail ratio to give estimated ending inventory at cost.

GUIDANCE ANSWER TO Judgement Call

Inventory Manager

Your recommendation is a difficult one. Increased profits may attract investors but they will also increase your bonus. The question becomes one of motivation. That is, would the change really be better for the investors or, would the change take place only because your bonus would increase? This presents the classic conflict of interests. Another problem is that profits can be manipulated by changing accounting methods, and if this is the motivation the profession would frown on the change.

GUIDANCE ANSWERS TO Flashback

1. The Bay.
2. Total cost is $12,180, computed as: $11,400 + $130 + $150 + $100 + $400.
3. The matching principle.
4. Specific identification exactly matches costs and revenues. Weighted average tends to smooth out price changes. FIFO assigns an amount to inventory that closely approximates current replacement cost. LIFO assigns the most recent costs incurred to cost of goods sold, and likely better matches current costs with revenues.
5. FIFO gives a lower cost of goods sold and a higher gross profit and higher net income when prices are rising.
6. Weighted average gives a lower inventory figure on the balance sheet as compared to FIFO. FIFO's inventory amount will approximate current replacement costs. Weighted average costs increase but more slowly because of the effect of averaging.
7. Cost of goods sold is understated by $10,000 in 2001 and overstated by $10,000 in 2002.
8. The reported inventory amount is $540, computed as (20 × $5) + (40 × $8) + (10 × $12).
9. The estimated ending inventory (at cost) is $327,000 and is computed as:

   Step 1: ($530,000 + $335,000) − $320,000 = $545,000

   Step 2: $\frac{\$324,000 + \$195,000}{\$530,000 + \$335,000} = 60\%$

   Step 3: $545,000 × 60% = $327,000

Demonstration Problem

Tale Company uses a perpetual inventory system and had the following beginning inventory and purchases during 2001:

Date		Item X Units		Unit Cost		Total Cost
Jan. 1	Inventory	400	×	$14	=	$5,600
Mar. 10	Purchase	200	×	15	=	3,000
May 9	Purchase	300	×	16	=	4,800
Sept. 22	Purchase	250	×	20	=	5,000
Nov. 1	Purchase	100	×	21	=	2,100
	Total units and cost of goods available for sale	1,250				$20,500

Sales of units were as follows:

Jan. 15	200 units at $30
April 1	200 units at $30
Nov. 28	300 units at $35
Total units sold	700

Additional data for use in applying the specific identification method:
The specific units sold were:

Jan. 15	200 units from the January 1 units on hand
Apr. 1	100 units from the January 1 units on hand, and 100 units from the March 10 purchase
Nov. 28	100 units from the January 1 units on hand, 100 units from the March 10 purchase, and 100 units from the November 1 purchase

Required

1. Using the preceding information, calculate the ending inventory and the cost of goods sold under a perpetual inventory system by applying each of the four different methods of inventory costing:
   a. FIFO,
   b. LIFO,
   c. Weighted average, and
   d. Specific identification.
2. In preparing the financial statements for 2001, the bookkeeper was instructed to use FIFO but failed to do so and computed the cost of goods sold according to LIFO. Determine the size of the misstatement of 2001's income from this error. Also determine the effect of the error on the 2002 income. Assume no income taxes.
3. The management of the company would like a report that shows how net income would change if the company changed from FIFO to another method. Prepare a schedule showing the costs of goods sold amount under each method. Calculate the amount by which each cost of goods sold total is different from the FIFO cost of goods to inform management how net income would change if another method were used.

Planning the Solution

- Prepare a perpetual FIFO schedule showing the composition of beginning inventory and how the composition of inventory changes after each purchase of inventory and after each sale.
- Prepare a perpetual LIFO schedule showing the composition of beginning inventory and how the composition of inventory changes after each purchase of inventory and after each sale.
- Make a schedule of purchases and sales recalculating the average cost of inventory after each purchase to arrive at the weighted average cost of ending inventory. Add up the average costs associated with each sale to determine the cost of goods sold using the weighted average method.
- Prepare a schedule showing the computation of the cost of goods sold and ending inventory using the specific identification method. Use the information provided to determine the cost of the specific units sold and which specific units remain in inventory.
- Compare the ending 2001 inventory amounts under FIFO and LIFO to determine the misstatement of 2001 income that resulted from using LIFO. The 2002 and 2001 errors are equal in amount but have opposite effects.
- Create a schedule showing the cost of goods sold under each method and how net income would differ from FIFO net income if an alternative method were to be adopted.

SOLUTION TO Demonstration Problem

1a. FIFO perpetual

Date	Purchases			Sales (at cost)			Inventory Balance		
	Units	Unit Cost	Total Cost	Units	Units Cost	Cost of Goods Sold	Units	Unit Cost	Total Cost
Jan. 1	Beginning inventory 400 @	$ 14	= $5,600				400 @	$ 14 =	$ 5,600
15				200 @	$ 14	= $2,800	200 @	$ 14 =	$ 2,800
Mar. 10	200 @	$ 15	= $3,000				200 @ 200 @ 400	$ 14 = 15 =	$ 2,800 3,000 $ 5,800
Apr. 1				200 @	$ 14	= $2,800	200 @	$ 15 =	$ 3,000
May 9	300 @	$ 16	= $4,800				200 @ 300 @ 500	$ 15 = 16 =	$ 3,000 4,800 $ 7,800
Sept. 22	250 @	$ 20	= $5,000				200 @ 300 @ 250 @ 750	$ 15 = 16 = 20 =	$ 3,000 4,800 5,000 $12,800
Nov. 1	100 @	$ 21	= $2,100				200 @ 300 @ 250 @ 100 @ 850	$ 15 = 16 = 20 = 21 =	$ 3,000 4,800 5,000 2,100 $14,900
28				200 @ 100 @ 300	$ 15 16	= $3,000 = 1,600 $4,600	200 @ 250 @ 100 @ 550	$ 16 = 20 = 21 =	$ 3,200 5,000 2,100 $10,300
Totals	**1,250**		**$20,500**	**700**		**$10,200**	**550**		**$10,300**

Cost of goods available for sale = *Cost of goods sold* + *Ending inventory*

(1) Under FIFO, units are assumed to be sold in the order acquired; therefore the 300 units sold on January 15 come from beginning inventory.

(2) The 200 units remaining in inventory after the January 15 sale are from beginning inventory.

(3) The 200 units sold on April 1 are assumed to be the 200 units remaining from beginning inventory.

(4) All of the units remaining in inventory after the April 1 sale are from the March 10 purchase.

1b. LIFO perpetual

Date	Purchases			Sales (at cost)			Inventory Balance		
	Units	Unit Cost	Total Cost	Units	Units Cost	Cost of Goods Sold	Units	Unit Cost	Total Cost
Jan. 1	Beginning inventory 400 @	$ 14	= $5,600				400 @	$ 14 =	$ 5,600
15				200 @	$ 14	= $2,800	200 @	$ 14 =	$ 2,800
Mar. 10	200 @	$ 15	= $3,000	①			200 @ 200 @ 400 ②	$ 14 = 15 =	$ 2,800 3,000 $ 5,800
Apr. 1				200 @	$ 15	= $3,000	200 @	$ 14 =	$ 2,800
May 9	300 @	$ 16	= $4,800				200 @ 300 @ 500	$ 14 = 16 =	$ 2,800 4,800 $ 7,600
Sept. 22	250 @	$ 20	= $5,000				200 @ 300 @ 250 @ 750	$ 14 = 16 = 20 =	$ 2,800 4,800 5,000 $12,600
Nov. 1	100 @	$ 21	= $2,100				200 @ 300 @ 250 @ 100 @ 850	$ 14 = 16 = 20 = 21 =	$ 2,800 4,800 5,000 2,100 $14,700
28				100 @ 200 @ 300	$ 21 20	= $2,100 = 4,000 $6,100	200 @ 300 @ 50 @ 550	$ 14 = 16 = 20 =	$ 2,800 4,800 1,000 $ 8,600
Totals	**1,250**		**$20,500**	**700**		**$11,900**	**550**		**$8,600**

Cost of goods available for sale = *Cost of goods sold* + *Ending inventory*

① Under LIFO, the most recently purchased units are assumed to be sold first. Therefore, the 200 units sold on April 1 are taken from the March 10 purchase.

② The 200 units remaining in inventory after the April 1 sale are from beginning inventory.

1c. Weighted average perpetual

Date	Purchases			Sales (at cost)			Inventory Balance		
	Units	Unit Cost	Total Cost	Units	Unit Cost	Cost of Goods Sold	(a) Total Cost	(b) Total Units	(a)÷(b) Average Cost/Unit
Jan. 1	Beginning inventory 400 @	$ 14	= $5,600				$5,600.00	÷ 400	= $14.00
15				200 @	$14.00	= $2,800.00	$2,800.00	÷ 200	= $14.00
Mar. 10	200 @	$ 15	= $3,000				$5,800.00	÷ 400	= $14.50
Apr. 1				200 @	$14.50	= $2,900.00	$2,900.00	÷ 200	= $14.50
May 9	300 @	$ 16	= $4,800				$ 7,700.00	÷ 500	= $15.40
Sept. 22	250 @	$ 20	= $5,000				$12,700.00	÷ 750	= $16.93
Nov. 1	100 @	$ 21	= $2,100				$14,800.00	÷ 850	= $17.41
28				300 @	$17.41	= $5,223.00	$9,577.00	÷ 550	= $17.41
Totals	**1,250**		**$20,500**	**700**		**$10,923.00**	**$9,577.00**	**550**	

Cost of goods available for sale = Cost of goods sold + Ending inventory

Inventory Balance Calculations

Units		Cost
400		$ 5,600.00
− 200	@ $14.00 =	− 2,800.00
200		$ 2,800.00
200		$ 2,800.00
+ 200	@ $15.00 =	+ 3,000.00
400		$ 5,800.00
400		$ 5,800.00
− 200	@ $14.50 =	− 2,900.00
200		$ 2,900.00
200		$ 2,900.00
+ 300	@ $16.00 =	+ 4,800.00
500		$ 7,700.00
500		$ 7,700.00
+ 250	@ $20.00 =	+ 5,000.00
750		$12,700.00
750		$12,700.00
+ 100	@ $21.00 =	+ 2,100.00
850		$14,800.00
850		$14,800.00
− 300	@ $17.41 =	− 1,000.00
550		$15,000.00

① The most current average cost per unit is assigned to the units sold.

② The beginning balance less the cost of the units sold equals the remaining inventory.

③ The total cost remaining in inventory divided by the total units remaining equals the average unit cost. Notice that the average unit cost does not change because of a sale.

1d. Specific identification perpetual

Date	Purchases			Sales (at cost)			Inventory Balance		
	Units	Unit Cost	Total Cost	Units	Units Cost	Cost of Goods Sold	Units	Unit Cost	Total Cost
Jan. 1	Beginning inventory 400 @	$ 14 =	$5,600				① 400 @	$ 14 =	$ 5,600
15				200 @	$ 14 =	$2,800	200 @	$ 14 =	$ 2,800
Mar. 10	200 @	$ 15 =	$3,000			②	200 @ 200 @ 400	$ 14 = 15 =	$ 2,800 3,000 $ 5,800
Apr. 1				100 @ 100 @ 200	$ 14 = 15 = =	$1,400 1,500 $2,900	100 @ 100 @ 200	$ 14 = 15 =	$ 1,400 1,500 $ 2,900
May 9	300 @	$ 16 =	$4,800				100 @ 100 @ 300 @ 500	$ 14 = 15 = 16 =	$ 1,400 1,500 4,800 $ 7,700
Sept. 22	250 @	$ 20 =	$5,000				100 @ 100 @ 300 @ 250 @ 750	$ 14 = 15 = 16 = 20 =	$ 1,400 1,500 4,800 5,000 $12,700
Nov. 1	100 @	$ 21 =	$2,100	②			100 @ 100 @ 300 @ 250 @ 100 @ 850	$ 14 = 15 = 16 = 20 = 21 =	$ 1,400 1,500 4,800 5,000 2,100 $14,800
28				100 @ 100 @ 100 @ 300	$ 14 = 15 = 21 =	$1,400 1,500 2,100 $5,000	300 @ 250 @ 550	$ 16 = 20 =	$ 4,800 5,000 $ 9,800
Totals	**1,250**		**$20,500**	**700**		**$10,700**	**550**		**$9,800**

Cost of goods available for sale = *Cost of goods sold* + *Ending inventory*

① 200 of the beginning inventory units were specifically identified as being sold on January 15. Therefore, the 200 units remaining on January 15 are identified as units from beginning inventory.

② The units sold on April 1 and November 28 are specifically identified. The units sold determines exactly which units remain in inventory.

2.

	2001 Correct Amount Using FIFO	2001 Incorrect Amount Using LIFO	
Cost of goods sold	$10,200	$11,900	Because cost of goods sold is overstated (too high) by $1,700, the net income will be understated (too low) by $1,700 in 2001.

	2001 Correct Amount Using FIFO	2001 Incorrect Amount Using LIFO	
Beginning inventory	$10,300	$8,600	Because the ending inventory for one period becomes the beginning inventory for the next period, the error in the 2001 ending inventory is carried forward to 2002. The result is that cost of goods sold will be understated (too low) by $1,700, causing 2002 net income to be overstated (too high) by $1,700

3. Analysis of the effects of alternative inventory methods:

	Cost of Goods Sold	Difference from FIFO Cost of Goods Sold	Effect on Net Income if adopted instead of FIFO
FIFO	$10,200	—	—
LIFO	11,900	+ $1,700	Net income would be $1,700 lower
Weighted Average	10,923	+ 723	Net income would be $723 lower
Specific Identification	10,700	+ 500	Net income would be $500 lower

Assigning Costs to Inventory—Periodic System

APPENDIX

LO8 Compute inventory in a periodic system using the methods of specific identification, weighted average, FIFO, and LIFO.

The aim of the periodic system is the same as the perpetual system: to assign costs to the inventory and the goods sold. The same four methods are used in assigning costs: specific identification; weighted average; first-in, first-out; and last-in, first-out. We use information from **Trekking** to describe how we assign costs using these four methods with a periodic system. Data for sales and purchases are reported in the chapter and are not repeated here.

Specific Identification

The amounts of cost assigned to inventory and cost of goods sold are the same under the perpetual and periodic systems. This is because specific identification precisely defines which units are in inventory and which are sold.

Weighted Average

The weighted average method of assigning cost involves three important steps, as illustrated in Exhibits 7A.1 and 7A.2. First, we multiply the per unit cost for beginning inventory and each particular purchase by their corresponding number of units. Second, we add these amounts and divide by the total number of units available for sale to find the *weighted average cost per unit.*

Exhibit 7A.1

Weighted Average Cost per Unit—Periodic

Step 1:	10 units	@ $ 91	=	$ 910	
	15 units	@ 106	=	1,590	
	20 units	@ 115	=	2,300	
	10 units	@ 119	=	1,190	
	55 units available for sale			**$5,990**	Total cost of goods available for sale
Step 2:	$5,990/55 = **$108.91** weighted average cost per unit				

The third step is to use the weighted average cost per unit to assign costs to inventory and to units sold:

Exhibit 7A.2

Weighted Average Computations—Periodic

Step 3:	
Total cost of 55 units available for sale	$5,990
Less: **Ending inventory** priced on a weighted average cost basis:	
12 units at $108.91 each	1,307*
Cost of goods sold (= 43 units x $108.91)	**$4,683***

**Rounded to nearest whole dollar.*

The assignment of costs to cost of goods sold and inventory using weighted average usually gives different results depending on whether a perpetual or periodic system is used. This is because weighted average under a perpetual system recomputes the per unit cost at the time of each sale. Under the periodic system, the per unit cost is only computed at the end of a period.

First-In, First-Out

The first-in, first-out (FIFO) method of assigning cost to inventory and goods sold using the periodic system is shown in Exhibit 7A.3.

Exhibit 7A.3

FIFO Computations—Periodic

Total cost of 55 units available for sale		$5,990
Less: **Ending inventory** priced using FIFO:		
10 units from August 28 purchase at $119 each	$1,190	
2 units from August 17 purchase at $115 each	230	
12 units in ending inventory		1,420*
Cost of goods sold		**$4,570***

Trekking's ending inventory reported on the balance sheet is $1,420 and its cost of goods sold reported on the income statement is $4,570. The assignment of costs to cost of goods sold and inventory using FIFO is the same for both the perpetual and periodic systems. This will always occur because the most recent purchases are in ending inventory under both systems.

Last-In, First-Out

The last-in, first-out (LIFO) method of assigning costs to the 12 remaining units in inventory and to cost of goods sold using the periodic system is shown in Exhibit 7A.4.

Exhibit 7A.4

LIFO Computations—Periodic

Total cost of 55 units available for sale		$5,990
Less: **Ending inventory** priced using LIFO:		
10 units in beginning inventory at $91 each	$910	
2 units from August 3 purchase at $106 each	212	
12 units in ending inventory		1,122
Cost of goods sold		**$4,868**

Trekking's ending inventory reported on the balance sheet is $1,122 and its cost of goods sold reported on the income statement is $4,868. The assignment of costs to cost of goods sold and inventory using LIFO usually gives different results depending on whether a perpetual or periodic system is used. This is because LIFO under a perpetual system assigns the most recent costs to goods sold at the time of each sale, whereas the periodic system waits to assign costs until the end of a period.

Exhibit 7A.5

Comparison of Inventory Methods—Periodic

	Specific Identification		Weighted Average		FIFO		LIFO	
	Units	$	Units	$	Units	$	Units	$
Cost of goods sold (or Cost of sales)	43	$4,586	43	$4,683	43	$4,570	43	$4,868
Ending inventory	12	1,404	12	1,307	12	1,420	12	1,122
Goods available for sale	55	$5,990	55	$5,990	55	$5,990	55	$5,990

When compared to the schedule in Exhibit 7.9 you can see that the figures for specific identification and FIFO are identical. However, the figures for Weighted Average and LIFO will differ between the perpetual and periodic methods.

10. A company uses a periodic inventory system and reports the following beginning inventory and purchases (and ends the period with 30 units on hand):

	Units	Cost per Unit
Beginning Inventory	100	$10
Purchases #1	40	12
#2	20	14

a. Compute ending inventory using FIFO.
b. Compute cost of goods sold using LIFO.

Answer—p. 364

APPENDIX

Using the Information

Merchandise Turnover and Days' Sales in Inventory

LO9 Assess inventory management using both merchandise turnover and days' sales in inventory.

This section describes how we use information about inventory to assess a company's short-term liquidity P. 220 and its management of inventory. Two measures useful for these assessments are defined and explained in this section.

Merchandise Turnover

A company's ability to pay its short-term obligations depends, in part, on how quickly it sells its merchandise inventory. The **merchandise turnover**, also called **inventory turnover**, is one ratio used to help analyze short-term liquidity. It is also used to assess whether management is doing a good job of controlling the amount of inventory on hand. The merchandise turnover is defined as shown in Exhibit 7B.1.

Exhibit 7B.1

Merchandise Turnover

$$\text{Merchandise turnover} = \frac{\text{Cost of goods sold}}{\text{Average merchandise inventory}}$$

Average merchandise inventory is usually computed by adding beginning and ending inventory amounts and dividing the total by two. If a company's sales vary within the year, it is often better to take an average of inventory amounts at the end of each quarter or month.

The merchandise turnover ratio tells us how many *times* a company turns its inventory over during a period. For example, Exhibit 7B.2 shows the merchandise turnover for Macrotronics, the company discussed in the Chapter 7 opening article, in comparison to Mark's Work Wearhouse for the year 2000.

Exhibit 7B.2

Merchandise Turnovers Compared for Macrotronics and Mark's Work Wearhouse for the Year 2000

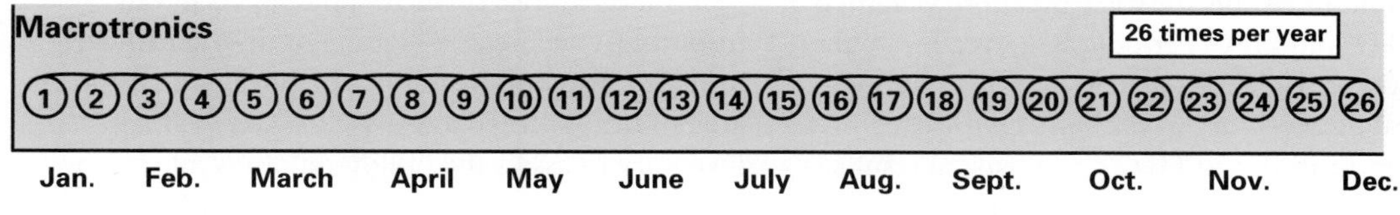

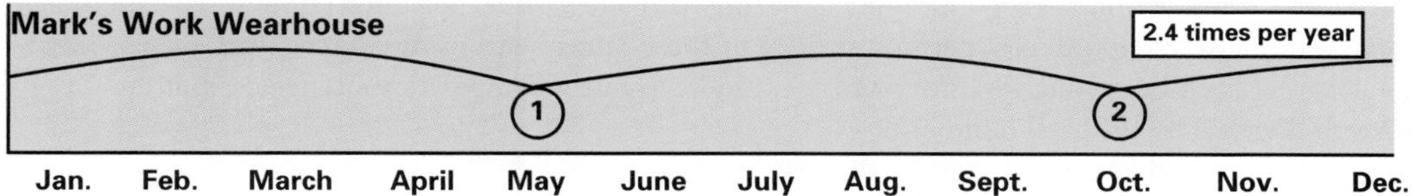

As Exhibit 7B.2 illustrates, Macrotronics' turnover ratio suggests that the amount of inventory on hand is low and that it is sold more quickly than that of Mark's Work Wearhouse. However, Macrotronics sells computer hardware, and is a different type of business than Mark's Work Wearhouse. As discussed in the opening article, Macrotronics is part of an industry where it is critical to move merchandise quickly because of the danger of obsolescence and rapidly changing costs. Mark's Work Wearhouse is in a different industry where merchandise turnovers of 2.4 times per year are typical. Ratio comparisons such as the preceding must be based on companies that are similar in order to be meaningful.

There is no simple rule with merchandise turnover, except to say that a high ratio is preferable provided inventory is adequate to meet demand.

Days' Sales in Inventory

To better interpret merchandise turnover, many users want a measure to determine if inventory levels can meet sales demand. **Days' sales in inventory**, also called **days' stock on hand**, is a ratio that estimates how many days it will take to convert inventory on hand into accounts receivable or cash. Days' sales in inventory is computed as shown in Exhibit 7B.3.

Exhibit 7B.3

Days' Sales in Inventory

$$\text{Days' sales in inventory} = \frac{\text{Ending inventory}}{\text{Cost of goods sold}} \times 365$$

Notice the different focus of days' sales in inventory and merchandise turnover. Days' sales in inventory focuses on ending inventory, whereas merchandise turnover focuses on average inventory.

Summary of Appendix 7A and Appendix 7B

LO8 **Compute inventory in a periodic system using the methods of specific identification, weighted average, FIFO, and LIFO.** Periodic systems allocate the cost of goods available for sale between cost of goods sold and ending inventory *at the end of a period.* Specific identification and FIFO give identical results whether the periodic or perpetual system is used. LIFO assigns cost to cost of goods sold assuming the last units purchased for the period are the first units sold. Weighted average cost computes cost per unit by taking the total cost of both beginning inventory and net purchases and dividing by the total number of units available. It then multiplies cost per unit by the number of units sold to give cost of goods sold.

LO9 **Assess inventory management using both merchandise turnover and days' sales in inventory.** We prefer a high merchandise turnover provided inventory is not out of stock and customers are not being turned away. We use days' sales in inventory to assess the likelihood of inventory being out of stock. We prefer a small number of days' sales in inventory provided we can serve customer needs and provide a buffer for uncertainties. Together, each of these ratios helps us assess inventory management and evaluate a company's short-term liquidity.

GUIDANCE ANSWER TO 

10. a. Ending inventory = (20 × \$14) + (10 × \$12) = \$400

b. Cost of goods sold = (20 × \$14) + (40 × \$12) + (70 × \$10) = \$1,460

Glossary

Average cost method See *weighted average inventory costing.* (p. 338)

Conservatism A shortened reference to the *conservatism principle.* (p. 347)

Conservatism principle The accounting principle that guides accountants to select the less optimistic estimate when two estimates of amounts to be received or paid are about equally likely. (p. 347)

Consignee One who receives and holds goods owned by another party for the purpose of selling the goods for the owner. (p. 333)

Consignor An owner of goods who ships them to another party who will then sell the goods for the owner. (p. 333)

Consistency principle The accounting requirement that a company use the same accounting methods period after period so that the financial statements of succeeding periods will be comparable. (p. 343)

Cost-to-benefit constraint See *materiality.* (p. 333)

Days' sales in inventory An estimate of how many days it will take to convert the inventory on hand at the end of the period into accounts receivable or cash; calculated by dividing the ending inventory by cost of goods sold and multiplying the result by 365. (p. 363)

Days' stock on hand See *days' sales in inventory.* (p. 363)

First-in, first-out inventory pricing (FIFO) The pricing of an inventory under the assumption that inventory items are sold in the order acquired; the first items received were the first items sold. (p. 339)

Full disclosure principle The GAAP that requires financial statements (including footnotes) to report all relevant information about the operations and financial position of the entity. (p. 341)

Gross profit method A procedure for estimating an ending inventory in which the past gross profit rate is used to estimate cost of goods sold, which is then subtracted from the cost of goods available for sale to determine the estimated ending inventory. (p. 348)

Gross profit ratio Measures how much of net sales is gross profit; calculated as gross profit divided by net sales; also known as the *gross margin ratio.* (p. 348)

Gross margin ratio See *gross profit ratio.*

Internal controls The policies and procedures used to protect assets, ensure reliable accounting, promote efficient operations, and urge adherence to company policies. (p. 334)

Inventory turnover See *merchandise turnover.* (p. 362)

Last-in, first-out inventory pricing (LIFO) The pricing of an inventory under the assumption that the most recent items purchased are sold first and their costs are charged to cost of goods sold. (p. 339)

Lower of cost or market (LCM) The required method of reporting merchandise inventory in the balance sheet where market value is reported when market is lower than cost; the market value may be defined as net realizable value or current replacement cost on the date of the balance sheet. (p. 347)

Market Defined as either *net realizable value* or *replacement cost.* (p. 347)

Materiality principle This GAAP states that an amount may be ignored if its affect on the financial statements is not important to their users; also called *cost-to-benefit constraint.*(p. 333)

Merchandise turnover The number of times a company's average inventory was sold during an accounting period, calculated by dividing cost of goods sold by the average merchandise inventory balance; also called *inventory turnover.* (p. 362)

Net realizable value The expected sales price of an item minus the cost of making the sale. (p. 333)

Physical count To count merchandise inventory for the purpose of reconciling goods actually on hand to the inventory control account in the general ledger. (p. 333)

Replacement cost Current cost of purchasing an item. (p. 347)

Retail The selling price of merchandise inventory. (p. 349)

Retail inventory method A method for estimating an ending inventory cost based on the ratio of the amount of goods for sale at cost to the amount of goods for sale at marked selling prices. (p. 349)

Specific identification The pricing of an inventory where the purchase invoice of each item in the ending inventory is identified and used to determine the cost assigned to the inventory. (p. 336)

Specific invoice inventory pricing See *specific identification.* (p. 336)

Taking an inventory See *physical count.* (p. 333)

Weighted average inventory costing An inventory pricing system in which the unit prices of the beginning inventory and of each purchase are weighted by the number of units in the beginning inventory and each purchase. The total of these amounts is then divided by the total number of units available for sale to find the unit cost of the ending inventory and of the units that were sold. (p. 338)

Questions

1. What accounts are used in a periodic inventory system but not in a perpetual inventory system?
2. What is meant when it is said that inventory errors correct themselves?
3. If inventory errors correct themselves, why be concerned when such errors are made?
4. Where is merchandise inventory disclosed in the financial statements?
5. Why are incidental costs often ignored in pricing an inventory? Under what accounting principle is this permitted?
6. Give the meanings of the following when applied to inventory: (a) FIFO, (b) LIFO, and (c) cost.
7. If prices are falling, will the LIFO or the FIFO method of inventory valuation result in the lower cost of goods sold?
8. May a company change its inventory pricing method each accounting period?
9. Does the accounting principle of consistency disallow any changes from one accounting method to another?
10. What effect does the full disclosure principle have if a company changes from one acceptable accounting method to another?
11. What guidance for accountants is provided by the principle of conservatism?
12. What is the usual meaning of the word *market* as it is used in determining the lower of cost or market for merchandise inventory?
13. Refer to WestJet's financial statements in Appendix I. On December 31, 1999 what percentage of WestJet's assets was represented by what would be WestJet's inventory? Is this merchandise inventory?

14. Refer to ClubLink's financial statements in Appendix I. Is it possible to determine a cost of sales figure for ClubLink? What is the cost of goods sold figure for ClubLink?

Quick Study

QS 7-1
Inventory ownership
LO1

1. At year-end Carefree Company has shipped, FOB destination, $500 of merchandise that is still in transit to Stark Company. Which company should include the $500 as part of inventory at year-end?
2. Carefree Company has shipped goods to Stark and has an arrangement that Stark will sell the goods for Carefree. Identify the consignor and the consignee. Which company should include any unsold goods as part of inventory?

QS 7-2
Inventory ownership
LO1

Crafts and More, a distributor of handmade gifts, operates out of owner Scott Arlen's home. At the end of the accounting period, Arlen tells us he has 1,500 units of products in his basement, 30 of which were damaged by water leaks and cannot be sold. He also has another 250 units in his van, ready to deliver to fill a customer order, terms FOB destination, and another 70 units out on consignment to a friend who owns a stationery store. How many units should be included in the end-of-period inventory?

QS 7-3
Inventory costs
LO2

A car dealer acquires a used car for $3,000. Additional costs in obtaining and offering the car for sale include $150 for transportation-in, $200 for import duties, $50 for insurance during shipment, $25 for advertising, and $250 for sales staff salaries. For computing inventory, what cost is assigned to the used car acquired? 340

QS 7-4
Inventory costs
LO2

Rigby & Son, antique dealers, purchased the contents of an estate for a bulk bid price of $37,500. The terms of the purchase were FOB shipping point, and the cost of transporting the goods to Rigby & Son's warehouse was $1,200. Rigby & Son insured the shipment at a cost of $150. Prior to placing the goods in the store, they cleaned and refurbished some merchandise at a cost of $490 for labour and parts. Determine the cost of the inventory acquired in the purchase of the estate's contents.

QS 7-5
Calculating cost of goods available for sale
LO3

A company has beginning inventory of 10 units at $50. Every week for four weeks an additional 10 units are purchased at respective costs of $51, $52, $55, and $60. Calculate the total cost of goods that were available for sale and the total units that were available for sale.

QS 7-6
Inventory costing methods—perpetual
LO3

A company had the following beginning inventory and purchases during January for a particular item. On January 28, 345 units were sold. What is the cost of the 140 units that remain in the ending inventory, assuming:

a. FIFO,
b. LIFO, and
c. Weighted average?

Round numbers to the nearest cent. Assume a perpetual inventory system.

	Units	Unit Cost	Total Cost
Beginning inventory on January 1	310	$3.00	$ 930.00
Purchase on January 9	75	3.20	240.00
Purchase on January 25	100	3.35	335.00
Total available for sale	485		$1,505.00

QS 7-7
Specific identification inventory method
LO3

Refer to the information in QS 7-6. Recall that 345 units were sold on January 28. The units specifically sold were:

- 250 units from beginning inventory
- 50 units from the January 9 purchase, and
- 45 units from the purchase on January 25.

Calculate cost of goods sold and the cost of ending inventory.

QS 7-8
Contrasting inventory costing methods
LO4

Identify the inventory costing method most closely related to each of the following statements, assuming a period of rising costs:

a. Matches recent costs against revenue.
b. Understates current value of inventory on a balance sheet.
c. Results in a balance sheet inventory closest to replacement costs.
d. Is best when each unit of product has unique features that affect cost.

QS 7-9
Inventory errors
LO5

The Weston Company performed a physical inventory count at the end of 2001. It was later determined that certain units were counted twice. Explain how this error affects the following:

a. 2001 cost of goods sold,
b. 2001 gross profit,
c. 2001 net income,
d. 2002 net income,
e. The combined two-year income, and
f. Income in years after 2002.

QS 7-10
Applying LCM to inventories
LO6

Thrifty Trading Co. has the following products in its ending inventory:

		Per Unit	
Product	Quantity	Cost	Market
Aprons	9	$6.00	$5.50
Bottles	12	3.50	4.25
Candles	25	8.00	7.00

Calculate lower of cost or market

a. For the inventory as a whole and
b. Applied separately to each product.

QS 7-11
Estimating inventories—gross profit method

LO7

The inventory of Bell Department Store was destroyed by a fire on September 10, 2001. The following 2001 data were found in the accounting records:

Jan. 1 inventory	$180,000
Jan. 1 – Sept. 10 purchases (net)	$342,000
Jan. 1 – Sept. 10 sales	$675,000
2001 estimated gross profit rate	42%

Determine the cost of the inventory destroyed in the fire.

QS 7-12
Estimating ending inventory—retail method

LO7

Best Stereo Centre showed the following selected information on August 31, 2001:

	Cost	Retail
Cost of goods available for sale	$67,600	$104,000
Net sales		$ 82,000

Using the retail method, estimate the cost of the ending inventory.

***QS 7-13**
Inventory costing methods—periodic

LO8

Refer to the information in QS 7-6. Determine the cost of the 140 units that remain in ending inventory, assuming:
a. FIFO
b. LIFO, and
c. Weighted average.
Round numbers to the nearest cent and use a periodic inventory system.

***QS 7-14**
Merchandise turnover

LO9

Huff Company and Mesa Company are similar firms that operate within the same industry. The following information is available.

	Huff			Mesa		
	2001	2000	1999	2001	2000	1999
Merchandise turnover	23.2	20.9	16.1	13.5	12.0	11.6

Required
Based on the information provided, which company is managing inventory more efficiently? Explain.

***QS 7-15**
Merchandise turnover and day's sales in inventory

LO9

Mixon Company showed the following selected information for the years ended December 31, 2001, 2000, and 1999:

	2001	2000	1999
Cost of goods sold	$410,225	$344,500	$312,600
Merchandise inventory (December 31)	56,195	82,500	111,500

Compute:
a. Days' sales in inventory and
b. Merchandise turnover for the year ended December 31, 2001.
Indicate if the change in the ratio from 2000 to 2001 is favourable (good) or unfavourable (not good).

An asterisk (*) identifies assignment material based on Appendix 7A or Appendix 7B.

Exercises

Exercise 7-1
Alternative cost flow assumptions—perpetual

LO3

Check Figures:
COGS a. $8,350.00;
b. $8,613.40;
c. $9,000.00

Parfour, Inc., made purchases of a particular product in the current year as follows:

Jan. 1	Beginning inventory	100 units	@	$10.00	=	$ 1,000
Mar. 14	Purchased	250 units	@	15.00	=	3,750
July 30	Purchased	400 units	@	20.00	=	8,000
Oct. 26	Purchased	600 units	@	25.00	=	15,000
	Units available for sale	1,350 units				
	Cost of goods available for sale					$27,750

Parfour, Inc., made sales on the following dates at a selling price of $40 a unit:

Jan. 10	90 units
Mar. 15	140 units
Oct. 5	300 units
Total	530 units

Required
The business uses a perpetual inventory system. Determine the costs that should be assigned to the ending inventory and to goods sold under:
a. FIFO
b. Weighted average
c. LIFO.
Also calculate the gross profit under each of the methods.

Exercise 7-2
Specific identification cost flow assumption

LO3

Check figures:
COGS = $8,650;
Gross profit = $12,550

Refer to the data in Exercise 7-1. Assume that Parfour uses the specific identification method to cost inventory. The 530 units were specifically sold as follows:

Jan. 10:	90	units from beginning inventory
Mar. 15:	10	units from beginning inventory, and
	130	units from the March 14 purchase
Oct. 5:	60	units from the March 14 purchase, and
	240	units from the July 30 purchase

Calculate cost of goods sold and the gross profit.

Exercise 7-3
Alternative cost flow assumptions—perpetual inventory system

LO3

Check figures:
COGS a. $4,092.75;
b. $4,245.00;
c. $3,940.00;

Trout, Inc., made purchases of a particular product in the current year (2001) as follows:

Jan. 1	Beginning inventory	120 units	@	$6.00	=	$ 720
Mar. 7	Purchased	250 units	@	5.60	=	1,400
July 28	Purchased	500 units	@	5.00	=	2,500
Oct. 3	Purchased	450 units	@	4.60	=	2,070
Dec. 19	Purchased	100 units	@	4.10	=	410
	Totals	1,420 units				$7,100

Trout, Inc., made sales on the following dates at a selling price of $15 per unit:

Jan. 10	70 units
Mar. 15	125 units
Oct. 5	600 units
Total	795 units

Required

The business uses a perpetual inventory system. Determine the share of the $7,100 cost of the units for sale that should be assigned to the ending inventory and to goods sold under:

a. A weighted-average cost basis,
b. FIFO,
c. LIFO.

Exercise 7-4

Specific identification cost flow assumption

Check figure:
COGS = $4,018

Use the information in Exercise 7-3. Assume that Trout, Inc. specifically sold the following units:

Jan. 10:	70 units from beginning inventory
Mar. 15:	25 units from beginning inventory, and
	100 units from the March 7 purchase
Oct. 5:	320 units from the July 28 purchase, and
	280 units from the October 3 purchase

Calculate cost to be assigned to ending inventory and cost of goods sold.

Exercise 7-5

Income statement effects of alternative cost flow assumptions

LO4

Use the data in Exercises 7-3 and 7-4 to construct comparative income statements for Trout, Inc. (year-end 2001), similar to those shown in Exhibit 7.10 in the chapter. Assume that operating expenses are $1,250.

1. Which method results in the highest net income?
2. Does the weighted average net income fall between the FIFO and LIFO net incomes?
3. If costs were rising instead of falling, which method would result in the highest net income?

Exercise 7-6

Analysis of inventory errors

LO5

Check figures:
1. 2001 = $380,000
   2002 = $420,000
   2003 = $400,000

Assume that The John Henry Company had $900,000 of sales during each of three consecutive years, and it purchased merchandise costing $500,000 during each of the years. It also maintained a $200,000 inventory from the beginning to the end of the three-year period. However, it made an error at the end of the first year, 2001, that caused its ending 2001 inventory to appear on its statements at $180,000 rather than the correct $200,000.

Required

1. State the actual amount of the company's gross profit in each of the years.
2. Prepare a comparative income statement like Exhibit 7.13 to show the effect of this error on the company's cost of goods sold and gross profit in 2001, 2002, and 2003.

Exercise 7-7

Lower of cost or market

LO6

Check figures:
a. $6,984
b. $6,896

Showtime Company's ending inventory includes the following items:

Product	Units on Hand	Unit Cost	Net Realizable Value per Unit
BB	22	$50	$54
FM	15	78	72
MB	36	95	91
SL	40	36	36

Net realizable value (NRV) is determined to be the best measure of market. Calculate lower of cost or market for the inventory:

a. As a whole, and
b. Applied separately to each product.

Exercise 7-8
Estimating ending inventory—retail method

LO7

Check figure:
$17,985.42

During 2001, Harmony Co. sold $130,000 of merchandise at marked retail prices. At the end of 2001, the following information was available from its records:

	At Cost	At Retail
Beginning inventory	$31,900	$64,200
Net purchases	57,810	98,400

Use the retail method to estimate Harmony's 2001 ending inventory at cost. Take all calculations to two decimal places.

Exercise 7-9
Reducing physical inventory to cost—retail method

LO7

Assume that in addition to estimating its ending inventory by the retail method, Harmony Co. of Exercise 7-8 also took a physical inventory at the marked selling prices of the inventory items at the end of 2001. Assume further that the total of this physical inventory at marked selling prices was $27,300.

a. Determine the amount of this inventory at cost.

b. Determine Harmony's 2001 inventory shrinkage from breakage, theft, or other causes at retail and at cost.

Round all calculations to two decimal places.

Exercise 7-10
Estimating ending inventory—gross profit method

LO7

On January 1, The Parts Store had a $450,000 inventory at cost. During the first quarter of the year, it purchased $1,590,000 of merchandise, returned $23,100, and paid freight charges on purchased merchandise totalling $37,600. During the past several years, the store's gross profit on sales has averaged 30%. Under the assumption the store had $2,000,000 of sales during the first quarter of the year, use the gross profit method to estimate its inventory at the end of the first quarter.

***Exercise 7-11**
Alternative cost flow assumptions–periodic

LO8

Check figure:
b. COGS = $3,230.00

Paddington Gifts, Inc. made purchases of a particular product in the current year as follows:

Jan. 1	Beginning inventory	120 units	@	$3.00	=	$ 360
Mar. 7	Purchased	250 units	@	2.80	=	700
July 28	Purchased	500 units	@	2.50	=	1,250
Oct. 3	Purchased	450 units	@	2.30	=	1,035
Dec.19	Purchased	100 units	@	2.05	=	205
	Totals	1,420 units				$3,550

Required

The business uses a periodic inventory system. Ending inventory consists of 150 units. Calculate the costs to be assigned to the ending inventory and to goods sold under:

a. A weighted-average cost basis,

b. FIFO, and

c. LIFO.

Which method provides the lowest net income?

An asterisk (*) identifies assignment material based on Appendix 7A or Appendix 7B.

*Exercise 7-12

Alternative cost flow assumptions—periodic

Check figure:
b. Ending inventory = $309.00

Jasper & Williams, Inc., made purchases of a particular product in the current year as follows:

Jan. 1	Beginning inventory................	120 units	@	$2.00	=	$ 240
Mar. 7	Purchased..............................	250 units	@	2.30	=	575
July 28	Purchased..............................	500 units	@	2.50	=	1,250
Oct. 3	Purchased..............................	450 units	@	2.80	=	1,260
Dec.19	Purchased..............................	100 units	@	2.96	=	296
	Totals	1,420 units				$3,621

Required
Ending inventory consists of 150 units. Assuming a periodic system, determine the costs to be assigned to cost of goods sold and ending inventory under:
a. FIFO
b. LIFO
c. Weighted average cost basis.
Which method provides the lowest net income?

*Exercise 7-13

Specific identification cost flow assumption—periodic

Check figure:
COGS = $3,280.50

Use the information in Exercise 7-12. Assume that the specific identification method is used to assign costs to cost of goods sold ending inventory. The units in ending inventory were specifically identified as follows:

- 80 units from beginning inventory,
- 7 units from the March 7 purchase,
- 48 units from the July 28 purchase, and
- 15 units from the December 19 purchase.

Required
Determine the cost to be assigned to ending inventory and cost of goods sold.

*Exercise 7-14

Merchandise turnover and days' sales in inventory

From the following information for Russo Merchandising Co., calculate merchandise turnover for 2003 and 2002 and days' sales in inventory at December 31, 2003 and 2002. Round answers to one decimal place.

	2003	2002	2001
Cost of goods sold..	$643,825	$426,650	$391,300
Merchandise inventory (December 31)	96,400	86,750	91,500

Comment on Russo's efficiency in using its assets to support increasing sales from 2002 to 2003.

An asterisk (*) identifies assignment material based on Appendix 7A or Appendix 7B.

Problems

Problem 7-1A
Alternative cost flows—perpetual

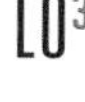

The Hall Company has the following inventory and purchases during the fiscal year ended December 31, 2001.

Beginning	500 units	@	$45/unit
Feb. 10	250 units	@	42/unit
Aug. 21	130 units	@	50/unit

Hall Company has two sales during the period. The units have a selling price of $75.00 per unit.

Sales	
Mar. 15	330 units
Sept.10	235 units

Hall Company employs a perpetual inventory system.

Required
1. Calculate cost of goods available for sale and units available for sale.
2. Calculate units remaining in ending inventory.
3. Calculate the dollar value of cost of goods sold and ending inventory using:
   a. FIFO
   b LIFO
   c. Weighted average.
   Round to two decimal places.
4. Calculate the dollar value of cost of goods sold and ending inventory using specific identification, assuming the sales were specifically identified as follows:

Mar. 15:	170	units from beginning inventory, and
	160	units from the February 10 purchase
Sept. 10:	165	units from beginning inventory, and
	20	units from the February 10 purchase, and
	50	units from the August 21 purchase

5. Calculate the gross profit earned by Hall Company under each of the costing methods in (3) and (4).

Analysis Component:

6. If the Hall Company's manager earns a bonus based on a percentage of gross profit, which method of inventory costing will she prefer?

Check figures:
1. Cost of goods available for sale = $39,500.00
3. Ending inventory
   a. $14,270.00
   b. $14,175.00
   c. $14,306.30

Problem 7-2A
Alternative cost flows—perpetual

LO3

The Lukich Company has the following inventory and purchases during the fiscal year ended December 31, 2001.

Beginning	300 units	@	$40/unit
Feb. 10	200 units	@	42/unit
Mar. 13	300 units	@	39/unit
Sept. 5	250 units	@	32/unit

Lukich Company has two sales during the period. The units have a selling price of $80 per unit.

Sales	
Feb. 20	350 units
Oct. 10	500 units

Lukich Company employs a perpetual inventory system.

Check figures:
1. Ending inventory
   a. $6,400.00
   b. $7,950.00
   c. $7,375.00

Required
1. Calculate the dollar value of ending inventory and cost of goods sold using:
   a. FIFO
   b. LIFO
   c. Weighted average.
   Round all amounts to two decimal places.
2. Calculate the gross profit under each of the costing methods in (1).

Problem 7-3A
Income statement comparisons and cost flow assumptions—perpetual

LO3, 4

Green Jeans, Inc., sold 2,500 units of its product on September 20 and 3,000 units on December 22, all at a price of $45 per unit (and all during 2001). Incurring operating expenses of $6 per unit sold, it began the year with and made successive purchases of the product as follows:

January 1 beginning inventory	600 units	@	$18 per unit
Purchases:			
February 20	1,500 units	@	$19 per unit
May 16	700 units	@	$20 per unit
December 11	3,300 units	@	$22 per unit
Total	6,100 units		

Check figure:
1. Net income, FIFO = $101,800

Required
Preparation component:
1. Prepare a comparative income statement for the company, showing in adjacent columns the net incomes earned from the sale of the product, assuming the company uses a perpetual inventory system and prices its ending inventory on the basis of:
   a. FIFO,
   b. LIFO, and
   c. Weighted average cost.
   Round all amounts to two decimal places.

Analysis component:
2. How would the results of the three alternatives change if Green Jeans had been experiencing declining prices in the acquisition of additional inventory?

Problem 7-4A
Analysis of inventory errors

LO5

Shockley Co. reported the following amounts in its financial statements:

	Financial Statements for Year Ended December 31		
	2001	2002	2003
(a) Cost of goods sold	$ 715,000	$ 847,000	$ 770,000
(b) Net income	220,000	275,000	231,000
(c) Total current assets	1,155,000	1,265,000	1,100,000
(d) Owner's equity	1,287,000	1,430,000	1,232,000

In making the physical counts of inventory, the following errors were made:
- Inventory on December 31, 2001: understated $66,000
- Inventory on December 31, 2002: overstated $30,000

Required
Preparation component:
1. For each of the preceding financial statement items—(a), (b), (c), and (d)—prepare a schedule similar to the following and show the adjustments that would have been necessary to correct the reported amounts.

	2001	2002	2003
Cost of goods sold:			
Reported			
Adjustments: Dec. 31/01 error			
Dec. 31/02 error			
Corrected			

Analytical component:

2. What is the error in the aggregate net income for the three-year period that resulted from the inventory errors? Explain why this result occurs. Also explain why the understatement of inventory by $66,000 at the end of 2001 resulted in an understatement of equity by the same amount that year.

Problem 7-5A
Analysis of inventory errors
LO5

While performing a detailed review of its financial records, Doors Unlimited noted the following ending inventory errors:

2001	2002	2003
Understated $55,000	Overstated $16,000	No errors

	2001	2002	2003
Ending inventory as reported	$ 345,000	$ 420,000	$ 392,000
Cost of goods sold as reported	1,300,00	1,750,000	2,100,000

Required
Calculate the corrected ending inventory and cost of goods sold amounts for each year by completing the following schedule:

	2001	2002	2003
Corrected ending inventory			
Corrected cost of goods sold			

Problem 7-6A
Lower of cost or market
LO6

The following information pertains to the physical inventory of Electronics Unlimited taken at December 31:

Product	Units on Hand	Per Unit Cost	Per Unit Market Value
Audio equipment:			
Receivers	335	$ 90	$ 98
CD players	250	111	100
Cassette decks	316	86	95
Turntables	194	52	41
Video equipment:			
Televisions	470	150	125
VCRs	281	93	84
Video cameras	202	310	322
Car audio equipment:			
Cassette radios	175	70	84
CD radios	160	97	105

Required
Calculate the lower of cost or market:
a. For the inventory as a whole,
b. For the inventory by major category, and
c. For the inventory, applied separately to each product.

Check figures:
a. $274,702
b. $270,332
c. $263,024

Problem 7-7A
Estimating ending inventory—gross profit method

LO7

The Navarre Company had a fire on February 10, 2001 that destroyed a major portion of its inventory. The salvaged accounting records contained the following information:

Sales, January 1 to February 10	$350,600
Net merchandise purchased Jan. 1 to Feb. 10	182,400
Additional information was determined from the 2000 annual report:	
Income statement:	
Sales	$3,200,225
Cost of goods sold	1,760,575
Balance sheet:	
Merchandise inventory	294,100

Navarre was able to salvage inventory with a cost of $106,200.

Check figure:
$177,470

Required
Determine the amount of inventory lost by Navarre as a result of the fire. Navarre has a December 31 year-end.

Problem 7-8A
Gross profit method

LO7

Walker Company wants to prepare interim financial statements for the first quarter of 2001 but would like to avoid making a physical count of inventory. During the last five years, the company's gross profit rate has averaged 35%. The following information for the year's first quarter is available from its records:

January 1 beginning inventory	$ 300,260
Purchases	945,200
Purchase returns	13,050
Transportation-in	6,900
Sales	1,191,150
Sales returns	9,450

Check figure:
$471,205

Required
Use the gross profit method to prepare an estimate of the company's March 31 inventory.

Problem 7-9A
Retail inventory method

LO7

The records of Basics Company provided the following information for the year ended December 31, 2001.

	At Cost	At Retail
January 1 beginning inventory	$ 471,350	$ 927,150
Purchases	3,328,830	6,398,700
Purchase returns	52,800	119,350
Sales		5,495,700
Sales returns		44,600

Check figure:
2. Loss at cost = $41,392

Required
1. Prepare an estimate of the company's year-end inventory by the retail method. Round all calculations to two decimal places.
2. Under the assumption the company took a year-end physical inventory at marked selling prices that totalled $1,675,800, prepare a schedule showing the store's loss from theft or other cause at cost and at retail.

Problem 7-10A
Retail inventory method

LO7

Macrotronics had a robbery on the weekend in which a large amount of inventory was taken. The loss is totally covered by insurance. A physical inventory count determined that the cost of the remaining merchandise is $234,000. The following additional information is available:

	At Cost	At Retail
Beginning merchandise inventory	$ 300,000	$ 375,000
Purchase returns and allowances	60,000	80,000
Purchases	5,100,000	6,925,000
Transportation-in	75,000	
Sales		6,570,000
Sales returns and allowances		72,000

Required

1. Prepare an estimate of ending merchandise inventory using the retail method.
2. Calculate the cost of the stolen inventory.

Check figure:
2. $307,500

***Problem 7-11A**
Alternative cost flows—periodic

LO8

Mill House Company began 2001 with 20,000 units of Product X in its inventory that cost $15 per unit, and it made successive purchases of the product as follows:

Mar. 7	28,000 units @ $18 each
May 25	30,000 units @ $22 each
Aug. 1	20,000 units @ $24 each
Nov. 10	33,000 units @ $27 each

The company uses a periodic inventory system. On December 31, 2001, a physical count disclosed that 35,000 units of Product X remained in inventory.

Required

1. Prepare a calculation showing the number and total cost of the units available for sale during 2001.
2. Prepare calculations showing the amounts that should be assigned to the 2001 ending inventory and to cost of goods sold, assuming:
   a. FIFO
   b. LIFO
   c. Weighted average cost basis.

Check figures:
2. Cost of goods sold
a. $1,896,000
b. $2,265,000
c. $2,077,557

***Problem 7-12A**
Income statement comparisons and cost flow assumptions—periodic

LO8

Use the data from Problem 7-3A and redo the problem assuming that Green Jeans, Inc. uses the periodic inventory method (round the average cost per unit to two decimal places).

Check figure:
1. Net income, LIFO = $98,600

An asterisk (*) identifies assignment material based on Appendix 7A or Appendix 7B.

Alternate Problems

Problem 7-1B

Alternative cost flows—perpetual

LO3

The Clinton Company has the following inventory purchases during the fiscal year ended December 31, 2001.

Beginning	600 units	@ $55/unit
Jan.10	450 units	@ 56/unit
Feb.13	200 units	@ 57/unit
July 21	230 units	@ 58/unit
Aug. 5	345 units	@ 59/unit

Clinton Company has two sales during the period. The units have a selling price of $90 per unit.

Sales	
Feb. 15	300 units
Aug. 10	335 units

Clinton Company employs a perpetual inventory system.

Check figures:
1. Cost of goods available for sale = $103,295.00
3. Ending inventory
   a. $68,335.00
   b. $66,530.00
   c. $67,569.70

Required
1. Calculate cost of goods available for sale and units available for sale.
2. Calculate units remaining in ending inventory.
3. Calculate the dollar value of cost of goods sold and ending inventory using
   a. FIFO
   b. LIFO
   c. Specific identification
   d. Weighted average method.
4. Calculate the dollar value of cost of goods sold and ending inventory using specific identification assuming the sales were specifically identified as follows:

Feb. 15:	175	units from beginning inventory
	80	units from the January 10 purchase
	45	units from the February 13 purchase
Aug. 10:	15	units from beginning inventory
	132	units from the January 10 purchase
	188	units from the August 5 purchase

5. Calculate the gross profit earned by Clinton Company under each of the cost methods in (3) and (4).

Analysis Component:

6. If the Clinton Company's manager earns a bonus based on a percentage of gross profit, which method of inventory costing will he prefer?

Problem 7-2B

Alternative cost flows—perpetual

LO3

The Moran Company has the following inventory and purchases during the fiscal year ended December 31, 2001.

Beginning	200 units	@ $60/unit
Feb. 15	300 units	@ 62/unit
Apr. 30	320 units	@ 58/unit
Sept. 21	200 units	@ 54/unit
Oct. 5	250 units	@ 50/unit

Moran Company has two sales during the period. The units have a selling price of $80 per unit.

Sales	
Feb. 20	450 units
Oct. 10	500 units

Moran Company employs a perpetual inventory system.

Required

1. Calculate the dollar value of ending inventory and cost of goods sold using:
   a. FIFO
   b. LIFO
   c. Weighted average method
   Round all values to the nearest dollar.
2. Calculate the gross profit under each of the costing methods in (1).

Check figures:
1. Ending inventory
   a. $16,280
   b. $18,660
   c. $17,530

Problem 7-3B

Income statement comparisons and cost flow assumptions—perpetual

LO3, 4

The Denney Company sold 1,200 units of its product on May 20 and 1,300 units on October 25, all at a price of $98 per unit (all during 2001). Incurring operating expenses of $14 per unit in selling the units, it began the year with, and made successive purchases of, units of the product as follows:

January 1 Beginning inventory	740 units costing $58 per unit		
Purchases:			
April 2	700 units	@	$59 per unit
June 14	600 units	@	$61 per unit
Aug. 29	500 units	@	$64 per unit
Nov. 18	800 units	@	$65 per unit
Total	3,340 units		

Required

Preparation component:

1. Prepare a comparative income statement for the company, showing in adjacent columns the net incomes earned from the sale of the product, assuming the company uses a perpetual inventory system and prices its ending inventory on the basis of:
   a. FIFO,
   b. LIFO, and
   c. Weighted average cost.

Analysis component:

2. How would the results of the three alternatives change if Denney had been experiencing decreasing prices in the acquisition of additional inventory?

Check figure:
1. Net income, LIFO = $59,500

Problem 7-4B

Analysis of inventory errors

LO5

Matchstick Company reported the following amounts in its financial statements:

	Financial Statements for Year Ended December 31		
	2001	2002	2003
(a) Cost of goods sold	$ 205,200	$ 212,800	$ 196,030
(b) Net income	174,800	211,270	183,910
(c) Total current assets	266,000	276,500	262,950
(d) Owner's equity	304,000	316,000	336,000

In making the physical counts of inventory, the following errors were made:

- Inventory on December 31, 2001: overstated $17,000
- Inventory on December 31, 2002: understated $25,000

Required

Preparation component:

1. For each of the preceding financial statement items—(a), (b), (c), and (d)—prepare a schedule similar to the following and show the adjustments that would have been necessary to correct the reported amounts.

	2001	2002	2003
Cost of goods sold			
Reported			
Adjustments: Dec. 31/01 error			
Dec. 31/02 error			
Corrected			

Analysis component:

2. What is the error in the aggregate net income for the three-year period that resulted from the inventory errors?

Problem 7-5B
Analysis of inventory errors

LO5

	Incorrect Income Statement Information For Years Ended December 31				Corrected Income Statement Information For Years Ended December 31			
	2001	%	2002	%	2001	%	2002	%
Sales	$1,350,000	100	$1,690,000	100				
Cost of goods sold	810,000	60	845,000	50				
Gross profit	$ 540,000	40	$ 845,000	50				

In comparing income statement information for the years ended December 31, 2001 and 2002, the owner noticed an increase in the gross profit. He was puzzled because he knew that inventory costs were increasing.

A detailed review of the records showed the following:

a. Goods with a cost of $75,000 were on consignment at another location. They were not included in the December 31, 2001 inventory in error.
b. $32,000 of merchandise inventory purchased on December 25, 2002 was shipped *FOB Shipping Point* and received on January 6, 2003. It was not included in inventory on December 31, 2002 in error.
c. While performing the physical inventory count on December 31, 2002, a calculation error was discovered that caused inventory on hand to be overstated by $49,000.

Required

1. Using the information provided, complete the schedule showing the corrected income statement information.
2. Does the new gross profit information reflect the owner's view of costs?

Problem 7-6B
Lower of cost or market

LO6

The following information pertains to the physical inventory of Office Outfitters taken at December 31:

Product	Units on Hand	Per Unit Cost	Per Unit Market Value
Office furniture:			
Desks	436	$261	$305
Credenzas	295	227	256
Chairs	587	49	43
Bookshelves	321	93	82
Filing cabinets:			
Two-drawer	214	81	70
Four-drawer	398	135	122
Lateral	175	104	118
Office equipment:			
Fax machines	430	168	200
Copiers	545	317	288
Typewriters	352	125	117

Required

Calculate the lower of cost or market for the:

a. Inventory as a whole,
b. Inventory by major category, and
c. Inventory, applied separately to each product.

Check figures:
a. $617,646
b. $607,707
c. $584,444

Problem 7-7B
Estimating ending inventory—gross profit method

LO7

The Toowong Company had a flood on July 5, 2002 that destroyed all of its inventory. The salvaged accounting records contained the following information:

Sales, January 1 to July 5	$1,475,300
Net merchandise purchased Jan. 1 to July 5	829,800
Additional information was determined from the 2001 annual report:	
Income statement:	
Sales	$4,245,100
Cost of goods sold	2,674,350
Balance sheet:	
Merchandise inventory	262,400

Toowong was unable to salvage any usable inventory after the water subsided.

Required

Determine the amount of inventory lost by Toowong as a result of the flood. Toowong has a December 31 year-end.

Check figure:
$162,761

Problem 7-8B
Gross profit method

LO7

Four Corners Equipment Co. wants to prepare interim financial statements for the first quarter of 2001. The company uses a periodic inventory system but would like to avoid making a physical count of inventory. During the last five years, the company's gross profit rate has averaged 30%. The following information for the year's first quarter is available from its records:

January 1 beginning inventory	$ 752,880
Purchases	2,132,100
Purchase returns	38,370
Transportation-in	65,900
Sales	3,710,250
Sales returns	74,200

Check figure:
$367,275

Required
Use the gross profit method to prepare an estimate of the company's March 31, 2001 inventory.

Problem 7-9B
Retail inventory method

LO7

The records of The R.E. McFadden Co. provided the following information for the year ended December 31, 2001:

	At Cost	At Retail
January 1 beginning inventory	$ 81,670	$ 114,610
Purchases	502,990	767,060
Purchase returns	10,740	15,330
Sales		786,120
Sales returns		4,480

Check figure:
2. Loss at cost = $4,074.30

Required
1. Prepare an estimate of the company's year-end inventory by the retail method. Round all calculations to two decimal places.
2. Under the assumption the company took a year-end physical inventory at marked selling prices that totalled $78,550, prepare a schedule showing the store's loss from theft or other causes at cost and at retail.

Problem 7-10B
Retail inventory method

LO7

JavCo just had a fire in its warehouse that destroyed all of its merchandise inventory. The insurance company covers 80% of the loss. The following information is available regarding the year ended March 31, 2001:

	At Cost	At Retail
Beginning merchandise inventory	$ 150,000	$ 250,000
Purchases	2,100,000	3,500,000
Purchase returns and allowances	250,000	400,000
Transportation-in	10,000	
Sales		2,715,000
Sales returns and allowances		35,000

Check figure:
Loss = $80,400

Required
Prepare an estimate of the company's loss using the retail method.

***Problem 7-11B**
Alternative cost flows—periodic

LO8

Sea Blue Co. began 2001 with 6,300 units of Product B in its inventory that cost $35 each, and it made successive purchases of the product as follows:

Jan. 4	10,500 units	@	$33 each
May 18	13,000 units	@	$32 each
July 9	12,000 units	@	$29 each
Nov. 21	15,500 units	@	$26 each

The company uses a periodic inventory system. On December 31, 2001, a physical count disclosed that 16,500 units of Product B remained in inventory.

Required

1. Prepare a calculation showing the number and total cost of the units available for sale during the year.
2. Prepare calculations showing the amounts that should be assigned to the ending inventory and to cost of goods sold assuming:
   a. A FIFO basis,
   b. A LIFO basis, and
   c. A weighted average cost basis (round the average unit cost to two decimal places).

Check figures:
2. Ending inventory
   a. $432,000
   b. $557,100
   c. $499,290

***Problem 7-12B**
Income statement comparisons and cost flow assumptions—periodic

LO8

Use the data from Problem 7-3B and redo the problem assuming that the Denney Company uses the periodic inventory method. (Round the average cost per unit to two decimal places.)

Check figure:
1. Net income, weighted average = $56,688.80

Analytical and Review Problems

A & R Problem 7-1

The following information is taken from the records of Bradford Company for four consecutive operating periods:

	Periods			
	1	2	3	4
Beginning inventory	$29,000	$41,000	$31,000	$37,000
Ending inventory	41,000	31,000	37,000	19,000
Net income	25,000	29,000	33,000	41,000

Assume that the company made the errors below:

Period	Error in Ending Inventory
1	Overstated $5,000
2	Understated 8,000
3	Overstated 6,000

An asterisk (*) identifies assignment material based on Appendix 7A or Appendix 7B.

Required

1. Compute the revised net income for each of the four periods.
2. Assuming that the company's ending inventory for Period 4 is correct, how would these errors affect the total net income for the four periods combined? Explain.

A & R Problem 7-2

The records of Thomas Company as of December 31, 2001, show the following:

	Net Purchases	Net Income	Accounts Payable	Inventory
Balance per company's books	$329,000	$22,100	$29,200	$20,500
(a)				
(b)				
(c)				
(d)				
(e)				
Correct balances				

The accountant of Thomas Company discovers in the first week of January 2002 that the following errors were made by his staff.

a. Goods costing $4,500 were in transit (FOB shipping point) and were not included in the ending inventory. The invoice had been received and the purchase recorded.

b. Damaged goods (cost $4,100) that were being held for return to the supplier were included in inventory. The goods had been recorded as a purchase and the entry for the return of these goods had also been made.

c. Inventory items costing $3,900 were incorrectly excluded from the final inventory. These goods had not been recorded as a purchase and had not been paid for by the company.

d. Goods that were shipped FOB destination had not yet arrived and were not included in inventory. However, the invoice had arrived on December 30, 2001, and the purchase for $2,700 was recorded.

e. Goods that cost $2,400 were segregated and not included in inventory because a customer expressed an intention to buy the goods. The sale of the goods for $4,200 had been recorded in December 2001.

Required

Using the format provided above, show the correct amount for net purchases, net income, accounts payable, and inventory for Thomas Company as at December 31, 2001.

CHAPTER 8

Accounting Information Systems

What's the Score?

Moncton, NB—It was the worst event in Marie Lanctot's early career as owner of Outdoors Unlimited. She'd lobbied hard to carry REV Sports products in her sporting goods store. Her rejection letter was harsh, and to the point. "The financial condition and records of Outdoors Unlimited do not support a business relationship at this time...," the letter said.

Marie knew she'd pushed the limit in keeping her own records. "I purchased the best accounting software according to small business magazines. But," says Marie. "I didn't have any idea how to use it." Marie thought she knew how to enter her store's sales and purchases data. Yet it turned out some data were entered in ledgers and not in journals, and vice versa. "The software created lovely reports, but I didn't know if they were correct," admits Marie. "Ledgers, journals, footings, crossfootings—it was all a confusion to me!" Most frustrating was that Marie knew her store was doing well, and for unknown reasons her financials weren't reflecting it.

Learning Objectives

LO1 Explain the relationship of the accounting information system to the management information system.

LO2 Explain the components, structure, and fundamental standards of accounting information systems.

LO3 Identify what technology-based systems have impacted accounting.

LO4 Explain the goals and uses of special journals.

LO5 Describe the use of controlling accounts and subsidiary ledgers.

LO6 Journalize and post transactions using special journals.

LO7 Prepare and test the accuracy of subsidiary ledgers.

"I ended up taking an evening course," says Marie. "I learned how to set up an accounting system and how to keep special journals. I set up my records as I went through the course." Marie now regularly creates schedules of accounts payable and accounts receivable. "I use ledgers and aging schedules to identify late paying customers. I also keep payable records to help me better time payments to suppliers." Marie also points out that Outdoors Unlimited now carries REV's products.

And what about that accounting software? "It's great software," says Marie. "But it ought to carry the warning: A lack of accounting knowledge can damage your company's health."

Chapter Preview

An organization collects and processes a wide range of information. The accounting information system is part of a larger system, the management information system. Accounting information systems must be efficient and effective in meeting the demands of the increasing complexity and volume of financial transactions. In this chapter, we take a brief look at where the accounting information system is positioned in the organization's total information system and how it is structured. We learn about fundamental standards guiding information systems, and we study components of these systems. We also explain procedures that use special journals and subsidiary ledgers to make accounting information systems more efficient. Our understanding of where the details of accounting reports come from makes us better decision makers when using financial information, and it improves our ability to analyze and interpret financial statements. Like Marie Lanctot says in the opening article, knowledge of these topics helps in running a company successfully.

Information Systems

Management Information Systems

LO1 Explain the relationship of the accounting information system to the management information system.

A **management information system (MIS)** is designed to collect and process data within an organization for the purpose of providing users with information. Within the MIS are subsystems: sales and marketing, production, finance, human resources, and accounting. These subsystems and their relationship to the MIS[1] and internal and external users P. 13/14 are shown in Exhibit 8.1. The arrows illustrate the exchange of information. Notice that each subsystem is both a user and provider of information.

Exhibit 8.1

Accounting Information System in Relation to Other Information Systems

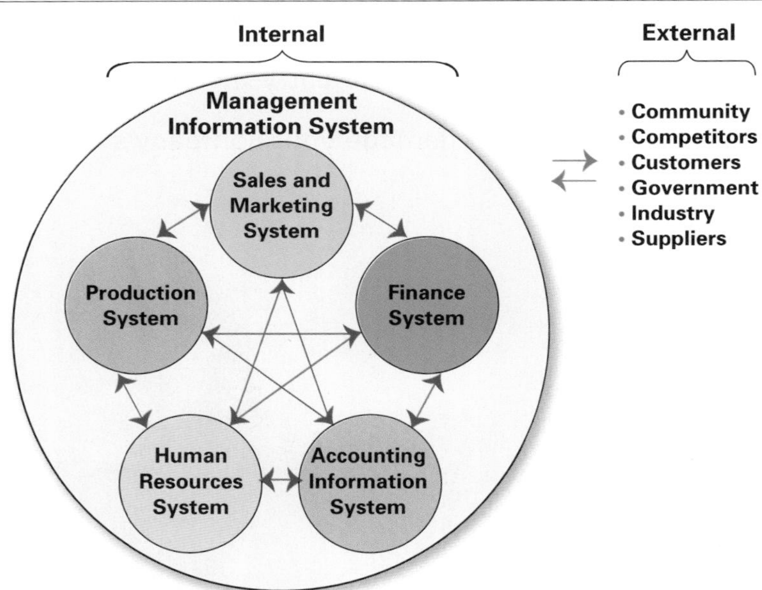

[1] There is discussion as to whether the accounting information system is a subsystem of the MIS or whether the two systems simply overlap. That discussion is beyond the scope of this textbook. Therefore, for the sake of brevity, the position taken here will be that the accounting information system is a subsystem of the MIS.

Accounting Information Systems

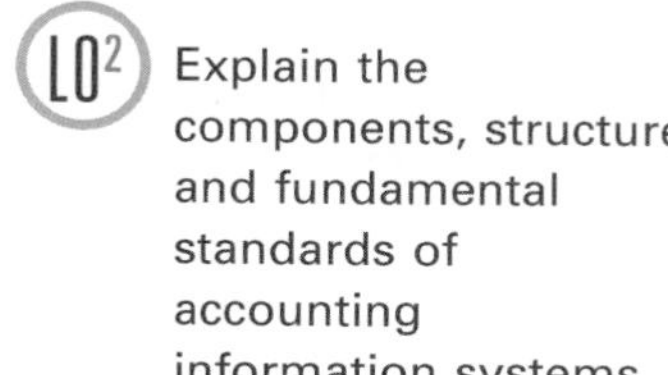

Explain the components, structure, and fundamental standards of accounting information systems.

An **accounting information system (AIS)** is a group of components that collect and process raw *financial* data into timely, accurate, relevant, and cost-effective information to meet the purposes of internal and external users. The primary components within an AIS are Accounts Payable, Accounts Receivable, and Payroll. Specialty components, such as Capital Assets, are often added dependent on the needs of the business. Exhibit 8.2 illustrates these components within the AIS.

Exhibit 8.2

Components of an AIS

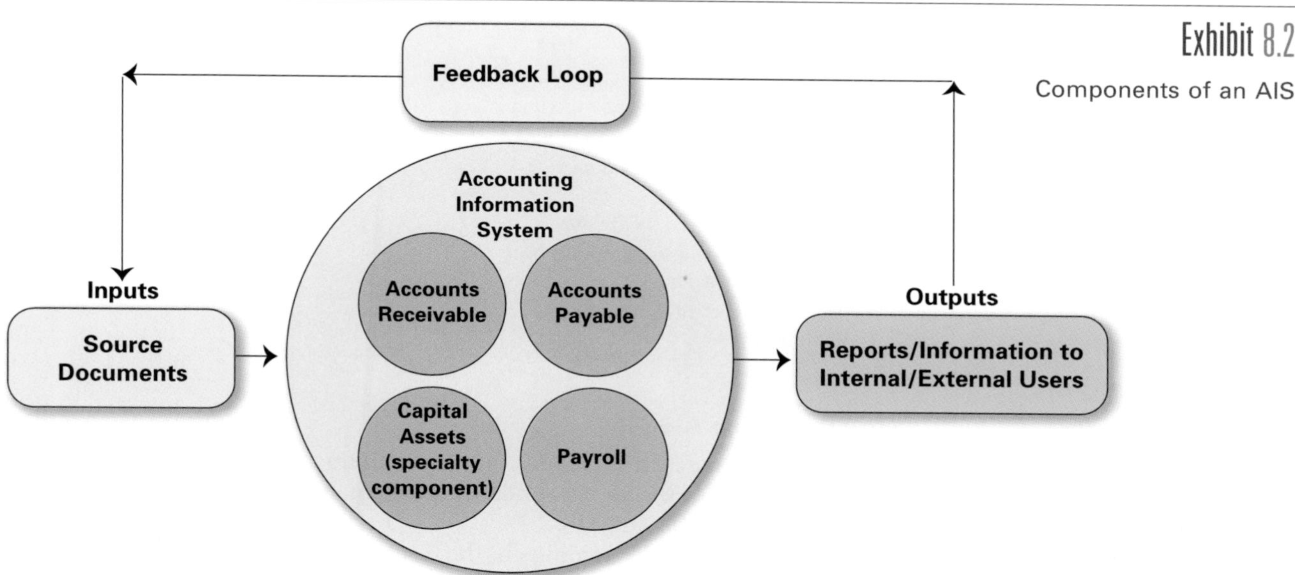

Other components of an AIS include people, data (inputs), software (accounting programs), hardware (computers), and reports (outputs). Most businesses, large and small, now depend on computers to provide support to the AIS.

Computers and the AIS

Basic accounting principles are the same whether the financial data are being processed manually or electronically. Prior to 1960, there were essentially no computer installations in business. Microcomputers began their widespread introduction in the early 1980s. Today, hundreds of thousands of computers have been put into operation in Canadian businesses. Of all the advances made over the years in the field of accounting, the computer has had the greatest impact. The use of computers in business began with the processing of payroll and inventory data but was restricted to large businesses because of the cost of computer systems. Today, even small firms process all or most of their accounting data using computers because it can now be done at a reasonable cost. There are advantages and disadvantages to using computers in an AIS. Exhibit 8.3 summarizes these.

Exhibit 8.3

Advantages and Disadvantages of Computerizing an AIS

Advantages	Disadvantages
• Time saved in processing data	• Unanticipated costs (related to testing, network and systems maintenance, security, and end-user retraining)
• More timely information	• Costs related to crashed/crashing systems
• Greater accuracy in processing data	
• Manipulates large volumes of data with ease	
• Greater range and detail of outputs available	
• Greater analytical ability	
• Financial information is immediately available for updating and reporting	
• Fewer paper accounting records	
• Lower cost of processing each transaction	
• More concise storage of data	
• More efficient retrieval /accessibility of data/information	
• Higher productivity for employees and managers	

Structure of an AIS

How the AIS is structured depends on the requirements of the users. A bank will have different needs than a restaurant or a steel manufacturer; however, the basic structure is similar for any AIS.

The journals and the accounts in the General Ledger form the foundation of the process that produces user reports. Whether the AIS is manual or computerized, the General Ledger system represents the primary database. Because the journal is the book of original entry, it serves as a check to the entries posted in the General Ledger accounts. The accounting components used for operating and financial controls are developed based on the journal and General Ledger systems. For example, the component used for accounts receivable control is related to sales and cash receipts.

Exhibit 8.4 shows the basic structural relationships. The sale of inventory (1) decreases inventory (requiring purchases to replenish stock), and (2) when on credit, creates accounts receivable and initiates the billing process. Accounts receivable are collected (cash receipts) and inventory purchases on account need to be paid (payment of accounts payable). These transactions, plus payroll activity, are posted into the General Ledger.

Exhibit 8.4

Accounting Information System Processing Cycle

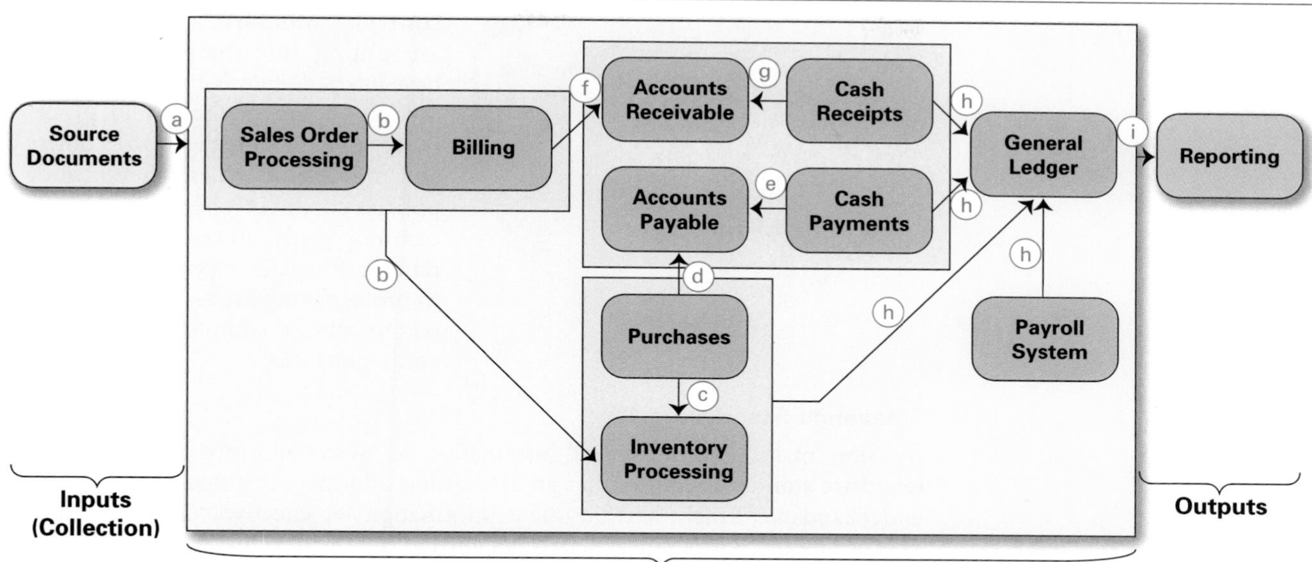

Explanation (not necessarily performed in this sequence):

(a) Source documents enter the Accounting Information System (AIS)

(b) Sales information is used to update records for both billing (Dr Accounts Receivable) and merchandise inventory (Cr Merchandise Inventory)

(c) Purchases are made based on sales information to maintain appropriate levels (Dr Merchandise Inventory)

(d) Purchases information is used to update Accounts Payable (Cr Accounts Payable)

(e) Purchases are paid when due and Accounts Payable is updated (Dr Accounts Payable)

(f) Accounts Receivable records are updated based on sales information (Dr Accounts Receivable)

(g) As cash is received from customers, Accounts Receivable is updated (Cr Accounts Receivable)

(h) All transactions are posted into the General Ledger at the end of the accounting period, including payroll transactions

(i) The AIS system generates financial statements at the end of the accounting period in addition to special purpose reports created as needed

Fundamental System Standards

In order for decision makers to structure an efficient and effective accounting information system, five fundamental standards must be incorporated. These are shown in Exhibit 8.5.

Exhibit 8.5

System Standards

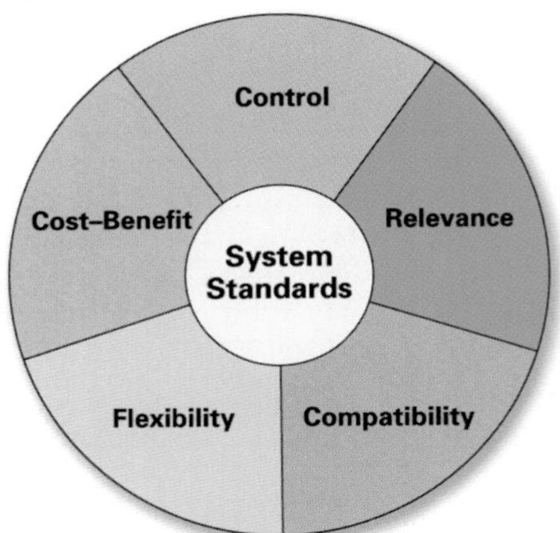

Control Standard

Managers need to control and monitor business activities. To this end, the **control standard** requires an accounting information system to have *internal controls.* Internal controls P. 334 are methods and procedures allowing managers to control and monitor activities. They include policies to direct operations toward common goals, procedures to ensure reliable financial reports, safeguards to protect company assets, and methods to achieve compliance with laws and regulations.

Relevance Standard

Decision makers need relevant information to make informed decisions. The **relevance standard** requires that an accounting information system report useful, understandable, timely, and pertinent information for effective decision making. This means an information system is designed to capture data that make a difference in decisions. To ensure this, it is important that all decision makers, both internal and external, be consulted when identifying relevant information for disclosure.

Compatibility Standard

Accounting information systems must be consistent with the aims of a company. The **compatibility standard** requires that an accounting information system conform to a company's activities, personnel, and structure. It must also adapt to the unique characteristics of a company. The system must not be intrusive but, rather, in harmony with and driven by company goals. Outdoors Unlimited described in the opening article, for example, needs a simple retail information system. Moore Corporation, on the other hand, demands a manufacturing information system that is able to assemble data from its global operations. (See p. 396 for more information on Moore Corporation.) These two systems are not compatible, yet they are effective for the two different companies.

Flexibility Standard

Accounting information systems must be able to adjust to change. The **flexibility standard** requires that an accounting information system adapt to changes in the company, business environment, and needs of decision makers. Technological advances, competitive pressures, consumer tastes, regulations, and company activities constantly change. A system must be designed to adapt.

Cost–Benefit Standard

Accounting information systems must balance costs and benefits. For each activity in an accounting information system the **cost–benefit standard** requires the benefits to outweigh the costs. The costs and benefits of an activity have an impact on the decisions of both external and internal information users. They also affect costs of computer systems, personnel, and other direct and indirect costs. Decisions regarding other systems standards (control, relevance, compatibility, and flexibility) are affected by the cost–benefit standard.

Accounting and Technology

LO3 Identify what technology-based systems have impacted accounting.

Source documents P. 85 provide the basic information processed by an accounting system. Examples are bank statements, cheques received for deposit, invoices from suppliers, billings to customers, and employee earnings records, to name a few. Source documents are often paper-based. Yet they are increasingly taking electronic form, such as those created by consumers using debit cards in lieu of cash to pay for goods purchased. Electronic funds transfer (EFT) capabilities allow employers to pay employees electronically by having funds transferred directly into the employee's bank account. More recently, e-commerce, or business conducted via the Internet, has taken financial transactions to cyberspace.

Computer hardware is the physical equipment in a computerized system. **Computer software** is the program that directs the operations of computer hardware. ACCPAC Plus® and Simply Accounting® are examples of accounting software used for small to medium-sized businesses. **Enterprise-application software** (such as SAP® and Oracle®) is an integrated program that manages a company's vital operations from order-taking to manufacturing to accounting, and is commonly used by the world's largest companies.

Flashback

1. Explain the difference between an MIS and an AIS.
2. Name the four basic components of an AIS.
3. Identify the five primary standards underlying an AIS.

Answers—p. 414

Public Accountant

You are a public accountant consulting with a client. This client's business has grown to the point where the accounting system must be updated to handle both the volume of transactions and management's needs for information. Your client requests your advice in purchasing new software for the accounting system. You have been offered a 10% commission by a software company for each purchase of its system by one of your clients. Do you think your evaluation of alternative software is affected by this commission arrangement? Do you think this commission arrangement is appropriate? Do you tell your client about the commission arrangement before making a recommendation?

Answers—p. 414

Special Journals in Accounting

Explain the goals and uses of special journals.

This section focuses both on *special journals* and *subsidiary ledgers*, the underlying operations of both manual and computerized accounting systems. These operations are set up to be efficient in processing transactions and events. They are part of all systems in various forms. They are also increasingly assisted by technology. But even in technologically advanced systems, an understanding of the operations we describe in this section will aid us in using, interpreting, and applying accounting information.

We describe how special journals are used to capture transactions, and we explain how subsidiary ledgers are set up to capture details of certain accounts. This section uses selected transactions of Outdoors Unlimited to illustrate these important points.

Since Outdoors Unlimited uses a *perpetual inventory* system P. 259, the special journals are set up using this system. Because the *periodic* inventory system P. 259 is still in use, we show in Appendix 8A the slight change in special journals when using a *periodic* system.

Basics of Special Journals—Perpetual Inventory System

A General Journal is an all-purpose journal where we can record any transaction. Yet using a General Journal means that each debit and each credit entered must be individually posted to its respective ledger account. The costs related to the time and effort of posting accounts can be reduced by organizing transactions into common groups and providing a separate special journal. A **special journal** is used in recording and posting transactions of similar type. Most transactions of a merchandiser, for instance, fall into four groups: sales on credit, purchases on credit, cash receipts, and cash disbursements. Exhibit 8.6 shows the special journals for these groups. This section assumes the use of these special journals along with the General Journal.

Exhibit 8.6

Using Special Journals with a General Journal

Sales Journal	Cash Receipts Journal	Purchases Journal	Cash Disbursement Journal	General Journal
For recording credit sales	For recording cash receipts	For recording credit purchases	For recording cash payments	For transactions not in special journals

The General Journal continues to be used for transactions not covered by special journals and for adjusting, closing, and correcting entries. We show in the following discussion how special journals are efficient tools for helping journalize and post transactions. This is done, for instance, by accumulating debits and credits of similar transactions, which allows us to post amounts entered in the columns as *column* totals rather than as individual amounts. The advantage of this system increases as the number of transactions increases. Special journals also allow an efficient division of labour. This can be an effective control procedure.

Subsidiary Ledgers

LO5 Describe the use of controlling accounts and subsidiary ledgers.

Accounting information systems must provide several detailed listings of amounts. One of the most important listings is the amounts due from customers, called *accounts receivable*, and amounts owed to creditors, called *accounts payable*. The Accounts Receivable account in the General Ledger (also known as Accounts Receivable Control) shows the total accounts receivable but it is difficult to extract information regarding one customer. To collect this information we often create a separate ledger called a *subsidiary ledger*.

A **subsidiary ledger** is a listing of individual accounts with a common characteristic. Using subsidiary ledgers removes unnecessary details from the General Ledger. Two common subsidiary ledgers are:

- **Accounts Receivable Ledger** for storing transaction data with individual customers.
- **Accounts Payable Ledger** for storing transaction data with individual creditors.

Accounts Receivable Ledger

When we recorded credit sales in prior transaction analysis, we debited Accounts Receivable. Yet when a company has more than one credit customer, the accounts receivable records must show how much *each* customer purchased, paid, and still owes. This information is collected for companies with credit customers by keeping a separate Account Receivable for each customer.

The General Ledger continues to keep a single Accounts Receivable account, called the **controlling account** because it controls the accounts receivable ledger. A subsidiary ledger is set up to keep a separate account for each customer. This subsidiary ledger is called the Accounts Receivable Ledger (also called *Accounts Receivable Subsidiary Ledger or Customers' Ledger*). Like a General Ledger, a subsidiary ledger can exist in electronic or paper form. Customer accounts in a subsidiary ledger are kept separate from the Accounts Receivable account in the General Ledger.

Exhibit 8.7 shows the relation between the Accounts Receivable controlling account and its related accounts in the subsidiary ledger. After all items are posted, the Accounts Receivable controlling account must equal the sum of balances in the customers' accounts in the Accounts Receivable Ledger.

Exhibit 8.7

Accounts Receivable Controlling Account and Subsidiary Ledger

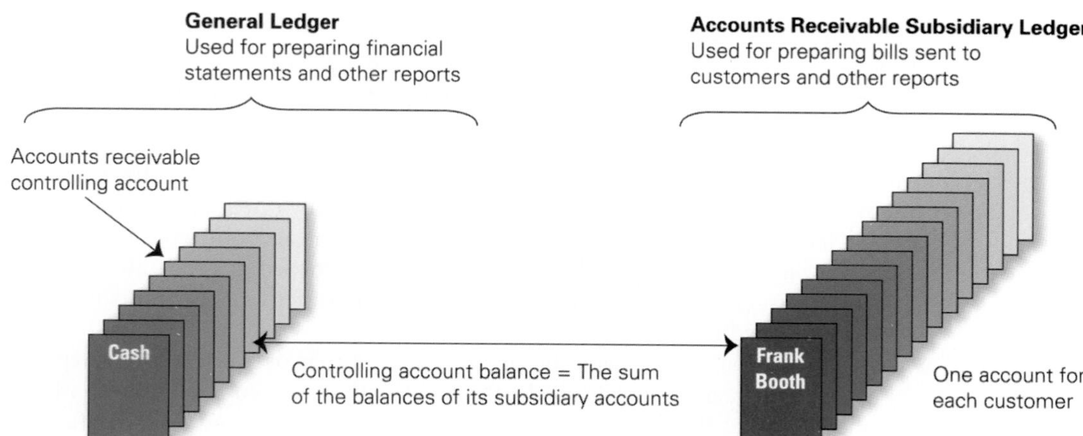

Accounts Payable Ledger

There are other controlling accounts and subsidiary ledgers. We know, for example, that many companies buy on credit from several suppliers. This means a company must keep a separate account for each creditor. It does this by keeping an Accounts Payable controlling account in the General Ledger and a separate account for each creditor in an Accounts Payable Ledger (also called *Accounts Payable Subsidiary Ledger or Creditors' Ledger*). The controlling account, subsidiary ledger, and columnar journal format described with accounts receivable also apply to Accounts Payable accounts.

Inventory Ledger

Merchandisers often have more than one type of item in inventory. Canadian Tire, for example, stocks thousands of different items from teapots to tents to tires. To manage such extensive stocks of inventory, companies using a perpetual inventory system record transactions affecting each type of inventory in a separate record. This group of individual inventory records makes up the *Inventory Ledger*. By keeping inventory information in separate records, detailed information about quantity, for example, is readily available. Exhibit 8.8 illustrates a typical Inventory Ledger record. This ledger is based on a FIFO P. 339 cost flow assumption.

Reitmans (Canada) Limited showed inventory on its January 29, 2000 balance sheet of $31.5 million. The $31.5 million is the balance in the Inventory account in the General Ledger and represents the total of the hundreds of individual inventory records in the Inventory Ledger. The total in the General Ledger is known as the controlling account. The balance of the Inventory controlling account must agree with the sum of the balances of the inventory records in the Inventory Ledger.

Exhibit 8.8

Subsidiary Inventory Record

Item: Leather Sports Bags — Location code: W18C2

Catalogue No.: LSB-117 — Units: Maximum 25 Minimum 5

		Purchases			Sales (at cost)			Balance		
Date	PR	Units	Unit Cost	Total Cost	Units	Unit Cost	Total Cost	Total Units	Unit Cost	Total Cost
2001 Aug. 1								10	$100	$1,000
12	S2				4	$100	$400	6	100	600
18	P3	20	$110	$2,200				6	100	
								20	110	2,800
30	S2				6	100	600			
					2	110	220	18	110	1,980
Totals		20		$2,200	12		$1,220			

Other Subsidiary Ledgers

Subsidiary ledgers are also common for several other accounts. A company with many items of equipment, for example, might keep only one Equipment account in its General Ledger. But this company's Equipment account would control a subsidiary ledger where each item of equipment is recorded in a separate account. Similar treatment is common with investments and other large accounts needing separate detailed records.

Moore Corporation, one of the largest manufacturers of business forms, reports in its 1999 annual report detailed sales information by geographic area, which included Canada, the United States, Europe, Latin America, and Asia Pacific. Yet Moore's accounting system most certainly keeps more detailed sales records than reflected in its annual report. Moore, for instance, sells hundreds of different products and is likely able to analyze the sales performance of each one of them. This detail can be captured by many different General Ledger sales accounts. But it is likely captured by using supplementary records that function like subsidiary ledgers. The concept of a subsidiary ledger can be applied in many different ways to ensure that our accounting system captures sufficient details to support analyses that decision makers need.

Mid-Chapter Demonstration Problem

Indicate in which journal each of the following transactions should be recorded:

a. Purchase of office supplies for cash.
b. Sale of merchandise on account.
c. Entry to record amortization expense for the period.
d. Purchase of merchandise on account.
e. Sale of scrap material for cash.
f. Collection of the amount of the sale in (b).

SOLUTION TO Mid-Chapter Demonstration Problem

a. Cash Disbursements Journal
b. Sales Journal
c. General Journal
d. Purchases Journal
e. Cash Receipts Journal
f. Cash Receipts Journal

LO6 Journalize and post transactions using special journals.

The next sections demonstrate the four common special journals: sales, cash receipts, purchases, and cash disbursements. While all of the transactions take place during the month of February, you will note that some of the General Ledger accounts have opening balances as of January 31. These balances are included for demonstration purposes only and to provide some continuity, where necessary. For simplicity, it has been assumed that the Accounts Receivable and Accounts Payable balances are zero at the beginning of February.

Sales Journal

A **Sales Journal** is used to record sales of merchandise on credit. Sales of merchandise for cash are not recorded in a Sales Journal, but instead are recorded in a Cash Receipts Journal. Sales of nonmerchandise assets on credit are recorded in the General Journal.

Journalizing

Credit sale transactions are recorded with information about each sale entered separately in a Sales Journal. This information is often taken from a copy of the sales ticket or invoice prepared at the time of sale. The top of Exhibit 8.9 shows a Sales Journal from a sporting goods merchandiser, Outdoors Unlimited. The Sales Journal in this exhibit is called a **columnar journal** because it has columns for recording the date, customer's name, invoice number, amount of each credit sale, and the cost of the merchandise sold.[2] A columnar journal is a journal with more than one column.

Exhibit 8.9

Sales Journal with Posting

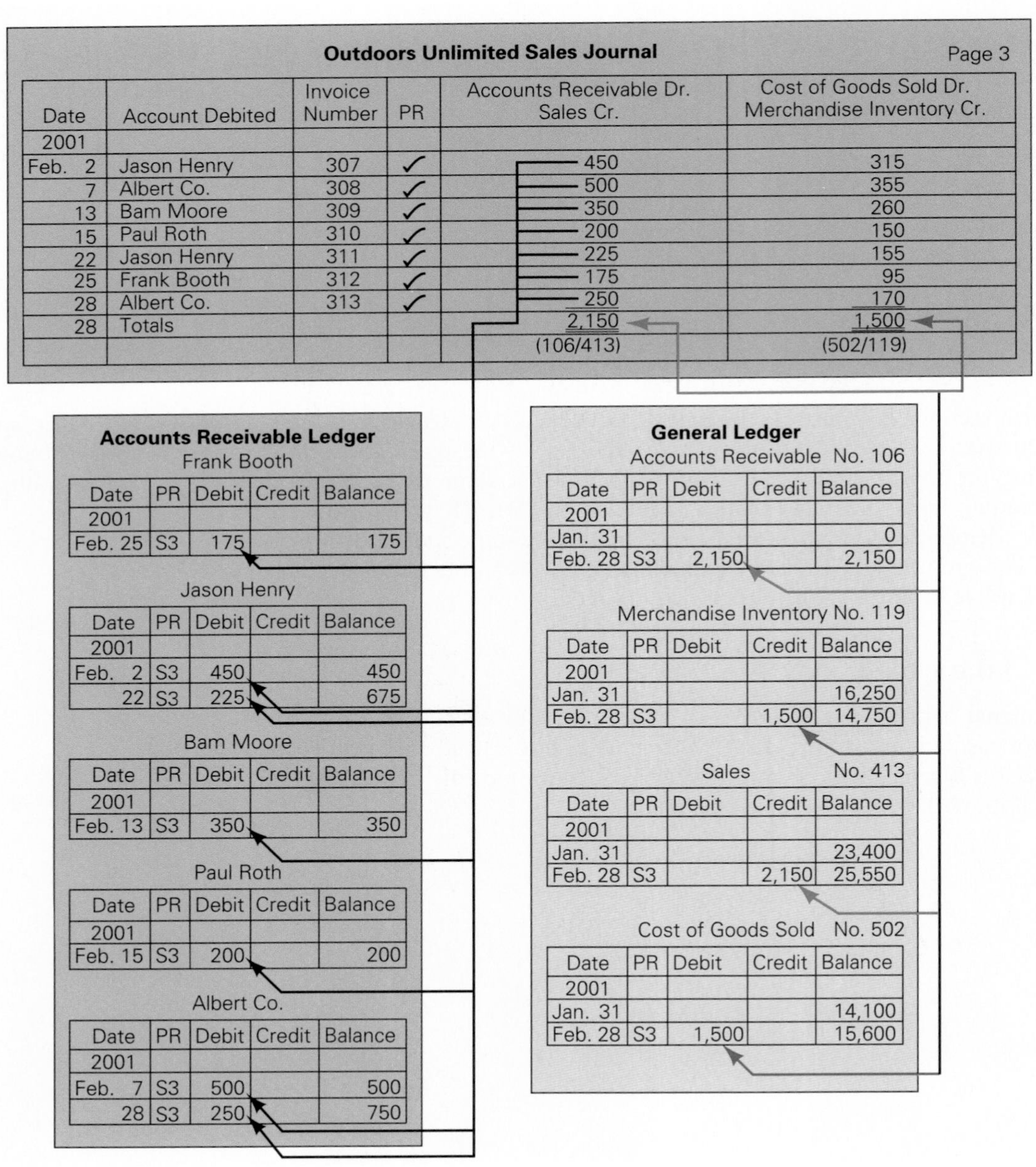

Outdoors Unlimited Sales Journal — Page 3

Date	Account Debited	Invoice Number	PR	Accounts Receivable Dr. Sales Cr.	Cost of Goods Sold Dr. Merchandise Inventory Cr.
2001					
Feb. 2	Jason Henry	307	✓	450	315
7	Albert Co.	308	✓	500	355
13	Bam Moore	309	✓	350	260
15	Paul Roth	310	✓	200	150
22	Jason Henry	311	✓	225	155
25	Frank Booth	312	✓	175	95
28	Albert Co.	313	✓	250	170
28	Totals			2,150	1,500
				(106/413)	(502/119)

Accounts Receivable Ledger

Frank Booth

Date	PR	Debit	Credit	Balance
2001				
Feb. 25	S3	175		175

Jason Henry

Date	PR	Debit	Credit	Balance
2001				
Feb. 2	S3	450		450
22	S3	225		675

Bam Moore

Date	PR	Debit	Credit	Balance
2001				
Feb. 13	S3	350		350

Paul Roth

Date	PR	Debit	Credit	Balance
2001				
Feb. 15	S3	200		200

Albert Co.

Date	PR	Debit	Credit	Balance
2001				
Feb. 7	S3	500		500
28	S3	250		750

General Ledger

Accounts Receivable No. 106

Date	PR	Debit	Credit	Balance
2001				
Jan. 31				0
Feb. 28	S3	2,150		2,150

Merchandise Inventory No. 119

Date	PR	Debit	Credit	Balance
2001				
Jan. 31				16,250
Feb. 28	S3		1,500	14,750

Sales No. 413

Date	PR	Debit	Credit	Balance
2001				
Jan. 31				23,400
Feb. 28	S3		2,150	25,550

Cost of Goods Sold No. 502

Date	PR	Debit	Credit	Balance
2001				
Jan. 31				14,100
Feb. 28	S3	1,500		15,600

[2] We do not record explanations in any of our special journals for brevity purposes.

Each transaction recorded in the Sales Journal yields a debit to Accounts Receivable and a credit to Sales, and a debit to Cost of Goods Sold and a credit to Merchandise Inventory. We only need two columns for these four accounts. An exception is when managers need more information about taxes, returns, departments, and other details of transactions. We describe these later in this section. We do not use the Posting Reference (PR) column P. 102 when entering transactions; instead this column is used when posting.

Posting

A Sales Journal is posted as shown in Exhibit 8.9. Individual transactions in the Sales Journal are typically posted each day to customer accounts in the Accounts Receivable Ledger. These postings keep customer accounts up to date. This is important for the person granting credit to customers, who needs to know the amount owed by credit-seeking customers. If this information in the customer's account is out of date, an incorrect decision can be made.

When sales recorded in the Sales Journal are individually posted to customer accounts in the Accounts Receivable Ledger, check marks are entered in the Sales Journal's Posting Reference column. Check marks are usually used rather than account numbers because customer accounts are not always numbered. Note that when debits (or credits) to Accounts Receivable are posted twice (once to the Accounts Receivable controlling account and once to the customer's account in the Accounts Receivable Ledger) this does not violate the accounting equation of debits equal credits. *The equality of debits and credits is always maintained in the General Ledger.* The Accounts Receivable Ledger is a subsidiary record with detailed information for each customer.

The Sales Journal's *amount* columns are totalled at the end of the period (month of February in this case). The total of the first amount column is debited to Accounts Receivable and credited to Sales. The credit records the period's revenue from sales on account. The debit records the increase in accounts receivable. The second amount column is debited to Cost of Goods Sold and credited to Merchandise Inventory. The debit records the cost of sales and the credit records the decrease in the inventory.

When a company uses more than one journal, it records in the Posting Reference column of the *ledgers* the journal and page number in the journal from which the amount is taken. We identify a journal by using an initial. Items posted from the Sales Journal carry the initial *S* before their journal page numbers in the Posting Reference columns. Likewise, items from the Cash Receipts Journal carry the initials *CR*, items from the Cash Disbursements Journal carry the initials *CD*, items from the Purchases Journal carry the initial *P*, and items from the General Journal carry the initial *G*.

There is a general rule for all postings to a subsidiary ledger and its controlling account: The controlling account is debited periodically for an amount or amounts equal to the sum of the debits to the subsidiary ledger, and it is credited periodically for an amount or amounts equal to the sum of the credits to the subsidiary ledger.

Prepare and test the accuracy of subsidiary ledgers.

Testing the Ledger

Account balances in the General Ledger and subsidiary ledgers are tested for accuracy after posting is complete. We do this by first preparing a trial balance P. 104 of the General Ledger to confirm debits equal credits. If debits equal credits in the trial balance, the accounts in the General Ledger, including the controlling accounts, are assumed to be correct. Second, we test the subsidiary ledgers by preparing a *schedule of accounts receivable.*

Exhibit 8.10

Schedule of Accounts Receivable

Outdoors Unlimited Schedule of Accounts Receivable February 28, 2001	
Frank Booth	$ 175
Jason Henry	675
Bam Moore	350
Paul Roth	200
Albert Co.	750
Total accounts receivable	$2,150

A **schedule of accounts receivable** is a listing of accounts from the Accounts Receivable Ledger with their balances and the sum of all balances. If this total equals the balance of the Accounts Receivable controlling account, the accounts in the Accounts Receivable Ledger are assumed correct. Exhibit 8.10 shows a schedule of accounts receivable drawn from the Accounts Receivable Ledger of Exhibit 8.9.

Sales Returns and Allowances

A company with only a few sales returns and allowances can record them in a General Journal with an entry like:

Mar. 7	Sales Returns and Allowances	414	10.00	
	Accounts Receivable—Robert Moore	106/✓		10.00
	Customer returned merchandise.			
7	Merchandise Inventory	119	6.00	
	Cost of Goods Sold	502		6.00
	The merchandise was returned to inventory.			

The debit in this entry is posted to the Sales Returns and Allowances account. The credit is posted to both the Accounts Receivable controlling account and to the customer's account in the subsidary ledger (posted daily). We also include the account number and the check mark, 106/✓, in the PR column on the credit line. This means both the Accounts Receivable controlling account in the General Ledger and the Robert Moore account in the Accounts Receivable Ledger are credited for $10.00. Both are credited because the balance of the controlling account in the General Ledger does not equal the sum of the customer account balances in the subsidiary ledger unless *both* are credited.

A company with a large number of sales returns and allowances can save costs by recording them in a special Sales Returns and Allowances Journal similar to Exhibit 8.11. A company can design and use a special journal for any group of similar transactions if there are enough transactions to warrant a journal. When using a Sales Returns and Allowances Journal to record returns, amounts in the journal are posted daily to customers' accounts. The journal total is posted as a debit to Sales Returns and Allowances and as a credit to Accounts Receivable at the end of the month.

Exhibit 8.11

Sales Returns and Allowances Journal

Outdoors Unlimited Sales Returns and Allowances Journal

Page 1

Date	Account Credited	Credit Memo No.	PR	Sales Returns & Allowances Dr. Accounts Receivable Cr.	Merchandise Inventory Dr. Cost of Goods Sold Cr.
2001					
Mar. 7	Robert Moore	203	✓	10	6
14	James Warren	204	✓	12	7
18	T.M. Jones	205	✓	6	4
23	Sam Smith	206	✓	18	11
31	Totals			46	28
				(414/106)	(502/119)

If the goods returned are in good condition and can be resold, then the cost of these items should be debited to Merchandise Inventory and credited to Cost of Goods Sold. If the returned goods are damaged or cannot be resold for some reason, the entry is not required since the goods are, in effect, lost and their costs should be included in the cost of goods sold and not be replaced into the Merchandise Inventory account.

4. When special journals are used, where are all cash payments by cheque recorded?
5. How does a columnar journal save posting time and effort?
6. How do debits and credits remain equal when credit sales to customers are posted twice (once to the Accounts Receivable controlling account and once to the customer's account in the subsidiary ledger)?
7. How do we identify the journal from which an amount in a ledger account was posted?

Answers—p. 415

Cash Receipts Journal

A **Cash Receipts Journal** records *all* receipts of cash. A Cash Receipts Journal must be a columnar journal because different accounts are credited when cash is received from different sources.

Journalizing

Cash receipts usually fall into one of three groups: (1) cash from credit customers in payment of their accounts, (2) cash from cash sales, and (3) cash from other sources. The Cash Receipts Journal in Exhibit 8.12 has a special column for credits when cash is received from one or more of these three sources. We describe how to journalize transactions for each of these three sources in this section. The next section describes how to post these transactions.[3]

[3] We include explanations in the Cash Receipts Journal to avoid listing the cash receipt transactions for February.

Cash from Credit Customers

To record cash received in payment of a customer's account, the customer's name is first entered in the Cash Receipts Journal's Accounts Credited column. Then the amounts debited to Cash and Sales Discounts, if any, are entered in their respective journal columns, and the amount credited to the customer's account is entered in the Accounts Receivable Credit column. Note that the Accounts Receivable Credit column contains only credits to customer accounts.

The posting procedure is twofold. First, individual amounts are posted to subsidiary ledger accounts. Second, column totals are posted to General Ledger accounts. Let's look at the Accounts Receivable Credit column as an example. First, individual credits are posted daily to customer accounts in the subsidiary Accounts Receivable Ledger. Second, the column total is posted at the end of the period as a credit to the Accounts Receivable controlling account.

Cash Sales

When cash sales are collected and totalled at the end of a day, the daily total is recorded with a debit to Cash and a credit to Sales. At the same time, the cost of sales is accumulated and recorded as a debit to Cost of Goods Sold and a credit to Merchandise Inventory. If we use a Cash Receipts Journal as in Exhibit 8.12, the debits to Cash are entered in the Cash Debit column, and the credits in a special column titled Sales Credit. By using a separate Sales Credit column, we can post the total cash sales for a month as a single amount, the column total. Cash sales are journalized weekly in Exhibit 8.12 for brevity.

Remember that in practice under a perpetual system these cash sales are recorded at the point of sale. To do that here would make this journal extremely lengthy since Outdoors Unlimited is a retailer with many cash sales every day. Note also that cash received from earlier credit sales does not result in amounts entered in the far right column. This is because the costs for these sales were recorded in the Sales Journal at the point of sale. The total of the Cost of Goods Sold and Merchandise Inventory amount column is posted to *both* of their General Ledger accounts at the end of the period.

Cash from Other Sources

Most cash receipts are from collections of accounts receivable and from cash sales. But other sources of cash include borrowing money from a bank, interest on account, or selling unneeded assets. The Other Accounts Credit column is for receipts that do not occur often enough to warrant a separate column. This means items entered in this column are few and are posted to a variety of General Ledger accounts. Postings are less apt to be omitted if these items are posted daily. The Cash Receipts Journal's Posting Reference column is used only for daily postings from the Other Accounts and Accounts Receivable columns. The account numbers in the Posting Reference column refer to items that are posted to General Ledger accounts.

Posting

At the end of a period, the amounts in the Cash, Sales Discounts, Accounts Receivable, Sales, Cost of Goods Sold and Merchandise Inventory columns of the Cash Receipts Journal are posted as column totals. The transactions recorded in all journals must result in equal debits and credits to general ledger accounts. To be sure that total debits and credits in a columnar journal are equal, we often *crossfoot* column totals before posting them. To **foot** a column of numbers is to

Exhibit 8.12

Cash Receipts Journal with Posting

Outdoors Unlimited Cash Receipts Journal

Page 2

Date	Accounts Credited	PR	Explanation	Cash Dr.	Sales Discount Dr.	Accounts Receivable Cr.	Sales Cr.	Other Accounts Cr.	Cost of Goods Sold Dr. Merchandise Inventory Cr.
2001									
Feb. 7	Sales		Cash sales	4,450			4,450		3,150
12	Jason Henry	✓	Invoice, Feb. 2	441	9	450			
14	Sales		Cash sales	3,925			3,925		2,950
17	Albert Co.	✓	Invoice, Feb. 7	490	10	500			
20	Notes Payable	245	Note to bank	750				750	
21	Sales		Cash sales	4,700			4,700		3,400
22	Interest Revenue	409	Bank account	250				250	
23	Bam Moore	✓	Invoice, Feb. 13	343	7	350			
25	Paul Roth	✓	Invoice, Feb. 15	196	4	200			
28	Sales		Cash sales	4,225			4,225		3,050
28	Totals			19,770	30	1,500	17,300	1,000	12,550
				(101)	(415)	(106)	(413)	(X)	(502/119)

Accounts Receivable Ledger

Frank Booth

Date	PR	Debit	Credit	Balance
2001				
Feb. 25	S3	175		175

Jason Henry

Date	PR	Debit	Credit	Balance
2001				
Feb. 2	S3	450		450
12	R2		450	-0-
22	S3	225		225

Bam Moore

Date	PR	Debit	Credit	Balance
2001				
Feb. 13	S3	350		350
23	R2		350	-0-

Paul Roth

Date	PR	Debit	Credit	Balance
2001				
Feb. 15	S3	200		200
25	R2		200	-0-

Albert Co.

Date	PR	Debit	Credit	Balance
2001				
Feb. 7	S3	500		500
17	R2		500	-0-
28	S3	250		250

General Ledger

Cash No. 101

Date	PR	Debit	Credit	Balance
2001				
Jan. 31				9,450
Feb. 28	R2	19,770		29,220

Accounts Receivable No. 106

Date	PR	Debit	Credit	Balance
2001				
Jan. 31				-0-
Feb. 28	S3	2,150		2,150
28	R2		1,500	650

Merchandise Inventory No. 119

Date	PR	Debit	Credit	Balance
2001				
Jan. 31				16,250
Feb. 28	S3		1,500	14,750
28	R2		12,550	2,200

Notes Payable No. 245

Date	PR	Debit	Credit	Balance
2001				
Jan. 31				-0-
Feb. 20	R2		750	750

Sales No. 413

Date	PR	Debit	Credit	Balance
2001				
Jan. 31				23,400
Feb. 28	S3		2,150	25,550
28	R2		17,300	42,850

Sales Discounts No. 415

Date	PR	Debit	Credit	Balance
2001				
Jan. 31				35
Feb. 28	R2	30		65

Interest Revenue No. 409

Date	PR	Debit	Credit	Balance
2001				
Jan. 31				260
Feb. 22	R2		250	510

Cost of Goods Sold No. 502

Date	PR	Debit	Credit	Balance
2001				
Jan. 31				14,100
Feb. 28	S3	1,500		15,600
28	R2	12,550		28,150

add it. To **crossfoot** we add the debit column totals and the credit column totals and compare the two sums for equality. Footing and crossfooting of the numbers in Exhibit 8.13 are as follows:

Exhibit 8.13

Footing and Crossfooting Journal Amounts

Debit Columns		Credit Columns	
Sales Discounts Debit	$ 30	Other Accounts Credit	$ 1,000
Cash Debit	19,770	Accounts Receivable Credit	1,500
Cost of Goods Sold Debit	12,550	Sales Credit	17,300
		Inventory Credit	12,550
Total	$32,350	Total	$32,350

After crossfooting the journal to confirm debits equal credits, we post the totals of all but the Other Accounts column as indicated by their column headings. Because individual items in the Other Accounts column are posted daily, this column total is not posted. We place an 'X' below the Other Accounts column to indicate that this *column total* is not posted. The account numbers of the accounts where the remaining column totals are posted are in parentheses below each column. Posting items daily from the Other Accounts column with a delayed posting of the offsetting total in the Cash column causes the General Ledger to be out of balance during the month. But this does not matter because posting the Cash column total causes the offsetting amounts to reach the General Ledger before the trial balance or other financial statements are prepared.

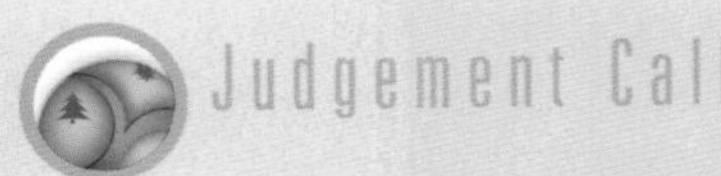

Answer—p. 414

Retailer

You are a retailer in computer equipment and supplies. You want to know how promptly customers are paying their bills. This information can help you in deciding whether to extend credit and in planning your own cash payments. Where might you look for this information?

Purchases Journal

A **Purchases Journal** is used to record *all* purchases on credit. Purchases for cash are recorded in the cash disbursements journal.

Journalizing

A Purchases Journal with one column for dollar amounts can be used to record purchases of merchandise on credit. But a Purchases Journal usually is more useful if it is a multicolumn journal where all credit purchases, not only merchandise, are recorded. Exhibit 8.14 shows a multicolumn Purchases Journal.

Purchase invoices or other source documents are used in recording transactions in the Purchases Journal. Journalizing is similar to the Sales Journal. We use the invoice date and terms to compute the date when payment for each purchase is due. The Merchandise Inventory Debit column is used for recording merchandise purchases. When a purchase involves an amount recorded in the Other Accounts Debit column, we use the Account column to identify the General Ledger account debited. Outdoors Unlimited also includes a separate column for credit purchases of office supplies. A separate column such as this is useful whenever several transactions involve debits to a specific account. Each company uses its own judgement in deciding on the number of separate columns necessary. The Other Accounts Debit column allows the Purchases Journal to be used for all purchase transactions involving credits to Accounts Payable. The Accounts Payable Credit column is used to record the amounts credited to each creditor's account.

Posting

The amounts in the Accounts Payable Credit column are posted daily to individual creditor accounts in a subsidiary Accounts Payable Ledger. Each line of the Account column in Exhibit 8.14 shows the subsidiary ledger account that is posted for these amounts in the Accounts Payable Credit column. Individual amounts in the Other Accounts Debit column usually are posted daily to their General Ledger accounts. At the end of the month, all column totals except the Other Accounts Debit column are posted to their General Ledger accounts. The balance in the Accounts Payable controlling account must equal the sum of the account balances in the subsidiary Accounts Payable Ledger after posting.

Testing the Ledger

Account balances in the General Ledger and subsidiary ledgers are tested for accuracy after posting of the Purchases Journal is complete. We perform two steps similar to the procedures followed for testing the ledger for the Sales Journal. First, we prepare a trial balance of the General Ledger to confirm debits equal credits. If debits equal credits in the trial balance, the accounts in the General Ledger, including the controlling accounts, are assumed to be correct. Second, we test the subsidiary ledgers by preparing a *schedule of accounts payable.* A **schedule of accounts payable** is a listing of accounts from the Accounts Payable Ledger with their balances and the sum of all balances. If this total equals the balance of the Accounts Payable controlling account, the accounts in the Accounts Payable Ledger are assumed to be correct.

Exhibit 8.14

Purchases Journal with Posting

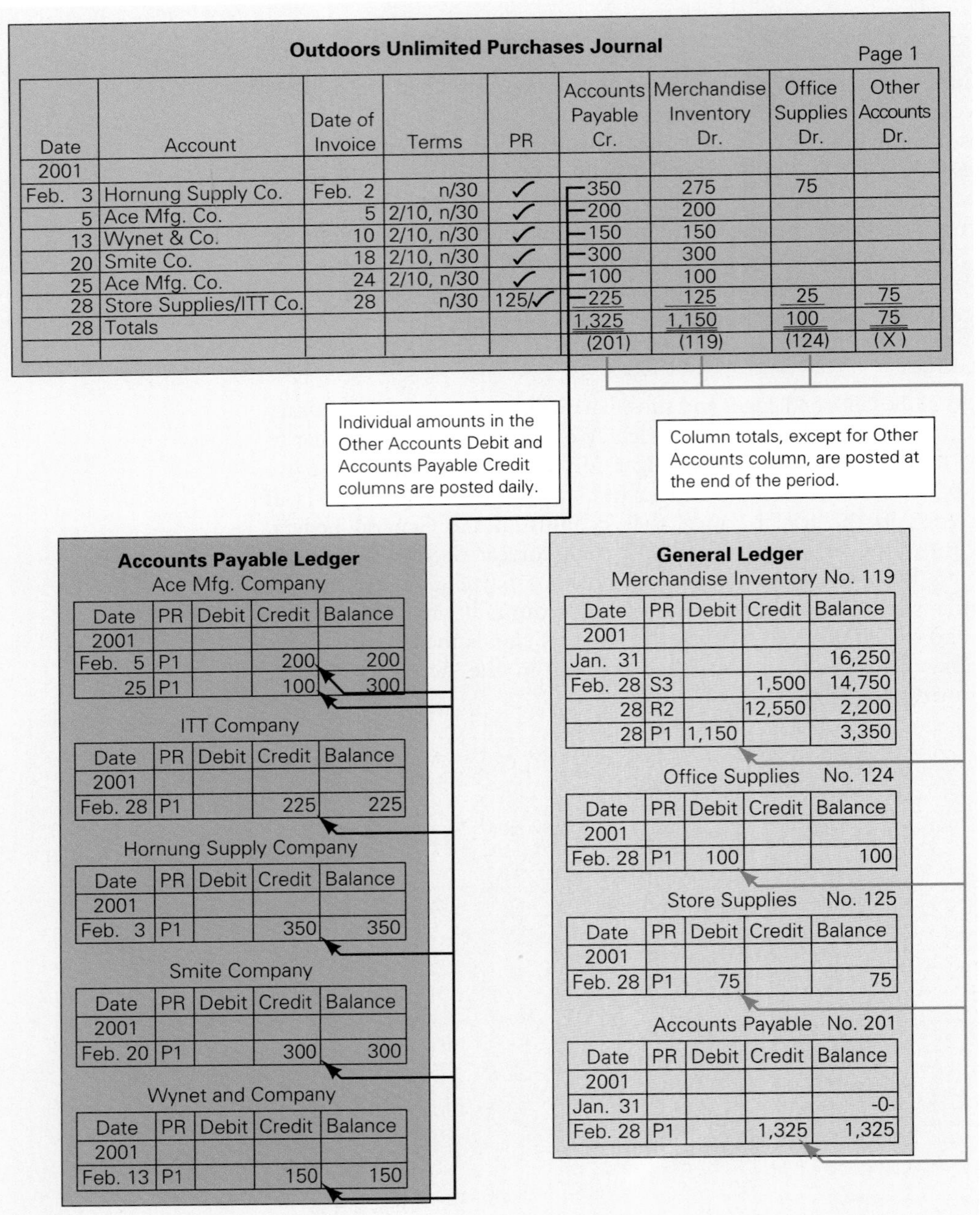

Outdoors Unlimited Purchases Journal Page 1

Date	Account	Date of Invoice	Terms	PR	Accounts Payable Cr.	Merchandise Inventory Dr.	Office Supplies Dr.	Other Accounts Dr.
2001								
Feb. 3	Hornung Supply Co.	Feb. 2	n/30	✓	350	275	75	
5	Ace Mfg. Co.	5	2/10, n/30	✓	200	200		
13	Wynet & Co.	10	2/10, n/30	✓	150	150		
20	Smite Co.	18	2/10, n/30	✓	300	300		
25	Ace Mfg. Co.	24	2/10, n/30	✓	100	100		
28	Store Supplies/ITT Co.	28	n/30	125/✓	225	125	25	75
28	Totals				1,325	1,150	100	75
					(201)	(119)	(124)	(X)

Individual amounts in the Other Accounts Debit and Accounts Payable Credit columns are posted daily.

Column totals, except for Other Accounts column, are posted at the end of the period.

Accounts Payable Ledger

Ace Mfg. Company

Date	PR	Debit	Credit	Balance
2001				
Feb. 5	P1		200	200
25	P1		100	300

ITT Company

Date	PR	Debit	Credit	Balance
2001				
Feb. 28	P1		225	225

Hornung Supply Company

Date	PR	Debit	Credit	Balance
2001				
Feb. 3	P1		350	350

Smite Company

Date	PR	Debit	Credit	Balance
2001				
Feb. 20	P1		300	300

Wynet and Company

Date	PR	Debit	Credit	Balance
2001				
Feb. 13	P1		150	150

General Ledger

Merchandise Inventory No. 119

Date	PR	Debit	Credit	Balance
2001				
Jan. 31				16,250
Feb. 28	S3		1,500	14,750
28	R2		12,550	2,200
28	P1	1,150		3,350

Office Supplies No. 124

Date	PR	Debit	Credit	Balance
2001				
Feb. 28	P1	100		100

Store Supplies No. 125

Date	PR	Debit	Credit	Balance
2001				
Feb. 28	P1	75		75

Accounts Payable No. 201

Date	PR	Debit	Credit	Balance
2001				
Jan. 31				-0-
Feb. 28	P1		1,325	1,325

Cash Disbursements Journal

A **Cash Disbursements Journal**, also called a *Cash Payments Journal*, is used to record *all* payments of cash. It is a multicolumn journal because cash payments are made for several different purposes.

Journalizing

A Cash Disbursements Journal is similar to a Cash Receipts Journal except that it has repetitive cash payments instead of receipts. Exhibit 8.15 shows the Cash Disbursements Journal for Outdoors Unlimited. We see repetitive credits to the Cash column of this journal. We also commonly see credits to Merchandise Inventory for purchases discounts and debits to the Accounts Payable account. Many companies purchase merchandise on credit and, therefore, a Merchandise Inventory Debit column is not often needed. Instead, the occasional cash purchase is recorded in the Other Accounts Debit column and Cash Credit column as shown for the February 5 transaction of Exhibit 8.15.

The Cash Disbursements Journal has a column titled Cheque Number (Ch. No.). For control over cash disbursements, all payments except for very small amounts are made by cheque.[4] Cheques should be prenumbered and entered in the journal in numerical order with each cheque's number in the column headed Ch. No. This makes it possible to scan the numbers in the column for omitted cheques. When a Cash Disbursements Journal has a column for cheque numbers, it is sometimes called a **Cheque Register**.

The treatment of purchase discounts and transportation-in under the perpetual system presents different posting options. These options are:

1. Post the amounts directly to the Merchandise Inventory account.
2. Post the amounts directly to Cost of Goods Sold.
3. Post the amounts first to a Discount account and Transportation account and then, at the end of the period, distribute the totals to Cost of Goods Sold and/or to Merchandise Inventory.

There are advantages and disadvantages for each. Exhibit 8.15 demonstrates the first option where purchase discounts and transportation-in are posted directly to the Merchandise Inventory account.

[4] We describe a system for controlling small cash payments in Chapter 9.

Exhibit 8.15

Cash Disbursements Journal with Posting

Outdoors Unlimited Cash Disbursements Journal

Page 2

Date	Ch. No.	Payee	Account Debited	PR	Cash Cr.	Merchandise Inventory Cr.	Other Accounts Dr.	Accounts Payable Dr.
2001								
Feb. 3	105	L & N Railroad	Inventory re transp-in	119	15		15	
5	106	East Sales Co.	Inventory	119	25		25	
13	107	Ace Mfg. Co.	Ace Mfg. Co.	✓	196	4		200
20	108	Jerry Hale	Salaries Expense	622	250		250	
25	109	Wynet & Co.	Wynet & Co.	✓	147	3		150
28	110	Smite Co.	Smite Co.	✓	294	6		300
28		Totals			927	13	290	650
					(101)	(119)	(X)	(201)

Column totals, except for Other Accounts column, are posted at the end of the period.

Individual amounts in the Other Accounts column and Accounts Payable column are posted daily.

General Ledger

Cash No. 101

Date	PR	Debit	Credit	Balance
2001				
Jan. 31	R2			9,450
Feb. 28	R2	19,770		29,220
28	D2		927	28,293

Inventory No. 119

Date	PR	Debit	Credit	Balance
2001				
Jan. 28				16,250
Feb. 3	D2	15		16,265
5	D2	25		16,290
28	S3		1,500	14,790
28	R2		12,550	2,240
28	P1	1,150		3,390
28	D2	13		3,403

Accounts Payable No. 201

Date	PR	Debit	Credit	Balance
2001				
Jan. 31				-0-
Feb. 28	P1		1,325	1,325
28	D2	650		675

Salaries Expense No. 622

Date	PR	Debit	Credit	Balance
2001				
Feb. 20	D2	250		250

Accounts Payable Ledger

Ace Mfg. Company

Date	PR	Debit	Credit	Balance
2001				
Feb. 5	P1		200	200
13	D2	200		-0-
25	P1		100	100

ITT Company

Date	PR	Debit	Credit	Balance
2001				
Feb. 28	P1		225	225

Hornung Supply Company

Date	PR	Debit	Credit	Balance
2001				
Feb. 3	P1		350	350

Smite Company

Date	PR	Debit	Credit	Balance
2001				
Feb. 20	P1		300	300
28	D2	300		-0-

Wynet & Company

Date	PR	Debit	Credit	Balance
2001				
Feb. 13	P1		150	150
25	D2	150		-0-

Posting

Individual amounts in the Other Accounts Debit column of a Cash Disbursements Journal are usually posted to their General Ledger accounts on a daily basis. Individual amounts in the Accounts Payable Debit column are also posted daily to the specific creditors' accounts in the subsidiary Accounts Payable Ledger. At the end of the period, we crossfoot column totals and post the Accounts Payable Debit column total to the Accounts Payable controlling account. Also at the end of the period the Merchandise Inventory Credit column total is posted to the Merchandise Inventory account and the Cash Credit column total is posted to the Cash account. The Other Accounts column total is not posted at the end of the period.

Exhibit 8.16 shows a schedule of accounts payable drawn from the Accounts Payable Ledger of Exhibit 8.15.

Exhibit 8.16

Schedule of Accounts Payable

Outdoors Unlimited Schedule of Accounts Payable February 28, 2001	
Ace Mfg. Company	$ 100
ITT Company	225
Hornung Supply Company	350
Total accounts payable	$ 675

Controller

You are a controller for a merchandising company. You want to analyze your company's cash payments to suppliers, including an analysis of purchases discounts. Where might you look for this information?

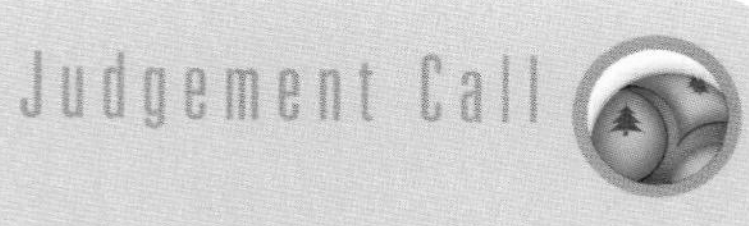

Answer—p. 414

8. What is the normal recording and posting procedure when using special journals and controlling accounts with subsidiary ledgers?
9. What is the rule for posting to a subsidiary ledger and its controlling account?
10. How do we test the accuracy of account balances in the General Ledger and subsidiary ledgers after posting?

Answers—p. 415

General Journal Transactions

When special journals are used, we still need a General Journal for adjusting, closing and correcting entries, and for special transactions not recorded in special journals. These special transactions include purchases returns and allowances, purchases of plant assets by issuing a note payable, sales returns if a Sales Returns and Allowances Journal is not used, and receiving a note receivable from a customer.

Additional Issue—Sales Tax

This section looks at the additional issue of recording sales taxes.

Most provinces and the federal government require retailers to collect sales taxes from customers and to send these taxes periodically to the appropriate agency. When using a columnar Sales Journal, we can have a record of taxes collected by adding columns to the journal as shown in Exhibit 8.17.

Exhibit 8.17

Sales Journal with Information on Sales Taxes

Outdoors Unlimited Sales Journal							Page 3
Date	Account Debited	Invoice No.	PR	Accounts Receivable Dr.	Sales Taxes Payable Cr.	Sales Cr.	Cost of Goods Sold Dr. Merchandise Inventory Cr.
2001 Feb. 2	Jason Henry	307		481.50	31.50	450.00	315.00

We described how column totals of a Sales Journal are commonly posted at the end of each period. This now includes crediting the Sales Taxes Payable account for the total of the Sales Taxes Payable column. Individual amounts in the Accounts Receivable column are posted daily to customer accounts in the Accounts Receivable Ledger. Individual amounts in the Sales Taxes Payable, Sales, and Cost of Goods Sold and Inventory columns are not posted. Companies that collect sales taxes on their cash sales can also use a special Sales Taxes Payable column in their Cash Receipts Journal.

Provincial Sales Tax

All provinces except Alberta (and the Territories) require retailers to collect a **provincial sales tax (PST)** from their customers and to remit this tax periodically to the appropriate provincial authority. When special journals are used, a column is provided for PST in the Sales Journal and the Cash Receipts Journal. A record of PST is obtained by recording in the PST column the appropriate amount of PST on cash sales (Cash Receipts Journal) and sales on account (Sales Journal). It should be noted that not all sales are subject to PST.[5]

PST may be paid on items that are not part of Merchandise Inventory for resale but will be consumed or are long-term assets. In these cases, the PST paid is not allocated to a separate account. Instead it is allocated as part of the expense or asset cost associated with the purchase.

Goods and Services Tax

The **goods and services tax (GST)** is a 7% tax on almost all goods and services provided in Canada. It is a federal tax on the consumer. However, unlike the PST, businesses pay GST up front but generally receive a full credit or refund for all GST paid. Ultimately, only the final consumer bears the burden of this tax. This is because businesses collect GST on sales, but since they receive full credit for GST paid on their purchases, they only remit the difference to the appropriate federal authority. PST and GST are accounted for under both perpetual and periodic inventory systems. To illustrate the collection and payment of GST, consider the following example.

[5] A detailed discussion of the liabilities created by PST and GST is found in Chapter 13.

LM Company sells riding mowers. On January 2, it pays $20,000 for merchandise inventory that is subject to GST of $1,400. LM pays the $1,400 to its suppliers, who remit the $1,400 to CCRA P. 13. LM now has a $1,400 GST debit, that is, a prepaid GST or input tax credit. The journal entry would be:

Jan. 2	Merchandise Inventory	20,000	
	GST Payable	1,400	
	Accounts Payable		21,400
	To record purchase of material.		

On January 8, LM sells several mowers to KD Company for $32,000 and collects $2,240 in GST. LM remits $840 ($2,240 minus the $1,400 input credit), that is, the GST paid to its suppliers. The entry to record the sale by LM is:

Jan. 8	Accounts Receivable—KD	34,240	
	GST Payable		2,240
	Sales		32,000
	To record sale to KD.		

To summarize:

	GST Paid	GST Collected	GST Remitted
Merchandise inventory supplier		$1,400	$1,400
LM Company	$1,400	2,240	840
KD Company (consumer)	2,240		$2,240

The final consumer, KD Company, bears the burden of the tax.

The total GST remitted is $2,240, the same amount that KD Company, the consumer, paid. The supplier and LM Company act as collection agents, collecting the tax along each stage of the process.

To facilitate the recording of GST, special GST (credit) columns must be provided not only in the Sales Journal and the Cash Receipts Journal, as in the case of PST, but also GST (debit) columns in the Purchases Journal and Cash Disbursements Journal. To illustrate, assume that Berlasty Company uses specialized journals shown in Exhibit 8.18. The following transactions were completed and recorded during December:

Dec. 1	Purchased merchandise inventory on account, $1,000 from Jason Supply (subject to 7% GST), terms n/30.
3	Paid transportation on the Dec. 1 purchase, $30 (subject to 7% GST).
9	Purchased merchandise inventory for cash, $500 (subject to 7% GST).
15	Cash sale, $1,200 (subject to 8% PST and 7% GST). Cost of sales $750.
28	Paid for the Dec. 1 purchase.
30	Sales to S. Burns on account, $2,000 ($1,500 subject to 8% PST and $2,000 subject to 7% GST). Cost of sales, $1,250.

Exhibit 8.18

Special Journals with PST and GST Columns as Applicable

Purchase Journal **Page 8**

Date	Account Credited	Terms	PR	Accounts Payable Cr.	Merchandise Inventory Dr.	Other Accounts Dr.	GST Payable Dr.
2001 Dec. 1	Jason Supply	n/30		1,070.00	1,000.00		70.00
31	Totals			1,070.00	1,000.00		70.00
							(225)

Cash Disbursements Journal **Page 6**

Date	Ch. No.	Account Debited	PR	Other Accounts Dr.	GST Payable Dr.	Accounts Payable Dr.	Merchandise Inventory Cr.	Cash Cr.
2001 Dec. 3	256	Transportation-in		30.00	2.10			32.10
9	257	Inventory		500.00	35.00			535.00
28	258	Accts. Pay/ Jason Supply				1,070.00		1,070.00
31		Totals		530.00	37.10	1,070.00		1,637.10
					(225)			

Sales Journal **Page 12**

Date	Account Debited	Invoice No.	PR	Acc Rec. Dr.	PST Payable Cr.	GST Payable Cr.	Sales Cr.	Cost of Goods Sold Dr. Merchandise Inventory Cr.
2001 Dec. 30	S. Burns	2734		2,260.00	120.00	140.00	2,000.00	1,250.00
							(224)	(225)

Cash Receipts Journal **Page 9**

Date	Account Credited	Explanation	PR	Other Accounts Cr.	Discount Cr.	PST Payable Cr.	GST Payable Cr.	Sales Cr.	Cash Dr.	Sales Discount. Dr.	Cost of Goods Sold/Dr. Merchandise Inventory/Cr.
2001 Dec. 15	Sales	Cash sale				96.00	84.00	1,200.00	1,380.00		750.00
						(224)	(225)				

After the posting is completed, as described earlier in the chapter, the PST and GST T-accounts would appear as follows:

PST			224
		S12	120.00
		CR9	96.00
		Balance	216.00

GST			225
P8	70.00	S12	140.00
CD6	37.10	CR9	84.00
		Balance	116.90

On December 31, PST Payable amounts to $216 and GST Payable amounts to $116.90.

The computation of GST is not uniform throughout the country. In some of the provinces, the computation is as illustrated above, that is, PST and GST are computed as a percentage of the selling price. In other provinces, PST is initially computed as a percentage of the selling price and GST is computed as a percentage of the total of the selling price plus the PST. It should also be noted that while GST is a 7% federal tax, thus uniform in each of the provinces, PST is a provincial tax and differs in percentage from province to province. Nova Scotia, New Brunswick, and Newfoundland charge a **harmonized sales tax (HST)** of 15% that comprises the 7% GST and the PST of 8%. The preceding discussion is based on Ontario's PST of 8%. Chapter 13 provides the detailed rates for each province.

Remittance of GST

The GST is administered by the Canada Customs and Revenue Agency (CCRA). Remittance is accompanied by a Goods and Services Tax Return.

Frequency of filing returns is dependent on the size of the business. Large businesses (annual sales in excess of $6 million) are required to file GST returns monthly. Medium-sized businesses (annual sales of $500,001 to $6 million) are required to file quarterly. Small businesses (annual sales up to $500,000) have the option of filing annually but paying quarterly installments. GST for a period must be remitted to CCRA by the end of the month following the month (quarter) collected.

11. How are sales taxes recorded in the context of special journals?
12. Why does a company need a General Journal when using special journals for sales, purchases, cash receipts, and cash disbursements?

Answers—p. 415

Summary

LO1 Explain the relationship of the accounting information system (AIS) to the management information system (MIS). The MIS includes the subsystems of Finance, Sales and Marketing, Human Resources, Production, and Accounting. Information systems collect and process data based on inputs for the purpose of generating useful information for both internal and external users.

LO2 Explain the components, structure, and fundamental standards of accounting information systems. An AIS collects financial data and processes it through the relevant component: Accounts Payable, Accounts Receivable, Payroll, or a specialty component such as Capital Assets. Computers are invaluable tools in processing data efficiently and effectively. Accounting information systems are guided by five fundamental standards in carrying out their tasks: control, relevance, compatibility, flexibility, and cost–benefit standards.

LO3 Identify what technology-based systems have impacted accounting. Source documents are evolving from paper-based to technology-based such as debit card, electronic funds transfer (EFT), and e-commerce transactions. General purpose accounting software is available for small to medium-sized businesses, whereas large businesses purchase enterprise-application software programs that can be customized to fit the specific needs of their operation.

LO4 Explain the goals and uses of special journals. Special journals are used for recording and posting transactions of similar type, each meant to cover one kind of transaction. Four of the most common special journals are the Sales Journal, Cash Receipts Journal, Purchases Journal, and Cash Disbursements Journal. Special journals are efficient and cost effective tools in helping to journalize and post transactions. In addition, special journals allow an efficient division of labour that is also an effective control procedure.

LO5 **Describe the use of controlling accounts and subsidiary ledgers.** A General Ledger keeps controlling accounts such as Accounts Receivable or Accounts Payable, but details on individual accounts making up the controlling account are kept in a subsidiary ledger (such as an Accounts Receivable Ledger). The balance in a controlling account must equal the sum of its subsidiary account balances after posting is complete.

LO6 **Journalize and post transactions using special journals.** Special journals are devoted to similar kinds of transactions. Transactions are journalized on one line of a special journal, with columns devoted to specific accounts, dates, names, posting references, explanations and other necessary information. Posting is threefold: (1) individual amounts in the Other Accounts column are posted to their General Ledger accounts on a regular (daily) basis, (2) individual amounts in a column that is posted in total to a controlling account at the end of a period (month) are posted regularly (daily) to its account in the subsidiary ledger, and (3) total amounts for all columns except the Other Accounts column are posted at the end of a period (month) to their column's account title.

LO7 **Prepare and test the accuracy of subsidiary ledgers.** Account balances in the General Ledger and its subsidiary ledgers are tested for accuracy after posting is complete. This procedure is twofold: (1) prepare a trial balance of the General Ledger to confirm debits equal credits, and (2) prepare a schedule of a subsidiary ledger to confirm that the controlling account's balance equals the subsidiary ledger's balance. A schedule is a listing of accounts from a ledger with their balances and the sum of all balances.

GUIDANCE ANSWER TO Judgement Call

Public Accountant

As a professional accountant, you are guided by the Professional Codes of Conduct described in Appendix II. You should recognize the main issue: whether commissions have an actual or perceived impact on the integrity and objectivity of your advice. The code says that you should not accept a commission if you either perform an audit or review of the client's financial statements or if you review prospective financial information for the client. The code also precludes a commission if you compile the client's statements, unless the compilation report discloses a lack of independence. Even in situations where a commission is allowed, the code requires you to tell the client of your commission arrangement. These suggested actions seem appropriate even if you are not bound by the code. Also, you need to seriously examine the merits of agreeing to a commission arrangement when you are in a position to exploit it.

Retailer

The Accounts Receivable Ledger has much of the information you need. It lists detailed information for each customer's account, including the amounts, dates for transactions, and dates of payments. It can be reorganized into an "aging schedule" to show how long customers wait in paying their bills. We describe an aging schedule in Chapter 10.

Controller

Much of the information you need is in the Accounts Payable Ledger. It contains information for each supplier, the amounts due, and when payments are made. This ledger, along with information on credit terms, should enable you to conduct your analyses.

GUIDANCE ANSWERS TO

1. An AIS is part of the MIS and collects and processes financial data for communication to users. The MIS collects and processes data from sales and marketing, finance, production, human resources, and accounting and provides information to these in turn and also to external users.
2. The four basic components of an AIS are Accounts Payable, Accounts Receivable, Payroll, and specialty components such as Capital Assets.
3. The five primary standards underlying an AIS are control, relevance, compatibility, flexibility, and cost–benefit.

4. All cash payments by cheque are recorded in the Cash Disbursements Journal.

5. Columnar journals allow us to accumulate repetitive debits and credits and post them as column totals rather than as individual amounts.

6. The equality of debits and credits is kept within the General Ledger. The subsidiary ledger keeps the customer's individual account and is used only for supplementary information.

7. An initial and page number of the journal from where the amount was posted is entered in the Posting Reference column of the ledger account next to the amount.

8. The normal recording and posting procedures are threefold. First, transactions are entered in a special journal column if applicable. Second, individual amounts are posted to the subsidiary ledger accounts. Third, column totals are posted to general ledger accounts.

9. The controlling account must be debited periodically for an amount or amounts equal to the sum of the debits to the subsidiary ledger, and it must be credited periodically for an amount or amounts equal to the sum of the credits to the subsidiary ledger.

10. Tests for accuracy of account balances in the General Ledger and subsidiary ledgers are twofold. First, we prepare a trial balance of the General Ledger to confirm that debits equal credits. Second, we test the subsidiary ledgers by preparing schedules of accounts receivable and accounts payable.

11. A separate column for Sales Taxes Payable is included in both the Cash Receipts Journal and the Sales Journal.

12. The General Journal is still needed for adjusting, closing and correcting entries, and for special transactions such as sales returns, purchases returns, plant asset purchases, and sales on credit of assets other than merchadise inventory.

Demonstration Problem

The Pepper Company completed these transactions during March, 2001:

Mar. 1	Merchandise inventory on hand was $28,400.
1	Adrian Pepper, Capital has an opening balance of $28,400.
4	Sold merchandise on credit to Jennifer Nelson, Invoice No. 954, $16,800 Cost, $10,100. *(Terms of all credit sales are 2/10, n/30.)*
6	Purchased office supplies on credit from Mack Company, $1,220. Invoice dated March 3, terms n/30.
6	Sold merchandise on credit to Dennie Hoskins, Invoice No. 955, $10,200. Cost, $6,200.
11	Received merchandise and an invoice dated March 11, terms 2/10, n/30, from Defore Industries, $52,600.
12	Borrowed $26,000 by giving Commerce Bank a long-term promissory note payable.
14	Received payment from Jennifer Nelson for the March 4 sale.
16	Received a credit memorandum from Defore Industries for unsatisfactory merchandise received on March 11 and returned for credit, $200.
16	Received payment from Dennie Hoskins for the March 6 sale.
18	Purchased store equipment on credit from Schmidt Supply, invoice dated March 15, terms n/30, $22,850.
20	Sold merchandise on credit to Marjorie Allen, Invoice No. 956, $5,600. Cost, $3,400.
21	Sent Defore Industries Cheque No. 516 in payment of its March 11 invoice.
22	Received merchandise and an invoice dated March 18, terms 2/10, n/30, from the Welch Company, $41,625.
26	Issued a credit memorandum to Marjorie Allen for defective merchandise sold on March 22 and returned for credit $600. The merchandise was scrapped and not returned to inventory.
31	Issued Cheque No. 517, payable to Payroll, in payment of sales salaries for the month, $15,900. Cashed the cheque and paid the employees.
31	Cash sales for the month were $134,680. (Normally, cash sales are recorded daily; however, they are recorded only once in this problem to reduce the repetitive entries.) Cost, $80,800.
31	Post to the customer and creditor accounts and post any amounts that should be posted as individual amounts to the General Ledger accounts.
31	Foot and crossfoot the journals and make the month-end postings.

Required

1. Open the following General Ledger accounts: Cash (101), Accounts Receivable (106), Merchandise Inventory (119), Office Supplies (124), Store Equipment (165), Accounts Payable (201), Long-Term Notes Payable (251), Adrian Pepper, Capital (301), Sales (413), Sales Returns and Allowances (414), Sales Discounts (415), Cost of Goods Sold (502), and Sales Salaries Expense (621).
2. Open the following Accounts Receivable Ledger accounts: Marjorie Allen, Dennie Hoskins, and Jennifer Nelson.
3. Open the following Accounts Payable Ledger accounts: Defore Industries, Mack Company, Schmidt Supply, and Welch Company.
4. Enter the transactions in a Purchases Journal, a Sales Journal, a Cash Receipts Journal, a Cash Disbursements Journal, and a General Journal similar to the ones illustrated in the chapter. Post at the end of the month.
5. Prepare a trial balance and test the accuracy of the subsidiary ledgers by preparing schedules of accounts receivable and payable.

Planning the Solution

- Set up the required General Ledger and subsidiary ledger accounts and the five required journals as illustrated in the chapter.
- First read and analyze each transaction and decide in which special journal (or General Journal) the transaction would be recorded.
- Now record each transaction in the proper journal.
- Once you have recorded all the transactions, total the journal columns.
- Now post from each journal to the appropriate ledger accounts.
- After you have completed posting, prepare a trial balance to prove the equality of the debit and credit balances in your General Ledger.
- Finally, prepare a schedule of accounts receivable and accounts payable. Compare the total of the schedules to the Accounts Receivable and Accounts Payable controlling account balances making sure that they agree.

SOLUTION TO Demonstration Problem

Sales Journal **Page 2**

Date	Account Debited	Invoice No.	PR	Accounts Receivable Dr. Sales Cr.	Cost of Goods Sold/Dr. Merchandise Inventory/Cr.
2001					
Mar. 4	Jennifer Nelson	954	✓	16,800	10,100
6	Dennie Hoskins	955	✓	10,200	6,200
20	Marjorie Allen	956	✓	5,600	3,400
31	Totals			32,600	19,700
				(106/413)	(502/119)

Purchases Journal **Page 3**

Date	Account	Date of Invoice	Terms	PR	Accounts Payable Cr.	Merchandise Inventory Dr.	Office Supplies Dr.	Other Accounts Dr.
2001								
Mar. 6	Office Supplies/Mack Co.	Mar. 3	n/30	✓	1,220		1,220	
11	Defore Industries	Mar. 11	2/10, n/30	✓	52,600	52,600		
18	Store Equipment/	Mar. 15	n/30	165/✓	22,850			22,850
	Schmidt Supp.							
22	Welch Company	Mar. 18	2/10, n/30	✓	41,625	41,625		
31	Totals				118,295	94,225	1,220	22,850
					(201)	(119)	(124)	(X)

Cash Receipts Journal **Page 3**

Date	Account Credited	Explanation	PR	Cash Dr.	Sales Discount Dr.	Accounts Receivable Cr.	Sales Cr.	Other Accounts Cr.	Cost of Goods Sold/Dr Merchandise Inventory/Cr.
2001									
Mar. 12	L.T. Notes Payable	Note to bank	251	26,000				26,000	
14	Jennifer Nelson	Invoice, Mar. 4	✓	16,464	336	16,800			
16	Dennie Hoskins	Invoice, Mar. 6	✓	9,996	204	10,200			
31	Sales	Cash sales		134,680			134,680		80,800
31	Totals			187,140	540	27,000	134,680	26,000	80,800
				(101)	(415)	(106)	(413)	(X)	(502/119)

Cash Disbursements Journal **Page 4**

Date	Ch. No.	Payee	Account Debited	PR	Cash Cr.	Merchandise Inventory Cr.	Other Accounts Dr.	Accounts Payable Dr.
2001								
Mar. 21	516	Defore Industries	Defore Industries	✓	51,352	1,048		52,400
31	517	Payroll	Sales Salaries Expense	621	15,900		15,900	
31		Totals			67,252	1,048	15,900	52,400
					(101)	(119)	(X)	(201)

General Journal **Page 2**

Mar. 16	Accounts Payable—Defore Industries	201/✓	200	
	Merchandise Inventory	119		200
	Credit memo regarding merchandise returned.			
26	Sales Returns and Allowances	414	600	
	Accounts Receivable—Marjorie Allen.....	106/✓		600
	Issued credit memo regarding mechandise returned and scrapped.			

Accounts Receivable Ledger

Marjorie Allen

Date	PR	Debit	Credit	Balance
2001 Mar. 20	S2	5,600		5,600
26	G2		600	5,000

Dennie Hoskins

Date	PR	Debit	Credit	Balance
2001 Mar. 6	S2	10,200		10,200
16	CR3		10,200	-0-

Jennifer Nelson

Date	PR	Debit	Credit	Balance
2001 Mar. 4	S2	16,800		16,800
14	CR3		16,800	-0-

General Ledger

Cash Acct. No. 101

Date	Explanation	PR	Debit	Credit	Balance
2001 Mar. 31		CR3	187,140		187,140
31		C4		67,252	119,888

Accounts Receivable 106

Date	Explanation	PR	Debit	Credit	Balance
2001 Mar. 26		G2		600	(600)
31		S2	32,600		32,000
31		CR3		27,000	5,000

Merchandise Inventory 119

Date	Explanation	PR	Debit	Credit	Balance
2001 Mar. 1	Opening Balance				28,400
16		G2		200	28,200
31		P3	94,225		122,425
31		S2		19,700	102,725
31		CR3		80,800	21,925
31		CD4		1,048	20,877

Office Supplies 124

Date	Explanation	PR	Debit	Credit	Balance
2001 Mar. 31		P3	1,220		1,220

Store Equipment 165

Date	Explanation	PR	Debit	Credit	Balance
2001 Mar. 18		P3	22,850		22,850

Accounts Payable 201

Date	Explanation	PR	Debit	Credit	Balance
2001 Mar. 16		G2	200		(200)
31		P3		118,295	118,095
31		CD4	52,400		65,695

Accounts Payable Ledger

Defore Industries

Date	PR	Debit	Credit	Balance
2001 Mar. 11	P3		52,600	52,600
16	G2	200		52,400
21	CD4	52,400		-0-

Mack Company

Date	PR	Debit	Credit	Balance
2001 Mar. 6	P3		1,220	1,220

Schmidt Supply

Date	PR	Debit	Credit	Balance
2001 Mar. 18	P3		22,850	22,850

Welch Company

Date	PR	Debit	Credit	Balance
2001 Mar. 22	P3		41,625	41,625

General Ledger

Long-Term Notes Payable Acct. No. 251

Date	Explanation	PR	Debit	Credit	Balance
2001 Mar. 12		CR3		26,000	26,000

Adrian Pepper, Capital 301

Date	Explanation	PR	Debit	Credit	Balance
2001 Mar. 1	Opening Balance				28,400

Sales 413

Date	Explanation	PR	Debit	Credit	Balance
2001 Mar. 31		S2		32,600	32,600
31		C2		134,680	167,280

Sales Returns and Allowances 414

Date	Explanation	PR	Debit	Credit	Balance
2001 Mar. 26		G2	600		600

Sales Discounts 415

Date	Explanation	PR	Debit	Credit	Balance
2001 Mar. 1		CR3	540		540

Cost of Goods Sold 502

Date	Explanation	PR	Debit	Credit	Balance
2001 Mar. 31		S2	19,700		19,700
31		CR3	80,800		100,500

Sales Salaries Expense 621

Date	Explanation	PR	Debit	Credit	Balance
2001 Mar. 31		CD4	15,900		15,900

Pepper Company
Trial Balance
March 31, 2001

Acct.	Title	Debit	Credit
101	Cash	$119,888	
106	Accounts receivable	5,000	
119	Merchandise inventory	20,877	
124	Office supplies	1,220	
165	Store equipment	22,850	
201	Accounts payable		$ 65,695
251	Long-term notes payable		26,000
301	Adrian Pepper, capital		28,400
413	Sales		167,280
414	Sales returns and allowances	600	
415	Sales discounts	540	
502	Cost of goods sold	100,500	
621	Sales salaries expense	15,900	
	Totals	$287,375	$287,375

Pepper Company
Schedule of Accounts Receivable
March 31, 2001

Marjorie Allen	$5,000
Total accounts receivable	$5,000

Pepper Company
Schedule of Accounts Payable
March 31, 2001

Mack Company	$ 1,220
Schmidt Supply	22,850
Welch Company	41,625
Total accounts payable	$65,695

The totals for both the Schedule of Accounts Receivable and Schedule of Accounts Payable agree to the respective controlling account balances in the trial balance.

APPENDIX

Special Journals Under a Periodic System

This appendix shows the special journals under a periodic inventory system. The Sales Journal and the Cash Receipts Journal each require one less column. The Purchases Journal replaces the *Inventory* column with a *Purchases Dr.* column in a periodic system. The Cash Disbursements Journal replaces the *Inventory Cr.* column with a *Purchases Discounts Cr.* column in a periodic system. These changes are illustrated below.

Sales Journal

LO8 Apply journalizing and posting of transactions using special journals in a periodic inventory system.

The Sales Journal for Outdoors Unlimited using the periodic inventory system is shown in Exhibit 8A.1. The difference in the Sales Journal between the perpetual and periodic system is the deletion of the cost of goods sold and merchandise inventory amounts for each sale. The periodic system does not record the increase in cost of goods sold and decrease in inventory at the time of sale.

Exhibit 8A.1
Sales Journal—Periodic System

Outdoors Unlimited Sales Journal Page 3

Date	Account Debited	Invoice Number	PR	Accounts Receivable Dr. Sales Cr.
2001				
Feb. 2	Jason Henry	307	✓	450
7	Albert Co.	308	✓	500
13	Bam Moore	309	✓	350
15	Paul Roth	310	✓	200
22	Jason Henry	311	✓	225
25	Frank Booth	312	✓	175
28	Albert Co.	313	✓	250
28	Total			2,150
				(106/413)

Cash Receipts Journal

The Cash Receipts Journal under the periodic system is shown in Exhibit 8A.2. Note the deletion of the column on the far right side to record debits to Cost of Goods Sold and credits to Merchandise Inventory for the cost of merchandise sold.

Consistent with the Cash Receipts Journal shown under the perpetual system in the chapter, we only show the weekly cash sale entries.

Exhibit 8A.2

Cash Receipts Journal—Periodic System

Outdoors Unlimited Cash Receipts Journal

Page 2

Date	Accounts Credited	Explanation	PR	Cash Dr.	Sales Discount Dr.	Accounts Receivable Cr.	Sales Cr.	Other Accounts Cr.
2001								
Feb. 7	Sales	Cash sales		4,450			4,450	
12	Jason Henry	Invoice, Feb. 2	✓	441	9	450		
14	Sales	Cash sales		3,925			3,925	
17	Albert Co.	Invoice, Feb. 7	✓	490	10	500		
20	Notes Payable	Note to bank	245	750				750
21	Sales	Cash sales		4,700			4,700	
22	Interest revenue	Bank account	409	250				250
23	Bam Moore	Invoice, Feb. 13	✓	343	7	350		
25	Paul Roth	Invoice, Feb.15	✓	196	4	200		
28	Sales	Cash sales		4,225			4,225	
28	Totals			19,770	30	1,500	17,300	1,000
				(101)	(415)	(106)	(413)	(X)

Purchases Journal

The Purchases Journal under the periodic system is shown in Exhibit 8A.3. This journal in a perpetual system includes the Merchandise Inventory column where the periodic system has the Purchases column. All else is identical under the two systems.

Exhibit 8A.3

Purchases Journal—Periodic System

Outdoors Unlimited Purchases Journal

Page 1

Date	Account	Date of Invoice	Terms	PR	Accounts Payable Cr.	Purchases Dr.	Office Supplies Dr.	Other Accounts Dr.
2001								
Feb. 3	Hornung Supply Co.	Feb. 2	n/30	✓	350	275	75	
5	Ace Mfg. Co.	5	2/10, n/30	✓	200	200		
13	Wynet & Co.	10	2/10, n/30	✓	150	150		
20	Smite Co.	18	2/10, n/30	✓	300	300		
25	Ace Mfg. Co.	24	2/10, n/30	✓	100	100		
28	Store Supplies/ITT Co.	28	n/30	125/✓	225	125	25	75
28	Totals				1,325	1,150	100	(75)
					(201)	(505)	(124)	(X)

Cash Disbursements Journal

The Cash Disbursements Journal in a periodic system is shown in Exhibit 8A.4. This journal includes the Purchases Discounts column where the perpetual system had the Merchandise Inventory column. All else is identical under the two systems. When a company has several cash purchases of inventory, it often adds a new column for Purchases Debit entries.

Exhibit 8A.4

Cash Disbursements Journal—Periodic System

Outdoors Unlimited Cash Disbursements Journal

Page 2

Date	Ch. No.	Payee	Account Debited	PR	Cash Cr.	Purchase Discounts Cr.	Other Accounts Dr.	Accounts Payable Dr.
2001								
Feb. 3	105	L & N Railroad	Transportation-In	508	15		15	
12	106	East Sales Co.	Purchases	505	25		25	
15	107	Ace Mfg. Co.	Ace Mfg. Co.	✓	196	4		200
15	108	Jerry Hale	Salaries Expense	622	250		250	
20	109	Wynet & Co.	Wynet & Co.	✓	147	3		150
28	110	Smite Co.	Smite Co.	✓	294	6		300
28		Totals			927	13	290	650
					(101)	(507)	(X)	(201)

Sales tax rules for GST and PST are incorporated in special journals under a periodic inventory system in an identical manner to that shown earlier for a perpetual system, by adding columns to the Sales, Purchases, Cash Receipts, and Cash Disbursements Journals.

Summary of Appendix 8A

LO8 **Apply journalizing and posting of transactions using special journals in a periodic inventory system.** Transactions are journalized and posted using special journals in a periodic system. The methods are similar to those in a perpetual system. The primary difference is that cost of goods sold and inventory do not need adjusting at the time of each sale. This normally results in the deletion of one or more columns in each special journal devoted to these accounts.

Glossary

Accounting information system The people, records, methods, and equipment that collect and process data from transactions and events, organize them in useful forms, and communicate results to decision makers. (p. 389)

Accounts Payable Ledger A subsidiary ledger listing individual credit supplier accounts. (p. 395)

Accounts Receivable Ledger A subsidiary ledger listing individual credit customer accounts. (p. 395)

Cash Disbursements Journal The special journal that is used to record all payments of cash; also called cash payments journal. (p. 407)

Cash Receipts Journal The special journal that is used to record all receipts of cash. (p. 401)

Cheque Register Another name for a Cash Disbursements journal when the journal has a column for cheque numbers. (p. 407)

Columnar journal A journal with more than one column. (p. 398)

Compatibility standard An information system standard requiring that an accounting information system conform with a company's activities, personnel, and structure. (p. 392)

Computer hardware The physical equipment in a computerized accounting information system. (p. 393)

Computer software The programs that direct the operations of computer hardware. (p. 393)

Controlling account A General Ledger account, the balance of which (after posting) equals the sum of the balances of the accounts in a related subsidiary ledger. (p. 395)

Control standard An information system standard requiring that an accounting information system aid managers in controlling and monitoring business activities. (p. 392)

Cost–benefit standard An information system standard requiring that the benefits from an activity in an accounting information system outweigh the costs of that activity. (p. 392)

Crossfoot To add debit and credit column totals and compare the sums for equality. (p. 404)

Enterprise-application software Programs that manage a company's vital operations, which range from order-taking programs to manufacturing to accounting. (p. 393)

Flexibility standard An information system standard requiring that an information system adapt to changes in the company, business environment, and needs of decisions makers. (p. 392)

Foot To add a column of numbers. (p. 402)

Goods and services tax (GST) A federal tax on the consumer on almost all goods and services. (p. 410)

Harmonized sales tax (HST) The sales tax in the Atlantic provinces, which is a combination of the GST and PST. (p. 413)

Management information system (MIS) Designed to collect and process data within an organization for the purpose of providing users with information. (p. 388)

Provincial sales tax (PST) A provincial tax collected by retailers on customer purchases. (p. 410)

Purchases Journal A journal that is used to record all purchases on credit. (p. 404)

Relevance standard An information system standard requiring that an accounting information system report useful, understandable, timely and pertinent information for effective decision-making. (p. 392)

Sales Journal A journal used to record sales of merchandise on credit. (p. 397)

Schedule of accounts payable A list of the balances of all the accounts in the Accounts Payable Ledger that is summed to show the total amount of accounts payable outstanding. (p. 405)

Schedule of accounts receivable A list of the balances of all the accounts in the Accounts Receivable Ledger that is summed to show the total amount of accounts receivable outstanding. (p. 400)

Special journal Any journal that is used for recording and posting transactions of a similar type. (p. 394)

Subsidiary ledger A listing of individual accounts with a common characteristic. (p. 395)

Questions

1. When special journals are used, separate special journals normally record each of four different types of transactions. What are these four types of transactions?
2. Why should sales to and receipts of cash from credit customers be recorded and posted daily?
3. Both credits to customer accounts and credits to miscellaneous accounts are individually posted from a Cash Receipts Journal similar to the one in Exhibit 8.12. Why not put both kinds of credits in the same column and save journal space?
4. When a General Journal entry is used to record a returned credit sale, the credit of the entry must be posted twice. Does this cause the trial balance to be out of balance? Why or why not?
5. What notations are entered into the Posting Reference column of a ledger account?
6. What are source documents? Give some examples.
7. Identify all of the special journals that Marie Lanctot is now likely keeping for Outdoors Unlimited. What does Marie mean when she says she now keeps an aging schedule on late paying customers.

Quick Study

Note 1: *End-of-chapter items do not include consideration of GST/PST unless stated otherwise.*

Note 2: *When opening General Ledger accounts, recall that a Chart of Accounts is provided at the end of the text, in Appendix III, to assist you in numbering your accounts.*

QS 8-1
Special journal identification

LO2

Refer to Exhibit 8-2. Identify which component of the AIS would process each of the following source documents:

	Accounts Payable (AP) Accounts Receivable (AR) Payroll (P)
1. Time cards from employees	______
2. Sales invoice; terms 2/10, n/30	______
3. Deposit slip regarding cash collections from credit customers	______
4. Cheque written to pay account with supplier	______

QS 8-2
Inputs and Outputs to AIS

LO2

Refer to Exhibit 8-4. Identify each of the following as an *input to* or an *output from* an AIS:

	Input (I) or Output (O)
1. Bank statement	______
2. Sales invoice issued to customer	______
3. Schedule of Accounts Payable	______
4. Income statement	______
5. Purchase order issued to supplier	______
6. Schedule detailing capital assets	______
7. Report detailing employee absences/minutes late	______
8. Memorandum issued by supplier regarding defective merchandise	______

QS 8-3
Accounting information system standards

LO2

Required

Match the system standards below with the statements that follow.

a. Control standard
b. Relevance standard
c. Compatibility standard
d. Flexibility standard
e. Cost–benefit standard

______ 1. The standard requiring the information system to adapt to the unique characteristics of the company.
______ 2. The standard that affects all other information system standards.
______ 3. The standard requiring the accounting information system to change in response to technological advances and competitive pressures.
______ 4. The standard requiring the accounting information system to help with monitoring activities.
______ 5. The standard requiring the system to provide timely information for effective decision making.

QS 8-4
Special journal identification
LO4

Trenton Iron Works uses a Sales Journal, a Purchases Journal, a Cash Receipts Journal, a Cash Disbursements Journal, and a General Journal. Trenton recently completed the following transactions. List the transaction letters and, next to each letter, give the name of the journal in which the transaction should be recorded.

a. Sold merchandise on credit.
b. Purchased shop supplies on credit.
c. Paid an employee's salary.
d. Paid a creditor.
e. Purchased merchandise on credit.
f. Borrowed money from the bank.
g. Sold merchandise for cash.

QS 8-5
Entries belonging to the General Journal—perpetual
LO3

The Nostalgic Book Shop uses a Sales Journal, a Purchases Journal, a Cash Receipts Journal, a Cash Disbursements Journal, and a General Journal. The following transactions occurred during the month of November. Journalize the November transactions that should be recorded in the General Journal, assuming a perpetual inventory system.

Nov. 2	Purchased merchandise on credit for $2,900 from the Ringdol Co., terms 2/10, n/30.
12	The owner, Jesse Cooke, contributed an automobile worth $15,000 to the business.
16	Sold merchandise on credit to R. Wyder for $1,100, terms n/30; cost, $700.
19	R. Wyder returned $150 (cost, $95) of merchandise originally purchased on November 16. The merchandise was returned to inventory.
28	Returned $170 of defective merchandise to the Ringdol Co. from the November 2 purchase.

QS 8-6
Accounts Receivable Subsidiary Ledger
LO5

Identify the effect caused by each of the following transactions on the Accounts Receivable Subsidiary Ledger:

	Debit (DR), Credit (CR), or No Effect (NE)
1. Sale of merchandise on credit.	__________
2. Purchase of merchandise on credit.	__________
3. Closing of revenue accounts at year-end.	__________
4. Receipt of cash from credit customer.	__________
5. Payment to supplier.	__________
6. Credit memo issued to customer regarding defective merchandise returned.	__________
7. Accrued wages payable at month-end.	__________

QS 8-7
Accounts Payable Subsidiary Ledger

LO5

Identify the effect caused by each of the following transactions on the Accounts Payable Subsidiary Ledger:

	Debit (DR), Credit (CR), or No Effect (NE)
1. Purchase of merchandise on credit.	______
2. Sale of merchandise on credit.	______
3. Purchase of office supplies on account.	______
4. Receipt of cash from credit customer.	______
5. Payment to supplier.	______
6. Memorandum issued by supplier regarding defective merchandise returned.	______
7. Closing of Income Summary to Capital at year-end.	______

Exercises

Exercise 8-1
The Sales Journal—perpetual

LO6

Spindle Corporation uses a Sales Journal, a Purchases Journal, a Cash Receipts Journal, a Cash Disbursements Journal, and a General Journal. The following transactions occurred during the month of February 2001:

Feb. 2	Sold merchandise to S. Mayer for $450 cash, invoice 5703. Cost, $200.
5	Purchased merchandise on credit from Camp Corp., $2,300.
7	Sold merchandise to J. Eason for $1,150, terms 2/10, n/30, invoice 5704. Cost, $700.
8	Borrowed $8,000 by giving a note to the bank.
12	Sold merchandise to P. Lathan for $320, terms n/30, invoice 5705. Cost, $170.
16	Received $1,127 from J. Eason to pay for the purchase of February 7.
19	Sold used store equipment to Whiten, Inc., for $900.
25	Sold merchandise to S. Summers for $550, terms n/30, invoice 5706. Cost, $300.

Required
On a sheet of notebook paper, draw a Sales Journal like the one that appears in Exhibit 8.9. Journalize the February transactions that should be recorded in the Sales Journal.

Exercise 8-2
The Cash Receipts Journal—perpetual

LO6

SeaMap Company uses a Sales Journal, a Purchases Journal, a Cash Receipts Journal, a Cash Disbursements Journal, and a General Journal. The following transactions occurred during the month of September 2001:

Sept. 3	Purchased merchandise on credit for $3,100 from Pacer Co.
7	Sold merchandise on credit to J. Namal for $900, subject to a 2% sales discount if paid by the end of the month. Cost, $500.
9	Borrowed $2,750 by giving a note to the bank.
13	Owner, Dale Trent, invested an additional $3,500 cash into the business.
18	Sold merchandise to B. Baird for $230 cash. Cost, $140.
22	Paid Pacer Co. $3,100 for the merchandise purchased on September 3.
27	Received $882 from J. Namal in payment of the September 7 purchase.
30	Paid salaries of $1,600.

Required
On a sheet of notebook paper, draw a multicolumn Cash Receipts Journal like the one that appears in Exhibit 8.12. Journalize the September transactions that should be recorded in the Cash Receipts Journal.

Exercise 8-3
The Purchases Journal–perpetual

LO6

Chem Corp. uses a Sales Journal, a Purchases Journal, a Cash Receipts Journal, a Cash Disbursements Journal, and a General Journal. The following transactions occurred during the month of July 2001:

July	1	Purchased merchandise on credit for $8,100 from Angler, Inc., terms n/30.
	8	Sold merchandise on credit to B. Harren for $1,500, subject to a $30 sales discount if paid by the end of the month. Cost, $820.
	10	The owner of Chem Corp., Pat Johnson, invested $2,000 cash.
	14	Purchased store supplies from Steck Company on credit for $240, terms 2/10, n/30.
	17	Purchased merchandise inventory on credit from Marten Company for $2,600, terms n/30.
	24	Sold merchandise to W. Winger for $630 cash. Cost, $350.
	28	Purchased merchandise inventory from Hadley's for $9,000 cash.
	29	Paid Angler, Inc., $8,100 for the merchandise purchased on July 1.

Required
On a sheet of notebook paper, draw a multicolumn Purchases Journal like the one that appears in Exhibit 8.14. Journalize the July transactions that should be recorded in the Purchases Journal.

Exercise 8-4
The Cash Disbursements Journal—perpetual

LO6

Aeron Supply uses a Sales Journal, a Purchases Journal, a Cash Receipts Journal, a Cash Disbursements Journal, and a General Journal. The following transactions occurred during the month of March 2001:

Mar.	3	Purchased merchandise for $2,750 on credit from Pace, Inc., terms 2/10, n/30.
	9	Issued cheque #210 to Narlin Corp. to buy store supplies for $450.
	12	Sold merchandise on credit to K. Camp for $670, terms n/30. Cost, $400.
	17	Issued cheque #211 for $1,500 to repay a note payable to City Bank.
	20	Purchased merchandise for $3,500 on credit from LeBaron, terms 2/10, n/30.
	29	Issued cheque #212 to LeBaron to pay the amount due for the purchase of March 20, less the discount.
	31	Paid salary of $1,700 to E. Brandon by issuing cheque #213.
	31	Issued cheque #214 to Pace, Inc., to pay the amount due for the purchase of March 3.

Required
On a sheet of notebook paper, draw a multicolumn Cash Disbursements Journal like the one that appears in Exhibit 8.15. Journalize the March transactions that should be recorded in the Cash Disbursements Journal.

Exercise 8-5
Special journal transactions—perpetual

LO6

Simon Pharmacy uses the following journals: Sales Journal, Purchases Journal, Cash Receipts Journal, Cash Disbursements Journal, and General Journal. On June 5, Simon purchased merchandise priced at $12,000, subject to credit terms of 2/10, n/30. On June 14, the pharmacy paid the net amount due. However, in journalizing the payment, the bookkeeper debited Accounts Payable for $12,000 and failed to record the cash discount. Cash was credited for the actual amount paid. In what journals would the transactions of June 5 and June 14 have been recorded? What procedure is likely to discover the error in journalizing the June 14 transaction?

Exercise 8-6
Errors related to the Purchases Journal

LO6

A company that records credit purchases in a Purchases Journal and records purchase returns in its General Journal made the following errors. List each error by letter and, opposite each letter, tell when the error should be discovered:

a. Made an addition error in determining the balance of a creditor's account.
b. Made an addition error in totalling the Office Supplies column of the Purchases Journal.
c. Posted a purchase return to the Accounts Payable account and to the creditor's account but did not post to the Purchases Returns and Allowances account.
d. Posted a purchases return to the Purchases Returns and Allowances account and to the Accounts Payable account but did not post to the creditor's account.
e. Correctly recorded a $4,000 purchase in the Purchases Journal but posted it to the creditor's account as a $400 purchase.

Exercise 8-7
Posting to subsidiary ledger accounts—perpetual

LO6, 7

At the end of May 2001, the Sales Journal of Camper Goods appeared as follows:

Sales Journal — **Page 4**

Date	Account Debited	Invoice Number	PR	A/R Dr. Sales Cr.	Cost of Goods Sold Dr. Merchandise Inventory Cr.
2001 May 6	Brad Smithers	190		2,880.00	1,600.00
10	Dan Holland	191		1,940.00	1,100.00
17	Sanders Farrell	192		850.00	500.00
25	Dan Holland	193		340.00	130.00
31	Totals			6,010.00	3,330.00

Camper had also recorded the return of merchandise with the following General Journal entry:

May 20	Sales Returns and Allowances	250	
	Accounts Receivable—Sanders Farrell ...		250
	Merchandise Inventory	130	
	Cost of Goods Sold................................		130
	Customer returned merchandise.		

Required

1. On a sheet of notebook paper, open a subsidiary Accounts Receivable Ledger that has a T-account for each customer listed in the Sales Journal. Post to the customer accounts the entries in the Sales Journal and any portion of the General Journal entry that affects a customer's account.
2. Open a General Ledger that has T-accounts for Accounts Receivable, Sales, and Sales Returns and Allowances. Post the Sales Journal and any portion of the General Journal entry that affects these accounts. Calculate the ending balance for each account.
3. Prepare a list or schedule of the accounts in the subsidiary Accounts Receivable Ledger and add their balances to show that the total equals the balance in the Accounts Receivable controlling account.

Exercise 8-8
Sales tax—perpetual

LO7

Fleming Industries is a metal fabricator. It is subject to GST of 7% on all sales and purchases, 8% PST is applied to all sales. Fleming Industries uses a perpetual inventory system.

Required
Journalize the following transactions from August 2001 in the appropriate special journal.

August 1	Purchased $5,000 of inventory from Arden Sheet Metal Suppliers; terms 2/10, n/30.
5	Sold $22,000 of merchandise to Jay Smith; terms 1/10, n/30, invoice 50. Cost of the goods sold was $10,500.
7	Purchased $3,000 of equipment for use in daily operations from JayCee Equipment; terms n/30.
10	Paid for the August 1 purchase; cheque #28.
11	Sold $17,000 of merchandise to Dee Oliver; terms 1/10, n/30; invoice 51. Cost of goods sold was $8,100.
20	Received payment from Jay Smith.
21	Received payment from Dee Oliver.

***Exercise 8-9**
Posting from special journals and subsidiary ledgers to T-accounts—periodic system

LO8

Following are the condensed journals of Tipper Trophies. The journal column headings are incomplete in that they do not indicate whether the columns are debit or credit columns. Assume a periodic inventory system.

Sales Journal		Purchases Journal	
Account	**Amount**	**Account**	**Amount**
Jack Hertz	3,700	Grass Corp.	5,400
Trudy Stone	8,400	Sulter, Inc.	4,500
Dave Waylon	1,000	McGrew Company	1,700
Total	13,100	Total	11,600

Sales Returns and Allowances	300.00	
Accounts Receivable—Jack Hertz		300.00
Customer returned merchandise.		
Accounts Payable—Grass Corp.	750.00	
Purchases Returns and Allowances		750.00
Returned merchandise.		

Cash Receipts Journal

Account	Other Accounts	Accounts Receivable	Sales	Sales Discounts	Cash
Jack Hertz		3,400		68	3,332
Sales			2,250		2,250
Notes Payable	4,500				4,500
Sales			625		625
Trudy Stone		8,400		168	8,232
Store Equipment	500				500
Totals	5,000	11,800	2,875	236	19,439

An asterisk (*) identifies assignment material based on Appendix 8A.

Cash Disbursements Journal				
Account	**Other Accounts**	**Accounts Payable**	**Purchase Discounts**	**Cash**
Prepaid Insurance....................	850			850
Sulter, Inc.		4,500	135	4,365
Grass Corp.		4,650	93	4,557
Store Equipment	1,750			1,750
Totals	2,600	9,150	228	11,522

Required

1. Prepare T-accounts on notebook paper for the following General Ledger and subsidiary ledger accounts. Separate the accounts of each ledger group as follows:

General Ledger Accounts	Accounts Receivable Ledger Accounts
Cash	Jack Hertz
Accounts Receivable	Trudy Stone
Prepaid Insurance	Dave Waylon
Store Equipment	
Accounts Payable	
Notes Payable	
Sales	**Accounts Payable Ledger Accounts**
Sales Discounts	Grass Corp.
Sales Returns and Allowances	McGrew Company
Purchases	Sulter, Inc.
Purchase Discounts	
Purchase Returns and Allowances	

2. Without referring to any of the illustrations in the chapter that show complete column headings for the journals, post the journals to the proper T-accounts.

***Exercise 8-10**
Accounts Receivable Ledger—periodic

LO8

Skillern Company uses a periodic inventory system and had the following credit sales, excluding sales taxes, during January. Sales are subject to a 10% Provincial Sales Tax and the 7% Goods and Services Tax.

Jan.	2	Jay Newton..................	$ 3,600
	8	Adrian Carr	6,100
	10	Kathy Olivas	13,400
	14	Lisa Mack......................	20,500
	20	Kathy Olivas	11,200
	29	Jay Newton..................	7,300
		Total sales on credit.....	$62,100

Check figure:
4. Schedule of accounts receivable = $72,657

Required

1. On a sheet of notebook paper, open a subsidiary Accounts Receivable Ledger having a T-account for each customer. Post the credit sales to the subsidiary ledger.
2. Give the General Journal entry to record the end-of-month total of the Sales Journal.
3. Open an Accounts Receivable controlling account and a Sales account and post the General Journal entry.
4. Prepare a list or schedule of the accounts in the subsidiary Accounts Receivable Ledger and add their balances to show that the total equals the balance in the Accounts Receivable controlling account.

An asterisk (*) identifies assignment material based on Appendix 8A.

Problems

Problem 8-1A
Special journals and subsidiary ledgers

LO 4, 5, 6

Moore Corporation is a major distributor of office supplies. All sales are on terms 1/10, n/15. During March, the following selected transactions occurred. For each transaction, identify into which special journal it should be journalized. Also indicate which subsidiary ledger is affected. Use the list of codes to label your answers. Moore Corporation uses a perpetual inventory system.

Special Journal	
Sales	S
Purchases	P
Cash Receipts	CR
Cash Disbursements	CD
General Journal	G

Subsidiary Ledger	
Accounts Receivable	AR
Accounts Payable	AP
Merchandise Inventory	MI
No Effect	NE

Date	Transaction	Special Journal	Subsidiary Ledger
Mar. 1	Sold merchandise on credit.		
2	Defective merchandise sold on March 1 was returned by the customer. It was scrapped.		
3	Purchased office equipment on credit.		
5	Received payment regarding the March 1 sale.		
10	Received a memorandum from the supplier regarding defective equipment purchased on March 3.		
14	Sold merchandise for cash.		
16	Purchased merchandise inventory on credit; terms 1/5, n/30.		
17	Paid the balance owing on the March 3 transaction.		
18	Purchased merchandise inventory for cash.		
21	Paid for the merchandise purchased on March 16.		
22	Sold old equipment for cash.		
30	Paid salaries for the month of March.		
30	Accrued utilities for the month of March.		
30	Closed the credit balance in the Income Summary to Capital.		

Problem 8-2A
Special journals—perpetual

LO6

Janish Supplies completed the transactions listed below during April 2001. *All sales are on terms 2/10, n/30.*

April 2	Sold merchandise to Tim Bennett for $35,000 on credit; invoice 306 (cost $22,750).
3	Cash sales for the day totalled $15,000; invoices 307 to 310 (cost $9,750).
4	Purchased $48,000 of merchandise from Wallace Brothers; terms 1/10, n/30.
5	Sold merchandise to Brian Kennedy for $42,000 on credit; invoice 311 (cost $27,300).
6	Returned $4,200 of defective merchandise purchased on April 4.
9	Purchased $230 of office supplies; cheque #620.
11	Purchased $56,000 of merchandise from McKinley & Sons; terms n/30.
12	Received payment from Tim Bennett regarding the sale of April 2.
13	Paid for the merchandise purchased on April 4; cheque #621.
16	Sold merchandise to Wynne Walsh for $14,000 on credit; invoice 312 (cost $9,100).
19	Issued a credit memo regarding a $3,000 allowance granted to Wynne Walsh to cover defective merchandise sold on April 16.
20	Received payment from Brian Kennedy for the sale of April 5.
23	Purchased $3,800 of equipment from Zardon Company; terms 1/15, n/30.
24	Sold merchandise to Brian Kennedy for $18,000 on credit; invoice 313 (cost $11,700).
26	Paid for the purchase of April 11; cheque #622.
27	Received payment from Wynne Walsh regarding the sale of April 16.
30	Paid April salaries; $36,000; cheque #623.

Required

1. Prepare a General Journal, Sales Journal, Purchases Journal, Cash Receipts Journal, and Cash Disbursements Journal like the ones illustrated in this chapter.
2. Journalize the April transactions into the appropriate journal *(do not post to the subsidiary ledgers or the General Ledger).*

Problem 8-3A
Special journals, subsidiary ledgers, schedule of accounts receivable—perpetual

LO6, 7

On March 31, 2001, Newton Company had a Merchandise Inventory balance of $95,000 and a balance in Jeff Newton, Capital of $95,000. Newton Company completed these transactions during April 2001. *The terms of all credit sales are 2/10, n/30.*

Apr. 2	Purchased merchandise on credit from Baskin Company, invoice dated April 2, terms 2/10, n/60, $13,300.
3	Sold merchandise on credit to Linda Hobart, invoice 760, $3,000. Cost, $1,800.
3	Purchased office supplies on credit from Eau Claire Inc., $1,380. Invoice dated April 2, terms n/10 EOM.
4	Issued cheque #587 to *The Record* for advertising expense, $999.
5	Sold merchandise on credit to Paul Abrams, invoice 761, $8,000. Cost, $4,500.
6	Received an $85 credit memorandum from Eau Claire Inc. for office supplies received on April 3 and returned for credit.
9	Purchased store equipment on credit from Frank's Supply, invoice dated April 9, terms n/10 EOM, $11,125.
11	Sold merchandise on credit to Kelly Schaefer, invoice 762, $9,500. Cost, $5,000.
12	Issued cheque #588 to Baskin Company in payment of its April 2 invoice.
13	Received payment from Linda Hobart for the April 3 sale.
13	Sold merchandise on credit to Linda Hobart, invoice 763, $4,100. Cost, $2,400.
14	Received payment from Paul Abrams for the April 5 sale.
16	Issued cheque #589, payable to Payroll, in payment of the sales salaries for the first half of the month, $9,750. Cashed the cheque and paid the employees.
16	Cash sales for the first half of the month were $50,840. Cost, $28,000. (Cash sales are usually recorded daily from the cash register readings. However, they are recorded only twice in this problem to reduce the repetitive transactions.)
17	Purchased merchandise on credit from Sprocket Company, invoice dated April 16, terms 2/10, n/30, $12,750.
18	Borrowed $50,000 from First Bank by giving a long-term note payable.
20	Received payment from Kelly Schaefer for the April 11 sale.
20	Purchased store supplies on credit from Frank's Supply, invoice dated April 19, terms n/10 EOM, $730.
23	Received a $400 credit memorandum from Sprocket Company for defective merchandise received on April 17 and returned.
23	Received payment from Linda Hobart for the April 13 sale.
25	Purchased merchandise on credit from Baskin Company, invoice dated April 24, terms 2/10, n/60, $10,375.
26	Issued cheque #590 to Sprocket Company in payment of its April 16 invoice.
27	Sold merchandise on credit to Paul Abrams, invoice 764, $3,070. Cost, $1,600.
27	Sold merchandise on credit to Kelly Schaefer, invoice 765, $5,700. Cost, $3,000.
30	Issued cheque #591, payable to Payroll, in payment of the sales salaries for the last half of the month, $9,750.
30	Cash sales for the last half of the month were $70,975. Cost, $37,000.

Required

Preparation component:

1. Open the following General Ledger accounts: Cash; Accounts Receivable; Merchandise Inventory; Long-Term Notes Payable; Jeff Newton, Capital Sales; Sales Discounts; and Cost of Goods Sold. Also open subsidiary Accounts Receivable Ledger accounts for Paul Abrams, Linda Hobart, and Kelly Schaefer. Enter the March 31 balances of Jeff Newton, Capital and Merchandise Inventory ($95,000 each).
2. Prepare a Sales Journal and a Cash Receipts Journal like the ones illustrated in this chapter.

Check figures:
6. Trial balance = \$300,185
7. Schedule of accounts receivable = \$8,770

3. Review the transactions of Newton Company and enter those transactions that should be journalized in the Sales Journal and those that should be journalized in the Cash Receipts Journal. *Ignore any transactions that should be journalized in a Purchases Journal, a Cash Disbursements Journal, or a General Journal.*
4. Post the items that should be posted as individual amounts from the journals.
5. Foot and crossfoot the journals and make the month-end postings.
6. Prepare a trial balance of the General Ledger and test the accuracy of the subsidiary ledger by preparing a schedule of accounts receivable.

Analysis component:

7. Assume that the sum of the account balances on the schedule of accounts receivable does not equal the balance of the controlling account in the General Ledger. Describe the steps you would go through to discover the error(s).

Problem 8-4A

Special journals, subsidiary ledgers, schedule of accounts payable—perpetual

LO6, 7

Check figures:
7. Trial balance = \$190,525; Schedule of accounts payable = \$23,525

On March 31, 2001, Newton Company had a cash balance of \$167,000 and a Long-Term Notes Payable balance of \$167,000. The April 2001 transactions of Newton Company are those listed in Problem 8-3A.

Required

1. Open the following General Ledger accounts: Cash; Merchandise Inventory; Office Supplies; Store Supplies; Store Equipment; Accounts Payable; Long-Term Notes Payable; Sales Salaries Expense; and Advertising Expense. Enter the March 31 balances of Cash and Long-Term Notes Payable.
2. Open subsidiary Accounts Payable Ledger accounts for Frank's Supply, Baskin Company, Sprocket Company, and Eau Claire Inc.
3. Prepare a General Journal and a Cash Disbursements Journal like the ones illustrated in this chapter. Prepare a Purchases Journal with a debit column for inventory, a debit column for other accounts, and a credit column for accounts payable.
4. Review the April transactions of Newton Company and enter those transactions that should be journalized in the General Journal, the Purchases Journal, or the Cash Disbursements Journal. *Ignore any transactions that should be journalized in a Sales Journal or Cash Receipts Journal.*
5. Post the items that should be posted as individual amounts from the journals. (Normally, such items are posted daily, but since they are few in number in this problem you are asked to post them only once.)
6. Foot and crossfoot the journals and make the month-end postings.
7. Prepare a trial balance and a schedule of accounts payable.

Problem 8-5A

Special journals, subsidiary ledgers, trial balance—perpetual

LO6, 7

(If the Working Papers that accompany this text are not being used, omit this problem.)

It is December 16, 2001, and you have just taken over the accounting work of Saskan Enterprises, whose annual accounting period ends each December 31. The company's previous accountant journalized its transactions through December 15 and posted all items that required posting as individual amounts, as an examination of the journals and ledgers in the Working Papers will show.

The company completed these transactions beginning on December 16, 2001:

Dec. 16	Sold merchandise on credit to Vickie Foresman, invoice 916, $7,700. Cost, $3,900. *Terms of all credit sales are 2/10, n/30.*
17	Received a $1,040 credit memorandum from Shore Company for merchandise received on December 15 and returned for credit.
17	Purchased office supplies on credit from Brown Supply Company, $615. Invoice dated December 16, terms n/10 EOM.
18	Received a $40 credit memorandum from Brown Supply Company for office supplies received on December 17 and returned for credit.
20	Issued a credit memorandum to Amy Ihrig for defective merchandise sold on December 15 and returned for credit, $500. The returned merchandise was scrapped.
21	Purchased store equipment on credit from Brown Supply Company, invoice dated December 21, terms n/10 EOM, $6,700.
22	Received payment from Vickie Foresman for the December 12 sale.
23	Issued cheque #623 to Sunshine Company in payment of its December 15 invoice.
24	Sold merchandise on credit to Bill Grigsby, invoice 917, $1,200. Cost, $700.
24	Issued cheque #624 to Shore Company in payment of its December 15 invoice.
25	Received payment from Amy Ihrig for the December 15 sale.
26	Received merchandise and an invoice dated December 25, terms 2/10, n/60, from Sunshine Company, $8,100.
29	Sold a neighbouring merchant five boxes of file folders (office supplies) for cash at cost, $50.
30	Ken Shaw, the owner of Saskan Enterprises, used cheque #625 to withdraw $2,500 cash from the business for personal use.
31	Issued cheque #626 to Jamie Green, the company's only sales employee, in payment of her salary for the last half of December, $2,020.
31	Issued cheque #627 to Countywide Electric Company in payment of the December electric bill, $710.
31	Cash sales for the last half of the month were $29,600. Cost, $16,300. *Cash sales are usually recorded daily but are recorded only twice in this problem to reduce the repetitive transactions.*

Required

1. Record the transactions in the journals provided.
2. Post to the customer and creditor accounts and also post any amounts that should be posted as individual amounts to the General Ledger accounts. (Normally, these amounts are posted daily, but they are posted only once by you in this problem because they are few in number.)
3. Foot and crossfoot the journals and make the month-end postings.
4. Prepare a December 31 trial balance and test the accuracy of the subsidiary ledgers by preparing schedules of accounts receivable and accounts payable.

Check figure:
4. Trial balance = $219,408

Problem 8-6A
Inventory Subsidiary Ledger—perpetual

LO 6, 7

The Turner Company sells a product called TurnUp for $25 each and uses a perpetual inventory system to account for its merchandise. The beginning balance of TurnUps and transactions during January 2001 were as follows:

Jan.	1	Balance: 25 units costing $8 each.
	3	Purchased from Curtis & Sons 50 units costing $9 each.
	7	Sold to G. Little 20 units, invoice 103.
	19	Sold to B. Moore 15 units, invoice 104.
	20	Purchased from Norton Industries 30 units costing $11 each.
	24	Sold to C. Woudstra 15 units, invoice 105.
	29	Sold to D. Isla 32 units, invoice 106.

Required
Journalize the January transactions in the Sales and Purchases Journal. *Assume all sales and purchases are on credit; terms n/30.* Under the assumption that the company keeps its records on a FIFO basis, enter the beginning balances and post the transactions on a subsidiary inventory record like the one illustrated in Exhibit 8.8.

Problem 8-7A
Sales tax

LO 7

Waterous Company operates a welding business. It is subject to GST of 7% on all sales and purchases and 8% PST on all sales.

Required
Assuming a perpetual inventory system, journalize the October 2001 transactions listed below in the appropriate special journal. Set up your special journals as illustrated in Exhibit 8.18.

Oct.	1	Purchased $4,000 of inventory from Lexor Suppliers; terms 2/10, n/30.
	5	Purchased $2,000 of inventory from Corning; paid cash, cheque #13.
	9	Recorded a cash sale of $1,200; invoice 105. Cost of sale: $740.
	10	Paid for the purchase of October 1; cheque #14.
	12	Sold $6,000 of merchandise to K-Company; terms 1/10, n/30; invoice 106. Cost of sales was $4,200.
	17	Sold merchandise for $7,000 to CanCor; terms 1/10, n/30; invoice 107. Cost of sales was $4,600.
	24	Received payment from CanCor regarding the October 17 transaction.
	26	Received payment from K-Company regarding the October 12 sale.
	27	Purchased $8,000 of inventory from Milton Suppliers; terms n/30.
	30	Sold $4,000 of merchandise to Delton Hardware; terms 1/10, n/30; invoice 108. Cost of sales was $2,900.

***Problem 8-8A**
Special journals, subsidiary ledgers, trial balance—periodic

LO8

The Bledsoe Company completed these transactions during March 2001. Sales are subject to 10% PST and 7% GST is applied to all sales and purchases. Bledsoe uses a periodic system to account for inventory. *Terms of all credit sales are 2/10, n/30.*

Mar.	2	Sold merchandise on credit to Leroy Hackett, invoice 854, $15,800.
	3	Purchased office supplies on credit from Arndt Company, $1,120. Invoice dated March 3, terms n/10 EOM.
	3	Sold merchandise on credit to Sam Snickers, invoice 855, $9,200.
	5	Received merchandise and an invoice dated March 3, terms 2/10, n/30, from Defore Industries, $42,600.
	6	Borrowed $72,000 by giving Commerce Bank a long-term promissory note payable.
	9	Purchased office equipment on credit from Jett Supply, invoice dated March 9, terms n/10 EOM, $20,850.
	10	Sold merchandise on credit to Marjorie Coble, invoice 856, $4,600.
	12	Received payment from Leroy Hackett for the March 2 sale.
	13	Sent Defore Industries cheque #416 in payment of its March 3 invoice.
	13	Received payment from Sam Snickers for the March 3 sale.
	14	Received merchandise and an invoice dated March 13, terms 2/10, n/30, from the Welch Company, $31,625.
	15	Issued cheque #417, payable to Payroll, in payment of sales salaries for the first half of the month, $15,900. Cashed the cheque and paid the employees.
	15	Cash sales for the first half of the month were $164,680. *Normally, cash sales are recorded daily; however, they are recorded only twice in this problem to reduce the repetitive entries.*
	15	*Post to the customer and creditor accounts and also post any amounts that should be posted as individual amounts to the General Ledger accounts. Normally, such items are posted daily, but you are asked to post them on only two occasions in this problem because they are few in number.*
	16	Purchased store supplies on credit from Arndt Company, $1,670. Invoice dated March 16, terms n/10 EOM.
	17	Received a credit memorandum from the Welch Company for unsatisfactory merchandise received on March 14 and returned for credit, $2,425.
	19	Received a credit memorandum from Jett Supply for office equipment received on March 9 and returned for credit, $630.
	20	Received payment from Marjorie Coble for the sale of March 10.
	23	Issued cheque #418 to the Welch Company in payment of its invoice of March 13.
	27	Sold merchandise on credit to Marjorie Coble, invoice 857, $13,910.
	28	Sold merchandise on credit to Sam Snickers, invoice 858, $5,315.
	31	Issued cheque #419, payable to Payroll, in payment of sales salaries for the last half of the month, $15,900. Cashed the cheque and paid the employees.
	31	Cash sales for the last half of the month were $174,590.
	31	*Post to the customer and creditor accounts and post any amounts that should be posted as individual amounts to the General Ledger accounts.*
	31	*Foot and crossfoot the journals and make the month-end postings.*

An asterisk (*) identifies assignment material based on Appendix 8A.

Required

1. Open the following General Ledger accounts: Cash; Accounts Receivable; Office Supplies; Store Supplies; Office Equipment; Accounts Payable; PST Payable; GST Payable; Long-Term Notes Payable; Sales; Sales Discounts; Purchases; Purchases Returns and Allowances; Purchases Discounts; and Sales Salaries Expense.
2. Open the following Accounts Receivable Ledger accounts: Marjorie Coble, Leroy Hackett, and Sam Snickers.
3. Open the following Accounts Payable Ledger accounts: Arndt Company, Defore Industries, Jett Supply, and the Welch Company.
4. Enter the transactions in a Sales Journal, a Purchases Journal, a Cash Receipts Journal, a Cash Disbursements Journal, and a General Journal similar to the ones illustrated in this chapter. Post when instructed to do so.
5. Prepare a trial balance and test the accuracy of the subsidiary ledgers by preparing schedules of accounts receivable and payable.

Check figure:
5. Trial balance = $547,916.15

Alternate Problems

Problem 8-1B

Special journals and subsidiary ledgers—perpetual

LO4,5,6

Lavender Gifts and Novelties uses a perpetual inventory system. All sales are on terms of 2/15, n/30. During May, the following selected transactions occurred. Identify into which special journal each transaction should be journalized. Also indicate which subsidiary ledger is affected. Use the list of codes to label your answers:

Special Journal	
Sales	S
Purchases	P
Cash Receipts	CR
Cash Disbursements	CD
General Journal	G

Subsidiary Ledger	
Accounts Receivable	AR
Accounts Payable	AP
Merchandise Inventory	MI
No Effect	NE

Date		Transaction	Special Journal	Subsidiary Ledger
May	1	The owner invested an automobile into the business.		
	2	Sold merchandise and received cash.		
	3	Purchased merchandise inventory on credit; terms 1/5, n/30.		
	4	Sold merchandise on credit.		
	5	The customer of May 4 returned defective merchandise; the merchandise was scrapped.		
	6	Regarding the May 3 purchase, received a memorandum from the supplier granting an allowance.		
	15	Paid mid-month salaries.		
	17	Purchased office supplies on credit; terms n/30.		
	19	Paid for the balance owing on the May 3 purchase.		
	22	Received payment on the May 4 sale.		
	25	Borrowed money from bank.		
	29	Purchased merchandise inventory; paid cash.		
	30	Accrued interest revenue.		
	30	Closed all revenue accounts to the Income Summary account.		

Problem 8-2B
Special journals and subsidiary ledgers—perpetual

LO6

Willaby Antiques completed the transactions listed below during June 2001. *All sales are on terms 2/10, n/30.*

June 1	Purchased equipment costing $45,000 from Exeter Equipment; terms n/30.
4	Purchased a collection of antiques for $85,000 from Whitby Co.; terms 1/5, n/15.
5	Sold a group of antiques to Martha Stohart for $102,000 on credit; invoice 347 (cost $51,000).
6	Sold an antique to Carol Larson for $8,200 on credit; invoice 348 (cost $5,700).
7	Received an allowance of $4,800 regarding the June 4 purchase due to damages that occurred during delivery.
8	Purchased office supplies of $1,800 from Suppliers Unlimited; terms 2/10, n/30.
11	Paid for the purchase of June 4; cheque #101.
12	Received payment from Carol Larson regarding the sale of June 6.
14	Paid mid-month salaries of $15,000; cheque #102.
18	Sold an antique to Lars Wilson for $6,000 on credit; invoice 349 (cost $4,900).
24	Received payment regarding the sale of June 5.
25	Sold a group of antiques to Nathan Blythe for $28,000 on credit; invoice 350 (cost $14,500).
26	Nathan Blythe returned one of the antiques purchased on June 25 for $2,800 because it was not suited to his home (cost $2,200). The item was returned to inventory.
27	Received payment on the sale of June 18.
28	Paid for the purchase of June 1; cheque #103.
29	Paid month-end salaries of $15,000; cheque #104.

Required

1. Prepare a General Journal, Sales Journal, Purchases Journal, Cash Receipts Journal, and Cash Disbursements Journal like the ones illustrated in this chapter.
2. Journalize the June transactions into the appropriate journal. *Do not post to the subsidiary ledgers or General Ledger.*

Problem 8-3B

Special journals, subsidiary ledgers, schedule of accounts receivable—perpetual

LO6, 7

On June 30, 2001, Eldridge Industries had a Merchandise Inventory balance of $175,000 and the Gene Eldridge, Capital account had a balance of $175,000. Eldridge Industries completed these transactions during July 2001. *The terms of all credit sales are 2/10, n/30.*

July	1	Purchased merchandise on credit from Beech Company, invoice dated June 30, terms 2/10, n/30, $6,300.
	3	Issued cheque #300 to *The Weekly Journal* for advertising expense, $575.
	5	Sold merchandise on credit to Karen Harden, invoice 918, $18,400. Cost, $10,200.
	6	Sold merchandise on credit to Paul Kane, invoice 919, $7,500. Cost, $4,100.
	7	Purchased store supplies on credit from Blackwater Inc., $1,050. Invoice dated July 7, terms n/10 EOM.
	8	Received a $150 credit memorandum from Blackwater Inc. for store supplies received on July 7 and returned for credit.
	9	Purchased store equipment on credit from Poppe's Supply, invoice dated July 8, terms n/10 EOM, $37,710.
	10	Issued cheque #301 to Beech Company in payment of its June 30 invoice.
	13	Sold merchandise on credit to Kelly Grody, invoice 920, $8,350. Cost, $4,600.
	14	Sold merchandise on credit to Karen Harden, invoice 921, $4,100. Cost, $2,300.
	15	Received payment from Karen Harden for the July 5 sale.
	15	Issued cheque #302, payable to Payroll, in payment of the sales salaries for the first half of the month, $30,620. Cashed the cheque and paid the employees.
	15	Cash sales for the first half of the month were $121,370. Cost, $66,700. *Cash sales are usually recorded daily from the cash register readings. However, they are recorded only twice in this problem to reduce the repetitive transactions.*
	16	Received payment from Paul Kane for the July 6 sale.
	17	Purchased merchandise on credit from Sprague Company, invoice dated July 17, terms 2/10, n/30, $8,200.
	20	Purchased office supplies on credit from Poppe's Supply, $750. Invoice dated July 19, terms n/10 EOM.
	21	Borrowed $20,000 from College Bank by giving a long-term note payable.
	23	Received payment from Kelly Grody for the July 13 sale.
	24	Received payment from Karen Harden for the July 14 sale.
	24	Received a $2,400 credit memorandum from Sprague Company for defective merchandise received on July 17 and returned.
	26	Purchased merchandise on credit from Beech Company, invoice dated July 26, terms 2/10, n/30, $9,770.
	27	Issued cheque #303 to Sprague Company in payment of its July 17 invoice.
	29	Sold merchandise on credit to Paul Kane, invoice 922, $28,090. Cost, $15,500.
	30	Sold merchandise on credit to Kelly Grody, invoice 923, $15,750. Cost, $8,700.
	31	Issued cheque #304, payable to Payroll, in payment of the sales salaries for the last half of the month, $30,620.
	31	Cash sales for the last half of the month were $79,020. Cost, $43,500.

Required

Preparation component:

1. Open the following General Ledger accounts: Cash; Accounts Receivable; Merchandise Inventory; Long-Term Notes Payable; Gene Eldridge, Capital; Sales; Sales Discounts; and Cost of Goods Sold. Also open subsidiary Accounts Receivable Ledger accounts for Kelly Grody, Karen Harden, and Paul Kane. Enter the June 30 balances of Merchandise Inventory and Gene Eldridge.

2. Prepare a Sales Journal and a Cash Receipts Journal similar to the ones illustrated in this chapter.
3. Review the transactions of Eldridge Industries and enter those transactions that should be journalized in the Sales Journal and those that should be journalized in the Cash Receipts Journal. *Ignore any transactions that should be journalized in a Purchases Journal, Cash Disbursements Journal, or a General Journal.*
4. Post the items that should be posted as individual amounts from the journals. *Normally, such items are posted daily; since they are few in number in this problem, you are asked to post them only once.*
5. Foot and crossfoot the journals and make the month-end postings.
6. Prepare a trial balance of the General Ledger and test the accuracy of the subsidiary ledger by preparing a schedule of accounts receivable.

Check figures:
6. Trial balance = $477,850
7. Schedule of accounts receivable = $43,840

Analysis component:

7. Assume that the sum of the account balances on the schedule of accounts receivable does not equal the balance of the controlling account in the General Ledger. Describe the steps you would go through to discover the error(s).

Problem 8-4B

Special journals, subsidiary ledgers, schedule of accounts payable—perpetual

LO 6, 7

On June 30, 2001, Eldridge Industries had a Cash balance of $165,600 and a Long-Term Notes Payable balance of $165,600. The July 2001 transactions of Eldridge Industries are those listed in Problem 8-3B.

Required

1. Open the following General Ledger accounts: Cash; Merchandise Inventory; Office Supplies; Store Supplies; Store Equipment; Accounts Payable; Long-Term Notes Payable; Sales Salaries Expense; and Advertising Expense. Enter the June 30 balances of Cash and Long-Term Notes Payable.
2. Open subsidiary Accounts Payable Ledger accounts for Beech Company, Blackwater Inc., Poppe's Supply, and Sprague Company.
3. Prepare a General Journal and a Cash Disbursements Journal like the ones illustrated in this chapter. Prepare a Purchases Journal with a debit column for purchases, a debit column for other accounts, and a credit column for accounts payable.
4. Review the July transactions of Eldridge Industries and enter those transactions that should be journalized in the General Journal, the Purchases Journal, or the Cash Disbursements Journal. *Ignore any transactions that should be journalized in a Sales Journal or Cash Receipts Journal.*
5. Post the items that should be posted as individual amounts from the journals. *Normally, such items are posted daily, but since they are few in number in this problem, you are asked to post them only once.*
6. Foot and crossfoot the journals and make the month-end postings.
7. Prepare a trial balance and a schedule of accounts payable.

Check figures:
7. Trial balance = $214,730
Schedule of Accounts Payable = $49,130

Problem 8-5B

Special journals, subsidiary ledgers, trial balance—perpetual

LO 6, 7

(If the Working Papers that accompany this text are not being used, omit this problem.)

It is December 16, 2001 and you have just taken over the accounting work of Starshine Products, whose annual accounting period ends December 31. The company's previous accountant journalized its transactions through December 15 and posted all items that required posting as individual amounts, as an examination of the journals and ledgers in the booklet of working papers will show.

The company completed these transactions beginning on December 16, 2001. *Terms of all credit sales are 2/10, n/30.*

Dec. 16	Purchased office supplies on credit from Green Supply Company, $765. Invoice dated December 16, terms n/10 EOM.
16	Sold merchandise on credit to Heather Flatt, invoice 916, $4,290. Cost, $2,460.
18	Issued a credit memorandum to Amy Izon for defective merchandise sold on December 15 and returned for credit, $200. The returned merchandise was scrapped.
19	Received a $640 credit memorandum from Walters Company for merchandise received on December 15 and returned for credit.
20	Received a $143 credit memorandum from Green Supply Company for office supplies received on December 16 and returned for credit.
20	Purchased store equipment on credit from Green Supply Company, invoice dated December 19, terms n/10 EOM, $7,475.
21	Sold merchandise on credit to Jan Wildman, invoice 917, $5,520. Cost, $3,000.
22	Received payment from Heather Flatt for the December 12 sale.
25	Received payment from Amy Izon for the December 15 sale.
25	Issued cheque #623 to Walters Company in payment of its December 15 invoice.
25	Issued cheque #624 to Sunshine Company in payment of its December 15 invoice.
28	Received merchandise with an invoice dated December 28, terms 2/10, n/60, from Sunshine Company, $6,030.
28	Sold a neighbouring merchant a carton of calculator tape (store supplies) for cash at cost, $58.
29	Marlee Levin, the owner of Starshine Products, used cheque #625 to withdraw $4,000 cash from the business for personal use.
30	Issued cheque #626 to Midwest Electric Company in payment of the December electric bill, $990.
30	Issued cheque #627 to Jamie Ford, the company's only sales employee, in payment of her salary for the last half of December, $2,620.
31	Cash sales for the last half of the month were $66,128. Cost, $36,400. *Cash sales are usually recorded daily but are recorded only twice in this problem to reduce the repetitive transactions.*

Required

1. Record the transactions in the journals provided.
2. Post to the customer and creditor accounts and also post any amounts that should be posted as individual amounts to the General Ledger accounts. *Normally, these amounts are posted daily, but they are posted only once by you in this problem because they are few in number.*
3. Foot and crossfoot the journals and make the month-end postings.
4. Prepare a December 31 trial balance and test the accuracy of the subsidiary ledgers by preparing schedules of accounts receivable and payable.

Check figure:
4. Trial balance = $255,598

Problem 8-6B
Inventory Subsidiary Ledger—perpetual
LO6, 7

The Record Company sells a product called ReCord for $30 each and uses a perpetual inventory system to account for its merchandise. The beginning balance of ReCords and transactions during July 2001 were as follows:

July	1	Balance: 30 units costing $12 each.
	4	Purchased from Tulsco Supply 45 units costing $10 each.
	9	Sold to W. Tilden 10 units, invoice 213.
	15	Sold to J. Samuelson 25 units, invoice 214.
	18	Purchased from Gentry Holdings 30 units costing $9 each.
	22	Sold to V. Nels 20 units, invoice 215.
	30	Sold to M. Bains 27 units, invoice 216.

Required
Journalize the July transactions in the sales and purchases journal. *Assume all sales and purchases are on credit; terms n/30.* Under the assumption that the company keeps its records on a weighted average basis, enter the beginning balances and post the transactions on a subsidiary inventory record like the one illustrated in Exhibit 8.8.

Problem 8-7B
Sales tax
LO7

Trenton Industries is an office furniture wholesaler. It is subject to GST of 7% on all sales and purchases and 8% PST on all sales.

Required
Assuming a perpetual inventory system, journalize the May 2001 transactions in the appropriate special journal. Set up your special journals as illustrated in Exhibit 8.18.

May	1	John Trenton the owner, invested cash of $9,000 into the business.
	3	Sold $6,000 of merchandise to Ajax Holdings; terms 1/10, n/30; invoice 361. Cost of sales was $3,200.
	5	Purchased merchandise inventory costing $1,600; paid by cheque #83.
	7	Purchased office supplies with a cost of $3,200 on credit from Moore Corporation; terms n/30.
	12	Received payment from Ajax Holdings.
	13	Sold $1,800 of merchandise for cash; invoice 362. Cost of sales was $1,100.
	15	Borrowed $5,000 from the bank.
	16	Purchased merchandise inventory costing $7,200 from London Company; terms 1/15, n/30.
	30	Paid for the office supplies purchased on May 7, cheque #84.
	30	Sold $3,700 of merchandise to Allendale Arena; terms 1/10, n/30; invoice 363. Cost of sales was $1,900.

***Problem 8-8B**
Special journals, subsidiary ledgers, trial balance—periodic

LO[8]

Crystal Company completed these transactions during November 2001. Sales are subject to 10% PST and 7% GST is applied to sales and purchases. Crystal Company uses a periodic inventory system. *Terms of all credit sales are 2/10, n/30.*

Nov.	1	Purchased office equipment on credit from Jett Supply, invoice dated November 1, terms n/10 EOM, $5,062.
	2	Borrowed $86,250 by giving Jefferson Bank a long-term promissory note payable.
	4	Received merchandise and an invoice dated November 3, terms 2/10, n/30, from Defore Industries, $11,400.
	5	Purchased store supplies on credit from Atlas Company, $1,020. Invoice dated November 5, terms n/10 EOM.
	8	Sold merchandise on credit to Leroy Holmes, invoice 439, $6,350.
	10	Sold merchandise on credit to Sam Spear, invoice 440, $12,500.
	11	Received merchandise and an invoice dated November 10, terms 2/10, n/30, from The Welch Company, $2,887.
	12	Sent Defore Industries cheque #633 in payment of its November 3 invoice.
	15	Issued cheque #634, payable to Payroll, in payment of sales salaries for the first half of the month, $8,435. Cashed the cheque and paid the employees.
	15	Cash sales for the first half of the month were $27,170. *Normally, cash sales are recorded daily; however, they are recorded only twice in this problem to reduce the number of repetitive entries.*
	15	Post to the customer and creditor accounts and also post any amounts that should be posted as individual amounts to the General Ledger accounts. *Normally, such items are posted daily, but you are asked to post them on only two occasions in this problem because they are few in number.*
	15	Sold merchandise on credit to Marjorie Cook, invoice 441, $4,250.
	16	Purchased office supplies on credit from Atlas Company, $559. Invoice dated November 16, terms n/10 EOM.
	17	Received a credit memorandum from The Welch Company for unsatisfactory merchandise received on November 10 and returned for credit, $487.
	18	Received payment from Leroy Holmes for the November 8 sale.
	19	Received payment from Sam Spear for the November 10 sale.
	19	Issued cheque #635 to The Welch Company in payment of its invoice of November 10.
	22	Sold merchandise on credit to Sam Spear, invoice 442, $2,595.
	24	Sold merchandise on credit to Marjorie Cook, invoice 443, $3,240.
	25	Received payment from Marjorie Cook for the sale of November 15.
	26	Received a credit memorandum from Jett Supply for office equipment received on November 1 and returned for credit, $922.
	30	Issued cheque #636, payable to Payroll, in payment of sales salaries for the last half of the month, $8,435. Cashed the cheque and paid the employees.
	30	Cash sales for the last half of the month were $35,703.
	30	*Post to the customer and creditor accounts and post any amounts that should be posted as individual amounts to the General Ledger accounts.*
	30	*Foot and crossfoot the journals and make the month-end postings.*

An asterisk (*) identifies assignment material based on Appendix 8A.

Required

1. Open the following General Ledger accounts: Cash; Accounts Receivable; Office Supplies; Store Supplies; Office Equipment; Accounts Payable; PST Payable; GST Payable; Long-Term Notes Payable; Sales; Sales Discounts; Purchases; Purchases Returns and Allowances; Purchases Discounts; and Sales Salaries Expense.
2. Open the following Accounts Receivable Ledger accounts: Marjorie Cook, Leroy Holmes, and Sam Spear.
3. Open the following Accounts Payable Ledger accounts: Atlas Company, Defore Industries, Jett Supply, and The Welch Company. Enter the transactions in a Sales Journal, a Purchases Journal, a Cash Receipts Journal, a Cash Disbursements Journal, and a General Journal similar to the ones illustrated in this chapter. Post when instructed to do so.
4. Prepare a trial balance and test the accuracy of the subsidiary ledgers by preparing schedules of accounts receivable and payable.

Check figure:
4. Trial balance = $199,181.36

Analytical and Review Problem—Perpetual

A & R Problem 8-1

The Williams Company sells a product called Mix-Right for $15 each and uses a perpetual inventory system to account for its merchandise. The beginning balance of Mix-Rights and transactions during October 2001 were as follows:

Oct.	1	Balance: 85 units costing $5 each.
	3	Purchased 100 units from Arnold Brothers costing $7.50 each.
	4	Returned 20 of the units purchased on October 3.
	9	Sold 75 units to Kitchen Club, invoice 210.
	15	Purchased 200 units from Arnold Brothers costing $7.75 each.
	18	Sold 150 units to Thorhild Co-op, invoice 211.
	19	Paid for the October 3 purchase; cheque #101.
	23	Paid for the October 15 purchase, cheque #102.
	24	Sold 50 units to Boyle Grocery, invoice 212.
	31	Purchased 75 units from Arnold Brothers costing $8.00 each.

Required

Journalize the October transactions in the sales, purchases, and cash disbursements journal. *Assume all sales and purchases are on credit; terms 2/10, n/30.* Under the assumption that the company keeps its records on a weighted average basis, enter the beginning balances and post the transactions on a subsidiary inventory record like the one illustrated below. Posting to other subsidiary ledgers is not required.

Date	PR	Purchases (Returns, Allowances and Discounts)			Sales (at cost)			Inventory Balance (a)	(b)	(a) ÷ (b)
		Units	Cost	Total Cost	Units	Cost	Total Cost	Total Cost	Total Units	Average Cost/Unit

Comprehensive Problem 8.1—Perpetual

Alpine Company

LO6, 7

(If the Working Papers that accompany this text are not available, omit this comprehensive problem.)

Assume it is Monday, May 1, 2001, the first business day of the month, and you have just been hired as the accountant for Alpine Company, which operates with monthly accounting periods. All of the company's accounting work has been completed through the end of April and its ledgers show April 30 balances. Alpine uses a perpetual system to account for inventory. *The terms of all credit sales are 2/10, n/30.* During your first month on the job, you record the following transactions:

May 1 Issued cheque #3410 to S&M Management Co. in payment of the May rent, $3,710. *Use two lines to record the transaction. Charge 80% of the rent to Rent Expense, Selling Space and the balance to Rent Expense, Office Space.*

2 Sold merchandise on credit to Essex Company, invoice 8785, $6,100. Cost $3,660.

2 Issued a $175 credit memorandum to Nabors, Inc., for defective merchandise sold on April 28 and returned to inventory (cost $105) for credit. The total selling price was $4,725.

3 Received a $798 credit memorandum from Parkay Products for merchandise received on April 29 and returned for credit.

4 Purchased on credit from Thompson Supply Co.: merchandise, $37,072; store supplies, $574; and office supplies, $83. Invoice dated May 4, terms n/10 EOM.

5 Received payment from Nabors, Inc. from the sale of April 28.

8 Issued cheque #3411 to Parkay Products to pay for the $7,098 of merchandise received on April 29.

9 Sold store supplies to the merchant next door at cost for cash, $350.

10 Purchased office equipment on credit from Thompson Supply Co., invoice dated May 10, terms n/10 EOM, $4,074.

11 Received payment from Essex Company for the May 2 sale.

11 Received merchandise and an invoice dated May 10, terms 2/10, n/30, from Gale, Inc., $8,800.

12 Received an $854 credit memorandum from Thompson Supply Co. for defective office equipment received on May 10 and returned for credit.

15 Issued cheque #3412, payable to Payroll, in payment of sales salaries, $5,320, and office salaries, $3,150. Cashed the cheque and paid the employees.

15 Cash sales for the first half of the month, $59,220. Cost $35,532. *Such sales are normally recorded daily. They are recorded only twice in this problem to reduce the repetitive entries.*

15 *Post to the customer and creditor accounts. Also, post individual items that are not included in column totals at the end of the month to the General Ledger accounts. Such items are normally posted daily, but you are asked to post them only twice each month because they are few in number.*

16 Sold merchandise on credit to Essex Company, invoice 8786, $3,990. Cost $2,394.

17 Received merchandise and an invoice dated May 14, terms 2/10, n/60, from Chandler Corp., $13,650.

19 Issued cheque #3413 to Gale, Inc. in payment of its May 10 invoice.

22 Sold merchandise to Oscar Services, invoice 8787, $6,850, terms 2/10, n/60. Cost $4,110.

23 Issued cheque #3414 to Chandler Corp. in payment of its May 14 invoice.

24 Purchased on credit from Thompson Supply Co.: merchandise, $8,120; store supplies, $630; and office supplies, $280. Invoice dated May 24, terms n/10 EOM.

25 Received merchandise and an invoice dated May 23, terms 2/10, n/30, from Parkay Products, $3,080.

26 Sold merchandise on credit to Deaver Corp., invoice 8788, $14,210. Cost $8,526.

26 Issued cheque #3415 to Trinity Power in payment of the April electric bill, $1,283.

29 The owner, Clint Barry, withdrew $7,000 from the business for personal use, using cheque #3416.

30 Received payment from Oscar Services for the May 22 sale.

30 Issued cheque #3417, payable to Payroll, in payment of sales salaries, $5,320, and office salaries, $3,150. Cashed the cheque and paid the employees.

31 Cash sales for the last half of the month were $66,052. Cost $39,630.

31 *Post to the customer and creditor accounts. Also, post individual items that are not included in column totals at the end of the month to the General Ledger accounts.*

31 *Foot and crossfoot the journals and make the month-end postings.*

Required

1. Enter the transactions in the appropriate journals and post when instructed to do so.
2. Prepare a trial balance in the Trial Balance columns of the provided work sheet form and complete the work sheet using the following information.
   a. Expired insurance, $553.
   b. Ending store supplies inventory, $2,632.
   c. Ending office supplies inventory, $504.
   d. Estimated amortization of store equipment, $567.
   e. Estimated amortization of office equipment, $329.
   f. Ending merchandise inventory, $191,000.
3. Prepare a May classified, multiple-step income statement P. 276, a May statement of owner's equity P. 38, and a May 31 classified balance sheet P. 208.
4. Prepare and post adjusting and closing entries (omit explanations).
5. Prepare a post-closing trial balance P. 203. Also prepare a list of the Accounts Receivable Ledger accounts and a list of the Accounts Payable Ledger accounts. Total the balances of each to confirm that the totals equal the balances in the controlling accounts.

*Comprehensive Problem 8.2—Periodic

Alphine Company

LO8

Required

Using information from Comprehensive Problem 8.1, complete the requirements assuming a periodic inventory system.

An asterisk (*) identifies assignment material based on Appendix 8A.

CHAPTER

Internal Control and Cash

Undercover Accountants

With "white collar" crime on the increase, demands on the Commercial Crime Division of the RCMP are growing. Dealing with a broad range of issues including technological fraud, securities and exchange irregularities, crimes against federal departments, and international fraud, RCMP investigating specialists like Corporal Gibson Glavin understand the sensitivity of assets and the resulting need for sound internal controls.

Many of the crimes investigated by the RCMP are related to internal control issues. In November 1999 the RCMP were involved in the investigation of a student-loan scam where the Ontario government was defrauded by a private business and technology school of some $18 million. How did it happen? Inadequate internal controls. In 1999, an Alberta pharmacist was convicted of defrauding Health Canada of $400,000 in false prescriptions. How did it happen? Controls were in place, according to Health Canada, that were subsequently enhanced with the expectation that this kind of wrongdoing would not go undetected in the future. Staff Sergeant Tim Turner, Supervisor of a Federal Commercial Crime Unit, indicated that his team has investigated several situations that involved an individual within an organization

Learning Objectives

- **LO1** Define, explain the purpose, and identify the principles of internal control.
- **LO2** Define cash and explain how it is reported.
- **LO3** Apply internal control to cash.
- **LO4** Explain and record petty cash fund transactions.
- **LO5** Identify control features of banking activities.
- **LO6** Prepare a bank reconciliation.

who was responsible for both writing cheques and preparing the bank reconciliation. The individual supplemented his income by writing cheques to himself and then later destroyed the cheques when returned by the bank. Staff Sergeant Turner is surprised that external auditors could miss this type of irregularity because it should be obvious through the use of a basic audit procedure: scrutinizing the sequence of cheque numbers.

In all of the above cases, the RCMP became involved because of concerns raised by members of the general public and not because the perpetrator was detected by the internal control system. The lesson, according to Staff Sergeant Tim Turner, is to ensure that your organization has a sound system of controls, including management review on a regular basis. Otherwise, in keeping with a longstanding Canadian tradition, the RCMP will have to put things right by always getting their man!

Chapter Preview

We are all aware of reports and experiences involving theft and fraud. These activities affect us and produce various actions, including locking doors, chaining bikes, reviewing sales receipts, and acquiring alarm systems. A company also takes action to safeguard, control, and manage what it owns. Experience tells us small companies are most vulnerable, usually due to weak internal controls. It is management's responsibility to set up policies and procedures to safeguard a company's assets, especially cash. To do so, management and employees must understand and apply principles of internal control. This chapter describes these principles and how we apply them. We learn about important internal control policies and procedures. We focus special attention on cash, because cash is easily transferable and is often at high risk of loss. Controls for cash are explained, including petty cash funds and reconciling bank accounts. Our understanding of these controls and procedures makes us more secure in carrying out business activities and in assessing those activities of companies. As Staff Sergeant Turner emphasizes in the opening article, internal controls are crucial for the successful operation of an organization.

Internal Control

This section describes internal control and its fundamental principles. We also discuss the impact of computing technology on internal control and the limitations of control procedures.

Purpose of Internal Control

Define, explain the purpose, and identify the principles of internal control.

Managers of small businesses often control the entire operation. They participate in all activities from hiring and managing employees to signing all cheques. These managers know from personal contact and observation whether the business is actually receiving the assets and services being paid for. The larger the operation, the more managers must delegate responsibilities and rely on formal procedures rather than personal contact in controlling and knowing all operations of the business.

These managers place a high priority on internal control systems to monitor and control operations. This is because these systems can prevent avoidable losses, help managers plan operations, and monitor company and human performance. An **internal control system** is all policies and procedures used to:

- Protect assets,
- Ensure reliable accounting,
- Promote efficient operations, and
- Encourage adherence to company policies.

Principles of Internal Control

Internal control policies and procedures depend on the nature and size of the business. The fundamental **principles of internal control** are:

1. **Establish responsibilities for each task clearly and for one person.**

   When two salesclerks share access to the same cash register, for instance, neither clerk can prove or disprove any alleged shortage. Instead, a company can use a register with separate cash drawers for each clerk.

2. **Maintain adequate records to help protect assets by ensuring that employees use prescribed procedures.**

   When detailed records of manufacturing equipment and tools are kept, for instance, lost or stolen items are readily noticed. Similarly, the use of a chart of accounts encourages the correct recording of transactions that improves the accuracy of reports.

   Preprinted forms and internal business papers are also designed and properly used in a good internal control system. For example, when sales slips are prenumbered and accounted for, a salesperson is not able to pocket cash by making a sale and destroying the sales slip. Computerized point-of-sale systems achieve the same control results.

3. **Insure assets and *bond* key employees to reduce risk of loss from casualty and theft.**

   To **bond** an employee is to purchase an insurance policy, or a bond, against losses from theft by that employee. Bonding reduces the risk of loss suffered from theft in addition to discouraging theft by the bonded employee.

4. **Separate recordkeeping from custody of assets so a person who controls or has access to an asset is not responsible for the maintenance of that asset's accounting records.**

   The risk of theft or waste is reduced since the person with control over the asset knows that records are kept by another person. The recordkeeper does not have access to the asset and has no reason to falsify records. In situations where recordkeeping is separate from the custody of assets, *collusion* is necessary to hide theft from the records. **Collusion** is not likely because it means two or more people must agree to commit a fraud.

5. **Divide responsibility for related transactions between two or more individuals or departments (also called *separation of duties*).**

   This is not a call for duplication of work but instead ensures that the work of one acts as a check on the other. An example is requiring two signatures on cheques to verify that disbursements are in conformance with policies and procedures. Other examples of transactions improved by dividing responsibility are placing purchase orders and receiving merchandise. Having an independent person check incoming goods for quality and quantity encourages more care and attention to detail than when checked by the person placing the order.

6. **Apply technological controls.**

   Cash registers with a locked-in tape or electronic file make a record of each cash sale. A time clock registers the exact time an employee both arrives on and departs from the job. Passwords limit access to sensitive information.

Mechanical change and currency counters can quickly and accurately count amounts. Personal identification scanners can limit access to only those individuals who are authorized. Each of these and other technological controls are effective parts of many internal control systems.

7. **Perform regular and independent reviews to ensure that internal control procedures are followed.**

   No internal control system is entirely effective, for various reasons such as changes in personnel and time pressures. Reviews are preferably done by internal auditors who are employees not directly involved in operations and who report directly to senior management. Their independent perspective encourages an evaluation of the efficiency as well as the effectiveness of the internal control system.

   Many companies also pay for audits by independent external auditors who are professional accountants. These external auditors test the company's financial records and then give an opinion as to whether the company's financial statements are presented fairly in accordance with generally accepted accounting principles. In the process of their evaluation, they often identify internal controls that need improvement.

Technology and Internal Control

The fundamental principles of internal control are relevant no matter what the technological state of the accounting system. This includes all systems from the purely manual to those that are fully automated with only electronic documentation. This section describes some technological impacts we must be alert to.

Reduced Processing Errors

Provided the software and data entries are correct, the risk of mechanical and mathematical errors is nearly eliminated because of technology. Yet mistakes happen and one must be alert to that possibly. The decreasing human involvement in later data processing can cause data entry errors to go undiscovered. Similarly, errors in software can produce consistent erroneous processing of transactions.

More Extensive Testing of Records

When accounting records are kept manually, auditors and others likely select only small samples of data to test during regular reviews. But when data are accessible with computer technology, then large samples or even complete data files can be quickly reviewed and analyzed.

Limited Evidence of Processing

Because many data processing steps are increasingly done by computer, fewer "hard copy" items of documentary evidence are available for review. Yet technologically advanced systems can store additional evidence. They can, for instance, record information such as who made the entries, the date and time, and the source of their entry. Technology can also be designed to require use of passwords or other identification before access to the system is granted. This means that internal control depends more on the design and operation of the information system and less on analysis of the documents left behind by the system.

Crucial Separation of Duties

Technological advances in accounting information systems are so efficient that they often require fewer employees. This reduction in workforce carries a risk that separation of crucial responsibilities is lost. Companies that use advanced technology also need employees with special skills to operate programs and equipment. The duties of these employees must be controlled and monitored to minimize risk of error and fraud. Better control is maintained if, for instance, the person designing and programming the system does not serve as the operator. Also the control over programs and files related to cash receipts and disbursements must be separated. Cheque-writing activities should not be controlled by a computer operator in order to avoid risk of fraud. Yet achieving acceptable separation of duties can be especially difficult in small companies with few employees.

Limitations of Internal Control

All internal control policies and procedures have limitations. Probably the most serious source of these limitations is the human element that we can categorize as either (1) human error, or (2) human fraud.

Human error is a factor whenever internal control policies and procedures are carried out by people. *Human error* can occur from negligence, fatigue, misjudgement or confusion. *Human fraud* involves intent by people to defeat internal controls for personal gain. This human element highlights the importance of establishing an *internal control environment* that conveys management's attitude and commitment to internal control.

Another important limitation of internal control is the *cost–benefit standard.* This means the costs of internal controls must not exceed their benefits. Analysis of costs and benefits must consider all factors, including the impact on morale. Most companies, for instance, have a legal right to read employees' e-mail. Yet companies seldom exercise that right unless confronted with evidence of potential harm to the company. The same holds for drug testing, phone tapping and hidden cameras. The bottom line is that no internal control system is perfect and that managers must establish internal control policies and procedures with a net benefit to the company.

The preceding discussion is an introduction to internal controls. The study of *auditing* takes a detailed look at internal controls.

Campaign Manager

You are leading a campaign to influence the government to improve the health care system. Your funding is limited and you try hiring people who are committed to your cause and will work for less. A systems analyst recently volunteered her services and put together a Web strategy to attract supporters. She also strongly encouraged you to force all employees to take at least one week of vacation per year. Why does she feel so strongly about a "forced vacation" policy?

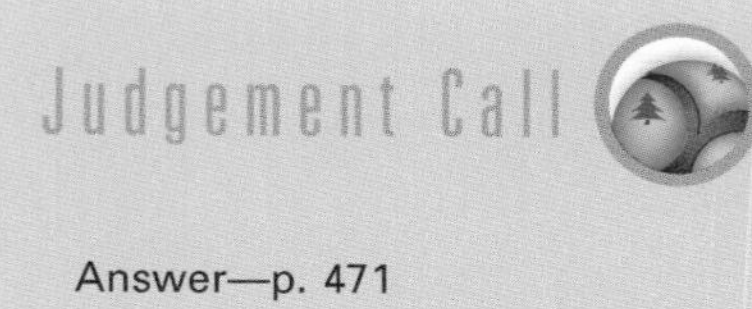

Answer—p. 471

1. Fundamental principles of internal control state that (choose the correct statement):
   a. Responsibility for a series of related transactions (such as placing orders for, receiving, and paying for merchandise) should be assigned to one person.
   b. Responsibility for specific tasks should be shared by more than one employee so that one serves as a check on the other.
   c. Employees who handle cash and negotiable assets are bonded.
2. What are some impacts of computing technology on internal control?

Answers—p. 472

Cash

Define cash and explain how it is reported.

Cash is an important asset for every company and must be managed. Companies also need to carefully control access to cash by employees and others who are inclined to take it for personal use. Good accounting systems support both goals by managing how much cash is on hand and controlling who has access to it.

Cash Defined

Cash includes currency, coins, and amounts on deposit in bank accounts, chequing accounts (also called *demand deposits*) and some savings accounts. Cash also includes items that are acceptable for deposit in these accounts, such as customers' cheques, cashier's cheques, certified cheques, money orders, and deposits made through electronic funds transfer (EFT).

Many companies invest idle cash in assets called *cash equivalents* or short-term investments to increase earnings. Because cash equivalents or short-term investments are similar to cash, many companies combine them with cash as a single item on the balance sheet. WestJet Airlines Ltd., for instance, reports the following on its December 31, 1999 balance sheet:

Cash and short-term investments............$50,740 (thousand)

Liquidity

Cash is the usual means of payment when paying for other assets, services, or liabilities. **Liquidity** refers to how easily an asset can be converted into another asset or used in paying for services or obligations. Cash and similar assets are called **liquid assets** because they are converted easily into other assets or used in paying for services or liabilities. A company must own some liquid assets, for example, so that bills are paid on time and purchases are made for cash when necessary.

Answer—p. 472

3. Why must a company own liquid assets?

Control of Cash

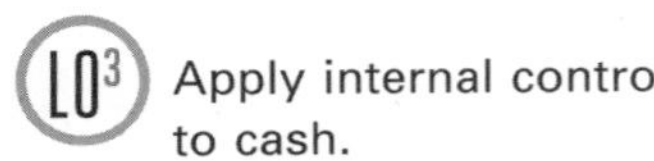
Apply internal control to cash.

It is important that we apply principles of good internal control to cash. Cash is the most liquid of all assets and is easily hidden and moved. A good system of internal control for cash provides adequate procedures for protecting both cash receipts and cash disbursements. These procedures should meet three basic guidelines:

1. Separate handling of cash from recordkeeping of cash.
2. Cash receipts are promptly (daily) deposited in a bank.
3. Cash disbursements are made by cheque.

The first guideline aims to minimize errors and fraud by a division of duties. When duties are separated, it requires two or more people to collude for cash to be stolen and the theft to be concealed in the accounting records. The second guideline aims to use immediate (daily) deposits of all cash receipts to produce a timely independent test of the accuracy of the count of cash received. It also reduces cash theft or loss, and it reduces the risk of an employee personally using the money before depositing it. The third guideline aims to use payments by cheque to develop a bank record of cash disbursements. This guideline also reduces the risk of cash theft. Often, two signatures are required to ensure that legitimate invoices are being paid.

One exception to the third guideline is to allow small disbursements of currency and coins from a petty cash fund. We describe a petty cash fund later in this section. Another important point is that the deposit of cash receipts and the use of cheques for cash disbursements allow a company to use bank records as a separate external record of cash transactions. We explain how to use bank records to confirm the accuracy of a company's own records later in this section.

Control of Cash Receipts

Internal control of cash receipts ensures that all cash received is properly recorded and deposited. Cash receipts arise from many transactions, including cash sales, collections of customers' accounts, receipts of interest and rent, bank loans, sale of assets, and owners' investments. This section explains internal control over two important types of cash receipts: over-the-counter and mail.

Over-the-Counter Cash Receipts

For purposes of internal control, over-the-counter cash sales should be recorded on a cash register at the time of each sale for internal control. To help ensure that correct amounts are entered, each register should be located so customers can read the amounts entered. The design of each cash register should provide a permanent, locked-in record of each transaction. Many software programs accept cash register transactions and enter them in accounting records. Less technology-dependent registers simply print a record of each transaction on a paper tape or electronic file locked inside the register.

Custody over cash should be separate from its recordkeeping; therefore the clerk who has access to cash in the register should not have access to its locked-in record. At the end of the clerk's work period, the clerk should count the cash in the register, record the amount, and turn over the cash and a record of its amount to an employee in the cashier's office. The employee in the cashier's office, like the clerk, has access to the cash and should not have access to accounting records (or the register tape or file). A third employee compares the record of total register transactions (or the register tape or file) with the cash receipts reported by the cashier's office. This record (or register tape or file) is the basis for a journal entry recording over-the-counter cash sales. Note that the third employee has access to the records for cash but not to the actual cash. The clerk and the employee from the cashier's office have access to cash but not to the accounting records. This means the accuracy of cash records and amounts are automatically checked. None of them can make a mistake or divert cash without the difference being revealed.

Cash Over and Short

Sometimes errors in making change are discovered when there is a difference between the cash in a cash register and the record of the amount of cash sales. This difference is reported in the **Cash Over and Short** account. This income statement account, shown under general and administrative expenses, records the income effects of cash overages and cash shortages from errors in making change and missing petty cash receipts. The journal entries to record cash over and short are illustrated later in this chapter.

Cash Receipts by Mail

Control of cash receipts that arrive through the mail starts with the person who opens the mail. In a large business, two people are assigned the task and are present when opening the mail. The person opening the mail makes a list (in triplicate) of money received. This list should contain a record of each sender's name, the amount, and an explanation for what purpose the money is sent. The first copy is sent with the money to the cashier. A second copy is sent to the accounting area. A third copy is kept by the clerk who opened the mail. The cashier deposits the money in the bank, and the recordkeeper records amounts received in the accounting records. In a small business, the owner should assume responsibility for cash.

Control of Cash Disbursements

Control of cash disbursements is especially important for companies. Most large thefts occur from payments of fictitious invoices. The key to controlling cash disbursements is to require that all expenditures be made by cheque, with two signatures if possible when not signed by the owner. The only exception is for small payments from petty cash. Another key is that when the authority to sign cheques is assigned to a person other than the owner, that person must not have access to the accounting records. This separation of duties helps prevent an employee from hiding fraudulent disbursements in the accounting records.

The manager of a small business often signs cheques and knows from personal contact that the items being paid for are actually received. This arrangement is impossible in large businesses. Instead, internal control procedures must be substituted for personal contact. These controls are achieved through a *voucher system.* Briefly, the **voucher system** of control requires that a number of procedures be performed and documents collected to support the validity of each disbursement. These procedures are designed to assure the cheque signer that the obligations recorded were properly incurred and should be paid. The voucher system is explained in detail in Appendix 9A.

The exact procedures used to achieve control over cash vary across companies. They depend on such factors as company size, number of employees, volume of cash transactions, and sources of cash. We must therefore view the procedures described in this section as illustrative of those in practice today.

Answer—p. 472

4. Good internal control procedures for cash receipts imply that (choose one):
   - **a.** All cash disbursements, other than those for very small amounts, are made by cheque.
   - **b.** An accounting employee should count cash received from sales and promptly deposit receipts.
   - **c.** Cash receipts by mail should be opened by an accounting employee who is responsible for recording and depositing receipts.

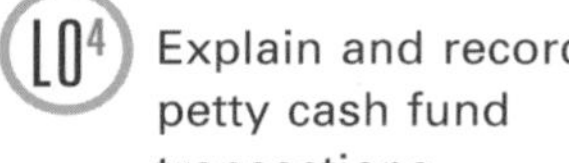

Explain and record petty cash fund transactions.

Petty Cash System of Control

A basic principle for controlling cash disbursements is that all payments are made by cheque. An exception to this rule is made for petty cash disbursements. Petty cash disbursements are the *small amount* payments required in most companies for items such as postage, courier fees, repairs, and supplies. To avoid writing cheques for small amounts, a company usually sets up a petty cash fund and uses the money in this fund to make small payments.

Operating a Petty Cash Fund

Establishing a petty cash fund requires estimating the total amount of small payments likely to be made during a short period such as a week or month. A cheque is then drawn by the company cashier's office for an amount slightly in excess of this estimate. To illustrate, assume Z-Mart established a petty cash fund on November 1, 2001 in the amount of $75. A $75 cheque was drawn, cashed, and the proceeds turned over to Jim Gibbs, an office employee designated as the *petty cashier* or *petty cash custodian.* The **petty cashier** is responsible for safekeeping of the cash, for making payments from this fund, and for keeping accurate records. The entry to record the set-up of this petty cash fund is:

Nov. 1	Petty Cash	75	
	Cash		75
	To establish a petty cash fund.		

This entry transfers $75 from the regular Cash account to the Petty Cash account. After the petty cash fund is established, the Petty Cash account is not debited or credited again unless the size of the total fund is changed.

The petty cashier should keep petty cash in a locked box in a safe place. As each disbursement is made, the person receiving payment signs a *petty cash receipt* or *petty cash ticket* as illustrated in Exhibit 9.1.

Exhibit 9.1

Petty Cash Receipt

Petty Cash Receipt No. 6
Z-Mart

For Delivery charges Date Nov.18/2001

Charge to Delivery expense Amount $5.00

Approved by *Jim Gibbs* Received by *Dick Fitch*

The petty cash receipt is then placed in the petty cashbox with the remaining money. When the cash is nearly gone, the fund should be reimbursed. When it is time to reimburse the petty cash fund, the petty cashier should sort the receipts by type and prepare a summary as shown in Exhibit 9.2.

Exhibit 9.2

Petty Cash Payments Report

Z-Mart Petty Cash Payments Report				
Office maintenance				
Nov.	2	Washing windows	$10.00	
	17	Washing windows	10.00	
	27	Computer repairs	26.50	$ 46.50
Transportation-in				
Nov.	5	Delivery of merchandise purchased	$ 6.75	
	20	Delivery of merchandise purchased	8.30	15.05
Delivery expense				
Nov.	18	Customer's package delivered		5.00
Office supplies				
Nov.	15	Purchased office supplies		4.75
Total				**$71.30**

To replenish Petty Cash:

Cash Required to Replenish Petty Cash = Fund Size − Cash Remaining

To calculate cash over/(short):

Cash Over/(Short) = Total of Petty Cash Receipts − Cash Required to Replenish Petty Cash

This summary and all petty cash receipts are presented to the company's cashier. The company's cashier stamps all receipts paid so they cannot be reused, files them for recordkeeping, records the reimbursement, and gives the petty cashier a cheque for a sum *equal to the fund size less the cash remaining.* In our example, Jim Gibbs had only $2.20 cash remaining in the fund at the end of November. Therefore, the reimbursement cheque is for $72.80 (= $75.00 − $2.20). Notice that Exhibit 9.2 shows total receipts for $71.30. The difference between the total receipts and the reimbursement cheque represents a cash shortage of $1.50 (= $71.30 − $72.80) due to an error. The reimbursement cheque is recorded as follows:

Nov. 27	Office Maintenance Expenses	46.50	
	Merchandise Inventory	15.05	
	Delivery Expense	5.00	
	Office Supplies	4.75	
	Cash Over and Short	1.50	
	Cash		72.80
	To reimburse petty cash.		

In the case of an overage in the petty cash fund, a credit to Cash Over and Short is recorded in the reimbursing entry.

When the reimbursement cheque is cashed and the money returned to the cashbox, the total money in the box is restored to its original amount of $75.00 (= $72.80 + $2.20). The fund is now ready to begin a new cycle of operations.

Increasing or Decreasing Petty Cash Fund

A decision to increase or decrease a petty cash fund is often made when the fund is being reimbursed. To illustrate, let us assume that Z-Mart decides to increase the petty cash fund by $25, from $75 to $100, on November 27 when it reimburses the fund. This is recorded as follows:

Nov. 27	Petty Cash	25.00	
	Office Maintenance Expenses	46.50	
	Merchandise Inventory	15.05	
	Delivery Expense	5.00	
	Office Supplies	4.75	
	Cash Over and Short	1.50	
	Cash		97.80
	To reimburse petty cash and increase it by $25.00.		

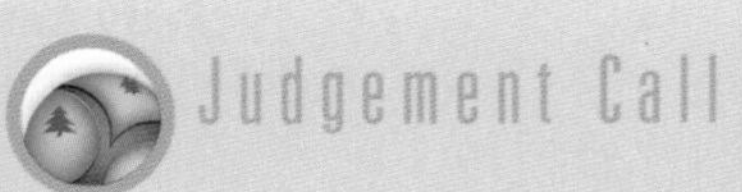

Answer—p. 471

Internal Auditor

You are an internal auditor for a company. You are currently making surprise counts of three $200 petty cash funds. You arrive at the office of one of the petty cashiers while she is on the telephone. You explain the purpose of your visit, and the petty cashier asks politely that you come back after lunch so that she can finish the business she's conducting by long distance. You agree and return after lunch. The petty cashier opens the petty cashbox and shows you nine new $20 bills with consecutive serial numbers plus receipts totalling $20. Do you take further action or comment on these events in your report to management?

5. Why are some cash payments made from a petty cash fund?
6. Why should a petty cash fund be reimbursed at the end of an accounting period?
7. What are three results of reimbursing the petty cash fund?

Answers—p. 472

Mid-Chapter Demonstration Problem

Castillo Company established a $250 petty cash fund on February 10. On February 28, the fund had $180.14 remaining in cash and receipts for these expenditures: postage due, $15.25; office supplies, $45.26; and repair expenses, $10.50. Prepare:

a. the February 10 entry to establish the fund,
b. the February 28 entry to record the fund transactions and replenish it, and
c. independent of (b), the February 28 entry to record the fund transactions and reduce the fund to $100.

Planning the Solution

- Total petty cash receipts
- Calculate cash required to replenish petty cash
- Calculate cash over/(short), if any
- Prepare journal entries as required

SOLUTION TO Mid-Chapter Demonstration Problem

a. Feb. 10	Petty Cash Fund	250.00	
	Cash		250.00
	To establish petty cash fund.		
b. 28	Postage Expense	15.25	
	Office Expense	45.26	
	Repair Expense	10.50	
	Cash Over and Short		1.15
	Cash		69.86
	To reimburse petty cash fund.		

Calculations:

Total of petty cash receipts = $15.25 + $45.26 + $10.50 = $71.01

Cash required to replenish petty cash = Fund size − Cash remaining
= $250 − $180.14
= $69.86

Cash over/(short) = Receipt totals − Cash required
= $71.01 − $69.86
= $1.15

c.	28	Cash	80.14	
		Postage Expense	15.25	
		Office Expense	45.26	
		Repair Expense	10.50	
		Cash Over and Short		1.15
		Petty Cash		150.00
		To reimburse petty cash fund and decrease it to $100.		

Calculations:

Cash required to replenish petty cash = New fund size − Cash remaining
= $100.00 − $180.14
= −$80.14 (therefore, instead of a credit to Cash, debit Cash)

Banking Activities as Controls

LO5 Identify control features of banking activities.

Banks are used by most companies for many different services. One of their most important services is helping companies control cash and cash transactions. Banks safeguard cash, provide detailed and independent records of cash transactions, and are a source of cash financing. This section describes services and documents provided by banking activities that increase managers' control over cash.

Basic Bank Services

This first section explains basic bank services. We include the bank account, bank deposits, and cheques. Each of these services contributes to either or both the control or safeguarding of cash.

Bank Account

A bank account is a record set up by a bank for a customer, permitting this customer to deposit money for safeguarding and cheque withdrawals. To control access to a bank account, all persons authorized to use a bank account must sign a signature card. A **signature card** includes the signatures of each person authorized to sign cheques from the account. Bank employees use signature cards to verify signatures on cheques. This lowers the risk of loss from forgery for both banks and customers. Many companies have more than one bank account. This is for various reasons including serving local needs and for special transactions such as payroll.

Bank Deposit

Each bank deposit is supported by a *deposit slip*. A **deposit slip** lists the items such as currency, coins, and cheques deposited along with each of their dollar amounts. The bank gives the customer a copy of the deposit slip or a deposit receipt as proof of the deposit. Exhibit 9.3 shows a deposit slip.

Bank Cheque

To withdraw money from an account, a customer uses a *cheque*. A **cheque** is a document signed by the depositor instructing the bank to pay a specified amount of money to a designated recipient. A cheque involves three parties: a *maker* who signs the cheque, a *payee* who is the recipient, and a *bank* on which the cheque is drawn. The bank provides a depositor with cheques that are serially numbered and imprinted with the name and address of both the depositor and bank. Both cheques and deposit slips are imprinted with identification codes in magnetic ink for computer processing. Exhibit 9.4 shows a cheque. This cheque is accompanied by an optional *remittance advice* giving an explanation for the payment. When a remittance advice is unavailable, the memo line is often used for a brief explanation.

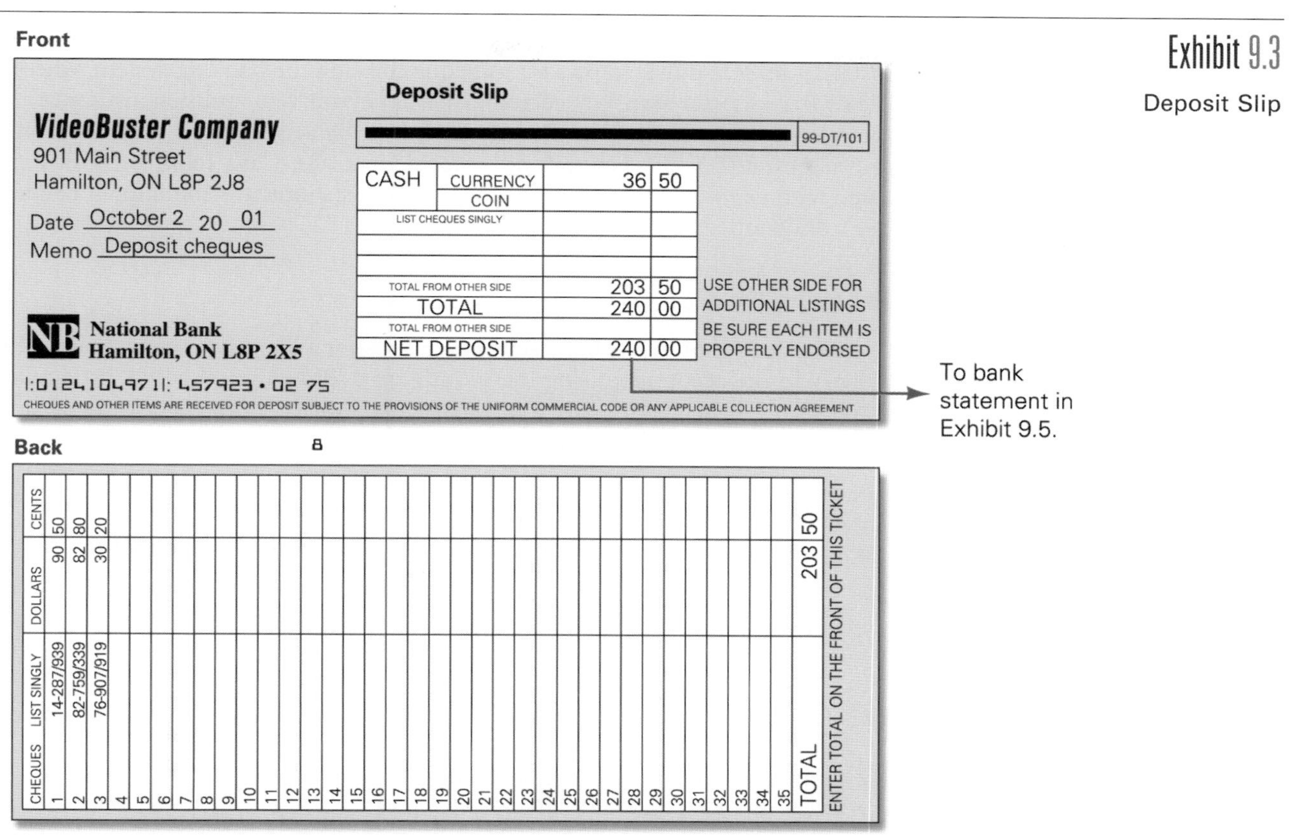

Exhibit 9.3

Deposit Slip

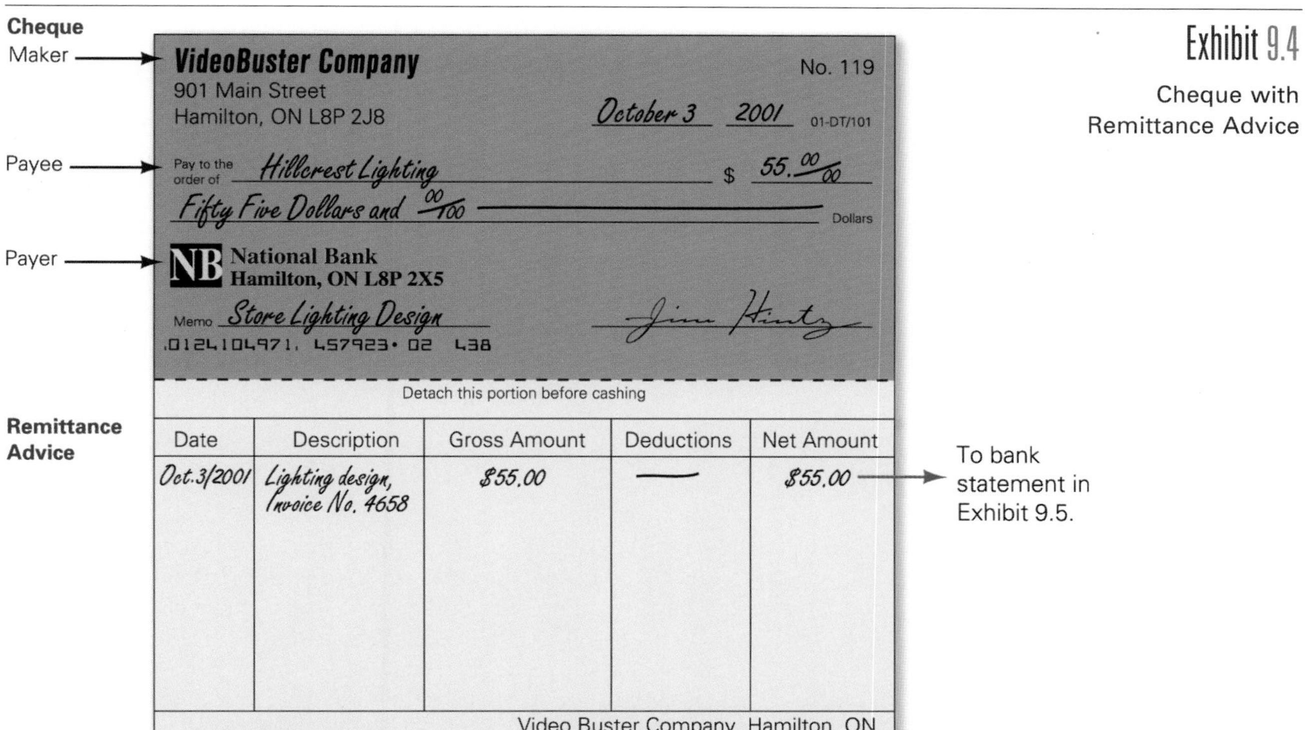

Exhibit 9.4

Cheque with Remittance Advice

Electronic Funds Transfer

Electronic funds transfer (EFT) is the use of electronic communication to transfer cash from one party to another. No paper documents are necessary. Banks simply transfer cash from one account to another with a journal entry. Companies are increasingly using EFT because of its convenience and low cost. It can cost, for instance, up to a dollar to process a cheque through the banking system, whereas the EFT cost is near zero. We see items such as payroll, rent, utilities, insurance and interest payments being handled by EFT. The bank statement lists cash withdrawals by EFT with cheques and other deductions. Cash receipts by EFT are listed with deposits and other additions. A bank statement is sometimes a depositor's only notice of an EFT.

Bank Statement

At least once a month, the bank sends the depositor a bank statement showing the activity in the accounts during the month, or a company can access its banking activity on-line at any time. Different banks use a variety of formats for their bank statements. Yet all of them include the following items of information:

1. Beginning-of-month balance of the depositor's account.
2. Cheques and other debits decreasing the account during the month.
3. Deposits and other credits increasing the account during the month.
4. End-of-month balance of the depositor's account.

This information reflects the bank's records. Exhibit 9.5 shows a bank statement.

A Summarizes changes in the account.

B Lists paid cheques in numerical order along with other debits (or decreases).

C Lists deposits and credits (increases) to the account.

D Shows the daily account balances.

Notice that 'Deposits' are called credits and 'Cheques' are called debits on the bank statement. This is because *a depositor's account is a liability on the bank's records since the money belongs to the depositor and not the bank.* When a depositor, Smith, puts money into the bank, the bank debits cash and ***credits*** the bank's liability account to Smith. Hence, ***credit memos*** show the bank's increasing liability to Smith. When Smith withdraws money from the bank, the bank records it as a credit to cash and *debits* the bank's liability account for Smith. Therefore, *debit memos* reflect decreases in the bank's liability to Smith.

Exhibit 9.5

Bank Statement

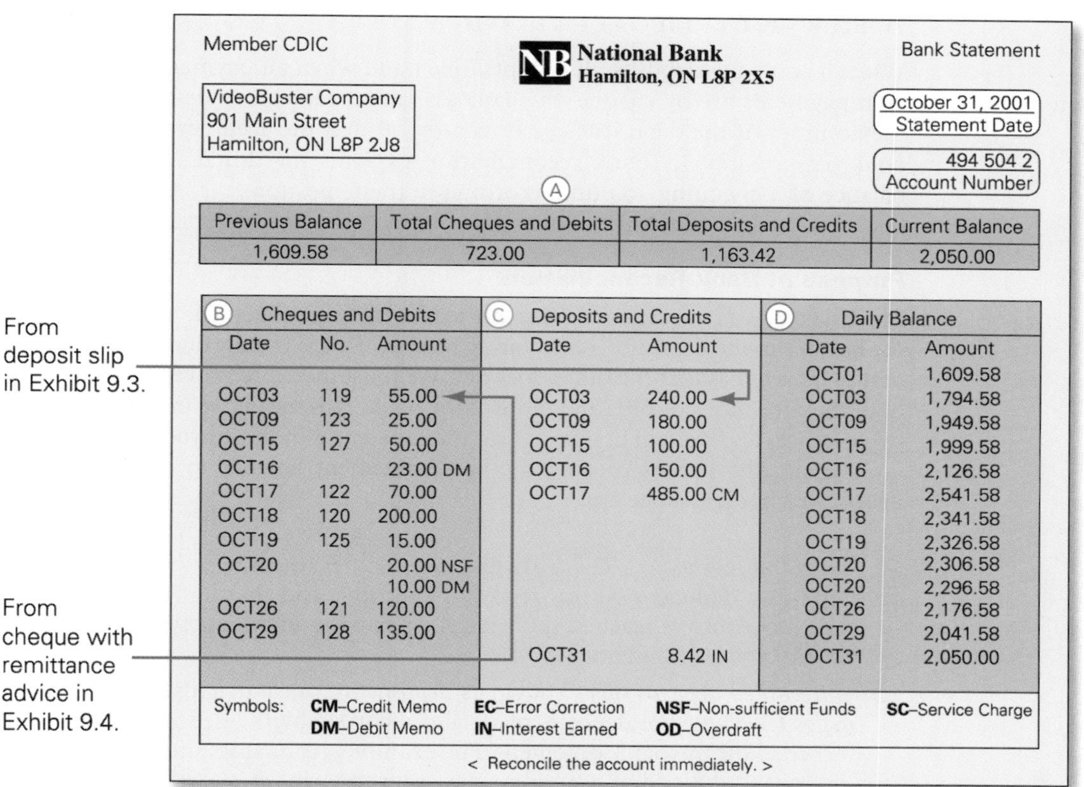

Member CDIC

NB National Bank
Hamilton, ON L8P 2X5

Bank Statement

VideoBuster Company
901 Main Street
Hamilton, ON L8P 2J8

October 31, 2001
Statement Date

494 504 2
Account Number

(A)

Previous Balance	Total Cheques and Debits	Total Deposits and Credits	Current Balance
1,609.58	723.00	1,163.42	2,050.00

(B) Cheques and Debits

Date	No.	Amount
OCT03	119	55.00
OCT09	123	25.00
OCT15	127	50.00
OCT16		23.00 DM
OCT17	122	70.00
OCT18	120	200.00
OCT19	125	15.00
OCT20		20.00 NSF
		10.00 DM
OCT26	121	120.00
OCT29	128	135.00

(C) Deposits and Credits

Date	Amount
OCT03	240.00
OCT09	180.00
OCT15	100.00
OCT16	150.00
OCT17	485.00 CM
OCT31	8.42 IN

(D) Daily Balance

Date	Amount
OCT01	1,609.58
OCT03	1,794.58
OCT09	1,949.58
OCT15	1,999.58
OCT16	2,126.58
OCT17	2,541.58
OCT18	2,341.58
OCT19	2,326.58
OCT20	2,306.58
OCT20	2,296.58
OCT26	2,176.58
OCT29	2,041.58
OCT31	2,050.00

Symbols: **CM**–Credit Memo **DM**–Debit Memo **EC**–Error Correction **IN**–Interest Earned **NSF**–Non-sufficient Funds **OD**–Overdraft **SC**–Service Charge

< Reconcile the account immediately. >

Enclosed with a bank statement are the depositor's cancelled cheques and any debit or credit memoranda affecting the account. **Cancelled cheques** are cheques the bank has paid and deducted from the customer's account during the month. Other deductions also often appear on a bank statement and include: (1) service charges and fees assessed by the bank, (2) customers' cheques deposited that are uncollectible, (3) corrections of previous errors, (4) withdrawals through automatic teller machines (ATM)[1], and (5) periodic payments arranged in advance by a depositor such as payments, insurance, and lease payments. Except for service charges, the bank notifies the depositor of each deduction with a debit memorandum when the bank reduces the balance. A copy of each debit memorandum is usually sent with the monthly statement.

While deposits increase a depositor's bank balance, there are other transactions that increase the depositor's account. Examples are amounts the bank collects on behalf of the depositor and corrections of previous errors. Credit

[1] Because of a desire to make all disbursements by cheque, most business chequing accounts do not allow ATM withdrawals.

memoranda notify the depositor of all increases recorded by the bank. A copy of each credit memorandum is often sent with the bank statement. Another item added to the bank balance is interest earned by the depositor. Many chequing accounts pay the depositor interest based on the average cash balance maintained in the account. The bank computes the amount of interest earned and credits it to the depositor's account each month. In Exhibit 9.5, for instance, the bank credits $8.42 of interest to the account of VideoBuster. We describe the methods used to compute interest in the next chapter.

Bank Reconciliation

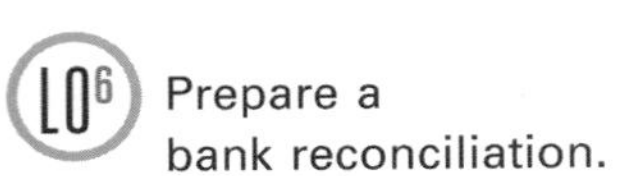

Prepare a bank reconciliation.

When a company deposits all receipts intact and when all payments except petty cash payments are by cheque, the bank statement serves as a device for proving the accuracy of the depositor's cash records. We test the accuracy by preparing a *bank reconciliation*. A **bank reconciliation** explains the difference between the balance of a chequing account according to the depositor's records and the balance reported on the bank statement.

Purpose of Bank Reconciliation

The balance of a chequing account reported on the bank statement is rarely equal to the balance in the depositor's accounting records. This is usually due to information that one party has that the other does not. We must therefore prove the accuracy of both the depositor's records and those of the bank. This means we must *reconcile* the two balances and explain or account for the differences in these two balances.

Among the factors causing the bank statement balance to differ from the depositor's book balance are:

1. *Outstanding cheques.* These are cheques written (or drawn) by the depositor, deducted on the depositor's records, and sent to the payees. But they have not yet reached the bank for payment and deduction at the time of the bank statement.
2. *Unrecorded deposits* (also known as *deposits in transit* or *outstanding deposits*). These are deposits made and recorded by the depositor but not recorded on the bank statement. For example, companies often make deposits at the end of a business day, after the bank is closed. A deposit in the bank's night depository on the last day of the month is not recorded by the bank until the next business day and does not appear on the bank statement for that month. Also, deposits mailed to the bank near the end of a month may be in transit and unrecorded when the statement is prepared.
3. *Deductions for uncollectible items and for services.* A company sometimes deposits a customer's cheque that is uncollectible. This usually is because the balance in the customer's account is not large enough to cover the cheque. This cheque is called a *nonsufficient funds (NSF)* cheque. The bank initially credited the depositor's account for the amount of the deposited cheque. When the bank learns that the cheque is uncollectible, it debits (reduces) the depositor's account for the amount of that cheque. The bank may also charge the depositor a fee for processing an uncollectible cheque and notify the depositor of the deduction by sending a debit memorandum. While each deduction should be recorded by the depositor when a debit memorandum is received, an entry is sometimes not made until the bank reconciliation is prepared.

   Other possible bank charges to a depositor's account reported on a bank statement include the printing of new cheques and a service charge for maintaining the account. Notification of these charges is *not* provided until the statement is mailed.

4. *Additions for collections and for interest.* Banks sometimes act as collection agents for their depositors by collecting notes and other items. Banks can also receive electronic funds transfers to the depositor's account. When a bank collects an item, it adds it to the depositor's account, less any service fee. It also sends a credit memorandum to notify the depositor of the transaction. When the memorandum is received, it should be recorded by the depositor. Yet these sometimes remain unrecorded until the time of the bank reconciliation.

   Many bank accounts earn interest on the average cash balance in the account during the month. If an account earns interest, the bank statement includes a credit for the amount earned during the past month. Notification of earned interest is provided by the bank statement.
5. *Errors.* Both banks and depositors can make errors. For example, a bank error might include a cheque written by *VideoBlaster* Company mistakenly charged against the account of *VideoBuster* Company or a deposit made by *VideoBuster* Company accidentally posted to the account of *Videon* Company. A depositor error might involve a cheque actually written for $102 but recorded in error in the cash disbursements journal as $120. These kinds of errors might not be discovered until the depositor prepares a bank reconciliation.

Steps in Reconciling a Bank Balance

The employee who prepares the bank reconciliation should not be responsible for cash receipts, processing cheques, or maintaining cash records. This employee needs to gather information from the bank statement and from other records. A reconciliation requires this person to:

- Compare deposits on the bank statement with deposits in the accounting records (Cash Receipts Journal and last month's bank reconciliation). Identify any discrepancies and determine which is correct. List any errors or unrecorded deposits.
- Inspect all additions (credits) on the bank statement and determine whether each is recorded in the books. These items include collections by the bank, correction of previous bank statement errors, and interest earned by the depositor. List any unrecorded items.
- Compare cancelled cheques on the bank statement with actual cheques returned with the statement. For each cheque, make sure the correct amount is deducted by the bank and the returned cheque is properly charged to the account. List any discrepancies or errors.
- Compare cancelled cheques on the bank statement with cheques recorded in the books (Cash Disbursements Journal). List any outstanding cheques. Also, while companies with good internal controls would rarely write a cheque without recording it, we should inspect and list any cancelled cheques that are unrecorded in the books.
- Identify any outstanding cheques listed on the previous month's bank reconciliation that are not included in the cancelled cheques on this month's bank statement. List these cheques that remain outstanding at the end of the current month. Send the list to the cashier's office for follow-up with the payees to see if the cheques were actually received.
- Inspect all deductions (debits) to the account on the bank statement and determine whether each is recorded in the books. These include bank charges for newly printed cheques, NSF cheques, and monthly service charges. List items not yet recorded.

When this information is gathered, the employee can complete the reconciliation.

Illustrating a Bank Reconciliation

We illustrate a bank reconciliation by preparing one for VideoBuster as of October 31. We use the guidelines listed above and follow nine specific steps. Follow each step to the corresponding Exhibits 9.5 to 9.8 to see where the information comes from and how it is shown on the bank reconciliation in Exhibit 9.9.

1. Identify the bank balance of the cash account at October 31 (balance per bank).
   - *Bank balance shown on the bank statement is $2,050 (from Exhibit 9.5).*
2. Identify and list any unrecorded deposits and any bank errors. Add them to the bank balance on the bank reconciliation.
   - *A $145 deposit was placed in the bank's night depository on October 31 and is not recorded on the bank statement (from Exhibit 9.6)*
3. Identify and list any outstanding cheques and any bank errors. Deduct them from the bank balance on the bank reconciliation.
   - *A comparison of cancelled cheques with the company's books showed two cheques outstanding: #124 for $150 and #126 for $200 (from Exhibit 9.7).*
4. Compute the *adjusted bank balance,* also called *corrected* or *reconciled* balance.
   - *See Exhibit 9.9.*
5. Identify the company's balance of the cash account (balance per book).
   - *Cash balance shown in the accounting records is $1,404.58 (from Exhibit 9.8).*
6. Identify and list any unrecorded credit memoranda from the bank, such as interest earned and errors. Add them to the book balance on the bank reconciliation.
   a. *Enclosed with the bank statement is a credit memorandum showing that the bank collected a note receivable for the company on October 17. The note's proceeds of $500 (minus a $15 collection fee) were credited to the company's account. This credit memorandum is not yet recorded by the company (from Exhibit 9.5).*
   b. *The bank statement shows a credit of $8.42 for interest earned on the average cash balance in the account. There was no prior notification of this item and it is not yet recorded on the company's books (from Exhibit 9.5).*

Exhibit 9.5

Bank Statement (repeated from e
for ease of refere

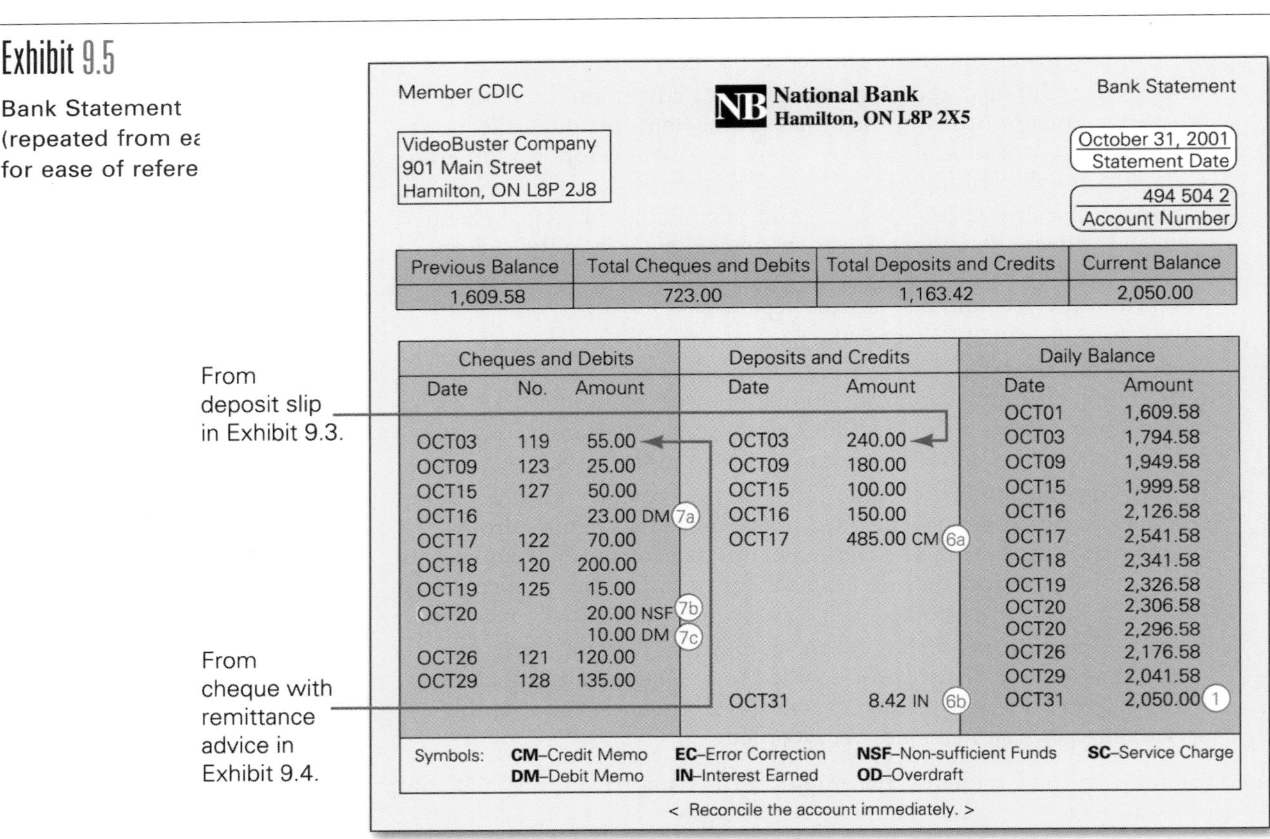

Member CDIC

NB National Bank
Hamilton, ON L8P 2X5

Bank Statement

VideoBuster Company
901 Main Street
Hamilton, ON L8P 2J8

October 31, 2001
Statement Date

494 504 2
Account Number

Previous Balance	Total Cheques and Debits	Total Deposits and Credits	Current Balance
1,609.58	723.00	1,163.42	2,050.00

Cheques and Debits			Deposits and Credits		Daily Balance	
Date	No.	Amount	Date	Amount	Date	Amount
					OCT01	1,609.58
OCT03	119	55.00	OCT03	240.00	OCT03	1,794.58
OCT09	123	25.00	OCT09	180.00	OCT09	1,949.58
OCT15	127	50.00	OCT15	100.00	OCT15	1,999.58
OCT16		23.00 DM (7a)	OCT16	150.00	OCT16	2,126.58
OCT17	122	70.00	OCT17	485.00 CM (6a)	OCT17	2,541.58
OCT18	120	200.00			OCT18	2,341.58
OCT19	125	15.00			OCT19	2,326.58
OCT20		20.00 NSF (7b)			OCT20	2,306.58
		10.00 DM (7c)			OCT20	2,296.58
OCT26	121	120.00			OCT26	2,176.58
OCT29	128	135.00			OCT29	2,041.58
			OCT31	8.42 IN (6b)	OCT31	2,050.00 (1)

Symbols: CM–Credit Memo DM–Debit Memo EC–Error Correction IN–Interest Earned NSF–Non-sufficient Funds OD–Overdraft SC–Service Charge

< Reconcile the account immediately. >

7. Identify and list any unrecorded debit memoranda from the bank, such as service charges and errors. Deduct them from the book balance on the bank reconciliation.
   - *Debits on the bank statement that are not recorded on the books include: (a) a $23 charge for cheques printed by the bank, and (b) an NSF cheque for $20 plus (c) a related $10 processing fee. The NSF cheque is from a customer, Frank Heflin, and was originally included as part of the October 16 deposit (from Exhibit 9.5).*
8. Compute the *adjusted book balance*, also called the *corrected* or *reconciled* balance.
   - *See Exhibit 9.9.*
9. Verify that the two adjusted balances from Steps 4 and 8 are equal. If so, they are reconciled. If not, check for mathematical accuracy and missing data.
   - *See Exhibit 9.9.*

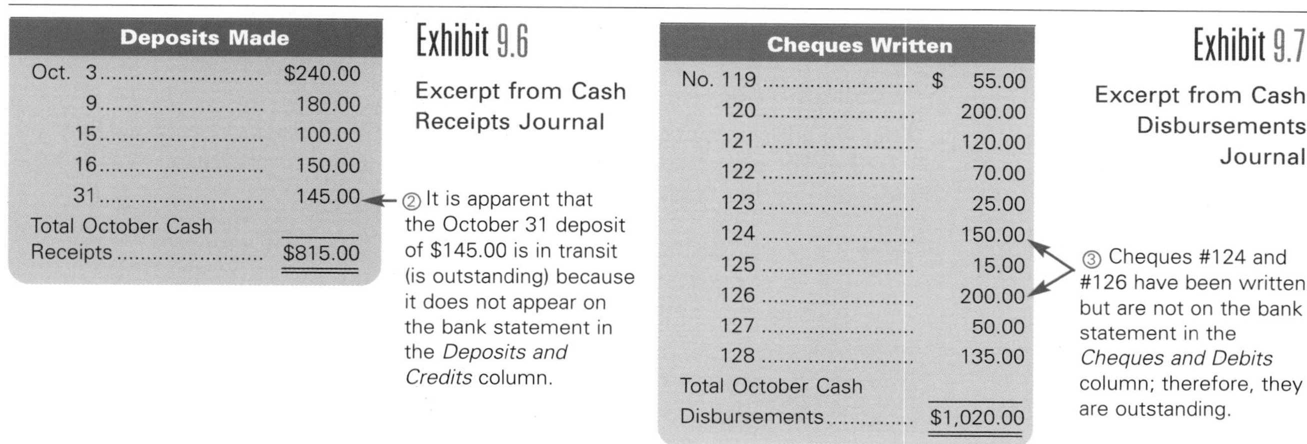

Exhibit 9.6

Excerpt from Cash Receipts Journal

Deposits Made	
Oct. 3	$240.00
9	180.00
15	100.00
16	150.00
31	145.00
Total October Cash Receipts	$815.00

② It is apparent that the October 31 deposit of $145.00 is in transit (is outstanding) because it does not appear on the bank statement in the *Deposits and Credits* column.

Exhibit 9.7

Excerpt from Cash Disbursements Journal

Cheques Written	
No. 119	$ 55.00
120	200.00
121	120.00
122	70.00
123	25.00
124	150.00
125	15.00
126	200.00
127	50.00
128	135.00
Total October Cash Disbursements	$1,020.00

③ Cheques #124 and #126 have been written but are not on the bank statement in the *Cheques and Debits* column; therefore, they are outstanding.

Exhibit 9.8

General Ledger Cash Account

Cash — Acct. No. 101

Date		Explanation	PR	Debit	Credit	Balance
2001						
Sept.	30	Balance				1,609.58
Oct.	31		CR6	815.00		2,424.58
	31		CD4		1,020.00	1,404.58 ⑤

Exhibit 9.9

Bank Reconciliation

VideoBuster Company
Bank Reconciliation
October 31, 2001

① Bank statement balance		$2,050.00	⑤ Book balance		$1,404.58
② Add:			⑥ Add:		
Deposit of Oct. 31 in transit		145.00	Collection of $500 note less $15 Collection fee	$485.00	
			Interest earned	8.42	493.42
		$2,195.00			$1,898.00
③ Deduct:			⑦ Deduct:		
Outstanding cheques:			Cheque printing charge	$ 23.00	
#124	$150.00		NSF cheque plus service		
#126	200.00	350.00	fee	30.00	53.00
④ Adjusted bank balance		$1,845.00	⑧ Adjusted book balance		$1,845.00

⑨ Balances are equal (reconciled)

When the reconciliation is complete, the employee sends a copy to the accounting department so that any needed journal entries are recorded. For instance, entries are needed to record any unrecorded debit and credit memoranda and any company mistakes. The entries resulting from VideoBuster's bank reconciliation are illustrated in the next section. Another copy goes to the cashier's office. This is especially important if the bank has made an error that needs correction.

Recording Adjusting Entries from the Bank Reconciliation

A bank reconciliation helps locate errors by either the bank or the depositor. It also identifies unrecorded items that need recording on the company's books. In VideoBuster's reconciliation, for instance, the adjusted balance of $1,845.00 is the correct balance as of October 31. But the company's accounting records show a $1,404.58 balance. We must prepare journal entries to adjust the book balance to the correct balance. It is important to remember that only the items reconciling the book balance side require adjustment. This means that the following four entries are required for VideoBuster:

1. Collection of Note

The first entry is to record the net proceeds of VideoBuster's note receivable collected by the bank, the expense of having the bank perform that service, and the reduction in the Notes Receivable account:

Oct. 31	Cash	485.00	
	Collection Expense	15.00	
	Notes Receivable		500.00
	To record collection fee and proceeds of a note collected by the bank.		

2. Interest Earned

The second entry records the interest credited to VideoBuster's account by the bank:

31	Cash	8.42	
	Interest Revenue		8.42
	To record interest earned on the average Cash balance in the chequing account.		

Interest earned is a revenue, and the entry recognizes both the revenue and the related increase in Cash.

3. NSF Cheque

The third entry records the NSF cheque that is returned as uncollectible. The $20 cheque was received from Heflin in payment of his account and deposited. When the cheque cleared the banking system, Heflin's bank account was found to have insufficient funds to cover the cheque. The bank charged $10 for handling the NSF cheque and deducted $30 total from VideoBuster's account. The company must reverse the entry made when the cheque was received and also record the $10 fee:

31	Accounts Receivable – Frank Heflin	30.00	
	Cash		30.00
	To charge Frank Heflin's account for his NSF cheque and the bank's fee.		

This entry reflects business practice by adding the NSF $10 fee to Heflin's account. The company will try to collect the entire $30 from Heflin.

4. Cheque Printing

The fourth entry debits Office Supplies Expense for the printing of cheques:

31	Office Supplies Expense	23.00	
	Cash		23.00
	Cheque printing charge.		

After these four entries are recorded, the balance of cash is increased to the correct amount of $1,845 (= $1,404.58 + $485 + $8.42 − $30 − $23).

Skyrocketing Bank Service Charges

On March 1, 2001, the Toronto-Dominion Bank adopted the Canada Trust account line-up, which doubled the monthly service charges paid by some customers. Some unhappy customers left the Toronto-Dominion and chose an alternative like President's Choice Financial, a partnership of the supermarket chain Loblaw Cos., and Canadian Imperial Bank of Commerce. There are always options. The financial services calculator offered by Industry Canada on its Consumer Connection Web site can help:
http://strategis.ic.gc.ca/SSG/ca00669e.html

SOURCE: http://archives.theglobeandmail.com

Answers—p. 472

8. What is a bank statement?
9. What is the meaning of the phrase to reconcile a bank balance?
10. Why do we reconcile the bank statement balance of cash and the depositor's book balance of cash?
11. List items affecting the bank side of a reconciliation and indicate if the items are added or subtracted.
12. List items affecting the book side of a reconciliation and indicate if the items are added or subtracted.

Summary

LO1 **Define, explain the purpose, and identify the principles of internal control.** An internal control system consists of the policies and procedures that managers use to protect assets, ensure reliable accounting, promote efficient operations, and encourage adherence to company policies. It is a key part of systems design, analysis and performance. It can prevent avoidable losses and help managers both plan operations and monitor company and human performance. Principles of good internal control include establishing responsibilities, maintaining adequate records, insuring assets and bonding employees, separating recordkeeping from custody of assets, dividing responsibilities for related transactions, applying technological controls, and performing regular independent reviews.

LO2 **Define cash and explain how it is reported.** Cash includes currency and coins, and amounts on deposit in bank, chequing and some savings accounts. It also includes items that are acceptable for deposit in these accounts. Cash equivalents or short-term investments are similar to cash, therefore most companies combine them with cash as a single item on the balance sheet. Cash and cash equivalents are liquid assets because they are converted easily into other assets or used in paying for services or liabilities.

LO3 **Apply internal control to cash.** Internal control of cash receipts ensures that all cash received is properly recorded and deposited. Cash receipts arise from many transactions including cash sales, collections of customers' accounts, receipts of interest and rent, bank loans, sale of assets, and owner investments. Attention is focused on two important types of cash receipts: over-the-counter and mail. The principles of internal control are applied in both cases. Good internal control for over-the-counter cash receipts includes use of a cash register, customer review, receipts, a permanent transaction record, and the separation of the custody of cash from its recordkeeping. Good internal control for cash receipts by mail includes at least two people being assigned to open the mail and prepare a list with each sender's name, amount of money received, and explanation.

LO4 **Explain and record petty cash fund transactions.** Petty cash disbursements are payments of small amounts for items such as postage, courier fees, repairs and supplies. To avoid writing cheques for small amounts, a company usually sets up one or more petty cash funds and uses the money to make small payments. A petty cash fund cashier is responsible for safekeeping of the cash, for making payments from this fund, and for keeping receipts and records. A Petty Cash account is debited when the fund is established or increased in size. The cashier presents all paid receipts to the company's cashier for reimbursement. Petty cash disbursements are recorded whenever the fund is replenished with debits to expense accounts reflecting receipts and a credit to cash. The petty cash fund is now restored to its full amount and is ready to cover more small expenditures.

LO5 **Identify control features of banking activities.** Banks offer several basic services that promote either or both the control or safeguarding of cash. These involve the bank account, the bank deposit, and chequing. A bank account is set up by a bank and permits a customer to deposit money for safeguarding and cheque withdrawals. A bank deposit is money contributed to the account with a deposit slip as proof. A cheque is a document signed by the depositor instructing the bank to pay a specified amount of money to a designated recipient. Electronic funds transfer (EFT) uses electronic communication to transfer cash from one party to another, and it decreases certain risks while exposing others. Companies increasingly use it because of its convenience and low cost.

LO6 **Prepare a bank reconciliation.** A bank reconciliation is prepared to prove the accuracy of the depositor's and the bank's records. In completing a reconciliation, the bank statement balance is adjusted for such items as outstanding cheques and unrecorded deposits made on or before the bank statement date but not reflected on the statement. The depositor's cash account balance also often requires adjustment. These adjustments include items such as service charges, bank collections for the depositor, and interest earned on the account balance.

GUIDANCE ANSWERS TO Judgement Call

Campaign Manager

A forced vacation policy is part of a system of good internal controls. When employees are forced to take vacations, their ability to hide any fraudulent behaviour decreases. This is because someone must take on the responsibilities of the person on vacation, and the replacement employee potentially can uncover fraudulent behaviour or records. A forced vacation policy is especially important for employees in more sensitive positions of handling money or other easily transferable assets.

Internal Auditor

Your problem is whether to accept the situation or to dig further to see if the petty cashier is abusing petty cash. Since you were asked to postpone your count and the fund consists of new $20 bills, you have legitimate concerns about whether money is being borrowed for personal use. You should conduct a further investigation. One result might show the most recent reimbursement of the fund was for $180 (=9 × $20) or more. In that case, this reimbursement can leave the fund with sequentially numbered $20 bills. But if the most recent reimbursement was for less than $180, the presence of nine sequentially numbered $20 bills suggests that the $180 of new $20 bills was obtained from a bank as replacement for bills that had been removed. Neither situation shows that the cashier is stealing money. Yet the second case indicates that the cashier "borrowed" the cash and later replaced it after the auditor showed up. In writing your report, you must not conclude that the cashier is unethical unless evidence along with your knowledge of company policies supports it. Your report must present facts according to the evidence.

GUIDANCE ANSWERS TO 

1. c
2. Technology reduces processing errors, allows more extensive testing of records, limits the amount of hard evidence of processing steps, and highlights the importance of maintaining separation of duties.
3. A company owns liquid assets so that it can purchase other assets, buy services, and pay obligations.
4. a
5. If all cash payments are made by cheque, numerous cheques for small amounts must be written. Because this practice is expensive and time consuming, a petty cash fund is established to make small cash payments.
6. If the petty cash fund is not reimbursed at the end of an accounting period, the transactions in petty cash are not yet recorded in the accounts and the petty cash asset is overstated. But these amounts are rarely large enough to affect users' decisions based on financial statements.
7. First, when the petty cash fund is reimbursed, the petty cash transactions are recorded in their proper accounts. Second, reimbursement also gives money that allows the fund to continue being used. Third, reimbursement identifies any cash shortage or overage in the fund.
8. A bank statement is a report prepared by the bank describing the activities in a depositor's account.
9. To reconcile a bank balance means to explain the difference between the cash balance in the depositor's accounting records and the balance on the bank statement.
10. The purpose of the bank reconciliation is to determine if any errors have been made by the bank or by the depositor and to determine if the bank has completed any transactions affecting the depositor's account that the depositor has not recorded. It is also an internal control mechanism to ensure that the company's cash system is operating properly.
11. Outstanding cheques—subtracted
Unrecorded deposits—added
12. Bank service charges—subtracted
Debit memos—subtracted
NSF cheques—subtracted
Interest earned—added
Credit memos—added

Demonstration Problem

Consider the following information and prepare a bank reconciliation, along with any resulting journal entries, for TJ Company for the month ended April 30, 2001.

The bank reconciliation prepared by TJ Company on March 31, 2001 follows:

TJ Company
Bank Reconciliation
March 31, 2001

Bank statement balance		$7,670	Book balance	$8,590
Add:				
Deposit of March 31 in transit		1,100		
		$8,770		
Deduct:				
Outstanding cheques:				
#797:	$ 60			
#804:	$120	180		
Adjusted bank balance		$8,590	Adjusted book balance	$8,590

The following bank statement is available for April:

Bank Statement					
To: TJ Company				April 30, 2001 Bank of Nova Scotia	
Cheques/Charges/Debits			Deposits/Credits		Balance
					7,670
#811	04/03	834	04/03	1,100	7,936
#807	04/07	375	04/07	810	8,371
#810	04/13	208	04/13	690	8,853
NSF	04/18	450	04/18	680	9,083
#808	04/23	850	04/23	355	8,588
#797	04/27	60	04/27	750	9,278
#814	04/30	550	04/30	620	9,348
#813	04/30	372	INT	47	9,023
#809	04/30	124			8,899
SC	04/30	32	04/30		**8,867**
NSF = Not Sufficient Funds		SC = Service Charge		INT = Interest	

A list of deposits made and cheques written during April, taken from the Cash Receipts Journal and Cash Disbursements Journal is shown below:

Deposits Made	
April 7	$ 810
13	690
18	680
23	355
27	750
30	620
30	770
Total April Cash Receipts	$4,675

Cheques Written	
No. 807	$ 375
808	850
809	124
810	208
811	348
812	207
813	372
814	550
815	405
816	602
Total April Cash Disbursements	$4,041

General Ledger Cash Account:

Cash					Acct. No. 101
Date	Explanation	PR	Debit	Credit	Balance
2001					
March 31	Balance				8,590.00
April 30		CR12	4,675.00		13,265.00
30		CD14		4,041.00	9,224.00

In reviewing cheques returned by the bank, the bookkeeper discovered that cheque #811, for delivery expense, was recorded in the Cash Disbursements Journal incorrectly as $348. The NSF cheque for $450 was that of customer A. Hussain, deposited in April.

Planning the Solution

- Set up a schedule like the following with a bank side and a book side for the reconciliation. Leave room on both sides to add several items and to deduct several items. Each column will result in a reconciled balance.

TJ Company
Bank Reconciliation
April 30, 2001

Bank statement balance		Book balance	
Add:		Add:	
Deduct:		Deduct	
Adjusted bank balance		Adjusted book balance	

- Follow the nine steps used in the chapter to prepare the bank reconciliation.
- For every reconciling item on the book side, prepare an appropriate adjusting entry. Any additions to the book side require an adjusting entry that debits cash. Conversely, any deduction on the book side will require an adjusting entry that credits cash.

SOLUTION TO Demonstration Problem

TJ Company
Bank Reconciliation
April 30, 2001

Bank statement balance		$8,867	Book balance		$9,224
Add:			Add:		
Deposit of April 30 in transit		770	Interest revenue		47
		$9,637			$9,271
Deduct:			Deduct:		
Outstanding cheques:			Error (Cheque #811 for delivery exp)	$486	
#804:	$120		NSF Cheque	450	
#812:	207		Service charge	32	968
#815:	405				
#816:	602	1,334			
Adjusted bank balance		$8,303	Adjusted book balance		$8,303

Required Adjusting Entries

April	30	Cash	47	
		Interest Revenue		47
		To record interest earned.		
	30	Delivery Expense	486	
		Cash		486
		To correct accounting error on cheque #811.		
	30	Accounts Receivable — A. Hussain	450	
		Cash		450
		To reinstate customer account due to NSF Cheque.		
	30	Bank Service Charges Expense	32	
		Cash		32
		To record bank service charges.		

APPENDIX

Voucher System of Control

9A

Apply the voucher system to control cash disbursements.

A voucher system is a set of procedures and approvals designed to control cash disbursements and acceptance of obligations. The voucher system of control establishes procedures for:

- Accepting obligations resulting in cash disbursements.
- Verifying, approving, and recording obligations.
- Issuing cheques for payment of verified, approved, and recorded obligations.
- Requiring obligations to be recorded when incurred.
- Treating each purchase as an independent transaction.

A good voucher system produces these results for every transaction. This applies even when many purchases are made from the same company during a period.

A voucher system's control over cash disbursements begins when a company incurs an obligation that will result in a payment of cash. A key factor in this system is that only approved departments and individuals are authorized to incur such obligations. The system also often limits the kinds of obligations that a department or individual can incur. In a large retail store, for instance, only a purchasing department should be authorized to incur obligations from merchandise purchases. Another key factor is that procedures for purchasing, receiving, and paying for merchandise are often divided among several departments. These departments include the one requesting the purchase, the purchasing department, the receiving department, and the accounting department. To coordinate and control the responsibilities of these departments, several different business papers are used. Exhibit 9A.1 shows how these papers are accumulated in a *voucher*. A **voucher** is an internal business paper (or "folder") that is used to accumulate other papers and information needed to control cash disbursements and to ensure that a transaction is properly recorded. We next discuss each document entering a voucher. This is to show how a company uses this system in controlling cash disbursements for merchandise purchases.

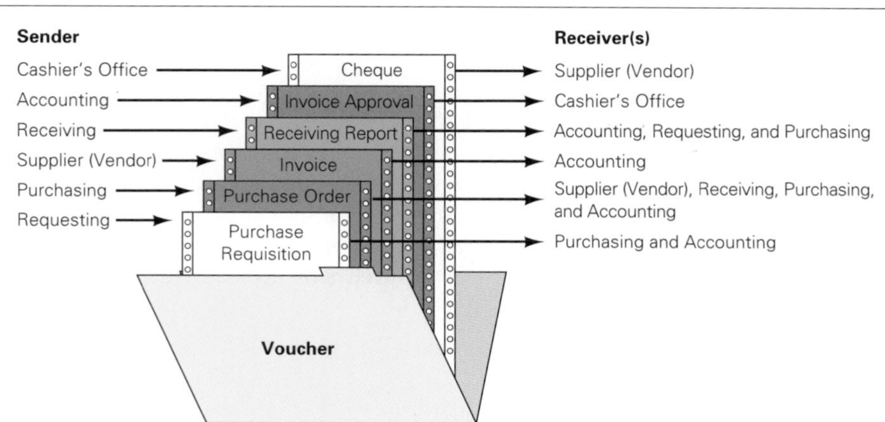

Exhibit 9A.1

Voucher and Business Documents

Purchase Requisition

Department managers in larger stores are usually not allowed to place orders directly with suppliers. If each manager dealt directly with suppliers, the merchandise purchased and the resulting liabilities would not be well controlled. To gain control over purchases and the resulting liabilities, department managers are often required to place all orders through a purchasing department. When merchandise is needed, a department manager must inform the purchasing department of its needs by preparing and signing a purchase requisition. A **purchase requisition** lists the merchandise needed by a department and requests that it be purchased—see Exhibit 9A.2. Two copies of the purchase requisition are sent to the purchasing department. The purchasing department sends one copy to the accounting department. When the accounting department receives a purchase requisition, it creates and maintains a voucher for this transaction. A third copy of the requisition is kept by the requesting department as back-up.

Exhibit 9A.2

Purchase Requisition

Purchase Requisition — No. 917

Z-Mart

From Sporting Goods Department — **Date** October 28, 2000

To Purchasing Department — **Preferred Vendor** Trex

Request purchase of the following item(s):

Model No.	Description	Quantity
CH 015	Challenger X7	1
SD 099	SpeedDemon	1

Reason for Request Replenish inventory

Approval for Request P.Z.

For Purchasing Department use only: Order Date Oct. 30/00 P.O. No. P98

Purchase Order

A **purchase order** is a business paper used by the purchasing department to place an order with a seller, also called a **vendor**. A vendor is usually a manufacturer or wholesaler. A purchase order authorizes a vendor to ship ordered merchandise at the stated price and terms—see Exhibit 9A.3. When the purchasing department receives a purchase requisition, it prepares at least four copies of a purchase order. The copies are distributed as follows: *Copy 1* is sent to the vendor as a purchase request and as authority to ship merchandise; *Copy 2* is sent, along with a copy of the purchase requisition, to the accounting department, where it is entered in the voucher and used in approving payment of the invoice; *Copy 3* is sent to the requesting department to inform its manager that action is being taken; *Copy 4* is sent to the receiving department; and *Copy 5* is retained on file by the purchasing department.

Exhibit 9A.3

Purchase Order

Purchase Order No. P98
Z-Mart
10 Prairie Street
Winnipeg, MB R3J 1G9

To: Trex
9797 Cherry Road
Windsor, ON N9G 2P5

Date Oct. 30/2000
FOB Destination
Ship by As soon as possible
Terms 2/15, n/30

Request shipment of the following item(s):

Model No.	Description	Quantity	Price	Amount
CH 015	Challenger X7	1	490	490
SD 099	SpeedDemon	1	710	710

All shipments and invoices must include purchase order number

Ordered by J.W.

Invoice

An **invoice** is an itemized statement of goods prepared by the vendor (seller) listing the customer's name, the items sold, the sales prices, and the terms of sale. An invoice is also a bill sent to the buyer by the seller. From the vendor's point of view, it is a *sales invoice*. The vendor sends the invoice to a buyer, or **vendee**, who treats it as a *purchase invoice*. When receiving a purchase order, the vendor ships the ordered merchandise to the buyer and includes or mails a copy of the invoice covering the shipment to the buyer. The invoice is sent to the buyer's accounting department, where it is placed in the voucher. Exhibit 6.6 on page 261 shows Z-Mart's purchase invoice.

Receiving Report

Many companies maintain a special department to receive all merchandise or other purchased assets. When each shipment arrives, this receiving department counts the goods and checks them for damage and agreement with the purchase order. It then prepares four or more copies of a receiving report. A **receiving report** is used within the company to notify the appropriate persons that ordered goods are received and to describe the quantities and condition of the goods. One copy is placed in the voucher. Copies are also sent to the requesting department and the purchasing department to notify them that goods arrived. The receiving department retains a copy in its files.

Invoice Approval

When a receiving report arrives, the accounting department should have copies of these papers on file in the voucher: purchase requisition, purchase order, invoice, and receiving report. With the information on these papers, the accounting department can record the purchase and approve its payment before the end of the discount period. In approving an invoice for payment, this department checks and compares information across all papers. To facilitate this checking and to ensure that no step is omitted, the department often uses an **invoice approval form**, also called *cheque authorization*. Exhibit 9A.4 shows an invoice approval form. An invoice approval is a checklist of steps necessary for approving an invoice for recording and payment. It is a separate business paper either filed in the voucher or preprinted on the voucher. It is sometimes stamped on the invoice. Exhibit 9A.4 shows the invoice approval as a separate document.

Exhibit 9A.4

Invoice Approval

Invoice Approval

	No.	By	Date
Purchase requisition	917	TZ	Oct. 28/00
Purchase order	P98	JW	Oct. 30/00
Receiving report	R85	SK	Nov. 3/00
Invoice:	1915		
Price		JK	Nov. 12/00
Calculations		JK	Nov. 12/00
Terms		JK	Nov. 12/00
Approved for payment		BC	Nov. 12/00

As each step in the checklist is approved, the clerk initials the invoice approval and records the current date. Approval implies that the following actions have been taken for each step:

1. *Requisition check* Items on invoice are requested, as shown on purchase requisition.
2. *Purchase order check* Items on invoice are ordered, as shown on purchase order.
3. *Receiving report check* Items on invoice are received, as shown on receiving report.
4. *Invoice check* *Price* Invoice prices are as agreed with the vendor (on purchase order).

   Calculations Invoice has no mathematical errors.

   Terms Terms are as agreed with the vendor (on purchase order).

The Voucher

Once an invoice is checked and approved, the voucher is complete. A complete voucher is a record summarizing a transaction. The voucher shows that a transaction is certified as correct and it authorizes recording an obligation for the buyer. A voucher also contains approval for paying the obligation on an appropriate date. The physical form of vouchers varies across companies. Many are designed so that the invoice and other related source documents are placed inside the voucher, which is often a folder.

Exhibit 9A.5

Inside of a Voucher

Z-Mart
Winnipeg, MB

Voucher No. 4657

Date Oct. 28, 2000
Pay to Trex
City Windsor Province Ontario

For the following: (attach all invoices and supporting papers)

Date of Invoice	Terms	Invoice Number and Other Details	Terms
Nov. 2, 2000	2/15, n/30	Invoice No. 1915	1,200
		Less discount	24
		Net amount payable	1,176

Payment approved
N.O. Neal
Auditor

Completion of a voucher usually requires a person to enter certain information required on the inside and outside of the voucher. Typical information required on the inside of a voucher is shown in Exhibit 9A.5, and that for the outside is shown in Exhibit 9A.6. The information is taken from the invoice and the supporting documents filed in the voucher. A complete voucher is sent to an authorized individual (often called an *auditor*). This person performs a final review, approves the accounts and amounts for debiting (called the *accounting distribution*), and authorizes recording of the voucher.

Exhibit 9A.6

Outside of a Voucher

Voucher No. 4657

Accounting Distribution

Account Debited	Amount
Merch. Inventory	1,200
Store Supplies	
Office Supplies	
Sales Salaries	
Other	
Total Vouch. Pay. Cr.	1,200

Due Date November 12, 2000
Pay to Trex
City Windsor
Province ON

Summary of charges:
Total charges 1,200
Discount 24
Net payment 1,176

Record of payment:
Paid
Cheque No.

When a voucher is approved and recorded, it is filed until its due date, when it is sent to the cashier's office for payment. The person issuing cheques relies on the approved voucher and its signed supporting documents as proof that an obligation is incurred and must be paid. The purchase requisition and purchase order confirm that the purchase is authorized. The receiving report shows that items are received, and the invoice approval form verifies that the invoice is checked for errors. There is little chance for error. There is even less chance for fraud without collusion, unless all of the documents and signatures are forged.

Expenses in a Voucher System

Obligations should be approved for payment and recorded as liabilities as soon as possible after they are incurred. This practice should be applied to all purchases. It should also be applied to all expenses. When a company receives a monthly telephone bill, for instance, the charges (especially long-distance and costly calls) should be checked for accuracy. A voucher is prepared and the telephone bill is filed inside the voucher. This voucher is then recorded with a journal entry. If the amount is due at once, a cheque is issued. If not, the voucher is filed for payment on its due date.

Requiring vouchers to be prepared for expenses when they are incurred helps ensure that every expense payment is valid. Yet invoices or bills for such items as repairs are often not received until weeks after work is done. If no records of repairs exist, it can be difficult to determine whether the invoice amount is correct. Also, if no records exist, it is possible for a dishonest employee to collude with a dishonest seller to get more than one payment for an obligation, or for payment of excessive amounts, or for payment for goods and services not received. An effective voucher system helps prevent each of these frauds.

Answer—p. 482

13. Do all companies require a voucher system? At what point in a company's growth do you recommend a voucher system?

Using the Information

APPENDIX 9B

Acid-Test Ratio

Compute the acid-test ratio and explain its use as an indicator of a company's liquidity.

We learned in Chapter 6 that merchandise inventory often makes up a large portion of current assets for merchandising companies. We know that merchandise inventory must be sold and any resulting accounts receivable need to be collected before cash is available. This often means that a large part of current assets is not readily available for paying liabilities because it is in the form of merchandise inventory.

We explained in Chapter 5 how the current ratio P. 220 is useful in assessing a company's ability to pay current liabilities. Because merchandise inventories are not readily available as a source of payment for current liabilities, we look to a measure other than the current ratio to obtain a more strict measure of a company's ability to cover current liabilities: the *acid-test ratio.*

The *acid-test ratio* differs from the current ratio by excluding current assets that are *less liquid,* such as inventory. The **acid-test ratio**, also called the ***quick ratio***, is defined as shown in Exhibit 9B.1.

Exhibit 9B.1

Acid-Test Ratio

$$\text{Acid-test ratio} = \frac{\text{Quick assets*}}{\text{Current liabilities}}$$

****Quick assets are cash, short-term investments, and receivables***

Exhibit 9B.2 shows both the acid-test and current ratios of Air Canada and WestJet.

Exhibit 9B.2

Current and Acid-Test Ratios Compared

	December 31, 1999	
	Current Ratio	Acid-Test Ratio
Air Canada	0.90	0.69
WestJet	1.21	1.12

The acid-test ratio is interpreted in a similar manner as the current ratio. WestJet's current ratio shows $1.21 of current assets available to cover each $1.00 of current liability as it comes due. As a more strict measure, the acid-test tells us WestJet had $1.12 of quick assets to cover each $1.00 of current obligations at December 31, 1999. An acid-test ratio equal to or greater than 1 is considered favourable (good). Both Air Canada's current and acid-test ratios are less than 1 at December 31, 1999, which indicates that it may have difficulty in covering obligations as they come due. It would be interesting to explore why these two companies, both in a similar industry, have such different current and acid-test ratios.

Summary of Appendix 9A and 9B

LO7 **Apply the voucher system to control cash disbursements.** A voucher system is a set of procedures and approvals designed to control cash disbursements and acceptance of obligations. The voucher system of control relies on several important documents including the voucher and many supporting files. A voucher system's control over cash disbursements begins when a company incurs an obligation that will result in payment of cash. A key factor in this system is that only approved departments and individuals are authorized to incur certain obligations. To coordinate and control responsibilities of these departments, several different business documents are used.

LO8 **Compute the acid-test ratio and explain its use as an indicator of a company's liquidity.** The acid-test ratio is computed as quick assets (cash, short-term investments, and receivables) divided by current liabilities. It is an indicator of a company's ability to pay its current liabilities with its existing quick assets. A ratio equal to or greater than 1 is often considered adequate.

GUIDANCE ANSWER TO 

13. Not necessarily. A voucher system is used when a manager can no longer control the purchasing procedures through personal supervision and direct participation in business activities.

Glossary

Acid-test ratio A ratio used to assess a company's ability to cover its current debts with existing assets calculated as quick assets (cash, short-term investments, and receivables) divided by current liabilities; also called *quick ratio.* (p. 481)

Bank reconciliation An analysis that explains the difference between the balance of a chequing account shown in the depositor's records and the balance reported on the bank statement. (p. 464)

Bond An insurance policy purchased by a company to protect against losses from theft by that employee. (p. 451).

Cancelled cheques Cheques that the bank has paid and deducted from the customer's account during the month. (p. 463)

Cash Includes currency, coins, and amounts on deposit in bank chequing or savings accounts. (p. 454)

Cash Over and Short account An income statement account used to record cash shortages and cash overages arising from omitted petty cash receipts and from errors in making change. (p. 455)

Cheque A document signed by the depositor instructing the bank to pay a specified amount of money to a designated recipient. (p. 461)

Collusion An act where two or more people agree to commit a fraud. (p. 451)

Deposit slip Lists the items such as currency, coins, and cheques deposited along with each of their dollar amounts. (p. 460)

Electronic funds transfer The use of electronic communication to transfer cash from one party to another. (p. 462)

Internal control system All the policies and procedures managers use to protect assets, ensure reliable accounting, promote efficient operations, and urge adherence to company policies. (p. 450)

Invoice An itemized statement of goods prepared by the vendor that lists the customer's name, the items sold, the sales prices, and the terms of sale. (p. 477)

Invoice approval form A document containing a checklist of steps necessary for approving an invoice for recording and payment; also called *cheque authorization form.* (p. 477)

Liquid asset An asset such as cash that is easily converted into other types of assets or used to buy services or to pay liabilities. (p. 454)

Liquidity A characteristic of an asset that refers to how easily the asset can be converted into cash or another type of asset or used in paying for services or obligations. (p. 454)

Petty cashier Employee responsible for safekeeping of the cash, making payments from this fund, and keeping accurate records. (p. 457)

Principles of internal control Fundamental principles of internal control that apply to all companies requiring management to establish responsibility, maintain adequate records, insure assets and bond key employees, separate recordkeeping from custody of assets, divide responsibility for related transactions, apply technological controls, and perform regular and independent reviews. (p. 451)

Purchase order A business paper used by the purchasing department to place an order with the seller (vendor); authorizes the vendor to ship the ordered merchandise at the stated price and terms. (p. 476)

Purchase requisition A business paper listing the merchandise needed by a department and requests that it be purchased. (p. 476)

Quick ratio See *acid-test ratio.* (p. 481)

Quick assets Those current assets that are most liquid, specifically cash, short-term investments, and receivables. (p. 481)

Receiving report A form used within a company to notify the appropriate persons that ordered goods are received and to describe the quantities and condition of the goods. (p. 477)

Separation of duties An internal control principle requiring the division of responsibility for related transactions between two or more individuals or departments. (p. 451)

Signature card Includes the signatures of each person authorized to sign cheques from the account. (p. 460)

Vendee The buyer or purchaser of goods or services. (p. 477)

Vendor The seller of goods or services, usually a manufacturer or wholesaler. (p. 476)

Voucher An internal business paper (or "folder") used to accumulate other papers and information needed to control cash disbursements and to ensure that the transaction is properly recorded. (p. 475)

Voucher system A set of procedures and approvals designed to control cash disbursements and acceptance of obligations. (p. 456)

Questions

1. Which of the following assets is most liquid and which is least liquid: merchandise inventory, building, accounts receivable, cash?
2. List the seven broad principles of internal control.
3. Why should the person who keeps the record of an asset not be the person responsible for custody of the asset?
4. Internal control procedures are important in every business, but at what stage in the development of a business do they become critical?
5. Why should responsibility for a sequence of related transactions be divided among different departments or individuals?
6. Why should all receipts be deposited intact on the day of receipt?
7. When merchandise is purchased for a large store, why are department managers not permitted to deal directly with suppliers?
8. What is a petty cash receipt? Who signs a petty cash receipt?
9. Refer to ClubLink's balance sheet in Appendix I. What is its cash balance as at December 31, 1999?

CLUBLINK CORPORATION

10. WestJet Airlines showed cash and short-term investments on December 31, 1999 of $50,740,000. What percentage is this of total assets?

Interi

Quick Study

QS 9-1
Internal control objectives

LO1

1. What is the main objective of internal control and how is it accomplished?
2. Why should recordkeeping for assets be separated from custody over the assets?

QS 9-2
Internal controls for cash

LO3

In a good system of internal control for cash that provides adequate procedures for protecting both cash receipts and cash disbursements, three basic guidelines should always be observed. What are these guidelines?

QS 9-3
Petty cash accounting

LO4

1. The petty cash fund of the Wee Ones Agency was established at $75. At the end of the month, the fund contained $12.74 and had the following receipts: film rentals, $19.40; refreshments for meetings, $22.81 (both expenditures to be classified as Entertainment Expense); postage, $6.95; and printing, $13.10. Prepare the journal entries to record (a) the establishment of the fund and (b) the reimbursement at the end of the month.
2. Explain when the Petty Cash account would be credited in a journal entry.

QS 9-4
Bank reconciliations

LO6

1. Identify whether each of the following items affects the bank or book side of the reconciliation and indicate if the amount represents an addition or a subtraction:
   a. Deposits in transit.
   b. Interest on average monthly balance.
   c. Credit memos.
   d. Bank service charges.
   e. Outstanding cheques.
   f. Debit memos.
   g. NSF cheques.
2. Which of the previous items require a journal entry?

***QS 9-5**
Acid-test ratio

LO8

Your company has a policy of granting credit only to customers whose acid-test ratio is greater than or equal to 1. Based on this policy, determine if the following companies should be granted credit. Why or why not?

	Company A	Company B
Cash	$1,200	$1,200
Accounts receivable	2,700	2,700
Inventory	5,000	5,000
Prepaid expenses	600	600
Accounts payable	3,100	4,750
Other current liabilities	250	950

Exercises

Exercise 9-1 ✓
Analyzing internal control

LO1

Lombard Company is a young business that has grown rapidly. The company's bookkeeper, who was hired two years ago, left town suddenly after the company's manager discovered that a great deal of money had disappeared over the past 18 months. An audit disclosed that the bookkeeper had written and signed several cheques made payable to the bookkeeper's brother and then recorded the cheques as salaries expense. The brother, who cashed the cheques but had never worked for the company, left town with the bookkeeper. As a result, the company incurred an uninsured loss of $84,000.

Evaluate Lombard Company's internal control system and indicate which principles of internal control appear to have been ignored in this situation.

An asterisk (*) identifies assignment material based on Appendix 9A or Appendix 9B.

Exercise 9-2
Recommending internal control procedures

LO1

What internal control procedures would you recommend in each of the following situations?

a. A concession company has one employee who sells T-shirts and sunglasses at the beach. Each day, the employee is given enough shirts and sunglasses to last through the day and enough cash to make change. The money is kept in a box at the stand.

b. An antique store has one employee who is given cash and sent to garage sales each weekend. The employee pays cash for merchandise to be resold at the antique store.

Exercise 9-3
Internal control over cash receipts

LO3

Some of Fannin Co.'s cash receipts from customers are sent to the company in the mail. Fannin's bookkeeper opens the letters and deposits the cash received each day. What internal control problem is inherent in this arrangement? What changes would you recommend?

Exercise 9-4
Petty cash fund

LO4

Eanes Co. established a $200 petty cash fund on January 1. One week later, on January 8, the fund contained $27.50 in cash and receipts for these expenditures: postage, $64.00; transportation-in, $19.00; store supplies, $36.50; and a withdrawal of $53.00 by Jim Eanes, the owner. Eanes uses the perpetual method to account for merchandise inventory.

Prepare the journal entries to (a) establish the fund on January 1 and (b) reimburse it on January 8. Now assume that the fund was not only reimbursed on January 8 but also increased to $500 because it was exhausted so quickly. (c) Give the entry to reimburse the fund and increase it to $500.

Exercise 9-5
Petty cash fund

LO4

Brady Company established a $400 petty cash fund on September 9. On September 30, the fund had $164.25 in cash and receipts for these expenditures: transportation-in, $32.45; office supplies, $113.55; and repairs expense, $87.60. Brady uses the perpetual method to account for merchandise inventory. The petty cashier could not account for the $2.15 shortage in the fund. Prepare (a) the September 9 entry to establish the fund and (b) the September 30 entry to reimburse the fund and reduce it to $300.

Exercise 9-6
Preparation of bank reconciliation

LO6

The bank reconciliation prepared by JenStar Holdings on June 30, 2001 appeared as follows:

JenStar Holdings
Bank Reconciliation
June 30, 2001

Bank statement balance	$4,000	Book balance	$3,740
Add:			
Deposit of June 30 in transit	340		
	$4,340		
Deduct:			
Outstanding cheque #14	600		
Adjusted bank balance	$3,740	Adjusted book balance	$3,740

The following bank statement is available for July:

Bank Statement

To: JenStar Holdings — July 31, 2001, Bank of Montreal

Cheques/Charges			Deposits/Credits		Balance
					4,000
NSF	07/02	120	07/02	340	4,220
#53	07/08	660	07/08	385	3,945
#96	07/11	280	07/11	664	4,329
			07/24	1,515	5,844
#52	07/31	920	07/31		4,924
NSF = Not Sufficient Funds		SC = Service Charge	PMT = Principal Payment		INT = Interest

The Cash account in the General Ledger appeared as follows on July 31:

Cash — Acct. No. 101

Date		Explanation	PR	Debit	Credit	Balance
2001						
June	30	Balance				3,740.00
July	31		CR3	2,850.00		6,590.00
	31		CD6		1,720.00	4,870.00

A list of deposits made and cheques written during July, taken from the Cash Receipts Journal and Cash Disbursements Journal is shown below:

Deposits Made

July	8	$ 385
	11	664
	24	1,515
	31	286
Total July Cash Receipts		$2,850

Cheques Written

No. 52	$ 920
53	660
54	140
Total July Cash Disbursements	$1,720

In reviewing cheques returned by the bank, the bookkeeper noted that cheque #96 written by JenCo Holdings in the amount of $280 was charged against our account in error by the bank. The NSF cheque was regarding a customer account, Jim Anderson.

Check figure:
1. Adjusted book balance = $4,750

Required

1. Prepare a bank reconciliation at July 31.
2. Prepare the necessary journal entries to bring the General Ledger Cash account into agreement with the adjusted balance on the bank reconciliation.

Exercise 9-7

Bank reconciliation

LO6

Check figure:
Adjusted book balance = $11,343

Medline Service Co. deposits all receipts intact on the day received and makes all payments by cheque. On July 31, 2001, after all posting was completed, its Cash account showed an $11,352 debit balance. However, Medline's July 31 bank statement showed only $10,332 on deposit in the bank on that day. Prepare a bank reconciliation for Medline, using the following information:

a. Outstanding cheques, $1,713.

b. Included with the July cancelled cheques returned by the bank was an $18 debit memorandum for bank services.

c. Cheque #919, returned with the cancelled cheques, was correctly drawn for $489 in payment of the utility bill and was paid by the bank on July 15. However, it had been recorded with a debit to Utilities Expense and a credit to Cash as though it were for $498.

d. The July 31 cash receipts, $2,724, were placed in the bank's night depository after banking hours on that date and were unrecorded by the bank at the time the July bank statement was prepared.

Exercise 9-8
Adjusting entries resulting from bank reconciliation
LO6

Give the journal entries that Medline Service Co. should make as a result of having prepared the bank reconciliation in the previous exercise.

Exercise 9-9
Bank reconciling items and required entries
LO6

Set up a table with the following headings for a bank reconciliation as of September 30:

Bank Balance		Book Balance			Not Shown on the Reconcil-iation
Add	Deduct	Add	Deduct	Must Adjust	

For each item that follows, place an X in the appropriate columns to indicate whether the item should be added to or deducted from the book or bank balance, or whether it should not appear on the reconciliation. If the book balance is to be adjusted, place a Dr. or Cr. in the Must Adjust column to indicate whether the Cash balance should be debited or credited.

1. Interest earned on the account.
2. Deposit made on September 30 after the bank was closed.
3. Cheques outstanding on August 31 that cleared the bank in September.
4. NSF cheque from customer returned on September 15 but not recorded by the company.
5. Cheques written and mailed to payees on September 30.
6. Deposit made on September 5 that was processed on September 8.
7. Bank service charge.
8. Cheques written and mailed to payees on October 5.
9. Cheques written by another depositor but charged against the company's account.
10. Principal and interest collected by the bank but not recorded by the company.
11. Special charge for collection of note in No. 10 on company's behalf.
12. Cheque written against the account and cleared by the bank; erroneously omitted by the bookkeeper.

***Exercise 9-10**
Acid-test ratio
LO8

Compute the acid-test ratio in each of the following cases:

	Case X	Case Y	Case Z
Cash	$ 800	$ 910	$1,100
Short-term investments			500
Receivables		990	800
Inventory	2,000	1,000	4,000
Prepaid expenses	1,200	600	900
Total current assets	$4,000	$3,500	$7,300
Current liabilities	$2,200	$1,100	$3,650

Which case is in the best position to meet short-term obligations most easily? Explain your choice.

An asterisk (*) identifies assignment material based on Appendix 9A or Appendix 9B.

Problems

Problem 9-1A
Principles of internal control

LO[1]

For the following five scenarios, identify the principle of internal control that is violated. Next, make a recommendation as to what the business should do to ensure adherence to principles of internal control.

1. At Stratford Iron Company, Jill and Joan alternate lunch hours. Normally Jill is the petty cash custodian, but if someone needs petty cash when Jill is at lunch, Joan fills in as custodian.
2. Nadine McDonald does all the posting of patient charges and payments at the Northampton Medical Clinic. Every night, Nadine backs up the computerized accounting system to a tape and stores the tape in a locked file at her desk.
3. Jack Mawben prides himself on hiring quality workers who require little supervision. As office manager, Jack gives his employees full discretion over their tasks and has seen no reason to perform independent reviews of their work for years.
4. Bill Clark's manager has told him to "reduce overhead" no matter what! Bill decides to raise the deductible on the plant's property insurance from $5,000 to $10,000. This cuts the property insurance premium in half. In a related move, he decides that bonding of the plant's employees is really a waste of money since the company has not experienced any losses due to employee theft. Bill saves the entire amount of the bonding insurance premium by dropping the bonding insurance.
5. Catherine Young records all incoming customer cash receipts for her employer and also posts the customer payments to their accounts.

Problem 9-2A
Establishing, reimbursing, and increasing the petty cash fund

LO[4]

Palladium Art Gallery completed the following petty cash transactions during February 2001:

Feb. 2	Drew a $300 cheque, cashed it, and gave the proceeds and the petty cash box to Nick Reed, the petty cashier.
5	Purchased paper for the copier, $10.13.
9	Paid $22.50 COD charges on merchandise purchased for resale. Assume Palladium uses the perpetual method to account for merchandise inventory.
12	Paid $9.95 postage to express mail a contract to a client.
14	Reimbursed Gina Barton, the manager of the business, $58.00 for business auto expenses.
20	Purchased stationery, $77.76.
23	Paid a courier $18.00 to deliver merchandise sold to a customer.
25	Paid $15.10 COD charges on merchandise purchased for resale.
28	Paid $64.00 for stamps.
28	Reed sorted the petty cash receipts by accounts affected and exchanged them for a cheque to reimburse the fund for expenditures. However, there was only $21.23 in cash in the fund. In addition, the size of the petty cash fund was increased to $400.

Required

1. Prepare a journal entry to record establishing the petty cash fund.
2. Prepare a summary of petty cash payments, similar to Exhibit 9.2, that has these categories: delivery expense, mileage expense, postage expense, transportation-in (merchandise inventory), and office supplies. Sort the payments into the appropriate categories and total the expenditures in each category.
3. Prepare the journal entry to record the reimbursement and the increase of the fund.

Problem 9-5A

Preparation of bank reconciliation

LO6

The bank reconciliation prepared by Primetech Electronics on March 31, 2001 appeared as follows:

Primetech Electronics Bank Reconciliation March 31, 2001				
Bank statement balance		$17,050	Book balance	$15,750
Add:				
Deposit of March 31 in transit		2,500		
		$19,550		
Deduct:				
Outstanding cheques:				
#79	$2,600			
#84:	1,200	3,800		
Adjusted bank balance		$15,750	Adjusted book balance	$15,750

The following bank statement is available for April:

Bank Statement To: Primetech Electronics					April 30, 2001 Bank of Montreal
Cheques/Charges			Deposits/Credits		Balance
					17,050
#93	04/02	849	04/03	2,500	18,701
#92	04/07	560	04/07	4,000	22,141
#84	04/13	1,200	04/13	560	21,501
NSF	04/18	412	04/18	3,200	24,289
#95	04/23	85	04/23	200	24,404
#99	04/27	129	04/27	1,800	26,075
#98	04/30	320	04/30	1,900	27,655
#97	04/30	240	04/30	INT 47	27,462
#94	04/30	1,550			25,912
PMT	04/30	2,100			23,812
INT	04/30	320			23,492
SC	04/30	40			23,452

NSF = Not Sufficient Funds | SC = Service Charge | PMT = Principal Payment | INT = Interest

The Cash account in the General Ledger appeared as follows on April 30:

Cash					Acct. No. 101
Date	Explanation	PR	Debit	Credit	Balance
2001					
March 31	Balance				15,750.00
April 30		CR11	11,660.00		27,410.00
30		CD14		5,952.00	21,458.00

A list of deposits made and cheques written during April, taken from the Cash Receipts Journal and Cash Disbursements Journal, is shown below:

Deposits Made	
April 7	$ 4,000
13	560
18	3,200
23	200
27	1,800
30	1,900
Total April Cash Receipts	$11,660

Cheques Written	
No. 91	$ 400
92	560
93	948
94	1,550
95	85
96	320
97	240
98	320
99	129
100	1,400
Total April Cash Disbursements	$5,952

In reviewing cheques returned by the bank, the bookkeeper discovered that cheque #93, for delivery expense, was recorded in the Cash Disbursements Journal incorrectly as $948. The NSF cheque for $412 was that of customer Jon Smith, deposited in April.

Check figure:
a. Adjusted book balance = $18,732

Required

a. Prepare a bank reconciliation at April 30.
b. Prepare the necessary journal entries to bring the General Ledger Cash account into agreement with the adjusted balance on the bank reconciliation.

Problem 9-6A

Preparation of bank reconciliation and recording adjustments

LO9

The following information was available to reconcile Archdale Company's book balance of Cash with its bank statement balance as of October 31, 2001:

a. After all posting was completed on October 31, the company's Cash account had a $26,193 debit balance, but its bank statement showed a $28,020 balance.
b. Cheques #3031 for $1,380 and #3040 for $552 were outstanding on the September 30 bank reconciliation. Cheque #3040 was returned with the October cancelled cheques, but cheque #3031 was not. It was also found that cheque #3065 for $336 and cheque #3069 for $2,148, both drawn in October, were not among the cancelled cheques returned with the statement.
c. In comparing the cancelled cheques returned by the bank with the entries in the accounting records, it was found that cheque #3056 for the October rent was correctly drawn for $1,250 but was erroneously entered in the accounting records as $1,230.
d. A credit memorandum enclosed with the bank statement indicated that the bank had collected a $9,000 non-interest-bearing note for Archdale, deducted a $45 collection fee, and credited the remainder to the account. This event was not recorded by Archdale before receiving the statement.
e. A debit memorandum for $805 listed a $795 NSF cheque plus a $10 NSF charge. The cheque had been received from a customer, Jefferson Tyler. Archdale had not recorded this bounced cheque before receiving the statement.
f. Also enclosed with the statement was a $15 debit memorandum for bank services. It had not been recorded because no previous notification had been received.
g. The October 31 cash receipts, $10,152, were placed in the bank's night depository after banking hours on that date and this amount did not appear on the bank statement.

Check figure:
1. Adjusted book balance = $34,308

Required

Preparation component:

1. Prepare a bank reconciliation for the company as of October 31, 2001.
2. Prepare the General Journal entries necessary to bring the company's book balance of cash into conformity with the reconciled balance.

Analysis component:

3. Assume that an October 31, 2001, bank reconciliation for the company has already been prepared and some of the items were treated incorrectly in preparing the reconciliation. For each of the following errors, explain the effect of the error on: (1) the final balance that was calculated by adjusting the bank statement balance, and (2) the final balance that was calculated by adjusting the Cash account balance.
   a. The company's Cash account balance of $26,193 was listed on the reconciliation as $26,139.
   b. The bank's collection of a $9,000 note less the $45 collection fee was added to the bank statement balance.

Problem 9-7A
Preparation of bank reconciliation and recording adjustments

LO[6]

Walburg Company reconciled its bank and book statement balances of Cash on August 31 and showed two cheques outstanding at that time, #5888 for $1,038.05 and #5893 for $484.25. The following information was available for the September 30, 2001, reconciliation:

From the September 30 bank statement

BALANCE OF PREVIOUS STATEMENT ON AUG. 31/01......	16,800.75
6 DEPOSITS AND OTHER CREDITS TOTALLING............	11,182.85
9 CHEQUES AND OTHER DEBITS TOTALLING................	9,620.05
CURRENT BALANCE AS OF SEPT. 30/01.........................	18,363.55

Chequing Account Transactions

Date	Amount	Transaction Description	Date	Amount	Transaction Description
Sept. 05	1,103.75	+Deposit	Sept. 25	2,351.70	+Deposit
12	2,226.90	+Deposit	30	22.50	+Interest
17	588.25	−NSF cheque	30	1,385.00	+Credit memo
21	4,093.00	+Deposit			

Date	Cheque No.	Amount	Date	Cheque No.	Amount
Sept. 03	5904	2,080.00	Sept. 22	5888	1,038.05
07	5901	1,824.25	24	5909	1,807.65
08	5905	937.00	28	5907	213.85
10	5903	399.10	29	5902	731.90

From Walburg Company's accounting records:

Deposits Made

Sept.	5	$ 1,103.75
	12	2,226,90
	21	4,093.00
	25	2,351.70
	30	1,582.75
Total Sept. Cash Receipts...		$11,358.10

Cheques Written

No. 5901	$1,824.25
5902	731.90
5903	399.10
5904	2,050.00
5905	937.00
5906	859.30
5907	213.85
5908	276.00
5909	1,807.65
Total Sept. Cash Disbursements.......................	$9,099.05

Cash — Acct. No. 101

Date		Explanation	PR	Debit	Credit	Balance
2001						
Aug.	31	Balance				15,278.45
Sept.	30		CR12	11,358.10		26,636.55
	30		CD23		9,099.05	17,537.50

Cheque #5904 was correctly drawn for $2,080 to pay for computer equipment; however, the bookkeeper misread the amount and entered it in the accounting records with a debit to Computer Equipment and a credit to Cash as though it were for $2,050.

The NSF cheque was originally received from a customer, Delia Hahn, in payment of her account. Its return was not recorded when the bank first notified the company. The credit memorandum resulted from the collection of a $1,400 note for Walburg Company by the bank. The bank had deducted a $15 collection fee. The collection has not been recorded.

Check figure:
1. Adjusted book balance, $18,326.75

Required

Preparation component:

1. Prepare a September 30 bank reconciliation for the company.
2. Prepare the general journal entries needed to adjust the book balance of cash to the reconciled balance.

Analysis component:

3. The preceding bank statement discloses three places where the cancelled cheques returned with the bank statement are not numbered sequentially. In other words, some of the prenumbered cheques in the sequence are missing. Several possible situations would explain why the cancelled cheques returned with a bank statement might not be numbered sequentially. Describe three possible explanations.

Problem 9-8A

Preparation of a bank reconciliation

LO[6]

Celtic Minerals, owned by Scott O'Donnell, showed the following bank reconciliation at March 31:

Celtic Minerals
Bank Reconciliation
March 31, 2001

Bank statement balance		$ 600	Book balance	$800
Add:				
Deposit of March 31 in transit		5,000		
		$5,600		
Deduct::				
Outstanding cheques:				
#14	$1,600			
#22	3,200	4,800		
Adjusted bank balance		$ 800	Adjusted book balance	$800

The following bank statement is available for April:

Bank Statement

To: Celtic Minerals — **April 30, 2001** **Bank of Canada**

Cheques/Charges			Deposits/Credits		Balance
					600
#31	04/03	820	04/03	5,000	4,780
#28	04/07	8,200	04/07	6,000	2,580
#26	04/13	230	04/13	1,400	3,750
NSF	04/18	4,000	04/18	2,000	1,750
#24	04/23	750	04/23	7,500	8,500
#23	04/27	1,800	04/27	1,450	8,150
#29	04/30	1,200	04/30	30,000	36,950
PMT	04/30	10,000			26,950
INT	04/30	500			26,450
SC	04/30	120			26,330
NSF = Not Sufficient Funds		SC = Service Charge	PMT = Payment of Principal on the Loan		INT = Interest on Bank Loan

A list of deposits made and cheques written during April, taken from the Cash Receipts Journal and Cash Disbursements Journal, is shown below:

Deposits Made	
April 7	$ 6,000
13	1,400
18	2,000
23	7,500
27	1,450
30	13,000
Total April Cash Receipts	$31,350

Cheques Written	
No. 23	$1,800
24	750
25	1,000
26	230
27	650
28	2,800
29	1,200
30	100
31	820
32	340
Total April Cash Disbursements	$9,690

Cash					Acct. No. 101
Date	Explanation	PR	Debit	Credit	Balance
2001					
Mar. 31	Balance				800.00
Apr. 30		CR17	31,350.00		32,150.00
30		CD13		9,690.00	22,460.00

In reviewing cheques returned by the bank, the bookkeeper discovered that cheque #28, for delivery expense, was recorded in the Cash Disbursements Journal correctly as $2,800. The NSF cheque for $4,000 was that of customer Don James, deposited in March.

On the bank statement, there is a deposit of $30,000 dated April 30. It is an investment made by the owner into the business (the bank transferred the funds electronically from the owner's personal account to his business account, which is why it was not recorded in the Cash Receipts Journal).

Required

a. Prepare a bank reconciliation for Celtic Minerals at April 30.
b. Prepare the necessary journal entries to bring the General Ledger Cash account into agreement with the adjusted balance on the bank reconciliation.

Check figure:
a. Adjusted book balance = $37,840

Problem 9-9A
Preparation of a bank reconciliation

LO6

Presented below is information related to Aswan Company. The balance according to the books at October 31, 2001 was $41,847.85; cash receipts recorded during November were $173,523.91; and cash disbursements recorded for November were $166,193.54. The balance according to the bank statement on November 30, 2001 was $56,274.20.

The following cheques were outstanding at November 30:

Cheque	Amount
#1224	1,635.29
#1230	2,468.30
#1232	3,625.15
#1233	482.17

Included with the November bank statement and not recorded by the company were a bank debit memo for $27.40 covering bank charges for the month, a debit memo for $372.13 for a customer's cheque (Trevor Clerk) returned and marked NSF, and a credit memo for $1,200 representing interest collected by the bank for Aswan Company. Cash on hand at November 30, which has been recorded and is awaiting deposit, amounted to $1,915.40.

Required

a. Prepare a bank reconciliation at November 30, 2001.
b. Prepare any journal entries required to adjust the Cash account at November 30.

Check figure:
a. Adjusted book balance = $49,978.69

Problem 9-10A

Preparation of a bank reconciliation

LO[6]

The following is information for Dundee Realty:

a. Balance per the bank statement dated October 31, 2001 is $48,260.
b. Balance of the Cash account on the company books as of October 31, 2001 is $38,535.
c. $5,500 of customer deposits were outstanding as of September 30; this amount had been deposited to Dundee's account in October.
d. Cheques written in October that had not cleared the bank as of October 31 were:
   #2033, $3,200
   #2099, $ 850
   #2300, $1,800
   #2345, $5,400.
e. The bank charged Dundee's account for a $1,700 cheque of the E-Zone Networks; the cheque was found among the cancelled cheques returned with the bank statement.
f. Bank service charges for October amount to $220.
g. A customer's cheque (Teresa Krant) for $15,800 had been deposited in the bank correctly but was recorded in the accounting records as $18,500.
h. Among the cancelled cheques is one for $890 given in payment of an account payable to Decker Company; the bookkeeper had recorded the cheque incorrectly at $980 in the company records.
i. The bank had collected a $5,000 note plus interest of $350. A fee of $45 was charged for this service.
j. A bank deposit of October 31 for $2,300 does not appear on the bank statement.

Required

1. Prepare a bank reconciliation statement as of October 31, 2001.
2. Prepare the necessary adjusting journal entries to make the Cash account agree with the bank reconciliation adjusted Cash balance as of October 31.

Check figure
1. Adjusted book balance = $41,010

Alternate Problems

Problem 9-1B

Principles of internal control

LO[1]

For the following five scenarios, identify the principle of internal control that is violated. Next, make a recommendation of what the business should do to ensure adherence to principles of internal control.

1. Tamerick Company is a fairly small organization but has segregated the duties of cash receipts and cash disbursements. However, the employee responsible for cash disbursements also reconciles the monthly bank account.
2. Stan Spencer is the most computer literate employee in his company. His boss has recently asked him to put password protection on all the office computers. Stan's main job at the company is to process payroll. Stan has put a password in place that now only allows his boss access to the file where pay rates are changed and personnel are added or deleted from the company payroll.
3. Starlight Theatre has a computerized order-taking system for its tickets. The system is active all week and backed up every Friday night.
4. Trek There Company has two employees handling acquisitions of inventory. One employee places purchase orders and pays vendors. The second employee receives the merchandise.
5. The owner of Holiday Helper uses a cheque protector to perforate cheques, making it difficult for anyone to alter the amount of the cheque. The cheque protector sits on the owner's desk in an office that houses company cheques and is often unlocked.

Problem 9-2B
Establishing, reimbursing, and increasing the petty cash fund

LO4

Dodge & Sons completed the following petty cash transactions during July 2001:

July 5	Drew a $200 cheque, cashed it, and turned the proceeds and the petty cash box over to Jackie Boone, the petty cashier.
6	Paid $14.50 COD charges on merchandise purchased for resale. Dodge & Sons uses the perpetual inventory method to account for merchandise inventory.
11	Paid $8.75 delivery charges on merchandise sold to a customer.
12	Purchased file folders, $12.13.
14	Reimbursed Collin Dodge, the manager of the business, $9.65 for office supplies purchased.
18	Purchased paper for printer, $22.54.
27	Paid $47.10 COD charges on merchandise purchased for resale.
28	Purchased stamps, $16.
30	Reimbursed Collin Dodge $58.80 for business car expenses.
31	Jackie Boone sorted the petty cash receipts by accounts affected and exchanged them for a cheque to reimburse the fund for expenditures. However, there was $11.53 in cash in the fund. In addition, the size of the petty cash fund was increased to $250.

Required
1. Prepare a General Journal entry to record establishing the petty cash fund.
2. Prepare a summary of petty cash payments that has these categories: delivery expense, mileage expense, postage expense, transportation-in, and office supplies. Sort the payments into the appropriate categories and total the expenses in each category.
3. Prepare the General Journal entry to record the reimbursement and the increase of the fund.

Problem 9-3B
Petty cash fund; reimbursement and analysis of errors

LO4

The accounting system used by The Thrifty Company requires that all entries be journalized in a General Journal. To facilitate payments for small items, Thrifty established a petty cash fund. The following transactions involving the petty cash fund occurred during February 2001.

Feb. 3	A company cheque for $150 was drawn and made payable to the petty cashier to establish the petty cash fund.
14	A company cheque was drawn to replenish the fund for the following expenditures made since February 3 and to increase the fund to $175. a. Purchased office supplies, $16.29. b Paid $17.60 COD charges on merchandise purchased for resale. Thrifty uses the perpetual method to account for merchandise inventory. c. Paid $36.57 to Data Services for minor repairs to computer. d. Paid $14.82 for postage expenses. e. Discovered that only $62.28 remained in the petty cash box.
28	The petty cashier noted that $48.81 remained in the fund, and decided that the February 14 increase in the fund was not large enough. A company cheque was drawn to replenish the fund for the following expenditures made since February 14, and to increase it to $250. f. Paid $40 to *The Smart Saver* for an advertisement in a monthly newsletter. g. Paid $28.19 for office supplies. h. Paid $58 to Best Movers for delivery of merchandise to a customer.

Required

Preparation component:

1. Prepare General Journal entries to record the establishment of the fund on February 3 and its replenishment February 14 and on February 28.

Analysis component:

2. Explain how the company's financial statements would be affected if the petty cash fund is not replenished and no entry is made on February 28. (Hint: The amount of Office Supplies that appears on a balance sheet is determined by a physical count of the supplies on hand.)

Problem 9-4B

Preparation of a bank reconciliation

LO6

Cindy Estelle, the controller of the Burnaby Corporation, provided the following information:

Burnaby Corporation
Bank Reconciliation
October 31, 2001

Bank statement balance		$ 9,843.80	Book balance		$10,054.69
Add:					
Deposit of Oct. 31 in transit		1,796.50			
		$11,640.30			
Deduct:			Deduct:		
Outstanding cheques:			NSF cheque plus		
#537	$948.24		service charge	$285.40	
#542	937.72	1,885.96	Bank service charges	14.95	300.35
Adjusted bank balance		$ 9,754.34	Adjusted book balance		$ 9,754.34

The following bank statement is available for November 2001:

Bank Statement

To: Burnaby Corporation — November 30, 2001, Bank of Canada

Cheques/Charges			Deposits/Credits		Balance
			10/31		**9,843.80**
#549	11/01	991.16	11/01	1,796.50	10,649.14
#543	11/02	1,800.00			8,849.14
#537	11/07	948.24			7,900.90
#551	11/09	699.36	11/09	1,908.56	9,110.10
#542	11/12	937.72			8,172.38
#544	11/14	679.12			7,493.26
#547	11/18	891.02	11/18	1,970.36	8,572.60
#545	11/20	921.84			7,650.76
#546	11/29	910.72			6,740.04
SC	11/30	36.50	11/30		**6,703.54**
NSF = Not Sufficient Funds		SC = Service Charge	PMT = Principal Payment		INT = Interest

A list of deposits made and cheques written during November, taken from the Cash Receipts Journal and Cash Disbursements journal, is shown below:

Deposits Made	
Nov. 9	$1,908.56
18	1,970.36
29	1,776.58
Total November Cash Receipts	$5,655.50

Cheques Written	
No. 543	$ 1,800.00
544	679.12
545	921.84
546	910.72
547	891.02
548	949.04
549	991.16
550	917.12
551	699.36
552	885.36
553	931.84
Total November Cash Disbursements	$10,576.58

Cash						Acct. No. 101
Date		Explanation	PR	Debit	Credit	Balance
2001						
Oct.	31	Balance				9,754.34
Nov.	30		CR7	5,655.50		15,409.84
	30		CD8		10,576.58	4,833.26

Required

Prepare a bank reconciliation for Burnaby Corporation for the month of November 2001.

Check figure: Adjusted book balance = $4,796.76

Problem 9-5B

Preparation of bank reconciliation

LO8

The bank reconciliation prepared by Arbour Glen Apartments on May 31, 2001 is shown below:

Arbour Glen Apartments
Bank Reconciliation
May 31, 2001

Bank statement balance		$1,030	Book balance	$4,370
Add:				
Deposit of May 31 in transit		4,800		
		$5,830		
Deduct:				
Outstanding cheques:				
#103	$940			
#120	520	1,460		
Adjusted bank balance		$4,370	Adjusted book balance	$4,370

The following bank statement is available:

Bank Statement					
To: Arbour Glen Apartments				June 30, 2001 Bank of Nova Scotia	
Cheques/Charges			Deposits/Credits		Balance
					1,030
#133	06/02	1,500	06/02	4,800	4,330
#136	06/05	3,900	06/05	1,700	2,130
#129	06/10	950	06/10	890	2,070
#130	06/15	1,200	06/15	1,100	1,970
#103	06/20	940	06/20	1,350	2,380
#134	06/27	1,640	06/27	30,000	30,740
#128	06/30	4,670	06/30	9,200	35,270
SC	06/30	200			35,070
NSF = Not Sufficient Funds		SC = Service Charge	PMT = Principal Payment		INT = Interest

The Cash account in the General Ledger appeared as follows on June 30:

Cash						Acct. No. 101
Date		Explanation	PR	Debit	Credit	Balance
2001						
May	31	Balance				4,370.00
June	30		CR21	45,040.00		49,410.00
	30		CD16		17,610.00	31,800.00

A list of deposits made and cheques written during June, taken from the Cash Receipts Journal and Cash Disbursements Journal, is shown below:

Deposits Made	
June 5	$ 1,700
10	890
15	1,100
20	1,350
27	30,000
30	2,900
30	7,100
Total June Cash Receipts	$45,040

Cheques Written	
No. 127	$ 1,700
128	4,670
129	950
130	1,200
131	225
132	1,175
133	1,500
134	1,640
135	650
136	3,900
Total June Cash Disbursements	$17,610

In reviewing deposits recorded by the bank, the bookkeeper discovered that the deposit from customer Darla Smith dated June 30, recorded in the Cash Receipts Journal incorrectly as $2,900, was recorded by the bank correctly as $9,200.

Check figure:
a. Adjusted book balance = $37,900

Required

a. Prepare a bank reconciliation at June 30.

b. Prepare the necessary journal entries to bring the General Ledger Cash account into agreement with the adjusted balance on the bank reconciliation.

Problem 9-6B

Preparation of bank reconciliation and recording adjustments

LO6

The following information was available to reconcile Bohannon Co.'s book cash balance with its bank statement balance as of December 31, 2001:

a. The December 31 Cash balance according to the accounting records was $31,743.70, and the bank statement balance for that date was $45,091.80.
b. Cheque #1273 for $1,084.20 and cheque #1282 for $390, both written and entered in the accounting records in December, were not among the cancelled cheques returned. Two cheques, #1231 for $2,289 and #1242 for $370.50, were outstanding on November 30 when the bank and book statement balances were last reconciled. Cheque #1231 was returned with the December cancelled cheques, but cheque #1242 was not.
c. When the December cheques were compared with entries in the accounting records, it was found that cheque #1267 had been correctly drawn for $2,435 to pay for office supplies, but was erroneously entered in the accounting records as though it were drawn for $2,453.
d. Two debit memoranda were included with the returned cheques and were unrecorded at the time of the reconciliation. One of the debit memoranda was for $749.50 and dealt with an NSF cheque for $732 that had been received from a customer, Tork Industries, in payment of its account. It also assessed a $17.50 fee for processing. The second debit memorandum covered cheque printing and was for $79. These transactions had not been recorded by Bohannon before receiving the statement.
e. A credit memorandum indicated that the bank had collected a $20,000 note receivable for the company, deducted a $20 collection fee, and credited the balance to the company's account. This transaction was not recorded by Bohannon before receiving the statement.
f. The December 31 cash receipts, $7,666.10, had been placed in the bank's night depository after banking hours on that date and did not appear on the bank statement.

Required

Preparation component:

1. Prepare a bank reconciliation for the company as of December 31.
2. Prepare the General Journal entries necessary to bring the company's book balance of Cash into conformity with the reconciled balance.

Analysis component:

3. Explain the nature of the messages conveyed by a bank to one of its depositors when the bank sends a debit memo and a credit memo to the depositor.

Check figure:
1. Adjusted book balance = $50,913,20

Problem 9-7B

Preparation of bank reconciliation and recording adjustments

LO6

Safety Systems reconciled its bank balance on April 30 and showed two cheques outstanding at that time, #1771 for $781 and #1780 for $1,325.90. The following information is available for the May 31, 2001, reconciliation:

From the May 31, 2001 bank statement:

BALANCE OF PREVIOUS STATEMENT ON APR 30/01 . . .	$ 18,290.70
5 DEPOSITS AND OTHER CREDITS TOTALLING	16,416.80
9 CHEQUES AND OTHER DEBITS TOTALLING.	12,898.90
CURRENT BALANCE AS OF THIS STATEMENT	21,808.60

Chequing Account Transactions

Date	Amount	Transaction Description	Date	Amount	Transaction Description
May 04	2,438.00	+Deposit	May 25	7,200.00	+Credit memo
14	2,898.00	+Deposit	26	2,079.00	+Deposit
18	431.80	−NSF cheque	31	12.00	−Service charge
22	1,801.80	+Deposit			

Date	Cheque No.	Amount	Date	Cheque No.	Amount
May 01	1784	1,449.60	May 26	1785	157.20
02	1783	195.30	28	1771	781.00
15	1787	8,032.50	29	1788	554.00
16	1782	1,285.50			

From Safety Systems' accounting records:

Deposits Made	
May 4	$ 2,438.00
14	2,898.00
22	1,801.80
26	2,079.00
31	2,526.30
Total May Cash Receipts	$11,743.10

Cheques Written	
No. 1782	$1,285.50
1783	195.30
1784	1,449.60
1785	157.20
1786	353.10
1787	8,032.50
1788	544.00
1789	639.50
Total May Cash Disbursements	$12,656.70

Cash						Acct. No. 101
Date		Explanation	PR	Debit	Credit	Balance
2001						
Apr.	30	Balance				16,183.80
May	31		CR7	11,743.10		27,926.90
	31		CD8		12,656.70	15,270.20

Cheque #1788 was correctly drawn for $554 to pay for May utilities; however, the bookkeeper misread the amount and entered it in the accounting records with a debit to Utilities Expense and a credit to Cash as though it were for $544. The bank paid and deducted the correct amount.

The NSF cheque was originally received from a customer, Gertie Mayer, in payment of her account. Its return was unrecorded. The credit memorandum resulted from a $7,300 note that the bank had collected for the company. The bank had deducted a $100 collection fee and deposited the remainder in the company's account. The collection has not been recorded.

Required

Preparation component:

1. Prepare a bank reconciliation for Safety Systems.
2. Prepare the General Journal entries needed to adjust the book balance of cash to the reconciled balance.

Analysis component:

3. The preceding bank statement discloses two places where the cancelled cheques returned with the bank statement are not numbered sequentially. In other words, some of the prenumbered cheques in the sequence are missing. Several possible situations would explain why the cancelled cheques returned with a bank statement might not be numbered sequentially. Describe three possible reasons why this might occur.

Check figure:
1. Adjusted book balance = $22,016.40

Problem 9-8B
Preparation of bank reconciliation and recording adjustments

LO6

Mountainview Co. reconciled its bank statement balances of Cash on October 31 and showed two cheques outstanding at that time, #1388 for $1,597 and #1393 for $745. The following information was available for the November 30, 2001 reconciliation:

From the November 30 bank statement:

BALANCE OF PREVIOUS STATEMENT ON OCT. 31/01	27,418.00
5 DEPOSITS AND OTHER CREDITS TOTALLING	17,176.00
9 CHEQUES AND OTHER DEBITS TOTALLING	16,342.00
CURRENT BALANCE AS OF NOVEMBER 30/01	28,252.00

Chequing Account Transactions

Date	Amount	Transaction Description	Date	Amount	Transaction Description
Nov. 05	1,698.00	+Deposit	Nov. 25	3,618.00	+Deposit
12	3,426.00	+Deposit	30	17.00	+Interest
17	905.00	−NSF cheque	30	2,120.00	+Credit memorandum
21	6,297.00	+Deposit			

Date	Cheque No.	Amount	Date	Cheque No.	Amount
Nov. 03	1402	1,126.00	Nov. 17	1409	2,781.00
04	1403	614.00	20	1405	1,442.00
08	1388	1,597.00	27	1407	329.00
12	1401	4,363.00	29	1404	3,185.00

From Mountainview Co's accounting records:

Cash Acct. No. 101

Date	Explanation	PR	Debit	Credit	Balance
2001					
Oct. 31	Balance				25,076.00
Nov. 30		CR12	17,474.00		42,550.00
30		CD23		15,537.00	27,013.00

Deposits Made

Nov. 5	$1,698.00
12	3,426.00
21	6,297.00
25	3,618.00
30	2,435.00
Total November Cash Receipts	$17,474.00

Cheques Written

No. 1401	$ 4,363.00
1402	1,126.00
1403	614.00
1404	3,135.00
1405	1,442.00
1406	1,322.00
1407	329.00
1408	425.00
1409	2,781.00
Total November Cash Disbursements	$15,537.00

Cheque #1404 was correctly drawn for $3,185 to pay for computer equipment: however, the bookkeeper misread the amount and entered it in the accounting records with a debit to Computer Equipment and a credit to Cash as though it were for $3,135.

The NSF cheque was originally received from a customer, Jerry Skyles in payment of his account. Its return was not recorded when the bank first notified the company. The credit memorandum resulted from the collection of a $2,150 note for Mountainview by the bank. The bank had deducted a $30 collection fee. The collection has not been recorded.

Required

1. Prepare a November 30 bank reconciliation for the company.
2. Prepare the General Journal entries needed to adjust the book balance of Cash to the reconciled balance.

Check figure:
1. Adjusted book balance = $28,195.00

Problem 9-9B

Preparation of a bank reconciliation

LO6

The following information was available to reconcile Emirates Company's book balance of Cash with its bank statement balance as of February 28, 2001.

a. The bank statement at February 28 indicated a balance of $9,600. The General Ledger account for Cash showed a balance at February 28 of $12,992.
b. Of the cheques issued in February, the following were still outstanding:

Cheque	Amount
#202	$1,600
#205	110
#213	35
#240	200

c. Two cheques, #136 for $120 and #200 for $330, were outstanding on Jan. 31 when the bank and book balances were last reconciled. Cheque #136 was returned with the February cancelled cheques but cheque #200 was not.
d. Included with the February bank statement was an NSF cheque for $435 that had been received from a customer, Mrs. Tahani Ahmad in payment of her account.
e. Cheque #219 was correctly drawn for $406 in payment for office supplies but was erroneously entered as $604 in the Cash Payments Journal.
f. A debit memorandum for $60 was enclosed with the bank statement. This charge was for printing the chequebook for Emirates Company.
g. Included with the bank statement was a $50 credit memorandum for interest earned on the bank account in February.
h. The February 28 cash receipts amounting to $6,300 had been placed in the bank's night depository after banking hours on that date and did not appear among the deposits on the February bank statement.
i. Included with the bank statement was a credit memorandum, which indicated that the bank had collected a $900 note receivable for the company, deducted a $20 collection fee, and credited the balance to the company's account.

Check figure:
1. Adjusted book balance = $13,625

Required

1. Prepare a bank reconciliation for the Emirates Company as of February 28, 2001.
2. Prepare the entries needed to adjust the book balance of Cash to the reconciled balance.

Problem 9-10B

Preparation of a bank reconciliation

LO6

The following is information for the HR Cafe:

a. Balance per the bank statement dated December 31, 2001 is $25,430.
b. Balance of the Cash account on the company books as of December 31, 2001 is $11,040.
c. A cheque from customer Della Armstrong for $840 that had been deposited in the bank was erroneously recorded by the bookkeeper as $930.
d. A cheque made out by Neon Company for $2,100 deposited on December 21 is returned by the bank marked NSF; no entry has been made on the company records to reflect the returned cheque.
e. Among the cancelled cheques is one for $345 given in payment of an account payable to CT Financial; the bookkeeper had incorrectly recorded the cheque at $480 in the company records.
f. Bank service charges for December amount to $50.
g. The bank erroneously charged the HR Cafe account for a $10,000 cheque of the HRD Company; the cheque was found among the cancelled cheques returned with the bank statement.
h. The bank had collected a $15,000 note plus accrued interest amounting to $75; $15,075 was credited to HR Cafe's account; a collection fee of $10 was debited to HR Cafe's account.
i. Bank deposit of December 31 for $1,570 does not appear on the bank statement.
j. Outstanding cheques as of December 31: #197, $4,000; #199, $9,000.

Check figure:
1. Adjusted book balance = $24,000

Required

1. Prepare a bank reconciliation statement as of December 31, 2001.
2. Prepare the necessary adjusting journal entries to make the Cash account agree with the bank reconciliation adjusted Cash balance as of December 31.

Analytical and Review Problems

A & R Problem 9-1

The bank statement for October arrived in Friday's mail. You were especially anxious to receive the statement as one of your assignments was to prepare a bank reconciliation for the Saturday meeting. You got around to preparing the reconciliation rather late in the afternoon and found all the necessary data with the exception of the bank balance. The bottom portion of the bank statement was smudged, and several figures, including the balance, were obliterated. A telephone call to the bank was answered by a recording with the information that the bank was closed until 10 a.m. Monday. Since the reconcilation had to be prepared, you decided to plug in the bank balance. In preparation, you assembled the necessary material as follows:

a. Cash balance per books was $6,800.
b. From the cancelled cheques returned by the bank, you determined that six cheques remained outstanding. The total of these cheques was $3,700.
c. In checking the cancelled cheques you noted that cheque #274 was properly made for $416 to Staples but was recorded in the Cash Disbursements Journal as $461. The cheque was in payment of an account.
d. Included with the bank statement were two memoranda; the credit memorandum was for collection of a note for $1,500 and $90 of interest thereon and the debit memorandum was for $12 of bank charges.
e. While you were sorting the cancelled cheques, one of the cheques caught your attention. You were astounded by the similarity of name with that of your company and the similarity of the cheques. The cheque was for $620 and was obviously in error charged to your company's account.
f. From the deposit book, you determined that a $2,500 deposit was made after hours on October 31.

Required

1. Prepare a bank reconciliation statement as of October 31 (plug in the indicated bank balance).
2. Prepare the necessary journal entries.

A & R Problem 9-2

Your assistant prepared the following bank reconciliation statement. It appears that the statement is unacceptable and the task of preparing a proper reconciliation falls upon you.

Brandon Company Bank Reconciliation May 31, 2001		
Balance per books May 31		$ 9,500
Add:		
Note collected	$1,000	
Interest on note	60	
Deposit in transit	2,455	3,515
		$13,015
Deduct:		
Bank charges	$ 10	
NSF cheque, Rhonda Teal	500	
Outstanding cheques	1,800	
Error in cheque #78 issued for $762 and recorded in the books as $726 (Delta Co.)	36	2,346
Indicated bank balance		$10,669
Balance per bank statement		9,359
Discrepancy		$ 1,310

Required

1. Prepare a proper bank reconciliation showing the true Cash balance.
2. Prepare the necessary journal entries.

A & R Problem 9-3

Wanda White acquired a sports equipment distribution business with a staff of six salespersons and two clerks. Because of the trust that Wanda had in her employees—after all, they were all her friends and just like members of the family—she believed that an honour system in regard to the operation of the petty cash fund was adequate. Consequently, Wanda placed $300 in a coffee jar, which, for convenience, was kept in a cupboard in the common room. All employees had access to the petty cash fund and withdrew amounts as required. No vouchers were required for withdrawals. As required, additional funds were placed in the coffee jar and the amount of the replenishment was charged to "miscellaneous selling expense."

Required

1. From the internal control point of view, discuss the weaknesses of the petty cash fund operation and suggest steps necessary for improvement.
2. Does the petty cash fund operation as described above violate any of the generally accepted accounting principles? If yes, which and how is the principle(s) violated?

CHAPTER

10 Receivables

Debt into Gold—or—Finlay!

Winnipeg, MB—Today's economy runs on credit sales. These credit sales produce accounts receivable that are often the largest current asset a company owns. But not all accounts receivable are paid. Some end up as "bad debts"—accounts that a company cannot collect.

Enter George and Lucille Finlay. The Finlays first started collecting on other companies' bad debt accounts in 1986 from their kitchen table in Brandon, Manitoba. They used something more powerful than technology and pressure tactics to collect money debtors owed; they used a philosophy of "respect for people." The Finlays personally know the psychology of debtors. They found themselves in a huge hole in 1986 after their business went belly up. "You've got to be sympathetic, you've got to listen with your heart as well as your head," says George Finlay.

The Finlays' "polite persistence" has paid off. Their entrepreneurial spirit led them to create Manitoba Collections Corp. (MCC),

Learning Objectives

LO1 Describe accounts receivable and how they occur and are recorded.

LO2 Apply the allowance method to account for accounts receivable.

LO3 Estimate uncollectibles using methods based on sales and accounts receivable.

LO4 Apply the direct write-off method to account for uncollectible accounts receivable.

LO5 Describe a note receivable and compute its maturity date and interest.

LO6 Record notes receivable.

a Winnipeg-based company that is now one of the largest purchasers of bad credit card debts. Their company earns in excess of $6 million annually. And their net profit margin is a cool 67%.

Through all of its success, MCC has maintained its reputation for ethical dealings in an industry still plagued by abusive and questionable tactics. The company keeps a down-to-earth management style. One example is if revenue targets are met, MCC will fly all employees and guests to a baseball game in Toronto. It's vintage Finlay: bold and flamboyant.

Chapter Preview

This chapter focuses on accounts receivable and short-term notes receivable. We describe each of these assets, their use in practice, and how they are accounted for and reported in financial statements. This knowledge helps us use accounting information to make better decisions. It can also help in predicting bad debts as shown in the opening article.

Accounts Receivable

A *receivable* refers to an amount due from another party. The two most common receivables are accounts receivable and notes receivable. Other receivables include interest receivable, rent receivable, tax refund receivable, and amounts due from other parties such as officers and employees.

Accounts receivable refers to amounts due from customers for credit sales. They are also referred to as **trade receivables** because they result from customers we *trade* with. This section begins by describing how accounts receivable arise and their various sources. These sources include sales when customers use credit cards issued by third parties, and when a company gives credit directly to customers. When a company extends credit directly to customers, it must (1) maintain a separate account receivable for each customer and (2) account for bad debts from credit sales.

Recognizing Accounts Receivable

LO1 Describe accounts receivable and how they occur and are recorded.

Accounts receivable arise from credit sales to customers. The amount of credit sales over cash sales has increased in recent years, reflecting several factors including an efficient banking system and a sound economy. Exhibit 10.1 shows the dollar amount of accounts receivable and its percent of total assets for five companies.

Exhibit 10.1

Accounts Receivable for Selected Companies

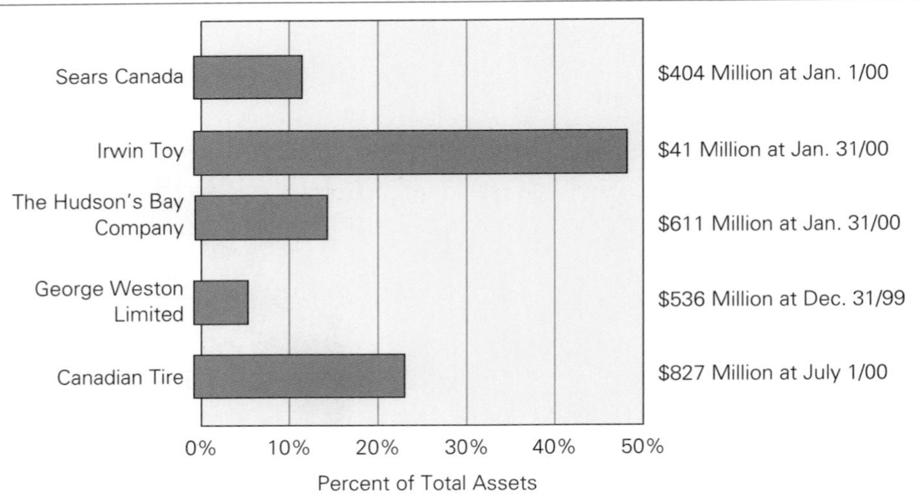

Sales on Credit

To review how accounts receivable from credit sales are recognized, we will record two transactions in the accounting records for TechCom, a small electronics wholesaler. TechCom's *Accounts Receivable controlling account* P. 395 in the General Ledger and subsidiary *Accounts Receivable Ledger* P. 395 prior to recording these transactions are illustrated in Exhibit 10.2.

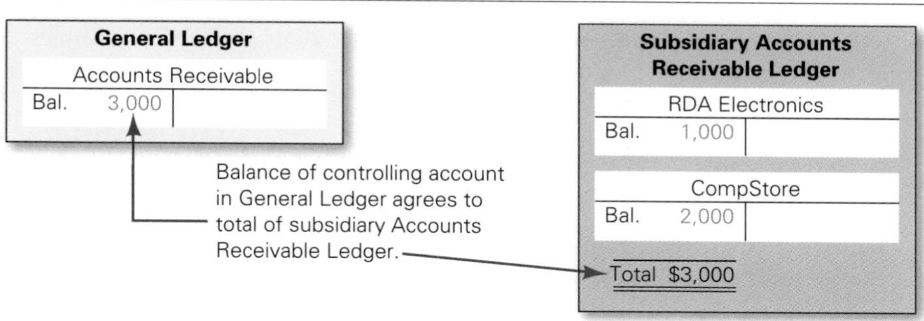

Exhibit 10.2

Accounts Receivable Account and the Subsidiary Accounts Receivable Ledger

The first transaction to be recorded on July 15 is a credit sale of $950 to CompStore (cost of sales to TechCom is $630 assuming a perpetual inventory system). The second is a collection of $720 from RDA Electronics from prior credit sales. Both transactions are reflected in Exhibit 10.3. Note that these transactions would typically be recorded in the appropriate Sales and Cash Receipts Journals. We use the General Journal format here for simplicity.

Exhibit 10.3

Accounts Receivable Transactions

Date	Account	Debit	Credit
July 15	Accounts Receivable—CompStore	950	
	Sales		950
	To record credit sales.		
15	Cost of Goods Sold	630	
	Merchandise Inventory		630
	To record cost of sales.		
15	Cash	720	
	Accounts Receivable—RDA Electronics		720
	To record collection of credit sales.		

Exhibit 10.4 shows the Accounts Receivable controlling account and the subsidiary Accounts Receivable Ledger after posting these two transactions.

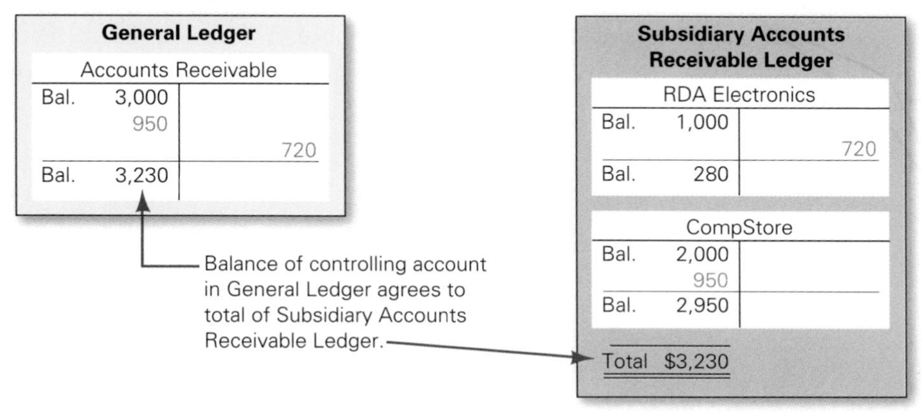

Exhibit 10.4

Accounts Receivable Account and the Subsidiary Accounts Receivable Ledger

Like many companies, TechCom grants credit directly to qualified customers. Many large retailers such as Canadian Tire and The Hudson's Bay Company maintain their own credit card. This allows them to grant credit to approved customers and to earn interest on any balance not paid within a specified period of time, as well as to avoid the fee charged by credit card companies. The entries in this case are the same as those above except for the possibility of added interest revenue. If a customer owes interest on the bill, then we debit Accounts Receivable and credit Interest Revenue for this amount.

Exhibit 10.5 shows the Hudson's Bay Company's credit card receivables as reported on its January 31, 2000 balance sheet.

Exhibit 10.5

Credit Card Receivables on the Balance Sheet of the Hudson's Bay Company

www.hbc.com

January 31 (thousands of dollars)	Notes	2000	1999
Current assets:			
Cash in stores		8,480	8,045
Short-term deposits		41,792	13,919
Credit card receivables	7	483,940	718,686

Credit Card Sales

Many companies allow customers to use credit cards such as Visa, Mastercard, or American Express to charge purchases.

The customer has the convenience of using the credit card instead of using cash or cheques. The retailer enjoys the benefits of being paid by the credit card company. The payment to the retailer normally occurs faster than if the retailer had to collect credit sales personally and the risk of credit customers who do not pay is transferred to the credit card company. The credit card company issues the customer a monthly statement detailing the customer's transactions. The customer pays the credit card company monthly based on the credit terms on the statement.

The seller pays a fee for the services provided by the credit card company. The fee covers the credit card company's costs, which include credit checks on credit card customers, collecting cash, reimbursing retailers, and, of course, a profit margin. Therefore, when the fee is deducted, the cash received by the retailer is less than 100% of the sales value of the transaction.

Bank Credit Card (such as Visa or Mastercard)

The retailer receives cash, net of the credit card fee, immediately upon deposit of the credit card sales receipt at the bank. For instance, if TechCom has $100 of credit card sales with a 4% fee and cash is received immediately, the entry is (assume cost of sales is $40):

Aug. 15	Cash	96	
	Credit Expense	4	
	Sales		100
	To record credit card sales less a 4% credit card expense.		
15	Cost of Goods Sold	40	
	Merchandise Inventory		40
	To record cost of sales.		

Non-bank Credit Card (such as EnRoute or Discovery)

When a non-bank credit card is used, the retailer mails the credit card sales receipts and awaits payment. For instance, if TechCom has a $300 credit card sale with a 2% fee and a non-bank credit card is used, the entry (assuming cost of sales is $120) is:

Aug. 15	Accounts Receivable—Credit Card Company.	300	
	Sales		300
	To record credit card sale.		
15	Cost of Goods Sold	120	
	Merchandise Inventory		120
	To record cost of sales.		

When cash is received from the credit card company, the entry is:

Sept. 15	Cash	294	
	Credit Card Expense	6	
	Accounts Receivable—		
	Credit Card Company..........................		300
	To record collection of amount due from Credit Card Company.		

Some firms report credit card expense in the income statement as a type of discount deducted from sales to get net sales. Other companies classify it as a selling expense or even as an administrative expense.

Debit Card Sales

The use of debit cards is becoming more common and popular with consumers. Payment for a purchase is electronically transferred from the customer's bank account to the vendor's bank account when authorized by the customer at the point of sale. Normally, the bank charges the retailer a fee for this service. The entries are identical to a bank credit card sale.

Entrepreneur

You are the owner of a small retail store. You are considering allowing customers to purchase merchandise using credit cards. Until now, your store only accepted cash and cheques. What forms of analysis do you use to make this decision.

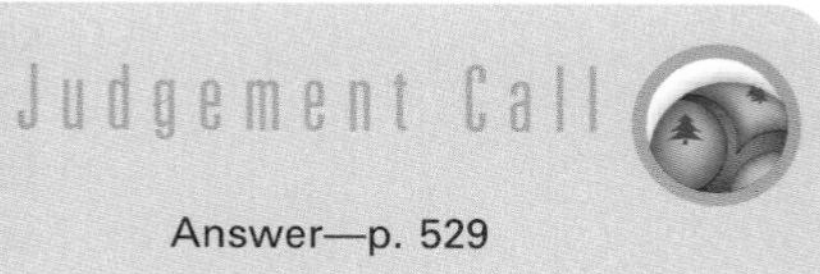

Answer—p. 529

1. In recording credit card sales, when do you debit Accounts Receivable and when do you debit Cash?

Answer—p. 530

Valuing Accounts Receivable

When a company grants credit to its customers, there are usually a few customers who do not pay what they promised. The accounts of these customers are **uncollectible accounts**, commonly called **bad debts**. The total amount of uncollectible accounts is an expense of selling on credit. Why do companies sell on credit if it is likely some accounts will prove uncollectible? Companies believe granting credit will increase revenues and profits to offset bad debts. They are willing to incur bad debt losses if the net effect is to increase sales and profits.

Two methods are used by companies to account for uncollectible accounts: (1) allowance method, and (2) direct write-off method. Exhibit 10.6 summarizes these methods.

Exhibit 10.6

Methods for Writing Off Bad Debts

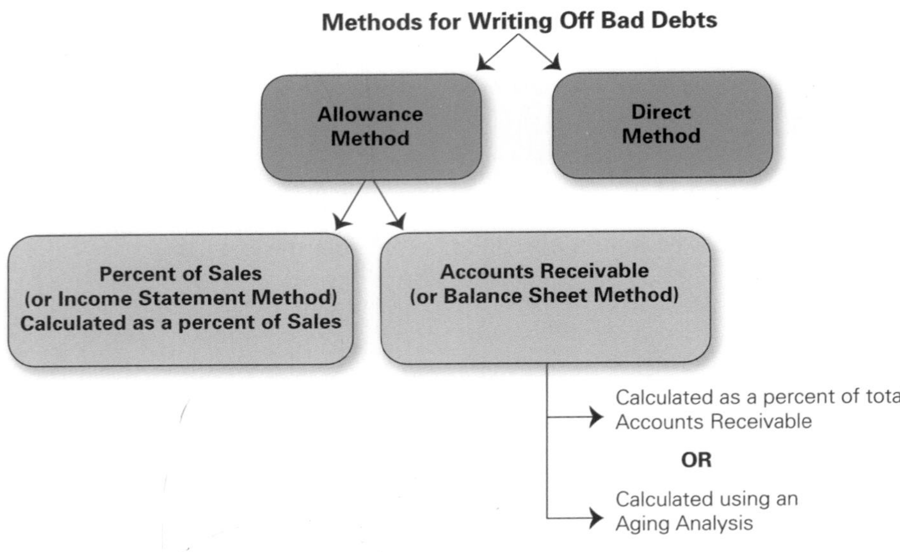

Allowance Method

LO2 Apply the allowance method to account for accounts receivable.

The matching principle P. 140 requires that expenses be reported in the same accounting period as the sales they helped produce. This means that if extending credit to customers helped produce sales, any bad debt expense linked to those sales should be matched and reported in the same period as the sales. The **allowance method** of accounting for bad debts satisfies the matching principle by matching the expected loss from uncollectible accounts receivable against the sales they helped produce in that period. How? Since the seller is unable to identify in advance which of the credit sales will become uncollectible, an estimate based on past experience and the experience of similar companies must be used. This means that at the end of each period, the total bad debts expected to result from that period's sales are estimated. An allowance is then recorded for this expected loss. As well as matching, the allowance method satisfies the requirement of the conservatism principle. To avoid overstatement, the allowance reduces accounts receivable on the balance sheet to an amount that is expected to be collected.

Recording Estimated Bad Debt Expense

The allowance method estimates bad debt expense at the end of each accounting period and records it with an adjusting entry P. 140. TechCom, for instance, had credit sales of approximately $300,000 during its first year of operations. At the end of the first year, $20,000 of credit sales remained uncollected. Based on the experience of similar businesses, TechCom estimated bad debt expense to be $1,500. This estimated expense is recorded with the following adjusting entry at the end of the accounting period:

Dec. 31	Bad Debt Expense	1,500	
	Allowance for Doubtful Accounts.........		1,500
	To record estimated bad debts.		

The debit in this entry means the estimated bad debt expense of $1,500 from selling on credit is matched on the income statement with the $300,000 sales it helped produce. The credit in this entry is to a contra account P. 144 called **Allowance for Doubtful Accounts**. A contra account is used because at the time of the adjusting entry, we do not know which customers will not pay. Because specific uncollectible accounts are not identifiable at the time of the adjusting entry, they cannot be removed from the subsidiary Accounts Receivable Ledger. Because the customer accounts are left in the subsidiary ledger, the controlling account for Accounts Receivable cannot be reduced. Instead, the Allowance for Doubtful Accounts account *must* be credited.

Bad Debts and Related Accounts in Financial Statements

Recall that TechCom has $20,000 of outstanding accounts receivable at the end of its first year of operations. After the bad debt adjusting entry is posted, TechCom's Accounts Receivable, Allowance for Doubtful Accounts, and Bad Debt Expense have balances as shown in Exhibit 10.7.

Exhibit 10.7

General Ledger Balances After Bad Debts Adjusting

Acounts Receivable			
Dec. 31	20,000		

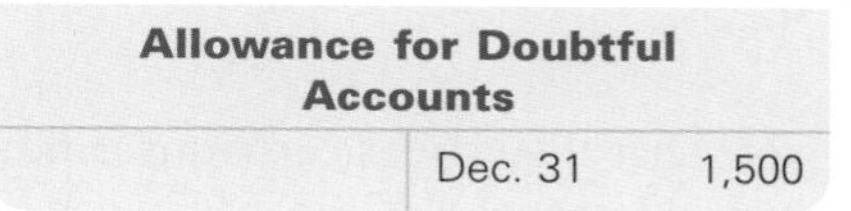

Allowance for Doubtful Accounts			
		Dec. 31	1,500

Accounts Receivable and *Allowance for Doubtful Accounts* are BOTH balance sheet accounts shown under current assets.

Bad Debt Expense			
Dec. 31	1,500		

Bad Debt Expense is an income statement account and is normally listed as a selling expense.

Although $20,000 is legally owed to TechCom by its credit customers, $18,500 (=20,000 – 1,500) is the **realizable value**, or amount to be realized in cash collections from customers.

In the balance sheet, the Allowance for Doubtful Accounts is subtracted from Accounts Receivable to show the realizable value. This information is often reported as shown in Exhibit 10.8.

Exhibit 10.8

Balance Sheet Presentation of Allowance for Doubtful Accounts

Current assets:		
Accounts receivable	$20,000	
Less: Allowance for doubtful accounts	1,500	18,500

Often the contra account to Accounts Receivable is not reported separately. This alternative presentation is shown in Exhibit 10.9.

Exhibit 10.9

Alternative Presentation of Allowance for Doubtful Accounts

Current assets:	
Accounts receivable (net of $1,500 estimated uncollectible accounts)	$18,500

Writing Off a Bad Debt

When specific accounts receivable are identified as uncollectible, they must be removed from accounts receivable. This is done by writing them off against the Allowance for Doubtful Accounts. For instance, after spending a year trying to collect from Jack Kent, TechCom finally decides that his $520 account is uncollectible and makes the following entry to write it off:

Jan. 23	Allowance for Doubtful Accounts	520	
	Accounts Receivable—Jack Kent		520
	To write off an uncollectible account.		

After this entry is posted, the General Ledger accounts appear as shown in Exhibit 10.10.

Exhibit 10.10

General Ledger Balances After Posting Write-Off

Accounts Receivable			
Dec. 31	20,000		
		Jan. 23	**520**
Balance	19,480		

Allowance for Doubtful Accounts			
		Dec. 31	1,500
Jan. 23	**520**		
		Balance	980

Note that the expense account is not debited, because bad debt expense is previously estimated and recorded with an adjusting entry at the end of the period in which the sale occurred. While the write-off removes the amount of the account receivable from the ledgers, it does not affect the estimated realizable value of TechCom's net accounts receivable as shown in Exhibit 10.11.

Exhibit 10.11

Realizable Value Before and After Write-off

	Before Write-off (Dec. 31)	After Write-off (Jan. 23)
Accounts receivable	$ 20,000	$ 19,480
Less: Allowance for doubtful accounts	1,500	980
Estimated realizable accounts receivable	$18,500	$18,500

Neither total assets nor net income is affected by the write-off of a specific account. But both total assets and net income are affected by recognizing the year's bad debts expense in the adjusting entry.

Recovery of a Bad Debt

When a customer fails to pay and the account is written off, his or her credit standing is jeopardized. The customer sometimes chooses to voluntarily pay all or part of the amount owed after the account is written off as uncollectible. This payment helps restore credit standing. When a recovery of a bad debt occurs, it is recorded in the customer's subsidiary account where this information is retained for use in future credit evaluation.

If on March 11 Jack Kent pays in full his account that TechCom previously wrote off, the entries to record this bad debt recovery are:

Mar. 11	Accounts Receivable—Jack Kent	520	
	Allowance for Doubtful Accounts.........		520
	To reinstate the account of Jack Kent previously written off.		
11	Cash	520	
	Accounts Receivable—Jack Kent.........		520
	In full payment of account.		

Jack Kent paid the entire amount previously written off, but in some cases a customer may pay only a portion of the amount owed. A question then arises of whether the entire balance of the account is returned to accounts receivable or just the amount paid. The answer is a matter of judgement. If we believe this customer will later pay in full, the entire amount owed is returned to accounts receivable. But only the amount paid is returned if we expect no further collection.

To summarize, the transactions discussed in this chapter[1] that cause changes in Accounts Receivable and Allowance for Doubtful Accounts are illustrated using T-accounts in Exhibit 10.12.

Exhibit 10.12 Summary of Accounts Receivable and Allowance for Doubtful Accounts Transactions

Accounts Receivable	
(a) Sales on credit	(b) Collections received from credit customers
	(c) Write-off of accounts receivable identified as uncollectible
(d) Recovery (reinstatement of accounts previously written off)	(e) Recovery (collection of reinstated accounts)

Allowance for Doubtful Accounts	
(c) Write-off of accounts receivable identified as uncollectible	
	(d) Recovery (reinstatement of accounts previously written off)
	(f) Adjusting entry to estimate uncollectible accounts

Answers—p. 530

2. Using the matching principle, why must bad debt expenses be estimated?
3. What term describes the balance sheet valuation of accounts receivable less the allowance for doubtful accounts?
4. Why is estimated bad debt expense credited to a contra account rather than to the Accounts Receivable controlling account?
5. Record entries for the following transactions:

January 10, 2001	The $300 account of customer Cool Jam is determined to be uncollectible.
April 12, 2001	Cool Jam pays in full its account that was deemed uncollectible on January 10, 2001.

[1] Remember that Sales Returns and Allowances also cause Accounts Receivable to decrease.

Estimate uncollectibles using methods based on sales and accounts receivable.

Estimating Bad Debt Expense

There are two general methods for estimating bad debt expense. These were introduced briefly in Exhibit 10.6.

Percent of Sales Method

The **percent of sales method** (or **income statement method**) uses income statement relations to estimate bad debts. It is based on the idea that a percentage of a company's credit sales for the period are uncollectible.[2] To demonstrate, assume MusicLand has credit sales of $400,000 in 2001. Based on experience, MusicLand estimates 0.6% of credit sales to be uncollectible. Using this prediction, MusicLand expects $2,400 of bad debt expense from 2001's sales ($400,000 × 0.006 = $2,400). The adjusting entry to record this estimated expense is:

Dec. 31	Bad Debt Expense	2,400	
	Allowance for Doubtful Accounts.........		2,400
	To record estimated bad debts.		

For demonstration purposes, assume that the Allowance for Doubtful Accounts (AFDA) had an unadjusted credit balance of $200 on December 31. Bad Debt Expense and Allowance for Doubtful Accounts would appear as in Exhibit 10.13 *after* the December 31 adjustment.

Exhibit 10.13

Accounts Receivable and Allowance for Doubtful Accounts Balances After the December 31 Adjustment

Bad Debt Expense		
Dec. 31 Adjustment	**2,400**	
Adjusted Balance Dec. 31	2,400	

Allowance for Doubtful Accounts		
	200	Unadjusted Balance Dec. 31
	2,400	**Dec. 31 Adjustment**
	2,600	Adjusted Balance Dec. 31

Note that the unadjusted balance of AFDA could be a zero balance, credit balance, or a debit balance depending on the circumstances. If MusicLand were in its first period of operations, the AFDA would have a zero beginning balance. In the next accounting periods, if write-offs are *greater* than what had been estimated, a *debit* unadjusted balance will result. If *fewer* write-offs occur than what was estimated, as in Exhibit 10.13, a *credit* unadjusted balance will result. If the estimate for bad debts is too high or too low, the percentage used to estimate bad debts can be adjusted in future periods.

Accounts Receivable Methods

The **accounts receivable method**, also known as the **balance sheet method**, uses balance sheet relations (Accounts Receivable and the Allowance for Doubtful Accounts) to estimate bad debts. It is based on the idea that some portion of the end-of-period accounts receivable balance is not collectible. The objective for the bad debt adjusting entry is to make the Allowance for Doubtful Accounts balance

[2] Note the focus is on *credit* sales. Cash sales do not produce bad debts, and they are generally not used in this estimation. But if cash sales are relatively small compared to credit sales, there is no major impact of including them.

equal to the portion of outstanding accounts receivable estimated to be uncollectible. To obtain this required balance for the Allowance for Doubtful Accounts account, we compare its balance before the adjustment with the required balance. The difference between the two is debited to Bad Debt Expense and credited to Allowance for Doubtful Accounts. Estimating this required balance for the allowance account is done in one of two ways:

1. By using a simple percent estimate of uncollectibles from the total outstanding accounts receivable, or
2. By aging accounts receivable.

Percent of Accounts Receivable Method

The **percent of accounts receivable method** assumes that a percent of a company's outstanding receivables is uncollectible. This estimated percent is based on past experience and the experience of similar companies. It also is impacted by current conditions such as recent economic conditions and difficulties faced by customers. The total dollar amount of all outstanding receivables is multiplied by an estimated percent to get the estimated dollar amount of uncollectible accounts. This is the amount to be reported in the balance sheet as the balance for Allowance for Doubtful Accounts. To accomplish this, we prepare the adjusting entry in the amount necessary to give us the required balance in Allowance for Doubtful Accounts.

Assume RGO, an office furniture supplier, has $50,000 of outstanding accounts receivable on December 31. Past experience suggests that 5% of outstanding receivables are uncollectible.

Therefore, we want the Allowance for Doubtful Accounts to show a $2,500 credit balance (5% of $50,000). Assume that the unadjusted balance in the Allowance for Doubtful Accounts at December 31 is currently $500.

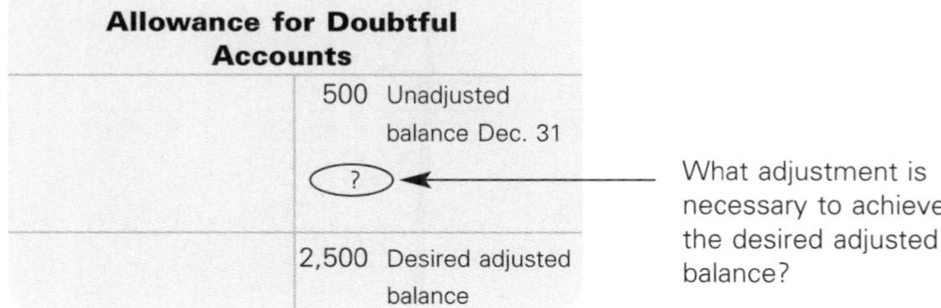

The adjusting entry to give the required $2,500 balance is:

Dec. 31	Bad Debt Expense	2,000	
	Allowance for Doubtful Accounts.........		2,000
	To record estimated bad debts.		

After this entry is posted the allowance has a $2,500 credit balance as shown in Exhibit 10.14.

Exhibit 10.14

Allowance for Doubtful Accounts after Bad Debt Adjusting Entry

Allowance for Doubtful Accounts		
	500	Unadjusted balance Dec. 31
	2,000	From Dec. 31 adjusting entry
	2,500	Adjusted balance Dec. 31

Accounts receivable would then be reported as follows on RGO's balance sheet:

Current assets:		
Accounts receivable	$50,000	
Less: Allowance for doubtful accounts	2,500	$47,500

or

Current assets:	
Accounts receivable (net of $2,500 estimated uncollectible accounts)	$47,500

Aging of Accounts Receivable Method

The **aging of accounts receivable** method examines each account receivable outstanding at the end of a period and classifies it according to how much time has passed since it was created. Classifications depend on the judgement of management but are often based on 30-day periods. Estimated rates of uncollectibility are applied to each class and totalled to get the required balance of the Allowance for Doubtful Accounts. This computation is illustrated in Exhibit 10.15 for DeCor, an interior design company whose total outstanding accounts receivable at December 31 were $49,900.

Exhibit 10.15

Aging of Accounts Receivable

DeCor
Schedule of Accounts Receivable by Age
December 31, 2001

Customer's Name	Total	Not Yet Due	1 to 30 Days Past Due	31 to 60 Days Past Due	61 to 90 Days Past Due	Over 90 Days Past Due
Charles Abbot	$ 450	$ 450				
Frank Allen	710			$ 710		
George Arden	500	300	$ 200			
Paul Baum	740				$ 100	$ 640
ZZ Services	1,000	810	190			
Totals	$49,900	$37,000	$6,500	$3,500	$1,900	$1,000
Percent Uncollectible		× 2%	× 5%	× 10%	× 25%	× 40%
Estimated Uncollectible Accounts	**$2,290**	$ 740	$ 325	$ 350	$ 475	$ 400

Notice the percent of uncollectibility increases with the age of the accounts to reflect the increasing risk of noncollection.

The total in the first column tells us the adjusted balance in DeCor's Allowance for Doubtful Accounts should be $2,290 (= $740 + $325 + $350 + $475 + $400). Because DeCor's allowance account as shown below has an unadjusted ***debit balance*** of $200, the required adjustment to the Allowance for Doubtful Accounts needs to be calculated as follows:

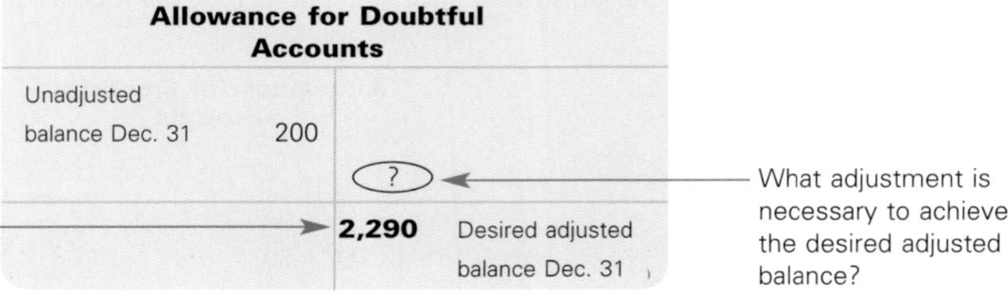

DeCor records the following adjusting entry:

Dec. 31	Bad Debt Expense	2,490	
	Allowance for Doubtful Accounts.........		2,490
	To record estimated bad debts; 2,290 + 200 = 2,490.		

On the balance sheet, DeCor's accounts receivable would be reported as follows:

Current assets:		
Accounts receivable	$49,900	
Less: Allowance for doubtful accounts........................	2,290	$47,610

or

Current assets:	
Accounts receivable (net of $2,290 estimated uncollectible accounts)........	$47,610

Exhibit 10.16 summarizes the principles guiding all three estimation methods and their focus of analysis.

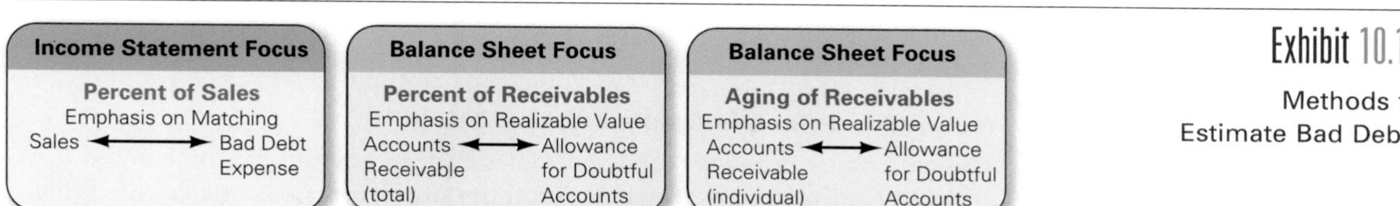

Exhibit 10.16
Methods to Estimate Bad Debts

The aging of receivables method is the most reliable of the three approaches because it is based on a more detailed examination of specific accounts.[3]

6. SnoBoard Company's end-of-period Dec. 31, 2001 balance in the Allowance for Doubtful Accounts is a credit of $440. It estimates from an aging of accounts receivable that $6,142 is uncollectible. Prepare SnoBoard's year-end adjusting entry for bad debts.

Answer—p. 530

High-tech Estimates

Technology can assist users in estimating bad debts. Both the sales-based and receivables-based methods of estimating bad debts are easily included in computerized information systems. Using current and past data in the system, estimates of bad debts are obtained with adjustments for different assumptions. Spreadsheet programs can also be used for estimating bad debts.

[3] In many cases, the aging analysis is supplemented with information about specific customers, allowing management to decide whether those accounts should be classified as uncollectible. This information is often supplied by the sales and credit department managers.

Direct Write-off Method

Apply the direct write-off method to account for uncollectible accounts receivable.

The **direct write-off method** of accounting for bad debts records the loss from an uncollectible account receivable at the time it is determined to be uncollectible. No attempt is made to estimate uncollectible accounts or bad debt expense. If TechCom determines on January 23 that it cannot collect $520 owed by an individual named Jack Kent, this loss is recognized using the direct write-off method in the following entry:

Jan. 23	Bad Debt Expense	520	
	Accounts Receivable—Jack Kent		520
	To write off uncollectible accounts under the direct write-off method.		

Companies must weigh at least two principles when considering use of the direct write-off method: (1) matching principle, and (2) materiality principle P. 333.

Matching Principle Applied to Bad Debts

The direct write-off method usually doesn't match revenues and expenses. This mismatch occurs because bad debt expense is not recorded until an account becomes uncollectible, which often does not occur during the same accounting period.

Materiality Principle Applied to Bad Debts

The *materiality principle* P. 333 states that an amount can be ignored if its effect on the financial statements is unimportant to users. The materiality principle permits the matching principle to be ignored and the direct write-off method to be used in accounting for expenses from bad debts when bad debt expenses are very small in relation to a company's other financial statement items, such as sales and net income. This requires that bad debt expense be unimportant for decisions made by users of the company's financial statements.

The allowance method has two advantages over the direct write-off method:

1. Bad debt expense is charged to the period when the related sales are recognized (matching principle), and
2. Accounts receivable are reported on the balance sheet at the estimated amount of cash to be collected (conservatism).

Answer—p. 529

Labour Union Chief

You are representing your employee union in contract negotiations with management. One week prior to contract discussions, management released financial statements showing zero growth in earnings. This is far below the 10% growth predicted earlier. In your review of the financial statements, you find the company increased its "allowance for uncollectible accounts" from 1.5% to 4.5% of accounts receivable. Apart from this change, earnings would show a 9% growth. Does this information impact your negotiations?

Mid-Chapter Demonstration Problem

Delcor Industries, a distributor of electrical supplies, had outstanding accounts receivable on December 31, 2002 of $450,000 aged as follows:

Delcor Industries Schedule of Accounts Receivable by Age December 31, 2002						
Customer's Name	**Total**	**Not Yet Due**	**1 to 30 Days Past Due**	**31 to 60 Days Past Due**	**61 to 90 Days Past Due**	**Over 90 Days Past Due**
Alton Group	$ 90,000		$ 90,000			
Filby's Electrical Service.....................	48,000			$22,000	$26,000	
GDP Servicing	162,000	$120,000	42,000			
Parker's Electrical	80,000	80,000				
Trenton Construction..	15,000					$15,000
Xeon Developments..	55,000	30,000	25,000			
Totals	$450,000	$230,000	$157,000	$22,000	$26,000	$15,000
Percent uncollectible		× 1%	× 4%	× 8%	× 25%	× 60%
Estimated uncollectible accounts						

During the year 2002, the company had sales of $3,720,000, of which $38,000 were cash sales. The Allowance for Doubtful Accounts had an unadjusted debit balance on December 31, 2002 of $3,050.

Required

Prepare the adjusting entry to estimate uncollectible accounts on December 31, 2002 under each of the following independent assumptions, and show the resulting balance sheet presentation for accounts receivable:

a. Bad debts are estimated to be 0.6% of credit sales.

b. Bad debts are estimated to be 4% of outstanding accounts receivable.

c. Bad debts are based on an aging analysis (part of the required information is provided in the schedule above).

SOLUTION TO Mid-Chapter Demonstration Problem

a. 0.6% × ($3,720,000 − $38,000 = $3,682,000 credit sales) = $22,092

Dec. 31	Bad Debt Expense	22,092	
	Allowance for Doubtful Accounts..........		22,092
	To record estimated bad debts.		

Current assets:		
Accounts receivable	$450,000	
Less: Allowance for doubtful accounts	19,042*	$430,958

or

Current assets:	
Accounts receivable (net of $19,042* estimated uncollectible accounts) ..	$430,958

**22,092 credit adjustment − 3,050 debit balance = 19,042.*

b. The required balance in the Allowance for Doubtful Accounts is $18,000 (= 4% × $450,000)

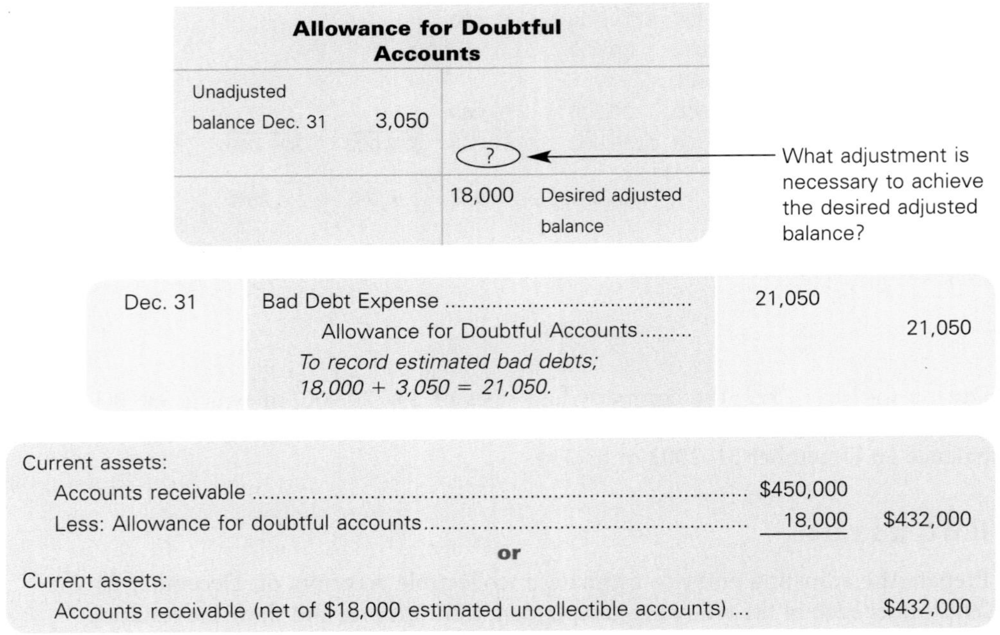

Allowance for Doubtful Accounts

Debit		Credit	
Unadjusted balance Dec. 31	3,050	?	
		18,000	Desired adjusted balance

Dec. 31	Bad Debt Expense	21,050	
	Allowance for Doubtful Accounts		21,050
	To record estimated bad debts; 18,000 + 3,050 = 21,050.		

Current assets:		
Accounts receivable	$450,000	
Less: Allowance for doubtful accounts	18,000	$432,000

or

Current assets:	
Accounts receivable (net of $18,000 estimated uncollectible accounts) ...	$432,000

c. First, calculate total estimated uncollectible accounts by completing the bottom of the aging schedule as follows:

Totals	$450,000	$230,000	$157,000	$22,000	$26,000	$15,000
Percent uncollectible		× 1%	× 4%	× 8%	× 25%	× 60%
Estimated uncollectible accounts	$25,840	$2,300	$6,280	$1,760	$6,500	$9,000

Allowance for Doubtful Accounts

Debit		Credit	
Unadjusted balance Dec. 31	3,050	?	
		25,840	Desired adjusted balance Dec. 31

What adjustment is necessary to achieve the desired adjusted balance?

Second, determine what adjustment is necessary to achieve the desired balance of $25,840 in the Allowance for Doubtful Accounts as follows:

Dec. 31	Bad Debt Expense	28,890	
	Allowance for Doubtful Accounts		28,890
	To record estimated bad debts; 25,840 + 3,050.		

Current assets:		
Accounts receivable	$450,000	
Less: Allowance for doubtful accounts	25,840	$424,160
or		
Current assets:		
Accounts receivable (net of $25,840 estimated uncollectible accounts)		$424,160

Notes Receivable

A **promissory note,** as illustrated in Exhibit 10.17, is a written promise to pay a specified amount of money either on demand or at a definite future date.

LO5 Describe a note receivable and compute its maturity date and interest.

Exhibit 10.17

Terminology Related to a Promissory Note

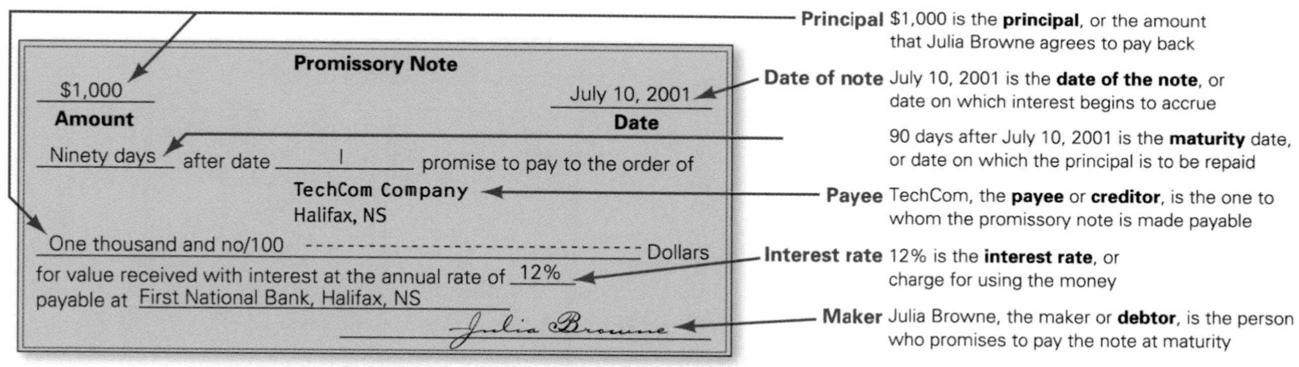

* Note: The ***due date*** of a note is also referred to as the **maturity date**. The **period** of this note is 90 days, the time from the *date of the note* to its *maturity date* or *due date*.

Computations for Notes

We need to know two computations related to notes:

1. How to determine the maturity date, and
2. How to calculate interest.

Maturity Date

A note dated on June 15 with a specified maturity date of June 20 is a five-day note (calculated as June 20 − June 15 = 5 days). A ten-day note dated June 15 would have a maturity date of June 25 (calculated as June 15 + 10 days = June 25). The promissory note in Exhibit 10.17 is a ninety-day note and the maturity date is computed as shown in Exhibit 10.18.

Exhibit 10.18

Maturity Date Computation

Days in July	31
Minus date of note	10
Days remaining in July	21
Add days in August	31
Add days in September	30
Days to equal 90 days or **Maturity Date, October 8**	8
Period of the note in days	90

The period of a note is sometimes expressed in months or years. When months are used, the note matures and is payable in the month of its maturity on the *same day of the month* as its original date. A three-month note dated July 10, for instance, is payable on October 10. The same analysis applies when years are used.

Interest Calculation

Interest is an annual rate unless otherwise stated. The formula for computing interest is shown in Exhibit 10.19.

Exhibit 10.19

Formula for Computing Interest

$$\text{Interest} = \begin{array}{c}\text{Principal}\\ \text{of the}\\ \text{note}\end{array} \times \begin{array}{c}\text{Annual}\\ \text{interest}\\ \text{rate}\end{array} \times \begin{array}{c}\text{Time}\\ \text{expressed}\\ \text{in years}\end{array} \quad \textbf{OR} \quad i = Prt$$

Interest on a $1,000, 12%, six-month note is computed as:

$$\$1{,}000 \times 12\% \times \frac{6}{12} = \underline{\underline{\$60}}$$

Using the promissory note in Exhibit 10.17 where the term of the note is in days, interest is computed as follows:

$$\text{Interest} = \text{Principal} \times \text{Rate} \times \frac{\text{Exact days}}{365}$$

OR

$$\$1{,}000 \times 12\% \times \frac{90}{365} = \underline{\underline{\$29.59}}$$

Unless otherwise instructed, you are to solve problems using the specific number of days and a 365-day year. Interest calculations should be rounded to the nearest whole cent.

Receipt of a Note

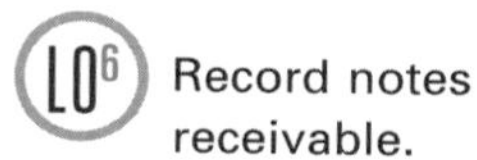

To illustrate recording the receipt of a note, we use the $1,000, 90-day, 12% promissory note in Exhibit 10.17. Assume that TechCom receives this note at the time of a product sale to Julia Browne (cost of sales $630). This transaction is recorded as:

July 10	Notes Receivable	1,000	
	Sales		1,000
	Sold merchandise in exchange for a 90-day, 12% note.		
10	Cost of Goods Sold	630	
	Merchandise Inventory		630
	To record cost of sales.		

A note receivable can also arise when a company accepts a note from an overdue customer as a way of granting a time extension on a past-due account receivable. When this occurs, a company may collect part of the past-due balance in cash. This partial payment forces a concession from the customer, reduces the customer's debt (and the seller's risk), and produces a note for a smaller amount. TechCom, for instance, agreed to accept $1,000 in cash and a $3,000, 60-day, 12% note from Jo Cook to settle her $4,000 past-due account. TechCom made the following entry to record receipt of this cash and note:

Dec. 16	Cash	1,000	
	Notes Receivable	3,000	
	Accounts Receivable—Jo Cook		4,000
	Received cash and note in settlement of account.		

End-of-Period Interest Adjustment

When notes receivable are outstanding at the end of an accounting period, accrued interest is computed and recorded. This recognizes both the interest revenue when it is earned and the added asset (interest receivable) owned by the note's holder. When TechCom's accounting period ends on December 31, $14.79 of interest accrues on the note dated December 16 ($3,000 × 12% × 15/365). The following adjusting entry records this revenue:

Dec. 31	Interest Receivable	14.79	
	Interest Revenue		14.79
	To record accrued interest.		

This adjusting entry means that interest revenue appears on the income statement of the period when it is earned. It also means that interest receivable appears on the balance sheet as a current asset.

Honouring a Note

When the note dated December 16 is paid on the maturity date of February 14, the maker of the note, Jo Cook, is **honouring** the note. TechCom's entry to record the cash receipt is:

Feb. 14	Cash	3,059.18	
	Interest Revenue		44.39
	Interest Receivable		14.79
	Notes Receivable		3,000.00
	Received payment of a note and its interest.		

Total interest earned on this note is \$59.18 (= \$3,000 × 12% × 60/365). On February 14, Interest Receivable is credited for \$14.79 to record the collection of the interest accrued on December 31. The interest revenue in this period is \$44.39 (= \$59.18 total interest less \$14.79 interest accrued on December 31) and reflects TechCom's revenue from holding the note from January 1 to February 14.

Dishonouring a Note

Sometimes the maker of a note does not pay the note at maturity; this is known as **dishonouring** the note. The act of dishonouring does not relieve the maker of the obligation to pay. The payee should use every legitimate means to collect. Assume Julia Browne did not pay the note dated July 10 when it matured on October 8. TechCom removes the amount of the note from the Notes Receivable account and charges it back to an account receivable from its maker as follows:

Oct. 8	Accounts Receivable—Julia Browne	1,029.59	
	Interest Revenue		29.59
	Notes Receivable		1,000.00
	To charge the account of Julia Browne for a dishonoured note including interest; 1,000 × 12% × 90/365.		

Charging a dishonoured note back to the account of its maker serves two purposes. First, it removes the amount of the note from the Notes Receivable account, leaving in the account only notes that have not matured, and records the dishonoured note in the maker's account. Second, and most important, if the maker of the dishonoured note applies for credit in the future, his or her account will show all past dealings, including the dishonoured note. Restoring the account also reminds the company to continue collection efforts for both principal and interest.

Answers—p. 530

7. Wiley purchases \$7,000 of merchandise from Stamford Company on December 16, 2002. Stamford accepts Wiley's \$7,000, 90-day, 12% note as payment. Stamford's annual accounting period ends on December 31 and it doesn't make reversing entries. Prepare entries for Stamford Company on December 16, 2002, and December 31, 2001.
8. Using the information in Flashback 7, prepare Stamford's March 16, 2003 entry if Wiley dishonours the note.

Summary

LO1 Describe accounts receivable and how they occur and are recorded. Accounts receivable refer to amounts due from customers for credit sales. The subsidiary ledger lists the amounts owed by individual customers. Credit sales arise from at least two sources: (1) sales on credit and (2) credit card sales. Sales on credit refers to a company granting credit directly to customers. Credit card sales involve use of a third party issuing a credit card.

LO2 Apply the allowance method to account for accounts receivable. Under the allowance method, bad debt expense is estimated at the end of the accounting period by debiting Bad Debt Expense and crediting the Allowance for Doubtful Accounts. When accounts are later identified as being uncollectible, they are written off by debiting the Allowance for Doubtful Accounts and crediting Accounts Receivable.

LO3 Estimate uncollectibles using methods based on sales and accounts receivable. Uncollectibles are estimated by focusing on either (a) the income statement relation between bad debt expense and credit sales or (b) the balance sheet relation between accounts receivable and the Allowance for Doubtful Accounts. The first approach emphasizes the matching principle for the income statement. The second approach can include either a simple percent relation with accounts receivable or the aging of accounts receivable. It emphasizes realizable value of accounts receivable for the balance sheet.

LO4 Apply the direct write-off method to account for uncollectible accounts receivable. The direct write-off method debits Bad Debt Expense and credits Accounts Receivable when accounts are determined to be uncollectible. This method is acceptable only when the amount of bad debt expense is immaterial.

LO5 Describe a note receivable and compute its maturity date and interest. A note receivable is a written promise to pay a specified amount of money either on demand or at a definite future date. The maturity date of a note is the day the note (principal and interest) must be repaid. Interest rates are typically stated in annual terms. When a note's time to maturity is more or less than one year, the amount of interest on a note is computed by expressing time as a fraction of one year and multiplying the note's principal by this fraction and the annual interest rate.

LO6 Record notes receivable. A note is recorded at its principal amount by debiting the Notes Receivable account. The credit amount is to the asset or service provided in return for the note. Interest is earned from holding a note. This interest is recorded for the time period it is held in the accounting period reported on. When a note is honoured, the payee debits the money received and credits both Notes Receivable and Interest Revenue. Dishonoured notes are credited to Notes Receivable and Interest Revenue and debited to Accounts Receivable.

GUIDANCE ANSWERS TO Judgement Call

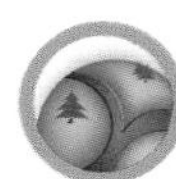

Entrepreneur

Your analysis of allowing credit card sales should estimate the benefits against the costs. The primary benefit is the potential to increase sales by attracting customers who prefer the convenience of credit cards. The primary cost is the fee charged by the credit card company for providing this service to your store. Your analysis should therefore estimate the expected increase in sales dollars from allowing credit card sales and then subtract (1) the normal costs and expenses, and (2) the credit card fees associated with this expected increase in sales dollars. If your analysis shows an increase in profit from allowing credit card sales, your store should probably allow them.

Labour Union Chief

Yes, this information is likely to impact your negotiations. The obvious question is why the company increased the allowance to such a large extent. This major increase in allowance means a substantial increase in bad debt expense *and* a decrease in earnings. Also, this change coming immediately prior to labour contract discussions raises concerns since it reduces the union's bargaining power for increased compensation. You want to ask management for supporting documentation justifying this increase. Also, you want data for two or three prior years, and similar data from competitors. These data should give you some sense of whether the change in the allowance for uncollectibles is justified or not.

GUIDANCE ANSWERS TO  Flashback

1. If cash is received as soon as copies of credit card sales receipts are deposited in the bank, the business debits Cash at the time of the sale. If the business does not receive payment until after it submits the receipts to the credit card company, it debits Accounts Receivable at the time of the sale.
2. Bad debt expense must be matched with the sales that gave rise to the accounts receivable. This requires that companies estimate bad debts before they learn which accounts are uncollectible.
3. Realizable value.
4. The estimated amount of bad debt expense cannot be credited to the Accounts Receivable account because the specific customer accounts that will prove uncollectible cannot be identified and removed from the subsidiary Accounts Receivable Ledger. If the controlling account were credited directly, its balance would not equal the sum of the subsidiary account balances.
5.

2001			
Jan. 10	Allowance for Doubtful Accounts........	300	
	Accounts Receivable—Cool Jam.....		300
	To record write-off of uncollectible account.		
Apr. 12	Accounts Receivable—Cool Jam.........	300	
	Allowance for Doubtful Accounts....		300
	To reinstate account previously written off.		
12	Cash..	300	
	Accounts Receivable—Cool Jam.....		300
	To record collection.		

6.

2001			
Dec. 31	Bad Debt Expense..............................	5,702	
	Allowance for Doubtful Accounts....		5,702
	To record estimated bad debts.		

7.

2002			
Dec. 16	Notes Receivable	7,000.00	
	Sales..		7,000.00
	To record 90-day, 12% note.		
31	Interest Receivable........................	34.52	
	Interest Revenue.....................		34.52
	To record accrued interest; $7,000 × 12% × 15/365.		

8.

2003			
Mar. 16	Accounts Receivable—Willey........	7,207.12	
	Interest Revenue		172.60
	Interest Receivable		34.52
	Notes Receivable		7000.00
	To record dishonour of a bad note; $7,000 × 12% × 90/365 = $207.12.		

Demonstration Problem

Garden Company had a number of transactions involving receivables during the year 2001. Each of them follows.

Required

Prepare journal entries to record these independent transactions on the books of Garden Company. Garden Company's year-end is December 31.

a. On November 15, 2001, Garden Company agreed to accept $500 in cash and a $2,000, 90-day, 8% note from Argo Company to settle its $2,500 past-due account. Determine the maturity date and record the entry on November 15, December 31, and on the date of maturity.

b. Garden Company held an $1,800, 6%, 45-day note of Altamira Industries. At maturity, December 15, Altamira dishonoured the note. Record the dishonouring of the Note Receivable.

c. On December 15, 2001, a customer used a credit card to pay Garden Company for services performed of $14,800. The receipt from the December 15 credit card transaction was mailed to the credit card company at the end of the following week, on December 21, along with additional receipts; total receipts mailed were $118,400. A cheque was received in the mail from the credit card company on December 28. The credit card company charges Garden Company 1.5% for its services. Prepare the entries for December 15, 21, and 28.

d. On December 20, 2001, Garden Company performed $12,000 of services. The customer paid using a credit card. The credit card company deposits the cash into Garden Company's account immediately and withholds a 2% fee. Prepare the entry on December 20.

e. Elko Purchasing Consultants estimates bad debts to be 3.5% of net credit sales. During 2001, total sales were $6,200,000, of which 35% were for cash. Sales returns and allowances for the year were $128,000, all related to credit sales. Accounts receivable in the amount of $130,000 were identified as uncollectible and written off during 2001. Calculate the adjusted balance in the allowance for doubtful accounts at December 31, 2001, assuming a balance on January 1, 2001 of $160,000.

Planning the Solution

- Examine each item to determine which accounts are affected and perform the required calculations.
- Prepare required journal entries.

SOLUTION TO Demonstration Problem

a.

Days in November	30
Minus date of note	15
Days remaining in November	15
Add days in December	31
	46
Add days in January	31
Days to equal 90 days or **Maturity date, February 13**	13
Period of the note in days	90

Date	Account	Debit	Credit
2001			
Nov. 15	Cash	500.00	
	Notes Receivable	2,000.00	
	Accounts Receivable—Argo Company		2,500.00
	Received cash and note in settlement of account.		
Dec. 31	Interest Receivable	20.16	
	Interest Revenue		20.16
	To record accrued interest; $2,000 × 46/365 × 8% = $20.16.		
2002			
Feb. 13	Cash	2,039.45	
	Interest Receivable		20.16
	Interest Revenue		19.29
	Notes Receivable		2,000.00
	Collected note with interest; $2,000 × 90/365 × 8% = $39.45.		

b.

Date	Account	Debit	Credit
2001			
Dec. 15	Accounts Receivable—Altamira	1,813.32	
	Interest Revenue		13.32
	Note Receivable		1,800.00
	To charge the account of Altamira for a dishonoured note including interest; $1,800 × 6% × 45/365 = $13.32.		

c.

Date	Account	Debit	Credit
2001			
Dec 15	Accounts Receivable—Credit Card Company	14,800.00	
	Service Revenue		14,800.00
	To record revenues earned.		
21	No entry		
28	Cash	116,624.00	
	Credit Card Expense	1,776.00	
	Accounts Receivable—Credit Card Company		118,400.00
	To record collection from Credit Card Company.		

d.

Date	Account	Debit	Credit
2001			
Dec. 20	Cash	11,760.00	
	Credit Card Expense	240.00	
	Service Revenue		12,000.00
	To record credit card sale, less 2% fee.		

e.

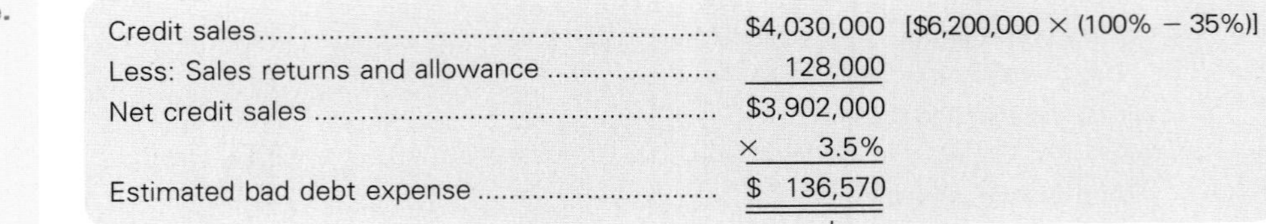

Credit sales	$4,030,000	[$6,200,000 × (100% − 35%)]
Less: Sales returns and allowance	128,000	
Net credit sales	$3,902,000	
	× 3.5%	
Estimated bad debt expense	$ 136,570	

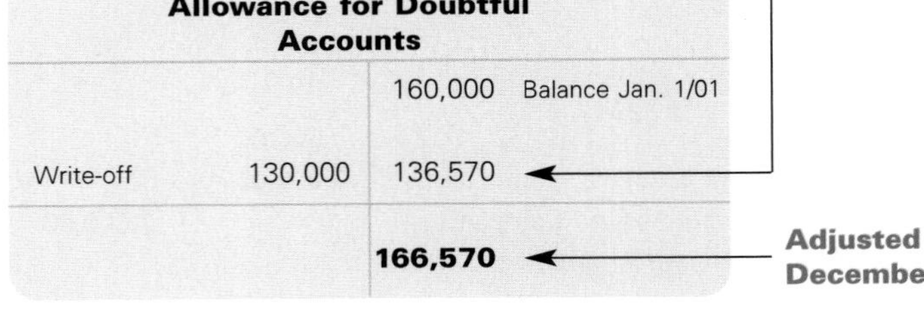

Allowance for Doubtful Accounts

	Debit	Credit	
		160,000	Balance Jan. 1/01
Write-off	130,000	136,570	
		166,570	**Adjusted balance December 31/01**

APPENDIX

Converting Receivables to Cash Before Maturity

Explain how receivables can be converted to cash before maturity.

Sometimes companies convert receivables to cash before they are due. Reasons for this include the need for cash or a desire not to be involved in collection activities. Converting receivables is usually done either (1) by selling them or (2) by using them as security for a loan. A recent survey showed that about 20% of large companies obtain cash from either the sale of receivables or the pledging of receivables as security. In some industries such as textiles and furniture, this is common practice. Recently, this practice has grown to other industries, especially the apparel industry. Also, many small companies use sales of receivables as an immediate source of cash. This is especially the case for those selling to companies and government agencies that often delay payment.

Selling Accounts Receivable

A company can sell its accounts receivable to a finance company or bank. The buyer, called a **factor**, charges the seller a *factoring fee* and then collects the receivables as they come due. By incurring a factoring fee, the seller receives cash earlier and passes the risk of bad debts to the factor. The seller also avoids costs of billing and accounting for the receivables.

If TechCom, for instance, sells $20,000 of its accounts receivable and is charged a 2% factoring fee, it records this sale as:

Aug. 15	Cash	19,600	
	Factoring Fee Expense	400	
	Accounts Receivable		20,000
	Sold accounts receivable for cash, less a 2% factoring fee.		

Pledging Accounts Receivable as Loan Security

A company can also raise cash by borrowing money and then *pledging* its accounts receivable as security for the loan. Pledging receivables does not transfer the risk of bad debts to the lender. The borrower retains ownership of the receivables. But if the borrower defaults on the loan, the lender has a right to be paid from cash receipts as the accounts receivable are collected. When TechCom borrowed $35,000 and pledged its receivables as security, it recorded this transaction as:

Aug. 20	Cash	35,000	
	Notes Payable		35,000
	Borrowed money with the note secured by pledging accounts receivable.		

Because pledged receivables are committed as security for a specific loan, the borrower's financial statements should disclose the pledging of accounts receivable. TechCom, for instance, includes the following note with its financial statements regarding its pledged receivables: "Accounts receivable in the amount of $40,000 are pledged as security for a $35,000 note payable to First National Bank."

Discounting Notes Receivable

Notes receivable can be converted to cash before they mature. Companies who may need cash sooner to meet their obligations can discount notes receivable at a financial institution or bank. TechCom, for instance, discounted a $3,000, 90-day, 10% note receivable at First National Bank. TechCom held the note for 50 of the 90 days before discounting it. The bank applied a 12% rate in discounting the note. TechCom received proceeds of $3,033.55 from the bank computed as:

Principal of Note	$3,000.00
+ Interest from Note ($3000 × 10% × 90/365)	73.97
= Maturity Value	$3,073.97
− Bank Discount ($3,073.97 × 12% × 40/365)	40.42
= Proceeds	$3,033.55

TechCom recorded the discounting of this note as:

Aug. 25	Cash	3,033.55	
	Interest Revenue		33.55
	Notes Receivable		3,000.00
	Discounted a note receivable.		

Computer programs are used in practice to compute bank proceeds easily. Notes receivable are discounted without recourse or with recourse. When a note is discounted *without recourse*, the bank assumes the risk of a bad debt loss and the original payee does not have a *contingent liability*. A **contingent liability** is an obligation to make a future payment if, and only if, an uncertain future event occurs. A note discounted without recourse is like an outright sale of an asset. If a note is discounted *with recourse* and the original maker of the note fails to pay the bank when it matures, the original payee of the note must pay for it. This means a company discounting a note with recourse has a contingent liability until the bank is paid. A company should disclose contingent liabilities in notes to its financial statements. TechCom included the following note: "The Company is contingently liable for a $3,000 note receivable discounted with recourse."

Full Disclosure

The disclosure of contingent liabilities in notes is consistent with the full-disclosure principle P. 341. Contingent liabilities are discussed in more detail in Chapter 13.

Answer—p. 537

9. A company needs cash and has substantial accounts receivable. What alternatives are available for getting cash from its accounts receivable prior to receiving payments from credit customers? Show the entry made for each alternative.

Using the Information

10B

APPENDIX

Accounts Receivable Turnover and Days' Sales Uncollected

Compute accounts receivable turnover and days' sales uncollected to analyze liquidity.

For a company selling on credit, we want to assess both the *quality* and *liquidity* of its accounts receivable. Quality of receivables refers to the likelihood of collection without loss. Experience shows that the longer receivables are outstanding beyond their due date, the lower the likelihood of collection. Liquidity of receivables refers to the speed of collection.

Accounts Receivable Turnover

The **accounts receivable turnover** is a measure of both the quality and liquidity of accounts receivable. It indicates how often, on average, receivables are received and collected during the period. Accounts receivable turnover also helps us evaluate how well management is doing in granting credit to customers in a desire to increase sales revenues. A high turnover in comparison with competitors suggests that management should consider using more liberal credit terms to increase sales. A low turnover suggests management should consider more strict credit terms and more aggressive collection efforts to avoid having its resources tied up in accounts receivable.

The formula for this ratio is shown in Exhibit 10B.1

Exhibit 10B.1

Accounts Receivable Turnover Formula

$$\text{Accounts receivable turnover} = \frac{\text{Net sales}}{\text{Average accounts receivable}}$$

Although the numerator of this ratio is more precise if credit sales are used, total net sales is usually used by external users because information about credit sales is typically not reported. The denominator includes accounts receivable and all short-term receivables (including notes receivable) from customers. Average accounts receivable is calculated by adding the balance at the beginning and end of the period and dividing the sum by two. Some users prefer using gross accounts receivable, before subtracting the allowance for doubtful accounts, but many balance sheets report only the net amount of accounts receivable.

Days' Sales Uncollected

We use the number of **days' sales uncollected** (also known as **days' sales in receivables**) to estimate how much time is likely to pass before we receive cash from credit sales equal to the current amount of accounts receivable. The formula for this ratio is shown in Exhibit 10B.2.

Exhibit 10B.2

Days' Sales Uncollected Formula

$$\text{Days' sales uncollected} = \frac{\text{Accounts receivable}}{\text{Net sales}} \times 365$$

Days' sales uncollected is more meaningful if we know the company's credit terms. A rough guideline is that days' sales uncollected should not exceed one and one-third times the days in its: (1) credit period, if discounts are not offered; (2) discount period, if discounts are offered.

Analysis

To perform an analysis using the receivable ratios, we select data from the 1999 annual reports of two airlines, Air Canada and WestJet as shown in Exhibit 10B.3.

Exhibit 10B.3

Comparison of Accounts Receivable Turnover and Days' Sales Uncollected for Air Canada and WestJet

		($ thousands) 1999	1998
Air Canada	Accounts receivable	$ 443,000	$ 405,000
	Net sales	6,509,000	5,932,000
WestJet	Accounts receivable	$ 5,168	$ 5,240
	Net sales	203,574	125,437

Results for 1999:

	Accounts Receivable Turnover	Days' Sales Uncollected
Air Canada	$\frac{\$6,509,000}{(\$443,000 + \$405,000)/2} = 15.35$ times	$\frac{\$443,000}{\$6,509,000} \times 365 = 24.84$ days
WestJet	$\frac{\$203,574}{(\$5,168 + \$5,240)/2} = 39.12$ times	$\frac{\$5,168}{\$203,574} \times 365 = 9.27$ days

WestJet's accounts receivable turnover of 39.12 times tells us that in 1999 it collected receivables more than twice as fast as Air Canada. The days' sales uncollected ratio indicates that Air Canada will take 24.84 days to collect the December 31, 1999 balance in accounts receivable as compared to WestJet's 9.27 days to collect its receivables balance on the same date.

Summary of Appendix 10A and 10B

LO7 **Explain how receivables can be converted to cash before maturity.** There are three usual means to convert receivables to cash before maturity. First, a company can sell accounts receivable to a factor, who charges a factoring fee. Second, a company can borrow money by signing a note payable that is secured by pledging the accounts receivable. Third, notes receivable can be discounted at a bank, with or without recourse. The full-disclosure principle requires companies to disclose the amount of receivables pledged and the contingent liability for notes discounted with recourse.

LO8 **Compute accounts receivable turnover and days' sales uncollected and use them to analyze liquidity.** Accounts receivable turnover and days' sales uncollected are measures of both the quality and liquidity of accounts receivable. The accounts receivable turnover measure indicates how often, on average, receivables are received and collected during the period and is computed as sales divided by average accounts receivable for the period. Days' sales uncollected is calculated as (accounts receivable divided by net sales) × 365 and is used to estimate how much time is likely to pass before cash receipts from net sales are received equal to the current amount of accounts receivable. Both ratios are compared to those for other companies in the same industry, and with prior years' estimates.

GUIDANCE ANSWER TO  Flashback

9. Alternatives are:

1. Selling their accounts receivable to a factor, and

2. Pledging accounts receivable as loan security.

The entries to record these transactions take the following form:

(1)	Cash	#	
	Factoring Fee Expense	#	
	Accounts Receivable		#
	Sold accounts receivable for cash.		
(2)	Cash	#	
	Notes Payable		#
	Borrowed money with the note secured by pledging accounts receivable.		

Glossary

Accounts receivable Amounts due from customers for credit sales. Also referred to as *trade receivables.* (p. 510)

Accounts receivable method A method of estimating bad debts using balance sheet relations. Also known as *Balance Sheet method.* (p. 518)

Accounts receivable turnover A measure of both the quality and liquidity of accounts receivable; it indicates how often, on average, receivables are received and collected during the period; computed by dividing credit sales (or net sales) by the average accounts receivable balance. (p. 535)

Aging of accounts receivable method A process of classifying accounts receivable in terms of how long they have been outstanding for the purpose of estimating the amount of uncollectible accounts. (p. 520)

Allowance for Doubtful Accounts A contra asset account with a balance equal to the estimated amount of accounts receivable that will be uncollectible; also called the *Allowance for Uncollectible Accounts.* (p. 515)

Allowance method of accounting for bad debts An accounting procedure that (1) estimates and reports bad debt expense from credit sales during the period of the sales, and (2) reports accounts receivable as the amount of cash proceeds that is expected from their collection (their estimated realizable value). (p. 514)

Bad debts The accounts of customers who do not pay what they have promised to pay; the amount is an expense of selling on credit; also called *uncollectible accounts.* (p. 513)

Balance sheet method See *Accounts receivable method.* (p. 518)

Contingent liability An obligation to make a future payment if, and only if, an uncertain future event actually occurs. (p. 534)

Creditor See *payee.* (p. 525)

Date of a note The date on which interest begins to accrue. (p. 525)

Days' sales uncollected A measure of the liquidity of receivables computed by taking the current balance of receivables and dividing by the credit (or net) sales over the year just completed, and then multiplying by 365 (the number of days in a year); also called *days' sales in receivables.* (p. 535)

Days' sales in receivables See *Days sales uncollected.* (p. 535)

Debtor See *maker of a note.* (p. 525)

Direct write-off method A method of accounting for bad debts that records the loss from an uncollectible account receivable at the time it is determined to be uncollectible; no attempt is made to estimate uncollectible accounts or bad debt expense. (p. 522)

Dishonouring a note When a note's maker is unable or refuses to pay at maturity. (p. 528)

Due date of a note See *maturity date.* (p. 525)

Factor The buyer of accounts receivable. (p. 533)

Honouring a Note Receivable When the maker of the note pays the note in full at maturity. (p. 528)

Income statement method See *percent of sales method.* (p. 518)

Interest The charge for using (not paying) money until a later date. (p. 525)

Maker of a note One who signs a note and promises to pay it at maturity. (p. 526)

Maturity date of a note The date on which a note and any interest are due and payable. (p. 525)

Payee of a note The one to whom a promissory note is made payable. (p. 525)

Percent of sales method Uses income statement relations to estimate bad debits. Also known as the *income statement method.* (p. 518)

Percent of accounts receivable method A method of estimating bad debts which assumes a percent of outstanding receivables is uncollectible. (p. 526)

Period of a note The time from the date of the note top its maturity date or due date. (p. 525)

Principal of a note The amount that the signer of a promissory note agrees to pay back when it matures, not including the interest. (p. 525)

Promissory note A written promise to pay a specified amount of money either on demand or at a definite future date. (p. 525)

Realizable value The expected proceeds from converting assets into cash. (p. 515)

Trade receivables See *accounts receivable.* (p. 510)

Uncollectible accounts See *bad debts.* (p. 513)

Questions

1. How do businesses benefit from allowing their customers to use credit cards?
2. Explain why writing off a bad debt against the Allowance Account does not reduce the estimated realizable value of a company's accounts receivable.
3. Why does the Bad Debt Expense account usually not have the same adjusted balance as the Allowance for Doubtful Accounts?
4. Why does the direct write-off method of accounting for bad debts commonly fail to match revenues and expenses?
5. What is the essence of the accounting principle of materiality?
6. Why might a business prefer a note receivable to an account receivable?
*7. What does it mean to sell a receivable without recourse?
8. Review the consolidated balance sheet for ClubLink in Appendix I. What is the amount of Loans Receivable?

An asterisk (*) identifies assignment material using Appendix 10A or Appendix 10B.

Quick Study

QS 10-1
Credit card transactions
LO1

Journalize the following transactions:

a. Sold $10,000 (costing $4,000) in merchandise on MasterCard credit cards, which are bank credit cards. The sales receipts were deposited in our business account. MasterCard charges us a 5% fee.

b. Sold $3,000 (costing $1,100) on miscellaneous non-bank credit cards. Cash will be received within 10 days and a 4% fee will be charged.

QS 10-2
Entries for sale on credit and subsequent collection
LO1

Journalize the following transaction for Kimmel Company:

a. On March 1, Kimmel Company sold $40,000 of merchandise costing $32,000 on credit terms of n/30 to JP Holdings.

b. On March 27, JP Holdings paid its account in full.

QS 10-3
Write-off of uncollectible account
LO2

On February 16, 2002, a detailed review of the subsidiary Accounts Receivable Ledger determined that the account of Jim Heatherington in the amount of $17,000 was uncollectible. Prepare the appropriate entry on February 16.

QS 10-4
Recovery of previously written-off receivable
LO2

Refer to the information in QS 10-3. On May 1, J. Heatherington paid $4,000 of the amount previously written off. He has confirmed it to be highly unlikely that he will make any additional payments against his written-off account. Prepare the entry for the recovery.

QS 10-5
Accounts receivable allowance method of accounting for bad debts
LO2

Duncan Company's year-end trial balance shows accounts receivable of $89,000, allowance for doubtful accounts of $500 (credit), and sales of $270,000. Uncollectibles are estimated to be 1.5% of outstanding accounts receivable.

a. Prepare the December 31 year-end adjustment.

b. What amount would have been used in the year-end adjustment if the allowance account had had a year-end debit balance of $200?

c. Assume the same facts, except that Duncan estimates uncollectibles as 1% of sales. What amount would be used in the adjustment?

QS 10-6
Adjusting entry to estimate bad debts — percent of receivables
LO3

Foster Corporation uses the allowance method to account for uncollectible accounts receivable. At year-end, December 31, the unadjusted balance in the Allowance for Doubtful Accounts was $450 credit. Based on past experience, it was estimated that 2.5% of the Accounts Receivable balance of $640,000 was uncollectible. Record the adjusting entry to estimate bad debts at December 31.

QS 10-7
Adjusting entry to estimate bad debts — percent of sales
LO3

Lexton Company uses the allowance method to account for uncollectible accounts receivable. At year-end, October 31, it was estimated that 0.6% of net credit sales were uncollectible based on past experience. Net sales were $690,000, of which 2/3 were on credit. Record the entry at year-end to estimate uncollectible receivables.

QS 10-8
Notes receivable
LO6

On August 2, 2001, SLM, Inc. received a $5,500, 90-day, 12% note from customer Will Carr as payment on his account. Prepare the August 2 and maturity date entries, assuming the note is honoured by Carr.

QS 10-9
Notes receivable
LO6

Seaver Company's December 31 year-end trial balance shows an $8,000 balance in Notes Receivable. This balance is from one note dated December 1, with a period of 45 days and 9% interest. Prepare the December 31 and maturity date entries, assuming the note is honoured.

QS 10-10
Dishonouring of a note receivable
LO6

Ajax Company had a $17,000, 7%, 30-day note of Beatrice Inc. At maturity, April 4, Beatrice dishonoured the note. Record the entry on April 4.

QS 10-11
Sale of accounts receivable
LO7

On June 4, Maltex sold $108,000 of its accounts receivable to a collection agency, which charges a 2.5% factoring fee. Record the entry on June 4.

***QS 10-12**
Discounting a note receivable
LO7

Tallcrest discounted a $50,000, 45-day, 8% note receivable on August 10 at the local bank, which applies an 11% discount rate. Tallcrest had held the note for 25 days before discounting it. Record the entry on August 10.

***QS 10-13**
Accounts receivable turnover and days' sales uncollected
LO8

Mega Company and Holton Company are similar firms that operate within the same industry. The following information is available:

		Mega Company			Holton Company		
	Industry Average	**2002**	**2001**	**2000**	**2002**	**2001**	**2000**
Accounts receivable turnover	12	14.9	12.2	11.5	10.6	13.1	13.5
Days' sales uncollected	30	24.5	29.9	31.7	34.4	27.9	27.1

a. Which company has the *most favourable* accounts receivable turnover in 2002?
b. Which company has the *greatest* number of days in uncollected accounts in 2002? Is this generally favourable or unfavourable?
c. Which company is showing an *unfavourable* trend in terms of managing accounts receivable?

An asterisk (*) identifies assignment material based on Appendix 10A or Appendix 10B.

Exercises

Exercise 10-1
Credit card transactions
LO1

Aston Corporation allows customers to use two credit cards in charging purchases. With the OmniCard, Aston receives an immediate credit when it deposits sales receipts in its chequing account. OmniCard assesses a 4% service charge for credit card sales. The second credit card that Aston accepts is Colonial Bank Card. Aston sends its accumulated receipts to Colonial Bank on a weekly basis and is paid by Colonial approximately 10 days later. Colonial Bank charges 2% of sales for using its card. Prepare entries in journal form to record the following credit card transactions of Aston Corporation (assume a perpetual inventory system):

Apr. 6	Sold merchandise costing $5,300 for $9,200, accepting the customers' OmniCards. At the end of the day, the OmniCard receipts were deposited in Aston's account at the bank.
10	Sold merchandise to a customer for $310 (cost: $160) and accepted the customer's Colonial Bank Card.
17	Mailed $5,480 of credit card receipts to Colonial Bank, requesting payment.
28	Received Colonial Bank's cheque for the April 17 billing, less the normal service charge.

Exercise 10-2
Subsidiary ledger accounts
LO1

Jenkins Inc. recorded the following transactions during November 2001:

Nov. 3	Accounts Receivable—ABC Shop	4,417	
	Sales*		4,417
8	Accounts Receivable—Colt Enterprises	1,250	
	Sales*		1,250
11	Accounts Receivable—Red McKenzie	733	
	Sales*		733
19	Sales Returns and Allowances*	189	
	Accounts Receivable—Red McKenzie		189
28	Accounts Receivable—ABC Shop	2,606	
	Sales*		2,606

**Cost of sales (or COGS) has been ignored for the purpose of maintaining focus on Accounts Receivable.*

Required

1. Open a General Ledger having T-accounts for Accounts Receivable, Sales, and Sales Returns and Allowances. Also, open a subsidiary Accounts Receivable Ledger having a T-account for each customer. Post the preceding entries to the General Ledger accounts and the customer accounts.
2. List the balances of the accounts in the subsidiary ledger, total the balances, and compare the total with the balance of the Accounts Receivable controlling account.

Exercise 10-3
Write-off and subsequent partial recovery
LO2

Foster Corporation uses the allowance method to account for uncollectibles. On October 31, it wrote off a $1,000 account of a customer, Gwen Rowe. On December 9, it received a $200 payment from Rowe.

a. Make the appropriate entry or entries for October 31.
b. Make the appropriate entry or entries for December 9.

Exercise 10-4

Allowance for doubtful accounts

LO[2,3]

At the end of its annual accounting period, Bali Company estimated its bad debts as one-half of 1% of its $875,000 of credit sales made during the year. On December 31, Bali made an addition to its Allowance for Doubtful Accounts equal to that amount. On the following February 1, management decided that the $420 account of Catherine Hicks was uncollectible and wrote it off as a bad debt. Four months later, on June 5, Hicks unexpectedly paid the amount previously written off. Give the journal entries required to record these events.

Exercise 10-5

Bad debt expense

LO[2,3]

Check figure:
b. Bad Debt Expense = $3,452

At the end of each year, Deutch Supply Co. uses the simplified balance sheet approach to estimate bad debts. On December 31, 2001, it has outstanding accounts receivable of $53,000 and estimates that 4% will be uncollectible.

Required

a. Give the entry to record bad debt expense for 2001 under the assumption that the Allowance for Doubtful Accounts has a $915 credit balance before the adjustment.

b. Give the entry under the assumption that the Allowance for Doubtful Accounts has a $1,332 debit balance before the adjustment.

Exercise 10-6

Analyzing receivables and allowance for doubtful accounts

LO[1,2,3]

Acounts Receivable

	Debit	Credit
Dec. 31/01 Balance	178,000	
	690,000	712,000
		5,800
	340	340
Dec. 31/02 Balance	150,200	

Allowance for Doubtful Accounts

Debit	Credit	
	6,000	Dec. 31/01 Balance
	340	
5,800	5,100	
	5,640	Dec. 31/02 Balance

Required

Analyzing the information presented in the T-accounts above, identify the dollar value related to each of the following:

a. Credit sales during the period.

b. Collection of credit sales made during the period.

c. Write-off of uncollectible account.

d. Recovery of account previously written off.

e. Adjusting entry to estimate bad debts.

Exercise 10-7

Analyzing receivables and allowance for doubtful accounts

LO[1,2,3]

Reproduced below from Farthington Supply's accounting records are the subsidiary Accounts Receivable Ledger along with selected General Ledger accounts.

General Ledger

Accounts Receivable

	Debit	Credit	
Dec. 31/02 Balance	159,000		
		7,000	Jan. 4/03
Credit sales in 2003	????	????	Collections in 2003
		14,000	July 15/03
Dec. 31/03 Balance	????		

Allowance for Doubtful Accounts

	Debit	Credit	
		350	Dec. 31/02 Balance
July 15/03	14,000		
		????	Dec. 31/03
		????	Dec. 31/03 Balance

Subsidiary Accounts Receivable Ledger

JenStar Company				*Indigo Developments*			
Dec. 31/02 Balance	48,000			Dec. 31/02 Balance	-0-		
		48,000	Jan. 20/03	Mar. 1/03	17,000	17,000	Mar. 20/03
Nov. 15/03	????			Nov. 28/03	39,000		
				Dec. 2/03	4,000		
Dec. 31/03 Balance	104,000			Dec. 31/03 Balance	43,000		

Lomas Industries				*PDQ Servicing*			
Dec. 31/02 Balance	????			Dec. 31/02 Balance	14,000		
		7,000	Jan. 4/03				
		????	Jan. 7/03				
Apr. 21/03	52,000	52,000	May 5/03			14,000	July 15/03
Dec. 7/03	21,000						
Dec. 31/03 Balance	21,000			Dec. 31/03 Balance	-0-		

During the year 2003, there were no recoveries of accounts previously written off. Only one account, that of PDQ Servicing, was identified as being uncollectible on July 15, 2003. On January 4, 2003, Farthington issued a $7,000 credit memo to Lomas Industries regarding damaged goods returned.

Required

Analyzing the accounts, determine the following amounts:

a. The December 31, 2002 balance in Lomas Industries' account.
b. The January 7, 2003 collection from Lomas Industries.
c. The December 31, 2003 balance in the Accounts Receivable controlling account.
d. The November 15, 2003 transaction in JenStar Company's account.
e. Collections during 2003.
f. Credit sales during 2003.
g. Adjusting entry on December 31, 2003 to estimate uncollectible accounts based on a rate of 2% of outstanding receivables.
h. The December 31, 2003 balance in the Allowance for Doubtful Accounts.
i. Show how accounts receivable should appear on the balance sheet on December 31, 2003.

Check figure:
g. Bad Debt Expense = $17,010

Exercise 10-8
Dishonouring a note
LO6

Prepare journal entries to record these transactions:

Mar.	21	Accepted a $3,100, six-month, 10% note dated today from Bradley Brooks in granting a time extension on his past-due account.
Sept.	21	Brooks dishonoured his note when presented for payment.
Dec.	31	After exhausting all legal means of collection, wrote off Brooks' account against the Allowance for Doubtful Accounts.

Exercise 10-9
Honouring a note
LO6

Prepare journal entries to record these transactions:

Oct.	31	Accepted a $5,000, six-month, 8% note dated today from Leann Grimes in granting a time extension on her past-due account.
Dec.	31	Adjusted the books for the interest due on the Grimes note.
Apr.	30	Grimes honoured her note when presented for payment.

Exercise 10-10
Accounting for notes receivable transactions
LO[6]

Following are transactions of The Barnett Company:

2001		
Dec.	16	Accepted an $8,600, 60-day, 7% note dated this day in granting Carmel Karuthers a time extension on her past-due account.
	31	Made an adjusting entry to record the accrued interest on the Karuthers note.
	31	Closed the Interest Revenue account.
2002		
Feb.	14	Received Karuthers' payment for the principal and interest on the note dated December 16.
Mar.	2	Accepted a $4,000, 8%, 90-day note dated this day in granting a time extension on the past-due account of ATW Company.
	17	Accepted a $1,600, 30-day, 9% note dated this day in granting Leroy Johnson a time extension on his past-due account.
May	31	Received ATW's payment for the principal and interest on the note dated March 2.

Required
Prepare journal entries to record The Barnett Company's transactions.

***Exercise 10-11**
Selling and pledging accounts receivable
LO[7]

On July 31, Konrad International had $125,900 of accounts receivable. Prepare journal entries to record the following August transactions. Also, prepare any footnotes to the August 31 financial statements that should be reported as a result of these transactions.

2001		
Aug.	2	Sold merchandise to customers on credit, $6,295. Cost of sales was $3,150.
	7	Sold $18,770 of accounts receivable to Fidelity Bank. Fidelity charges a 1.5% fee.
	15	Received payments from customers, $3,436.
	25	Borrowed $10,000 from Fidelity Bank, pledging $14,000 of accounts receivable as security for the loan.

***Exercise 10-12**
Discounting notes receivable
LO[7]

Check figure:
Feb. 19: Interest Revenue = $243.79

Prepare journal entries to record the following transactions by Ericton Industries:

2001		
Jan.	20	Accepted an $85,000, 90-day, 9% note dated this day in granting a time extension on the past due account of Steve Soetart.
Feb.	19	Discounted the Steve Soetart note at the bank at 11.5%.

An asterisk (*) identifies assignment material based on Appendix 10A or Appendix 10B.

***Exercise 10-13**
Accounts receivable turnover and days' sales uncollected
LO8

The following information was taken from the December 31, 2002 annual report of WestCon Developments.

	($ millions) 2002	2001
Net sales	$7,280	$5,410
Accounts receivable	598	486

	Industry Average
Accounts receivable turnover	16.2
Days' sales uncollected	21.0

Required

1. Calculate the accounts receivable turnover and days' sales uncollected for the year 2002.
2. Compare your calculations in (1) to the industry average and comment on WestCon's relative performance as F (Favourable) or U (Unfavourable).

Problems

Problem 10-1A
Credit sales and credit card sales
LO1

Accessories Unlimited allows a few customers to make purchases on credit. Other customers may use either of two credit cards.

- Express Bank deducts a 3% service charge for sales on its credit card but credits the chequing accounts of its commercial customers immediately when credit card receipts are deposited. Accessories Unlimited deposits the Express Bank credit card receipts at the close of each business day.
- When customers use UniCharge credit cards, Accessories Unlimited accumulates the receipts for several days before submitting them to UniCharge for payment. UniCharge deducts a 2% service charge and usually pays within one week of being billed.

Accessories Unlimited completed the following transactions during the month of May (assume a perpetual inventory system):

May 4	Sold merchandise costing $214 on credit to Anne Bismarck for $565. *The terms of all credit sales are 2/15, n/30.*
5	Sold merchandise costing $2,250 for $5,934 to customers who used their Express Bank credit cards. Sold merchandise costing $1,800 for $4,876 to customers who used their UniCharge cards.
8	Sold merchandise costing $1,220 for $3,213 to customers who used their UniCharge credit cards.
10	The UniCharge card receipts accumulated since May 5 were submitted to the credit card company for payment.
17	Received the amount due from UniCharge.
18	Received Bismarck's cheque paying for the purchase of May 4.

Required

Prepare journal entries to record the preceding transactions and events.

An asterisk (*) identifies assignment material based on Appendix 10A or Appendix 10B.

Problem 10-2A
Estimating bad debt expense

LO2,3

On December 31, 2001, SysComm Corporation's records showed the following results for the year:

Cash sales	$1,803,750
Credit sales	3,534,000

In addition, the unadjusted trial balance included the following items:

Accounts receivable	$1,070,100 debit
Allowance for doubtful accounts	15,750 debit

Check figure:
1c. Bad Debt Expense = $69,255

Required

1. Prepare the adjusting entry needed in SysComm's books to recognize bad debts under each of the following independent assumptions:
   a. Bad debts are estimated to be 2% of credit sales.
   b. Bad debts are estimated to be 1% of total sales.
   c. An analysis suggests that 5% of outstanding accounts receivable on December 31, 2001 will become uncollectible.
2. Show how Accounts Receivable and the Allowance for Doubtful Accounts would appear on the December 31, 2001 balance sheet given the facts in requirement 1(a).
3. Show how Accounts Receivable and the Allowance for Doubtful Accounts would appear on the December 31, 2001 balance sheet given the facts in requirement 1(c).

Problem 10-3A
Aging accounts receivable

LO2,3

Jewell, Inc. had credit sales of $2.6 million in 2001. On December 31, 2001, the company's Allowance for Doubtful Accounts had a credit balance of $13,400. The accountant for Jewell has prepared a schedule of the December 31, 2001 accounts receivable by age and, on the basis of past experience, has estimated the percentage of the receivables in each age category that will become uncollectible. This information is summarized as follows:

December 31, 2001 Accounts Receivable	Age of Accounts Receivable	Expected Percentage Uncollectable
$730,000	Not due (under 30 days)	1.25 %
354,000	1 to 30 days past due	2.00
76,000	31 to 60 days past due	6.50
48,000	61 to 90 days past due	32.75
12,000	Over 90 days past due	68.00

Check figure:
2. Bad Debt Expense = $31,625

Required

Preparation component:

1. Compute the amount that should appear in the December 31, 2001 balance sheet as the allowance for doubtful accounts.
2. Prepare the journal entry to record bad debt expense for 2001.

Analysis component:

3. On June 30, 2002, Jewell, Inc. concluded that a customer's $3,750 receivable (created in 2001) was uncollectible and that the account should be written off. What effect will this action have on Jewell's 2002 net income? Explain your answer.

Problem 10-4A
Accounts receivable transactions and bad debt adjustments

LO1,2,3

Luxton Supplies showed the following selected adjusted balances at its December 31, 2001 year-end:

Accounts Receivable	
Dec. 31/01 Balance 249,000	

Allowance for Doubtful Accounts	
	8,340 Dec. 31/01 Balance

During the year 2002, the following selected transactions occurred:

a. Sales totalled $1,480,000, of which 25% were cash sales.
b. Sales returns and allowances were $57,000, half regarding credit sales.
c. An account for $12,000 was recovered.
d. Several accounts were written off; $19,500.
e. Collections from credit customers totalled $940,000 (excluding the recovery in (c) above).

Part 1

Required

a. Prepare the December 31, 2002 adjusting entry to estimate bad debts assuming that uncollectible accounts are estimated to be 1% of net credit sales.
b. Show how accounts receivable will appear on the December 31, 2002 balance sheet.
c. What will bad debt expense be on the income statement for the year ended December 31, 2002?

Check figures:
1a. Bad Debt Expense = $10,815
2d. Bad Debt Expense = $10,290

Part 2

Required

d. Prepare the December 31, 2002 adjusting entry to estimate bad debts assuming that uncollectible accounts are estimated to be 3% of outstanding receivables.
e. Show how accounts receivable will appear on the December 31, 2002 balance sheet.
f. What will bad debt expense be on the income statement for the year ended December 31, 2002?

Problem 10-5A

Recording accounts receivable transactions and bad debt adjustments

LO2,3

Harrell Industries began operations on January 1, 2001. During the next two years, the company completed a number of transactions involving credit sales, accounts receivable collections, and bad debts. These transactions are summarized as follows:

2001

a. Sold merchandise on credit for $1,144,500, terms n/30 (COGS = $620,000).
b. Wrote off uncollectible accounts receivable in the amount of $17,270.
c. Received cash of $667,100 in payment of outstanding accounts receivable.
d. In adjusting the accounts on December 31, concluded that 1.5% of the outstanding accounts receivable would become uncollectible.

2002

e. Sold merchandise on credit for $1,423,800, terms n/30 (COGS = $796,000).
f. Wrote off uncollectible accounts receivable in the amount of $26,880.
g. Received cash of $1,103,900 in payment of outstanding accounts receivable.
h. In adjusting the accounts on December 31, concluded that 1.5% of the outstanding accounts receivable would become uncollectible.

Check figures:
d. Bad Debt Expense = $24,171.95
h. Bad Debt Expense = $31,275.30

Required

Prepare journal entries to record Harrell's 2001 and 2002 summarized transactions and the adjusting entries to record bad debt expense at the end of each year.

Problem 10-6A

Bad debt expense

LO3

The following is information taken from the June 30, 2001 balance sheet of Abbacas Company:

Accounts receivable	$680,000	
Less: Allowance for doubtful accounts	27,000	$653,000

Check figures:
1. Bad Debt Expense = $17,350
2. Bad Debt expense = $11,250

Part 1

During July, Abbacas Company recorded total sales of $1,800,000, all on credit. There were $65,000 of sales returns and allowances. Collections during July were $1,920,000. Total receivables identified as being uncollectible and written off during July were $31,000. Abbacas estimates bad debts as 1% of net credit sales.

Required

Prepare the adjusting entry to record estimated bad debts for July.

Part 2

During August, total sales of $1,690,000 were recorded, all on credit. Sales returns and allowances totalled $33,000. Collections during the month were $1,420,000, which included the recovery of $3,900 from a customer account written off in a previous month. No accounts were written off during August. Abbacas Company changed its method of estimating bad debts to the balance sheet approach because the new accountant said it more accurately reflected uncollectible accounts. The resulting aging analysis determined total estimated uncollectible accounts at August 30 to be $28,500.

Required

Prepare the adjusting entry to record estimated bad debts on August 31.

Problem 10-7A
Estimating bad debts

The following information is available regarding the outstanding accounts receivable of QuickFix Servicing at September 30, 2001:

	Month of Credit Sale*				
Customer	**May**	**June**	**July**	**Aug.**	**Sept.**
B. Axley	$14,000	$ -0-	$ -0-	$ -0-	$ -0-
T. Holton	-0-	-0-	36,000	12,000	7,000
W. Nix	-0-	9,000	-0-	2,000	6,000
C. Percy	-0-	-0-	2,000	-0-	5,000
K. Willis	-0-	-0-	-0-	-0-	48,000

**All services are performed on terms of n/30.*

QuickFix estimates bad debts using the following rates:

Not yet due	1 to 30 days past due	31 to 60 days past due	61 to 90 days past due	91 to 120 days past due	Over 120 days past due
0.5%	1%	4%	10%	20%	50%

Check figure:
a. Total estimated uncollectible accounts = $5,690

Required

a. Complete a Schedule of Accounts Receivable by Age at September 30, 2001 (similar to Exhibit 10.15).

b. The allowance for doubtful accounts showed an unadjusted balance on September 30, 2001 of $800. Record the adjusting entry at September 30, 2001 to estimate uncollectible accounts.

Problem 10-8A
Notes receivable

LO[5,6]

Lendrum Holdings showed the following information regarding its notes receivable:

Note	Date of Note	Principal	Interest Rate	Term	Maturity Date	Days of Accrued Interest at Dec. 31, 2001	Accrued Interest at Dec. 31, 2001*
1	Nov. 1/00	$120,000	7%	180 days			
2	Jan. 5/01	50,000	8%	90 days			
3	Nov. 20/01	45,000	10%	45 days			
4	Dec. 10/01	60,000	12%	30 days			

**Round calculations to the nearest whole cent.*

Required

For each note:

a. Determine the maturity date.

b. Calculate the *days* of accrued interest, if any, at December 31, 2001 (Lendrum Holdings' year-end).

c. Calculate the *amount* of accrued interest, if any, at December 31, 2001.

For Note 3:

d. Prepare the entry to record the accrued interest at December 31, 2001.

e. Prepare the entry to record the collection on the maturity date. Assume that both interest and principal are collected at maturity.

Check figures:
d. Interest Revenue = $505.48
e. Interest Revenue = $49.32

Problem 10-9A
Accrued interest computation and dishonouring note receivable

LO5,6

Following are transactions of The Perry-Finch Company:

2001	
Dec. 16	Accepted a $9,600, 60-day, 9% note dated this day in granting Hal Krueger a time extension on his past-due account.
31	Made an adjusting entry to record the accrued interest on the Krueger note.
31	Closed the Interest Revenue account.
2002	
Feb. 14	Received Krueger's payment for the principal and interest on the note dated December 16.
Mar. 2	Accepted a $5,120, 10%, 90-day note dated this day in granting a time extension on the past-due account of ARC Company.
17	Accepted a $1,600, 30-day, 9% note dated this day in granting Penny Bobek a time extension on her past-due account.
Apr. 16	Bobek dishonoured her note when presented for payment.

Required

a. Prepare journal entries to record Perry-Finch's transactions.

b. Determine the maturity date of the note dated March 2. Prepare the entry on the maturity date, assuming ARC Company honours the note.

*Problem 10-10A
Discounting notes receivable

LO7

Prepare General Journal entries to record these transactions and events experienced by Ethyl Company:

Mar. 2	Accepted a $5,120, 10%, 90-day note dated this day in granting a time extension on the past-due account of JNC Company.
Apr. 21	Discounted, with recourse, the JNC Company note at BancFirst at a cost of $50.
June 2	Received notice from BancFirst that JNC Company defaulted on the note due May 31. Paid the bank the principal plus interest due on the note. *(Hint: Create an account receivable for the maturity value of the note.)*
July 16	Received payment from JNC Company for the maturity value of its dishonoured note plus interest for 45 days beyond maturity at 10%.
Sept. 3	Accepted a $2,080, 60-day, 10% note dated this day in granting Cecile Duval a time extension on her past-due account.
18	Discounted, without recourse, the Duval note at BancFirst at a cost of $25.

Required

Preparation component:

Prepare journal entries to record Ethyl Company's transactions.

Analysis component:

What reporting is necessary when a business discounts notes receivable with recourse and these notes have not reached maturity by the end of the fiscal period? Explain the reason for this requirement and what accounting principle is being satisfied.

An asterisk (*) identifies assignment material based on Appendix 10A and Appendix 10B.

***Problem 10-11A**
Discounting notes receivable

LO[7]

Check figures:
Jan. 10/02: Cash = $7,559.95
Mar. 29/02: Cash = $2,256.79

Required

Prepare General Journal entries to record the following transactions of Waterloo Company:

2001	
Dec. 11	Accepted a $7,500, 12%, 60-day note dated this day in granting Fred Calhoun a time extension on his past-due account.
31	Made an adjusting entry to record the accrued interest on the Fred Calhoun note.
31	Closed the Interest Revenue account.
2002	
Jan. 10	Discounted the Fred Calhoun note at the bank at 14%.
Feb. 10	Received notice protesting the Fred Calhoun note. Paid the bank the maturity value of the note plus a $30 protest fee.
Mar. 5	Accepted a $2,250, 11%, 60-day note dated this day in granting a time extension on the past-due account of Donna Reed.
29	Discounted the Donna Reed note at the bank at 15%.
May 7	Because no notice protesting the Donna Reed note had been received, assumed that it had been paid.
June 9	Accepted a $3,375, 60-day, 10% note dated this day in granting a time extension on the past-due account of Jack Miller.
Aug. 8	Received payment of the maturity value of the Jack Miller note.
11	Accepted a $4,000, 60-day, 10% note dated this day in granting Roger Addison a time extension on his past-due account.
31	Discounted the Roger Addison note at the bank at 13%.
Oct. 12	Received notice protesting the Roger Addison note. Paid the bank the maturity value of the note plus a $30 protest fee.
Nov. 19	Received payment from Roger Addison of the maturity value of his dishonoured note, the protest fee, and interest on both for 40 days beyond maturity at 10%.
Dec. 23	Wrote off the Fred Calhoun account against Allowance for Doubtful Accounts.

Alternate Problems

Problem 10-1B
Credit sales and credit card sales

LO[1]

Ace Office Supply Co. allows a few customers to make purchases on credit. Other customers may use either of two credit cards. Commerce Bank deducts a 3% service charge for sales on its credit card, but immediately credits the chequing account of its commercial customers when credit card receipts are deposited. Ace deposits the Commerce Bank credit card receipts at the close of each business day.

When customers use the Fortune card, Ace accumulates the receipts for several days and then submits them to the Fortune Credit Company for payment. Fortune deducts a 2% service charge and usually pays within one week of being billed.

Ace completed the following transactions in July (assume a perpetual inventory system).

July 2	Sold merchandise costing $1,660 on credit to J.R. Lacey for $2,780. *Terms of all credit sales are 2/10, n/30; all sales are recorded at the gross price.*
8	Sold merchandise costing $1,950 for $3,248 to customers who used their Commerce Bank credit cards. Sold merchandise costing $665 for $1,114 to customers who used their Fortune cards.
12	Received Lacey's cheque paying for the purchase of July 2.
13	Sold merchandise costing $1,775 for $2,960 to customers who used their Fortune cards.
16	The Fortune card receipts accumulated since July 8 were submitted to the credit card company for payment.
23	Received the amount due from Fortune Credit Company.

Required

Prepare journal entries to record the preceding transactions.

An asterisk (*) identifies assignment material based on Appendix 10A or Appendix 10B.

Problem 10-2B
Estimating bad debt expense

LO2,3

On December 31, 2001, Genie Service Corp.'s records showed the following results for the year:

Cash sales	$1,015,000
Credit sales	1,241,000

In addition, the unadjusted trial balance included the following items:

Accounts receivable	$475,000 debit
Allowance for doubtful accounts	5,200 credit

Required

1. Prepare the adjusting entry on the books of Genie Service Corp. to estimate bad debts under each of the following independent assumptions:
   a. Bad debts are estimated to be 2.5% of credit sales.
   b. Bad debts are estimated to be 1.5% of total sales.
   c. An analysis suggests that 6% of outstanding accounts receivable on December 31, 2001 will become uncollectible.
2. Show how Accounts Receivable and the Allowance for Doubtful Accounts would appear on the December 31, 2001, balance sheet given the facts in requirement 1(a).
3. Show how Accounts Receivable and the Allowance for Doubtful Accounts would appear on the December 31, 2001, balance sheet given the facts in requirement 1(c).

Check figure:
1c. Bad Debt Expense = $23,300

Problem 10-3B
Aging accounts receivable

LO2,3

NutraMade Corporation had credit sales of $3.5 million in 2001. On December 31, 2001, the company's Allowance for Doubtful Accounts had a debit balance of $4,100. The accountant for NutraMade has prepared a schedule of the December 31, 2001 accounts receivable by age and, on the basis of past experience, has estimated the percentage of the receivables in each age category that will become uncollectible. This information is summarized as follows:

December 31, 2001 Accounts Receivable	Age of Accounts Receivable	Expected Percentage Uncollectible
$296,400	Not due (under 30 days)	2.0%
177,800	1 to 30 days past due	4.0
58,000	31 to 60 days past due	8.5
7,600	61 to 90 days past due	39.0
3,700	Over 90 days past due	82.5

Required

Preparation component:

1. Compute the amount that should appear in the December 31, 2001 balance sheet as the Allowance for Doubtful Accounts.
2. Prepare the journal entry to record bad debt expense for 2001.

Check figure:
2. Bad Debt Expense = $28,086.50

Analysis component:

3. On July 31, 2002, NutraMade concluded that a customer's $2,345 receivable (created in 2001) was uncollectible and that the account should be written off. What effect will this action have on NutraMade's 2002 net income? Explain your answer.

Problem 10-4B
Accounts receivable transactions and bad debt adjustments

LO1,2,3

Jaxton Supplies showed the following selected adjusted balances at its December 31, 2001 year-end:

Accounts Receivable	
Dec. 31/01 Balance 980,000	

Allowance for Doubtful Accounts	
	24,920 Dec. 31/01 Balance

During the year 2002, the following selected transactions occurred:

a. Sales totalled $3,450,000, of which 85% were credit sales.
b. Sales returns and allowances were $98,000, all regarding credit sales.
c. An account for $58,000 was recovered.
d. Several accounts were written off, including one very large account; the total was $265,000.
e. Collected accounts receivable of $3,001,500 (excluding the recovery in (c) above). Sales discounts of $52,000 were taken. *(Hint: Journalize the entry for clarity.)*

Check figures:
1a. Bad Debt Expense = $222,600
2d. Bad Debt Expense = $206,740

Part 1

Required

a. Prepare the December 31, 2002 adjusting entry to estimate bad debts, assuming uncollectible accounts are estimated to be 8% of net credit sales.
b. Show how accounts receivable will appear on the December 31, 2002 balance sheet.
c. What will bad debt expense be on the income statement for the year ended December 31, 2002?

Part 2

Required

d. Prepare the December 31, 2002 adjusting entry to estimate bad debts, assuming uncollectible accounts are estimated to be 4.5% of outstanding receivables.
e. Show how accounts receivable will appear on the December 31, 2002 balance sheet.
f. What will bad debt expense be on the income statement for the year ended December 31, 2002?

Problem 10-5B

Recording accounts receivable transactions and bad debt adjustments

LO2,3

Check figures:
d. Bad Debt Expense = $10,609.10
h. Bad Debt Expense = $10,387.90

Spring Products Co. began operations on January 1, 2001, and completed a number of transactions during 2001 and 2002 that involved credit sales, accounts receivable collections, and bad debts. Assume a perpetual inventory system. These transactions are summarized as follows:

2001

a. Sold merchandise on credit for $673,490, terms n/30 (COGS = $486,000).
b. Received cash of $437,250 in payment of outstanding accounts receivable.
c. Wrote off uncollectible accounts receivable in the amount of $8,330.
d. In adjusting the accounts on December 31, concluded that 1% of the outstanding accounts receivable would become uncollectible.

2002

e. Sold merchandise on credit for $930,100, terms n/30 (COGS = $716,000).
f. Received cash of $890,220 in payment of outstanding accounts receivable.
g. Wrote off uncollectible accounts receivable in the amount of $10,090.
h. In adjusting the accounts on December 31, concluded that 1% of the outstanding accounts receivable would become uncollectible.

Required

Prepare General Journal entries to record the 2001 and 2002 summarized transactions of Spring Products Co., and the adjusting entries to record bad debt expense at the end of each year.

Problem 10-6B

Bad debt expense

LO3

The following is information regarding adjusted account balances at September 30, 2001:

Accounts Receivable	
320,000	

Allowance for Doubtful Accounts	
	4,800

Part 1

During October, Leonardo Painters recorded $2,300,000 in total revenues, all on credit. Collections during October were $2,025,000, which included the recovery of $65,000 from a customer account written off in September. Total receivables identified as being uncollectible and written off during October were $25,000. Leonardo Painters estimates bad debts to be 0.5% of net credit revenues.

Required

Prepare the adjusting entry to record estimated bad debts for October.

Part 2

During November, revenues totalled $1,975,000, all on credit. Collections during the month were $1,865,000. An account for $28,000 was identified as being uncollectible and written off on November 28. It was recommended to Leonardo Painters that the method of estimating bad debts be changed to the balance sheet approach. As a result, it was estimated that 5% of the November 30 accounts receivable balance was uncollectible.

Required

Prepare the adjusting entry to record estimated bad debts on November 30.

Check figures:
1. Bad Debt Expense = $11,500
2. Bad Debt Expense = $7,550

Problem 10-7B
Estimating bad debts
LO3

The following information is available regarding the accounts receivable of Touchstone Holdings at August 31, 2001:

	Month of Credit Sale*				
Customer	**April**	**May**	**June**	**July**	**Aug.**
A. Leslie	$ -0-	$12,000	$ -0-	$29,000	$ -0-
T. Meston	26,000	-0-	-0-	-0-	-0-
P. Obrian	-0-	-0-	-0-	52,000	21,000
L. Timms	-0-	63,000	26,000	-0-	14,000
W. Victor	-0-	-0-	83,000	61,000	32,000

**All services are performed on terms of n/60.*

Touchstone estimates uncollectibility of accounts receivable using the following rates:

Not yet due	1 to 30 days past due	31 to 60 days past due	61 to 90 days past due	91 to 120 days past due	Over 120 days past due
1%	2%	5%	20%	35%	50%

Required

a. Complete a Schedule of Accounts Receivable by Age at August 31, 2001 similar to Exhibit 10.15.

b. The allowance for doubtful accounts showed an unadjusted balance on August 31, 2001 of $6,300 (debit). Record the adjusting journal entry at August 31, 2001 to estimate uncollectible accounts.

Check figure:
a. Total estimated uncollectible accounts = $13,220

Problem 10-8B
Notes receivable
LO5,6

Qualico showed the following details regarding its notes receivable:

Note	Date of Note	Principal	Interest Rate	Term	Maturity Date	Days of Accrued Interest at Dec. 31, 2001	Accrued Interest at Dec. 31, 2001
1	Sept. 20/00	$245,000	7%	120 days			
2	June 01/01	120,000	9%	45 days			
3	Nov. 23/01	82,000	9%	90 days			
4	Dec. 18/01	60,000	10%	30 days			

**Round calculations to the nearest whole cent.*

Required

For each note:

a. Determine the maturity date.

b. Calculate the *days* of accrued interest, if any, at December 31, 2001, Qualico's year-end.

c. Calculate the *amount* of accrued interest, if any, at December 31, 2001.

For Note 4:

d. Prepare the entry to record the accrued interest at December 31, 2001.

e. Prepare the entry to record the collection on the maturity date. Assume that interest and principal are collected at maturity.

Check figures:
d. Interest Revenue = $213.70
e. Interest Revenue = $279.45

Problem 10-9B
Accrued interest computation and dishonouring note receivable

LO 5,6

Following are transactions of Metro, Inc.:

2001	
Nov. 16	Accepted a $3,700, 90-day, 12% note dated this day in granting Bess Parker a time extension on her past-due account.
Dec. 31	Made an adjusting entry to record the accrued interest on the Parker note.
31	Closed the Interest Revenue account.
2002	
Feb. 14	Received Parker's payment for the principal and interest on the note dated November 16.
28	Accepted a $12,400, 9%, 30-day note dated this day in granting a time extension on the past-due account of The Simms Co.
Mar. 1	Accepted a $5,100, 60-day, 10% note dated this day in granting Bedford Holmes a time extension on his past-due account.
30	The Simms Co. dishonoured its note when presented for payment.

Required

a. Prepare journal entries to record Metro's transactions.

b. Determine the maturity date of the note dated March 1. Prepare the entry at maturity assuming Bedford Holmes honours the note.

Check figure:
b. Interest Revenue = $83.84

*Problem 10-10B
Discounting notes receivable

Prepare General Journal entries to record these transactions and events experienced by Trontelli Company:

Mar. 1	Accepted a $5,100, 60-day, 10% note dated this day in granting Bolton Company a time extension on its past-due account.
23	Discounted, without recourse, the Bolton note at Security Bank at a cost of $50.
June 21	Accepted a $9,300, 90-day, 12% note dated this day in granting Vince Soto a time extension on his past-due account.
July 5	Discounted, with recourse, the Soto note at Security Bank at a cost of $200.
Sept. 25	Received notice from Security Bank that the Soto note had been paid.

Required

Preparation component:
Prepare journal entries to record Trontelli Company's transactions.

Analysis component:
What reporting is necessary when a business discounts notes receivable with recourse and these notes have not reached maturity by the end of the fiscal period? Explain the reason for this requirement and what accounting principle is being satisfied.

An asterisk (*) identifies assignment material based on Appendix 10A and Appendix 10B.

*Problem 10-11B

Discounting notes receivable

LO[7]

Required

Prepare General Journal entries to record the following transactions of Dexton Company.

2001	
Jan 10	Accepted a $3,000, 60-day, 12% note dated this day in granting a time extension on the past-due account of David Huerta.
Mar. 14	David Huerta dishonoured his note when presented for payment.
19	Accepted a $2,100, 90-day, 10% note dated this day in granting a time extension on the past-due account of Rose Jones.
28	Discounted the Rose Jones note at the bank at 16%.
Jun. 20	Since notice protesting the Rose Jones note had not been received, assumed the note had been paid.
27	Accepted $700 in cash and a $1,300, 60-day, 12% note dated this day in granting a time extension on the past-due account of Jake Thomas.
July 24	Discounted the Jake Thomas note at the bank at 14%.
Aug. 29	Received notice protesting the Jake Thomas note. Paid the bank the maturity of the note plus a $20 protest fee.
Sept. 4	Accepted a $1,500, 60-day, 11% note dated this day in granting a time extension on the past-due account of Ginnie Bauer.
Oct. 13	Discounted the Ginnie Bauer note at the bank at 14%.
Nov. 6	Received notice protesting the Ginnie Bauer note. Paid the bank the maturity value of the note plus a $20 protest fee.
Dec. 6	Received payment from Ginnie Bauer of the maturity value of her dishonoured note; the protest fee, and interest at 11% on both for 30 days beyond maturity.
28	Decided the accounts of David Huerta and Jake Thomas were uncollectible and wrote them off against Allowance for Doubtful Accounts.

Check figures:
Mar. 28: Cash = $2,075.38
July 24: Cash = $1,308.86

Analytical and Review Problem

A & R Problem 10-1

The Tor-Mont Company has been in business three years and has applied for a significant bank loan. Prior to considering the applications, the bank asks you to conduct an audit for the last three years. Concerning accounts receivable, you find that the company has been charging off receivables as they finally proved uncollectible and treating them as expenses at the time of write-off.

Your investigation indicates that receivable losses have approximated (and can be expected to approximate) 2% of net sales. Until this first audit, the company's sales and direct receivable write-off experience was:

Year of Sales	Amount of sales	Accounts written off in: 2000	2001	2002
2000	$450,000	$1,500	$6,000	$1,800
2001	600,000	—	3,000	7,200
2002	750,000	—	—	4,500

Required

1. Indicate the amount by which net income was understated or overstated each year because the company used the direct write-off method rather than the generally acceptable allowance method.
2. Prepare all entries for each of the three years that would have been made if Tor-Mont had used the allowance method from the start of the business.
3. Which of the entries in (2) are year-end adjusting entries?

An asterisk (*) identifies assignment material based on Appendix 10A or Appendix 10B.

CHAPTER

11 Payroll Liabilities

Guilty

Shelburne, January 9, 2001—A Shelburne County fishing company has been fined a total of $3,000 for failing to remit tax deducted from employees' pay cheques. The crown prosecutor told the court that the charge was laid after a Canada Customs and Revenue Agency (CCRA) investigation showed that the company failed to remit federal income tax totalling over $25,800 deducted from employee wages for periods in August and December 1999 and January 2000.

Quebec City, December 13, 2000—A restaurant owner and administrator pleaded guilty to charges of tax evasion and was fined a total of $14,000. The owner was charged with failing to remit $3,663 in payroll source deductions on the salaries of his employees, at both restaurants, for each of September through December 1999.

Stellarton, December 4, 2000—A Pictou County construction company has been fined a total of $5,000 for failing to remit tax deducted from employees' pay cheques. The crown prosecutor told the court that the charge was laid after a CCRA investigation

showed that the company failed to remit federal income tax totalling over $24,600 deducted from employee wages from January to May 2000.

In all of the above cases, unpaid deductions must be paid in addition to the fines. Failure to do so will result in imprisonment. The CCRA takes non-payment of source deductions very seriously, as the amounts deducted from employees are deemed to be held in trust until remitted to CCRA on their behalf. People who deliberately evade taxes force honest Canadians to pay more than their fair share. Canadians have to be confident that the tax system is fair, and know that CCRA will prosecute those individuals who cheat.

LO1 List the taxes and other items frequently withheld from employees' wages.

LO2 Make the calculations necessary to prepare a Payroll Register and prepare the entry to record payroll liabilities.

LO3 Prepare journal entries to record the payments to employees and explain the operation of a payroll bank account.

LO4 Calculate the payroll costs levied on employers and prepare the entries to record the accrual and payment of these amounts.

LO5 Calculate and record employee fringe benefit costs and show the effect of these items on the total cost of employing labour.

Chapter Preview

Wages or salaries generally amount to one of the largest expenses incurred by a business. Accounting for employees' wages and salaries is one task that is shared by almost all business entities.

Payroll accounting:

- Records cash payments to employees.
- Provides valuable information regarding labour costs.
- Accounts for amounts withheld from employees' pay.
- Accounts for employee (fringe) benefits and payroll costs paid by the employer.
- Provides the means to comply with governmental regulations on employee compensation.

As you study this chapter, you will learn the general processes that all businesses follow to account for these items.

Items Withheld from Employees' Wages

LO1 List the taxes and other items frequently withheld from employees' wages.

An understanding of payroll accounting and the design and use of payroll records requires some knowledge of the laws and programs that affect payrolls. Many of these require **payroll deductions,** amounts withheld from the wages of employees. Consequently, the more pertinent of these are discussed in the first portion of this chapter before the subject of payroll records is introduced.

Withholding Employees' Income Tax

With few exceptions, employers are required to calculate, collect, and remit to the Receiver General for Canada the income taxes of their employees. Historically, when the first federal income tax law became effective in 1917, it applied to only a few individuals having high earnings. It was not until World War II that income taxes were levied on substantially all wage earners. At that time Parliament recognized that many individual wage earners could not be expected to save sufficient money with which to pay their income taxes once each year. Consequently, Parliament instituted a system of pay-as-you-go withholding of taxes at their source each payday. This pay-as-you-go withholding of employee income taxes requires an employer to act as a tax collecting agent of the federal government. Failure to cooperate results in severe consequences, as illustrated in the opening article.

The amount of income taxes to be withheld from an employee's wages is determined by his or her wages and the amount of **personal tax credits.** Each individual is entitled, in 2000, to some or all of the following annual amounts that are subject to tax credits (as applicable):

1. Basic Personal Amount $7,231
2. Married or Equivalent 6,140
   (with maximum earnings stipulated)

The total of each taxpayer's personal tax credits is deducted from income to determine the level of income tax deductions from the individual's gross pay. For example, based on rates effective July 1, 2000, a Saskatchewan resident with a gross weekly salary of $500 and personal tax credits of $7,231 (2000 net claim code 1 on the TD1 form) would have $89.40 of income taxes withheld. Another individual with the same gross salary but with personal tax credits of $13,371 (claim code 5) would have $61.50 withheld.

Employers withhold income tax owed by each employee every payday based on an employee's completed Personal Tax Credit Return, Form TD1. The taxpayer must file a revised Form TD1 each time the exemptions change during a year. The electronic TD1 form is shown in Exhibit 11.1.

In determining the amounts of income taxes to be withheld from the wages of employees, employers normally use payroll deductions tables provided by Canada Customs and Revenue Agency (CCRA) P. 13. The to-be-withheld amounts include both federal and provincial income taxes except for the province of Quebec, which levies and collects its own income tax and its own pension plan contributions. Provincial income tax rates vary from province to province. Therefore, for consistency, all examples and problems making use of tax tables will be based on Saskatchewan's tables. Calculation of deductions is simplified for computer users if they request "tables on diskette" from CCRA. In addition to determining and withholding income taxes from each employee's wages every payday, employers are required to remit the withheld taxes to the Receiver General for Canada each month.

Canada Pension Plan (CPP)

Every working person between the ages of 18 and 70 with few exceptions must make contributions in required amounts to the **Canada Pension Plan** (CPP).

Contributions are based on earnings as follows:

	Canada Pension Plan Contributions	
Effective July 1, 2000	Employee Contributions	Employer Contributions
Rate	3.9%*	3.9%*
Maximum	$1,329.90	$1,329.90

**3.9% of earnings greater than $3,500 and less than $37,600.*

Employers are responsible for making the proper deductions from their employees' earnings. They remit these deductions each month, together with their own contributions, to the Receiver General for Canada.

Self-employed individuals pay the combined rate for employees and employers, or 7.8% on annual earnings between $3,500 and the exempt ceiling of $37,600.

Employment Insurance (EI)

To alleviate hardships caused by interruptions in earnings through unemployment, the federal government, with the concurrence of all provincial governments, implemented an employee/employer-financed unemployment insurance plan. Under the Employment Insurance Act, 1996, compulsory **employment insurance** coverage was extended to all Canadian workers who are not self-employed. As of January 1, 2000, over 13.5 million employees, including teachers, hospital workers, and top-level executives, were covered by the insurance plan.

Exhibit 11.1

Electronic TDI Form

Payroll Deductions - Effective July 1, 2000 - TD1(E)1

File View Forms Options Window Help

TD1(E)1

Last name (capital letters)	Usual first name and initials	Employee number
Address	For non-residents only - country of permanent residence	Social Insurance Number
Postal Code		Date of Birth YYYY-MM-DD

1. Basic personal amount
2. Spousal amount
3. Equivalent-to-spouse amount
4. Amount for infirm dependents age 18 or older
5. Amount for eligible pension income
6. Age amount

Tuition fees and education amount

7. Full time
8. Part Time

Amounts transferred from your spouse, or dependants

11. Age amount
12. Amount for eligible pension income
13. Disability amount
14. Tuition fees and education amount

9. Disability amount
10. Caregiver amount

Additional tax to be deducted

Deduction for living in a prescribed zone

Number of dependants under age 18 (optional) for (ON, MB, SK or BC)

Total of credits ☐ No tax witholding required Claim code

NUM

Start Corel CAPTURE 7.0 : 1 Adobe Photoshop Payroll Deductions - ... 4:41 PM

The employment insurance fund from which benefits are paid is jointly financed by employees and their employers. Employers are required to deduct from their employees' wages 2.4% of insured earnings, to add a contribution of 1.4 times the amount deducted from employees' wages, and to remit both amounts to the Receiver General for Canada. The system is summarized as follows:

Employment Insurance Contributions		
Effective July 1, 2000	Employee Contributions	Employer Contributions
Rate	2.4%	1.4 times employee rate
Maximum	$936.00	$1,310.40

Note: Maximum insurable earnings for 2000 are $39,000.

Insured earnings, in most instances, refer to gross earnings. An employee may receive taxable benefits or allowances that would be included in gross earnings but would not be considered insurable earnings. However, in this text, gross earnings will be insurable earnings.

The Employment Insurance Act also requires that an employer complete a "Record of Employment" because of termination of employment, illness, injury, or pregnancy and keep a record for each employee that shows among other things wages subject to employment insurance and taxes withheld.

Use of Withholding Tables

Employers may use **wage bracket withholding tables** in determining Canada Pension Plan and employment insurance to be withheld from employees' gross earnings. These tables are also available in electronic form for computer applications on disk from CCRA or at www.ccra-adrc.gc.ca.

Determining the amount of withholdings from an employee's gross wages is quite easy when electronic tables are used. Exhibit 11.2 shows the screens used to determine withholding amounts. First the gross pay is entered in the "Gross income for the pay period" area. Then the "View Deductions" button is clicked. The "Payroll Deductions for Regular Salary" automatically appears.

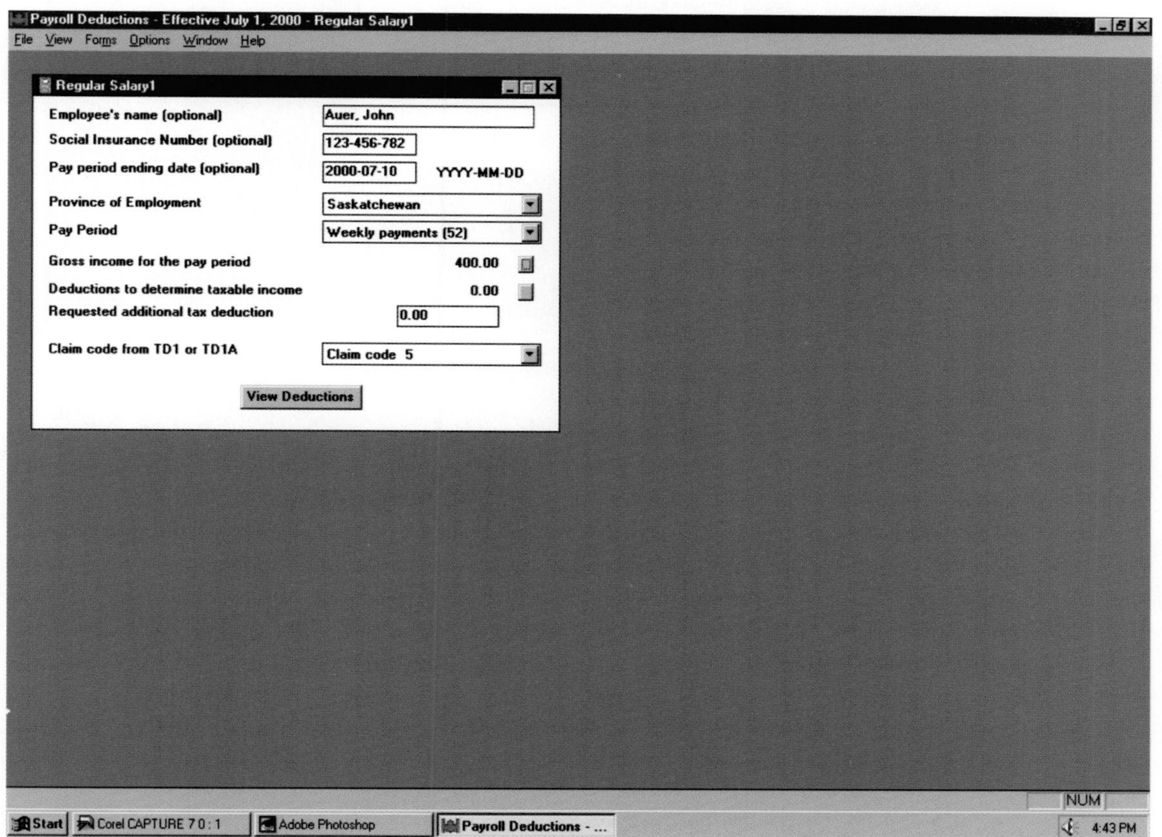

Exhibit 11.2

2000 Electronic Tables Screens

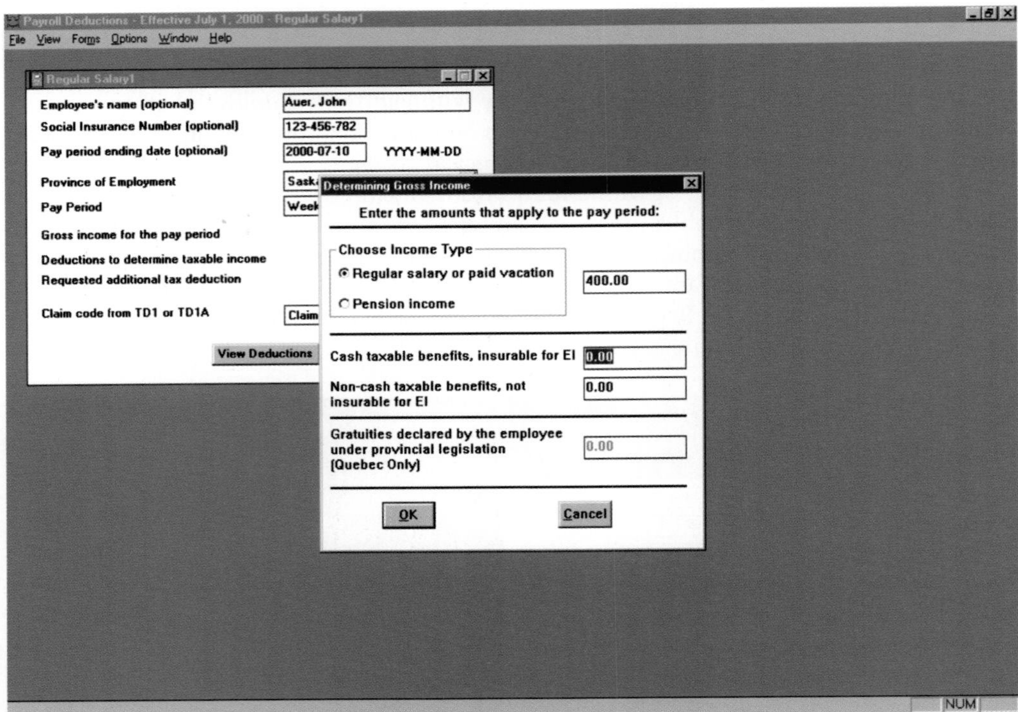

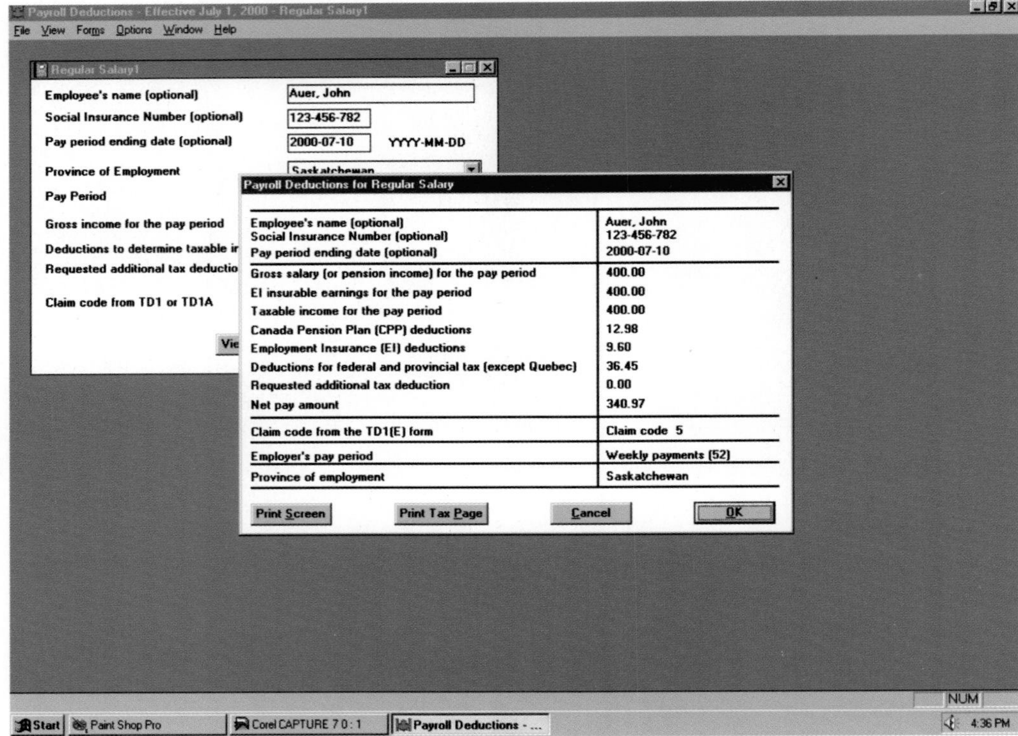

The T-4 Form

Employers are required to report wages and deductions both to each employee and to the local office of CCRA. On or before the last day of February, the employer must give each employee a T-4 summary, a statement that tells the employee:

- Total wages for the preceding year.
- Taxable benefits received from the employer.
- Income taxes withheld.
- Deductions for registered pension plan.
- Canada Pension Plan contributions.
- Employment insurance deductions.

On or before the last day of February the employer must forward to the district taxation office copies of the employee's T-4 statements plus a T-4 that summarizes the information contained on the employee's T-4 statements. The T-4 form is shown in Exhibit 11.3.

Wages, Hours, and Union Contracts

All provinces have laws establishing maximum hours of work and minimum pay rates. And, while the details vary with each province, generally employers are required to pay an employee for hours worked in excess of 40 in any one week at the employee's regular pay rate plus an overtime premium of at least one-half of his or her regular rate. In addition, employers commonly operate under contracts with their employees' union that provide even better terms.

In addition to specifying working hours and wage rates, union contracts often provide that the employer shall deduct dues from the wages of each employee and remit the amounts deducted to the union.

Other Payroll Deductions

Employees may individually authorize additional deductions such as:

1. Deductions to accumulate funds for the purchase of Canada Savings Bonds.
2. Deductions to pay health, accident, hospital, or life insurance premiums.
3. Deductions to repay loans from the employer or the employees' credit union.
4. Deductions to pay for merchandise purchased from the company.
5. Deductions for donations to charitable organizations such as the United Way.

Exhibit 11.3

2000 T-4 Form

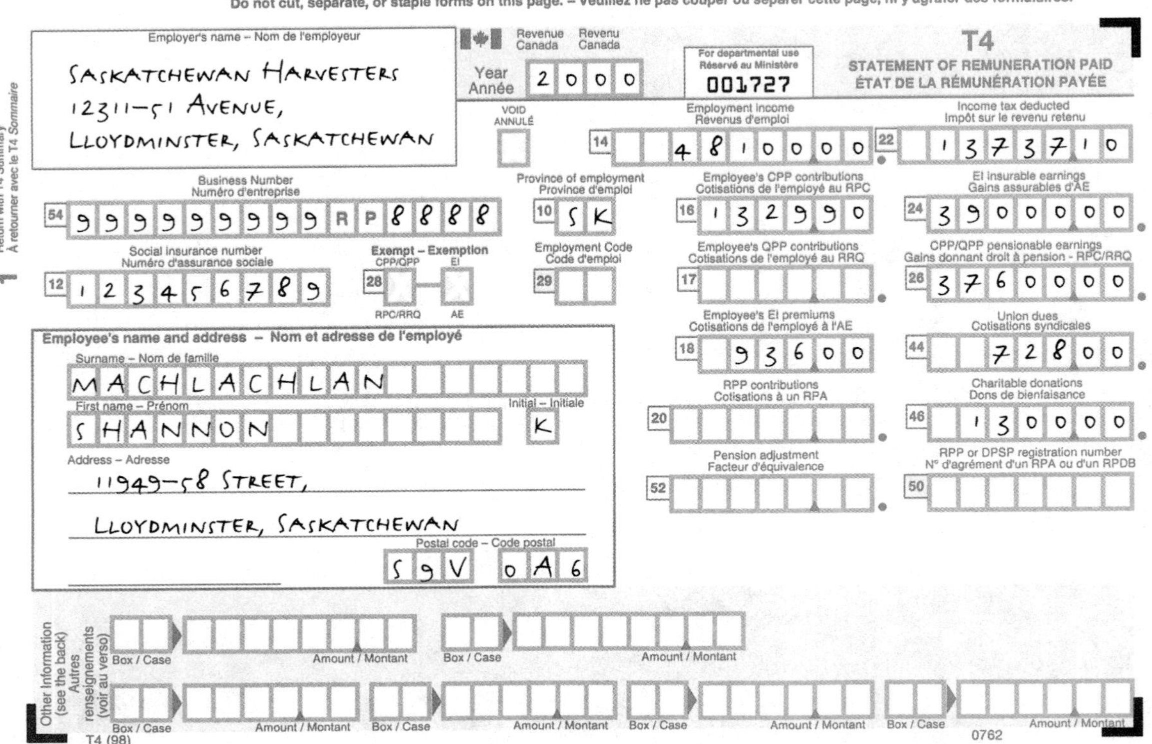

Do not cut, separate, or staple forms on this page. – Veuillez ne pas couper ou séparer cette page, ni y agrafer des formulaires.

1 Return with T4 Summary / À retourner avec le T4 Sommaire

Revenue Canada / Revenu Canada

T4 — STATEMENT OF REMUNERATION PAID / ÉTAT DE LA RÉMUNÉRATION PAYÉE

Employer's name – Nom de l'employeur:
SASKATCHEWAN HARVESTERS
12311–51 AVENUE,
LLOYDMINSTER, SASKATCHEWAN

Year / Année: 2000

For departmental use / Réservé au Ministère: 001727

VOID / ANNULÉ

Box	Description	Entry
14	Employment income / Revenus d'emploi	48100.00
22	Income tax deducted / Impôt sur le revenu retenu	13737.10
54	Business Number / Numéro d'entreprise	999999999 RP 8888
10	Province of employment / Province d'emploi	SK
16	Employee's CPP contributions / Cotisations de l'employé au RPC	1329.90
24	EI insurable earnings / Gains assurables d'AE	39000.00
12	Social insurance number / Numéro d'assurance sociale	123456789
28	Exempt – Exemption: CPP/QPP, EI / RPC/RRQ, AE	
29	Employment Code / Code d'emploi	
17	Employee's QPP contributions / Cotisations de l'employé au RRQ	
26	CPP/QPP pensionable earnings / Gains donnant droit à pension - RPC/RRQ	37600.00
18	Employee's EI premiums / Cotisations de l'employé à l'AE	936.00
44	Union dues / Cotisations syndicales	728.00
20	RPP contributions / Cotisations à un RPA	
46	Charitable donations / Dons de bienfaisance	1300.00
52	Pension adjustment / Facteur d'équivalence	
50	RPP or DPSP registration number / N° d'agrément d'un RPA ou d'un RPDB	

Employee's name and address – Nom et adresse de l'employé

Surname – Nom de famille: MACHLACHLAN
First name – Prénom: SHANNON
Initial – Initiale: K
Address – Adresse: 11949–58 STREET, LLOYDMINSTER, SASKATCHEWAN
Postal code – Code postal: S9V 0A6

Other Information (see the back) / Autres renseignements (voir au verso): Box / Case — Amount / Montant

T4 (98) 0762

Timekeeping

Compiling a record of the time worked by each employee is called **timekeeping.** The method used to compile such a record depends on the nature of the company's business and the number of its employees. In a very small business, timekeeping may consist of no more than notations of each employee's working time made in a memorandum book by the manager or owner. In many companies, however, time clocks are used to record on **clock cards** each employee's time of arrival and departure. At the beginning of each payroll period, a clock card for each employee (see Exhibit 11.4) is placed in a rack for use by the employee. Upon arriving at work, each employee takes his or her card from the rack and places it in a slot in the time clock. This activates the clock to stamp the date and arrival time on the card. The employee then returns the card to the rack. Upon leaving the plant, store, or office for lunch or at the end of the day, the procedure is repeated. The employee takes the card from the rack, places it in the clock, and the time of departure is automatically stamped, As a result, at the end of each period, the card shows the hours the employee was at work.

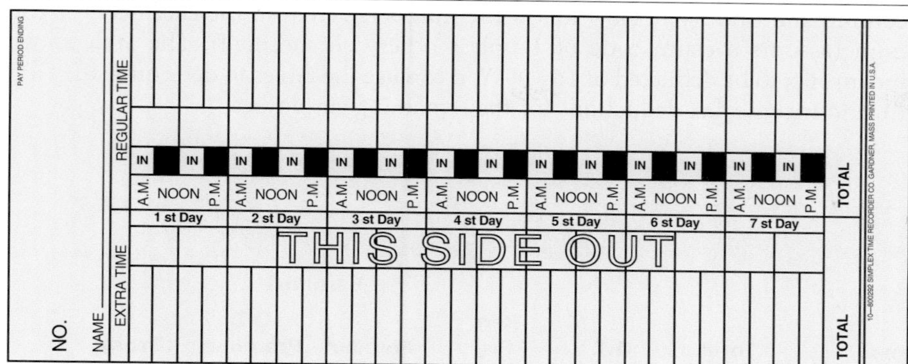

Exhibit 11.4

Employee's Clock Card

1. What is the purpose of the federal Employment Insurance scheme?
2. When must T-4 statements be given to employees?
3. What are other typical nonmandatory payroll deductions?

Answers—p. 578

The Payroll Register

Make the calculations necessary to prepare a Payroll Register and prepare the entry to record payroll liabilities.

Each pay period the total hours worked as compiled on clock cards or by other means are summarized in a Payroll Register, an example of which is shown in Exhibit 11.5. The illustrated register is for a weekly pay period and shows the payroll data for each employee on a separate line.

In Exhibit 11.5, the columns under the heading Daily Time show the hours worked each day by each employee. The total of each employee's hours is entered in the column headed Total Hours. If hours include overtime hours, these are entered in the column headed O.T. Hours.

The Regular Pay Rate column shows the hourly pay rate of each employee. Total hours worked multiplied by the regular pay rate equals regular pay. Overtime hours multiplied by the overtime premium rate (50% in this case) equals overtime premium pay. And regular pay plus overtime premium pay is the **employee's gross pay.**

The amounts withheld from each employee's gross pay are recorded in the Deductions columns of the payroll register. For example, you determine the income tax deductions by matching the gross pay of each employee to the tax deduction tables and then enter the results in the tax deduction column. Income tax deductions are based on the gross pay less the amounts deducted for employment insurance and Canada Pension Plan. The tax tables allow for these adjustments and separate books are available for each province. Exhibit 11.5 assumes that income tax deductions are based on the employees being resident in Saskatchewan.

For example, you can use the tables in Exhibit 11.6 to determine the appropriate CPP, EI, and Income Tax deductions for John Auer's $400 pay. In the CPP table, under the *Pay* column, find $400. The CPP deduction according to the table is $12.98 for the pay range $400.00–$400.24. Using the EI table, go to the *Insurable Earnings* column and find $400. The table shows that the EI deduction for the range $399.80–$400.20 is $9.60. Finally, using the income tax table, go to the Pay column and find $400. Now follow the numbers across to the claim code 1 column (assume a claim code of 1 unless otherwise specified). The table shows income tax to be deducted of $64.00. You can use the tables to determine the CPP, EI, and Income Tax deductions for the remaining employees.

Exhibit 11.5

Payroll Register

Payroll Week Ended

Employees	Clock Card No.	M	T	W	T	F	S	S	Total Hours	O.T. Hours	Reg. Pay Rate	Regular Pay	O.T. Premium Pay	Gross Pay	
		Daily Time									Earnings				
Auer, John	118	8	8	8	8	8			40		10.00	400.00		400.00	1
Cheung, Joen	109	0	8	8	8	8	8		40		12.00	480.00		480.00	2
Daljit, Moe	121	8	8	8	8	8	8	4	52	12	15.00	780.00	90.00	870.00	3
Lee, Shannon	104	8	8		8	8	8	4	44	4	14.00	616.00	28.00	644.00	4
Prasad, Sunil	108		8	8	8	8	4	8	44	4	15.00	660.00	30.00	690.00	5
Rupert, Allan	105	8	8	8	8	8			40		12.00	480.00		480.00	6
Totals												3,416.00	148.00	3,564.00	

Register July 14, 2000

	Gross Pay	EI Premium	Income Taxes	Hospital Insurance	CPP	Total Deductions	Net Pay	Cheque Number	Sales Salaries	Office Salaries
		Deductions					Payment		Distribution	
1	400.00	9.60	64.00	18.00	12.98	104.58	295.42	754	400.00	
2	480.00	11.52	83.30	18.00	16.10	128.92	351.08	755	480.00	
3	870.00	20.88	216.00	24.00	31.24	292.12	577.88	756		870.00
4	644.00	15.46	132.75	18.00	22.49	188.70	455.30	757		644.00
5	690.00	16.56	147.25	24.00	24.29	212.10	477.90	758	690.00	
6	480.00	11.52	83.30	18.00	16.10	128.92	351.08	759	480.00	
	3,564.00	85.54	726.60	120.00	123.20	1,055.34	2,508.66		2,050.00	1,514.00

The column headed Hospital Insurance shows the amounts withheld to pay for hospital insurance for the employees and their families. The total withheld from all employees is a current liability of the employer until paid to the insurance company. Likewise, the total withheld for employees' union dues is a current liability until paid to the union.

Additional columns may be added to the Payroll register for any other deductions that occur sufficiently often to warrant special columns. For example, a company that regularly deducts amounts from its employees' pay for Canada Savings bonds may add a special column for this deduction.

An employee's gross pay less total deductions is the **employee's net pay** and is entered in the Net Pay column. The total of this column is the amount the employees are to be paid. The numbers of the cheques used to pay the employees are entered in the column headed Cheque Number.

The Distribution columns are used to classify the various salaries in terms of different kinds of expense. Here you enter each employee's gross salary in the proper column according to the type of work performed. The column totals then indicate the amounts to be debited to the salary expense accounts.

Exhibit 11.6

Excerpts From CPP, EI, and Income Tax Tables Effective July 1, 2000. Register July 14, 2000

Canada Pension Plan Contributions — Cotisations au Régime de pensions du Canada
Weekly (52 pay periods a year) — Hebdomadaire (52 périodes de paie par année)

Pay Rémunération From - De	To - À	CPP RPC	Pay Rémunération From - De	To - À	CPP RPC	Pay Rémunération From - De	To - À	CPP RPC	Pay Rémunération From - De	To - À	CPP RPC	Pay Rémunération From - De	To - À	CPP RPC
399.48	399.73	12.96	477.95	478.19	16.02	641.79	642.04	22.41	687.95	688.19	24.21	783.33	793.32	28.12
399.74	399.99	12.97	478.20	478.45	16.03	642.05	642.29	22.42	688.20	688.45	24.22	793.33	803.32	28.51
400.00	400.24	12.98	478.46	478.71	16.04	642.30	642.55	22.43	688.46	688.71	24.23	803.33	813.32	28.90
400.25	400.50	12.99	478.72	478.96	16.05	642.56	642.81	22.44	688.72	688.96	24.24	813.33	823.32	29.29
400.51	400.76	13.00	478.97	479.22	16.06	642.82	643.06	22.45	688.97	689.22	24.25	823.33	833.32	29.68
400.77	401.01	13.01	479.23	479.47	16.07	643.07	643.32	22.46	689.23	689.47	24.26	833.33	843.32	30.07
401.02	401.27	13.02	479.48	479.73	16.08	643.33	643.58	22.47	689.48	689.73	24.27	843.33	853.32	30.46
401.28	401.53	13.03	479.74	479.99	16.09	643.59	643.83	22.48	689.74	689.99	24.28	853.33	863.32	30.85
401.54	401.78	13.04	480.00	480.24	16.10	643.84	644.09	22.49	690.00	690.24	24.29	863.33	873.32	31.24
401.79	402.04	13.05	480.25	480.50	16.11	644.10	644.35	22.50	690.25	690.50	24.30	873.33	883.32	31.63
402.05	402.29	13.06	480.51	480.76	16.12	644.36	644.60	22.51	690.51	690.76	24.31	883.33	893.32	32.02
402.30	402.55	13.07	480.77	481.01	16.13	644.61	644.86	22.52	690.77	691.01	24.32	893.33	903.32	32.41
402.56	402.81	13.08	481.02	481.27	16.14	644.87	645.12	22.53	691.02	691.27	24.33	903.33	913.32	32.80
402.82	403.06	13.09	481.28	481.53	16.15	645.13	645.37	22.54	691.28	691.53	24.34	913.33	923.32	33.19
403.07	403.32	13.10	481.54	481.78	16.16	645.38	645.63	22.55	691.54	691.78	24.35	923.33	933.32	33.58
403.33	403.58	13.11	481.79	482.04	16.17	645.64	645.88	22.56	691.79	692.04	24.36	933.33	943.32	33.97
403.59	403.83	13.12	482.05	482.29	16.18	645.89	646.14	22.57	692.05	692.29	24.37	943.33	953.32	34.36
403.84	404.09	13.13	482.30	482.55	16.19	646.15	646.40	22.58	692.30	692.55	24.38	953.33	963.32	34.75
404.10	404.35	13.14	482.56	482.81	16.20	646.41	646.65	22.59	692.56	692.81	24.39	963.33	973.32	35.14
404.36	404.60	13.15	482.82	483.06	16.21	646.66	646.91	22.60	692.82	693.06	24.40	973.33	983.32	35.53
404.61	404.86	13.16	483.07	483.32	16.22	646.92	647.17	22.61	693.07	693.32	24.41	983.33	993.32	35.92
404.87	405.12	13.17	483.33	483.58	16.23	647.18	647.42	22.62	693.33	693.58	24.42	993.33	1003.32	36.31
405.13	405.37	13.18	483.59	483.83	16.24	647.43	647.68	22.63	693.59	693.83	24.43	1003.33	1013.32	36.70
405.38	405.63	13.19	483.84	484.09	16.25	647.69	647.94	22.64	693.84	694.09	24.44	1013.33	1023.32	37.09
405.64	405.88	13.20	484.10	484.35	16.26	647.95	648.19	22.65	694.10	694.35	24.45	1023.33	1033.32	37.48
405.89	406.14	13.21	484.36	484.60	16.27	648.20	648.45	22.66	694.36	694.60	24.46	1033.33	1043.32	37.87
406.15	406.40	13.22	484.61	484.86	16.28	648.46	648.71	22.67	694.61	694.86	24.47	1043.33	1053.32	38.26

Employment Insurance Premiums — Cotisations à l'assurance-emploi

Insurable Earnings Rémunération assurable From - De	To - À	EI premium Cotisation d'AE	Insurable Earnings Rémunération assurable From - De	To - À	EI premium Cotisation d'AE	Insurable Earnings Rémunération assurable From - De	To - À	EI premium Cotisation d'AE	Insurable Earnings Rémunération assurable From - De	To - À	EI premium Cotisation d'AE	Insurable Earnings Rémunération assurable From - De	To - À	EI premium Cotisation d'AE
390.21	390.62	9.37	468.96	469.37	11.26	637.71	638.12	15.31	678.96	679.37	16.30	869.80	870.20	20.88
390.63	391.04	9.38	469.38	469.79	11.27	638.13	638.54	15.32	679.38	679.79	16.31	870.21	870.62	20.89
391.05	391.45	9.39	469.80	470.20	11.28	638.55	638.95	15.33	679.80	680.20	16.32	870.63	871.04	20.90
391.46	391.87	9.40	470.21	470.62	11.29	638.96	639.37	15.34	680.21	680.62	16.33	871.05	871.45	20.91
391.88	392.29	9.41	470.63	471.04	11.30	639.38	639.79	15.35	680.63	681.04	16.34	871.46	871.87	20.92
392.30	392.70	9.42	471.05	471.45	11.31	639.80	640.20	15.36	681.05	681.45	16.35	871.88	872.29	20.93
392.71	393.12	9.43	471.46	471.87	11.32	640.21	640.62	15.37	681.46	681.87	16.36	872.30	872.70	20.94
393.13	393.54	9.44	471.88	472.29	11.33	640.63	641.04	15.38	681.88	682.29	16.37	872.71	873.12	20.95
393.55	393.95	9.45	472.30	472.70	11.34	641.05	641.45	15.39	682.30	682.70	16.38	873.13	873.54	20.96
												873.55	873.95	20.97
393.96	394.37	9.46	472.71	473.12	11.35	641.46	641.87	15.40	682.71	683.12	16.39	873.96	874.37	20.98
394.38	394.79	9.47	473.13	473.54	11.36	641.88	642.29	15.41	683.13	683.54	16.40	874.38	874.79	20.99
394.80	395.20	9.48	473.55	473.95	11.37	642.30	642.70	15.42	683.55	683.95	16.41	874.80	875.20	21.00
395.21	395.62	9.49	473.96	474.37	11.38	642.71	643.12	15.43	683.96	684.37	16.42	875.21	875.62	21.01
395.63	396.04	9.50	474.38	474.79	11.39	643.13	643.54	15.44	684.38	684.79	16.43	875.63	876.04	21.02
396.05	396.45	9.51	474.80	475.20	11.40	643.55	643.95	15.45	684.80	685.20	16.44	876.05	876.45	21.03
396.46	396.87	9.52	475.21	475.62	11.41	643.96	644.37	15.46	685.21	685.62	16.45	876.46	876.87	21.04
396.88	397.29	9.53	475.63	476.04	11.42	644.38	644.79	15.47	685.63	686.04	16.46	876.88	877.29	21.05
397.30	397.70	9.54	476.05	476.45	11.43	644.80	645.20	15.48	686.05	686.45	16.47	877.30	877.70	21.06
397.71	398.12	9.55	476.46	476.87	11.44	645.21	645.62	15.49	686.46	686.87	16.48	877.71	878.12	21.07
398.13	398.54	9.56	476.88	477.29	11.45	645.63	646.04	15.50	686.88	687.29	16.49	878.13	878.54	21.08
398.55	398.95	9.57	477.30	477.70	11.46	646.05	646.45	15.51	687.30	687.70	16.50	878.55	878.95	21.09
398.96	399.37	9.58	477.71	478.12	11.47	646.46	646.87	15.52	687.71	688.12	16.51	878.96	879.37	21.10
399.38	399.79	9.59	478.13	478.54	11.48	646.88	647.29	15.53	688.13	688.54	16.52	879.38	879.79	21.11
399.80	400.20	9.60	478.55	478.95	11.49	647.30	647.70	15.54	688.55	688.95	16.53	879.80	880.20	21.12
400.21	400.62	9.61	478.96	479.37	11.50	647.71	648.12	15.55	688.96	689.37	16.54	880.21	880.62	21.13
400.63	401.04	9.62	479.38	479.79	11.51	648.13	648.54	15.56	689.38	689.79	16.55	880.63	881.04	21.14
401.05	401.45	9.63	479.80	480.20	11.52	648.55	648.95	15.57	689.80	690.20	16.56	881.05	881.45	21.15

Saskatchewan (July 1, 2000)
Federal and Provincial Tax Deductions
Weekly (52 pay periods a year)

(Le 1er juillet 2000) Saskatchewan
Retenues d'impôt fédéral et provincial
Hebdomadaire (52 périodes de paie par année)

Pay Rémunération		If the employee's claim code from the TD1(E) form is / Si le code de demande de l'employé selon le formulaire TD1(F) est										
		0	1	2	3	4	5	6	7	8	9	10
From De	Less than Moins de		Deduct from each pay / Retenez sur chaque paie									
396.	400	99.05	63.00	59.05	51.20	43.35	35.45	23.45	15.60	7.75		
400.	404	100.05	64.00	60.05	52.20	44.30	36.45	24.65	16.80	8.90	1.05	.10
404.	408	101.10	64.95	61.05	53.15	45.30	37.45	25.80	17.95	10.10	2.20	.30
408.	412	102.10	65.95	62.00	54.15	46.30	38.40	27.00	19.15	11.30	3.40	.55
412.	416	103.10	66.95	63.00	55.15	47.25	39.40	28.20	20.35	12.45	4.60	.80
476.	484	119.90	83.30	79.25	71.35	63.50	55.60	47.70	39.85	32.00	24.10	16.25
484.	492	121.95	85.30	81.25	73.30	65.45	57.60	49.70	41.85	34.00	26.10	18.25
492.	500	124.00	87.35	83.30	75.30	67.40	59.55	51.70	43.80	35.95	28.10	20.20
500.	508	126.00	89.40	85.35	77.25	69.40	61.50	53.65	45.80	37.90	30.05	22.20
508.	516	128.05	91.45	87.35	79.25	71.35	63.50	55.60	47.75	39.90	32.00	24.15
636.	644	166.50	129.90	125.80	117.70	109.60	101.45	93.35	85.20	77.10	69.20	61.30
644.	652	169.40	132.75	128.70	120.60	112.45	104.35	96.25	88.10	80.00	71.95	64.10
652.	660	172.30	135.65	131.60	123.50	115.35	107.25	99.10	91.00	82.85	74.75	66.90
660.	668	175.20	138.55	134.50	126.40	118.25	110.10	102.00	93.90	85.75	77.65	69.70
668.	676	178.05	141.45	137.40	129.25	121.15	113.00	104.90	96.80	88.65	80.55	72.50
676.	684	180.95	144.35	140.30	132.15	124.05	115.90	107.80	99.65	91.55	83.40	75.30
684.	692	183.85	147.25	143.15	135.05	126.90	118.80	110.70	102.55	94.45	86.30	78.20
692.	700	186.75	150.10	146.05	137.95	129.80	121.70	113.55	105.45	97.35	89.20	81.10
700.	708	189.65	153.00	148.95	140.85	132.70	124.60	116.45	108.35	100.20	92.10	83.95
708.	716	192.50	155.90	151.85	143.70	135.60	127.45	119.35	111.25	103.10	95.00	86.85
836.	844	241.30	203.90	199.85	191.70	183.60	175.45	167.35	159.25	151.10	143.00	134.85
844.	852	244.45	206.90	202.85	194.75	186.60	178.50	170.35	162.25	154.15	146.00	137.90
852.	860	247.60	209.95	205.90	197.75	189.65	181.50	173.40	165.25	157.15	149.05	140.90
860.	868	250.80	212.95	208.90	200.80	192.65	184.55	176.40	168.30	160.15	152.05	143.90
868.	876	253.95	216.00	211.95	203.80	195.70	187.55	179.45	171.30	163.20	155.05	146.95
876.	884	257.15	219.00	214.95	206.85	198.70	190.60	182.45	174.35	166.20	158.10	149.95
884.	892	260.30	222.05	217.95	209.85	201.70	193.60	185.50	177.35	169.25	161.10	153.00
892.	900	263.50	225.15	221.00	212.85	204.75	196.60	188.50	180.40	172.25	164.15	156.00
900.	908	266.65	228.30	224.05	215.90	207.75	199.65	191.55	183.40	175.30	167.15	159.05
908.	916	269.80	231.50	227.25	218.90	210.80	202.65	194.55	186.45	178.30	170.20	162.05

Recording the Payroll

Generally, a Payroll Register such as the one shown is a supplementary memorandum record. As such, you do not post its information directly to the accounts. Instead, you must first record the payroll with a General Journal entry, which is then posted to the accounts. The entry to record the payroll shown in Exhibit 11.5 is:

July 14	Sales Salaries Expense	2,050.00	
	Office Salaries Expense	1,514.00	
	Employment Insurance Payable		85.54
	Employees' Income Taxes Payable		726.60
	Employees' Hospital Insurance Payable		120.00
	Canada Pension Plan Payable		123.20
	Payroll Payable		2,508.66
	To record the July 14 payroll.		

The debits of the entry were taken from the Payroll Register's distribution column totals. They charge the employees' gross earnings to the proper salary expense accounts. The credits to EI Payable, Employees' Income Taxes Payable, Employees' Hospital Insurance Payable, and CPP Payable record these amounts as current liabilities. The credit to Payroll Payable (also called Salaries Payable, Wages Payable, or Accrued Salaries Payable, etc.) records as a liability the net amount to be paid to the employees.

4. What constitutes the employee's gross pay?
5. What is the employee's net pay?

Answers—p. 578

Paying the Employees

Prepare journal entries to record the payments to employees and explain the operation of a payroll bank account.

Almost every business pays its employees by cheque or through electronic funds transfer (EFT). In a company that has few employees, these amounts are often drawn on the regular bank account and entered in a Cash Disbursements Journal (or Cheque Register) like the one described in Chapter 8. Since each payment is debited to the Payroll Payable account, posting labour can be saved by adding a Payroll Payable column in the journal. If such a column is added, entries to pay the employees shown in the Exhibit 11.5 payroll will appear as in Exhibit 11.7. Most employers furnish each employee an earnings statement each payday. The statement gives the employee a record of hours worked, gross pay, deductions, and net pay. If payment is by cheque, the statement often takes the form of a detachable paycheque portion that is removed before the cheque is cashed. A paycheque earnings statement is reproduced in Exhibit 11.8.

Lawn Worker

You take a summer job working for a family friend who runs a small lawn mowing service. When the time arrives for your first paycheque, the owner slaps you on the back, gives you full payment in cash, winks, and adds: "No need to pay those high taxes, eh?" What are your responsibilities in this case? Do you take any action?

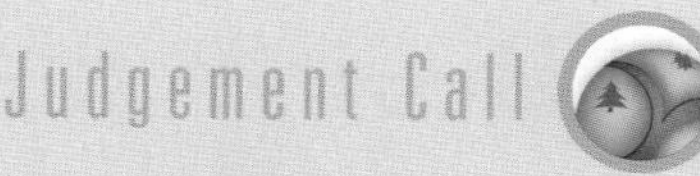

Answers—p. 578

Payroll Bank Account

A business with many employees will often use a special **payroll bank account** to pay its employees. When such an account is used, one cheque for the total payroll is drawn on the regular bank account and deposited in the special payroll bank account.

Exhibit 11.7

Cash Disbursements Journal

Cash Disbursments Journal									
Date	Cheque No.	Payee	Account Debited	PR	Other Accts. Debit	Accts. Pay. Debit	Payroll Payable Debit	Merch. Inv. Credit	Cash Credit
July 14	754	John Auer	Payroll Pay				295.42		295.42
	755	Joan Cheung	"				351.08		351.08
	756	Moe Daljit	"				577.88		577.88
	757	Shannon Lee	"				455.30		455.30
	758	Sunil Prasad	"				477.90		477.90
	759	Allan Rupert	"				351.08		351.08

Then individual payroll cheques are drawn on this special account. Because only one cheque for the payroll total is drawn on the regular bank account each payday, use of a special payroll bank account simplifies internal control, especially the reconciliation of the regular bank account. It may be reconciled without considering the payroll cheques outstanding. Many financial institutions offer a payroll service whereby the employees' net pay is transferred electronically into their accounts. The employer simply transfers the net amount of the payroll to the institution along with the employees' names and the accounts to be credited.

Exhibit 11.8

A Payroll Cheque

John Auer	*40*		*10.00*	*400.00*		*400.00*	*9.60*	*64.00*	*12.98*	*18.00*	*104.58*	*295.42*
Employee	Total Hours	O.T. Hours	Reg. Pay Rate	Regular Pay	O.T. Prem. Pay	Gross Pay	EI Premium	Income Taxes	CP Plan	Hosp. Ins.	Total Deductions	Net Pay

STATEMENT OF EARNINGS AND DEDUCTIONS FOR EMPLOYEE'S RECORDS—DETACH BEFORE CASHING CHEQUE

GRASSLAND INDUSTRIES
Loon Lake, Saskatchewan

No. 1517

PAY TO THE ORDER OF *John Auer* Date *July 14, 2000* $ *295.42*

Two hundred ninety - five - forty two cents - - - - - - - - - - - - - - - -

Lloydminster Credit Union
Lloydminster, Saskatchewan

GRASSLAND INDUSTRIES

Jane R. Morris

When a company uses a special payroll account, it must complete the following steps to pay the employees:

1. Record the information shown on the payroll Register in the usual manner with a General Journal entry similar to the one previously illustrated. This entry causes the sum of the employees' net pay to be credited to the liability account (Salaries Payable).
2. Have a single cheque written that is payable to Payroll Bank account for the total amount of the payroll and enter the payment in the Cash Disbursements Journal. This requires a debit to Salaries Payable and a credit to Cash.
3. Have the cheque deposited in the payroll bank account. This transfers an amount of money equal to the payroll total from the regular bank account to the special payroll bank account.
4. Have individual payroll cheques drawn on the special payroll bank account and delivered to the employees. As soon as all employees cash their cheques, the funds in the special account will be exhausted. Typically, companies will arrange for the bank to charge all service costs to the regular bank account.

A special Payroll Cheque Register may be used in connection with a payroll bank account. However, most companies do not use such a register. Instead, the payroll cheque numbers are entered in the Payroll Register so that it serves as a Cheque Register.

Employee's Individual Earnings Record

An **Employee's Individual Earnings Record,** as shown in Exhibit 11.9, provides for each employee, in one record, a full year's summary of the employee's working time, gross earnings, deductions, and net pay. In addition, it accumulates information that:

1. Serves as a basis for the employer's payroll tax returns.
2. Indicates when an employee's earnings have reached the maximum amounts for CPP and EI deductions.
3. Supplies data for the T4 slip, which must be given to the employee at the end of the year.

The payroll information on an Employee's Individual Earnings Record is taken from the Payroll Register. The information as to earnings, deductions, and net pay is first recorded on a single line in the Payroll Register. Then, each pay period the information is posted from the Payroll Register to the earnings record. Note the last column of the record. It shows an employee's cumulative earnings and is used to determine when the earnings reach the maximum amounts taxed and are no longer subject to the various payroll taxes.

Exhibit 11.9

Employee's Individual Earnings Record

Employee's Name *John Auer* SIN No. *123-456-789* Employee No. *114*

Home Address *Box 68, Loon Lake* Notify in Case of Emergency *Margaret Auer* Phone No. *964-9834*

Employed *May 15, 1999* Date of Termination ______ Reason ______

Date of Birth *June 6, 1972* Date Becomes 65 *June 6, 2037* Male (X) Female ( ) Married ( ) Single (X) Number of Exemptions 0 Pay Rate $10.00

Occupation *Clerk* Place *Warehouse*

Date		Time Lost		Time Worked												
Per. Ends	Paid	Hrs.	Reason	Total	O.T. Hours	Reg. Pay	O.T. Pay	Gross Pay	EI Prem	Income Taxes	Hosp. Ins.	CPP	Total Deductions	Net Pay	Cheque No.	Cumulative Earnings
7-Jan	7-Jan			40		400.00		400.00	9.60	64.00	18.00	12.98	104.58	295.42	673.00	400.00
14-Jan	14-Jan			40		400.00		400.00	9.60	64.00	18.00	12.98	104.58	295.42	701.00	800.00
21-Jan	21-Jan			40		400.00		400.00	9.60	64.00	18.00	12.98	104.58	295.42	743.00	1,200.00
28-Jan	28-Jan	4	Sick	36		360.00		360.00	8.64	54.15	18.00	11.42	92.21	267.79	795.00	1,560.00
4-Feb	4-Feb			40		400.00		400.00	9.60	64.00	18.00	12.98	104.58	295.42	839.00	1,960.00
11-Feb	11-Feb			40		400.00		400.00	9.60	64.00	18.00	12.98	104.58	295.42	854.00	2,360.00
18-Feb	18-Feb			40		400.00		400.00	9.60	64.00	18.00	12.98	104.58	295.42	893.00	2,760.00
25-Feb	25-Feb			40		400.00		400.00	9.60	64.00	18.00	12.98	104.58	295.42	932.00	3,160.00
14-Jul	14-Jul			40		400.00		400.00	9.60	64.00	18.00	12.98	104.58	295.42		9.560.00

6. Why would a company use a special payroll bank account?
7. What is the purpose of the employee's earnings record?

Answers—p. 578

Mid-Chapter Demonstration Problem

On January 7, the end of its first weekly pay period in the year, Saskat Company's payroll record showed that its one office employee and two sales employees had earned $688 (claim code 4), $880 (claim code 1), and $648 (claim code 2) respectively. Each employee has $40 of hospital insurance premiums withheld plus $15 of union dues.

Required

a. Prepare a schedule similar to the register in Exhibit 11.5 to summarize deductions by employee and in total. Use the tables in Exhibit 11.6 to determine the appropriate CPP, EI, and income tax to be withheld.

b. Give the journal entry to record the payroll on January 7.

SOLUTION TO Mid-Chapter Demonstration Problem

a.

		Deductions						Payment	Distribution	
	Gross Pay	EI Premium	Income Taxes	Hospital Insurance	CPP	Union Dues	Total Deductions	Net Pay	Sales Salaries	Office Salaries
1	688.00	16.51	126.90	40.00	24.21	15.00	222.62	465.38	688.00	
2	880.00	21.12	219.00	40.00	31.63	15.00	326.75	553.25		880.00
3	648.00	15.55	128.70	40.00	22.65	15.00	221.90	426.10		648.00
	2,216.00	53.18	474.60	120.00	78.49	45.00	771.27	1,444.73	688.00	1,528.00

b.

July 7	Office Salaries Expense	688.00	
	Sales Salaries Expense	1,528.00	
	EI Payable		53.18
	Employees' Income Taxes Payable		474.60
	Employees' Hospital Insurance Payable		120.00
	CPP Payable		78.49
	Employees' Union Dues Payable		45.00
	Payroll Payable		1,444.73
	To record payroll deductions for pay period ending January 7.		

Payroll Deductions Required of the Employer

LO4 Calculate the payroll costs levied on employers and prepare the entries to record the accrual and payments of these amounts.

Under the previous discussion of the Canada Pension Plan, it was pointed out that pension deductions are required in like amounts on both employed workers and their employers. A covered employer is required by law to deduct from the employees' pay the amounts of their Canada Pension Plan, but in addition, the employer must pay an amount equal to the sum of the employees' Canada pension. Commonly, the amount deducted by the employer is recorded at the same time as the payroll to which it relates is recorded. Also, since both the employees' and employer's shares are reported on the same form and are paid in one amount, the liability for both is normally recorded in the same liability account, the Canada Pension Plan Payable account.

In addition to the Canada Pension Plan, an employer is required to pay employment insurance that is 1.4 times the sum of the employees' employment insurance deductions. Most employers record both of these payroll deductions with a journal entry that is made at the time of recording the payroll to which they relate. For example, the entry to record the employer's amounts on the payroll in Exhibit 11.5 is:

July 14	EI Expense (1.4 × $85.54)	119.76	
	CPP Expense...	123.20	
	Employment Insurance Payable...........		119.76
	Canada Pension Plan Payable		123.20
	To record the employer's payroll taxes.		

The debit of the entry records as an expense the payroll taxes levied on the employer, and the credits record the liabilities for the taxes.

Paying the Payroll Deductions

Income tax, Employment Insurance, and Canada Pension Plan amounts withheld each payday from the employees' pay plus the employer's portion of employment insurance and Canada Pension Plan are current liabilities until paid to the Receiver General for Canada. The normal method of payment is to pay the amounts due at any chartered bank or remit directly to the Receiver General for Canada. Payment of these amounts is usually required to be made before the 15th of the month following the month that deductions were made from the earnings of the employees. Large employers are required to remit on the 10th and 25th of each month.

For simplicity, we assume the payment of the July 14 amounts recorded above is made the following day. Recall, however, that the employer must remit the amounts withheld from the employee as determined in Exhibit 11.5 *plus* the employer's portion recorded above. The following T-accounts summarize all of these amounts:

EI Payable	
	85.54*
	119.76**
	205.30

Employees' Income Taxes Payable	
	726.60*

Hospital Insurance Payable	
	120.00*

CPP Payable	
	123.20*
	123.20**
	246.40

**Employees' portion per Exhibit 11.5* ***Employer's portion*

The entry to record remittance to the Receiver General for Canada is then:

July 15	Employment Insurance Payable	205.30	
	Employees' Income Taxes Payable	726.60	
	Canada Pension Plan Payable	246.40	
	Cash		1,178.30
	To record the remittance of payroll liabilities to the Receiver General for Canada.		

The entry to record remittance to the hospital insurance plan authority is then:

July 15	Employment Hospital Insurance Payable	120.00	
	Cash		120.00
	To record the remittance of employees' hospital insurance premiums.		

Notice that the payment of payroll liabilities is recorded in the same manner as payment of any other liabilities.

Accruing Payroll Deductions on Wages

Mandatory payroll deductions are levied *only on wages actually paid.* Accrued wages are not subject to payroll deductions until they are paid. However, to satisfy the matching principle P. 140, both, accrued wages and the related accrued deductions should be recorded at the end of an accounting period. In reality, because the amounts of such deductions vary little from one accounting period to the next and often are small in amount, many employers apply the materiality principle P. 333 and do not accrue payroll deductions.

8. When are the payments for employee deductions due to the Receiver General for Canada?

Answers—p. 578

Employee (Fringe) Benefit Costs

Calculate and record employee fringe benefit costs and show the effect of these items on the total cost of employing labour.

Many companies pay for a variety of benefits called **employee fringe benefits** in addition to the wages earned by employees and the related amounts paid by the employer. For example, an employer may pay for part (or all) of the employees' medical insurance, life insurance, and disability insurance. Another typical employee benefit involves employer contributions to a retirement income plan. Workers' compensation and vacation pay are required to be paid by employers according to the legislation in each province.

Workers' Compensation

Legislation is in effect in all provinces for payments to employees for an injury or disability arising out of or in the course of their employment. Under the provincial workers' compensation acts, employers are, in effect, required to insure their employees against injury or disability that may arise as a result of employment. Premiums are normally based on (1) accident experience of the industrial classification to which each business is assigned and (2) the total payroll.

Procedures for payment are as follows:

1. At the beginning of each year, every covered employer is required to submit to the Workers' Compensation Board[1] an estimate of his or her expected payroll for the coming year.
2. Provisional premiums are then established by the board relating estimated requirements for disability payments to estimated payroll. Provisional premium notices are then sent to all employers.
3. Provisional premiums are normally payable in three to six installments during the year.
4. At the end of each year, actual payrolls are submitted to the board, and final assessments are made based on actual payrolls and actual payments. Premiums are normally between 1% and 3% of gross payroll and are borne by the employer.

Employer Contributions to Employee Insurance and Retirement Plans

The entries to record employee benefits costs depend on the nature of the benefit. Some employee retirement plans are quite complicated and involve accounting procedures that are too complex for discussion in this introductory course. In other cases, however, the employer simply makes periodic cash contributions to a retirement fund for each employee and records the amounts contributed as expense. Other employee benefits that require periodic cash payments by the employer include employer payments of insurance premiums for employees.

In the case of employee benefits that simply require the employer to make periodic cash payments, the entries to record the employer's obligations are similar to those used for payroll deductions.[2] For example, assume that an employer with five employees has agreed to pay medical insurance premiums of $40 per month for each employee. The employer will also contribute 10% of each employee's salary to a retirement program. If each employee earns $2,500 per month, the entry to record these employee benefits for the month of July is:

July 31	Benefits Expense	1,450	
	Employees' Medical Insurance Payable		200
	Employees' Retirement Program Payable [($2,500 x 5) × 10%]		1,250
	To record employee benefits.		

Vacation Pay

Employers are required to allow their employees paid vacation time (at a minimum rate of 4% of gross earnings) as a benefit of employment. For example,

[1] In Ontario, the Workers' Compensation Board has been renamed as the Workplace Safety and Insurance Board (WSIB).

[2] Some payments of employee benefits must be added to the gross salary of the employee for the purpose of calculating income tax, CPP, and EI payroll deductions. However, in this chapter and in the problems at the end of the chapter, the possible effect of employee benefit costs on payroll taxes is ignored to avoid undue complexity in the introductory course.

many employees receive two weeks' vacation in return for working 50 weeks each year. The effect of a two-week vacation is to increase the employer's payroll expenses by 4% (2/50 = 0.04). After five years of service, most employees are entitled to a three-week vacation (i.e., 3/49 = 6.12%). However, new employees often do not begin to accrue vacation time until after they have worked for a period of time, perhaps as much as a year. The employment contract may say that no vacation is granted until the employee works one year, but if the first year is completed, the employee receives the full two weeks. Contracts between the employer and employee may allow for vacation pay in excess of the 4% minimum.

To account for vacation pay, an employer should estimate and record the additional expense during the weeks the employees are working and earning the vacation time. For example, assume that a company with a weekly payroll of $20,000 grants two weeks' vacation after one year's employment. The entry to record the estimated vacation pay is:

Date	Benefits Expense	800	
	Estimated Vacation Pay Liability ($20,000 × 0.04)		800
	To record estimated vacation pay.		

As employees take their vacations and receive their vacation pay, the entries to record the vacation payroll take the following general form:

Date	Estimated Vacation Pay Liability	XXX	
	Employees' EI and CPP Payable		XXX
	Employees' Income Taxes Payable		XXX
	Other Withholding Liability Accounts Such as Employees' Hospital Insurance Payable		XXX
	Payroll Payable		XXX
	To record payroll.		

Mandatory payroll deductions and employee benefits costs are often a major category of expense incurred by a company. They may amount to well over 25% of the salaries earned by employees.

9. How is the cost of Workers' Compensation determined?

Answers—p. 578

Computerized Payroll Systems

Manually prepared records like the ones described in this chapter are used in many small companies. However, an increasing number of companies use computers to process their payroll. The computer programs are designed to take advantage of the fact that the same calculations are performed each pay period. Also, much of the same information must be entered for each employee in the Payroll Register, on the employee's earnings record, and on the employee's paycheque. The computers simultaneously store or print the information in all three places.

Summary

LO1 List the taxes and other items frequently withheld from employees' wages. Amounts withheld from employees' wages include federal income taxes, Canada Pension Plan and employment insurance. Payroll costs levied on employers include employment insurance and Canada Pension.

An employee's gross pay may be the employee's specified wage rate multiplied by the total hours worked plus an overtime premium rate multiplied by the number of overtime hours worked. Alternatively, it may be the given periodic salary of the employee. Taxes withheld and other deductions for items such as union dues, insurance premiums, and charitable contributions are subtracted from gross pay to determine the net pay.

LO2 Make the calculations necessary to prepare a Payroll Register and prepare the entry to record payroll liabilities. A Payroll Register is used to summarize all employees' hours worked, regular and overtime pay, payroll deductions, net pay, and distribution of gross pay to expense accounts during each pay period. It provides the necessary information for journal entries to record the accrued payroll and to pay the employees.

LO3 Prepare journal entries to record the payments to employees and explain the operation of a payroll bank account. A payroll bank account is a separate account that is used solely for the purpose of paying employees. Each pay period, an amount equal to the total net pay of all employees is transferred from the regular bank account to the payroll bank account. Then cheques are drawn against the payroll bank account for the net pay of the employees.

LO4 Calculate the payroll costs levied on employers and prepare the entries to record the accrual and payment of these amounts. When a payroll is accrued at the end of each pay period, payroll deductions and levies should also be accrued with debits and credits to the appropriate expense and liability accounts.

LO5 Calculate and record employee fringe benefit costs and show the effect of these items on the total cost of employing labour. Fringe benefit costs that involve simple cash payments by the employer should be accrued with an entry similar to the one used to accrue payroll levies. Legislated employee benefits related to Workers' Compensation and vacation pay are paid for by the employer.

GUIDANCE ANSWER TO Judgement Call

Lawn Worker

You need to be concerned about being an accomplice to unlawful payroll activities. Not paying federal and provincial taxes on wages earned is unlawful and unethical. Such payments won't provide CPP and EI contributions. The best course of action is to request payment by cheque. If this fails to change the owner's payment practices, you must consider quitting this job.

GUIDANCE ANSWERS TO Flashback

1. Employment insurance is designed to alleviate hardships caused by interruptions in earnings through unemployment.
2. On or before the last day in February.
3. Deductions for Canada Savings Bonds, health or life insurance premiums, loan repayments, and donations to charitable organizations.
4. Regular pay plus overtime pay.
5. Gross pay less all the deductions.
6. A payroll bank account simplifies the payments to the employees and the internal control.
7. An employee's earnings record serves as a basis for the employer's tax returns, indicates when the maximum CPP and EI deductions have been reached and supplies the data for the employees' T-4 slips.
8. Normally by the 15th of the following month; large employers must remit on the 10th and 25th of each month.
9. Premiums are based on the accident experience in the specific industry and on the size of the employer's payroll.

Demonstration Problem

Presented below are various items of information about three employees of the Deluth Company for the week ending November 24, 2000.

	Billings	Dephir	Singe
Wage rate (per hour)	$ 15	$ 30	$ 18
Overtime premium	50%	50%	50%
Annual vacation	2.5 weeks	2.5 weeks	2.5 weeks
Cumulative wages as of November 17, 2000	$28,500	$52,600	$14,800
For the week (pay period) ended November 24, 2000:			
Hours worked	40	44	48
Medical insurance:			
Deluth's contribution	$ 25	$ 25	$ 25
Withheld from employee	18	18	18
Union dues withheld	50	70	50
Income tax withheld	127	479	269
Employment insurance withheld	14	—	22
Canada Pension withheld	21	—	34
Payroll deduction rates:			
Employment insurance	2.4% to an annual maximum of $936.00		
Canada Pension Plan	3.9% less annual exemption of $3,500; maximum per year is $1,329.90		

Required

In solving the following requirements, *round all amounts to the nearest whole dollar.* Prepare schedules that determine, for each employee and for all employees combined, the following information:

1. Wages earned for the regular 40-hour week, total overtime pay, and gross wages.
2. Vacation pay accrued for the week.
3. Costs imposed on the employer.
4. Employees' net pay for the week.
5. Employer's total payroll-related cost (wages, mandatory deductions, and fringe benefits).

Present journal entries to record the following:

6. Payroll expense.
7. Payroll deductions and employees' benefits expense.

Planning the Solution

- Calculate the gross pay for each employee.
- Compute the amounts deducted for all employees and their net pay.
- Compute the employer's share of payroll deductions.
- Prepare the necessary journal entries.

SOLUTION TO Demonstration Problem

1. The gross wages (including overtime) for the week:

	Billings	Dephir	Singe	Total
Regular wage rate	$ 15	$ 30	$ 18	
Regular hours	× 40	× 44	× 48	
Regular pay	$600	$1,320	$864	$2,784
Overtime premium	$ 7.5	$ 15	$ 9	
Overtime hours	-0-	× 4	× 8	
Total overtime pay	$ -0-	$ 60	$ 72	$ 132
Gross wages	$600	$1,380	$936	$2,916

2. The vacation pay accrued for the week:

	Billings	Dephir	Singe	Total
Annual vacation	2.5 weeks	2.5 weeks	2.5 weeks	
Weeks worked in year	49.5 weeks	49.5 weeks	49.5 weeks	
Vacation pay as a percentage of regular pay	5.05%	5.05%	5.05%	
Regular pay this week	× $600	× $1,380	× $936	
Vacation pay this week	$30	$70	$47	$147

The information in the following table is needed for part 3:

			Earnings Subject to	
Employees	Earnings Through November 17	Earnings This Week	CPP	Employment Insurance
Billings	$28,500	$ 600	$ 533*	$ 600
Dephir[1]	52,600	1,380	—	—
Singe[2]	14,800	936	869*	936
Totals		2,916	1,402	1,536

** Recall that the first $3,500 of income is exempt from CPP. This represents $67/week (=3,500/52 weeks).*

3. The costs imposed on the employer.

	Billings	Dephir	Singe	Total
CPP (1.0)	$21	—	$34	$ 55
Employment Insurance (1.4)	20	—	31	51
Totals	41	—	65	106

[1] Dephir's earnings have exceeded the CPP maximum of $37,600 and EI maximum of $39,000 and the maximum deductions of $1,329.90 (CPP) and $936.00 (EI). Therefore, neither CPP nor EI is deducted.

[2] EI deduction calculations from the diskette ignore the maximum weekly earnings of $750. Deductions would cease when the yearly maximum deduction of $936 is reached.

4. The net amount paid to the employees:

	Billings	Dephir	Singe	Total
Regular pay	$600	$1,320	$864	$2,784
Overtime pay	-0-	60	72	132
Gross pay	$600	$1,380	$936	$2,916
Withholdings:				
Income tax withholding	$127	$ 479	$269	$ 875
CPP withholding	21	—	34	55
EI withholding	14	—	22	36
Medical insurance	18	18	18	54
Union dues	50	70	50	170
Total withholdings	$230	$ 567	$393	$1,190
Net pay to employees	$370	$ 813	$543	$1,726

5. The total payroll-related cost to the employer.

	Billings	Dephir	Singe	Total
Regular pay	$600	$1,320	$ 864	$2,784
Overtime pay	-0-	60	72	132
Gross pay	$600	$1,380	$ 936	$2,916
Deductions and fringe benefits:				
CPP	$ 21	$ —	$ 34	$ 55
EI	20	—	31	51
Vacation	30	70	47	147
Medical insurance	25	25	25	75
Total deductions and fringe benefits	$ 96	$ 95	$ 137	$ 328
Total payroll-related cost	$696	$1,475	$1,073	$3,244

6. Journal entry for payroll expense:

2000			
Nov. 24	Salary Expense	2,916	
	Employees' Income Taxes Payable		875
	Employees' CPP Payable		55
	Employees' EI Payable		36
	Employees' Medical Insurance Payable		54
	Employees' Union Dues Payable		170
	Payroll Payable		1,726
	To record payroll expense.		

7. Journal entry for payroll deductions and employees' benefit expense:

2000			
Nov. 24	EI Expense	51	
	CPP Expense	55	
	Benefits Expense	222	
	Employees' CPP Payable		55
	Employees' EI Payable		51
	Accrued Vacation Pay Payable		147
	Employees' Medical Insurance Payable		75
	To record employer's share of payroll deductions and benefits expense.		

Glossary

Canada Pension Plan A national contributory retirement pension scheme. (p. 559)

Clock card A card issued to each employee that the employee inserts in a time clock to record the time of arrival to and departure from work. (p. 564)

Employee fringe benefits Payments by an employer, in addition to wages and salaries, that are made to acquire employee benefits such as insurance coverage and retirement income. (p. 575)

Employment insurance An employment/employer-financed unemployment insurance plan. (p. 559)

Employee's gross pay The amount an employee earns before any deductions for taxes or other items such as union dues or insurance premiums. (p. 565)

Employee's Individual Earnings Record A record of an employee's hours worked, gross pay, deductions, net pay, and certain personal information about the employee. (p. 571)

Employee's net pay The amount an employee is paid, determined by subtracting from gross pay all deductions for taxes and other items that are withheld from the employee's earnings. (p. 566)

Payroll bank account A special bank account a company uses solely for the purpose of paying employees by depositing in the account each pay period an amount equal to the total employees' net pay and drawing the employees' payroll cheques on the account. (p. 570)

Payroll deduction An amount deducted from an employee's pay, usually based on the amount of an employee's gross pay. (p. 558)

Personal tax credits Amounts that may be deducted from an individual's income taxes and that determine the amount of income taxes to be withheld. (p. 558)

Timekeeping The process of recording the time worked by each employee. (p. 564)

Wage bracket withholding table A table showing the amounts to be withheld from employees' wages at various levels of earnings. (p. 561)

Questions

1. Who pays the contributions to the Canada Pension Plan?
2. Who pays premiums under the workers' compensation laws?
3. Who pays federal employment insurance? What is the rate?
4. What are the objectives of employment insurance laws?
5. To whom and when are payroll deductions remitted?
6. What determines the amount that must be deducted from an employee's wages for income taxes?
7. What is a tax withholding table?
8. What is the Canada Pension Plan deduction rate for self-employed individuals?
9. How is a clock card used in recording the time an employee is on the job?
10. How is a special payroll bank account used in paying the wages of employees?
11. At the end of an accounting period a firm's special payroll bank account has a $562.35 balance because the payroll cheques of two employees have not cleared the bank. Should this $562.35 appear on the firm's balance sheet? If so, where?
12. What information is accumulated on an employee's individual earnings record? Why must this information be accumulated? For what purposes is the information used?
13. What payroll charges are levied on the employer? What amounts are deducted from the wages of an employee?
14. What are employee fringe benefits? Name some examples.

Quick Study

QS 11-1
Payroll expenses
LO1

A company deducts $260 in Employment Insurance and $205 in Canada Pension from the weekly payroll of its employees. How much is the company's expense for these items for the week?

QS 11-2
Preparing payroll journal entries
LO2

Tracon Co. has six employees, each of whom earns $3,000 per month. Income taxes are 20% of gross pay and the company deducts EI and CPP. Prepare the March 31 journal entry to record payroll for the month.

QS 11-3
Paying employees
LO3

Use the information in QS 11-2 to record the payment of the wages to the employees for March assuming that Tracon uses a payroll bank account.

QS 11-4
Completing a payroll register
LO2

		Deductions				Pay	Distribution	
Employee	Gross Pay	EI Premium	Income Taxes	CPP	Total Deductions	Net Pay	Office Salaries	Sales Salaries
Johnson, S.	1,200.00	28.80	389.10	44.11				
Waverley, N.	530.00	12.72	103.10	18.05				
Zender, B.	675.00	16.20	155.90	23.70				
Totals								

Required
Prairie Rigging's three employees are paid weekly. Waverley works in the office and Johnson and Zender are sales representatives. Complete the payroll register above for the week ended October 27, 2000.

QS 11-5
Completing a payroll register using tables
LO2

		Deductions				Pay	
Employee	Gross Pay	EI Premium	Income Taxes	CPP	Total Deductions	Net Pay	Salaries Expense
Bentley, A.	2,010.00						
Craig, T.	2,115.00						
Totals							

Required
Meadow Lake Groceries has two employees who are paid monthly. Using the tables beginning on page 592, complete the payroll register above for the month ended September 30, 2000 assuming both employees' TD1 claim code is 1.

QS 11-6
Completing a payroll register by calculating deductions
LO2

		Deductions				Pay	Distribution	
Employee	Gross Pay	EI Premium	Income Taxes	CPP	Total Deductions	Net Pay	Office Salaries	Sales Salaries
Withers, S.	2,500.00						2,500.00	
Volt, C.	1,800.00							1,800.00
Totals								

Required
Maidstone Plumbing Services' two employees are paid bi-weekly. Assuming a tax rate of 30%, complete the payroll register above for the two-week period ended November 17, 2000.

QS 11-7
Payroll journal entry
LO3

Racon Co. has eight employees, each of whom earns $3,500 per month. Income taxes are 20% of gross pay and the company deducts EI and CPP. Prepare the September 30, 2000 journal entry to record Racon's payroll expenses for the month.

QS 11-8
Payroll journal entry
LO3

Chandler Tailors pays its three employees monthly. The following information is available for the September 2000 payroll:

		Deductions				Pay	Distribution	
Employee	**Gross Pay**	**EI Premium**	**Income Taxes**	**CPP**	**Total Deductions**	**Net Pay**	**Office Salaries**	**Sales Salaries**
Berkley, M.	575.00	13.80	114.00	19.80	147.60	427.40	575.00	
Cander, O.	840.00	20.16	226.25	20.07	266.48	573.52		840.00
Meister, P.	720.00	17.28	175.25	25.46	217.99	502.01		720.00
Totals	2,135.00	51.24	515.50	65.33	632.07	1,502.93	575.00	1,560.00

Required
Prepare the journal entry to record payroll expenses for the month.

QS 11-9
Recording employer's payroll deductions
LO4

Refer to the information in QS 11-8. Prepare a journal entry to record Chandler Tailors' share of payroll deductions.

QS 11-10
Payment of payroll deductions
LO4

Refer to the information in QS 11-8 and QS 11-9. Prepare a journal entry to record payment by Chandler Tailors to the Receiver General for Canada.

QS 11-11
Recording fringe benefit costs
LO5

Racon Co. (see QS 11-7) contributes 8% of an employee's salary to a retirement program, medical insurance premiums of $60 per employee, and vacation allowance equivalent to 5% of the employee's salary. Prepare a journal entry to record the fringe benefit costs for September.

Exercises

Exercise 11-1
Calculating gross and net pay
LO1

Check figure:
Net pay = $1,700.45

Julie Leung, an employee of the Import Company Limited, worked 172 hours during the month of October 2000. Her pay rate is $12.50 per hour, and her wages are subject to no deductions other than income taxes, employment insurance, and Canada Pension Plan. The overtime premium is 50% and is applicable to any time greater than 160 hours per month. Calculate her regular pay, overtime premium pay, gross pay, total deductions, and net pay. Use the tables beginning on page 592 to determine the EI, CPP, and income tax decductions (assume claim code 1).

Exercise 11-2
Calculating payroll deductions and recording the payroll

LO2

The following information as to earnings and deductions for the pay period ended July 14 was taken from a company's payroll records:

Employees' Names	Weekly Gross Pay	Earnings to End of Previous Week	Income Taxes	Health Insurance Deductions
Hellena Chea	$ 720	$12,510	$ 175.25	$ 24.00
Joseph Lim	610	10,320	130.10	24.00
Dino Patelli	830	15,500	219.20	36.00
Sharl Qulnata	1,700	29,500	641.50	24.00
	$3,860		$1,166.05	$108.00

Calculate the employees' EI and CPP withholdings, the amounts paid to each employee, and prepare a General Journal entry to record the payroll. Assume all employees work in the office.

Check figure:
Total CPP withholding = $140.02

Exercise 11-3
Completing a payroll register

LO2

Lendrum Servicing's four employees are paid every two weeks. Akerley runs the office and the remaining employees are sales representatives.

		Deductions					Pay	Distribution	
Employee	Gross Pay	EI Premium	Income Taxes	United Way	CPP	Total Deductions	Net Pay	Admin. Salaries	Sales Salaries
Akerley, D.	1,900.00	45.60	549.50	80.00	68.90				
Nesbitt, M.	1.260.00	30.24	273.10	50.00	43.89				
Trent, F.	1,680.00	40.32	452.50	40.00	60.32				
Vacon, M.	3,000.00	72.00	1,079.65	300.00	111.80				
Totals									

Required
Complete the payroll register above for the bi-weekly period ended December 29, 2000.

Check figure:
Total deductions = $3,297.82

Exercise 11-4
Completing a payroll register using tables

LO2

D&D Stockyards' four employees are paid monthly. Each employee donates 5% to the United Way through payroll deductions. Crimson and Peterson purchase Canada Savings Bonds through monthly payroll deductions of $150 and $200 respectively.

		Deductions						Pay	Distribution	
Employee	Gross Pay	EI Premium	Income Taxes	Canada Savings Bonds	CPP	United Way	Total Deductions	Net Pay	Office Salaries	Sales Salaries
Crimson, L.	1,995.00								1,995.00	
Long, M.	2,040.00									2,040.00
Morris, P.	2,000.00									2,000.00
Peterson, B.	2,280.00									2,280.00
Totals										

Required
Using the tables beginning on page 592, complete the payroll register above for the month ended August 31, 2000 assuming the following TD1 claim codes for each employee: Crimson (2), Long (1), Morris (1), and Peterson (3).

Check figure:
Total EI premiums = $199.56

Exercise 11-5
Completing a payroll register by calculating deductions

LO2

		Deductions						Pay	Distribution	
Employee	Gross Pay	EI Premium	Income Taxes	Medical Ins.	CPP	United Way	Total Deductions	Net Pay	Office Salaries	Guide Salaries
Crimson, L.	1,995.00			65.00		40.00				1,995.00
Long, M.	2,040.00			65.00		100.00			2,040.00	
Morris, P.	2,000.00			65.00		-0-				2,000.00
Peterson, B.	2,350.00			65.00		50.00				2,350.00
Totals										

Check figure:
Total deductions = $3,448.24

Required
Piperel Lake Resort's four employees are paid monthly. Assuming a tax rate of 30%, complete the payroll register above for the month ended November 30, 2000.

Exercise 11-6
Other payroll deductions

LO3

Sharon Von Hatton is the only employee of a self-employed businessperson. She earned a monthly salary of $2,050 in December 2000, her first month of employment. In response to a citywide effort to obtain charitable contributions to the local United Way programs, Von Hatton has requested that her employer withhold 2% of her salary (net of CPP, EI, and income taxes).

Required
Prepare the journal entry to record payroll expenses for the month of December 2000. Use the tables beginning on page 592 to determine CPP, EI, and income tax deductions (assume claim code 1).

Check figure:
Monthly United Way contribution = $31.55

Exercise 11-7
Payroll journal entry

LO3

Paradise Hills Berry Farm has 25 employees who are paid bi-weekly. The payroll register showed the following payroll deductions for the pay period ending August 25, 2000.

Gross Pay	EI Premium	Income Taxes	CPP	Medical Ins.	United Way
65,950.00	1,582.75	22,458.75	2,444.00	1,150.00	1,319.00

Required
Using the information provided, prepare the journal entry to record the payroll expenses.

Exercise 11-8
Recording employer's payroll deductions

LO4

Refer to the information in Exercise 11-7. Prepare a journal entry to record the employer's share of payroll deductions.

Exercise 11-9
Payment of payroll deductions

LO4

Refer to the information in Exercise 11-7 and Exercise 11-8. Prepare a journal entry to record payment by the employer to the Receiver General for Canada.

Exercise 11-10
Calculating and recording payroll deductions

LO4

Use the information provided in Exercise 11-2 to complete the following requirements:

1. Prepare a General Journal entry to record the employer's payroll costs resulting from the payroll.
2. Prepare a General Journal entry to record the following employee benefits incurred by the company: (a) health insurance costs equal to the amounts contributed by each employee and (b) contributions equal to 10% of gross pay for each employee's retirement income program.

Exercise 11-11
Analyzing total labour costs

LO4, 5

O'Riley Company's payroll costs and fringe benefit expenses include the normal CPP and EI contributions, retirement fund contributions of 10% of total earnings, and health insurance premiums of $120 per employee per month. Given the following list of employees' annual salaries, payroll costs and fringe benefits are what percentage of salaries?

Doherty	$ 36,000
Fane	61,000
Kahan	59,000
Martin	37,000
Poon	48,000
Total	$241,000

Check figure:
Total CPP contributions = $6,563.70

Exercise 11-12
Calculating and recording payroll costs (using tables)

LO2, 3, 4, 5

Milly's Drive-In's 12 employees earn a gross pay of $2,080 each per month. Milly's Drive-In contributes 8% of gross pay to a retirement program for employees and pays a medical insurance premium of $50 per month per employee.

Required

Prepare the entries to record the employer's payroll costs for the month of October 2000. Use the tables beginning on page 592 to determine CPP, EI, and income tax deductions (assume claim code 1).

Exercise 11-13
Calculating fringe benefits costs

LO5

Bellward Corporation grants vacation time of two weeks to those employees who have worked for the company one complete year. After 10 years of service, employees receive four weeks of vacation. The monthly payroll for January totals $320,000, of which 70% is payable to employees with 10 or more years of service. On January 31, record the January expense arising from the vacation policy of the company.

Problems

Problem 11-1A
The Payroll Register, the payroll bank account, and payroll deductions

LO2, 3, 4

The payroll records of Brownlee Corporation provided the following information for the weekly pay period ended December 21, 2000:

												Payroll Week Ended
	Clock Card	Daily Time							Pay	Hospital	Union	Earnings to End of Previous
Employees	No.	M	T	W	T	F	S	S	Rate	Insurance	Dues	Week
Ray Loran	11	8	8	8	8	8	4	0	20.00	40.00	16.00	42,000
Kathy Sousa	12	7	8	6	7	8	4	0	18.00	40.00	15.00	46,000
Gary Smith	13	8	8	0	8	8	4	4	16.00	40.00	14.00	21,000
Nicola Parton	14	8	8	8	8	8	0	0	20.00	40.00	16.00	32,000
Diana Wood	15	0	6	6	6	6	8	8	18.00	40.00	15.00	36,000
Totals										200.00	76.00	

Check figure:
Total deductions = $1,164.19

Required

1. Enter the relevant information in the proper columns of a Payroll Register and complete the register; calculate CPP and EI deductions. Charge the wages of Kathy Sousa to Office Salaries Expense and the wages of the remaining employees to Service Wages Expense. Calculate income tax deductions at 20% of gross pay. Employees are paid an overtime premium of 50% for all hours in excess of 40 per week.
2. Prepare a General Journal entry to record the Payroll Register information.
3. Make the entry in the Cash Disbursements journal (Cheque No. 399) to transfer funds equal to the payroll from the regular bank account to the payroll bank account under the assumption that the company uses special payroll cheques and a payroll bank account in paying its employees. Assume that the first payroll cheque is numbered 530 and enter the payroll cheque numbers in the Payroll Register.
4. Prepare a General Journal entry to record the employer's payroll costs resulting from the payroll.

Problem 11-2A

The Payroll Register and the payroll bank account

LO3

On January 5, at the end of the first weekly pay period of the year, a company's Payroll Register showed that its employees had earned $19,570 of sales salaries and $6,230 of office salaries. Withholdings from the employees' salaries were to include $740 of EI, $660 of CPP, $5,310 of income taxes, $930 of hospital insurance, and $420 of union dues.

Required

1. Prepare the General Journal entry to record the January 6 payroll.
2. Prepare a General Journal entry to record the employer's payroll expenses resulting from the January 6 payroll.
3. Under the assumption that the company uses a payroll bank account and special payroll cheques in paying its employees, give the entry in the Cash Disbursements journal (Cheque No. 542) to transfer funds equal to the payroll from the regular bank account to the payroll bank account.
4. After the Cheque Register entry is made and posted, are additional debit and credit entries required to record the payroll cheques for the employees?

Problem 11-3A

Journal entries — payroll taxes, and employee fringe benefits

LO3, 4, 5

A company showed the following information in its Payroll Register:

Deductions						Pay	Distribution		
EI Premium	CPP	Income Taxes	Medical Ins.	Union Dues	Total Deductions	Net Pay	Sales Salaries Expense	Office Salaries Expense	Shop Salaries Expense
0.00	0.00	219.20	30.00	20.00	269.00	558.80	828.00		
0.00	0.00	143.00	28.00	18.00	189.00	451.00			640.00
13.44	19.22	111.60	25.00	16.00	185.26	374.74			560.00
17.28	25.46	175.25	30.00	20.00	267.99	452.01		720.00	
30.72	**44.68**	**649.05**	**113.00**	**74.00**	**911.45**	**1,836.55**	**828.00**	**720.00**	**1,200.00**

1. Prepare a General Journal entry to record the Payroll Register information.
2. Make the Cheque Register entry to transfer funds equal to the payroll from the regular bank account (Cheque No. 522) under the assumption that the company uses special payroll cheques and a payroll bank account in paying its employees. Assume that the first payroll cheque is numbered 230 and enter the payroll cheque numbers in the Payroll Register.
3. Prepare a General Journal entry to record the employer's payroll deductions resulting from the payroll.
4. Prepare General Journal entries to accrue employee fringe benefit costs for the week. Assume that the company matches the employees' payments for medical insurance and contributes an amount equal to 8% of each employee's gross pay to a retirement program. Also, each employee accrues vacation pay at the rate of 6% of the wages and salaries earned. The company estimates that all employees eventually will be paid their vacation pay.

Problem 11-4A
Journal entries for payroll transactions
LO3, 4, 5

A company has three employees, each of whom has been employed since January 1, earns $2,600 per month, and is paid on the last day of each month. On March 1, the following accounts and balances appeared in its ledger.

a. Employees' Income Taxes Payable, $1,480 (liability for February only).
b. Employment Insurance Payable, $475 (liability for February).
c. Canada Pension Plan Payable, $390 (liability for February).
d. Employees' Medical Insurance Payable, $908 (liability for January and February).

During March and April, the company completed the following related to payroll.

Mar. 12 Issued Cheque No. 320 payable to Receiver General for Canada. The cheque was in payment of the February employee income taxes, EI and CPP amounts due.

30 Prepared a General Journal entry to record the March Payroll Record, which had the following column totals:

Income Taxes	EI	CPP	Medical Insurance	Total Deductions	Net Pay	Office Salaries	Shop Wages
$1,460	$187	$270	$260	$2,177	$5,623	$2,600	$5,200

30 Recorded the employer's $260 liability for its 50% contribution to the medical insurance plan of employees and 4% vacation pay accrued to the employees.

30 Prepared a General Journal entry to record the employer's costs resulting from the March payroll.

Apr. 13 Issued Cheque No. 375 payable to the Receiver General for Canada in payment of the March mandatory deductions.

13 Issued Cheque No. 376 payable to All Canadian Insurance Company in payment of the employee medical insurance premiums for the first quarter.

Required
Prepare the entries to record the transactions.

Alternate Problems

Problem 11-1B
The Payroll Register, the payroll bank account, and payroll deductions
LO2, 3, 4

The payroll records of Wailee Corporation provided the following information for the weekly pay period ended December 22, 2000:

												Payroll Week Ended
Employees	Clock Card No.	Daily Time M	T	W	T	F	S	S	Pay Rate	Hospital Insurance	Union Dues	Earnings to End of Previous Week
Ben Amoko	31	8	8	8	8	8	0	0	17.00	30.00	12.00	28,000
Auleen Carson	32	7	8	8	7	8	4	0	18.00	30.00	12.00	36,000
Mitali De	33	8	8	0	8	8	4	4	18.00	30.00	12.00	28,000
Gene Deszca	34	8	8	8	8	8	0	0	15.00	30.00	12.00	32,000
Ysong Tan	35	0	6	6	6	6	8	8	15.00	30.00	12.00	36,000
Totals										150.00	60.00	

Check figure:
Total deductions = $2,289.78

Required
1. Enter the relevant information in the proper columns of a Payroll Register and complete the register; calculate CPP and EI deductions. Charge the wages of Auleen Carson to Office Salaries Expense and the wages of the remaining employees to Service Wages Expense. Calculate income tax deductions at 20% of gross pay.
2. Prepare a General Journal entry to record the Payroll Register information.
3. Make the entry in the Cash Disbursements journal (Cheque No. 753) to transfer funds equal to the payroll from the regular bank account to the payroll bank account under the assumption the company uses special payroll cheques and a payroll bank account in paying its employees. Assume that the first cheque is numbered 530 and enter the payroll cheque numbers in the Payroll Register.
4. Prepare a General Journal entry to record the employer's payroll costs resulting from the payroll.

Problem 11-2B
The Payroll Register and the payroll bank account

LO3

On January 5, at the end of the first weekly pay period of the year, a company's Payroll Register showed that its employees had earned $23,400 of sales salaries and $5,820 of office salaries. Withholdings from the employees' salaries were to include $860 of EI, $710 of CPP, $6,180 of income taxes, $920 of hospital insurance, and $490 of union dues.

Required
1. Prepare the General Journal entry to record the January 5 payroll.
2. Prepare a General Journal entry to record the employer's payroll expenses resulting from the January 5 payroll.
3. Under the assumption that the company uses a payroll bank account and special payroll cheques in paying its employees, give the Cheque Register entry (Cheque No. 874) to transfer funds equal to the payroll from the bank account to the payroll bank account.
4. After the entry in the Cash Disbursements journal is made and posted, are additional debit and credit entries required to record the payroll cheques and pay the employees?

Problem 11-3B
Journal entries — payroll taxes, and employee fringe benefits

LO3, 4, 5

A company showed the following information in its Payroll Register:

Deductions						Pay	Distribution		
EI Premium	CPP	Income Taxes	Medical Ins.	Union Dues	Total Deductions	Net Pay	Sales Salaries Expense	Office Salaries Expense	Shop Salaries Expense
0.00	0.00	208.60	30.00	20.00	258.60	541.40	800.00		
0.00	0.00	123.65	25.00	18.00	166.65	425.35			592.00
18.24	26.95	191.85	25.00	18.00	280.04	479.96			760.00
17.28	25.46	175.25	30.00	20.00	267.99	452.01		720.00	
35.52	**52.41**	**699.35**	**110.00**	**76.00**	**973.28**	**1,898.72**	**800.00**	**720.00**	**1,352.00**

1. Prepare a General Journal entry to record the Payroll register information.
2. Make the Cheque Register entry to transfer funds equal to the payroll from the regular bank account to the payroll bank account (Cheque No. 412) under the assumption that the company uses special payroll cheques and a payroll bank account in paying its employees. Assume that the first payroll cheque is numbered 630 and enter the payroll cheque numbers in the Payroll Register.
3. Prepare a General Journal entry to record the employer's payroll deductions resulting from the payroll.
4. Prepare General Journal entries to accrue employee fringe benefits costs for the week. Assume that the company matches the employees' payments for medical insurance and contributes an amount equal to 8% of each employee's gross pay to a retirement program. Also, each employee accrues vacation pay at the rate of 6% of the wages and salaries earned. The company estimates that all employees eventually will be paid their vacation pay.

Problem 11-4B
General Journal entries for payroll transactions
LO3, 4, 5

A company has three employees', each of whom has been employed since January 1, earns $2,300 per month, and is paid on the last day of each month. On March 1, the following accounts and balances appeared in its ledger:

a. Employees Income Taxes Payable, $1,290 (liability for February only).
b. Unemployment Insurance Payable, $460 (liability for February).
c. Canada Pension Plan Payable, $340 (liability for February).
d. Employees' Medical Insurance Payable, $935 (liability for January and February).

During March and April, the company completed the following transactions related to payroll:

Mar. 11 Issued Cheque No. 635 payable to Receiver General for Canada. The cheque was in payment of the February employee income taxes, EI and CPP amounts due.

31 Prepared a General Journal entry to record the March Payroll Record, which had the following column totals:

Income Taxes	EI	CPP	Medical Insurance	Total Deductions	Net Pay	Office Salaries	Shop Wages
$1,190	$166	$235	$225	$1,816	$5,084	$2,300	$4,600

31 Recorded the employer's $225 liability for its 50% contribution to the medical insurance plan of employees and 4% vacation pay accrued to the employees.

31 Prepared a General Journal entry to record the employer's payroll costs resulting from the March payroll.

Apr. 13 Issued Cheque No. 764 payable to the Receiver General for Canada in payment of the March mandatory deductions.

13 Issued Cheque No. 765 payable to National Insurance Company in payment of the employee medical insurance premiums for the first quarter.

Required
Prepare the entries to record the transactions.

Analytical and Review Problems

A & R Problem 11-1

Using the current year's withholding tables for Canada Pension Plan, employment insurance and income tax, update the Payroll Register of Exhibit 11.5. In computing income tax withholdings, state your assumption as to each employee's personal deductions. Assume that hospital insurance deductions continue at the same amounts as in Exhibit 11.5.

A & R Problem 11-2

The following data were taken from the Payroll Register of Eastcoastal Company:

Gross Salary	xxx
Employee's Income Tax Deductions	xxx
EI Deductions	xxx
CPP Deductions	xxx
Hospital Insurance Deductions	xxx
Union Dues Deductions	xxx

Eastcoastal contributes an equal amount to the hospital insurance plan, in addition to the statutory payroll taxes, and 6% of the gross salaries to a pension program.

Required
Record in General Journal form the payroll, payment of the employees, and remittance to the appropriate authority amounts owing in connection with the payroll. (Note: All amounts are to be indicated as xxx.)

Canada Pension Plan Contributions
Monthly (12 pay periods a year)

Cotisations au Régime de pensions du Canada
Mensuel (12 périodes de paie par année)

Pay Rémunération From - De	To - À	CPP RPC	Pay Rémunération From - De	To - À	CPP RPC	Pay Rémunération From - De	To - À	CPP RPC	Pay Rémunération From - De	To - À	CPP RPC
1990.00	1990.24	66.24	2008.46	2008.71	66.96	2026.92	2027.17	67.68	2045.38	2045.63	68.40
1990.25	1990.50	66.25	2008.72	2008.96	66.97	2027.18	2027.42	67.69	2045.64	2045.89	68.41
1990.51	1990.76	66.26	2008.97	2009.22	66.98	2027.43	2027.68	67.70	2045.90	2046.14	68.42
1990.77	1991.01	66.27	2009.23	2009.48	66.99	2027.69	2027.94	67.71	2046.15	2046.40	68.43
1991.02	1991.27	66.28	2009.49	2009.73	67.00	2027.95	2028.19	67.72	2046.41	2046.65	68.44
1991.28	1991.53	66.29	2009.74	2009.99	67.01	2028.20	2028.45	67.73	2046.66	2046.91	68.45
1991.54	1991.78	66.30	2010.00	2010.24	67.02	2028.46	2028.71	67.74	2046.92	2047.17	68.46
1991.79	1992.04	66.31	2010.25	2010.50	67.03	2028.72	2028.96	67.75	2047.18	2047.42	68.47
1992.05	1992.30	66.32	2010.51	2010.76	67.04	2028.97	2029.22	67.76	2047.43	2047.68	68.48
1992.31	1992.55	66.33	2010.77	2011.01	67.05	2029.23	2029.48	67.77	2047.69	2047.94	68.49
1992.56	1992.81	66.34	2011.02	2011.27	67.06	2029.49	2029.73	67.78	2047.95	2048.19	68.50
1992.82	1993.07	66.35	2011.28	2011.53	67.07	2029.74	2029.99	67.79	2048.20	2048.45	68.51
1993.08	1993.32	66.36	2011.54	2011.78	67.08	2030.00	2030.24	67.80	2048.46	2048.71	68.52
1993.33	1993.58	66.37	2011.79	2012.04	67.09	2030.25	2030.50	67.81	2048.72	2048.96	68.53
1993.59	1993.83	66.38	2012.05	2012.30	67.10	2030.51	2030.76	67.82	2048.97	2049.22	68.54
1993.84	1994.09	66.39	2012.31	2012.55	67.11	2030.77	2031.01	67.83	2049.23	2049.48	68.55
1994.10	1994.35	66.40	2012.56	2012.81	67.12	2031.02	2031.27	67.84	2049.49	2049.73	68.56
1994.36	1994.60	66.41	2012.82	2013.07	67.13	2031.28	2031.53	67.85	2049.74	2049.99	68.57
1994.61	1994.86	66.42	2013.08	2013.32	67.14	2031.54	2031.78	67.86	2050.00	2050.24	68.58
1994.87	1995.12	66.43	2013.33	2013.58	67.15	2031.79	2032.04	67.87	2050.25	2050.50	68.59
1995.13	1995.37	66.44	2013.59	2013.83	67.16	2032.05	2032.30	67.88	2050.51	2050.76	68.60
1995.38	1995.63	66.45	2013.84	2014.09	67.17	2032.31	2032.55	67.89	2050.77	2051.01	68.61
1995.64	1995.89	66.46	2014.10	2014.35	67.18	2032.56	2032.81	67.90	2051.02	2051.27	68.62
1995.90	1996.14	66.47	2014.36	2014.60	67.19	2032.82	2033.07	67.91	2051.28	2051.53	68.63
1996.15	1996.40	66.48	2014.61	2014.86	67.20	2033.08	2033.32	67.92	2051.54	2051.78	68.64
1996.41	1996.65	66.49	2014.87	2015.12	67.21	2033.33	2033.58	67.93	2051.79	2052.04	68.65
1996.66	1996.91	66.50	2015.13	2015.37	67.22	2033.59	2033.83	67.94	2052.05	2052.30	68.66
1996.92	1997.17	66.51	2015.38	2015.63	67.23	2033.84	2034.09	67.95	2052.31	2052.55	68.67
1997.18	1997.42	66.52	2015.64	2015.89	67.24	2034.10	2034.35	67.96	2052.56	2052.81	68.68
1997.43	1997.68	66.53	2015.90	2016.14	67.25	2034.36	2034.60	67.97	2052.82	2053.07	68.69
1997.69	1997.94	66.54	2016.15	2016.40	67.26	2034.61	2034.86	67.98	2053.08	2053.32	68.70
1997.95	1998.19	66.55	2016.41	2016.65	67.27	2034.87	2035.12	67.99	2053.33	2053.58	68.71
1998.20	1998.45	66.56	2016.66	2016.91	67.28	2035.13	2035.37	68.00	2053.59	2053.83	68.72
1998.46	1998.71	66.57	2016.92	2017.17	67.29	2035.38	2035.63	68.01	2053.84	2054.09	68.73
1998.72	1998.96	66.58	2017.18	2017.42	67.30	2035.64	2035.89	68.02	2054.10	2054.35	68.74
1998.97	1999.22	66.59	2017.43	2017.68	67.31	2035.90	2036.14	68.03	2054.36	2054.60	68.75
1999.23	1999.48	66.60	2017.69	2017.94	67.32	2036.15	2036.40	68.04	2054.61	2054.86	68.76
1999.49	1999.73	66.61	2017.95	2018.19	67.33	2036.41	2036.65	68.05	2054.87	2055.12	68.77
1999.74	1999.99	66.62	2018.20	2018.45	67.34	2036.66	2036.91	68.06	2055.13	2055.37	68.78
2000.00	2000.24	66.63	2018.46	2018.71	67.35	2036.92	2037.17	68.07	2055.38	2055.63	68.79
2000.25	2000.50	66.64	2018.72	2018.96	67.36	2037.18	2037.42	68.08	2055.64	2055.89	68.80
2000.51	2000.76	66.65	2018.97	2019.22	67.37	2037.43	2037.68	68.09	2055.90	2056.14	68.81
2000.77	2001.01	66.66	2019.23	2019.48	67.38	2037.69	2037.94	68.10	2056.15	2056.40	68.82
2001.02	2001.27	66.67	2019.49	2019.73	67.39	2037.95	2038.19	68.11	2056.41	2056.65	68.83
2001.28	2001.53	66.68	2019.74	2019.99	67.40	2038.20	2038.45	68.12	2056.66	2056.91	68.84
2001.54	2001.78	66.69	2020.00	2020.24	67.41	2038.46	2038.71	68.13	2056.92	2057.17	68.85
2001.79	2002.04	66.70	2020.25	2020.50	67.42	2038.72	2038.96	68.14	2057.18	2057.42	68.86
2002.05	2002.30	66.71	2020.51	2020.76	67.43	2038.97	2039.22	68.15	2057.43	2057.68	68.87
2002.31	2002.55	66.72	2020.77	2021.01	67.44	2039.23	2039.48	68.16	2057.69	2057.94	68.88
2002.56	2002.81	66.73	2021.02	2021.27	67.45	2039.49	2039.73	68.17	2057.95	2058.19	68.89
2002.82	2003.07	66.74	2021.28	2021.53	67.46	2039.74	2039.99	68.18	2058.20	2058.45	68.90
2003.08	2003.32	66.75	2021.54	2021.78	67.47	2040.00	2040.24	68.19	2058.46	2058.71	68.91
2003.33	2003.58	66.76	2021.79	2022.04	67.48	2040.25	2040.50	68.20	2058.72	2058.96	68.92
2003.59	2003.83	66.77	2022.05	2022.30	67.49	2040.51	2040.76	68.21	2058.97	2059.22	68.93
2003.84	2004.09	66.78	2022.31	2022.55	67.50	2040.77	2041.01	68.22	2059.23	2059.48	68.94
2004.10	2004.35	66.79	2022.56	2022.81	67.51	2041.02	2041.27	68.23	2059.49	2059.73	68.95
2004.36	2004.60	66.80	2022.82	2023.07	67.52	2041.28	2041.53	68.24	2059.74	2059.99	68.96
2004.61	2004.86	66.81	2023.08	2023.32	67.53	2041.54	2041.78	68.25	2060.00	2060.24	68.97
2004.87	2005.12	66.82	2023.33	2023.58	67.54	2041.79	2042.04	68.26	2060.25	2060.50	68.98
2005.13	2005.37	66.83	2023.59	2023.83	67.55	2042.05	2042.30	68.27	2060.51	2060.76	68.99
2005.38	2005.63	66.84	2023.84	2024.09	67.56	2042.31	2042.55	68.28	2060.77	2061.01	69.00
2005.64	2005.89	66.85	2024.10	2024.35	67.57	2042.56	2042.81	68.29	2061.02	2061.27	69.01
2005.90	2006.14	66.86	2024.36	2024.60	67.58	2042.82	2043.07	68.30	2061.28	2061.53	69.02
2006.15	2006.40	66.87	2024.61	2024.86	67.59	2043.08	2043.32	68.31	2061.54	2061.78	69.03
2006.41	2006.65	66.88	2024.87	2025.12	67.60	2043.33	2043.58	68.32	2061.79	2062.04	69.04
2006.66	2006.91	66.89	2025.13	2025.37	67.61	2043.59	2043.83	68.33	2062.05	2062.30	69.05
2006.92	2007.17	66.90	2025.38	2025.63	67.62	2043.84	2044.09	68.34	2062.31	2062.55	69.06
2007.18	2007.42	66.91	2025.64	2025.89	67.63	2044.10	2044.35	68.35	2062.56	2062.81	69.07
2007.43	2007.68	66.92	2025.90	2026.14	67.64	2044.36	2044.60	68.36	2062.82	2063.07	69.08
2007.69	2007.94	66.93	2026.15	2026.40	67.65	2044.61	2044.86	68.37	2063.08	2063.32	69.09
2007.95	2008.19	66.94	2026.41	2026.65	67.66	2044.87	2045.12	68.38	2063.33	2063.58	69.10
2008.20	2008.45	66.95	2026.66	2026.91	67.67	2045.13	2045.37	68.39	2063.59	2063.83	69.11

 Employee's maximum CPP contribution for the year 2000 is $1329.90 La cotisation maximale de l'employé au RPC pour l'année 2000 est de 1329,90 $

Canada Pension Plan Contributions
Monthly (12 pay periods a year)

Cotisations au Régime de pensions du Canada
Mensuel (12 périodes de paie par année)

Pay Rémunération From - De	To - À	CPP RPC	Pay Rémunération From - De	To - À	CPP RPC	Pay Rémunération From - De	To - À	CPP RPC	Pay Rémunération From - De	To - À	CPP RPC
2063.84	2064.09	69.12	2082.31	2082.55	69.84	2100.77	2101.01	70.56	2119.23	2119.48	71.28
2064.10	2064.35	69.13	2082.56	2082.81	69.85	2101.02	2101.27	70.57	2119.49	2119.73	71.29
2064.36	2064.60	69.14	2082.82	2083.07	69.86	2101.28	2101.53	70.58	2119.74	2119.99	71.30
2064.61	2064.86	69.15	2083.08	2083.32	69.87	2101.54	2101.78	70.59	2120.00	2120.24	71.31
2064.87	2065.12	69.16	2083.33	2083.58	69.88	2101.79	2102.04	70.60	2120.25	2120.50	71.32
2065.13	2065.37	69.17	2083.59	2083.83	69.89	2102.05	2102.30	70.61	2120.51	2120.76	71.33
2065.38	2065.63	69.18	2083.84	2084.09	69.90	2102.31	2102.55	70.62	2120.77	2121.01	71.34
2065.64	2065.89	69.19	2084.10	2084.35	69.91	2102.56	2102.81	70.63	2121.02	2121.27	71.35
2065.90	2066.14	69.20	2084.36	2084.60	69.92	2102.82	2103.07	70.64	2121.28	2121.53	71.36
2066.15	2066.40	69.21	2084.61	2084.86	69.93	2103.08	2103.32	70.65	2121.54	2121.78	71.37
2066.41	2066.65	69.22	2084.87	2085.12	69.94	2103.33	2103.58	70.66	2121.79	2122.04	71.38
2066.66	2066.91	69.23	2085.13	2085.37	69.95	2103.59	2103.83	70.67	2122.05	2122.30	71.39
2066.92	2067.17	69.24	2085.38	2085.63	69.96	2103.84	2104.09	70.68	2122.31	2122.55	71.40
2067.18	2067.42	69.25	2085.64	2085.89	69.97	2104.10	2104.35	70.69	2122.56	2122.81	71.41
2067.43	2067.68	69.26	2085.90	2086.14	69.98	2104.36	2104.60	70.70	2122.82	2123.07	71.42
2067.69	2067.94	69.27	2086.15	2086.40	69.99	2104.61	2104.86	70.71	2123.08	2123.32	71.43
2067.95	2068.19	69.28	2086.41	2086.65	70.00	2104.87	2105.12	70.72	2123.33	2123.58	71.44
2068.20	2068.45	69.29	2086.66	2086.91	70.01	2105.13	2105.37	70.73	2123.59	2123.83	71.45
2068.46	2068.71	69.30	2086.92	2087.17	70.02	2105.38	2105.63	70.74	2123.84	2124.09	71.46
2068.72	2068.96	69.31	2087.18	2087.42	70.03	2105.64	2105.89	70.75	2124.10	2124.35	71.47
2068.97	2069.22	69.32	2087.43	2087.68	70.04	2105.90	2106.14	70.76	2124.36	2124.60	71.48
2069.23	2069.48	69.33	2087.69	2087.94	70.05	2106.15	2106.40	70.77	2124.61	2124.86	71.49
2069.49	2069.73	69.34	2087.95	2088.19	70.06	2106.41	2106.65	70.78	2124.87	2125.12	71.50
2069.74	2069.99	69.35	2088.20	2088.45	70.07	2106.66	2106.91	70.79	2125.13	2125.37	71.51
2070.00	2070.24	69.36	2088.46	2088.71	70.08	2106.92	2107.17	70.80	2125.38	2125.63	71.52
2070.25	2070.50	69.37	2088.72	2088.96	70.09	2107.18	2107.42	70.81	2125.64	2125.89	71.53
2070.51	2070.76	69.38	2088.97	2089.22	70.10	2107.43	2107.68	70.82	2125.90	2126.14	71.54
2070.77	2071.01	69.39	2089.23	2089.48	70.11	2107.69	2107.94	70.83	2126.15	2126.40	71.55
2071.02	2071.27	69.40	2089.49	2089.73	70.12	2107.95	2108.19	70.84	2126.41	2126.65	71.56
2071.28	2071.53	69.41	2089.74	2089.99	70.13	2108.20	2108.45	70.85	2126.66	2126.91	71.57
2071.54	2071.78	69.42	2090.00	2090.24	70.14	2108.46	2108.71	70.86	2126.92	2127.17	71.58
2071.79	2072.04	69.43	2090.25	2090.50	70.15	2108.72	2108.96	70.87	2127.18	2127.42	71.59
2072.05	2072.30	69.44	2090.51	2090.76	70.16	2108.97	2109.22	70.88	2127.43	2127.68	71.60
2072.31	2072.55	69.45	2090.77	2091.01	70.17	2109.23	2109.48	70.89	2127.69	2127.94	71.61
2072.56	2072.81	69.46	2091.02	2091.27	70.18	2109.49	2109.73	70.90	2127.95	2128.19	71.62
2072.82	2073.07	69.47	2091.28	2091.53	70.19	2109.74	2109.99	70.91	2128.20	2128.45	71.63
2073.08	2073.32	69.48	2091.54	2091.78	70.20	2110.00	2110.24	70.92	2128.46	2128.71	71.64
2073.33	2073.58	69.49	2091.79	2092.04	70.21	2110.25	2110.50	70.93	2128.72	2128.96	71.65
2073.59	2073.83	69.50	2092.05	2092.30	70.22	2110.51	2110.76	70.94	2128.97	2129.22	71.66
2073.84	2074.09	69.51	2092.31	2092.55	70.23	2110.77	2111.01	70.95	2129.23	2129.48	71.67
2074.10	2074.35	69.52	2092.56	2092.81	70.24	2111.02	2111.27	70.96	2129.49	2129.73	71.68
2074.36	2074.60	69.53	2092.82	2093.07	70.25	2111.28	2111.53	70.97	2129.74	2129.99	71.69
2074.61	2074.86	69.54	2093.08	2093.32	70.26	2111.54	2111.78	70.98	2130.00	2130.24	71.70
2074.87	2075.12	69.55	2093.33	2093.58	70.27	2111.79	2112.04	70.99	2130.25	2130.50	71.71
2075.13	2075.37	69.56	2093.59	2093.83	70.28	2112.05	2112.30	71.00	2130.51	2130.76	71.72
2075.38	2075.63	69.57	2093.84	2094.09	70.29	2112.31	2112.55	71.01	2130.77	2131.01	71.73
2075.64	2075.89	69.58	2094.10	2094.35	70.30	2112.56	2112.81	71.02	2131.02	2131.27	71.74
2075.90	2076.14	69.59	2094.36	2094.60	70.31	2112.82	2113.07	71.03	2131.28	2131.53	71.75
2076.15	2076.40	69.60	2094.61	2094.86	70.32	2113.08	2113.32	71.04	2131.54	2131.78	71.76
2076.41	2076.65	69.61	2094.87	2095.12	70.33	2113.33	2113.58	71.05	2131.79	2132.04	71.77
2076.66	2076.91	69.62	2095.13	2095.37	70.34	2113.59	2113.83	71.06	2132.05	2132.30	71.78
2076.92	2077.17	69.63	2095.38	2095.63	70.35	2113.84	2114.09	71.07	2132.31	2132.55	71.79
2077.18	2077.42	69.64	2095.64	2095.89	70.36	2114.10	2114.35	71.08	2132.56	2132.81	71.80
2077.43	2077.68	69.65	2095.90	2096.14	70.37	2114.36	2114.60	71.09	2132.82	2133.07	71.81
2077.69	2077.94	69.66	2096.15	2096.40	70.38	2114.61	2114.86	71.10	2133.08	2133.32	71.82
2077.95	2078.19	69.67	2096.41	2096.65	70.39	2114.87	2115.12	71.11	2133.33	2133.58	71.83
2078.20	2078.45	69.68	2096.66	2096.91	70.40	2115.13	2115.37	71.12	2133.59	2133.83	71.84
2078.46	2078.71	69.69	2096.92	2097.17	70.41	2115.38	2115.63	71.13	2133.84	2134.09	71.85
2078.72	2078.96	69.70	2097.18	2097.42	70.42	2115.64	2115.89	71.14	2134.10	2134.35	71.86
2078.97	2079.22	69.71	2097.43	2097.68	70.43	2115.90	2116.14	71.15	2134.36	2134.60	71.87
2079.23	2079.48	69.72	2097.69	2097.94	70.44	2116.15	2116.40	71.16	2134.61	2134.86	71.88
2079.49	2079.73	69.73	2097.95	2098.19	70.45	2116.41	2116.65	71.17	2134.87	2135.12	71.89
2079.74	2079.99	69.74	2098.20	2098.45	70.46	2116.66	2116.91	71.18	2135.13	2135.37	71.90
2080.00	2080.24	69.75	2098.46	2098.71	70.47	2116.92	2117.17	71.19	2135.38	2135.63	71.91
2080.25	2080.50	69.76	2098.72	2098.96	70.48	2117.18	2117.42	71.20	2135.64	2135.89	71.92
2080.51	2080.76	69.77	2098.97	2099.22	70.49	2117.43	2117.68	71.21	2135.90	2136.14	71.93
2080.77	2081.01	69.78	2099.23	2099.48	70.50	2117.69	2117.94	71.22	2136.15	2136.40	71.94
2081.02	2081.27	69.79	2099.49	2099.73	70.51	2117.95	2118.19	71.23	2136.41	2136.65	71.95
2081.28	2081.53	69.80	2099.74	2099.99	70.52	2118.20	2118.45	71.24	2136.66	2136.91	71.96
2081.54	2081.78	69.81	2100.00	2100.24	70.53	2118.46	2118.71	71.25	2136.92	2137.17	71.97
2081.79	2082.04	69.82	2100.25	2100.50	70.54	2118.72	2118.96	71.26	2137.18	2137.42	71.98
2082.05	2082.30	69.83	2100.51	2100.76	70.55	2118.97	2119.22	71.27	2137.43	2137.68	71.99

Employee's maximum CPP contribution for the year 2000 is $1329.90   La cotisation maximale de l'employé au RPC pour l'année 2000 est de 1329,90 $

Canada Pension Plan Contributions
Monthly (12 pay periods a year)

Cotisations au Régime de pensions du Canada
Mensuel (12 périodes de paie par année)

Pay Rémunération From - De	To - À	CPP RPC	Pay Rémunération From - De	To - À	CPP RPC	Pay Rémunération From - De	To - À	CPP RPC	Pay Rémunération From - De	To - À	CPP RPC
2137.69	2137.94	72.00	2156.15	2156.40	72.72	2174.61	2174.86	73.44	2193.08	2193.32	74.16
2137.95	2138.19	72.01	2156.41	2156.65	72.73	2174.87	2175.12	73.45	2193.33	2193.58	74.17
2138.20	2138.45	72.02	2156.66	2156.91	72.74	2175.13	2175.37	73.46	2193.59	2193.83	74.18
2138.46	2138.71	72.03	2156.92	2157.17	72.75	2175.38	2175.63	73.47	2193.84	2194.09	74.19
2138.72	2138.96	72.04	2157.18	2157.42	72.76	2175.64	2175.89	73.48	2194.10	2194.35	74.20
2138.97	2139.22	72.05	2157.43	2157.68	72.77	2175.90	2176.14	73.49	2194.36	2194.60	74.21
2139.23	2139.48	72.06	2157.69	2157.94	72.78	2176.15	2176.40	73.50	2194.61	2194.86	74.22
2139.49	2139.73	72.07	2157.95	2158.19	72.79	2176.41	2176.65	73.51	2194.87	2195.12	74.23
2139.74	2139.99	72.08	2158.20	2158.45	72.80	2176.66	2176.91	73.52	2195.13	2195.37	74.24
2140.00	2140.24	72.09	2158.46	2158.71	72.81	2176.92	2177.17	73.53	2195.38	2195.63	74.25
2140.25	2140.50	72.10	2158.72	2158.96	72.82	2177.18	2177.42	73.54	2195.64	2195.89	74.26
2140.51	2140.76	72.11	2158.97	2159.22	72.83	2177.43	2177.68	73.55	2195.90	2196.14	74.27
2140.77	2141.01	72.12	2159.23	2159.48	72.84	2177.69	2177.94	73.56	2196.15	2196.40	74.28
2141.02	2141.27	72.13	2159.49	2159.73	72.85	2177.95	2178.19	73.57	2196.41	2196.65	74.29
2141.28	2141.53	72.14	2159.74	2159.99	72.86	2178.20	2178.45	73.58	2196.66	2196.91	74.30
2141.54	2141.78	72.15	2160.00	2160.24	72.87	2178.46	2178.71	73.59	2196.92	2197.17	74.31
2141.79	2142.04	72.16	2160.25	2160.50	72.88	2178.72	2178.96	73.60	2197.18	2197.42	74.32
2142.05	2142.30	72.17	2160.51	2160.76	72.89	2178.97	2179.22	73.61	2197.43	2197.68	74.33
2142.31	2142.55	72.18	2160.77	2161.01	72.90	2179.23	2179.48	73.62	2197.69	2197.94	74.34
2142.56	2142.81	72.19	2161.02	2161.27	72.91	2179.49	2179.73	73.63	2197.95	2198.19	74.35
2142.82	2143.07	72.20	2161.28	2161.53	72.92	2179.74	2179.99	73.64	2198.20	2198.45	74.36
2143.08	2143.32	72.21	2161.54	2161.78	72.93	2180.00	2180.24	73.65	2198.46	2198.71	74.37
2143.33	2143.58	72.22	2161.79	2162.04	72.94	2180.25	2180.50	73.66	2198.72	2198.96	74.38
2143.59	2143.83	72.23	2162.05	2162.30	72.95	2180.51	2180.76	73.67	2198.97	2199.22	74.39
2143.84	2144.09	72.24	2162.31	2162.55	72.96	2180.77	2181.01	73.68	2199.23	2199.48	74.40
2144.10	2144.35	72.25	2162.56	2162.81	72.97	2181.02	2181.27	73.69	2199.49	2199.73	74.41
2144.36	2144.60	72.26	2162.82	2163.07	72.98	2181.28	2181.53	73.70	2199.74	2199.99	74.42
2144.61	2144.86	72.27	2163.08	2163.32	72.99	2181.54	2181.78	73.71	2200.00	2200.24	74.43
2144.87	2145.12	72.28	2163.33	2163.58	73.00	2181.79	2182.04	73.72	2200.25	2200.50	74.44
2145.13	2145.37	72.29	2163.59	2163.83	73.01	2182.05	2182.30	73.73	2200.51	2200.76	74.45
2145.38	2145.63	72.30	2163.84	2164.09	73.02	2182.31	2182.55	73.74	2200.77	2201.01	74.46
2145.64	2145.89	72.31	2164.10	2164.35	73.03	2182.56	2182.81	73.75	2201.02	2201.27	74.47
2145.90	2146.14	72.32	2164.36	2164.60	73.04	2182.82	2183.07	73.76	2201.28	2201.53	74.48
2146.15	2146.40	72.33	2164.61	2164.86	73.05	2183.08	2183.32	73.77	2201.54	2201.78	74.49
2146.41	2146.65	72.34	2164.87	2165.12	73.06	2183.33	2183.58	73.78	2201.79	2202.04	74.50
2146.66	2146.91	72.35	2165.13	2165.37	73.07	2183.59	2183.83	73.79	2202.05	2202.30	74.51
2146.92	2147.17	72.36	2165.38	2165.63	73.08	2183.84	2184.09	73.80	2202.31	2202.55	74.52
2147.18	2147.42	72.37	2165.64	2165.89	73.09	2184.10	2184.35	73.81	2202.56	2202.81	74.53
2147.43	2147.68	72.38	2165.90	2166.14	73.10	2184.36	2184.60	73.82	2202.82	2203.07	74.54
2147.69	2147.94	72.39	2166.15	2166.40	73.11	2184.61	2184.86	73.83	2203.08	2203.32	74.55
2147.95	2148.19	72.40	2166.41	2166.65	73.12	2184.87	2185.12	73.84	2203.33	2203.58	74.56
2148.20	2148.45	72.41	2166.66	2166.91	73.13	2185.13	2185.37	73.85	2203.59	2203.83	74.57
2148.46	2148.71	72.42	2166.92	2167.17	73.14	2185.38	2185.63	73.86	2203.84	2204.09	74.58
2148.72	2148.96	72.43	2167.18	2167.42	73.15	2185.64	2185.89	73.87	2204.10	2204.35	74.59
2148.97	2149.22	72.44	2167.43	2167.68	73.16	2185.90	2186.14	73.88	2204.36	2204.60	74.60
2149.23	2149.48	72.45	2167.69	2167.94	73.17	2186.15	2186.40	73.89	2204.61	2204.86	74.61
2149.49	2149.73	72.46	2167.95	2168.19	73.18	2186.41	2186.65	73.90	2204.87	2205.12	74.62
2149.74	2149.99	72.47	2168.20	2168.45	73.19	2186.66	2186.91	73.91	2205.13	2205.37	74.63
2150.00	2150.24	72.48	2168.46	2168.71	73.20	2186.92	2187.17	73.92	2205.38	2205.63	74.64
2150.25	2150.50	72.49	2168.72	2168.96	73.21	2187.18	2187.42	73.93	2205.64	2205.89	74.65
2150.51	2150.76	72.50	2168.97	2169.22	73.22	2187.43	2187.68	73.94	2205.90	2206.14	74.66
2150.77	2151.01	72.51	2169.23	2169.48	73.23	2187.69	2187.94	73.95	2206.15	2206.40	74.67
2151.02	2151.27	72.52	2169.49	2169.73	73.24	2187.95	2188.19	73.96	2206.41	2206.65	74.68
2151.28	2151.53	72.53	2169.74	2169.99	73.25	2188.20	2188.45	73.97	2206.66	2206.91	74.69
2151.54	2151.78	72.54	2170.00	2170.24	73.26	2188.46	2188.71	73.98	2206.92	2207.17	74.70
2151.79	2152.04	72.55	2170.25	2170.50	73.27	2188.72	2188.96	73.99	2207.18	2207.42	74.71
2152.05	2152.30	72.56	2170.51	2170.76	73.28	2188.97	2189.22	74.00	2207.43	2207.68	74.72
2152.31	2152.55	72.57	2170.77	2171.01	73.29	2189.23	2189.48	74.01	2207.69	2207.94	74.73
2152.56	2152.81	72.58	2171.02	2171.27	73.30	2189.49	2189.73	74.02	2207.95	2208.19	74.74
2152.82	2153.07	72.59	2171.28	2171.53	73.31	2189.74	2189.99	74.03	2208.20	2208.45	74.75
2153.08	2153.32	72.60	2171.54	2171.78	73.32	2190.00	2190.24	74.04	2208.46	2208.71	74.76
2153.33	2153.58	72.61	2171.79	2172.04	73.33	2190.25	2190.50	74.05	2208.72	2208.96	74.77
2153.59	2153.83	72.62	2172.05	2172.30	73.34	2190.51	2190.76	74.06	2208.97	2209.22	74.78
2153.84	2154.09	72.63	2172.31	2172.55	73.35	2190.77	2191.01	74.07	2209.23	2209.48	74.79
2154.10	2154.35	72.64	2172.56	2172.81	73.36	2191.02	2191.27	74.08	2209.49	2209.73	74.80
2154.36	2154.60	72.65	2172.82	2173.07	73.37	2191.28	2191.53	74.09	2209.74	2209.99	74.81
2154.61	2154.86	72.66	2173.08	2173.32	73.38	2191.54	2191.78	74.10	2210.00	2210.24	74.82
2154.87	2155.12	72.67	2173.33	2173.58	73.39	2191.79	2192.04	74.11	2210.25	2210.50	74.83
2155.13	2155.37	72.68	2173.59	2173.83	73.40	2192.05	2192.30	74.12	2210.51	2210.76	74.84
2155.38	2155.63	72.69	2173.84	2174.09	73.41	2192.31	2192.55	74.13	2210.77	2211.01	74.85
2155.64	2155.89	72.70	2174.10	2174.35	73.42	2192.56	2192.81	74.14	2211.02	2211.27	74.86
2155.90	2156.14	72.71	2174.36	2174.60	73.43	2192.82	2193.07	74.15	2211.28	2211.53	74.87

 Employee's maximum CPP contribution for the year 2000 is $1329.90   La cotisation maximale de l'employé au RPC pour l'année 2000 est de 1329,90 $

Canada Pension Plan Contributions
Monthly (12 pay periods a year)

Cotisations au Régime de pensions du Canada
Mensuel (12 périodes de paie par année)

Pay Rémunération		CPP RPC	Pay Rémunération		CPP RPC	Pay Rémunération		CPP RPC	Pay Rémunération		CPP RPC
From - De	To - À		From - De	To - À		From - De	To - À		From - De	To - À	
2211.54	2211.78	74.88	2230.00	2230.24	75.60	2248.46	2248.71	76.32	2266.92	2267.17	77.04
2211.79	2212.04	74.89	2230.25	2230.50	75.61	2248.72	2248.96	76.33	2267.18	2267.42	77.05
2212.05	2212.30	74.90	2230.51	2230.76	75.62	2248.97	2249.22	76.34	2267.43	2267.68	77.06
2212.31	2212.55	74.91	2230.77	2231.01	75.63	2249.23	2249.48	76.35	2267.69	2267.94	77.07
2212.56	2212.81	74.92	2231.02	2231.27	75.64	2249.49	2249.73	76.36	2267.95	2268.19	77.08
2212.82	2213.07	74.93	2231.28	2231.53	75.65	2249.74	2249.99	76.37	2268.20	2268.45	77.09
2213.08	2213.32	74.94	2231.54	2231.78	75.66	2250.00	2250.24	76.38	2268.46	2268.71	77.10
2213.33	2213.58	74.95	2231.79	2232.04	75.67	2250.25	2250.50	76.39	2268.72	2268.96	77.11
2213.59	2213.83	74.96	2232.05	2232.30	75.68	2250.51	2250.76	76.40	2268.97	2269.22	77.12
2213.84	2214.09	74.97	2232.31	2232.55	75.69	2250.77	2251.01	76.41	2269.23	2269.48	77.13
2214.10	2214.35	74.98	2232.56	2232.81	75.70	2251.02	2251.27	76.42	2269.49	2269.73	77.14
2214.36	2214.60	74.99	2232.82	2233.07	75.71	2251.28	2251.53	76.43	2269.74	2269.99	77.15
2214.61	2214.86	75.00	2233.08	2233.32	75.72	2251.54	2251.78	76.44	2270.00	2270.24	77.16
2214.87	2215.12	75.01	2233.33	2233.58	75.73	2251.79	2252.04	76.45	2270.25	2270.50	77.17
2215.13	2215.37	75.02	2233.59	2233.83	75.74	2252.05	2252.30	76.46	2270.51	2270.76	77.18
2215.38	2215.63	75.03	2233.84	2234.09	75.75	2252.31	2252.55	76.47	2270.77	2271.01	77.19
2215.64	2215.89	75.04	2234.10	2234.35	75.76	2252.56	2252.81	76.48	2271.02	2271.27	77.20
2215.90	2216.14	75.05	2234.36	2234.60	75.77	2252.82	2253.07	76.49	2271.28	2271.53	77.21
2216.15	2216.40	75.06	2234.61	2234.86	75.78	2253.08	2253.32	76.50	2271.54	2271.78	77.22
2216.41	2216.65	75.07	2234.87	2235.12	75.79	2253.33	2253.58	76.51	2271.79	2272.04	77.23
2216.66	2216.91	75.08	2235.13	2235.37	75.80	2253.59	2253.83	76.52	2272.05	2272.30	77.24
2216.92	2217.17	75.09	2235.38	2235.63	75.81	2253.84	2254.09	76.53	2272.31	2272.55	77.25
2217.18	2217.42	75.10	2235.64	2235.89	75.82	2254.10	2254.35	76.54	2272.56	2272.81	77.26
2217.43	2217.68	75.11	2235.90	2236.14	75.83	2254.36	2254.60	76.55	2272.82	2273.07	77.27
2217.69	2217.94	75.12	2236.15	2236.40	75.84	2254.61	2254.86	76.56	2273.08	2273.32	77.28
2217.95	2218.19	75.13	2236.41	2236.65	75.85	2254.87	2255.12	76.57	2273.33	2273.58	77.29
2218.20	2218.45	75.14	2236.66	2236.91	75.86	2255.13	2255.37	76.58	2273.59	2273.83	77.30
2218.46	2218.71	75.15	2236.92	2237.17	75.87	2255.38	2255.63	76.59	2273.84	2274.09	77.31
2218.72	2218.96	75.16	2237.18	2237.42	75.88	2255.64	2255.89	76.60	2274.10	2274.35	77.32
2218.97	2219.22	75.17	2237.43	2237.68	75.89	2255.90	2256.14	76.61	2274.36	2274.60	77.33
2219.23	2219.48	75.18	2237.69	2237.94	75.90	2256.15	2256.40	76.62	2274.61	2274.86	77.34
2219.49	2219.73	75.19	2237.95	2238.19	75.91	2256.41	2256.65	76.63	2274.87	2275.12	77.35
2219.74	2219.99	75.20	2238.20	2238.45	75.92	2256.66	2256.91	76.64	2275.13	2275.37	77.36
2220.00	2220.24	75.21	2238.46	2238.71	75.93	2256.92	2257.17	76.65	2275.38	2275.63	77.37
2220.25	2220.50	75.22	2238.72	2238.96	75.94	2257.18	2257.42	76.66	2275.64	2275.89	77.38
2220.51	2220.76	75.23	2238.97	2239.22	75.95	2257.43	2257.68	76.67	2275.90	2276.14	77.39
2220.77	2221.01	75.24	2239.23	2239.48	75.96	2257.69	2257.94	76.68	2276.15	2276.40	77.40
2221.02	2221.27	75.25	2239.49	2239.73	75.97	2257.95	2258.19	76.69	2276.41	2276.65	77.41
2221.28	2221.53	75.26	2239.74	2239.99	75.98	2258.20	2258.45	76.70	2276.66	2276.91	77.42
2221.54	2221.78	75.27	2240.00	2240.24	75.99	2258.46	2258.71	76.71	2276.92	2277.17	77.43
2221.79	2222.04	75.28	2240.25	2240.50	76.00	2258.72	2258.96	76.72	2277.18	2277.42	77.44
2222.05	2222.30	75.29	2240.51	2240.76	76.01	2258.97	2259.22	76.73	2277.43	2277.68	77.45
2222.31	2222.55	75.30	2240.77	2241.01	76.02	2259.23	2259.48	76.74	2277.69	2277.94	77.46
2222.56	2222.81	75.31	2241.02	2241.27	76.03	2259.49	2259.73	76.75	2277.95	2278.19	77.47
2222.82	2223.07	75.32	2241.28	2241.53	76.04	2259.74	2259.99	76.76	2278.20	2278.45	77.48
2223.08	2223.32	75.33	2241.54	2241.78	76.05	2260.00	2260.24	76.77	2278.46	2278.71	77.49
2223.33	2223.58	75.34	2241.79	2242.04	76.06	2260.25	2260.50	76.78	2278.72	2278.96	77.50
2223.59	2223.83	75.35	2242.05	2242.30	76.07	2260.51	2260.76	76.79	2278.97	2279.22	77.51
2223.84	2224.09	75.36	2242.31	2242.55	76.08	2260.77	2261.01	76.80	2279.23	2279.48	77.52
2224.10	2224.35	75.37	2242.56	2242.81	76.09	2261.02	2261.27	76.81	2279.49	2279.73	77.53
2224.36	2224.60	75.38	2242.82	2243.07	76.10	2261.28	2261.53	76.82	2279.74	2279.99	77.54
2224.61	2224.86	75.39	2243.08	2243.32	76.11	2261.54	2261.78	76.83	2280.00	2280.24	77.55
2224.87	2225.12	75.40	2243.33	2243.58	76.12	2261.79	2262.04	76.84	2280.25	2280.50	77.56
2225.13	2225.37	75.41	2243.59	2243.83	76.13	2262.05	2262.30	76.85	2280.51	2280.76	77.57
2225.38	2225.63	75.42	2243.84	2244.09	76.14	2262.31	2262.55	76.86	2280.77	2281.01	77.58
2225.64	2225.89	75.43	2244.10	2244.35	76.15	2262.56	2262.81	76.87	2281.02	2281.27	77.59
2225.90	2226.14	75.44	2244.36	2244.60	76.16	2262.82	2263.07	76.88	2281.28	2281.53	77.60
2226.15	2226.40	75.45	2244.61	2244.86	76.17	2263.08	2263.32	76.89	2281.54	2281.78	77.61
2226.41	2226.65	75.46	2244.87	2245.12	76.18	2263.33	2263.58	76.90	2281.79	2282.04	77.62
2226.66	2226.91	75.47	2245.13	2245.37	76.19	2263.59	2263.83	76.91	2282.05	2282.30	77.63
2226.92	2227.17	75.48	2245.38	2245.63	76.20	2263.84	2264.09	76.92	2282.31	2282.55	77.64
2227.18	2227.42	75.49	2245.64	2245.89	76.21	2264.10	2264.35	76.93	2282.56	2282.81	77.65
2227.43	2227.68	75.50	2245.90	2246.14	76.22	2264.36	2264.60	76.94	2282.82	2283.07	77.66
2227.69	2227.94	75.51	2246.15	2246.40	76.23	2264.61	2264.86	76.95	2283.08	2283.32	77.67
2227.95	2228.19	75.52	2246.41	2246.65	76.24	2264.87	2265.12	76.96	2283.33	2283.58	77.68
2228.20	2228.45	75.53	2246.66	2246.91	76.25	2265.13	2265.37	76.97	2283.59	2283.83	77.69
2228.46	2228.71	75.54	2246.92	2247.17	76.26	2265.38	2265.63	76.98	2283.84	2284.09	77.70
2228.72	2228.96	75.55	2247.18	2247.42	76.27	2265.64	2265.89	76.99	2284.10	2284.35	77.71
2228.97	2229.22	75.56	2247.43	2247.68	76.28	2265.90	2266.14	77.00	2284.36	2284.60	77.72
2229.23	2229.48	75.57	2247.69	2247.94	76.29	2266.15	2266.40	77.01	2284.61	2284.86	77.73
2229.49	2229.73	75.58	2247.95	2248.19	76.30	2266.41	2266.65	77.02	2284.87	2285.12	77.74
2229.74	2229.99	75.59	2248.20	2248.45	76.31	2266.66	2266.91	77.03	2285.13	2285.37	77.75

Employee's maximum CPP contribution for the year 2000 is $1329.90 La cotisation maximale de l'employé au RPC pour l'année 2000 est de 1329,90 $

Employment Insurance Premiums — Cotisations à l'assurance-emploi

Insurable Earnings Rémunération assurable		EI premium Cotisation d'AE	Insurable Earnings Rémunération assurable		EI premium Cotisation d'AE	Insurable Earnings Rémunération assurable		EI premium Cotisation d'AE	Insurable Earnings Rémunération assurable		EI premium Cotisation d'AE	Insurable Earnings Rémunération assurable		EI premium Cotisation d'AE
From - De	To - À		From - De	To - À		From - De	To - À		From - De	To - À		From - De	To - À	
1980.21 -	1980.62	47.53	2010.21 -	2010.62	48.25	2040.21 -	2040.62	48.97	2070.21 -	2070.62	49.69	2100.21 -	2100.62	50.41
1980.63 -	1981.04	47.54	2010.63 -	2011.04	48.26	2040.63 -	2041.04	48.98	2070.63 -	2071.04	49.70	2100.63 -	2101.04	50.42
1981.05 -	1981.45	47.55	2011.05 -	2011.45	48.27	2041.05 -	2041.45	48.99	2071.05 -	2071.45	49.71	2101.05 -	2101.45	50.43
1981.46 -	1981.87	47.56	2011.46 -	2011.87	48.28	2041.46 -	2041.87	49.00	2071.46 -	2071.87	49.72	2101.46 -	2101.87	50.44
1981.88 -	1982.29	47.57	2011.88 -	2012.29	48.29	2041.88 -	2042.29	49.01	2071.88 -	2072.29	49.73	2101.88 -	2102.29	50.45
1982.30 -	1982.70	47.58	2012.30 -	2012.70	48.30	2042.30 -	2042.70	49.02	2072.30 -	2072.70	49.74	2102.30 -	2102.70	50.46
1982.71 -	1983.12	47.59	2012.71 -	2013.12	48.31	2042.71 -	2043.12	49.03	2072.71 -	2073.12	49.75	2102.71 -	2103.12	50.47
1983.13 -	1983.54	47.60	2013.13 -	2013.54	48.32	2043.13 -	2043.54	49.04	2073.13 -	2073.54	49.76	2103.13 -	2103.54	50.48
1983.55 -	1983.95	47.61	2013.55 -	2013.95	48.33	2043.55 -	2043.95	49.05	2073.55 -	2073.95	49.77	2103.55 -	2103.95	50.49
1983.96 -	1984.37	47.62	2013.96 -	2014.37	48.34	2043.96 -	2044.37	49.06	2073.96 -	2074.37	49.78	2103.96 -	2104.37	50.50
1984.38 -	1984.79	47.63	2014.38 -	2014.79	48.35	2044.38 -	2044.79	49.07	2074.38 -	2074.79	49.79	2104.38 -	2104.79	50.51
1984.80 -	1985.20	47.64	2014.80 -	2015.20	48.36	2044.80 -	2045.20	49.08	2074.80 -	2075.20	49.80	2104.80 -	2105.20	50.52
1985.21 -	1985.62	47.65	2015.21 -	2015.62	48.37	2045.21 -	2045.62	49.09	2075.21 -	2075.62	49.81	2105.21 -	2105.62	50.53
1985.63 -	1986.04	47.66	2015.63 -	2016.04	48.38	2045.63 -	2046.04	49.10	2075.63 -	2076.04	49.82	2105.63 -	2106.04	50.54
1986.05 -	1986.45	47.67	2016.05 -	2016.45	48.39	2046.05 -	2046.45	49.11	2076.05 -	2076.45	49.83	2106.05 -	2106.45	50.55
1986.46 -	1986.87	47.68	2016.46 -	2016.87	48.40	2046.46 -	2046.87	49.12	2076.46 -	2076.87	49.84	2106.46 -	2106.87	50.56
1986.88 -	1987.29	47.69	2016.88 -	2017.29	48.41	2046.88 -	2047.29	49.13	2076.88 -	2077.29	49.85	2106.88 -	2107.29	50.57
1987.30 -	1987.70	47.70	2017.30 -	2017.70	48.42	2047.30 -	2047.70	49.14	2077.30 -	2077.70	49.86	2107.30 -	2107.70	50.58
1987.71 -	1988.12	47.71	2017.71 -	2018.12	48.43	2047.71 -	2048.12	49.15	2077.71 -	2078.12	49.87	2107.71 -	2108.12	50.59
1988.13 -	1988.54	47.72	2018.13 -	2018.54	48.44	2048.13 -	2048.54	49.16	2078.13 -	2078.54	49.88	2108.13 -	2108.54	50.60
1988.55 -	1988.95	47.73	2018.55 -	2018.95	48.45	2048.55 -	2048.95	49.17	2078.55 -	2078.95	49.89	2108.55 -	2108.95	50.61
1988.96 -	1989.37	47.74	2018.96 -	2019.37	48.46	2048.96 -	2049.37	49.18	2078.96 -	2079.37	49.90	2108.96 -	2109.37	50.62
1989.38 -	1989.79	47.75	2019.38 -	2019.79	48.47	2049.38 -	2049.79	49.19	2079.38 -	2079.79	49.91	2109.38 -	2109.79	50.63
1989.80 -	1990.20	47.76	2019.80 -	2020.20	48.48	2049.80 -	2050.20	49.20	2079.80 -	2080.20	49.92	2109.80 -	2110.20	50.64
1990.21 -	1990.62	47.77	2020.21 -	2020.62	48.49	2050.21 -	2050.62	49.21	2080.21 -	2080.62	49.93	2110.21 -	2110.62	50.65
1990.63 -	1991.04	47.78	2020.63 -	2021.04	48.50	2050.63 -	2051.04	49.22	2080.63 -	2081.04	49.94	2110.63 -	2111.04	50.66
1991.05 -	1991.45	47.79	2021.05 -	2021.45	48.51	2051.05 -	2051.45	49.23	2081.05 -	2081.45	49.95	2111.05 -	2111.45	50.67
1991.46 -	1991.87	47.80	2021.46 -	2021.87	48.52	2051.46 -	2051.87	49.24	2081.46 -	2081.87	49.96	2111.46 -	2111.87	50.68
1991.88 -	1992.29	47.81	2021.88 -	2022.29	48.53	2051.88 -	2052.29	49.25	2081.88 -	2082.29	49.97	2111.88 -	2112.29	50.69
1992.30 -	1992.70	47.82	2022.30 -	2022.70	48.54	2052.30 -	2052.70	49.26	2082.30 -	2082.70	49.98	2112.30 -	2112.70	50.70
1992.71 -	1993.12	47.83	2022.71 -	2023.12	48.55	2052.71 -	2053.12	49.27	2082.71 -	2083.12	49.99	2112.71 -	2113.12	50.71
1993.13 -	1993.54	47.84	2023.13 -	2023.54	48.56	2053.13 -	2053.54	49.28	2083.13 -	2083.54	50.00	2113.13 -	2113.54	50.72
1993.55 -	1993.95	47.85	2023.55 -	2023.95	48.57	2053.55 -	2053.95	49.29	2083.55 -	2083.95	50.01	2113.55 -	2113.95	50.73
1993.96 -	1994.37	47.86	2023.96 -	2024.37	48.58	2053.96 -	2054.37	49.30	2083.96 -	2084.37	50.02	2113.96 -	2114.37	50.74
1994.38 -	1994.79	47.87	2024.38 -	2024.79	48.59	2054.38 -	2054.79	49.31	2084.38 -	2084.79	50.03	2114.38 -	2114.79	50.75
1994.80 -	1995.20	47.88	2024.80 -	2025.20	48.60	2054.80 -	2055.20	49.32	2084.80 -	2085.20	50.04	2114.80 -	2115.20	50.76
1995.21 -	1995.62	47.89	2025.21 -	2025.62	48.61	2055.21 -	2055.62	49.33	2085.21 -	2085.62	50.05	2115.21 -	2115.62	50.77
1995.63 -	1996.04	47.90	2025.63 -	2026.04	48.62	2055.63 -	2056.04	49.34	2085.63 -	2086.04	50.06	2115.63 -	2116.04	50.78
1996.05 -	1996.45	47.91	2026.05 -	2026.45	48.63	2056.05 -	2056.45	49.35	2086.05 -	2086.45	50.07	2116.05 -	2116.45	50.79
1996.46 -	1996.87	47.92	2026.46 -	2026.87	48.64	2056.46 -	2056.87	49.36	2086.46 -	2086.87	50.08	2116.46 -	2116.87	50.80
1996.88 -	1997.29	47.93	2026.88 -	2027.29	48.65	2056.88 -	2057.29	49.37	2086.88 -	2087.29	50.09	2116.88 -	2117.29	50.81
1997.30 -	1997.70	47.94	2027.30 -	2027.70	48.66	2057.30 -	2057.70	49.38	2087.30 -	2087.70	50.10	2117.30 -	2117.70	50.82
1997.71 -	1998.12	47.95	2027.71 -	2028.12	48.67	2057.71 -	2058.12	49.39	2087.71 -	2088.12	50.11	2117.71 -	2118.12	50.83
1998.13 -	1998.54	47.96	2028.13 -	2028.54	48.68	2058.13 -	2058.54	49.40	2088.13 -	2088.54	50.12	2118.13 -	2118.54	50.84
1998.55 -	1998.95	47.97	2028.55 -	2028.95	48.69	2058.55 -	2058.95	49.41	2088.55 -	2088.95	50.13	2118.55 -	2118.95	50.85
1998.96 -	1999.37	47.98	2028.96 -	2029.37	48.70	2058.96 -	2059.37	49.42	2088.96 -	2089.37	50.14	2118.96 -	2119.37	50.86
1999.38 -	1999.79	47.99	2029.38 -	2029.79	48.71	2059.38 -	2059.79	49.43	2089.38 -	2089.79	50.15	2119.38 -	2119.79	50.87
1999.80 -	2000.20	48.00	2029.80 -	2030.20	48.72	2059.80 -	2060.20	49.44	2089.80 -	2090.20	50.16	2119.80 -	2120.20	50.88
2000.21 -	2000.62	48.01	2030.21 -	2030.62	48.73	2060.21 -	2060.62	49.45	2090.21 -	2090.62	50.17	2120.21 -	2120.62	50.89
2000.63 -	2001.04	48.02	2030.63 -	2031.04	48.74	2060.63 -	2061.04	49.46	2090.63 -	2091.04	50.18	2120.63 -	2121.04	50.90
2001.05 -	2001.45	48.03	2031.05 -	2031.45	48.75	2061.05 -	2061.45	49.47	2091.05 -	2091.45	50.19	2121.05 -	2121.45	50.91
2001.46 -	2001.87	48.04	2031.46 -	2031.87	48.76	2061.46 -	2061.87	49.48	2091.46 -	2091.87	50.20	2121.46 -	2121.87	50.92
2001.88 -	2002.29	48.05	2031.88 -	2032.29	48.77	2061.88 -	2062.29	49.49	2091.88 -	2092.29	50.21	2121.88 -	2122.29	50.93
2002.30 -	2002.70	48.06	2032.30 -	2032.70	48.78	2062.30 -	2062.70	49.50	2092.30 -	2092.70	50.22	2122.30 -	2122.70	50.94
2002.71 -	2003.12	48.07	2032.71 -	2033.12	48.79	2062.71 -	2063.12	49.51	2092.71 -	2093.12	50.23	2122.71 -	2123.12	50.95
2003.13 -	2003.54	48.08	2033.13 -	2033.54	48.80	2063.13 -	2063.54	49.52	2093.13 -	2093.54	50.24	2123.13 -	2123.54	50.96
2003.55 -	2003.95	48.09	2033.55 -	2033.95	48.81	2063.55 -	2063.95	49.53	2093.55 -	2093.95	50.25	2123.55 -	2123.95	50.97
2003.96 -	2004.37	48.10	2033.96 -	2034.37	48.82	2063.96 -	2064.37	49.54	2093.96 -	2094.37	50.26	2123.96 -	2124.37	50.98
2004.38 -	2004.79	48.11	2034.38 -	2034.79	48.83	2064.38 -	2064.79	49.55	2094.38 -	2094.79	50.27	2124.38 -	2124.79	50.99
2004.80 -	2005.20	48.12	2034.80 -	2035.20	48.84	2064.80 -	2065.20	49.56	2094.80 -	2095.20	50.28	2124.80 -	2125.20	51.00
2005.21 -	2005.62	48.13	2035.21 -	2035.62	48.85	2065.21 -	2065.62	49.57	2095.21 -	2095.62	50.29	2125.21 -	2125.62	51.01
2005.63 -	2006.04	48.14	2035.63 -	2036.04	48.86	2065.63 -	2066.04	49.58	2095.63 -	2096.04	50.30	2125.63 -	2126.04	51.02
2006.05 -	2006.45	48.15	2036.05 -	2036.45	48.87	2066.05 -	2066.45	49.59	2096.05 -	2096.45	50.31	2126.05 -	2126.45	51.03
2006.46 -	2006.87	48.16	2036.46 -	2036.87	48.88	2066.46 -	2066.87	49.60	2096.46 -	2096.87	50.32	2126.46 -	2126.87	51.04
2006.88 -	2007.29	48.17	2036.88 -	2037.29	48.89	2066.88 -	2067.29	49.61	2096.88 -	2097.29	50.33	2126.88 -	2127.29	51.05
2007.30 -	2007.70	48.18	2037.30 -	2037.70	48.90	2067.30 -	2067.70	49.62	2097.30 -	2097.70	50.34	2127.30 -	2127.70	51.06
2007.71 -	2008.12	48.19	2037.71 -	2038.12	48.91	2067.71 -	2068.12	49.63	2097.71 -	2098.12	50.35	2127.71 -	2128.12	51.07
2008.13 -	2008.54	48.20	2038.13 -	2038.54	48.92	2068.13 -	2068.54	49.64	2098.13 -	2098.54	50.36	2128.13 -	2128.54	51.08
2008.55 -	2008.95	48.21	2038.55 -	2038.95	48.93	2068.55 -	2068.95	49.65	2098.55 -	2098.95	50.37	2128.55 -	2128.95	51.09
2008.96 -	2009.37	48.22	2038.96 -	2039.37	48.94	2068.96 -	2069.37	49.66	2098.96 -	2099.37	50.38	2128.96 -	2129.37	51.10
2009.38 -	2009.79	48.23	2039.38 -	2039.79	48.95	2069.38 -	2069.79	49.67	2099.38 -	2099.79	50.39	2129.38 -	2129.79	51.11
2009.80 -	2010.20	48.24	2039.80 -	2040.20	48.96	2069.80 -	2070.20	49.68	2099.80 -	2100.20	50.40	2129.80 -	2130.20	51.12

Employment Insurance Premiums **Cotisations à l'assurance-emploi**

Insurable Earnings Rémunération assurable From - De	To - À	EI premium Cotisation d'AE	Insurable Earnings Rémunération assurable From - De	To - À	EI premium Cotisation d'AE	Insurable Earnings Rémunération assurable From - De	To - À	EI premium Cotisation d'AE	Insurable Earnings Rémunération assurable From - De	To - À	EI premium Cotisation d'AE	Insurable Earnings Rémunération assurable From - De	To - À	EI premium Cotisation d'AE
2130.21	2130.62	51.13	2160.21	2160.62	51.85	2190.21	2190.62	52.57	2220.21	2220.62	53.29	2250.21	2250.62	54.01
2130.63	2131.04	51.14	2160.63	2161.04	51.86	2190.63	2191.04	52.58	2220.63	2221.04	53.30	2250.63	2251.04	54.02
2131.05	2131.45	51.15	2161.05	2161.45	51.87	2191.05	2191.45	52.59	2221.05	2221.45	53.31	2251.05	2251.45	54.03
2131.46	2131.87	51.16	2161.46	2161.87	51.88	2191.46	2191.87	52.60	2221.46	2221.87	53.32	2251.46	2251.87	54.04
2131.88	2132.29	51.17	2161.88	2162.29	51.89	2191.88	2192.29	52.61	2221.88	2222.29	53.33	2251.88	2252.29	54.05
2132.30	2132.70	51.18	2162.30	2162.70	51.90	2192.30	2192.70	52.62	2222.30	2222.70	53.34	2252.30	2252.70	54.06
2132.71	2133.12	51.19	2162.71	2163.12	51.91	2192.71	2193.12	52.63	2222.71	2223.12	53.35	2252.71	2253.12	54.07
2133.13	2133.54	51.20	2163.13	2163.54	51.92	2193.13	2193.54	52.64	2223.13	2223.54	53.36	2253.13	2253.54	54.08
2133.55	2133.95	51.21	2163.55	2163.95	51.93	2193.55	2193.95	52.65	2223.55	2223.95	53.37	2253.55	2253.95	54.09
2133.96	2134.37	51.22	2163.96	2164.37	51.94	2193.96	2194.37	52.66	2223.96	2224.37	53.38	2253.96	2254.37	54.10
2134.38	2134.79	51.23	2164.38	2164.79	51.95	2194.38	2194.79	52.67	2224.38	2224.79	53.39	2254.38	2254.79	54.11
2134.80	2135.20	51.24	2164.80	2165.20	51.96	2194.80	2195.20	52.68	2224.80	2225.20	53.40	2254.80	2255.20	54.12
2135.21	2135.62	51.25	2165.21	2165.62	51.97	2195.21	2195.62	52.69	2225.21	2225.62	53.41	2255.21	2255.62	54.13
2135.63	2136.04	51.26	2165.63	2166.04	51.98	2195.63	2196.04	52.70	2225.63	2226.04	53.42	2255.63	2256.04	54.14
2136.05	2136.45	51.27	2166.05	2166.45	51.99	2196.05	2196.45	52.71	2226.05	2226.45	53.43	2256.05	2256.45	54.15
2136.46	2136.87	51.28	2166.46	2166.87	52.00	2196.46	2196.87	52.72	2226.46	2226.87	53.44	2256.46	2256.87	54.16
2136.88	2137.29	51.29	2166.88	2167.29	52.01	2196.88	2197.29	52.73	2226.88	2227.29	53.45	2256.88	2257.29	54.17
2137.30	2137.70	51.30	2167.30	2167.70	52.02	2197.30	2197.70	52.74	2227.30	2227.70	53.46	2257.30	2257.70	54.18
2137.71	2138.12	51.31	2167.71	2168.12	52.03	2197.71	2198.12	52.75	2227.71	2228.12	53.47	2257.71	2258.12	54.19
2138.13	2138.54	51.32	2168.13	2168.54	52.04	2198.13	2198.54	52.76	2228.13	2228.54	53.48	2258.13	2258.54	54.20
2138.55	2138.95	51.33	2168.55	2168.95	52.05	2198.55	2198.95	52.77	2228.55	2228.95	53.49	2258.55	2258.95	54.21
2138.96	2139.37	51.34	2168.96	2169.37	52.06	2198.96	2199.37	52.78	2228.96	2229.37	53.50	2258.96	2259.37	54.22
2139.38	2139.79	51.35	2169.38	2169.79	52.07	2199.38	2199.79	52.79	2229.38	2229.79	53.51	2259.38	2259.79	54.23
2139.80	2140.20	51.36	2169.80	2170.20	52.08	2199.80	2200.20	52.80	2229.80	2230.20	53.52	2259.80	2260.20	54.24
2140.21	2140.62	51.37	2170.21	2170.62	52.09	2200.21	2200.62	52.81	2230.21	2230.62	53.53	2260.21	2260.62	54.25
2140.63	2141.04	51.38	2170.63	2171.04	52.10	2200.63	2201.04	52.82	2230.63	2231.04	53.54	2260.63	2261.04	54.26
2141.05	2141.45	51.39	2171.05	2171.45	52.11	2201.05	2201.45	52.83	2231.05	2231.45	53.55	2261.05	2261.45	54.27
2141.46	2141.87	51.40	2171.46	2171.87	52.12	2201.46	2201.87	52.84	2231.46	2231.87	53.56	2261.46	2261.87	54.28
2141.88	2142.29	51.41	2171.88	2172.29	52.13	2201.88	2202.29	52.85	2231.88	2232.29	53.57	2261.88	2262.29	54.29
2142.30	2142.70	51.42	2172.30	2172.70	52.14	2202.30	2202.70	52.86	2232.30	2232.70	53.58	2262.30	2262.70	54.30
2142.71	2143.12	51.43	2172.71	2173.12	52.15	2202.71	2203.12	52.87	2232.71	2233.12	53.59	2262.71	2263.12	54.31
2143.13	2143.54	51.44	2173.13	2173.54	52.16	2203.13	2203.54	52.88	2233.13	2233.54	53.60	2263.13	2263.54	54.32
2143.55	2143.95	51.45	2173.55	2173.95	52.17	2203.55	2203.95	52.89	2233.55	2233.95	53.61	2263.55	2263.95	54.33
2143.96	2144.37	51.46	2173.96	2174.37	52.18	2203.96	2204.37	52.90	2233.96	2234.37	53.62	2263.96	2264.37	54.34
2144.38	2144.79	51.47	2174.38	2174.79	52.19	2204.38	2204.79	52.91	2234.38	2234.79	53.63	2264.38	2264.79	54.35
2144.80	2145.20	51.48	2174.80	2175.20	52.20	2204.80	2205.20	52.92	2234.80	2235.20	53.64	2264.80	2265.20	54.36
2145.21	2145.62	51.49	2175.21	2175.62	52.21	2205.21	2205.62	52.93	2235.21	2235.62	53.65	2265.21	2265.62	54.37
2145.63	2146.04	51.50	2175.63	2176.04	52.22	2205.63	2206.04	52.94	2235.63	2236.04	53.66	2265.63	2266.04	54.38
2146.05	2146.45	51.51	2176.05	2176.45	52.23	2206.05	2206.45	52.95	2236.05	2236.45	53.67	2266.05	2266.45	54.39
2146.46	2146.87	51.52	2176.46	2176.87	52.24	2206.46	2206.87	52.96	2236.46	2236.87	53.68	2266.46	2266.87	54.40
2146.88	2147.29	51.53	2176.88	2177.29	52.25	2206.88	2207.29	52.97	2236.88	2237.29	53.69	2266.88	2267.29	54.41
2147.30	2147.70	51.54	2177.30	2177.70	52.26	2207.30	2207.70	52.98	2237.30	2237.70	53.70	2267.30	2267.70	54.42
2147.71	2148.12	51.55	2177.71	2178.12	52.27	2207.71	2208.12	52.99	2237.71	2238.12	53.71	2267.71	2268.12	54.43
2148.13	2148.54	51.56	2178.13	2178.54	52.28	2208.13	2208.54	53.00	2238.13	2238.54	53.72	2268.13	2268.54	54.44
2148.55	2148.95	51.57	2178.55	2178.95	52.29	2208.55	2208.95	53.01	2238.55	2238.95	53.73	2268.55	2268.95	54.45
2148.96	2149.37	51.58	2178.96	2179.37	52.30	2208.96	2209.37	53.02	2238.96	2239.37	53.74	2268.96	2269.37	54.46
2149.38	2149.79	51.59	2179.38	2179.79	52.31	2209.38	2209.79	53.03	2239.38	2239.79	53.75	2269.38	2269.79	54.47
2149.80	2150.20	51.60	2179.80	2180.20	52.32	2209.80	2210.20	53.04	2239.80	2240.20	53.76	2269.80	2270.20	54.48
2150.21	2150.62	51.61	2180.21	2180.62	52.33	2210.21	2210.62	53.05	2240.21	2240.62	53.77	2270.21	2270.62	54.49
2150.63	2151.04	51.62	2180.63	2181.04	52.34	2210.63	2211.04	53.06	2240.63	2241.04	53.78	2270.63	2271.04	54.50
2151.05	2151.45	51.63	2181.05	2181.45	52.35	2211.05	2211.45	53.07	2241.05	2241.45	53.79	2271.05	2271.45	54.51
2151.46	2151.87	51.64	2181.46	2181.87	52.36	2211.46	2211.87	53.08	2241.46	2241.87	53.80	2271.46	2271.87	54.52
2151.88	2152.29	51.65	2181.88	2182.29	52.37	2211.88	2212.29	53.09	2241.88	2242.29	53.81	2271.88	2272.29	54.53
2152.30	2152.70	51.66	2182.30	2182.70	52.38	2212.30	2212.70	53.10	2242.30	2242.70	53.82	2272.30	2272.70	54.54
2152.71	2153.12	51.67	2182.71	2183.12	52.39	2212.71	2213.12	53.11	2242.71	2243.12	53.83	2272.71	2273.12	54.55
2153.13	2153.54	51.68	2183.13	2183.54	52.40	2213.13	2213.54	53.12	2243.13	2243.54	53.84	2273.13	2273.54	54.56
2153.55	2153.95	51.69	2183.55	2183.95	52.41	2213.55	2213.95	53.13	2243.55	2243.95	53.85	2273.55	2273.95	54.57
2153.96	2154.37	51.70	2183.96	2184.37	52.42	2213.96	2214.37	53.14	2243.96	2244.37	53.86	2273.96	2274.37	54.58
2154.38	2154.79	51.71	2184.38	2184.79	52.43	2214.38	2214.79	53.15	2244.38	2244.79	53.87	2274.38	2274.79	54.59
2154.80	2155.20	51.72	2184.80	2185.20	52.44	2214.80	2215.20	53.16	2244.80	2245.20	53.88	2274.80	2275.20	54.60
2155.21	2155.62	51.73	2185.21	2185.62	52.45	2215.21	2215.62	53.17	2245.21	2245.62	53.89	2275.21	2275.62	54.61
2155.63	2156.04	51.74	2185.63	2186.04	52.46	2215.63	2216.04	53.18	2245.63	2246.04	53.90	2275.63	2276.04	54.62
2156.05	2156.45	51.75	2186.05	2186.45	52.47	2216.05	2216.45	53.19	2246.05	2246.45	53.91	2276.05	2276.45	54.63
2156.46	2156.87	51.76	2186.46	2186.87	52.48	2216.46	2216.87	53.20	2246.46	2246.87	53.92	2276.46	2276.87	54.64
2156.88	2157.29	51.77	2186.88	2187.29	52.49	2216.88	2217.29	53.21	2246.88	2247.29	53.93	2276.88	2277.29	54.65
2157.30	2157.70	51.78	2187.30	2187.70	52.50	2217.30	2217.70	53.22	2247.30	2247.70	53.94	2277.30	2277.70	54.66
2157.71	2158.12	51.79	2187.71	2188.12	52.51	2217.71	2218.12	53.23	2247.71	2248.12	53.95	2277.71	2278.12	54.67
2158.13	2158.54	51.80	2188.13	2188.54	52.52	2218.13	2218.54	53.24	2248.13	2248.54	53.96	2278.13	2278.54	54.68
2158.55	2158.95	51.81	2188.55	2188.95	52.53	2218.55	2218.95	53.25	2248.55	2248.95	53.97	2278.55	2278.95	54.69
2158.96	2159.37	51.82	2188.96	2189.37	52.54	2218.96	2219.37	53.26	2248.96	2249.37	53.98	2278.96	2279.37	54.70
2159.38	2159.79	51.83	2189.38	2189.79	52.55	2219.38	2219.79	53.27	2249.38	2249.79	53.99	2279.38	2279.79	54.71
2159.80	2160.20	51.84	2189.80	2190.20	52.56	2219.80	2220.20	53.28	2249.80	2250.20	54.00	2279.80	2280.20	54.72

Saskatchewan (July 1, 2000)
Federal and Provincial Tax Deductions
Monthly (12 pay periods a year)

(Le 1er juillet 2000) Saskatchewan
Retenues d'impôt fédéral et provincial
Mensuel (12 périodes de paie par année

Pay Rémunération		If the employee's claim code from the TD1(E) form is / Si le code de demande de l'employé selon le formulaire TD1(F) est										
		0	1	2	3	4	5	6	7	8	9	10
From De	Less than Moins de		Deduct from each pay / Retenez sur chaque paie									
1344.	1362	335.35	181.65	153.10	119.00	84.90	46.65	9.95				
1362.	1380	339.80	186.10	158.40	124.35	90.25	51.95	12.80				
1380.	1398	344.20	190.50	163.75	129.65	95.55	57.30	15.70				
1398.	1416	348.65	194.95	169.05	135.00	100.90	62.60	18.55				
1416.	1434	353.05	199.35	174.40	140.30	106.20	67.95	21.40				
1434.	1452	357.55	203.75	179.70	145.65	111.50	73.25	24.30	1.25			
1452.	1470	362.15	208.20	185.05	150.95	116.85	78.60	27.15	4.10			
1470.	1488	366.70	212.60	190.35	156.30	122.15	83.90	30.00	7.00			
1488.	1506	371.30	217.05	195.70	161.60	127.50	89.25	34.30	9.85			
1506.	1524	375.85	221.45	201.00	166.95	132.80	94.55	39.65	12.70			
1524.	1542	380.45	225.90	206.35	172.25	138.15	99.85	44.95	15.60			
1542.	1560	385.00	230.30	211.65	177.60	143.45	105.20	50.30	18.45			
1560.	1578	389.60	234.75	217.00	182.90	148.80	110.50	55.60	21.55			
1578.	1596	394.20	239.15	222.10	188.05	153.95	115.85	60.95	26.85	1.15		
1596.	1614	398.75	243.60	226.55	192.45	158.35	121.15	66.25	32.20	4.00		
1614.	1632	403.35	248.00	230.95	196.90	162.80	126.50	71.60	37.50	6.90		
1632.	1650	407.90	252.45	235.40	201.30	167.20	131.80	76.90	42.85	9.75		
1650.	1668	412.50	256.85	239.80	205.75	171.60	137.15	82.25	48.15	14.05		
1668.	1686	417.10	261.30	244.25	210.15	176.05	141.95	87.55	53.50	19.40		
1686.	1704	421.65	265.70	248.65	214.60	180.45	146.35	92.90	58.80	24.70		
1704.	1722	426.25	270.10	253.10	219.00	184.90	150.80	98.20	64.10	30.05		
1722.	1740	430.80	274.55	257.50	223.45	189.30	155.20	103.55	69.45	35.35	1.25	
1740.	1758	435.40	278.95	261.95	227.85	193.75	159.65	108.85	74.75	40.70	6.60	.75
1758.	1776	439.95	283.40	266.35	232.30	198.15	164.05	114.15	80.10	46.00	11.90	1.85
1776.	1794	444.55	287.80	270.80	236.70	202.60	168.50	119.50	85.40	51.35	17.25	2.95
1794.	1812	449.15	292.25	275.20	241.10	207.00	172.90	124.80	90.75	56.65	22.55	4.00
1812.	1830	453.70	296.65	279.65	245.55	211.45	177.35	130.15	96.05	61.95	27.90	5.10
1830.	1848	458.30	301.10	284.05	249.95	215.85	181.75	135.45	101.40	67.30	33.20	6.15
1848.	1866	462.85	305.50	288.50	254.40	220.30	186.20	140.80	106.70	72.60	38.55	7.25
1866.	1884	467.45	309.95	292.90	258.80	224.70	190.60	146.10	112.05	77.95	43.85	9.75
1884.	1902	472.00	314.35	297.30	263.25	229.15	195.05	151.45	117.35	83.25	49.15	15.05
1902.	1920	476.60	318.80	301.75	267.65	233.55	199.45	156.75	122.70	88.60	54.50	20.40
1920.	1938	481.20	323.20	306.15	272.10	238.00	203.85	162.10	128.00	93.90	59.80	25.70
1938.	1956	485.75	327.65	310.60	276.50	242.40	208.30	167.40	133.35	99.25	65.15	31.05
1956.	1974	490.35	332.05	315.00	280.95	246.80	212.70	172.75	138.65	104.55	70.45	36.35
1974.	1992	494.90	336.50	319.45	285.35	251.25	217.15	178.05	143.95	109.90	75.80	41.70
1992.	2010	499.50	340.90	323.85	289.80	255.65	221.55	183.40	149.30	115.20	81.10	47.00
2010.	2028	504.10	345.40	328.30	294.20	260.10	226.00	188.70	154.60	120.55	86.45	52.35
2028.	2046	508.65	349.95	332.70	298.65	264.50	230.40	194.05	159.95	125.85	91.75	57.65
2046.	2064	513.25	354.55	337.15	303.05	268.95	234.85	199.35	165.25	131.20	97.10	62.95
2064.	2098	519.85	361.15	343.55	309.45	275.35	241.25	207.05	172.95	138.85	104.75	70.65
2098.	2132	528.50	369.80	352.20	317.80	283.70	249.60	215.50	181.45	147.35	113.25	79.15
2132.	2166	537.15	378.45	360.85	326.15	292.05	257.95	223.85	189.80	155.70	121.60	87.50
2166.	2200	545.80	387.10	369.50	334.50	300.40	266.30	232.20	198.15	164.05	129.95	95.85
2200.	2234	554.45	395.75	378.15	343.00	308.75	274.65	240.60	206.50	172.40	138.30	104.20
2234.	2268	563.10	404.40	386.80	351.65	317.10	283.00	248.95	214.85	180.75	146.65	112.55
2268.	2302	571.75	413.05	395.45	360.30	325.45	291.35	257.30	223.20	189.10	155.00	120.90
2302.	2336	580.40	421.70	404.10	368.95	333.80	299.70	265.65	231.55	197.45	163.40	129.25
2336.	2370	589.05	430.35	412.75	377.60	342.35	308.05	274.00	239.90	205.85	171.75	137.60
2370.	2404	597.70	439.00	421.40	386.25	351.00	316.45	282.35	248.25	214.20	180.10	146.00
2404.	2438	606.35	447.65	430.05	394.90	359.65	324.80	290.70	256.65	222.55	188.45	154.35
2438.	2472	615.00	456.30	438.70	403.55	368.30	333.15	299.05	265.00	230.90	196.80	162.70
2472.	2506	623.65	464.95	447.35	412.20	376.95	341.75	307.40	273.35	239.25	205.15	171.05
2506.	2540	632.30	473.60	456.00	420.85	385.60	350.40	315.80	281.70	247.60	213.50	179.40
2540.	2574	643.35	484.65	467.05	431.90	396.65	361.45	326.45	292.40	258.30	224.20	190.10

APPENDIX

I Financial Statement Information

This appendix includes financial statement information from (a) ClubLink Corporation and (b) WestJet Airlines Ltd. All of this information is taken from their annual reports. An **annual report** is a summary of the financial results of a company's operations for the year and its future plans. It is directed at external users of financial information, but also affects actions of internal users.

An annual report is also used by a company to showcase itself and its products. Many include attractive pictures, diagrams and illustrations related to the company. But the *financial section* is its primary objective. This section communicates much information about a company, with most data drawn from the accounting information system.

The layout of each annual report's financial section that is included in this appendix is:

- Auditor's Report
- Financial Statements
- Notes to Financial Statements
- List of Directors and Managers

This appendix provides this information for ClubLink Corporation and WestJet Airlines Ltd. This appendix is organized as follows:

- ClubLink: I-1 to I-20
- WestJet: I-21 to I-38

Many assignments at the end of each chapter refer to information in this appendix. We encourage readers to spend extra time with these assignments as they are especially useful in reinforcing and showing the relevance and diversity of financial reporting.

CLUBLINK

ClubLink

ClubLink Corporation 1999 Annual Report

ClubLink

Auditors' Report TO THE SHAREHOLDERS OF CLUBLINK CORPORATION

We have audited the consolidated balance sheets of ClubLink Corporation as at December 31, 1999 and 1998, and the consolidated statements of income, retained earnings and cash flows for the years then ended. These financial statements are the responsibility of the corporation's management. Our responsibility is to express an opinion on these financial statements based on our audits.

We conducted our audits in accordance with generally accepted auditing standards. Those standards require that we plan and perform an audit to obtain reasonable assurance whether the financial statements are free of material misstatement. An audit includes examining, on a test basis, evidence supporting the amounts and disclosures in the financial statements. An audit also includes assessing the accounting principles used and significant estimates made by management, as well as evaluating the overall financial statement presentation.

In our opinion, these consolidated financial statements present fairly, in all material respects, the financial position of the corporation as at December 31, 1999 and 1998, and the results of its operations and its cash flows for the years then ended in accordance with generally accepted accounting principles.

Pannell Kerr Forster

PANNELL KERR FORSTER
(ALSO OPERATING AS PKF HILL LLP)
CHARTERED ACCOUNTANTS
TORONTO, ONTARIO
MARCH 17, 2000

Consolidated Statements of Cash Flows FOR THE YEARS ENDED DECEMBER 31

(THOUSANDS OF DOLLARS – EXCEPT PER SHARE AMOUNTS)	1999	1998
OPERATING ACTIVITIES		
Net income	$ 7,391	$ 10,626
Add (subtract) items not involving cash:		
Amortization of capital assets	6,661	4,208
Amortization of deferred financing costs	560	127
Amortization of deferred marketing costs	375	-
Loss on sale of capital assets	500	-
Loss on sale of long-term portfolio investments	1,398	-
Unrealized foreign exchange loss (gain)	1,058	(808)
Deferred income taxes	1,700	1,850
Cash flow from operations	19,643	16,003
Net change in non-cash working capital (NOTE 16)	(2,813)	3,602
Membership fees receivable, long-term	(2,728)	(3,432)
Deferred revenue	2,978	5,430
CASH FLOW FROM OPERATING ACTIVITIES	17,080	21,603
INVESTING ACTIVITIES		
Loans receivable	(20,141)	(17,364)
Long-term portfolio investments	5,175	(16,185)
Development assets	(47,920)	(47,858)
Capital assets	(53,011)	(77,827)
Deferred charges	(716)	(2,623)
CASH FLOW FROM INVESTING ACTIVITIES	(116,613)	(161,857)
FINANCING ACTIVITIES		
Instalment receipt receivable	35,200	(35,200)
Deferred financing costs	(3,265)	(1,570)
Bank indebtedness	(43,609)	43,609
Long-term debt	75,443	11,292
Capital lease obligations	3,984	6,697
Convertible debentures	(4,714)	86,631
Share capital	51,408	14,214
CASH FLOW FROM FINANCING ACTIVITIES	114,447	125,673
NET INCREASE (DECREASE) IN CASH DURING THE YEAR	14,914	(14,581)
CASH, BEGINNING OF YEAR	–	14,581
CASH, END OF YEAR	$ 14,914	$ -
CASH FLOW FROM OPERATIONS PER SHARE	$ 0.93	$ 1.00

SEE ACCOMPANYING NOTES

ClubLink

ClubLink

Notes to Consolidated Financial Statements

FOR THE YEARS ENDED DECEMBER 31, 1999 AND 1998

NOTE 1. SUMMARY OF SIGNIFICANT ACCOUNTING POLICIES

The consolidated financial statements of ClubLink Corporation ("ClubLink") have been prepared by management in accordance with generally accepted accounting principles, the more significant of which are outlined below. In addition, the accounting policies and financial disclosure requirements relating to development assets are in accordance with the policies of the Canadian Institute of Public Real Estate Companies.

PRINCIPLES OF CONSOLIDATION

The accompanying consolidated financial statements include the accounts of ClubLink and its subsidiaries. Joint ventures are accounted for using the proportionate consolidation method.

USE OF ESTIMATES

The preparation of financial statements that conform with generally accepted accounting principles requires management to make estimates and assumptions that affect the amounts reported in the financial statements and accompanying notes. Actual results could differ from those estimates.

INVENTORIES

Inventories are stated at the lower of cost and net realizable value and consist of food, beverages and merchandise with cost determined on a weighted average basis.

LONG-TERM PORTFOLIO INVESTMENTS

Long-term portfolio investments are accounted for by the cost method. The carrying value is written down only in the event of a permanent impairment in value.

DEVELOPMENT ASSETS

Properties under construction, development and held for future development are recorded at the lower of cost and net realizable value. ClubLink capitalizes all direct costs relating to the acquisition, development and construction of these properties, including interest and direct general and administrative expenses.

CAPITAL ASSETS

Capital assets are recorded at cost. These capital assets include operating Golf Clubs and Golf Resorts, including land and improvements thereto, buildings and related equipment.

Capital assets are amortized on a straight-line basis over their estimated useful lives as follows:

Buildings, fixtures and related improvements	–	40 years
Roads, cart paths and irrigation	–	20 years
Maintenance equipment	–	10 years
Furnishings	–	10 years
Golf carts	–	5 years
Office and data processing equipment	–	5 years

Leased golf course land is amortized on a straight-line basis over the term of the lease.

In the first year of operation, capital assets are amortized at one-half of the stated rate.

DEFERRED CHARGES

The costs of securing ClubLink's long-term debt are deferred and amortized on a straight-line basis over the term of the related debt.

Deferred debenture interest represents interest on the final instalment of debentures, the proceeds of which were received one year from the date the debentures were issued. This portion of interest is being amortized over the term of the debentures.

Investments in the marketing campaign to establish ClubLink's corporate identity and market concept within the Daily Fee golf market are being amortized on a straight-line basis over three years, ending in 2000.

Costs associated with the development of a strategy and organization for operations in the U.S. market have been deferred.

Deferred charges are carried at cost less accumulated amortization.

ACQUISITION COSTS

Direct costs incurred in respect of completed acquisitions are allocated to the net assets acquired. Direct costs related to acquisitions not completed are charged to income.

SHARE ISSUE COSTS

The costs of issuing shares, net of income tax recoveries thereon, are applied to reduce the stated value of such shares.

REVENUE RECOGNITION

Membership fee revenue is recognized as the cash is received. ClubLink offers its Members financing on their Membership fees. When a financing option is selected, the Membership fee is recorded as deferred revenue and is matched by a corresponding receivable. Annual dues paid in advance are also recorded as deferred revenue.

DEFERRED INCOME TAXES

ClubLink follows the deferral method of tax allocation to account for income taxes. Under this method, timing differences between accounting income and taxable income result in the recording of deferred income taxes.

TRANSLATION OF FOREIGN CURRENCIES

Monetary assets denominated in foreign currencies are translated at the exchange rate in effect at the year-end dates. Gains and losses are deferred and amortized to income on a straight-line basis over the term of the related item.

ClubLink

ClubLink

NOTE 2. ACQUISITIONS

During 1999, ClubLink purchased Glen Abbey Golf Club, Cedarbrook Golf Club and a 50% investment in Les Quatre Domaines. During 1998, ClubLink acquired nine 18-hole golf courses, three 9-hole academy golf courses and a golf dome, in addition to six resort properties. Consideration included:

(THOUSANDS OF DOLLARS)	1999	1998
Cash	$ 42,930	$ 57,793
Assumption of debt	1,670	14,579
Common shares issued	-	5,100
	$ 44,600	$ 77,472

NOTE 3. LOANS RECEIVABLE

(THOUSANDS OF DOLLARS)	1999	1998
GolfSouth Holdings LLC and related entities	$ 46,169	$ 33,967
Vendor take-back mortgages and loans	7,941	1,827
Sonar Financial debenture	1,582	-
Senior officer loans	248	467
Other	104	700
	56,044	36,961
Less: current portion	39,110	1,260
	$ 16,934	$ 35,701

Secured loans receivable from GolfSouth Holdings LLC and related entities ("GolfSouth") are repayable in U.S. funds and earn interest at effective annual rates ranging from 11% to 14%. Pursuant to the terms of the loans, ClubLink has an option (expiring March 2003) to acquire control of GolfSouth. The loans are repayable in the amounts of US$31,989,000 (1998 – US$22,186,000). Interest revenue recognized during the year amounts to Cdn$4,705,000 (1998 – Cdn$3,081,000). The current portion of the GolfSouth loans reflects the portion of the loans that were repaid in cash during the first quarter of 2000.

The vendor take-back mortgages and loans have various terms attached to them and are due over varying periods ending in 2009.

The Sonar Financial debenture represents amounts advanced in conjunction with the acquisition, which occurred subsequent to year end, of Greenhills Golf Club, and earned interest at 12% per annum.

The senior officer loans are due in instalments over a seven-year period ending in 2003 and earn interest at 4.75% per annum.

NOTE **4.** LONG-TERM PORTFOLIO INVESTMENTS

Long-term portfolio investments are carried at cost and consist of the following:

(THOUSANDS OF DOLLARS)	1999	1998
THE LINKS GROUP, INC.		
4,080,417 Series AA convertible (to common), 15% preferred shares	$ 9,612	$ 9,409
OTHER LONG-TERM INVESTMENTS	-	6,776
	$ 9,612	$ 16,185

The Links Group, Inc., is a private U.S. company that operates ten and one-half 18-hole golf courses in South Carolina and one in Georgia.

NOTE **5.** DEVELOPMENT ASSETS

Development assets consist of golf, resort and residential real estate properties in the following stages of development:

(THOUSANDS OF DOLLARS)	1999	1998
Properties under construction	$ 29,296	$ 46,344
Properties under development	26,638	22,834
Properties held for future development	23,255	21,585
	$ 79,189	$ 90,763

Interest in the amount of $5,494,000 (1998 – $4,843,000), project development and management costs in the amount of $2,211,000 (1998 – $2,875,000) and corporate general and administrative costs in the amount of $nil (1998 – $1,325,000) have been capitalized to development assets. The 1999 amounts are net of $1,200,000 of capitalized interest and $1,300,000 of capitalized corporate general and administrative costs which were expensed as part of the $2,500,000 charge against development assets described in note 13.

Certain development assets are being held as security for long-term debt (see note 9).

NOTE **6.** CAPITAL ASSETS

Capital assets consist of the following asset classifications:

(THOUSANDS OF DOLLARS)			1999	1998
	COST	ACCUMULATED AMORTIZATION	NET	NET
Land and improvements	$ 174,660	$ –	$ 174,660	$ 115,387
Leased golf course land	1,343	66	1,277	1,326
Buildings, fixtures and related improvements	75,276	4,913	70,363	39,078
Roads, cart paths and irrigation	20,702	2,264	18,438	11,371
Maintenance equipment	12,996	3,570	9,426	7,264
Furnishings	10,125	2,889	7,236	4,808
Golf carts	4,932	1,145	3,787	2,583
Office and data processing equipment	8,180	2,493	5,687	3,713
	$ 308,214	$ 17,340	$ 290,874	$ 185,530

Maintenance equipment, golf carts and office and data processing equipment include assets under capital leases in the amount of $16,715,000 (1998 – $11,236,000) with related accumulated amortization of $5,069,000 (1998 – $2,778,000). Amortization in the amount of $2,291,000 (1998 – $1,297,000) of assets recorded as capital leases is included in amortization expense.

Certain capital assets are being held as security for bank indebtedness (see note 8) and long-term debt (see note 9).

NOTE 7. DEFERRED CHARGES

Deferred charges consists of the following:

(THOUSANDS OF DOLLARS)	1999	1998
Financing costs	$ 2,976	$ 875
6% Convertible debenture interest (NOTE 11)	1,866	1,262
Daily Fee golf marketing costs	375	750
U.S. organizational costs	2,589	1,873
	$ 7,806	$ 4,760

NOTE 8. BANK INDEBTEDNESS

Bank indebtedness consists of the following:

(THOUSANDS OF DOLLARS)	1999	1998
Demand overdraft facility, secured by a general security agreement, first ranking specific assignment of the instalment payment from the 6% convertible debentures, in addition to charges on golf properties	$ –	$ 28,000
Demand operating line of credit, secured by security agreements on accounts receivable and inventory and charges on golf properties	–	5,000
Demand term revolving credit facility, security as described in the operating line of credit above	–	10,609
	$ –	$ 43,609

At year end, outstanding letters of credit amounted to $689,000 (1998 – $1,519,000).

Notes to Consolidated Financial Statements

NOTE **9.** LONG-TERM DEBT

Long-term debt consists of the following:

(THOUSANDS OF DOLLARS)	1999	1998
9.655% Series A Secured Debenture due August 31, 2002, no principal repayments until maturity, interest payable monthly	$ 5,000	$ 5,000
9.655% Series B Secured Debenture due August 31, 2002, principal repayments of $350,000 on a semi-annual basis, interest payable monthly	4,900	5,600
8.05% Mortgage due January 1, 2004, blended payments of principal and interest payable monthly	8,011	8,140
8.75% Mortgage due May 1, 2004, blended payments of principal and interest payable monthly	6,619	6,776
7.77% Mortgage due September 6, 2009, blended payments of principal and interest payable monthly	24,912	–
30-day LIBOR plus 3.0% floating line of credit due September 12, 2004, blended payments of principal and interest payable monthly	64,823	–
Prime plus 0.5% floating mortgage, due April 1, 2001	–	6,900
Other mortgages and long-term debt, varying terms	5,899	12,305
	120,164	44,721
Less: current portion	4,631	7,442
	$ 115,533	$ 37,279

The long-term debt is secured by real property.

Minimum principal repayments over the next five years and thereafter are as follows:

(THOUSANDS OF DOLLARS)	
2000	$ 4,631
2001	3,300
2002	14,946
2003	2,806
2004	72,799
Thereafter	21,682
	$ 120,164

Interest for the year on long-term debt amounted to $5,022,000 (1998 – $2,567,000).

ClubLink

Notes to Consolidated Financial Statements

ClubLink

NOTE 10. CAPITAL LEASE OBLIGATIONS

ClubLink has committed to the following capital lease obligations:

(THOUSANDS OF DOLLARS)	1999	1998
TOTAL MINIMUM LEASE PAYMENTS	$ 15,831	$ 11,730
Less: amount representing interest at an approximate average rate of 7.4% (1998 – 7.5%)	1,917	1,800
CAPITAL LEASE OBLIGATIONS	13,914	9,930
Less: current portion	3,290	2,509
	$ 10,624	$ 7,421

Future minimum lease payments in respect of capital lease obligations are as follows :

(THOUSANDS OF DOLLARS)	
2000	$ 4,832
2001	5,047
2002	3,488
2003	1,496
2004	968
	$ 15,831

Interest for the year on capital lease obligations amounted to $909,000 (1998 – $588,000).

NOTE 11. CONVERTIBLE DEBENTURES

Convertible debentures consists of the following:

(THOUSANDS OF DOLLARS)			1999	1998
	LIABILITY COMPONENT	EQUITY COMPONENT	TOTAL	TOTAL
6.5% Debentures mature April 30, 2004, are convertible into common shares prior to February 2, 2004, at $13.50 per share and redeemable at par under certain conditions	$ 2,449	$ 7,727	$ 10,176	$ 10,166
6.0% Debentures mature May 15, 2008, are convertible into common shares at $20.00 per share and redeemable at par under certain conditions	–	86,071	86,071	88,000
	$ 2,449	$ 93,798	$ 96,247	$ 98,166

With respect to the 6.5% convertible debentures, the liability component was determined by discounting the stream of future interest payments at the prevailing market rate. The liability component will increase over the term to maturity through charges to earnings and decrease through the semi-annual payment of interest, so that at maturity it will be nil. The equity component was calculated at inception as the difference between the debenture principal obligation and the amount of the liability component. The equity component will increase over the term to maturity through charges to retained earnings, so that at maturity it will equal the original issued amount of the debenture.

With respect to the 6.0% debentures, 60% of the issue proceeds ($52,800,000) were received in May 1998, while the remaining 40% ($35,200,000) were received in May 1999. Interest payable to the debenture holders was determined on the full $88,000,000 outstanding from the date of issue. Deferred debenture interest (see note 7) represents the portion of interest relating to the final instalment, from the date of issue until May 15, 1999, which is being amortized over the term of the debentures. ClubLink has the option (subject to regulatory approval) to pay interest or principal in common shares. Accordingly, these debentures are included as part of shareholders' equity and the interest is charged to retained earnings.

During the year, ClubLink purchased $1,929,000 face value of 6.0% debentures on the open market in accordance with a normal course issuer bid. These debentures were purchased at a total cost of $1,349,000 and were subsequently cancelled. The difference between the cost amount and the original face value is included in share capital in the amount of $580,000 (see note 12).

NOTE 12. SHARE CAPITAL

(a) Authorized and issued share capital

The authorized share capital is an unlimited number of common shares and preferred shares. As at December 31, 1999, no preferred shares have been issued.

(THOUSANDS OF DOLLARS)	COMMON SHARES		AMOUNT
BALANCE AT DECEMBER 31, 1997	15,354,831	$	133,855
Exercise of common share purchase warrants	706,000		6,356
Issued on the acquisition of properties	398,715		5,100
Exercise of stock options	493,344		4,406
Costs related to debenture issue (net of tax)	–		(1,648)
BALANCE AT DECEMBER 31, 1998	16,952,890		148,069
Private placement (see (b) below)	3,300,000		34,011
Rights offering (see (c) below)	1,488,518		15,298
Exercise of stock options	29,000		230
Purchase and cancellation of 6.0% convertible debentures (note 11)	–		580
BALANCE AT DECEMBER 31, 1999	21,770,408	$	198,188

(b) Private placement

ClubLink issued 3,300,000 treasury shares to ClubCorp, Inc., by way of a private placement at $10.40 per share.

(c) Rights offering

Subsequent to the private placement to ClubCorp, Inc., ClubLink initiated a rights offering whereby shareholders had the option of buying ClubLink stock at $10.40 per share. ClubLink issued 1,488,518 shares under the rights offering.

ClubLink

(d) Stock options

ClubLink has a stock option plan under which options may be granted to its employees in respect of a maximum of 4,000,000 common shares. The exercise price of stock options under the plan is equal to the weighted average closing market price of the five trading days preceding the date of grant. The vesting period of the options vary from three to five years. Option grants are administered by the Compensation Committee of the Board of Directors.

	1999			1998		
FIXED OPTIONS	SHARES		WEIGHTED AVERAGE EXERCISE PRICE	SHARES		WEIGHTED AVERAGE EXERCISE PRICE
Balance at beginning of year	2,258,850	$	11.44	1,647,200	$	9.57
Granted	414,000		8.29	1,141,500		12.98
Exercised	(29,000)		7.93	(493,344)		8.93
Forfeited/expired	(134,600)		10.93	(36,506)		9.05
Balance at end of year	2,509,250	$	10.99	2,258,850	$	11.44
Options in the money at year end	427,600			756,500		

NOTE 13. REORGANIZATION AND OTHER ITEMS

Reorganization costs and other items consist of the following:

(THOUSANDS OF DOLLARS)		1999		1998
Charge against development assets	$	2,500	$	–
Loss on sale of long-term portfolio investment		1,398		–
Reorganization costs		1,400		–
Unrealized foreign exchange loss (gain)		1,058		(808)
Loss on sale of capital assets		500		–
	$	6,856	$	(808)

NOTE 14. INCOME TAXES

The income tax provision differs from the combined federal and provincial standard rates as follows:

(THOUSANDS OF DOLLARS)	1999			1998		
		AMOUNT	RATE %		AMOUNT	RATE %
Income tax expense computed at statutory rate	$	5,482	44.6	$	8,686	44.6
Federal surtax recovery		(135)	(1.1)		(214)	(1.1)
Effect of United States tax rates		(165)	(1.3)		(166)	(0.9)
Permanent differences		(311)	(2.5)		(36)	(0.2)
Large corporations tax		730	5.9		580	3.0
Benefits of losses and other tax assets not previously recognized		(701)	(5.7)		–	–
	$	4,900	39.9	$	8,850	45.4

NOTE 15. EARNINGS PER SHARE

The calculation of basic earnings per share is based on the weighted average number of common shares outstanding for the year. Earnings used in the calculation are net income for the year, reduced by the amortization of the equity component of 6.5% convertible debentures and interest on the 6.0% convertible debentures.

(THOUSANDS OF DOLLARS – EXCEPT PER SHARE AMOUNTS)		1999		1998
Net income	$	7,391	$	10,626
Amortization of equity component of 6.5% convertible debentures		(244)		(231)
Interest on 6.0% convertible debentures		(2,551)		(1,155)
	$	4,596	$	9,240
Weighted average number of common shares		21,153,330		16,019,001
Basic earnings per share	$	0.22	$	0.58

NOTE 16. NOTES TO THE STATEMENTS OF CASH FLOWS

Net change in non-cash working capital consists of the following:

(THOUSANDS OF DOLLARS)		1999		1998
Accounts receivable	$	582	$	(1,184)
Membership fees receivable		(1,294)		(2,391)
Inventories and prepaid expenses		(774)		637
Accounts and taxes payable		(4,797)		4,763
Accrued interest		571		105
Accrued liabilities		2,899		1,672
	$	(2,813)	$	3,602

During the year, income taxes paid amounted to $6,044,000 (1998 – $623,000).

NOTE 17. FINANCIAL INSTRUMENTS

(a) Fair value

ClubLink has various financial instruments including accounts and Membership fees receivable, instalment receipt receivable, loans receivable, long-term portfolio investments, bank indebtedness, accounts and taxes payable, accrued interest, accrued liabilities, long-term debt, capital lease obligations and convertible debentures. Due to their short-term maturity, or, in the case of long-term debt, capital lease obligations and convertible debentures, their market comparable interest rates, book values approximate fair market value.

ClubLink

(b) Credit risk

ClubLink does not have a significant credit exposure to any individual customer or Member. ClubLink takes into consideration a new Member's financial background and capacity before extending credit. ClubLink's exposure to credit risk is mitigated by its Membership revenue recognition policy whereby Membership fees are recognized as revenue when received.

In addition, ClubLink is not exposed to any significant credit risk on the loans receivable at year end, because they are adequately secured.

(c) Exchange risk

ClubLink is subject to exchange risk on its investments and loans which are held in foreign denominations. The value of these instruments may fluctuate depending upon the fluctuation of the related denomination.

NOTE 18. SEGMENTED OPERATIONS

ClubLink has two reportable segments: Golf Club operations and Golf Resort operations. The Golf Club operations segment represents all aspects of operating ClubLink's Member and Daily Fee golf courses including annual dues, guest fees and food and beverage revenue. The Golf Resort operations segment represents all aspects of operating ClubLink's resorts, including room revenue, food and beverage and golf revenue. All other operations, including interest revenue, membership sales and real estate sales, are included under Development, Corporate & Unallocated.

The accounting policies of the segments are the same as those described in the summary of significant accounting policies. Any inter-segment transfers are recorded at cost.

ClubLink's reportable segments are strategic business units that offer different services and/or products. They are managed separately because each segment requires different strategies and involves different aspects of management expertise.

ClubLink

Notes to Consolidated Financial Statements

(THOUSANDS OF DOLLARS)				1999
	GOLF CLUB OPERATIONS	GOLF RESORT OPERATIONS	DEVELOPMENT, CORPORATE & UNALLOCATED	TOTAL
REVENUE				
Operating	$ 62,520	$ 18,210	$ 7,439	$ 88,169
Membership fees	–	–	12,545	12,545
	62,520	18,210	19,984	100,714
EXPENSES				
Cost of goods sold	9,456	2,311	406	12,173
Operating	34,029	11,010	–	45,039
Membership sales and marketing	–	–	6,476	6,476
General and administrative	–	–	7,724	7,724
Capital taxes	–	–	922	922
	43,485	13,321	15,528	72,334
EBITDA	19,035	4,889	4,456	28,380
Amortization	4,402	1,148	1,671	7,221
Interest	–	–	2,012	2,012
Reorganization and other items	–	–	6,856	6,856
Income taxes	–	–	4,900	4,900
	4,402	1,148	15,439	20,989
NET INCOME (LOSS)	$ 14,633	$ 3,741	$ (10,983)	$ 7,391
Capital assets	$ 232,022	$ 51,588	$ 7,264	$ 290,874
Development assets	34,628	23,440	21,121	79,189
Loans receivable	–	–	56,044	56,044
Membership fees receivable	–	–	22,077	22,077
Long-term portfolio investments	–	–	9,612	9,612
Other assets	–	–	29,436	29,436
TOTAL ASSETS	$ 266,650	$ 75,028	$ 145,554	$ 487,232

ClubLink

(THOUSANDS OF DOLLARS)				1998
	GOLF CLUB OPERATIONS	GOLF RESORT OPERATIONS	DEVELOPMENT, CORPORATE & UNALLOCATED	TOTAL
REVENUE				
Operating	$ 41,517	$ 11,740	$ 11,454	$ 64,711
Membership fees	–	–	9,485	9,485
	41,517	11,740	20,939	74,196
EXPENSES				
Cost of goods sold	5,919	2,116	5,851	13,886
Operating	22,176	6,596	–	28,772
Membership sales and marketing	–	–	2,236	2,236
General and administrative	–	–	4,489	4,489
Capital taxes	–	–	781	781
	28,095	8,712	13,357	50,164
EBITDA	13,422	3,028	7,582	24,032
Amortization	2,721	634	980	4,335
Interest	–	–	1,029	1,029
Reorganization and other items	–	–	(808)	(808)
Income taxes	–	–	8,850	8,850
	2,721	634	10,051	13,406
NET INCOME (LOSS)	$ 10,701	$ 2,394	$ (2,469)	$ 10,626
Capital assets	$ 147,825	$ 33,375	$ 4,330	$ 185,530
Development assets	43,307	26,045	21,411	90,763
Loans receivable	–	–	36,961	36,961
Membership fees receivable	–	–	18,055	18,055
Long-term portfolio investments	–	–	16,185	16,185
Other assets	–	–	46,484	46,484
TOTAL ASSETS	$ 191,132	$ 59,420	$ 143,426	$ 393,978

NOTE 19. CONTINGENCIES

The Year 2000 Issue arises because many computerized systems use two digits rather than four to identify a year. Date-sensitive systems may recognize the year 2000 as 1900 or some other date, resulting in errors when information using year 2000 dates is processed. In addition, similar problems may arise in some systems which use certain dates in 1999 to represent something other than a date. Although the change in date has occurred, it is not possible to conclude that all aspects of the Year 2000 Issue that may affect the entity, including those related to customers, suppliers or other third parties, have been fully resolved.

To date, ClubLink has not experienced any year 2000 computer problems.

NOTE 20. COMPARATIVE AMOUNTS

Certain comparative amounts have been reclassified from those previously presented to conform to the presentation of the 1999 consolidated financial statements.

ClubLink

Management's Discussion and Analysis

Board of Directors

PATRICK S. BRIGHAM(2)(4)
PRESIDENT OF HARTAY ENTERPRISES INC.

JUSTIN A. CONNIDIS
PRESIDENT & CHIEF OPERATING OFFICER,
QUEBEC/EASTERN ONTARIO
SENIOR VICE PRESIDENT, CORPORATE DEVELOPMENT

ROBERT H. DEDMAN, JR.
PRESIDENT & CHIEF EXECUTIVE OFFICER OF
CLUBCORP, INC.

ROBERT M. FRANKLIN(1)(2)(3)
CHAIRMAN OF THE CORPORATION
CHAIRMAN OF PLACER DOME INC.

CHRISTOPHER J.F. HARROP(1)(3)
SENIOR VICE PRESIDENT & DIRECTOR OF
CANACCORD CAPITAL CORPORATION

JAMES M. HINCKLEY
CHIEF OPERATING OFFICER OF CLUBCORP, INC.

MICHAEL W. MANLEY(2)(4)
BARRISTER & SOLICITOR

BRUCE S. SIMMONDS
PRESIDENT & CHIEF EXECUTIVE OFFICER

JACK D. WINBERG(1)(3)(4)
PRESIDENT & CHIEF EXECUTIVE OFFICER OF
ROCKPORT GROUP
CHAIRMAN OF REVENUE PROPERTIES CO. LTD.

(1) AUDIT COMMITTEE
(2) COMPENSATION COMMITTEE
(3) GOVERNANCE COMMITTEE
(4) ENVIRONMENTAL COMMITTEE

ClubLink

Officers

BRUCE S. SIMMONDS
PRESIDENT & CHIEF EXECUTIVE OFFICER

JUSTIN A. CONNIDIS
PRESIDENT & CHIEF OPERATING OFFICER,
QUEBEC/EASTERN ONTARIO
SENIOR VICE PRESIDENT, CORPORATE DEVELOPMENT

SUSAN J. HODKINSON
SENIOR VICE PRESIDENT,
OPERATIONS & HUMAN RESOURCES

JIM MOLENHUIS
VICE PRESIDENT, GOLF DEVELOPMENT &
TURF OPERATIONS

ROBERT VISENTIN
CHIEF FINANCIAL OFFICER

I. KEVIN COUTTS
VICE PRESIDENT, US ACQUISITIONS
CLUBLINK US CORPORATION

SCOTT A. DAVIDSON
VICE PRESIDENT, SYSTEMS,
ADMINISTRATION & RETAIL

CHARLES F. LORIMER
VICE PRESIDENT,
GOLF BUSINESS DEVELOPMENT

DAREN G. SELFE
VICE PRESIDENT, FINANCE

IAN G. WETHERLY
VICE PRESIDENT, ACQUISITIONS
QUEBEC/EASTERN ONTARIO

ClubLink

Corporate Information

LEGAL COUNSEL

BLAKE, CASSELS & GRAYDON

AUDITORS

PANNELL KERR FORSTER

TRANSFER AGENT

CIBC MELLON TRUST COMPANY

LISTINGS

TSE: LNK

TSE: LNK.DB

HEAD OFFICE

15675 DUFFERIN STREET
KING CITY, ONTARIO
L7B 1K5

TEL: (905) 841-3730
FAX: (905) 841-1134

PLEASE VISIT OUR WEB SITE AT
WWW.CLUBLINK.CA

ANNUAL SHAREHOLDERS MEETING

CLUBLINK CORPORATION'S ANNUAL MEETING OF SHAREHOLDERS WILL BE HELD WEDNESDAY, JUNE 28, 2000 AT 10:00 A.M. AT:

KING'S RIDING GOLF CLUB
14700 BATHURST STREET
KING CITY, ONTARIO

Embracing
the Future!
WestJet Airlines 1999 Annual Report
WestJet

WestJet

Auditors Report to the Shareholders

We have audited the balance sheets of WestJet Airlines Ltd. as at December 31, 1999 and 1998 and the statements of operations and retained earnings and cash flows for the years then ended. These financial statements are the responsibility of the Corporation's management. Our responsibility is to express an opinion on these financial statements based on our audits.

We conducted our audits in accordance with Canadian generally accepted auditing standards. Those standards require that we plan and perform an audit to obtain reasonable assurance whether the financial statements are free of material misstatement. An audit includes examining, on a test basis, evidence supporting the amounts and disclosures in the financial statements. An audit also includes assessing the accounting principles used and significant estimates made by management, as well as evaluating the overall financial statement presentation.

In our opinion, these financial statements present fairly, in all material respects, the financial position of the Corporation as at December 31, 1999 and 1998 and the results of its operations and its cash flows for the years then ended in accordance with Canadian generally accepted accounting principles.

KPMG LLP

Calgary, Canada

February 24, 2000

WestJetter Kevin of our Flight Operations team.

Flight Attendants Deanna and Marla, along with First Officer Don and Captain Roger, outside a WestJet 737.

WestJet

WestJet

December 31, 1999 and 1998 (Stated in Thousands of Dollars)

	1999	1998
Assets		
Current assets:		
Cash and short-term investments	$ 50,740	$ 13,500
Accounts receivable	5,168	5,240
Prepaid expenses and deposits	4,123	3,479
Inventory	462	500
	60,493	22,719
Capital assets (note 2)	121,974	85,523
Other long-term assets (note 3)	4,131	-
	$ 186,598	$ 108,242
Liabilities and Shareholders' Equity		
Current liabilities:		
Accounts payable and accrued liabilities	$ 21,059	$ 14,663
Income taxes payable	7,410	-
Advance ticket sales	10,907	7,218
Non-refundable passenger credits	3,863	2,940
Current portion of long-term debt (note 4)	6,550	4,051
Current portion of obligations under capital lease (note 5)	137	78
	49,926	28,950
Long-term debt (note 4)	29,341	21,861
Obligations under capital lease (note 5)	335	322
Deferred income tax	12,509	7,748
	92,111	58,881
Shareholders' equity:		
Share capital (note 6)	69,039	39,536
Obligation to issue share capital (note 6)	-	209
Retained earnings	25,448	9,616
	94,487	49,361
Commitments (notes 5 and 8)		
Subsequent events (note 11)		
	$ 186,598	$ 108,242

See accompanying notes to financial statements.

On behalf of the Board:

Stephen Smith
Director

Wilmot Matthews
Director

Lou is responsible for Accounts Payable with our Accounting Team.

Statements of Operations and Retained Earnings

Years ended December 31, 1999 and 1998
(Stated in Thousands of Dollars, Except Per Share Data)

		1999		1998
Revenues:				
Passenger revenues	$	193,715	$	118,612
Charter and other		9,859		6,825
		203,574		125,437
Expenses:				
Passenger services		43,955		31,386
Maintenance		31,854		22,129
Aircraft fuel		30,480		20,490
Sales and marketing		13,907		9,452
Reservations		9,550		4,917
General and administration		9,410		6,545
Flight operations		8,826		5,709
Inflight		7,531		3,465
Employee profit share provision		6,633		1,702
Aircraft leasing		2,687		1,448
Depreciation		8,272		5,087
		173,105		112,330
Earnings from operations		30,469		13,107
Non-operating income (expense):				
Interest income		1,657		453
Interest expense		(2,871)		(1,137)
Gain on disposal of assets		93		8
		(1,121)		(676)
Earnings before income taxes		29,348		12,431
Income taxes (note 7):				
Current		7,696		335
Deferred		5,820		5,579
		13,516		5,914
Net earnings		15,832		6,517
Retained earnings, beginning of year		9,616		3,099
Retained earnings, end of year	$	25,448	$	9,616
Earnings per share:				
Basic	$	0.63	$	0.28
Fully diluted	$	0.58	$	0.28

See accompanying notes to financial statements.

WestJet

WestJet

Statements of Cash Flow

Years ended December 31, 1999 and 1998
(Stated in Thousands of Dollars)

	1999	1998
Cash provided by (used in):		
Operations:		
Net earnings	$ 15,832	$ 6,517
Items not involving cash:		
Depreciation	8,272	5,087
Gain on disposal of capital assets	(93)	(8)
Deferred income tax	5,820	5,579
Cash flow from operations	29,831	17,175
Increase in non-cash working capital	17,948	6,759
	47,779	23,934
Financing:		
Increase in long-term debt	15,314	20,759
Repayment of long-term debt	(5,335)	(2,422)
Issuance of common shares	30,591	2,144
Share issuance costs	(2,356)	(87)
Issuance of performance shares	-	12
Increase in other long-term assets	(4,195)	-
Decrease in obligations under capital lease	(96)	(75)
	33,923	20,331
Investments:		
Aircraft additions	(39,318)	(42,717)
Other capital asset additions	(5,350)	(4,933)
Other capital asset disposals	206	99
	(44,462)	(47,551)
Net change in cash	37,240	(3,286)
Cash, beginning of year	13,500	16,786
Cash, end of year	$ 50,740	$ 13,500

Cash is defined as cash and short-term investments.
See accompanying notes to financial statements.

Gareth, our Vice President of Technical Services.

Notes to Financial Statements
WestJet Airlines
18
1999 Annual Report

WestJet

WestJet

Years ended December 31, 1999 and 1998
(Tabular Amounts are Stated in Thousands of Dollars)

1. Significant accounting policies:

(a) Revenue recognition

Passenger revenue is recognized when air transportation is provided. The value of unused tickets is included in the balance sheet as advance ticket sales under current liabilities.

(b) Non-refundable passenger credits:

The Corporation, under certain circumstances, may issue future travel credits which are non-refundable and which expire one year from the date of issue. These passenger credits are recorded at a discount of their face value. The utilization of passenger credits are recorded as revenue when flown.

(c) Foreign currency:

Monetary assets and liabilities, denominated in foreign currencies, are translated into Canadian dollars at rates of exchange in effect at the balance sheet date. Other assets and revenue and expense items are translated at rates prevailing when they were acquired or incurred.

Exchange gains and losses arising on the translation of long-term monetary items that are denominated in foreign currencies are deferred and amortized on a straight-line basis over the remaining term of the related monetary item.

(d) Inventory:

Materials and supplies are valued at the lower of cost and replacement value. Aircraft expendables and consumables are expensed as incurred.

(e) Deferred costs:

Sales and marketing and reservation expenses attributed to the advance ticket sales are deferred and expensed in the period the related revenue is recognized. Included in prepaid expenses are $1,169,000 (1998 - $873,000) of deferred costs.

(f) Capital assets:

Capital assets are to be depreciated over their estimated useful lives at the following rates and methods.

Asset	Basis	Rate
Aircraft net of estimated residual value	Flight hours	Hours flown
Computer hardware and software	Straight-line	5 years
Equipment	Straight-line	5 years
Leasehold improvements	Straight-line	Over the term of the lease

(g) Maintenance costs:

Maintenance costs related to the cost of acquiring the aircraft and preparation for service are capitalized and included in aircraft costs.

Heavy maintenance ("D" check) costs incurred on aircraft are deferred and amortized over the remaining useful service life of the aircraft.

All other maintenance costs are expensed as incurred.

(h) Deferred income taxes:

The Corporation follows the deferral method of tax allocation accounting under which the provision for corporate income taxes is based on the earnings reported in the accounts and takes into account the tax effects of timing differences between financial statement income and taxable income.

(i) Financial instruments:

The Corporation manages its foreign exchange exposure through the use of options, forward contracts and cross currency swaps. Resulting gains and losses are accrued as exchange rates change to offset gains and losses resulting from the underlying hedged transactions. Premiums and discounts are amortized over the term of the contracts.

The Corporation manages its exposure to jet fuel price volatility through the use of fixed price and fixed ceiling price agreements. Premiums and discounts are amortized over the term of the contracts.

(j) Comparative figures:

Certain prior period balances have been reclassified to conform with current presentation.

2. Capital assets:

1999		Cost		Accumulated depreciation		Net book value
Aircraft	$	117,084	$	14,385	$	102,699
Spare engines and parts		14,331		-		14,331
Computer hardware and software		3,539		1,148		2,391
Computer hardware under capital lease		643		230		413
Equipment		2,484		787		1,697
Leasehold improvements		979		536		443
	$	139,060	$	17,086	$	121,974
Aircraft	$	77,766	$	7,188	$	70,578
Spare engines and parts		11,521		-		11,521
Computer hardware and software		2,404		709		1,695
Computer hardware under capital lease		476		116		360
Equipment		1,584		493		1,091
Leasehold improvements		592		314		278
	$	94,343	$	8,820	$	85,523

During the year capital assets were acquired at an aggregate cost of $168,000 by means of capital leases.

WestJet

WestJet

3. Other long-term assets:

Included in other long-term assets are pre-payments of premiums for long-term contracts with fuel suppliers of $3,333,000, deposits on long-term operating lease agreements of $603,000, and a loan to an officer of the Corporation of $195,000. The loan to an officer of the Corporation is unsecured and non-interest bearing. The loan will be repaid out of the officer's future compensation.

4. Long-term debt:

		1999		1998
$7,500,000 bank term loan repayable in monthly instalments of $154, 000 including interest at 8.50%, maturing November 2002, secured by two aircraft	$	4,754	$	6,133
$7,500,000 bank term loan repayable in monthly instalments of $153,000 including interest at 8.13%, maturing April 2003, secured by two aircraft		5,330		6,667
$5,117,000 term loan repayable in monthly instalments of $76,000 including interest at 8.29% and $2,383,000 term loan repayable in monthly instalments of $36,000 including interest at 8.36%, maturing October 2005, secured by one aircraft		6,645		7,399
$5,759,000 term loan repayable in monthly instalments of $87,000 including interest at 8.42%, and $1,614,000 term loan repayable in monthly instalments of $25,000 including interest at 8.49%, maturing October 2005, secured by one aircraft		6,606		5,713
$4,257,000 term loan repayable in monthly instalments of $66,000 including interest at 8.39% and $2,943,000 term loan repayable in monthly instalments of $47,000 including interest at 8.81%, maturing October 2005, secured by one aircraft		6,681		-
$6,500,000 bank term loan repayable in monthly instalments of $133,000 including interest at 8.38%, maturing May 2004, secured by two aircraft		5,875		-
		35,891		25,912
Less current portion		6,550		4,051
	$	29,341	$	21,861

Future scheduled repayment of long-term debt is as follows:

2000	$	6,550
2001		7,124
2002		7,590
2003		5,237
2004 and thereafter		9,390
	$	35,891

The Corporation has available a facility with a chartered bank of $2,000,000 for letters of guarantee and U.S. $7,000,000 for forward foreign exchange contracts. At December 31, 1999, letters of guarantee totaling $725,000 have been issued under these facilities. The credit facilities are secured by a fixed first charge on one aircraft, a general security agreement and an assignment of insurance proceeds.

The cash interest paid in the year was $2,860,000.

5. Leases:

The Corporation has entered into operating leases for aircraft, buildings, computer hardware and software licenses and capital leases relating to computer hardware. The obligations on a calendar-year basis, are as follows:

		Capital Lease		Operating Leases
2000	$	171	$	7,506
2001		171		7,196
2002		149		7,148
2003		53		5,155
2004 and thereafter		-		3,600
Total lease payments		544	$	30,605
Less imputed interest at 8.12%		72		
Net minimum lease payments		472		
Current portion of obligations under capital lease		137		
Obligations under capital lease	$	335		

6. Share capital:

The non-voting common shares and the non-voting preferred shares are subject to limitations to be fixed by the directors of the Corporation.

(a) Authorized:

Unlimited number of voting common shares

700,000 non-voting performance shares

Unlimited number of non-voting shares

Unlimited number of non-voting first preferred shares

Unlimited number of non-voting second preferred shares

Unlimited number of non-voting third preferred shares.

Victoria

With over 1,000 fluttering beauties, Victoria's Butterfly Gardens is one of the largest butterfly conservation in Canada.

Vancouver

Vancouver's reputation as "Hollywood North" is well deserved. The city hosts almost $1 billion of television and film production annually.

Abbotsford

Abbotsford is home to an annual garlic festival, where the "stinky flower" is celebrated for two straight days.

Grande Prairie

Grande Prairie is no ugly duckling. The city's many lakes are home to one of North America's largest populations of trumpeter swans.

WestJet

WestJet

6. Share capital cont:

(b) Issued:

	1999		1998	
	Number	Amount	Number	Amount
Common shares:				
Balance, beginning of year	23,337,530	$ 39,523	22,665,398	$ 37,513
Initial Public Offering	2,750,000	27,500	-	-
Exercise of options	744,772	2,138	-	-
Employee share purchase	370,248	1,742	554,184	2,061
Conversion of performance shares	103,502	3	119,990	-
Cancellation of shares	(2,053)	(5)	(2,042)	(3)
Share issuance costs	-	(2,356)	-	(87)
Tax benefit of issue costs	-	1,059	-	39
	27,303,999	69,604	23,337,530	39,523
Less: Due from shareholder	-	(575)	-	-
Balance, end of year	27,303,999	69,029	23,337,530	39,523
Performance shares:				
Balance, beginning of year	437,146	13	542,500	1
Issued	-	-	38,000	12
Converted to common shares	(103,502)	(3)	(119,990)	-
Surrendered	-	-	(23,364)	-
Balance, end of year	333,644	10	437,146	13
		$ 69,039		$ 39,536

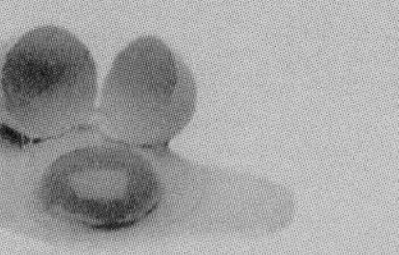

Calgary
Visitors and staff at the annual Calgary Stampede consume two tonnes of bacon and sausage, 5000 bottles of pancake syrup and 85,000 containers of juice. And that's just breakfast, pardner.

Saskatoon
Saskatoon gets more sunshine than any other city in Canada.

Winnipeg
No need to dream of a white Christmas. Winnipeg is one of four major Canadian cities to guarantee snow for Santa's annual run.

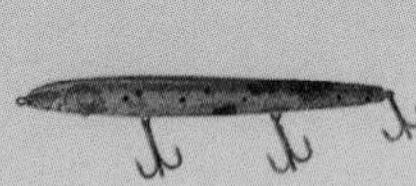

Thunder Bay
Thunder Bay sits on the shores of Lake Superior, the world's largest freshwater Lake.

Pato, a member of WestJet's dedicated Maintenance team.

(c) Performance shares:

The performance shares are held by management and key employees of the Corporation. These performance shares are convertible at the option of the holder into common shares of the Corporation on the basis of one performance share for each $1.86 of convertible amount. The convertible amount is calculated as being 5% of the net earnings of the Corporation up to maximum net earnings of $25,668,000. Net earnings is defined as net income after tax for each fiscal year as per the audited financial statements in accordance with generally accepted accounting principles, less an imputed interest charge on new equity invested.

The interest charge is calculated as the aggregate of 20% times each amount of new equity invested, times the number of days that the new equity was available to the Corporation, divided by the number of days in the year. At the Annual and Special Meeting of the Shareholders held on June 21, 1999, the shareholders approved a six month deferral of this calculation with respect to any new equity funds raised. The holders of the performance shares shall, on a cumulative basis, be entitled to convert to a maximum of one-third of the performance shares following each of the three fiscal years, beginning with the completion of the 1997 fiscal year. The cumulative convertible amount is to be allocated in proportion to the holders' percentage of outstanding performance shares. The right to convert expires 90 days following issuance of audited financial statements on the third fiscal year from the commencement date, termination of employment or the death of the shareholder.

As at December 31, 1999, 333,644 (1998 - 118,252) performance shares are eligible for conversion. These shares must be converted by June 2000 or the right to convert expires.

WestJet

WestJet

(d) Share option plan:

The Corporation has a share option plan, whereby up to a maximum of 2,650,000 common shares may be issued to directors, officers and employees of the Corporation subject to the following limitations:

(i) the number of common shares reserved for issuance to any one optionee will not exceed 5% of the issued and outstanding common shares at any time;

(ii) the number of common shares reserved for issuance to insiders shall not exceed 10% of the issued and outstanding common shares; and

(iii) the number of common shares issuable under the Plan which may be issued within a one year period shall not exceed 10% of the issued and outstanding common shares at any time.

Changes in the number of options, with their weighted average exercise prices, are summarized below:

	1999			1998		
	Number of options		Weighted average exercise price	Number of options		Weighted average exercise price
Stock options outstanding, beginning of year	2,265,503	$	3.16	1,825,500	$	2.87
Granted	649,653		6.50	567,920		4.00
Exercised	(744,772)		2.87	-		-
Cancelled	(22,167)		4.09	(127,917)		2.76
Stock options outstanding, end of year	2,148,217	$	4.26	2,265,503	$	3.16
Exercisable at year end	550,478	$	2.91	432,166	$	3.00

The following table summarizes the stock options outstanding and exercisable at December 31, 1999 and the year of expiry:

Outstanding				Exercisable Options			
	Exercise Price	Number Outstanding	Year of Vesting	Exercisable		Exercise Price	Year of Expiry
$	2.50	200,761	1999	200,761	$	2.50	2000
$	3.00	751,217	one third per year beginning 1998	299,717	$	3.00	One year after vesting
$	4.00	552,086	2001	-	$	4.00	2002
$	4.00	50,000	1999	50,000	$	4.00	2003
$	6.00	488,583	2002	-	$	6.00	2003
$	10.00	105,570	2002	-	$	10.00	2003
$	4.26	2,148,217		550,478	$	2.91	

Upon filing the Corporation's initial public offering, 105,570 options were re-priced from $6.00 per share to $10.00 per share. In 1999, the Corporation has committed to the holders of the options that it will pay the differential up to $4.00 per share upon exercise of those options.

6. Share capital cont:

(e) Employee share purchase plan:

Under the terms of the Employee Share Purchase Plan, employees may contribute up to a maximum of 20% of their gross pay and acquire common shares of the Corporation at the current fair market value of such shares. The Corporation matches the employee contributions and shares may be withdrawn from the Plan after being held in trust for one year. Employees may offer to sell common shares at any time to the Corporation for 50% of the then current market price.

As at December 31, 1998, $209,000 was held in Trust representing employee and employer contributions under the Plan and the Company had an obligation to issue 52,331 common shares at $4.00 per share. After July, 1999, the Corporation has not issued the shares from Treasury but purchased these shares off of the open market.

(f) Due from shareholder:

The advance to purchase common shares of the Corporation consists of promissory notes of $575,000 as at December 31, 1999 due from a shareholder who is an officer of the Corporation. The amount repayable on or before March 31, 2000 is $275,000 and on or before May 31, 2000 is $300,000.

7. Income taxes:

Income taxes vary upon the amount that would be computed by applying the basic Federal and Provincial tax rate of 45% to earnings before taxes as follows:

	1999	1998
Expected income tax provision	$ 13,207	$ 5,544
Add (deduct):		
Non-deductible expenses	55	35
Capital taxes	264	335
Other	(10)	-
	$ 13,516	$ 5,914

8. Commitments:

(a) Employee profit share:

The Corporation has an employee profit sharing plan whereby eligible employees will participate in the pre-tax operating income of the Corporation. The profit share ranges from a minimum of 10% to a maximum of 20% of earnings before employee profit share and income taxes. The amounts paid under the plan are subject to approval by the Board of Directors.

(b) Building lease:

The Corporation entered into a 10 year lease agreement for additional office space. The building, which is expected to be ready for occupancy by September 2000, will result in the consolidation of all head office, administration and accounting functions. The aggregate payments under this lease agreement were included in the Corporation's commitments as at December 31, 1999 (see note 5).

(c) Hushkit requirements:

In accordance with Canadian Aviation Regulations (C.A.R.s) requirements, the Corporation is required to install hushkits on its aircraft fleet in order to conform to noise emission standards. The C.A.R.s requirement to hushkit Boeing 737 aircraft is as follows:

	Percentage of fleet to be hushkitted (rounded down)
December 31, 1999	75%
October 1, 2001	85%
April 1, 2002	100%

As at December 31, 1999, the Corporation had 11 of its 15 operational aircraft equipped with hushkits and was in compliance with C.A.R.'s requirements.

WestJet

WestJet

9. Risk management:

(a) Interest rate risk:

The Corporation has entered into fixed rate debt agreements in order to manage its interest rate exposure on debt instruments. These agreements are described in note 3.

(b) Foreign currency exchange risk:

The Corporation is exposed to foreign currency fluctuations as certain ongoing expenses are referenced to U.S. dollar denominated prices. The Corporation periodically uses financial instruments, including forward exchange contracts and options, to manage its exposure. At December 31, 1999 there was a forward contract to purchase U.S. $2 million. The fair value of the contract outstanding at December 31, 1999 was not materially different than carrying value.

(c) Credit risk:

The Corporation does not believe it is subject to any significant concentration of credit risk. Most of the Corporation's receivables result from tickets sold to individual passengers through the use of major credit cards and travel agents. These receivables are short-term, generally being settled shortly after the sale.

(d) Fuel risk management:

The Corporation has managed its exposure to jet fuel price volatility through the use of long-term fixed price contracts and contracts with a fixed ceiling price which it has entered into with various fuel suppliers. Any premiums paid to enter into these long-term fuel arrangements are recorded as other long-term assets and amortized to fuel expense over the term of the contracts. As of December 31, 1999, the Corporation had entered into fixed price fuel contracts that are in effect through to June 2000, as well as a contract with a fixed ceiling price for the period July 2000 to June 2003. Based on historical and anticipated volumes of fuel usage, these contracts represent approximately 66% of the Corporation's projected 2000 fuel requirements.

(e) Fair value of financial instruments:

The carrying amounts of financial instruments included in the balance sheet, other than long-term debt, approximate their fair value due to their short-term to maturity.

At December 31, 1999, the fair value of the long-term debt was approximately $35,058,000, based on market prices of debt with comparable remaining maturities.

10. Uncertainty due to the Year 2000 Issue:

The Year 2000 Issue arises because many computerized systems use two digits rather than four to identify a year. Date-sensitive systems may recognize the year 2000 as 1900 or some other date, resulting in errors when information using year 2000 dates is processed. In addition, similar problems may arise in some systems which use certain dates in 1999 to represent something other than a date. Although the change in date has occurred, it is not possible to conclude that all aspects of the Year 2000 Issue that may affect the entity, including those related to customers, suppliers, or other third parties, have been fully resolved.

11. Subsequent events:

(a) Subsequent to year end, the Corporation has reached an agreement with Boeing Corporation to acquire 20 new 737-600 or 737-700 series aircraft, with an option to acquire an additional 30 aircraft prior to 2008. In addition, the Corporation also entered into an agreement for the lease of 10 of the same aircraft type with the option to lease a further 10. The purchase price of 20 Boeing 737-600 or 737-700's will be approximately $900 million including spares.

(b) Subsequent to year end, the Corporation has entered into letter agreements for the acquisition of four Boeing 737-200 aircraft for a total purchase price of approximately U.S. $17 million. The delivery dates for these aircraft are expected to be between March and October 2000.

(c) Subsequent to year end, the Corporation entered into a settlement agreement to discontinue its claim against a California corporation (the "defendant") in exchange for a net payment of U.S. $275,000. The settlement also includes the discontinuance of the defendant's counter-claim against the Corporation in the amount of $10 million. The amount of the settlement will be recorded as other income in fiscal 2000.

(d) Subsequent to year end, the Corporation's Board of Directors approved a stock split on the basis of three common shares for each two common shares held. The stock split is subject to shareholders' approval and will be proposed at the Corporation's Annual and Special Meeting on May 4, 2000.

Larry, an Aircraft Mechanic at the Winnipeg airport.

Corporate Information

Board of Directors

Clive J. Beddoe – Executive Chairman
President
Hanover Group of Companies

Stephen C. Smith
President and Chief Executive Officer
WestJet Airlines Ltd.

Ron Greene
President
Tortuga Investment Corp.

Wilmot Matthews
President
Marjad Inc.

Murph N. Hannon
President
Murcon Development Ltd.

Brian Gibson
Portfolio Manager, Canadian Equities
Ontario Teachers' Pension Plan Board

Tim Morgan
Senior Vice President, Operations
WestJet Airlines Ltd.

Donald A. MacDonald
President
Sanjel Corporation

Larry Pollock
President and Chief Executive Officer
Canadian Western Bank and Canadian Western Trust

Officers

Clive J. Beddoe
Executive Chairman

Stephen C. Smith
President and Chief Executive Officer

Alexander (Sandy) J. Campbell
Senior Vice President, Finance
Chief Financial Officer

Tim Morgan
Senior Vice President, Operations

Donald Bell
Senior Vice President, Customer Service

Auditors

KPMG LLP
1200, 205-5 Avenue SW
Calgary, AB T2P 4B9

Legal Counsel

Burnett, Duckworth and Palmer
1400, 350-7 Avenue SW
Calgary, AB T2P 3N9

WestJet

WestJet

WESTJET

35 McTavish Place N.E., Calgary, Alberta T2E 7J7 Telephone: 403.735.2600 Facsimile: 403.571.5367 Website: www.westjet.com

Codes of Professional Conduct

APPENDIX II

Selections from the ICAO Rules of Professional Conduct[1]

Principles

- A member or student shall conduct himself or herself at all times in a manner that will maintain the good reputation of the profession and its ability to serve the public interest.
- A member or student shall perform his or her professional services with integrity and care and accept an obligation to sustain his or her professional competence by keeping himself or herself informed of, and complying with, developments in professional standards.
- A member who is engaged in an attest function such as an audit or review of financial statements shall hold himself or herself free of any influence, interest or relationship, in respect of his or her client's affairs, which impairs his or her professional judgement or objectivity or which, in the view of a reasonable observer, would impair the member's professional judgement or objectivity.
- A member or student has a duty of confidence in respect of the affairs of any client and shall not disclose, without proper cause, any information obtained in the course of his or her duties, nor shall he or she in any way exploit such information to his or her advantage.
- The development of a member's practice shall be founded upon a reputation for professional excellence. The use of methods of advertising that do not uphold professional good taste, that could be characterized as self-promotion, and that solicit, rather than inform, is not in keeping with this principle.
- A member shall act in relation to any member with the courtesy and consideration due between professional colleagues and which, in turn, he or she would wish to be accorded by the other member.

[1] ICAO, *Rules of Professional Conduct* (Toronto: Institute of Chartered Accountants of Ontario). Other provincial institutes have similar provisions.

Standards of Conduct Affecting the Public Interest

201	Maintenance of reputation of profession
202	Integrity and due care
203	Professional competence
204	Objectivity
205	False or misleading documents and oral representations
206	Compliance with professional standards
207	Informing clients and associates of possible conflicts of interest
208	Unauthorized benefits
209	Improper use of confidential information
210	Confidentiality of information
211	Duty to report breach of rules of professional conduct
212	Handling of trust funds and other property
213	Unlawful activity
214	Fee quotations
215	Contingency fees and services without fees
216	Payment or receipt of commissions
217	General advertising
218	Retention of documentation and working papers

Compliance with the ICAO Rules of Professional Conduct depends primarily on a member's understanding and voluntary actions. However, there are provisions for reinforcement by peers and the public through public opinion, and ultimately by disciplinary proceedings, where necessary. Adherence to the Rules helps ensure individual and collective ethical behaviour by CAs.

Selections from the Code of Professional Ethics for Management Accountants[2]

Introduction

- Professional Ethics is the behaviour of a professional toward peers, other professionals and members of the public. It concerns the performance of professional duties in accordance with recognized standards of accounting and professional integrity.

[2] The Society of Management Accountants of Ontario, *Management Accountants Handbook.* (Toronto: SMAC).

- The codes of professional ethics vary from province to province in certain details in order to comply with provincial legislation and the by-laws of the provincial societies. The following discussion covers the elements common to these codes. Reference should be made to the relevant code of ethics for specific information.
- Every member of the Society is duty bound to uphold and increase the competence and prestige of the accounting profession. In keeping with high standards of ethical conduct, members will conduct their professional work with honesty, impartiality, courtesy, and personal honour. Any breach of the principles of professional ethics will constitute discreditable conduct. The offending member will be liable to disciplinary measures the by-laws of the Society consider appropriate.
- A professional approach to resolving a problem of ethics requires that the rules of behaviour establish minimum, not maximum standards. Where the rules are silent, an even greater burden of responsibility falls upon the member to ensure that the course of action followed is consistent with general standards established by the Society.

General

- Members shall, in exercising their professional responsibilities, subordinate personal interest to that of the public, the employer, the Society and the profession.
- Any member convicted of any criminal offence or who has been a party to any fraud or improper business practice may be charged with professional misconduct and be required to appear before a Society disciplinary tribunal. If found guilty of such charges by the tribunal, the member may be subject to dismissal from membership in the Society and to forfeiture of the right to use the CMA designation, or to other penalties provided in the by-laws.
- A certificate of conviction in any court in Canada shall be sufficient evidence of a criminal conviction.
- No member shall report any false or misleading fact in a financial statement, or knowingly misrepresent any statement.

Relations with the Public

- Subject to provincial legislation, a Certified Management Accountant may offer services to the public as a management or cost accountant or consultant with the status of proprietor, partner, director, officer, or shareholder of an incorporated company and may associate with non-members for this purpose. A member associated with any company must abide by the rules of professional conduct of the Society. Certified members may use the initials CMA on the letterhead, professional cards or announcement in any public forum of the businesses with which they are associated.
- The right of Certified Management Accountants to sign an audit certificate or perform a review engagement varies from jurisdiction to jurisdiction across Canada. Members of the Society must comply with local legislation.

- No person except a Certified member shall on letterhead, nameplates, professional cards or announcements claim membership in the Society.
- When practising as a management accountant in preparing or expressing an opinion on financial statements intended to inform the public or management, a member shall disclose all material facts, require all and sufficient information to warrant expression of opinion, and will report all material misstatements or departures from generally accepted accounting principles.
- Improper use by a member of a client's or employer's confidential information or affairs is discreditable conduct.
- The member will treat as confident any information obtained concerning a client's affairs. The member also has a duty to inform the client of any member interest, affiliation or other matter of which the client ought reasonably to be informed, or which might influence the member's judgement.

Relations with Employers

- No member shall use an employer's confidential information or business affairs to acquire any personal interest, property or benefit.
- A member shall treat as confidential any information or documents concerning the employer's business affairs and shall not disclose or release such information or documents without the consent of the employer, or the order of lawful authority.
- A member shall inform the employer of any business connections, affiliations or interests of which the employer might reasonably expect to be informed.
- No member shall knowingly be a party to any unlawful act of the employer.

Relations with Professional Accountants

- No member shall criticize the professional work of another professional accountant except with the knowledge of that accountant unless the member reviews the work of others as a normal responsibility.
- Members will uphold the principle of appropriate and adequate compensation for work and will endeavour to provide opportunities for professional development and advancement for accountants employed by them or under their supervision.

Chart of Accounts

APPENDIX

Assets

Current Assets

101 Cash
102 Petty Cash
103 Cash equivalents
104 Temporary investments
105 Allowance to reduce temporary investments to market
106 Accounts receivable
107 Allowance for doubtful accounts
108 Legal fees receivable
109 Interest receivable
110 Rent receivable
111 Notes receivable
115 Subscription receivable, common shares
116 Subscription receivable, preferred shares
119 Merchandise inventory
120 ____________ inventory
121 ____________ inventory
124 Office supplies
125 Store supplies
126 ________ supplies
128 Prepaid insurance
129 Prepaid interest
131 Prepaid rent
132 Raw materials inventory
133 Goods in process inventory, ________
134 Goods in process inventory, ________
135 Finished goods inventory

Long-Term Investments

141 Investment in ____ shares
142 Investment in ____ bonds
144 Investment in _______
145 Bond sinking fund

Capital Assets

151 Automobiles
152 Accumulated amortization, automobiles
153 Trucks
154 Accumulated amortization, trucks
155 Boats
156 Accumulated amortization, boats
157 Professional library
158 Accumulated amortization, professional library
159 Law library
160 Accumulated amortization, law library
161 Furniture
162 Accumulated amortization, Furniture
163 Office equipment
164 Accumulated amortization, office equipment
165 Store equipment
166 Accumulated amortization, store equipment
167 ________ equipment
168 Accumulated amortization, ________ equipment
169 Machinery
170 Accumulated amortization, machinery
173 Building ________
174 Accumulated amortization, building ________
175 Building ________
176 Accumulated amortization, building ________
179 Land improvements, _______
180 Accumulated amortization, land improvements ________
181 Land improvements_____
182 Accumulated amortization, land improvements _____
183 Land

Natural Resources

185 Mineral deposit
186 Accumulated depletion, mineral deposit

Intangible Assets

191 Patents
192 Leasehold
193 Franchise
194 Copyright
195 Leasehold improvements
196 Organization costs
197 Deferred income tax debits

Liabilities

Current Liabilities

201 Accounts payable
202 Insurance payable
203 Interest payable
204 Legal fees payable
205 Short-term notes payable
206 Discount on short-term notes payable
207 Office salaries payable
208 Rent payable
209 Salaries payable
210 Wages payable
211 Accrued payroll payable
214 Estimated warranty liability
215 Income taxes payable
216 Common dividends payable
217 Preferred dividends payable
218 UI payable
219 CPP payable
221 Employees' medical insurance payable
222 Employees' retirement program payable
223 Employees' union dues payable
224 PST payable
225 GST payable

226 Estimated vacation pay liability

Unearned Revenues

230 Unearned consulting fees
231 Unearned legal fees
232 Unearned property management fees
233 Unearned ________ fees
234 Unearned ________
235 Unearned janitorial revenue
236 Unearned _____ revenue
238 Unearned rent ________

Long-Terms Liabilities

251 Long-term notes payable
252 Discount on notes payable
253 Long-term lease liability
254 Discount on lease liability
255 Bonds payable
256 Discount on bonds payable
257 Premium on bonds payable
258 Deferred income tax credit

Equity

Owners' Equity

301 ________ , capital
302 ________ , withdrawals
303 ________ , capital
304 ________ , withdrawals
305 ________ , capital
305 ________ , withdrawals

Corporate Contributed Capital

307 Common shares
309 Common shares subscribed
310 Common share dividends distributable
313 Contributed capital from the retirement of common shares
315 Preferred shares
317 Preferred shares subscribed

Retained Earnings

318 Retained earnings
319 Cash dividends declared
320 Share dividends declared

Revenues

401 ________ fees earned
402 ________ fees earned
403 ________ services revenue
404 ________ services revenue
405 Commission earned
406 Rent earned
407 Dividends earned
408 Earnings from investment in ________
409 Interest earned
410 Sinking fund earnings
413 Sales
414 Sales returns and allowances
415 Sales discounts

Cost of Sales

501 Amortization of patents
502 Cost of goods sold
503 Depletion of mine deposit
505 Purchases
506 Purchases returns and allowances
507 Purchases discounts
508 Transportation-in

Manufacturing Accounts

520 Raw materials purchases
521 Freight-in on raw materials
530 Factory payroll
531 Direct labour
540 Factory overhead
541 Indirect materials
542 Indirect labour
543 Factory insurance expired
544 Factory supervision
545 Factory supplies used
546 Factory utilities
547 Miscellaneous production costs
548 Property taxes on factory building
550 Rent on factory building
551 Repairs, factory equipment
552 Small tools written off
560 Amortization of factory equipment
561 Amortization of factory building

Standard Cost Variance Accounts

580 Direct material quantity variance
581 Direct material price variance
582 Direct labour quantity variance
583 Direct labour price variance
584 Factory overhead volume variance
585 Factory overhead controllable variance

Expenses

Amortization and Depletion

602 Amortization expense, copyrights
603 Amortization expense, ________
604 Amortization expense, boats
605 Amortization expense, automobiles
606 Amortization expense, building ________
607 Amortization expense, building ________
608 Amortization expense, land improvements ________
609 Amortization expense, land improvements ________
610 Amortization expense, law library
611 Amortization expense, trucks
612 Amortization expense, ________ equipment
613 Amortization expense, ________ equipment
614 Amortization expense, ________
615 Amortization expense, ________

Employee Related Expense

620 Office salaries expense
621 Sales salaries expense
622 Salaries expense
623 ________ wages expense
624 Employees' benefits expense
625 Payroll taxes expense

Financial Expenses

630 Cash over and short
631 Discounts lost
633 Interest expense

Insurance Expenses

635 Insurance expense, delivery equipment
636 Insurance expense, office equipment
637 Insurance expense, ________

Rental Expenses

640 Rent expense
641 Rent expense, office space
642 Rent expense, selling space
643 Press rental expense
644 Truck rental expense
645 ________ rental expense

Supplies Expense

650 Office supplies expense
651 Store supplies expense
652 __________ supplies expense
653 __________ supplies expense

Miscellaneous Expenses

655 Advertising expense
656 Bad debts expense
657 Blueprinting expense
658 Boat expense
659 Collection expense
661 Concessions expense
662 Credit card expense
663 Delivery expense
664 Dumping expense
667 Equipment expense
668 Food and drinks expense
669 Gas, oil, and repairs expense
671 Gas and oil expense
672 General and administrative expense
673 Janitorial expense
674 Legal fees expense
676 Mileage expense
677 Miscellaneous expenses
678 Mower and tools expense
679 Operating expenses
681 Permits expense
682 Postage expense
683 Property taxes expense
684 Repairs expense, ________
685 Repairs expense, ________
687 Selling expenses
688 Telephone expense
689 Travel and entertaining expense
690 Utilities expense
691 Warranty expense
695 Income taxes expense

Gains and Losses

701 Gain on retirement of bonds
702 Gain on sale of machinery
703 Gain on sale of temporary investments
704 Gain on sale of trucks
705 Gain on ________
801 Loss on disposal of machinery
802 Loss on exchange of equipment
803 Loss on exchange of ________
804 Loss on market decline of temporary investments
805 Loss on retirement of bonds
806 Loss on sale of investments
807 Loss on sale of machinery
808 Loss on sale of __________
809 Loss on __________
810 Loss or gain from liquidation

Clearing Accounts

901 Income summary
902 Manufacturing summary

Credits

Chapter 1, page 3, photo courtesy of London Drugs

Chapter 2, page 35, photo © Duomo Photography Inc./Chris Cole, The Image Bank

Chapter 3, page 83, photo © Jon Riley/Tony Stone Images

Chapter 4, page 137, photo © Mitch Sembaliuk

Chapter 5, page 191, photo © Frank Siteman/Tony Stone Images

Chapter 6, page 255, photo © Comstock Photofile Limited

Chapter 7, page 331, photo courtesy of Macrotronics

Chapter 8, page 387, photo © Tim Brown/Tony Stone Images

Chapter 9, page 449, photo © Tilly Jensen

Chapter 10, page 509, photo © Laurence Dutton/Tony Stone Images

Chapter 11, page 557, photo © John Edwards/Tony Stone Images

Index